Population density and major urban areas

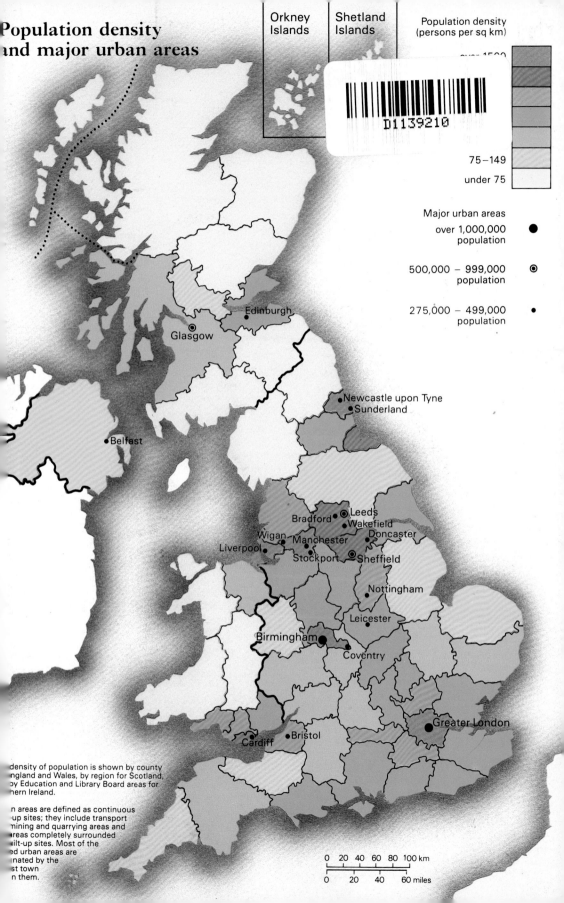

Orkney Islands	Shetland Islands

D1139210

Population density (persons per sq km)

over 1500

75–149

under 75

Major urban areas

over 1,000,000 population ●

500,000 – 999,000 population ◉

275,000 – 499,000 population ·

Edinburgh
Glasgow

Newcastle upon Tyne
· Sunderland

· Belfast

Bradford ◉ Leeds
· Wakefield
Wigan · · Manchester · Doncaster
Liverpool · · Stockport ◉ Sheffield

Nottingham

Leicester

Birmingham ●
· Coventry

Cardiff · Bristol

● Greater London

density of population is shown by county
ngland and Wales, by region for Scotland,
by Education and Library Board areas for
hern Ireland.

n areas are defined as continuous
-up sites; they include transport
mining and quarrying areas and
areas completely surrounded
ilt-up sites. Most of the
ed urban areas are
nated by the
st town
n them.

0	20	40	60	80	100 km

0	20	40	60 miles

NATIONAL STATISTICS

R

REF

This boo
available fo

Prepared by the Office for National Statistics

If you wish to reproduce any items in this publication, contact ONS Copyright Enquiries, Zone B1/04, 1 Drummond Gate, London, SW1V 2QQ. Tel 0171-533 5674 or fax 0171-533 5689.

ISBN 0 11 620941 0

London: The Stationery Office

Published by The Stationery Office and available from:

The Publications Centre
(mail, telephone and fax orders only)
PO Box 276, London SW8 5DT
General enquiries 0171 873 0011
Telephone orders 0171 873 9090
Fax orders 0171 873 8200

The Stationery Office Bookshops
59–60 Holborn Viaduct, London EC1A 2FD
temporary until mid 1998
(counter service and fax orders only)
Fax 0171 831 1326
68–69 Bull Street, Birmingham B4 6AD
0121 236 9696   Fax 0121 236 9699
33 Wine Street, Bristol BS1 2BQ
0117 9264306 Fax 0117 9294515
9–21 Princess Street, Manchester M60 8AS
0161 834 7201 Fax 0161 833 0634
16 Arthur Street, Belfast BT1 4GD
01232 238451 Fax 01232 235401
The Stationery Office Oriel Bookshop
The Friary, Cardiff CF1 4AA
01222 395548 Fax 01222 384347
71 Lothian Road, Edinburgh EH3 9AZ
(counter service only)

Customers in Scotland may
mail, telephone or fax their orders to:
Scottish Publications Sales
South Gyle Crescent, Edinburgh EH12 9EB
0131 228 4181 Fax 0131 622 7017

The Stationery Office's Accredited Agents
(see Yellow Pages)

and through good booksellers

Contents

List of Illustrations

Diagrams

Maps

Photographs

Acknowledgments for photographs
Diana, Princess of Wales: p. 1, British Forces Germany; p. 2, Jayne Fincher/Photographers International (x 2); p. 3, Gavin Kent/Mirror Syndication International; p. 4, Tim Graham Picture Library. **Expeditions and Anniversaries**: p. 1, Round the World in 97 (x 2); p. 2, Peter Smith Photography, Malton; p. 3, Roger Crowley, Barry Amateur Radio Society; p. 4, The Polar Travel Co./McVitie's Penguin Polar Relay (x 2). **Interiors**: p. 1, CADW: Welsh Historic Monuments; p. 2, Ulster Carpet Mills; p. 3, Shannon Tofts; p. 4, Richard Kalina (exterior) and John Tramper (*Henry V*). **Government Art Collection**: Copyright credits: Illustrations © The artists or their estates. Work by Barbara Hepworth, 'Conoid, Sphere and Hollow III' (back cover) © Alan Bowness, Hepworth Estate. Work by Patrick Heron, 'Horizontal Painting with Soft Black Squares' © Patrick Heron 1997: All Rights Reserved DACS. Photographic credits © Crown Copyright: UK Government Art Collection. Photography by the Department of the Environment, Eileen Tweedy and A.A. Barnes Photography. **Images of Europe**: Foreign & Commonwealth Office (UK Presidency logo); Remote Sensing Group of the Plymouth Marine Laboratory (satellite images). **Flora and Fauna**: p. 1, Dr Peter Merrett (spider) and English Nature (habitat); p. 2, Matthew Shepherd/White Cliffs Countryside Project (x 2); p. 3, Tendring District Council (x 2); p. 4, Northumberland County Council. **Fifty Years of the National Health Service**: Popperfoto (all photographs).

The Office for National Statistics works in partnership with others in the Government Statistical Service to provide Parliament, government and the wider community with the statistical information, analysis and advice needed to improve decision-making, stimulate research and inform debate. It also registers key life events. It aims to provide an authoritative and impartial picture of society and a window on the work and performance of government, allowing the impact of government policies and actions to be assessed.

Foreword

Britain 1998 is the 49th in the series of annual Handbooks, which go back to the 1940s, but the first to be prepared by the Office for National Statistics (ONS). Up to 1997, *The Britain Handbook* was produced by the Central Office of Information, but the staff working on it were transferred to the ONS in April 1997 and have now settled into their new home in Pimlico, central London. See opposite for the new address.

Drawing on a wide range of official and other authoritative sources, *The Britain Handbook* provides a factual and up-to-date overview of the state of Britain, while also covering government policy in all the nation's spheres of activity. It is widely recognised as an established work of reference, both in Britain itself, and overseas, where it is an important element of the information service provided by British diplomatic posts. It is sold by The Stationery Office and its agents throughout the world.

Special features

As always, the text, charts, tables and graphs have all been fully updated and revised. This year has been a particularly interesting one because of the historic General Election in May 1997, which brought a Labour Government to power—with its largest ever majority—after 18 years of Conservative rule, the longest period of administration by one party since 1830. As a result, the policy changes now being implemented, or proposed, are more fundamental and wide-ranging than they have been for many years.

In this edition we celebrate the 50th anniversary of the National Health Service (NHS), a ground-breaking development in British medicine which has since influenced the organisation of health services all over the world. The introductory essay by Alan Langlands, Chief Executive of the NHS Executive in England, describes the history and evolution of this national institution, the problems it has faced and overcome, its many achievements, and what the future might have in store. Within the main body of the book, chapter 24 also gives comprehensive coverage of the current organisation of the NHS.

In addition, we have included a special feature on the Government Art Collection (see photograph and caption opposite). This comprises an eight-page colour section in the centre of the book and three images on the cover. The cover images are:

● *front cover*—Richard Ernst Eurich: 'The Rescue' (1971–4) (detail);

● *back cover*—Barbara Hepworth: 'Conoid Sphere and Hollow III' (1937); and

● *spine*—Robert Adams: 'Tall Spike Form' (1956).

Another innovation which we hope readers will find useful is the inclusion of individual country maps in the chapters on England, Northern Ireland, Scotland and Wales, which give the county, district, council and unitary authority boundaries at 1 April 1998. We have also expanded the list of historical dates in chapter 1.

Finally, we remember Diana, Princess of Wales (see photographs between pp. 64 and 65, and obituary on p. 539).

Coverage

Every effort is made to ensure that the information given in *The Britain Handbook* is accurate at the time of going to press. The text is generally based on information available up to September 1997.

As far as possible, the book applies to Britain as a whole, as the title suggests. However, care should be taken when using it to note whether the information given refers to:

● Britain, formally the United Kingdom of Great Britain and Northern Ireland;

- Great Britain, which comprises England, Wales and Scotland;

- England and Wales, which are still grouped together for many administrative and other purposes; or, in some instances,

- England alone.

Acknowledgments

Britain 1998 has been compiled with the full co-operation of around 250 organisations, including other government departments and agencies. The editor would like to thank all the people from these organisations who have taken so much time and care to ensure that the book's high standards of accuracy have been maintained. Their contributions and comments have been extremely valuable.

The book was researched, written, edited and proofread by an in-house team of four, backed up by a pool of experienced freelances. The in-house team comprised Nigel Pearce, Christine Winfield, Stephen Peace and Paul Webb; the main freelances were Henry Langley, Richard German, John Collis, Jole Cosgrove, Anthony Osley and Oliver Metcalf. The cover was designed by Michelle Franco of ONS Design, and the photographic sections and most of the other artwork by Ray Martin.

Readers' Comments

We welcome readers' comments and suggestions on *The Britain Handbook*. These should be sent to:

The Editor, The Britain Handbook Unit,
Office for National Statistics,
1 Drummond Gate, London SW1V 2QQ.

'Iona', by James McIntosh Patrick.

The works of art reproduced in this volume are part of the Government Art Collection of the United Kingdom, first established 100 years ago by HM Treasury, in 1898. Guided by an Advisory Committee, the Collection acquires historical, modern and contemporary British art, and commissions art for specific sites such as diplomatic missions overseas. It aims to promote understanding and appreciation of British culture and history, and provide a showcase for Britain's creative talent. The core of the Collection consists of some 12,000 works, displayed in 500 locations around the world.

The first in a series of summary catalogues devoted to the holdings of the Collection was published in April 1997, covering works of art created during the 20th century: *Government Art Collection of the United Kingdom: The Twentieth Century* (ISBN 0 9516468 3 4), Merrell Holberton Publishers Ltd, Willcox House, 42 Southwark Street, London SE1 1UN.

Fifty Years of the National Health Service in Britain

by Alan Langlands

Alan Langlands joined the National Health Service (NHS) as a graduate trainee in 1974 and is now the Chief Executive of the NHS Executive in England and Britain's most senior health service manager. As well as managing major teaching hospitals in London during his career, he has run a Regional Health Authority and been responsible for a major review of the top management of the NHS. Today, in recognition of his achievements, he is an honorary Professor at the University of Warwick Business School and an honorary Fellow of the Faculty of Public Health Medicine of the Royal College of Physicians. What follows is his personal account of the past, present and future of the NHS as it celebrates its 50th Anniversary in 1998.

Alan Langlands

Your new National Health Service begins on 5th July. It will provide you with all medical, dental, and nursing care. Everyone—rich or poor, man, woman or child—can use it or any part of it. There are no charges, except for a few special items. There are no insurance qualifications. But it is not a "charity". You are all paying for it, mainly as taxpayers, and it will relieve your money worries in time of illness.

—from a leaflet issued by the Ministry of Health, February 1948

On a typical day in Britain in 1998 nearly 700,000 people will visit their family doctor and about 130,000 people will visit their dentist. Over 130,000 people will be treated in hospital outpatient clinics, pharmacists will dispense about one-and-a-half million items on prescription, and around 2,000 babies will be delivered.

In over 300 district general hospitals surgeons will perform around 220 hip replacement and other arthroplasty of the hip operations, 750 operations on the heart and 2,100 kidney operations. Ambulances will make 8,000 emergency journeys. And 10,000 people will donate blood.

In the community, around 540,000 people will receive help at home from the NHS. District nurses will make over 100,000 visits and chiropodists will provide some 6,000 sessions each day in patients' homes.

Impressive as they are, statistics like these represent only a fraction of what is routinely achieved every day by the National Health Service. It is the same routine, more or less, that has been re-run twenty-four hours a day every day for the last fifty years. The scale on which the NHS operates today, and the financial and technical resources at its disposal, may have been undreamed of back in the 1940s, but its underlying principles have remained unchanged since the day it was founded.

Since 5 July 1948 the NHS has been charged with providing comprehensive healthcare for every person in the United Kingdom, young and old, men and women, rich and poor, and for improving the nation's health as a whole. Everyone born in this country has been, or will be, touched by the NHS at some point in their lives. As an institution it is one of the nation's greatest assets and success stories.

Indeed, the NHS is such an integral part of life in this country that many of us now take it for granted, until we need it and suddenly remember how reassuring its existence has become. But it has not always been like this, and as we celebrate its first fifty years it is worth reminding ourselves why the NHS began and what it set out to do.

Healthcare Before the NHS

The NHS was founded on the principle that healthcare should be provided according to a person's clinical need, not on their ability to pay. It is difficult today to imagine what life must have been like without free healthcare, and the difference it must have made to people's lives when it was first introduced. Fifty years ago, healthcare was a luxury not everyone could afford. Poor people often went without medical treatment, relying instead on often dubious (and sometimes dangerous) home remedies, or on the charity of doctors who gave their services free to their poorest patients.

The need for free healthcare was widely recognised, but it was impossible to achieve without the support or the resources of the state. Throughout the 19th century philanthropists and social reformers working in isolation had tried to provide free medical care for the poor. One such was William Marsden, a young surgeon, who in 1828 opened a 'dispensary for advice and medicines'. Marsden's grandly named London General Institution for the Gratuitous Cure of Malignant Diseases, an ordinary four-storey house in one of the poorest parts of the city, was conceived as 'a hospital to which the only passport should be poverty and disease', and where treatment would be provided free of charge to any destitute or sick person who asked for it.

The demand for Marsden's free services was overwhelming. By 1844 his dispensary, now renamed the Royal Free Hospital, was treating 30,000 patients a year. With consultant medical staff giving their services free of charge, and with money from legacies, donations, subscriptions and fund-raising events, the Royal Free (in much expanded premises) struggled to fulfil Marsden's vision until 1920 when, teetering on the edge of bankruptcy, it, too, was finally forced to ask patients to pay whatever they could towards their treatment, just like every other voluntary hospital in the country.

The Role of the Local Authorities

Alongside the charitable and voluntary hospitals, which mainly dealt with serious illnesses, the local authorities of large towns provided 'municipal' hospitals: maternity hospitals, hospitals for infectious diseases like tuberculosis and smallpox, and hospitals for the elderly, mentally ill and mentally handicapped. Many of these were a mixed blessing.

Mentally ill and mentally handicapped people were locked away in large forbidding institutions, not always for their own benefit but to save other people from embarrassment. Conditions were often so bad that many patients became worse, not better.

Older people who were no longer able to look after themselves also fared badly. Many ended their lives in the workhouse, a Victorian institution feared by everyone, where paupers did unpaid work in return for food and shelter. Workhouses changed their name to Public Assistance Institutions in 1929, but their character, and the stigma attached to them, remained.

The Birth of the NHS

With the voluntary hospitals permanently on the verge of financial collapse and the municipal hospitals almost universally loathed, there was no shortage of pressure for change. The first call for a national health service is usually attributed to Beatrice Webb, who argued the case for a 'state medical service' in a submission to the Royal Commission on the Poor Law in 1909. Over the next thirty years the case for reform was taken up and developed in a succession of key reports from the Ministry of Health, the British Medical Association and others, culminating in the ground-breaking Beveridge report of 1942.

Sir William Beveridge had been appointed by the Government to chair an inter-departmental committee to look into the existing national insurance schemes. He made no detailed recommendations about how a national health service should be run, but by identifying healthcare as one of the three basic prerequisites for a viable social security system, he laid the foundations for the NHS as we know it today.

The Beveridge report was followed by a White Paper, *A National Health Service*, published in 1944, which stated: 'Everybody, irrespective of means, age, sex or occupation, shall have equal opportunity to benefit from the best and most up-to-date medical and allied services available.' It said the services should be comprehensive and free of charge, and should promote good health as well as treating sickness and disease.

In 1945 came a second White Paper. The NHS Bill of March 1946 proposed the nationalisation of all the voluntary and municipal hospitals and the creation of 14 regional hospital boards to control them.

The National Health Service Act, steered through Parliament by Aneurin Bevan, the Minister of Health, became law on 6 November 1946. It laid the ground rules for the modern NHS: it was to be 'a comprehensive health service designed to secure improvements in the physical and mental health of the people of England and Wales and the prevention, diagnosis and treatment of illness', funded through general taxation rather than national insurance contributions.

Early Difficulties in Establishing the NHS

The NHS became reality on 5 July 1948. To appreciate the scale of the achievement it is worth remembering that Britain was at war with the Axis powers throughout the final years in which the organisation was being pieced together. (In fact, it was the Second World War which demonstrated that a centrally controlled health service could be run effectively.)

The NHS brought hospital services, family practitioner services (doctors, pharmacists, opticians, dentists) and community-based services into one organisation for the first time. But it had not been easy. Holding everything together and keeping everyone on board continued to be an administrative nightmare (Bevan described it as 'the chief headache') for years to come.

However, the difficulties of administering the new system paled in comparison to its financial problems, which became apparent almost immediately. It was impossible to predict the day-to-day costs of the new service, and public expectations rose. Spending in the first nine months was two-thirds higher than anticipated. 'The sea of unmet need', as one commentator has described it, threatened to engulf the new service. Other uncontrollable costs added to the burden: medical and technological progress—in new therapies, diagnostic techniques and equipment—was gathering pace all the time, and scarce new drugs, such as penicillin and other antibiotics, for which there was a huge demand, were still disproportionately expensive.

Within three years of its creation, the NHS, which had been conceived as being available to everyone free of direct charges, was forced to introduce some modest fees. Prescription charges of one shilling (5p), which had been legislated for as early as 1949 but had not been implemented, were introduced in June 1952. A flat rate of £1 for ordinary dental treatment was also introduced at that time.

Many of the difficulties that emerged in the early days of the NHS have challenged its senior management, and successive governments, ever since. Today the NHS has a workforce of over one million people and a budget of some £42 billion a year; it is a sophisticated modern organisation with all the advantages of state-of-the-art technology at its disposal. Yet the fundamental questions that tested Bevan and his colleagues—how best to organise and manage the service, how to fund it adequately, how to keep the often conflicting demands and expectations of patients, staff and taxpayers in check, how to ensure that finite resources are targeted where they are most needed—exercise us all to this day. Bevan foresaw all this. 'We never shall have all we need,' he said. 'Expectations will always exceed capacity. The service must always be changing, growing and improving: it must always appear inadequate.'

The Advantages to the Public of the New NHS System

Despite the problems that had been experienced in setting it up, the NHS transformed healthcare. The new arrangements enabled health professionals to work as teams in hospitals, health centres and people's homes and offer a complete range of care for each patient. The level of co-operation may have been rudimentary by today's standards of multi-disciplinary care, but it was revolutionary at the time.

The cornerstone of the new service was the family doctor or general practitioner (GP). 'Everyone aged 16 and over can choose his or her own doctor,' explained the Ministry of Health in 1948. 'You will visit his surgery, or he will call on you, as may be necessary. The difference is that the doctor will be paid by the Government, out of funds provided by everybody.'

Then, as now, the family doctor acted as 'gate-keeper' to the rest of the NHS, referring patients where appropriate to hospital or specialist treatment, and prescribing medicines, drugs 'and all necessary appliances'. In addition, expectant mothers could have the services of 'a doctor who undertakes maternity work, and of a midwife, as well as general care before and after confinement'. Today there are 29,000 GPs, mostly working in group practices and supported by a team of practice nurses and other staff.

Some of the services the family doctor could arrange were provided by the local authorities—county councils and county borough councils—who were charged with making special provision for the care of expectant and nursing mothers and children under five, and for providing midwifery services, home nursing, all necessary vaccination or immunisation, and a health visitor service 'to deal with problems of illness in the home, especially tuberculosis'.

The family doctor also arranged hospital care. Patients were entitled to all forms of in-patient and out-patient treatment in general or special hospitals, including maternity care, sanatorium treatment, care of mental health, and all surgical operations, plus the help of consultants and specialists of all kinds, 'whether at hospital, at special health centres, or at your home'.

Dental services consisted of check-ups and all necessary fillings and dentures. There was a school dental service and a special priority service for expectant and nursing mothers and young children which was organised by the local authorities. Eye tests were provided by ophthalmic opticians on production of a GP referral note; if a person needed glasses, the NHS could provide 'several kinds of spectacles of different types'.

A major innovation was the notion of the community health centre—'special premises' with accommodation and equipment supplied from public funds to enable family doctors, dentists and others to work together to provide a range of services on the spot. There were also specialist ear clinics at which the patient would get 'an expert opinion upon deafness' and, if necessary, 'a new hearing aid invented by a special committee of the Medical Research Council'.

What the NHS has Achieved

In its first fifty years the NHS has ushered in dramatic improvements in healthcare: it has introduced national immunisation programmes that have all but eradicated potentially fatal diseases such as measles, polio, meningitis, diphtheria and tuberculosis; it has presided over the first combined heart, lung, liver and kidney transplants, and operations to replace hips and other joints that have given thousands of people a second lease of life; it has delivered the first babies born by *in vitro* fertilisation. The list of major achievements in medicine and science goes on and on.

An equally important, though often overlooked, achievement has been the way the NHS has provided much of that care; how its willingness and ability to adapt to the changing needs of the population and changing attitudes in society have enabled it to find ways of keeping up with, for example, an ageing population, advances in technology, and changes in clinical practice.

For some people the type of care they receive has changed beyond recognition under the NHS. New drug regimes and the growth of networks of community-based health and social services—provided in collaboration with local authorities, housing associations and voluntary organisations—have given people with a mental illness or learning disability the chance to live as independently as possible in their own neighbourhoods, where they are able to make the kinds of day-to-day choices and decisions that institutional life usually denied them. Older people have benefited from the development of community-based services from district nurses, physiotherapists, chiropodists and others who give them the care and support they need to live with dignity in their own homes for as long as possible. Closing down the crumbling Victorian asylums and long-stay hospitals—considered by many to be a national disgrace—is probably the greatest legacy the NHS has made to future generations.

In surgery, developments such as shorter-acting anaesthetics and 'keyhole' or endoscopic procedures have had a wide-ranging impact on the way hospital care is provided. Even ten years ago, a three-week stay after a routine operation was common, adding to the traditional image of the hospital as a dormitory or hotel as much as a provider of treatment.

Nowadays, shorter recovery times and shorter stays mean that people are able to resume their everyday lives much more quickly. For most people, going into hospital no longer means taking weeks off work or being away from friends and loved ones for extended periods. In 1994–95, 24 per cent of all people treated in hospital were day cases and the proportion is expected to increase further. This year every health authority is expected to provide at least 60 per cent of all non-urgent ('elective') surgery on a day basis.

Developments such as these are encouraging the growing trend away from healthcare provided in hospitals to primary care that is provided in the local community, closer to where people live or in their own homes.

Health Promotion and Prevention of Illness

Treating ill-health and its consequences is only one part of what the NHS does. It is also charged with promoting good health, and in recent years has introduced a wide range of initiatives to encourage people to stay fit and healthy. Anti-smoking campaigns alone have saved thousands of people from lung cancer, bronchitis, emphysema, strokes and heart disease, whilst campaigns extolling the benefits of a well-balanced diet and plenty of exercise have led to a healthier lifestyle for many. National screening programmes have been introduced to screen all women aged between 20 and 64 for cervical cancer at least every five years, and all women aged between 50 and 64 for breast cancer every three years.

Preventing disease rather than waiting to cure people once they are ill makes good sense for several reasons:

● it stops people becoming seriously ill, and so reduces the need for hospital services;

● it reduces the number of working days lost through sickness absence (estimated to cost Britain some £13 billion a year);

- the cost of preventing illness is cheaper than treating it with drugs or surgery; and
- for some diseases, such as AIDS, there is no alternative to prevention.

Since 1992 NHS policy on disease prevention and health promotion has been driven by targets laid down in *The Health of the Nation*, a strategy to improve health in England by the year 2000, which the new Government has said it will extend and update radically. Similar strategies are in place for Scotland, Wales and Northern Ireland. As we approach the Millennium it is clear that, while excellent progress has been made towards many of the targets, there are still areas—such as teenage smoking—where more work needs to be done.

The Cost of Healthcare

The medical advances which have taken place in the past fifty years have revolutionised healthcare and greatly increased our understanding of the causes of illness and disease. Today, we can treat more diseases than ever before, and in many cases prevent them occurring in the first place. Men and women now live longer; more babies survive the critical period just before or just after birth; and it is rare for people to catch diseases such as poliomyelitis, diphtheria and tuberculosis, let alone die from them.

Future developments in healthcare look even more promising. Advances in cell and molecular science and advanced bio-engineering foresee treatments for chronic conditions such as psychiatric illness, multiple sclerosis and arthritis.

Today clinicians can do more, try more, than ever. And as each new breakthrough takes root, the public's expectations of the NHS grow even greater. Pressure on services is rising inexorably. In 1994–95 there were around 10.5 million new referrals to hospital and 18 million people were treated at accident and emergency departments. Surgeons performed over 3.6 million operations and hospitals provided around 13 million completed episodes of care. Last year in England demand for non-elective services rose by 4.5 per cent, and demand for mental health services rose by 5 per cent.

Statistics like these help to explain why the NHS is now the second largest spending programme in the country. Over the past 20 years successive governments have raised NHS expenditure in Britain by an average of 3 per cent per annum in real terms. In 1997–98 the total cost of the NHS was £36 billion in England and £42 billion for Britain as a whole—more than £1,700 for every household in the country. Ninety-four per cent of this money is raised from direct taxation, through either income tax or National Insurance contributions. This ensures that employers in Britain benefit from low direct costs, in contrast to schemes based on private insurance (as in the USA) or social insurance (adopted in some countries in Europe).

Managers and senior clinicians in the NHS are responsible for ensuring that these huge resources are spent as effectively and efficiently as possible whilst making sure that health services are available to everyone on the basis of clinical need. Maintaining this delicate balance at a time when people rightly expect high-quality services which are organised and run around their individual needs rather than the convenience of the system is the enduring challenge of the NHS.

The fact that the NHS continues to meet the challenge is a tribute to the dedication and professionalism of all those who work in it; in fact, in a recent report from the OECD the NHS was recognised as 'a remarkably cost-effective institution'. It achieves health outcomes comparable to those achieved in other countries with similar or higher incomes, and at a cost in terms of share of national income (5.5 per cent of UK Gross Domestic Product in 1996–97) that is significantly lower than in most other countries. Furthermore, productivity across the NHS has risen by more than 40 per cent over the past twenty years, broadly in line with trends across the economy as a whole. In the 1990s the service has delivered average increases in efficiency of 2 per cent a year including, since 1994–95, reductions in management costs of some £350 million.

Shortly after taking office the present Government announced a comprehensive spending review. One of the things the review will consider is the contribution the NHS makes to the well-being of the economy as a whole, something that has never been fully investigated. This is surprising, given that the NHS is responsible for helping to keep Britain at work—literally. It is the biggest single employer in Europe, one of the cornerstones of the British pharmaceutical industry, has a huge capital investment programme, and spends some £440 million a year on research and development. After fifty years in existence, the idea that the NHS is a giant sponge that simply soaks up public money and gives nothing back to the economy looks like being laid to rest at last.

Two Decades of Change

One of the myths about the NHS is that it has been in a state of organisational turmoil since the day it was created. In truth, there was relative stability for the first thirty years. But in the 1970s two major reorganisations within a decade saw different administrative layers come and go.

The 1974 reorganisation introduced a three-tier management system to England, consisting of regional health authorities, 90 area health authorities and 206 district management teams, each of which would manage its affairs collectively ('consensus management'). Community health services that had previously been provided by local authorities—such as district nurses, immunisation and vaccination, school health and ambulance services—were transferred to the NHS. Five years later the Government decided to remove the area tier and create 192 new district health authorities in its place.

In 1983 the Government asked a leading businessman, Sir Roy Griffiths, to scrutinise the NHS's management procedures. 'If Florence Nightingale were carrying her lamp through the corridors of the NHS today, she would almost certainly be searching for the people in charge,' he wrote. Griffiths recommended abandoning decision-making by consensus and replacing administrators with general managers with clear performance targets. Doctors would be involved in running their budgets, and treatments would be evaluated to make sure they were cost-efficient and clinically effective. The ideas that emerged from Griffiths—the insistence on value for money, and on the link between funding and the quality and quantity of healthcare—have guided the development of the NHS ever since.

It was against this background that, in 1988, there began a fundamental review of every aspect of the NHS, from the way services were delivered to the way they were paid for. The resulting White Paper, *Working for Patients*, introduced the concept of the internal market whereby, from 1991, the 'providers' of healthcare were to be separated from the 'purchasers' of healthcare. The idea was that by giving the purchasers the freedom to choose where to buy the best care, including the private sector, the system would place competitive pressure on the providers to offer greater quality, efficiency and value for money.

Fundamental changes had to be made to the traditional relationships between the various parts of the NHS to make the new system work. Health authorities ceased to run the service directly and became 'purchasers' of healthcare on behalf of their populations from a range of 'providers' (hospitals, community services, ambulance services) who, in turn, were given the opportunity of becoming NHS Trusts—self-governing bodies with the freedom to decide things like staff numbers, rates of pay and what to charge for their services. (Though independent of health authority control, Trusts remain part of the NHS and are ultimately accountable to the Secretary of State for Health.)

A central role in the new system was reserved for family doctors who, for the first time, were offered budgets to buy a range of services for their own patients, such as elective (non-emergency) surgery, out-patient treatment and specialist nursing care. Family doctors could become 'fundholders' and negotiate annual contracts with providers of healthcare, making them competitors with health authorities as purchasers of healthcare.

To its supporters, like some of the fundholders themselves, this meant unprecedented freedom to obtain the best for patients, control budgets and shape what hospitals did. Opponents believed it was creating a two-tier system, in which patients of non-fundholders had to wait longer for hospital treatment than patients of fundholders, and which placed fundholders under pressure to buy cheap care before effective care.

Looking to the Future: What Next?

The Government elected on 1 May 1997 pledged itself to ending the internal market and developing an alternative organisational model. It has recommitted itself unequivocally to the principle of universality in healthcare and has stated that, 'if you are ill or injured there will be a National Health Service there to help; and access to it will be based on need and need alone, not on your ability to pay, or on who your GP happens to be, or on where you live.' The new system will reinforce the underlying values of equity, efficiency and responsiveness, and will take account of the need to provide incentives that will ensure an integrated approach to health and social care, with financial control systems that maintain clear lines of public and parliamentary accountability. It will also be flexible enough to deal with changing circumstances and to encourage innovation at local level.

The Government has also committed itself to increasing NHS spending every year, to achieving higher-quality standards in the provision of care, and to maintaining a leading role for primary care. These commitments will drive NHS policy for the next five years.

As Chief Executive of the NHS Executive in England, it is my job to make sure that the Government's objectives are met, so that during the next five to ten years the NHS will provide genuinely integrated preventative care, treatment and after-care; that we will plan and deliver healthcare which is more effective and responsive to people's needs; that we will provide good services at a local level, serving people in or as close as possible to their homes, but offering treatment and care in more specialist centres where this is required. My colleagues in Scotland, Wales and Northern Ireland will be working towards the same ends. Our approach will be based on the flexible working of health and social care professionals rather than one which revolves around institutions.

The NHS has come a long way in its first fifty years. Its very existence is the mark of a civilised society. Yet no society has the ability to provide every treatment that patients would wish. How, and to what extent, the NHS will be funded in future is, as ever, a matter of ongoing debate. One thing is clear: difficult choices will have to be made about patient and service priorities, and ultimately they will have to carry public support. I am equally clear that the first duty of the NHS is to respond to those in greatest need.

The NHS has retained the allegiance of the people to an extent that cannot be matched by other public systems: a 1996 public opinion poll found that 86 per cent of people believed that the NHS is the most important of our public services for them and their families. Furthermore, throughout the world, no better model than the NHS has been found for adapting to change and for making the best use of available resources to meet the demand for healthcare. As it celebrates its fiftieth anniversary, that is probably the best tribute it could receive.

1 Introduction

Britain comprises Great Britain (England, Wales and Scotland) and Northern Ireland, and is one of the 15 member states of the European Union (EU). Its full name is the United Kingdom of Great Britain and Northern Ireland.

Physical Features

Britain constitutes the greater part of the British Isles. The largest of the islands is Great Britain. The next largest comprises Northern Ireland, and the Irish Republic. Western Scotland is fringed by the large island chain known as the Hebrides, and to the north east of the Scottish mainland are the Orkney and Shetland Islands. All these, along with the Isle of Wight, Anglesey and the Isles of Scilly, have administrative ties with the mainland, but the Isle of Man in the Irish Sea and the Channel Islands between Great Britain and France are largely self-governing, and are not part of the United Kingdom.

With an area of about 242,000 sq km (93,000 sq miles), Britain is just under 1,000 km (about 600 miles) from the south coast to the extreme north of Scotland and just under 500 km (around 300 miles) across at the widest point.

Channel Islands and Isle of Man

Although the Channel Islands and the Isle of Man are not part of the United Kingdom, they have a special relationship with it. The Channel Islands were part of the Duchy of Normandy in the 10th and 11th centuries and remained subject to the English Crown after the final loss of Normandy to the French in the 15th century. The Isle of Man was under the nominal sovereignty of Norway until 1266, and eventually came under the direct administration of the British Crown in 1765. Today the territories have their own legislative assemblies and systems of law; the Isle of Man also has its own system of taxation. The British Government is responsible for their international relations and external defence.

Geographical Facts

- Highest mountain: Ben Nevis, in the highlands of Scotland, at 1,343 m (4,406 ft)
- Longest river: the Severn, 354 km (220 miles) long, which rises in central Wales and flows through Shrewsbury, Worcester and Gloucester in England to the Bristol Channel
- Largest lake: Lough Neagh, Northern Ireland, at 396 sq km (153 sq miles)
- Highest waterfall: Eas a'Chual Aluinn, from Glas Bheinn, in the highlands of Scotland, with a drop of 200 m (660 ft)
- Deepest cave: Ogof Ffynnon Ddu, Wales, at 308 m (1,010 ft) deep
- Most northerly point on the British mainland: Dunnet Head, north-east Scotland
- Most southerly point on the British mainland: Lizard Point, Cornwall
- Closest point to mainland continental Europe: Dover, Kent. The Channel Tunnel, which links England and France, is a little over 31 miles (50 km) long, of which nearly 24 miles (38 km) are actually under the Channel.

Climate and Wildlife

The climate in Britain is generally mild and temperate. Prevailing winds are south-westerly and the weather from day to day is mainly influenced by depressions moving eastwards across the Atlantic. The weather is subject to frequent changes. In general, there are few extremes of temperature; it rarely rises above 32°C (90°F) or falls below –10°C (14°F).

Average annual rainfall is more than 1,600 mm (over 60 inches) in the mountainous areas of the west and north but less than 800 mm (30 inches) over central and eastern parts. Rain is fairly well distributed throughout the year but, on average, March to June are the driest months and September to January the wettest. During May, June and July (the months of longest daylight) the mean daily duration of sunshine varies from five hours in northern Scotland to eight hours in the Isle of Wight. During the months of shortest daylight (November, December and January) sunshine is at a minimum, with an average of an hour a day in northern Scotland and two hours a day on the south coast of England.

As in much of the rest of the world, the temperatures in Britain have been rising over recent years. The 12-month period from November 1994 to October 1995 was the warmest in the 330-year temperature record for central England; and the 24 months from May 1995 to April 1997 were the driest two-year period in the 230-year rainfall record for England and Wales. These changes in climate may be arising partly from increasing emissions of greenhouse gases, although it is still too early to be certain about this.

Meanwhile, there is some evidence to suggest that the British spring is arriving on average one week earlier in the 1990s than it did in the 1970s. Certainly, some 20 bird species have been laying their eggs earlier each year since 1971 (although the stock dove is laying significantly later).

Britain is home to a great variety of wildlife, with an estimated 30,000 animal species, as well as marine and microscopic life; about 2,800 species of 'higher' plants; and many thousands of mosses, fungi and algae. However, the unusual weather of recent years—together with other factors, such as changes in farming methods—has put pressure on a number of species. There are currently 116 separate biodiversity species action plans being implemented by the Government, with the aim of conserving species and their habitats. In January 1997, the Joint Nature Conservation Committee recommended that a further 33 species—including the water vole, basking shark, marsh fritillary butterfly, bluebell and sandy stilt puffball—be given added protection to ensure their continued survival in Britain (see pp. 361–3).

Historical Outline

The name 'Britain' derives from Greek and Latin names probably stemming from a Celtic original. Although in the prehistoric timescale the Celts were relatively late arrivals in the British Isles, only with them does Britain emerge into recorded history. The term 'Celtic' is often used rather generally to distinguish the early inhabitants of the British Isles from the later Anglo-Saxon invaders.

After two expeditions by Julius Caesar in 55 and 54 BC, contact between Britain and the Roman world grew, culminating in the Roman invasion of AD 43. Roman rule was gradually extended from south-east England to include Wales and, for a time, the lowlands of Scotland. The final Roman withdrawal in 409 followed a period of increasing disorder during which the island began to be raided by Angles, Saxons and Jutes from northern Europe. It is from the Angles that the name 'England' derives. The raids turned into settlement and a number of small English kingdoms were established. The Britons maintained an independent existence in the areas now known as Wales and Cornwall. Among these kingdoms more powerful ones emerged, claiming overlordship over the whole country, first in the north (Northumbria), then in the midlands (Mercia) and finally in the south (Wessex). However, further raids and settlement by the Vikings from Scandinavia occurred, although in the 10th century the Wessex dynasty defeated the invading Danes and established a wide-ranging authority in England. In 1066 England was invaded by the Normans (see p. 6), who then settled along with others from France.

Dates of some of the main events in Britain's history are given below and on the next page. The early histories of England, Wales, Scotland and Northern Ireland are included in chapters 2 to 5, which also deal with the main aspects of their social, economic and political life. Additional material is included on the political situation in Northern Ireland. Table 1.1 (see p. 5) gives a selection of some of the main statistics for each of the four lands.

Significant Dates

55 and 54 BC: Julius Caesar's expeditions to Britain

AD 43: Roman conquest begins under Claudius

122–38: Hadrian's Wall built

c.409: Roman army withdraws from Britain

450s onwards: foundation of the Anglo-Saxon kingdoms

597: arrival of St Augustine to preach Christianity to the Anglo-Saxons

664: Synod of Whitby opts for Roman Catholic rather than Celtic church

789–95: first Viking raids

832–60: Scots and Picts merge under Kenneth Macalpin to form what is to become the kingdom of Scotia

860s: Danes overrun East Anglia, Northumbria and eastern Mercia

871–99: reign of Alfred the Great in Wessex

1066: William the Conqueror defeats Harold Godwinson at Hastings and takes the throne

1215: King John signs Magna Carta to protect feudal rights against royal abuse

13th century: first Oxford and Cambridge colleges founded

1301: Edward of Caernarvon (later Edward II) created Prince of Wales

1314: battle of Bannockburn ensures survival of separate Scottish kingdom

1337: Hundred Years War between England and France begins

1348–49: Black Death (bubonic plague) wipes out a third of England's population

1381: Peasants' Revolt in England, the most significant popular rebellion in English history

c.1387–c.1394: Geoffrey Chaucer writes *The Canterbury Tales*

1400–c.1406: Owain Glyndŵr (Owen Glendower) leads the last major Welsh revolt against English rule

1411: St Andrews University founded, the first university in Scotland

1455–87: Wars of the Roses between Yorkists and Lancastrians

1477: first book to be printed in England, by William Caxton

1534–40: English Reformation; Henry VIII breaks with the Papacy

1536–42: Acts of Union integrate England and Wales administratively and legally and give Wales representation in Parliament

1547–53: Protestantism becomes official religion in England under Edward VI

1553–58: Catholic reaction under Mary I

1558: loss of Calais, last English possession in France

1588: defeat of Spanish Armada

1558–1603: reign of Elizabeth I; moderate Protestantism established

c.1590–c.1613: plays of Shakespeare written

1598: first undisputed reference to the game of cricket

1603: union of the two crowns under James VI of Scotland

1642–51: Civil Wars between King and Parliament

1649: execution of Charles I

1653–58: Oliver Cromwell rules as Lord Protector

1660: monarchy restored under Charles II

1660: founding of the Royal Society for the Promotion of Natural Knowledge

1663: John Milton finishes *Paradise Lost*

1665: the Great Plague, the last major epidemic of plague in England

1666: the Great Fire of London

1686: Isaac Newton unveils his laws of motion and the idea of universal gravitation

1688: Glorious Revolution; accession of William and Mary

1707: Act of Union unites England and Scotland

1721–42: Robert Walpole, first British Prime Minister

1745–46: Bonnie Prince Charlie's failed attempt to retake the British throne for the Stuarts

c.1760s–c.1830s: Industrial Revolution

1761: opening of the Bridgewater Canal ushers in Canal Age

1775–83: American War of Independence leads to loss of the Thirteen Colonies

1801: Act of Union unites Great Britain and Ireland

1805: Battle of Trafalgar, the decisive naval battle of the Napoleonic Wars

1815: Battle of Waterloo, the final defeat of Napoleon

1821: John Constable paints 'The Haywain'

1825: opening of the Stockton and Darlington Railway, the world's first passenger railway

1829: Catholic emancipation

1832: First Reform Act extends the franchise (increasing the number of those entitled to vote by about 50 per cent)

1833: Abolition of slavery in the British Empire (the slave *trade* having been abolished in 1807)

1837–1901: reign of Queen Victoria

1836–70: Charles Dickens writes his novels

1859: Charles Darwin publishes *On the Origin of Species by Means of Natural Selection*

1868: founding of the Trades Union Congress (TUC)

1907: Henry Royce and C. S. Rolls build and sell their first Rolls-Royce (the Silver Ghost)

1910–36: during the reign of George V, the British Empire reaches its territorial zenith

1914–18: First World War

1918: the vote given to women over 30

1921: Anglo-Irish Treaty establishes the Irish Free State; Northern Ireland remains part of the United Kingdom

1926: John Logie Baird gives the first practical demonstration of television

1928: voting age for women reduced to 21, on equal terms with men

1928: Alexander Fleming discovers penicillin

1936: Jarrow Crusade, the most famous of the hunger marches in the 1930s

1939–45: Second World War

1943: Max Newman, Donald Michie and Alan Turing build the first electronic computer, Colossus I, which was used for breaking enemy communications codes in the Second World War

1947: Independence for India and Pakistan: Britain begins to dismantle its imperial structure

1948: the National Health Service comes into operation, offering free medical care to the whole population

1952: accession of Elizabeth II

1953: Francis Crick and his colleague James Watson of the United States discover the structure of DNA

1958: Empire Day is renamed Commonwealth Day

1963: The Beatles top the British charts (Hit Parade) for the first time and go on to achieve worldwide fame

1973: Britain enters European Community (now the European Union)

1979–90: Margaret Thatcher, Britain's first woman Prime Minister

1997: General Election: the Labour Party returns to power with its largest ever parliamentary majority

1997: In separate referendums, Scotland and Wales vote for devolution

Table 1.1: General Statistics

	England	Wales	Scotland	Northern Ireland	Britain
Population (1996)('000)	49,089	2,921	5,149	1,663	58,823
Area (sq km)*	130,423	20,766	77,080	13,483	241,752
Population density (persons per sq km)	376	141	67	123	243
Gross domestic product (£ per head, 1995)	10,324	8,440	9,873	8,410	10,134
Employees (LFS) ('000, spring 1997)	19,395	1,038	2,014	556	23,003
Percentage of employees (spring 1997) in:					
services	72.8	69.9	71.6	70.6	72.5
manufacturing	20.6	22.9	18.4	19.6	20.5
construction	4.5	4.9	6.3	7.3	4.7
energy & water	1.0	1.5	2.5	0.9	1.2
agriculture & fishing	0.9	0.8	1.2	0.8	0.9
Unemployment rate (LFS) (per cent, not seasonally adjusted, spring 1997)	6.9	8.4	8.5	7.5	7.5

Source: Office for National Statistics
*Figures for area are not on a strictly comparable basis; those for England and Wales include inland water, while those for Scotland and Northern Ireland are for the land area only.

Further reading

Statlas UK: A Statistical Atlas of the United Kingdom. HMSO, 1995.
Annual Abstract of Statistics, ONS. The Stationery Office, 1998.

2   England

England is predominantly a lowland country, although there are upland regions in the north (the Pennine Chain, the Cumbrian mountains and the Yorkshire moorlands) and in the South West, in Cornwall, Devon and Somerset. The greatest concentrations of population are in London and the South East, South and West Yorkshire, Greater Manchester and Merseyside, the West Midlands conurbation, the north-east conurbations on the rivers Tyne and Tees, and along parts of the Channel coast. England's population is expected to rise from 48.9 million in 1995 to 51.2 million in 2016.

Early History

The name 'England' is derived from the Angles, one of the Germanic tribes which established monarchies in lowland Britain in the 5th century, after the final withdrawal of the Romans in 409. The Anglo–Saxon kingdoms were initially fairly small and numerous, but gradually larger entities emerged. Eventually Wessex came to dominate, following its leading role in resisting the Danish invasions of the 9th century. Athelstan (924–39) used the title of 'King of all Britain', and from 954 there was a single Kingdom of England. The present Royal Family is descended from the old royal house of Wessex.

In 1066 the last successful invasion of England took place. Duke William of Normandy defeated the English at the Battle of Hastings, and Normans and others from France came to settle. French became the language of the nobility for the next three centuries, and the legal and social structures were influenced by those prevailing across the Channel.

Almost all the English Crown's possessions in France were lost during the late Middle Ages. The union of England and Scotland took place in 1707, leaving England as the most populous part of the British nation state.

Government

In contrast to Wales, Scotland and Northern Ireland, England has no government minister or department exclusively responsible for its central administration. Instead, there are a number of government departments, whose responsibilities in some cases also cover aspects of affairs in Wales and Scotland (see Appendix 1). A network of ten Government Offices for the Regions (GORs—see p. 9) is responsible for the implementation of several government programmes in the English regions.[1]

---

[1] However, for statistical purposes, Merseyside and the North West are sometimes treated as one region. This is because of the difficulties associated with obtaining the full range of data for Merseyside alone, since it is a relatively small area.

England: Counties and Unitary Authorities, 1 April 1998

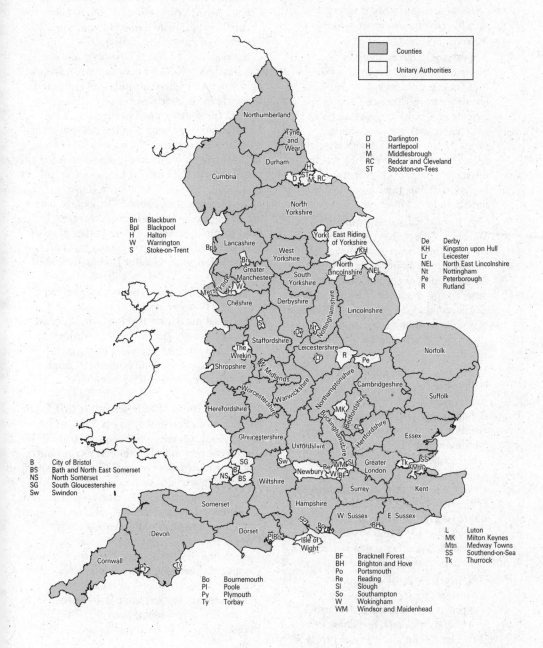

Counties

Unitary Authorities

Northumberland

Tyne and Wear

Durham

Cumbria

D Darlington
H Hartlepool
M Middlesbrough
RC Redcar and Cleveland
ST Stockton-on-Tees

North Yorkshire

Bn Blackburn
Bpl Blackpool
H Halton
W Warrington
S Stoke-on-Trent

Lancashire

West Yorkshire

York

East Riding of Yorkshire

KH

Bpl

Bn

Greater Manchester

South Yorkshire

North Lincolnshire

NEL

De Derby
KH Kingston upon Hull
Lr Leicester
NEL North East Lincolnshire
Nt Nottingham
Pe Peterborough
R Rutland

Merseyside

W

H

Cheshire

Derbyshire

De

Nt

Lincolnshire

The Wrekin

Staffordshire

Leicestershire

Lr

R

Pe

Norfolk

Shropshire

W. Midlands

Worcestershire

Warwickshire

Northamptonshire

Cambridgeshire

Suffolk

Herefordshire

MK

Bedfordshire

Gloucestershire

Oxfordshire

Buckinghamshire

Hertfordshire

Essex

B City of Bristol
BS Bath and North East Somerset
NS North Somerset
SG South Gloucestershire
Sw Swindon

SG

B

Sw

WM

SI

Re

W

BF

Greater London

Tk

Mtn

SS

NS

BS

Wiltshire

Newbury

Surrey

Kent

Somerset

Hampshire

W. Sussex

E. Sussex

Devon

Dorset

So

Po

Pl

Bo

Isle of Wight

BH

L Luton
MK Milton Keynes
Mtn Medway Towns
SS Southend-on-Sea
Tk Thurrock

Cornwall

Py

Ty

BF Bracknell Forest
BH Brighton and Hove
Po Portsmouth
Re Reading
SI Slough
So Southampton
W Wokingham
WM Windsor and Maidenhead

Bo Bournemouth
Pl Poole
Py Plymouth
Ty Torbay

History Around Us

A large number of important archaeological discoveries were made in England during 1997, of which the following are some of the most notable:

- A royal Anglo-Saxon tomb in Northamptonshire, dating from the mid-7th century. Archaeologists have unearthed a steel-surfaced iron sword, a ceremonial bowl, and an iron helmet with nose guard, crescent-shaped cheek guards and a wild boar-shaped crest. This 'boar helmet', of a type often mentioned in Old English literature, is only the second ever to have been found in Europe.

- Two Roman villas near Swindon in Wiltshire. One of them, to the north of the town, may prove to be the largest villa in Britain dating from the final century of Roman occupation. The other site, to the south of Swindon, has already produced a double-handled jar, probably for holding beer, and the finely carved bone handle of a folding razor.

- What appears to be a platform, walkway or raft, over 6,400 years old, in Hayling Bay, Hampshire. The same diving team that located the Tudor warship, the *Mary Rose*, 17 years ago has discovered a large structure at the edge of where the sea level was at the time, by the ancient river Solent. The structure is certainly worked timber rather than natural wood. If it turns out to be a raft, it would be one of the oldest ships ever found anywhere in the world, but either way it is a find of great archaeological significance.

- The largest series of dinosaur footprints ever found in Britain. The footprints were discovered by chance in a quarry in Dorset, on National Trust land. The series is made up of 52 prints, the biggest of which is 1.13 metres (44 inches) in diameter. They belong to sauropods, vegetarian dinosaurs who lived in the area over 140 million years ago.

Following a boundary review in 1995, there are now 529 English parliamentary constituencies represented in the House of Commons. After the General Election of 1 May 1997, England had 328 Labour Members of Parliament (MPs), 165 Conservative, 34 Liberal Democrat and one independent.[2] Conservative support tends to be strongest in suburban and rural areas, and the party has a large number of parliamentary seats in the southern half of England. The Labour Party has tended in the past to derive its main support from the big cities and areas associated with traditional industry, but it won many seats in the General Election that had previously been considered safe Conservative constituencies. The Liberal Democrats, who are strong in the South West, have recently been gaining greater support in other parts of England, and the party now has a third of its 34 English seats in Greater London and the South East.

Local government is mainly administered through a two-tier system of counties subdivided into districts. However, there are a number of single-tier, or unitary, authorities —especially in larger cities. The current restructuring of local government in England, now well advanced, will be completed in 1998 (see p. 80).

England elects 71 representatives (MEPs) to the European Parliament (see p. 116), which meets in full session in Strasbourg for about one week every month, although its committee work normally takes place in Brussels.

The English legal system comprises on the one hand a historic body of conventions known as 'common law' and 'equity', and, on the other, parliamentary and European Community (EC) legislation. In the formulation of common law since the Norman Conquest, great reliance has been placed on precedent. Equity law—law outside the scope of the common law or statute law—derives from the practice of petitioning the Lord Chancellor in cases not covered by common law.

---

[2] The Speaker of the House of Commons, who presides over the debates there (see pp. 59 and 64), traditionally does not vote along party lines and so is not counted towards the strength of the party for which he or she was originally elected. The independent MP is the former journalist Martin Bell, who won what had been the safe Conservative seat of Tatton in Cheshire.

The Church of England, which was separated from the Roman Catholic Church at the time of the Reformation in the early 16th century, is the Established Church (that is, the official religion of England). The Sovereign must always be a member of the Church and appoints its two archbishops and 42 other diocesan bishops (see pp. 460–1).

The Regions of England Covered by the GORs

The Economy

Considerable changes in the economy of England have occurred during the 20th century. In the past 50 years, jobs in service industries have grown and now account for three-quarters of employees in employment, with expansion having been particularly noticeable in financial and business services. Services account for three-quarters of gross domestic product (GDP) in London and the South East, and over a quarter of employees in Greater London work in financial services. London is one of the world's leading centres of banking, insurance and other financial services.

Manufacturing, although declining as a proportion of the employment base, remains important in a number of areas. In terms of GDP, it is most significant in the West Midlands (where manufacturing accounted for 31 per cent of the region's GDP in 1995, as opposed to 22 per cent in the country as a whole), the North and the East Midlands.

In agriculture, dairying is most common in the west of England; sheep and cattle are reared in the hilly and moorland areas of the North and South West. Arable farming, pig and poultry farming and horticulture are concentrated in the east and south.

As part of its plans to devolve more power to the regions, the new Government intends to set up Regional Development Agencies which,

Table 2.1: Population and Population Density Mid-1996

GOR*	Population	Area (sq km)	People per sq km
North East	2,600,500	8,592	303
North West	5,470,800	13,510	405
Merseyside	1,420,400	655	2,169
Yorkshire and the Humber	5,035,500	15,411	327
East Midlands	4,141,500	15,627	265
West Midlands	5,316,600	13,004	409
Eastern	5,292,600	19,120	277
London	7,074,300	1,578	4,483
South East	7,895,300	19,096	413
South West	4,841,500	23,829	203
England	**49,089,100**	**130,423**	**376**

Source: Office for National Statistics
*The region covered by each Government Office for the Region in England.

Table 2.2: Percentage Change in Population, Housing Stock and Employment

	Population 1981–95	Housing stock 1981–95	Employment[a] 1981–95
North East	−1.2	7.8	−7.3
North West	1.0	8.9	−1.0
Merseyside	−6.2	4.1	−20.6
Yorkshire and the Humber	2.3	9.8	1.8
East Midlands	7.0	15.2	5.5
West Midlands	2.3	10.6	−0.7
Eastern	8.3	18.1	8.5
London	3.0	11.6	−10.3
South East	8.3	17.2	9.4
South West	10.2	18.5	12.8
England	**4.4**	**13.0**	**0.6**

Source: *Regional Trends*, Office for National Statistics
[a]Employees in employment only; figures do not include the self-employed.

among other things, would promote regeneration, inward investment and small businesses in their regions (see p. 371).

Transport

The motorway network comprises four long-distance routes linking London and the cities of the Midlands, the North and North West, and the South West; the London orbital route (M25); and over 30 shorter motorways. In all, there are about 2,800 km (1,750 miles) of motorway in England, plus about 7,700 km (4,800 miles) of other trunk roads.

Virtually the entire railway system has now been privatised. The Government plans to strengthen regulation of the private train-operating companies, and of the infrastructure company, Railtrack, which was floated on the Stock Exchange in May 1996.

Cultural and Social Affairs

London and the other large cities have a wealth of cultural centres, including major art galleries, many renowned museums, theatres, ballet and opera houses, and concert halls. Many theatres outside London are used for touring by the national theatre, dance and opera companies. Popular culture also thrives in England, as elsewhere in Britain: there are numerous kinds of pop music, theatre styles such as pantomime and musicals, jazz festivals

and performances by comedians. Safari, wildlife and theme parks all offer family activities and entertainment. Some of the proceeds from the National Lottery (see p. 47) are allocated to arts projects.

Many regions and towns have associations with great English writers, artists and musicians: such as Stratford-upon-Avon (William Shakespeare), the Lake District (William Wordsworth), Stoke-on-Trent (Arnold Bennett), Haworth (the Brontë sisters), Dorset (Thomas Hardy), and the Cotswolds (Laurie Lee); Essex and Suffolk (John Constable) and Salford (L.S. Lowry); and Worcestershire (Edward Elgar) and Aldeburgh (Benjamin Britten).

The Environment

Despite its relatively high population density and degree of urbanisation, England still has many unspoilt rural and coastal areas. There are now nine National Parks, six forest parks, 36 designated 'areas of outstanding natural beauty', 22 environmentally sensitive areas, over 200 country parks approved by the Countryside Commission, more than 1,000 km (625 miles) of designated heritage coastline, and about 2,000 historic buildings and some 3,600 gardens open to the public. There are also nearly 200 National Nature Reserves.

Table 2.3: Attendances at some English Tourist Attractions, 1996–97

millions

Blackpool Pleasure Beach	F	7.5*
British Museum	F	6.8
National Gallery	F	5.0
Palace Pier, Brighton	F	4.3*
Alton Towers	P	2.7
Madame Tussaud's	P	2.7
Westminster Abbey	F	2.5*
Tower of London	P	2.5
Eastbourne Pier	F	2.3*
York Minster	F	2.2*
St Paul's Cathedral	P	2.0**
Pleasureland, Southport	F	2.0*
Tate Gallery (in London only)	F	2.0
Canterbury Cathedral	P	1.7
Chessington World of Adventures	P	1.7

Source: British Tourist Authority, Department for Culture, Media and Sport
F   Free admission
P   Paid-for admission
*   Estimated visitor numbers
** Including some free admissions

Further Reading

Regional Trends, annual report, Office for National Statistics. The Stationery Office.

3 Northern Ireland

About half of the 1.6 million people in Northern Ireland are settled in the eastern coastal region, the centre of which is the capital, Belfast. Most industry is sited in this part of the Province. Northern Ireland is at its nearest point only 21 km (13 miles) from Scotland. It has a 488-km (303-mile) border with the Irish Republic.

According to the 1991 Census, 50.6 per cent of the people regarded themselves as Protestants and 38.4 per cent as Roman Catholics. Most of the Protestants are descendants of Scots or English settlers who crossed to north-eastern Ireland; they are British by culture and tradition and committed to remaining part of Britain. The Roman Catholic population is mainly Irish by culture and history, and the majority of them favour a united Ireland. Northern Ireland has a younger population with proportionately more children and fewer pensioners than any other region in Britain.

History

During the tenth century Ireland was dominated by the Vikings. In 1169 Henry II of England launched an invasion of Ireland. He had been granted its overlordship by the English Pope Adrian IV, who was anxious to bring the Irish church into full obedience to Rome. Although a large part of the country came under the control of Anglo-Norman nobles, little direct authority was exercised from England during the Middle Ages.

The Tudor monarchs showed a much greater tendency to intervene in Ireland. During the reign of Elizabeth I, a series of campaigns was waged against Irish insurgents. The main focus of resistance was the northern province of Ulster. After the collapse of this resistance in 1607 and the flight of its leaders, Ulster was settled by immigrants from Scotland and England.

The English civil wars (1642–51) led to further risings in Ireland, which were crushed by Oliver Cromwell. More fighting took place after the overthrow of the Roman Catholic James II in 1688. During the Battle of the Boyne in Ireland in 1690 the forces of James II, who was trying to regain the throne, starting in Ireland, were defeated by those of the Protestant William of Orange (William III).

Throughout most of the 18th century there was uneasy peace. In 1782 the Irish Parliament (dating from medieval times) was given legislative independence; the only constitutional tie with Great Britain was the Crown. The Parliament, however, represented only the privileged Anglo-Irish minority, and Roman Catholics were excluded from it. In 1798 an abortive rebellion took place, led by Wolfe

Northern Ireland: Districts, 1 April 1998

Cf	Carrickfergus
Cr	Castlereagh
ND	North Down
Nta	Newtownabbey

Tone's United Irishmen movement. Three years later Ireland was unified with Great Britain; under the 1801 Act of Union the Irish Parliament was abolished and Irish members sat in both Houses of the Westminster Parliament in London.

The Irish question was one of the major issues of British politics during the 19th century. In 1886 the Liberal Government introduced a Home Rule Bill designed to give a new Irish Parliament devolved authority over most internal matters while Britain maintained control over foreign and defence policy. This led to a split in the Liberal Party and the failure of the Bill. In 1893 a second Home Rule Bill was approved by the House of Commons but rejected by the House of Lords.

The issue returned to the political agenda in 1910 because Asquith's Liberal administration was dependent, for its political survival, on support from the pro–Home Rule Irish Parliamentary Party. The controversy intensified as unionists and nationalists in Ireland formed private armies. In 1914 Home Rule was approved in the Government of Ireland Act. Implementation, however, was delayed by the outbreak of the First World War.

A nationalist rising in Dublin in 1916 was suppressed and its leaders executed. Two years later the nationalist Sinn Fein party won a large majority of the Irish seats in elections to the Westminster Parliament. Its members refused to attend the House of Commons and, instead, formed the Dail Eireann in Dublin. A nationalist guerrilla force called the Irish Republican Army began operations against the British administration in 1919.

The 1920 Government of Ireland Act provided for the establishment of two Home Rule parliaments, one in Dublin and the other in Belfast. The Act was implemented in 1921 in Northern Ireland, when six of the nine counties of the province of Ulster received their own Parliament and remained represented in, and subject to the supreme authority of, the British Parliament.

In the South the guerrillas continued to fight for independence. A truce was agreed in June 1921, followed by negotiations between the British Government and Sinn Fein. These were concluded in December 1921 with the

Table 3.1: General Election Results, 1 May 1997

Party	Total votes	Share of votes	Change from 1992	Candidates	MPs elected
Ulster Unionist	258,349	32.7%	−1.9%	16	10
Social Democratic and Labour	190,814	24.1%	0.6%	18	3
Sinn Fein	126,921	16.1%	6.1%	17	2
Democratic Unionist	107,348	13.6%	0.5%	9	2
Alliance	62,972	8.0%	−0.8%	17	–
United Kingdom Unionist	12,817	1.6%	1.6%	1	1
Progressive Unionist	10,934	1.4%	1.4%	3	–
Conservative	9,858	1.2%	−4.4%	8	–
Workers	2,766	0.3%	−0.2%	8	–
Natural Law	2,208	0.3%	0.0%	18	–
Green	539	0.1%	0.1%	1	–
Others	5,252	0.7%	−3.0%	9	–
Total	790,778	100.0%	–	125	18

Source: House of Commons Library

signature of the Anglo-Irish Treaty establishing the Irish Free State, which became a republic in 1949.

From its creation in 1921, Northern Ireland's Parliament had a consistent unionist majority from which government ministers were drawn. The nationalist minority resented this persistent domination and their effective exclusion from political office and influence.

An active and articulate civil rights movement emerged during the 1960s. Although reforms were made in response, sectarian disturbances developed. This led to the introduction in 1969 of British Army support for the police. These sectarian divisions were subsequently exploited by terrorists from both sides, most notably by the Provisional Irish Republican Army (IRA), which claimed to be protecting the Roman Catholic minority.

Because of increased terrorism and inter-communal violence, the British Government took over responsibility for law and order in 1972. The Northern Ireland unionist Government resigned in protest at this decision and direct rule from London began.

Government

Under the system of direct rule, the United Kingdom Parliament approves all laws, and Northern Ireland's government departments are controlled by the Secretary of State—a Cabinet minister—and a ministerial team.

Northern Ireland elects 18 Members of Parliament (MPs) to the House of Commons. In the most recent general election in May 1997 the Ulster Unionists won 10 seats, the nationalist Social Democratic and Labour Party (SDLP) 3, the Democratic Unionists 2, Sinn Fein 2,[1] and the United Kingdom Unionist 1. The Alliance Party, offering an alternative to Unionists and Nationalists, received 8 per cent of the vote but no seats. (See Table 3.1 for a full breakdown of the results.) Northern Ireland elects three representatives to the European Parliament.

Local Government

In Northern Ireland government departments and a range of public bodies provide important services which are normally the responsibility of local authorities elsewhere in Britain. The Province's 26 district councils have limited executive functions together with certain consultative and representational roles. Various statutory bodies administer regional services, such as education and libraries,

---

[1] The Sinn Fein members have not taken their seats.

health and personal social services, housing, drainage and fire services. In June 1997 the Government announced a number of initiatives to strengthen local government in the Province. They included the possibility of legislation to give councils 'a power of general competence' to do what they consider appropriate in the interests of their district and its people; proposals to increase the representation of councillors on public bodies; and a fuller consultation between district councils and central government, particularly in planning.

Efforts to Achieve Devolved Government

Throughout the period of direct rule, successive British Governments have favoured a devolved administration widely acceptable to both unionist and nationalist political traditions. In 1974 a unionist-nationalist coalition Executive was formed but soon collapsed as a result of a protest strike by those unionists opposed to power sharing. In 1982 an Assembly was elected by proportional representation but was dissolved four years later because no agreement could be reached between the parties on a devolved administration.

In 1991 and 1992 the four main constitutional parties (Ulster Unionists, Democratic Unionists, Alliance Party, and Social Democratic and Labour Party) held a series of talks with the Government and, where appropriate, the Irish Government, to see whether they could reach an agreement taking into account the three sets of relationships relevant to the Northern Ireland problem—within Northern Ireland itself; within the island of Ireland; and between the British and Irish Governments. The talks ended without agreement.

Since then, the British Government has been engaged in a series of bilateral talks with the Northern Ireland parties in order to explore the basis on which they might come together for further discussions. This work led to the launch of the negotiations which started in June 1996 (see p. 16). The aim of all these discussions was to produce a settlement attracting widespread agreement among the two political traditions in the North.

Relations with the Irish Republic

The British and Irish Governments have worked closely together in order to bring peace to Northern Ireland. The 1985 Anglo-Irish Agreement created an Intergovernmental Conference in which both governments discuss issues such as improved cross-border co-operation and security. Under the Agreement, the Irish Government can put forward views and proposals on matters related to Northern Ireland provided that these are not the responsibility of a devolved administration in Belfast.

Recent Developments

● The Downing Street Declaration, signed by the British and Irish Governments in 1993, set out the views of the two Governments on ways towards a future settlement based on the fundamental principles that the consent of a majority of people in Northern Ireland would be required before any constitutional change could come about.

● In August 1994 the IRA announced a ceasefire; this was followed in October 1994 by a similar ceasefire on the part of the loyalist paramilitary organisations. Shortly afterwards the British Government began separate exploratory talks with Sinn Fein and with the Progressive Unionist and Ulster Democratic parties, in order to explore the basis on which they could be admitted to the talks process and stressing the need for the decommissioning of illegally held weapons before these parties could take part in multi-party negotiations.

● In February 1995 the British and Irish Governments published two documents, together called Frameworks for the Future, outlining what an overall settlement might look like. Their aim was to serve as an aid to discussion and negotiation between the parties.

● In November 1995 the two Governments established an independent International Body to assess the issue of decommissioning illegal weapons. Chaired by former US Senator George Mitchell, the International Body reported in January 1996. It concluded that there should be some decommissioning during the talks and set out six principles of democracy and non-violence to which it said all parties should adhere. It also proposed an elected body for further negotiations to 'contribute to the building of confidence'.

● The IRA announced the end of its ceasefire in February 1996 and subsequently carried out bomb attacks both on mainland Britain and in Northern Ireland. At the end of February the British and Irish Governments agreed that all-party negotiations should begin in June 1996 and that there could be no question of ministerial meetings with Sinn Fein or of Sinn Fein's participation in the negotiations until there was an unequivocal restoration of the IRA ceasefire.

● Following an election in Northern Ireland on 30 May 1996 to provide delegates from whom participants in all-party negotiations could be chosen, 110 representatives were returned: 5 from each of the 18 parliamentary constituencies and 2 from each of the 10 most successful parties across the Province. The representatives took their seats in a deliberative forum whose purpose is to discuss issues relevant to promoting dialogue and understanding within Northern Ireland. Sinn Fein were entitled to attend the forum but have never done so. The parties represented in the forum—except for Sinn Fein—were invited to select negotiating teams to participate in the all-party talks which had begun on 10 June. As agreed between the Governments in February 1996, Sinn Fein's participation required an unequivocal restoration of the IRA ceasefire.

● The two Governments invited members of the independent International Body which examined the decommissioning issue to chair those aspects of the talks requiring independent chairmanship. The all-party talks and the forum were temporarily suspended in March 1997, following the announcement of the British General Election in May and local government elections in Northern Ireland.

● The Government which took office in May 1997 is seeking to secure a political settlement acceptable to all sections of the community. It is pursuing this objective through all-party talks (see below). The Government has stated that it considers the key elements of a political settlement would be: devolution in Northern Ireland, including an Assembly elected and operating on a widely acceptable basis; sensible cross-border arrangements between Northern Ireland and the Irish Republic; and new arrangements between Britain and the Irish Republic, including formal constitutional acceptance of the principle of consent and a new more broadly based Anglo–Irish Agreement.

● In June 1997 the British and Irish Governments jointly put forward proposals for resolving the decommissioning of illegal weapons. By September 1997 these had so far failed to secure sufficient consensus, but the two Governments have stated that they believe the proposals represent a broadly acceptable way forward, reflecting the approach set out in the Mitchell Report. They have been extensively clarified and the two Governments have stated that they consider they meet the concerns of all sides. An Independent Commission to make proposals for decommissioning and to monitor its implementation has since been established.

● On 19 July 1997 the IRA announced a restoration of its ceasefire. After careful consideration of all the circumstances following the IRA announcement, the Secretary of State announced on 29 August 1997 that she had decided to invite Sinn Fein to enter the talks. Sinn Fein would be required to make their commitment to the principles of democracy and non-violence set out in the Mitchell Report. The talks resumed on 9 September when Sinn Fein reaffirmed their commitment to the six Mitchell principles of democracy and non-violence.

● A major breakthrough occurred on 24 September 1997 when the participants in the all-party negotiations, meeting in plenary session, launched the three strands of substantive political negotiations. They also agreed to establish means to help make further progress on decommissioning and other confidence-building measures.

● The Government has proposed that substantive talks conclude by May 1998. Any agreement reached would have to command a broad measure of support among the parties representing each of the main communities.

It would also be put to a referendum of all people in Northern Ireland alongside a concurrent referendum in the Irish Republic. The settlement would also require the approval of Parliament at Westminster.

Human Rights

Economic and social deprivation persists on both sides of the Northern Ireland community. However, on all major social and economic indicators, Roman Catholics generally experience higher levels of disadvantage than Protestants, leading to feelings of discrimination and alienation which in turn influence attitudes to political and security issues. Government guidelines aim to promote fair treatment by ensuring that policies and programmes do not discriminate unjustifiably against, for example, people of different religious beliefs or political opinion, women, disabled people, ethnic minorities and people of different sexual orientation. The Government also provides grant aid to local government programmes designed to encourage mutual understanding and appreciation of cultural diversity; support is also given to the Cultural Traditions Programme, which attempts to show that different cultures do not have to lead to division. The aim of these initiatives is to encourage a more pluralistic and tolerant society with equal esteem for unionist and nationalist traditions.

The Standing Advisory Commission on Human Rights advises the Secretary of State on the effectiveness of anti-discrimination laws and measures. The Commission published a report on employment equality in June 1997. It finds that the fair employment legislation passed in 1989 has had a positive impact on employment equality and makes radical proposals for changes to policies and procedures in education, training, and the government initiatives on targeting social need. The Government is studying its recommendations.

Direct or indirect discrimination in employment on grounds of religious belief or political opinion is unlawful. All public authorities and all private employers with more than ten employees are required to register with the Fair Employment Commission. There is also compulsory monitoring of the religious composition of workforces, continual review of recruitment, training and promotion procedures, and affirmative action if fair employment is not provided. Criminal penalties and economic sanctions exist for defaulting employers. The Fair Employment Tribunal deals with individual complaints about discrimination.

An independent Chief Electoral Officer maintains the accuracy of the electoral register, while electoral boundaries for parliamentary constituencies are determined by impartial statutory procedures conducted by the Boundary Commission for Northern Ireland. The Northern Ireland Ombudsman and Commissioner for Complaints deal with complaints by the public against government departments and local authorities. An independent commission supervises police investigations into the more serious complaints against police officers and, at its discretion, the investigation of other matters (see p. 95).

The Parades Commission

The Parades Commission is an independent body whose role is to help resolve disputes over contentious parades in Northern Ireland. It was established in March 1997 in response to the recommendations of an independent review,[2] appointed to examine the whole question of parades and associated public order issues. The Government is to introduce legislation later in 1997 to provide a statutory role for the Commission and to give it specific functions, in particular, the power to make decisions on contentious parades.

Over 75 per cent of parades each year are organised by the Protestant/Unionist community, especially the 'Loyal Orders'. Most take place during the 'marching season', which runs from around Easter to the end of September.

---

[2] Report of the Independent Review of Parades and Marches (the North Report), 1997.

Security Policy

In order to protect the public, legislation gives the authorities exceptional powers to deal with and prevent terrorist activities. These include special powers of arrest for those suspected of certain serious terrorist offences, non-jury courts to try terrorist offences (see p. 98) and the banning of terrorist organisations. The legislation is subject to annual independent review and to annual approval by Parliament. The Government has stated that, once a lasting peace is established, there will be no need for these exceptional powers and is keeping the requirement for them under continuing review.

An Independent Commissioner observes and reports on the conditions under which terrorist suspects are detained by the security forces in police offices known as Holding Centres. The Commissioner submits an annual report to the Secretary of State which is published.

Statutory codes of practice apply to the detention, treatment, questioning and identification of suspects. A breach of any of the codes' provisions by a police officer is a disciplinary offence.

The Economy

Trends in output and employment tend to reflect those in Britain. In 1996 Northern Ireland lost 35 days for every 1,000 employees because of labour disputes, a better record than in any other region of Britain.

Some 74 per cent of employees work in service industries and 17.7 per cent in manufacturing. The largest industrial employer is Short Brothers, owned by the Canadian company Bombardier, with some 6,000 employees engaged on the manufacture of aircraft and their components, guided missiles and related products and services. The shipbuilder Harland and Wolff employs 1,768 people.

In 1995–96 the value of exports increased by 18 per cent to £3,100 million. Exports account for 77 per cent of product sales. The Irish Republic is the most important market outside Britain, taking 8 per cent of exports in 1995–96.

Agriculture accounts for 4.9 per cent of gross domestic product or 8 per cent if ancillary industries are included—higher percentages than in any other region in Britain. Some 10 per cent of the workforce is employed in agriculture, forestry, fishing and ancillary industries.

Tourism, which is promoted throughout the world by the Northern Ireland Tourist Board, sustains about 12,500 jobs. In 1996, 1.4 million people visited Northern Ireland, generating £206 million in revenue.

Overseas and other companies are important investors. Northern Ireland attracted almost 5 per cent of all new investment jobs in Britain in 1996–97 even though it accounted for only 3 per cent of the British population. Around 200 externally owned companies employ around 45,000 people, nearly half the manufacturing labour force. US-owned companies, for example, employ over 14,000 people in the Province. Many overseas companies use the region as a base for operations in the ever-increasing European market. In June 1997, for example, Seagate Technology, a US computer software manufacturer, announced a further investment of £149 million in its operations at Londonderry in a project expected to provide 1,125 new jobs by the year 2002. This brings the total amount committed by Seagate to Londonderry to some £323 million.

The Industrial Development Board (IDB) encourages industrial development and new international investment. In 1996–97, 6,000 new jobs were created by new and established companies. In the same year the IDB successfully negotiated 35 new investments or expansions by externally owned companies; these are expected to result in 4,640 new jobs.

The Local Enterprise Development Unit and local enterprise agencies run by people with business skills and expertise assist the establishment and growth of small businesses as well as expertise. In 1996–97 the Unit recorded an 11 per cent increase in employment among its small business clients. In the same year 42 per cent of its financial commitment—£14 million—was directed towards disadvantaged areas.

Considerable public expenditure has been devoted to improving conditions in urban and rural areas. Since 1974 there has been a 92 per cent reduction in housing unfitness levels in Belfast.

The recently completed cross-harbour road and rail bridges have transformed Belfast's infrastructure at a cost of £89 million. The telecommunications firm BT has started work on its new £30 million riverside Laganside headquarters. Other important Laganside developments include Belfast City Council's new concert hall and conference centre, and a 182-bedroom Hilton International hotel, a £24 million project on which construction work began in 1996. Over 250 economic, social and environmental projects in the city's disadvantaged areas have been supported in a bid to improve education, training for adults, and job-finding services for unemployed people.

Northern Ireland currently receives around £1,300 million under the EU Structural Funds Programme (see p. 199). Over the period 1995–99 some £200 million of this comes from the Special Support Programme for Peace and Reconciliation. The five areas eligible for funding are: employment; urban and rural regeneration; cross-border development; social inclusion; and productive investment and industrial development. Under the Programme up to 80 per cent of funds are allocated to Northern Ireland, and the remainder to the border counties of the Irish Republic. At least 15 per cent of the total must be spent on cross-border activities.

The Government makes a contribution of over £3,000 million a year to maintain social services at the level of those in Great Britain, to meet the cost of security measures and to compensate for the natural disadvantages of geography and lack of resources.

In 1986 the British and Irish Governments established the International Fund for Ireland. Some three-quarters is spent in Northern Ireland, the rest going to border areas in the Republic. Programmes cover business enterprise, tourism, community relations, urban development, agriculture and rural development. Donors include the United States, the European Union, Canada and New Zealand.

Cultural and Social Affairs

Northern Ireland's cultural heritage is preserved and portrayed by the Ulster Museum in Belfast, the Ulster Folk and Transport Museum in County Down and the Ulster-American Folk Park in Omagh, which specialises in the history of Irish emigration to America. Plans to merge these three museums into a single National Museum of Northern Ireland are in progress. The merger is expected to take effect by April 1998. There are also several local museums and heritage centres, mainly funded by local district councils.

Local arts festivals are an important feature of the arts calendar, the highlight being the Belfast festival, based at Queen's University. The Ulster Orchestra has a notable reputation. Government support for the arts is channelled through the Arts Council of Northern Ireland, which gives financial help and advice to opera and drama companies, orchestras and festivals, arts centres, galleries, theatres, writers and artistic groups.

Local district councils provide leisure facilities, including leisure centres and swimming pools. The Government finances the Sports Council for Northern Ireland, which promotes sport and physical recreation. Proceeds from the National Lottery provide an additional source of funding for arts and sport in Northern Ireland.

Health and personal social services correspond fairly closely to those in the rest of Britain. Although the figures have been falling in recent years, Northern Ireland still has a high birth rate relative to the rest of Britain, imposing heavy demands on maternity and child care expenditure. Northern Ireland's elderly population is also increasing and the demands made on geriatric services are growing. On average over a fifth of the income of households comes from social security benefits, a higher proportion than in any other region of Britain.

Although publicly financed schools must be open to children from all religions, in practice Roman Catholic and Protestant children are mainly educated in separate schools. There are now 33 integrated schools for both Protestant and Roman Catholic children out of a total of 1,158 publicly financed primary, secondary and grammar schools, and this process of integration is being encouraged by the Government (see p. 438.)

Most housing is owner occupied. The Housing Executive (see p. 385) allocates public housing to those in greatest need.

Further Reading

A Shorter Illustrated History of Ulster. Bardon, Jonathon. Blackstaff Press, 1997.

Northern Ireland (2nd edn). Aspects of Britain series, HMSO, 1995.

Northern Ireland Annual Abstract of Statistics. No 15—1997. Northern Ireland Statistics and Research Agency.

Northern Ireland Expenditure Plans and Priorities. The Government's Expenditure Plans 1997–98 to 1999–2000. The Stationery Office, 1997.

Regional Trends 32: 1997 edition. The Stationery Office.

Omnibus. A thrice-yearly magazine published by the Northern Ireland Information Service.

4 Scotland

Three-quarters of the population of Scotland and most of the industrial towns are in the central lowlands. The chief cities are Edinburgh (the capital), Glasgow, Aberdeen and Dundee. Scotland contains large areas of unspoilt and wild landscape, and the majority of Britain's highest mountains, including Ben Nevis (1,343 m, 4,406 ft), the highest peak in Britain. Scotland is to have its own Parliament, while remaining part of the United Kingdom and having continued representation in the Parliament at Westminster (London). A referendum in September 1997 approved this by a substantial majority.

Early History

At the time of the Roman invasion of Britain, what is now Scotland was mainly inhabited by the Picts. Despite a long campaign, Roman rule was never permanently extended to most of Scotland. In the sixth century, the Scots from Ireland settled in what is now Argyll, giving their name to the present-day Scotland.

War between the kingdoms of England and Scotland was frequent in the Middle Ages. There were, though, strong links between the kingdoms: several Scottish kings held land and titles in England and there was intermarriage between the Scottish and English royal families. Despite reverses such as the defeat of William Wallace's uprising in 1298, Robert the Bruce's victory over Edward II of England at Bannockburn in 1314 ensured the survival of a separate kingdom of Scotland.

The two crowns were eventually united when Elizabeth I of England was succeeded in 1603 by James VI of Scotland (James I of England), who was her nearest heir. Even so, England and Scotland remained separate political entities during the 17th century, apart from an enforced period of unification under Oliver Cromwell in the 1650s. In 1707 both countries, opting for closer political and economic union, agreed on a single parliament for Great Britain.

Devolution

Devolution in Scotland (and Wales) is an important part of the Government's

Scotland: New Council Areas, 1 April 1998

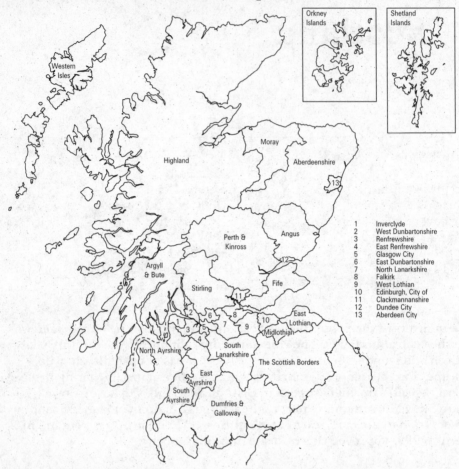

Orkney Islands

Shetland Islands

Western Isles

Moray

Highland

Aberdeenshire

13

Perth &
Kinross

Angus

Argyll
& Bute

Fife

Stirling

11

12

2
6
8
1
3
5
7
9
10
4

East
Lothian

Midlothian

North Ayrshire

South
Lanarkshire

The Scottish Borders

East
Ayrshire

South
Ayrshire

Dumfries &
Galloway

1	Inverclyde
2	West Dunbartonshire
3	Renfrewshire
4	East Renfrewshire
5	Glasgow City
6	East Dunbartonshire
7	North Lanarkshire
8	Falkirk
9	West Lothian
10	Edinburgh, City of
11	Clackmannanshire
12	Dundee City
13	Aberdeen City

programme of constitutional reform (see chapter 7). The Government's proposals were set out in a White Paper—*Scotland's Parliament*—in July 1997. The new Parliament will have significantly greater powers than those envisaged in the 1979 Scottish Assembly,[1] including powers over economic development and assistance to industry.

A referendum in September 1997 endorsed the Parliament by 1,775,045 votes (74.3 per cent) to 614,400 (25.7 per cent). A second question in the referendum on the Parliament's tax-raising powers (see p. 23) was also supported, by 1,512,889 votes (63.5 per cent) to 870,263 (36.5 per cent).

---

[1] Proposals to establish a Scottish Assembly were endorsed in a referendum in 1979, but the proportion of the total electorate voting in favour of the Assembly was below the required level of 40 per cent.

Scottish Parliament

Legislation to establish a Scottish Parliament is to be introduced as soon as possible. Elections will be held in the first half of 1999, and it is expected that the Parliament will become fully operational in 2000.

Electoral Arrangements

There will be 129 Members of the Scottish Parliament (MSPs), who will be elected for a fixed four-year period:

- 73 MSPs representing single-member constituencies, which will be the same as the parliamentary constituencies (except that Orkney and Shetland will be split into two seats); and

Table 4.1: Population

	Population at 30 June 1996	Population density (people per sq km)	Population change 1991-96 (%)
Cities			
Aberdeen	217,260	1,169	1.1
Dundee	150,250	2,306	-3.8
Edinburgh	448,850	1,711	2.1
Glasgow	616,430	3,522	-2.4
Least densely populated areas			
Argyll and Bute	90,840	13	-3.0
Highland	208,700	8	2.3
Orkney Islands	19,800	20	1.2
Scottish Borders	106,100	22	1.9
Shetland Islands	23,020	16	2.1
Western Isles	28,880	9	-1.8
Scotland	**5,128,000**	**66**	**0.4**

Source: General Register Office for Scotland

● 56 MSPs from party lists elected on the additional member system of proportional representation—seven from each of the eight European parliamentary constituencies.

Each elector will have two votes: one for a constituency MSP and one for a party list.

Functions

Responsibilities to be transferred to the Scottish Parliament include: health; education and training; local government; housing; economic development; the law and home affairs; transport; the environment; agriculture, fisheries and forestry; and sport and the arts.

Where it has responsibility, the Scottish Parliament will be able to amend or repeal existing Acts of Parliament and to pass new legislation. Among the areas where responsibility will remain with the Government in Westminster are overseas affairs, defence and national security, overall economic and monetary policy, employment legislation, social security, and most aspects of transport safety and regulation.

The Parliament will be located in Edinburgh. There will be a Scottish Executive, headed by a First Minister who will normally be the leader of the party able to command majority support in the Parliament. The Secretary of State for Scotland will represent Scottish interests within the British Government.

The Scottish Parliament and Executive will have an important role in scrutinising those aspects of European Union (EU) business which affect the devolved responsibilities. Like other regional governments in the EU, Scotland will be able to have its own representative office in Brussels.

The Scottish Executive will have responsibility for all public bodies whose functions and services will be devolved— around 95 organisations—and will be accountable to the Parliament for them. An independent review will examine how to build the most effective relationship between the Parliament/Executive and local authorities.

Financial Arrangements

The Scottish Parliament will have a budget broadly equivalent to that currently controlled by the Secretary of State—£14,274 million in 1997–98. Once the amount of the budget has been determined, the Parliament will be free to allocate resources across the expenditure programmes.

The Parliament will have the power to increase or decrease the basic rate of income tax—currently 23 pence in the pound—by a maximum of 3 pence. Liability will be based on residence. A person will be resident in Scotland if he or she is a British resident for tax purposes and either spends 50 per cent or more of the tax year in Scotland or has his or her only or principal home in Scotland.

The Parliament will be responsible for determining the form of local taxation and, if it considers it wise to do so, will be able to alter both the council tax and business rates.

Current Government Arrangements

Scottish administration is at present the responsibility of the Secretary of State for Scotland, working through the Scottish Office. Separate Acts of Parliament are passed for Scotland where appropriate.

There are 72 Scottish seats in the House of Commons. At the May 1997 General Election, Labour strengthened its position as the largest party, gaining six seats, while the Conservative Party lost all its 10 seats. In October 1997 Labour had 55 Members of Parliament (MPs), Liberal Democrats 10 and the Scottish National Party 6, with one vacant seat following the death of a Labour MP. The Government announced in the White Paper *Scotland's Parliament* that there would be a statutory requirement for a minimum number of Scottish seats in the House of Commons. The Parliamentary Boundary Commission (see p. 59) will take this into account in its next full review of constituency boundaries; any change would affect the number of constituencies in the Scottish Parliament.

In 1996 a single-tier structure of 29 local authorities replaced 62 regional and district councils (see map on p. 22).

The principles and procedures of the Scottish legal system differ in many respects from those of England and Wales. These differences stem, in part, from the adoption of elements from other European legal systems, based on Roman law, during the 16th century. For example, a Scottish jury can give a verdict of 'not proven' as an alternative to 'not guilty' when the accused is acquitted. Scotland has its own prosecution, prison and police services.

Industry

As traditional industries such as coal, steel and shipbuilding have declined, there has been growth in high-technology industries, such as chemicals, electronic engineering and information technology, and in the service industries. Scotland has one of the biggest concentrations of the electronics industry in Western Europe, with around 200 plants employing some 39,000 workers. The industry accounts for around 18 per cent of manufacturing output in Scotland and is the biggest export sector.

Some traditional industries, such as high-quality tweeds and other textiles, and food and drink products, remain important. There are 92 whisky distilleries in operation, mostly in the north east, employing 10,700 people. Whisky exports, valued at £2,300 million in 1996, are Scotland's second largest export trade.

Services

Services now employ over 70 per cent of the workforce. The Scottish financial sector is the sixth largest in Europe in terms of equity funds under management, with the total funds managed being £172,000 million in 1995. There are four Scottish-based clearing banks, which have limited rights to issue their own banknotes.

Tourism and leisure make a significant contribution to the economy, accounting in 1996 for around 177,000 tourism-related jobs. In 1996 expenditure by tourists was valued at £2,400 million; there were 12.5 million tourist trips, including those originating in Scotland.

Industrial Development

Government support for enterprise and training is channelled through Scottish Enterprise and Highlands and Islands Enterprise, which both have general functions in economic development, training and environmental improvement in the Scottish lowlands and the Highlands and Islands respectively. They contract with 22 Local Enterprise Companies (LECs, led by the private sector), which arrange the provision of training and business support.

Investment by overseas companies has made a significant contribution to the growth of modern industry. In 1996–97, Locate in Scotland and the Scottish Office helped to attract 86 inward investment projects to Scotland, involving planned investment of over £3,100 million. The projects are expected to create or safeguard nearly 14,300 jobs.

Agriculture, Forestry and Fishing

About 80 per cent of the land area of Scotland is devoted to agriculture. Output of Scottish agriculture in 1996 was over £2,000 million, of which two-thirds came from livestock and livestock products. The principal crop is barley, which is used in the making of whisky.

Scotland accounts for over half of Britain's forest area and for just under half of timber production. Forestry is continuing to expand and many new woodlands are being created, including native pine forests. In the last ten years there has been significant international and local investment in timber panel production and in pulp and paper processing.

Fishing is important, particularly in the north east and the islands. Scotland accounts for over 60 per cent by value of the fish landed in Britain by British vessels.

Energy and Water Resources

Offshore oil and gas production continues to make a significant contribution to the economy, and production has been increasing. Nuclear and hydro–electric generation supply a higher proportion of electricity than in any other part of Britain.

With abundant rainfall, there is an extensive supply of water from upland sources. Three public water authorities are responsible for water and sewerage services. A review of the structure of the industry is in progress, examining a range of options designed to strengthen local democratic control and improve efficiency.

Transport

The roads programme is being reviewed as part of the Government's plans to develop an integrated transport policy (see chapter 19). A White Paper on transport in Scotland is planned for early 1998.

The current road construction programme includes completion of the Central Scotland motorway network and of the upgrading to motorway standard of the A74 from Carlisle to Glasgow. A bridge linking the Scottish mainland to the island of Skye was opened in 1995 and is one of the world's longest span balanced cantilever bridges.

Natural Heritage

Scotland's countryside contains a rich variety of wildlife, with some species not found elsewhere in Britain. There are 70 National Nature Reserves and 1,400 Sites of Special Scientific Interest. Four regional parks and 40 National Scenic Areas cover 13 per cent of the land surface. Five of the 17 forest parks in Great Britain are in Scotland, and a sixth spans the border between Scotland and England.

Over 100 sites have been identified as possible Special Areas of Conservation under the European Community (EC) Habitats Directive. Under the EC's Wild Birds Directive, 77 sites have been classified as Special Protection Areas because of their importance to rare and migratory birds.

Housing and Urban Regeneration

In Scotland a much higher proportion of housing is rented from the public sector— around 30 per cent—than in Britain as a whole (19 per cent). Home ownership is increasing but, at just under 60 per cent, is still lower than in most other areas of Britain.

In 12 Priority Partnership Areas and 11 Regeneration Programme Areas regeneration partnerships have been set up to tackle the causes of social and economic decline: unemployment, crime, poor housing and a degraded environment. Each partnership comprises the local council, Scottish Homes, the appropriate LEC, other relevant agencies and representatives from the private sector, the community and the voluntary sector (see p. 375).

Health

Although life expectancy has increased, Scotland's health record is not as good as elsewhere in Britain or other industrialised countries. A range of initiatives has been introduced to improve the situation, such as reducing smoking and alcohol misuse, and improving diet and exercise levels. In July 1997 three priority areas were set for the National Health Service in Scotland in 1997–98: mental health, cancer, and coronary heart disease/strokes.

Education

The Scottish education system has a number of distinctive features (see chapter 26). Three of the 13 universities—St Andrews, Glasgow and Aberdeen—were established in the 15th century, and Edinburgh was founded in the 16th century. Record numbers of students are now entering higher education.

A new University of the Highlands and Islands is planned, bringing together a network of further education colleges. A grant of £33 million from the Millennium Commission (see p. 47), together with government funding of over £15 million, is contributing towards the project's development.

Raising education standards in schools is a key government priority. In June 1997 the Early Intervention Programme, a series of measures costing £24 million, was announced with the intention of improving standards of reading, writing and numeracy for children aged 5 and 6. A new system of courses and awards for education after 16, 'Higher Still', is to be introduced in 1999.

Cultural and Social Affairs

Gaelic, a language of ancient Celtic origin, is spoken by some 70,000 people, many of whom live in the islands of the Hebrides. Government support for Gaelic covers three main areas: education, Gaelic organisations and television broadcasting.

The annual Edinburgh International Festival is one of the world's leading cultural events. Held in August, it brings about £70 million into the Scottish economy each year, and is the largest arts festival in Britain. Scotland possesses several major collections of the fine and applied arts, such as the Burrell Collection in Glasgow and the Scottish National Gallery of Modern Art, in Edinburgh. A new Museum of Scotland is being built in Edinburgh to house the National Museums' Scottish collection. Each spring, Edinburgh hosts the International Science Festival, the world's biggest science festival in a single city.

The predominant Church of Scotland is a Protestant church which is Presbyterian in form. It is governed by a hierarchy of church courts, each of which includes lay people.

The sport of golf originated in Scotland, and there are over 400 golf courses, including St Andrews, Gleneagles, Turnberry, Muirfield, Troon and Prestwick, which are internationally renowned. Many other outdoor activities, such as mountaineering, hill walking and fishing, are also pursued. Winter sports are increasingly popular in the Cairngorm Mountains, Glencoe and elsewhere.

Further Reading

Scotland (2nd edn). Aspects of Britain series, The Stationery Office, 1997.
Scotland's Parliament. Cm 3658. The Stationery Office, 1997.

5 Wales

Two-thirds of the population of Wales live in the southern valleys and the lower-lying coastal areas. The chief urban centres are Cardiff (with a population of 315,000), Swansea and Newport in the south and Wrexham in the north. Much of Wales is hilly or mountainous. The highest peak is Snowdon (1,085 m, 3,560 ft). The Welsh name of the country is Cymru.

The Government is proposing to create a new democratically elected Assembly for Wales. A referendum in September 1997 approved this by a majority of 6,700. Wales will continue to have full representation in the Parliament at Westminster in London.

Early History

After the collapse of Roman rule in Britain (see p. 2), Wales remained a Celtic stronghold, although often during Norman times within the English sphere of influence. In 1282 Edward I completed a successful campaign to bring Wales under English rule. The series of great castles that he built in north Wales remain among Britain's finest historic monuments (see p. 369). Edward I's eldest son—later Edward II—was born at Caernarfon in 1284 and was given the title Prince of Wales, which continues to be borne by the eldest son of the reigning monarch.

Continued strong Welsh national feeling culminated in the unsuccessful rising led by Owain Glyndŵr at the beginning of the 15th century. The Tudor dynasty, which ruled England from 1485 to 1603, was of Welsh ancestry. The Acts of Union of 1536 and 1542 united England and Wales administratively, politically and legally.

Devolution

Since the mid-1960s, when the Welsh Office and the office of Secretary of State for Wales were established, greater administrative responsibility has been devolved to Wales. The Secretary of State has responsibility for a range of public services, which are funded from an annual budget of nearly £7,000 million. Services are run by the Welsh Office and through local authorities, health authorities and non-departmental public bodies.

The Government's view is that the people of Wales will benefit by having an elected body and that this will be better placed to promote economic prosperity and

Wales: Unitary Authorities, 1 April 1998

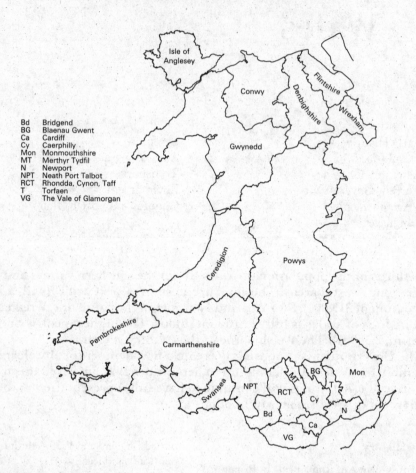

Bd   Bridgend
BG   Blaenau Gwent
Ca   Cardiff
Cy   Caerphilly
Mon   Monmouthshire
MT   Merthyr Tydfil
N   Newport
NPT   Neath Port Talbot
RCT   Rhondda, Cynon, Taff
T   Torfaen
VG   The Vale of Glamorgan

an improved quality of life across Wales. A White Paper published in July 1997 set out the Government's proposals for devolution, involving the creation of a directly elected Assembly for Wales.

A referendum in September 1997 endorsed the Government's proposals by 559,419 (50.3 per cent) to 552,698 (49.7 per cent).

Assembly for Wales

The Government intends to introduce a Bill before the end of 1997, which would provide for the establishment of the Assembly.

Electoral System

Elections to the Assembly will be held every four years, with the first election expected in May 1999. Electors will have two votes: one for a candidate in their local constituency and one for a party list. The Assembly will have 60 elected members, of whom 40 will be elected from local constituencies (which will be the same as the House of Commons constituencies). The remaining 20—four for each of the five European parliamentary constituencies—will be elected by the additional member system of proportional representation.

Functions

The Assembly will take over virtually all the functions currently exercised by the Secretary of State for Wales, in areas such as: economic development; agriculture, forestry, fisheries and food; industry and training; education; local government; health and personal social services; housing; the environment; planning; transport and roads; arts, culture and the Welsh language; the built heritage; and sport and recreation.

Among the functions that will remain the sole responsibility of the Government in London are foreign affairs, defence, taxation, overall economic policy, social security and broadcasting. The office of Secretary of State for Wales will continue, with a seat in the Cabinet.

The headquarters of the Assembly will be in Cardiff. It will have powers to make secondary legislation (see p. 67), be responsible for setting the policy within which Welsh public bodies operate, and be able to issue guidance and directions, for example, to local authorities and the National Health Service.

The working arrangements of the Assembly will comply with the principles of maximum openness and public accountability. It will treat the English and Welsh languages equally in all its work.

The leadership of the Assembly will be provided by an Executive Committee, made up of the leaders of each of its subject committees. It will operate in a way similar to the Cabinet (see p. 72) and will normally be formed by members of the Assembly's majority party. Regional committees will be established to ensure the involvement of all parts of Wales.

The Assembly will work in partnership with local authorities and other public bodies. It will be expected to respect the powers of local government, with the emphasis on local decisions being taken at a local level. The Assembly will control non-departmental public bodies—there are over 80 in Wales, spending more than £2,000 million a year. In most cases, it will have powers to reform or merge them, or to transfer their functions to itself, or to local authorities.

Economic Development

The Assembly will provide a new economic agenda for Wales, with distinct policies to meet the economy's particular needs. A new economic development agency will be established in advance of the Assembly. This will be an expanded Welsh Development Agency (see p. 31), incorporating the Development Board for Rural Wales (see p. 375) and the Land Authority for Wales (see p. 375). The new body will develop partnerships with the Assembly, local authorities, industry, Training and Enterprise Councils, further and higher education bodies, the voluntary sector and other organisations, and will have a strengthened regional structure. Business Connect, the advice and support network for small and medium-size enterprises in Wales, will also be strengthened.

Current Government Arrangements

Wales elects 40 Members of Parliament (MPs) to the House of Commons. Labour has usually had a majority of seats. In the General Election in May 1997 it gained seven seats from the Conservative Party, so that it now has 34 MPs, with four seats being held by Plaid Cymru (Welsh Nationalist) and two by the Liberal Democrats.

Arrangements for consideration of Welsh affairs in Parliament include a House of Commons Select Committee (see p. 68) on Welsh Affairs and the Welsh Grand Committee, whose function is to consider matters relating exclusively to Wales. Following the creation of the Assembly, the future of the Committees is likely to be considered by the House of Commons.

Local government has been reorganised, and 22 unitary authorities succeeded the two-tier structure of eight county councils and 37 district councils in 1996.

The legal system is identical to that in England.

Language

At the time of the 1991 census 19 per cent of the population said that they spoke Welsh. In much of the rural north and west, Welsh remains the first language of most of the population.

The Government has reaffirmed its commitment to enhancing Welsh culture and developing greater use of the Welsh language. Welsh is compulsory in the National Curriculum for Wales, and this arrangement will be fully implemented by 1999. Bilingual education in schools is encouraged (see p. 32). Welsh is now more widely used for official purposes and in broadcasting, while most road signs are bilingual.

The Welsh Language Act 1993 established the principle that, in the context of public business and the administration of justice in Wales, Welsh and English should be treated on the basis of equality. The Welsh Language Board aims to promote and facilitate the use of the Welsh language; in 1997–98 its gross expenditure will be over £5.7 million.

In December 1996 the Board published its strategy for the future of the Welsh language.

Its main priorities include:

- increasing the number of people able to speak Welsh;
- providing more opportunities to use the language; and
- strengthening Welsh as a community language.

Economy

Recent decades have seen fundamental changes in the Welsh economy. It is now much less dependent on heavy industry— coalmining and steelmaking—although steelmaking remains important, with Wales accounting for over a third of Britain's steel

Table 5.1: Population Mid-1996

	Population (thousands)	Population density (people per sq km)	Change in population 1991–1996 (%)
Blaenau Gwent	73	670	0.0
Bridgend (Pen-y-bont ar Ogwr)[a]	130	528	0.6
Caerphilly (Caerffili)	169	608	−1.4
Cardiff (Caerdydd)	315	2,250	5.0
Carmarthenshire (Sir Gaerfyrddin)	169	71	−0.8
Ceredigion	70	39	4.5
Conwy	111	98	1.9
Denbighshire (Sir Ddinbych)	92	109	0.5
Flintshire (Sir y Fflint)	145	331	1.6
Gwynedd	118	46	1.5
Isle of Anglesey (Ynys Môn)	67	94	−3.4
Merthyr Tydfil (Merthyr Tudful)	58	523	−3.0
Monmouthshire (Sir Fynwy)	87	102	8.0
Neath Port Talbot (Castell-nedd Port Talbot)	140	317	0.0
Newport (Casnewydd)	137	721	−0.1
Pembrokeshire (Sir Benfro)	114	72	0.6
Powys	124	24	3.6
Rhondda, Cynon, Taff (Rhondda, Cynon, Taf)	240	566	1.2
Swansea (Abertawe)	230	608	−0.6
Torfaen (Tor-faen)	91	722	−0.9
Vale of Glamorgan (Bro Morgannwg)	119	355	0.1
Wrexham (Wrecsam)	123	247	0.3
Wales (Cymru)	**2,921**	**141**	**1.0**

Sources: Office for National Statistics and Welsh Office.
[a] Welsh-language place names are given in parenthesis if they differ from the English names.

output. The most notable features have been expansion in service industries and the development of a more diverse range of manufacturing industries, including many at the forefront of technology.

Wales is an important centre for consumer electronics, information technology, automotive components, chemicals and materials, and food and drink. Around 35,000 people are employed in the manufacture of optical and electrical equipment, and over 20,000 in the automotive components sector, where annual sales are about £1,700 million.

In the service sector the most marked growth has been in financial and business services, and leisure services. Expenditure by tourists was about £1,900 million in 1996, and the industry employs directly or indirectly about 100,000 people. The Wales Tourist Board seeks to develop tourism in ways which will yield the optimum economic benefit for the people of Wales.

Although south Wales remains the principal industrial area, new industries and firms have been introduced in north-east Wales and light industry attracted to the towns in rural mid- and north Wales.

LG of Korea is undertaking a £1,700 million project at Newport, the largest inward investment scheme into Europe. It involves the construction of two factories—one producing semiconductors and the other wide-screen television sets and components. The first phase should be operational by the end of 1997. Over 6,100 new jobs are being directly created, with many thousands more expected in supporting industries.

Inward Investment

Wales has been particularly successful in attracting investment from overseas companies and from elsewhere in Britain. Since 1983 the Welsh Development Agency (WDA) has recorded 1,680 projects, bringing in total investment of £11,000

million and the creation or safeguarding of over 160,000 jobs. Overseas-owned manufacturing companies employ more than 75,000 people.

Economic Development

The economic programmes of the Welsh Office are complemented by the work of the WDA and the Development Board for Rural Wales, which have wide powers to promote economic, industrial and environmental change. In 1997–98 these bodies plan to undertake programmes involving expenditure of £130 million and £20 million respectively. One of the main areas of activity is providing accommodation for business.

The south Wales valleys have been particularly affected by the decline in traditional industries. A second five-year Programme for the Valleys was launched in 1993 to improve the economic, social and environmental conditions in the area.

The redevelopment of the Cardiff Bay area is one of the biggest regeneration projects in Britain. A new barrage being built across the harbour mouth should be completed in October 1998. It is expected that about 29,000 new jobs will be created in the Cardiff Bay area, 5,900 new homes built, 1.15 million sq m of business space created and over £1,500 million of private sector investment attracted.

Agriculture and Forestry

Agriculture occupies about 81 per cent of the land area. The main activities are sheep and cattle rearing in the hill regions and dairy farming in the lowlands. About 12 per cent of Wales is covered by woodland.

Transport

Motorway links to England and the rest of Europe were considerably improved when the second motorway bridge crossing the Severn and associated motorway links were opened in 1996. The bridge, which cost £300 million, was built and is operated by a private sector company, Severn River Crossing plc. A review of the roads programme in Wales is in progress, in conjunction with the development of an integrated transport policy (see chapter 19).

Ferry services to Ireland operate from Fishguard, Pembroke Dock and Swansea in south Wales, and from Holyhead in north Wales. More than 3.8 million passengers travelled through these ports in 1996. Passenger traffic at Cardiff International Airport has increased from 624,000 in 1990–91 to just over 1 million in 1996–97.

Environment

Wales has a rich and diverse natural heritage. About one-quarter of Wales is designated as a National Park or Area of Outstanding Natural Beauty (see p. 364). As well as three National Parks—Snowdonia, the Brecon Beacons and the Pembrokeshire Coast—and five Areas of Outstanding Natural Beauty, there are two national trails, 31 country parks and large stretches of heritage coast. There are 56 National Nature Reserves and over 900 Sites of Special Scientific Interest. In addition, there are a number of internationally important nature conservation sites in Wales. There are 36 sites proposed for designation as Special Areas of Conservation under the European Community (EC) Habitat Directive, 12 Special Protection Areas classified under the EC Wild Birds Directive and eight Ramsar Wetlands of international importance designated under the Ramsar Convention (see p. 366).

Cultural and Social Affairs

Welsh literature is one of the oldest in Europe. The Welsh people have strong musical traditions and Wales is well known for its choral singing, while the Welsh National Opera has an international reputation. Special festivals, known as eisteddfodau, encourage Welsh literature and music. The largest is the annual Royal National Eisteddfod, consisting of competitions in music, singing, prose and poetry entirely in Welsh. Artists from all over the world come to Llangollen for the annual International Musical Eisteddfod.

An active local press includes several Welsh language publications. The fourth television channel, Sianel Pedwar Cymru (S4C), broadcasts in Welsh during peak viewing hours and is required to ensure that a significant proportion of its output is in Welsh.

A White Paper setting out the Government's proposals for raising standards in schools in Wales was published in July 1997. In schools Welsh is taught—as a first or second language—to most pupils between the ages of 5 and 16. In addition, subjects are taught in Welsh in about 500 schools, in both the primary and secondary sectors. The majority of these are in the traditionally Welsh-speaking, largely rural areas. However, in recent years there has also been a significant growth in Welsh-medium education in other areas where the dominant language of the community is English. There are 14 higher education institutions, of which eight form the collegiate University of Wales (founded in 1893), and 26 further education colleges.

Among many sporting activities, there is particular interest in rugby union football, which has come to be regarded as the Welsh national game. A new national rugby stadium, costing some £114 million, is being built in Cardiff. It will host the final of the 1999 Rugby World Cup.

Further Reading

Statistical Focus on Wales. Welsh Office, 1996.

A Voice for Wales: The Government's Proposals for a Welsh Assembly. Cm 3718. The Stationery Office, 1997.

Wales. Aspects of Britain series, HMSO, 1993.

6 The Social Framework

Among the main social changes during the second half of the 20th century are longer life expectancy and a lower birth rate, reflected in a growing proportion of elderly people; a higher divorce rate; much greater participation by women in the workforce; wider educational opportunities; and a higher standard of living.

POPULATION

Britain's population in mid-1996 was estimated at 58.8 million, the 18th largest in the world. The population has increased by over 2.4 million since 1981. On mid-1994–based projections, it is forecast to rise to 59.5 million in 2001 and 60.5 million in 2011, reaching a peak of around 61.2 million in the 2020s. Population is likely to start falling from about 2025, owing to fewer births and an increase in the number of deaths in the elderly population—reflecting a peak in births in the post-war 'baby boom'.

Birth Rates

In 1996 there were 733,300 live births in Britain. The total period fertility rate (an indication of average family size) remains below 2.1, the level leading to the long-term replacement of the population, although it is projected that it will increase from 1.71 in 1995 to 1.8 for women born in or after 1980.

Contributory factors to the relatively low birth rate in recent years (12.5 live births per 1,000 population in 1996) include:

- the trends towards later marriage and postponing having children, which have led to an increase in the average age of women giving birth—28.6 years in England and Wales in 1996, compared with 26.8 in 1981;

- a preference for smaller families than in the past, which has led to a significant decline in the proportion of families with four or more children; and

- more widespread and effective contraception, making it easier to plan families, and the greater prevalence of voluntary sterilisation for both men and women.

Mortality

At birth the expectation of life for a man in Britain is now over 74 years and for a woman nearly 80 years, compared with 49 years for men and 52 years for women in 1901.

There were 638,900 deaths in 1996, a death rate of just under 11 per 1,000 population. There has been a decline in mortality at most ages, particularly among children. The infant mortality rate (deaths of children under one year old per 1,000 live births) was 6.1 in 1996; neonatal mortality (deaths of infants under four weeks old per 1,000 live births) was 4.1; and maternal mortality is about 0.07 per 1,000 total births. The decline in the mortality rate reflects many factors, including better nutrition, rising standards of living, advances in medical science, better working conditions, and the smaller size of families.

Deaths caused by circulatory diseases (including heart attacks and strokes) now account for over two-fifths of all deaths, and mortality from heart disease remains high compared with that of other developed countries. The next largest cause of death is cancer, which is responsible for around a quarter of deaths.

Cigarette smoking is the greatest single cause of preventable illness and death in Britain, and is associated with around 120,000 deaths each year (nearly a fifth of all deaths). Smoking has declined among adults—around 29 per cent of adult males and 28 per cent of adult females smoked cigarettes in 1996, compared with 52 and 41 per cent respectively in 1972—although recently there has been an increase in smoking among children. A survey conducted in December 1996 for the Department of Health found that 69 per cent of smokers would like to stop smoking. Government action to tackle smoking includes a proposed ban on tobacco advertising (see p. 408).

The level of good health varies quite significantly in some parts of the country and sections of the community. The Government is planning to reduce such inequality and to tackle the underlying causes of ill health, and it is developing a new public health strategy (see chapter 24). In addition, an independent review of the latest available information on health inequalities and expectation of life in England will identify priority areas for future policy development.

Households and Families

The number of households in Great Britain rose by more than 7 million between 1961 and 1995–96, to 23.5 million. Average household size fell during this period from 3.1 to 2.4, and has nearly halved during the 20th century. Fewer people are living in the traditional family of a married couple with dependent children (see Table 6.1), while many more

people are living on their own—12 per cent of adults—and 28 per cent of households in 1995–96 comprised one person. The declining average household size also reflects growth in the elderly and in lone-parent families, and the preference for smaller families. Other features are a big increase in cohabitation, fewer marriages and higher levels of divorce.

Table 6.1: Families in Britain by Type[a]

	Per cent 1990–91	Per cent 1995–96
Married couples	77	73
of which, those with:		
dependent children	44	41
non-dependent children only	11	9
no children	22	23
Cohabiting couples	8	11
of which, those with:		
dependent children	3	4
no children	5	7
Lone parents	15	16
of which, those with:		
dependent children	12	13
non-dependent children only	4	3

Source: ONS—*Social Focus on Families*
[a] Head of family aged 16 to 59.

Marriage, Divorce and Cohabitation

Fewer people are getting married, and the number of marriages—322,200 in 1995 (the latest year for which information is available)—has been falling. First marriages, of which there were 201,000 in 1994, have declined by nearly a half compared with the peak reached in 1970. A significant proportion of marriages—over a third—represent remarriages of one or both parties.

Separation and divorce have become much more common in recent decades, and Britain has the highest divorce rate in the European Union (EU). In 1995, 170,000 divorces were granted in Britain. There were 13.4 divorces for every 1,000 married couples in England and Wales; divorce rates for Scotland and Northern Ireland are lower. Nearly three-quarters of divorces are granted to wives. The average age at the time of divorce in England and Wales is now about 39.6 for men and 37.0 for women. Many divorced people do eventually remarry, with men more likely than women to remarry following separation.

As in many other Western European countries, cohabitation has become much more common. Between 1981 and 1995–96 the proportion of non-married women aged 18–49 who were cohabiting doubled, to 25 per cent. Cohabitation before marriage is increasingly widespread—around two-thirds of women who first married in 1993 had cohabited with their future husband before marriage, compared with 4 per cent of those first married in 1966.

Age and Sex Structure

The most significant changes in the age structure of the population have been the growing numbers of elderly people and the decline in the proportion of young people. Between 1971 and 1995 the proportion of young people aged under 15 fell from 24.1 per cent of the population to 19.4 per cent. The proportion of elderly people (those aged 65 and over) increased from 13.2 to 15.7 per cent, and the proportion over the normal retirement ages (60 or 65 years and over for women and men respectively) grew to 18.2 per cent in 1995. Among the elderly the number aged over 85 has more than doubled since 1971 and now exceeds 1 million.

There is a ratio of about 104 females to every 100 males in the population as a whole. There are about 3 per cent more male than female births every year. However, because of the higher mortality of men at all ages, there is a turning-point, at about 50 years of age, beyond which the number of women exceeds the number of men.

Distribution of Population

The population density is about 243 inhabitants per sq km, which is well above the EU average of about 116 per sq km. Of the four lands, England is by far the most densely populated, with 376 people per sq km.

Scotland is the least densely populated, with 66 people per sq km. Wales and Northern Ireland have 141 and 123 people per sq km respectively.

Since the 19th century there has been a trend for people to move away from congested urban centres into the suburbs. Between 1981 and 1995 a number of the large urban areas, such as Manchester, Merseyside, Sheffield, Glasgow and Dundee, experienced decreases in population, one of the largest being in Glasgow (13 per cent). Among the cities where the population rose in this period were London, Cardiff and Belfast. The regions with the highest rates of increase in population between 1981 and 1995, all in England, were the South West (10 per cent), South East (excluding London) and Eastern (8 per cent). Retirement migration is also a feature of population movement, the main recipient areas being the south coast of England and East Anglia.

International Migration

From 1991 to 1995 some 1.06 million people left Britain (excluding the Channel Islands and the Isle of Man) to live abroad. About 1.19 million came from overseas to live in Britain, so that net immigration increased the population by about 130,000. These figures exclude migration to and from the Irish Republic, and are also likely to exclude people admitted as visitors who were subsequently granted an extension of stay for a year or more.

In 1995 the total inflow of people intending to stay in Britain for one year or more was 245,000, while the outflow of people leaving to live abroad was 192,000 (see Table 6.2).

Nationality

Under the British Nationality Act 1981 there are three main forms of citizenship:

- British citizenship for people closely connected with Britain;

- British Dependent Territories citizenship for people connected with the dependent territories (see p. 121); and

- British Overseas citizenship for those citizens of the United Kingdom and

Table 6.2: International Migration 1995

	Inflow	Outflow	Balance
European Union	71,000	55,000	+16,000
Australia, Canada, New Zealand and South Africa	43,000	49,000	−5,000
Other Commonwealth countries	55,000	25,000	+30,000
United States	27,000	28,000	–
Middle East	11,000	9,000	+3,000
Other countries	37,000	27,000	+10,000
All countries	**245,000**	**192,000**	**+54,000**

Source: ONS (estimates derived from the *International Passenger Survey*)

Notes: 1. Differences between totals and the sums of their component parts are due to rounding.
2. Figures exclude migration between Britain and the Irish Republic.

Colonies who did not acquire either of the other citizenships when the 1981 Act came into force.

British citizenship is acquired automatically at birth by a child born in Britain if his or her mother or, if born legitimate, father is a British citizen or is settled in Britain. A child adopted in Britain by a British citizen is also a British citizen. A child born abroad to a British citizen born, adopted, naturalised or registered in Britain is generally a British citizen by descent. The Act safeguards the citizenship of a child born abroad to a British citizen in Crown service, certain related services, or in service under a European Union institution.

British citizenship may also be acquired:

- by registration for certain children, including those born in Britain who do not automatically acquire such citizenship at birth, or who have been born abroad to a parent who is a citizen by descent;

- by registration for British Dependent Territories citizens, British Overseas citizens, British subjects under the Act, British Nationals (Overseas) and British protected persons after five years' residence in Britain, except for people from Gibraltar, who may be registered without residence;

- by registration for stateless people and those who have previously renounced British nationality; and

- by naturalisation for all other adults aged 18 or over.

Naturalisation is at the Home Secretary's discretion. Requirements include five years' residence, or three years if the applicant's spouse is a British citizen. Those who are not married to a British citizen are also required to have a sufficient knowledge of English, Welsh or Scottish Gaelic; they must also intend to have their main home in Britain or be employed by the Crown, or by an international organisation of which Britain is a member, or by a company or association established in Britain.

Special arrangements covering certain Hong Kong residents have been made:

- the British Nationality (Hong Kong) Act 1990 made provision for the registration as British citizens before 30 June 1997 (when the territory returned to the People's Republic of China—see p. 131) of up to 50,000 people who were able to meet certain criteria, together with their spouses and any children who were still minors; and

- the British Nationality (Hong Kong) Act 1997 provided for the registration of solely British nationals after 1 July 1997.

In 1996, 43,154 people were granted British citizenship.

Immigration

Immigration into Britain is largely governed by the Immigration Act 1971 and the Immigration Rules made under it. The Rules set out the requirements to be met by those who are subject to immigration control and seek entry to, or leave to remain in, Britain. New Immigration Rules came into effect in 1994. British citizens and those Commonwealth citizens who had the right of abode before January 1983 maintain the right of abode and are not subject to immigration control.

In 1996, 10.3 million foreign and Commonwealth nationals (excluding nationals of the European Economic Area—see below) were admitted to Britain. Some 61,700 people were accepted for settlement.

Under the Immigration Rules nationals of certain specified countries or territorial entities must obtain a visa before they can enter Britain. Other nationals subject to immigration control require entry clearance when coming to work or settle in Britain. Visas and other entry clearances are normally obtained from the nearest or other specified British diplomatic post in a person's home country.

Nationals of the European Economic Area (EEA)—EU member states plus Norway, Iceland and Liechtenstein—are not subject to substantive immigration control. They may work in Britain without restriction. Provided they are working or able to support themselves financially, EEA nationals have a right to reside in Britain.

New Government Changes

With the intention of making the immigration system fairer for marriage partners of British citizens, the new Government has abolished the 'primary purpose' immigration rule introduced in 1980. Under this, a person wanting to marry a British citizen was refused entry to Britain if it was judged by an immigration officer that the primary purpose of the marriage was to settle in Britain. The rule was abolished in June 1997. The Government has stated that it considers that the rule penalised genuine marriages, divided families, and unnecessarily increased the administrative burden on the immigration system, and that its abolition will enable resources to be better focused on the other requirements regulating the entry of spouses to Britain.

In addition, work is in progress for a scheme to control unscrupulous immigration advisers.

Asylum

Britain has traditionally granted asylum to those fleeing persecution and respects its obligations under the United Nations Convention and Protocol relating to the Status of Refugees. These provide that refugees lawfully resident should enjoy treatment at least as favourable as that accorded to the indigenous population. In recent years there has been a significant change in both the numbers and the motivation of those seeking asylum in Britain, with many asylum seekers apparently motivated by economic rather than political factors. Between 1984 and 1995 the number of asylum seekers rose from 4,000 to 55,000 (including dependants); of whom only 6 per cent were accepted as being genuine refugees. However, in 1996 the total fell to 3,700, following the withdrawal of entitlement to social welfare benefits from those who claim asylum after entering Britain (see chapter 25). In common with other European countries,

Table 6.3: Acceptances for Settlement 1986 and 1996		
	1986	*1996*
Pakistan	5,530	6,250
India	4,140	4,620
United States	3,740	4,030
Turkey	400	3,720
Nigeria	560	3,220
Bangladesh	4,760	2,720
Sri Lanka	800	2,180
Australia	2,850	2,120
Ghana	520	1,970
Japan	890	1,780
Iran	1,640	1,720
Iraq	430	1,580
Jamaica	490	1,420
New Zealand	2,510	1,360
Hong Kong	860	1,240
People's Republic of China	100	1,180
South Africa	730	1,040
Uganda	80	1,040
Philippines	990	1,030
Canada	1,200	970

Source: Home Office

Britain has also reviewed its procedures. The Asylum and Immigration Act 1996, introduced under the previous Government, created the power to designate countries of destination as not generally giving rise to a serious risk of persecution. It made appeals against return to EU, and certain other, safe third countries exercisable only after removal from Britain; and made it a criminal offence for an employer to employ someone who does not have permission to reside or work in Britain.

In 1996, 38,960 asylum decisions were made, of which around 6 per cent were grants of asylum. The main nationalities applying for asylum were people from Nigeria, India, Somalia, Pakistan, Turkey, and countries formerly part of the Soviet Union.

In August 1997 the new Government announced details of an inter-departmental study of the asylum process. The study will look at all aspects of the process across government, including the provision of accommodation and support to asylum seekers. The aim is to identify more effective arrangements for handling asylum claims and the provision of support consistent with the Government's commitment to ensure swift and fair decisions on asylum cases and to meet its obligations under the United Nations Convention. In addition, a Special Immigration Appeals Bill is before Parliament. Its main provisions are to provide a right of appeal for individuals liable to deportation on grounds of national security; and to set up a new body with decision-making powers to consider such appeals.

LANGUAGE

English is the main language spoken in Britain, and is also one of the most widely used in the world.[1] Recent estimates suggest that 310 million people speak it as their first language, with a similar number speaking it as a second language. It is an official language in a large number of overseas countries, and is widely used internationally as the main language for purposes such as air traffic control, international maritime communications and academic gatherings.

Modern English derives primarily from one of the dialects of Old English (or Anglo-Saxon), itself made up of several Western Germanic dialects taken to Britain in the early 5th century. However, it has been very greatly influenced by other languages, particularly Latin, the language of learning and religion from the time of Old English and, following the Norman conquest, by French, the language of court, government and the nobility for many years after 1066. The re-emergence of English as the standard language of England was signified by such events as the Statute of Pleading in 1362, which laid down that English was to replace French as the language of law. The 14th century saw the first major English literature since Anglo-Saxon days, with works such as *Piers Plowman* by William Langland and the *Canterbury Tales* by Geoffrey Chaucer. However, there remained great regional variations in the language, and spellings were not always standardised.

Following the introduction of the printing press to England by William Caxton in the late 15th century, there was a considerable flowering of English literature in the 16th and early 17th centuries. William Shakespeare, Edmund Spenser and Christopher Marlowe produced work that is still famous today. Cranmer's prayerbook and the Authorised ('King James') Version of the Bible, which have had a profound effect on literature down to modern times, also date from this period. About this time, too, translations of Latin, Italian and other European works into English vastly expanded the English language. The work of early lexicographers, of whom the most famous was Samuel Johnson (1709–84), led to greater standardisation in matters such as spelling.

ETHNIC AND NATIONAL MINORITIES

For centuries people from overseas have settled in Britain, either to escape political or religious persecution or in search of better economic opportunities.

The Irish have long formed a large section of the population. Jewish refugees who came to Britain towards the end of the 19th century

---

[1] For the Welsh language see p. 29; for Gaelic see p. 26.

and in the 1930s were followed by other European refugees after 1945. Substantial immigration from the Caribbean and the South Asian subcontinent date principally from the 1950s and 1960s, while many people of Asian descent moved to this country from eastern Africa. In recent years, the number of people coming from the South Asian subcontinent has remained roughly stable, but there has been a rise in immigration from some African countries, such as Ghana, Nigeria and Somalia (see Table 6.3).

The 1991 census included for the first time a question on ethnic grouping. This found that 94.5 per cent of the population belonged to the 'White' group, while just over 3 million people (5.5 per cent) described themselves as belonging to another ethnic group (see Table 6.4).

Overall, just under half of the ethnic minority population was born in Britain. A higher proportion was under 16 than for the White group (respectively 33 per cent and 19 per cent), but a much lower proportion was over pensionable age (respectively 3 per cent and about 17 per cent).

Members of ethnic minority groups were heavily concentrated in industrial and urban areas, and over half lived in the South East, especially in London. The highest proportion was in the London borough of Brent: nearly 45 per cent of the local population. Ethnic

minority groups also accounted for over a third of the population in the London boroughs of Newham, Tower Hamlets and Hackney. Outside London the main concentrations were in Leicester, Slough, Luton, Bradford, the West Midlands and the Pennine conurbation. Regional concentrations varied among the ethnic groups. About three-fifths (60 per cent) of people from black ethnic groups lived in London, compared with about two-fifths (41 per cent) of Indians and just under one fifth (18 per cent) of Pakistanis, who were concentrated in other metropolitan areas such as the West Midlands and West Yorkshire.

According to the Labour Force Survey (see chapter 12), in 1996:

- 2.1 million people of working age (6 per cent) belonged to ethnic minority groups.

- Economic activity rates varied widely between ethnic groups; these variations were greatest among women. In 1996, working age White and Black Caribbean women had economic activity rates of 73 per cent compared with 22–24 per cent for Bangladeshi and Pakistani women (who also had the lowest employment rates at 17 per cent).

- Ethnic minority groups had lower employment rates than the White population and higher unemployment rates for both men and women but the variation between rates for minority groups was greater than that between White rates and the closest minority groups.

- The unemployment rates for Black African (28 per cent) and Pakistani men (27 per cent) were three times that for White men (9 per cent). Black African (24 per cent) and Pakistani (30 per cent) women had unemployment rates four times that of White women (6 per cent) .

Table 6.4: Resident Population by Ethnic Group, 1991, Great Britain

	Number of people (000s)	Per cent
White	51,874	94.5
All ethnic minority groups	3,015	5.5
Black groups	891	1.6
Black Caribbean	500	0.9
Black African	212	0.4
Black other	178	0.3
Indian	840	1.5
Pakistani	477	0.9
Bangladeshi	163	0.3
Chinese	157	0.3
Other groups	488	0.9
All groups	54,889	100.0

Source: Office for National Statistics

Alleviating Racial Disadvantage

Although many members of the Black and Asian communities are concentrated in the inner cities, where there are problems of deprivation and social stress, progress has been made over the last 20 years in tackling racial disadvantage in Britain.

Many individuals have achieved distinction in their careers and in public life, and the proportion of ethnic minority members occupying professional and managerial positions is increasing. There are at present nine Black and Asian Members of Parliament, and the number of ethnic minority councillors in local government is growing. There has also been an expansion of commercial enterprise, and there are numerous self-help projects in ethnic minority communities. Black competitors have represented Britain in a range of sports (such as athletics, cricket and football), and ethnic minority talents in the arts and in entertainment have increasingly been recognised.

Economic, environmental, educational and health programmes of central government and local authorities exist to combat disadvantage. There are also special allocations, mainly through grants from the Home Office and Department of the Environment, Transport and the Regions, which channel extra resources into projects of specific benefit to ethnic minorities. These include, for example, the provision of specialist teachers for children needing English language tuition. Cultural and recreational schemes and the health and personal social services also take account of the particular needs of ethnic minorities.

The Government is promoting equal opportunities for ethnic minorities through training programmes, including greater provision for unemployed people who need training in English as a second language. A Race Relations Forum is to be set up to advise on the issues affecting ethnic minority communities.

Race Relations Legislation

The Race Relations Act 1976, which applies to England, Scotland and Wales, strengthened previous legislation passed in the 1960s. It makes discrimination unlawful on grounds of colour, race, nationality or ethnic or national origin in the provision of goods, facilities and services, in employment, in housing, in education and in advertising. The 1976 Act also gave complainants direct access to civil courts and, for employment complaints, to industrial tribunals. It is a criminal offence to incite racial hatred under the provisions of the Public Order Act 1986.

Parallel legislation was introduced for Northern Ireland in August 1997.

In order to protect ethnic minority communities from intimidation, the Government proposes to create a new offence of racial harassment and a new crime of racially motivated violence. It also proposes to introduce court orders which prohibit named individuals from harassing the community at large, including racially motivated harassment. A consultation paper is to be issued shortly and a Crime and Disorder Bill will be published later in 1997.

Commission for Racial Equality

The Commission for Racial Equality was established by the 1976 Act. It has power to investigate unlawful discriminatory practices and to issue non-discrimination notices requiring such practices to cease. It has an important educational role and has issued codes of practice in employment, education, healthcare, maternity services and housing. It also provides advice to the general public about the Race Relations Act and may help individuals with their complaints about racial discrimination. In 1996 the Commission registered 1,750 applications for assistance and successfully handled 142 litigation cases (this includes 101 cases settled on terms, and 41 successful after hearing). It can also undertake or fund research.

The Commission supports the work of 84 racial equality councils. These are autonomous voluntary bodies set up in most areas with a significant ethnic minority population to promote equality of opportunity and good relations at the local level. The Commission helps pay the salaries of officers employed by the racial equality councils, most of whom also receive funds from their local authorities. It also gives grants to ethnic minority self-help groups and to other projects run by or for the benefit of the minority communities.

A Commission for Racial Equality for Northern Ireland was established in August 1997, with powers similar to that for England, Wales and Scotland.

THE ECONOMIC AND SOCIAL PATTERN

Marked improvements in the standard of living have taken place during the 20th century. According to a United Nations report on human development published in 1997, Britain ranked 15th out of 175 countries on a human development index that combines life expectancy, education levels and basic purchasing power. Britain's gross domestic product (GDP) per head is around the average for the 15 EU nations.

Income and Wealth

Wages and salaries remain the main source of household income for most people, although the proportion they contribute has declined, from 68 per cent in 1971 to 56 per cent in 1995. During this period income from private

Despite the rise in real wealth, inequalities remain in income and in areas such as health. The gap between those with high and low incomes has tended to grow over time, especially during the 1980s, although during the 1990s this gap has stabilised. In August 1997 the Government announced the establishment of a Social Exclusion Unit in the Cabinet Office to draw up a strategy for tackling problems of poverty, homelessness, public health and crime.

pensions and annuities has more than doubled, to 11 per cent of household income in 1995, partly as a result of the growing number of elderly people and the increased likelihood of them having occupational pensions. In 1995 other main sources of household income included self-employment

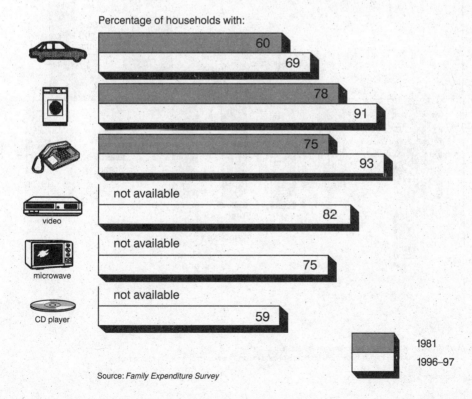

Availability of Certain Durable Goods

Percentage of households with:

	1981	1996-97
car	60	69
washing machine	78	91
telephone	75	93
video	not available	82
microwave	not available	75
CD player	not available	59

1981
1996–97

Source: *Family Expenditure Survey*

(10 per cent), rent, dividend and interest payments (7 per cent) and social security benefits (13 per cent). Direct taxes and social security contributions consume a lower proportion of personal income than in most other G7 countries.

The value of wealth held by the personal sector in Britain was £2,830,000 million in 1995. Investment in life assurance and pension funds accounted for 34 per cent, double the proportion in 1981. The proportion of wealth in dwellings declined rapidly during the 1990s, to 26 per cent in 1995, reflecting substantial falls in house prices. Nevertheless, a large proportion of households—67 per

cent—own their own homes. About two-fifths of these households own their property outright, while the remainder have a mortgage.

Wealth is less evenly distributed than income, with the richest 10 per cent of the population having 48 per cent of marketable wealth in 1993. The inclusion of 'non-marketable' wealth, such as rights in occupational and state pension schemes, reduces this share substantially, to 33 per cent.

The proportion of net wealth held in stocks, shares and unit trusts nearly doubled between 1981 and 1995, to 15 per cent. Prior to 1997, about 10 million people—22 per cent

Changes in Average Household Food Consumption 1986–1996

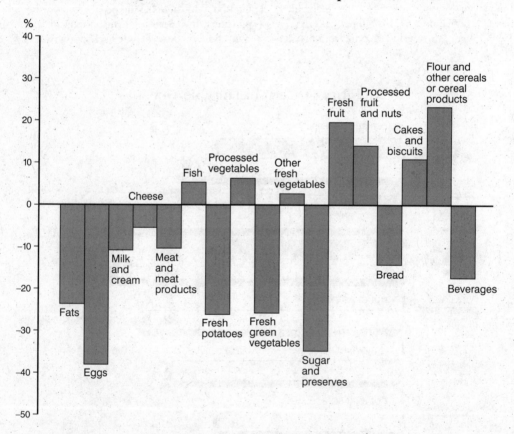

Note: Average household food consumption may be affected by changes in such factors as household composition and income as well as changes in eating habits.

Source: National Food Survey, MAFF

of the adult population in Great Britain—owned shares, but this has increased considerably during 1997 as a result of the conversion of five large building societies to banks (see chapter 16).

Eating and Drinking Habits

The general level of nutrition remains high. There has been a significant shift in eating patterns over the last decade, reflecting greater emphasis on health, frozen and convenience foods. Changes in household consumption of selected foods between 1986 and 1996 are shown in the diagram on p. 42. Consumption of several items, such as sugar, eggs, fresh potatoes and fresh green vegetables, has declined substantially. Other changes include:

- a long-term decline in consumption of red meats—beef, lamb and pork—while at the same time consumption of poultry has been rising;

- a rise in fish consumption, accompanied by a switch away from fresh white fish towards fat fish, canned fish and shellfish;

- an increase in purchases of semi-skimmed milks, with skimmed milk now constituting more than half of the total household consumption of liquid milk;

- a decline in the total consumption of cooking and spreading fats, with large falls in butter and lard usage being partly offset by rapid rises in the consumption of vegetable and salad oils and low and reduced-fat spreads;

- a long-term rise in consumption of fresh fruit, such as bananas; and

- a large increase in fruit juice consumption.

In 1996 there was a particularly large fall in beef and veal consumption, of over 16 per cent, reflecting concern over the safety of eating beef (see p. 280).

Average mineral and nutrient intakes are generally above the daily amounts recommended by the Department of Health. Health considerations appear to be influencing food consumption, for example, in the fall in red meat sales, the move away from whole milk and the growth in low fat spread consumption.

There has been an increase in the number of meals eaten away from home, for example, in restaurants or at work, and a growth in the consumption of food from 'take-away' and 'fast food' shops.

Alcohol consumption has changed little in recent years, although it rose by about 5 per cent in 1996. Beer is the most popular drink among male drinkers, whose overall consumption is significantly higher than that of women. A high proportion of beer is drunk in public houses ('pubs'), traditional social centres for many people, and in clubs. Lager is estimated to account for over half of all beer sales. The largest consumers of alcohol are those aged 18 to 24, with consumption generally declining with age. Consumption of table wine has grown, although there has been a slight decline in the consumption of higher strength wines such as sherry and port.

Women

The economic and domestic lives of women have been transformed in the 20th century, partly as a result of women obtaining many political and legal rights previously open only to men. The growth of part-time and flexible working patterns has allowed more women to combine raising a family with paid employment. Women now make up around 46 per cent of the workforce in employment, with about 850,000 running their own businesses. However, women are still under-represented in some occupations and at senior levels. For example, fewer than 5 per cent of company directors are women.

The Government supports 'Opportunity 2000', an employer-led initiative to increase the participation of women in the workforce and to promote family-friendly employment policies. Membership stands at over 300 employers, with organisations employing about a quarter of the workforce being committed to the campaign.

Responsibility for co-ordinating government policy lies with the two Ministers for Women (one of whom is the Secretary of State for Social Security) and a Cabinet Sub-committee on Women's Issues. This is chaired by the Secretary of State for Social Security.

At the May 1997 General Election the number of women MPs nearly doubled to 120: 101 Labour, 13 Conservative, three Liberal Democrat, two Scottish National Party and the Speaker. Women's representation at ministerial level in the Government is now at a record level, with five women in the Cabinet and 17 other women ministers.

The Government is seeking to improve communications with women's organisations. It has launched a review of the Women's National Commission, which has traditionally been the mechanism for consultation and communication between the Government and women's organisations. About 50 of the main national women's organisations are represented on the Commission. The review aims to ensure that there is a strong, independent organisation suitable for the 21st century.

The Government wants women to make their full contribution to the economy and to improve the living standards and quality of life of their families. It is taking action in a number of areas to enable more women to join or rejoin the labour force, including:

- launching the New Deal for Lone Parents in a number of areas in July 1997—it will be available throughout the country in October 1998. It is part of the Welfare-to-Work programme (see p.173), and is intended to help more lone parents (the vast majority of whom are women) to get back to work by giving them jobsearch help and advice and training, and help with childcare. Lone parents whose youngest child has reached school age will get help and advice on jobsearch, training and childcare from a personal adviser;

- promoting family-friendly employment policies, which enable women to balance successfully their home and work commitments;

- changing the benefits system to help those in work who are on low incomes to pay for childcare (see p. 429);

- providing funding through the National Lottery for out-of-school activities for children; and

- helping to increase the supply of childcare, through voluntary organisations training more people under the New Deal for young people (see p. 173).

The Government is developing a National Childcare Strategy, which will help to ensure that sufficient childcare places are available to match the requirements of the labour market. This will extend the Out of School Childcare Initiative, which offers parents with children of school age the chance to participate more fully in the labour market; around 74,000 childcare places in Great Britain are available under the initiative

The Ministers for Women are also co-ordinating work on tackling violence against women.

The Government is also taking steps to ensure that women's concerns are at the centre of policy-making, and that women's perspectives are automatically considered when policy is formulated.

Equal Opportunities

The Sex Discrimination Acts 1975 and 1986 make discrimination between men and women unlawful, with certain limited exceptions, in employment, education, training and the provision of housing, goods, facilities and services. Discriminatory job recruitment advertisements are unlawful. Complaints of discrimination concerning employment are dealt with by industrial tribunals; other complaints are taken before county courts in England and Wales or the Sheriff Court in Scotland. Under the Equal Pay Act 1970, as amended in 1984, women in Great Britain are entitled to equal pay with men when doing work that is the same or broadly similar, work which is rated as equivalent, or work which is of equal value. Parallel legislation on sex discrimination and equal pay applies in Northern Ireland.

The Equal Opportunities Commission (EOC), an independent statutory body, has the duties of working towards the elimination of sex discrimination and promoting equality of opportunity. The EOC may advise people of their rights under the Acts and may give assistance to help individuals conduct a case. It is empowered to carry out formal investigations and issue notices requiring discriminatory practices to stop. The EOC runs an 'Equality Exchange', with around 500 members, which enables employers to exchange information on good practice.

The Voluntary Sector

There is a long tradition in Britain of voluntary service to the community. Hundreds of thousands of voluntary organisations exist, ranging from national bodies to small local groups. Voluntary organisations may be staffed by professional workers, but most rely on the efforts of volunteers at some level. It has been estimated that up to half of all adults take part in some form of organised voluntary work in the course of a year. Many volunteers are involved in work which improves the quality of life in their local communities or, more widely, give their time to help organise events or groups in areas as diverse as social welfare, education, sport, heritage and the arts. A very large number of volunteers are involved in activities to protect or improve the environment, working, for example, for the National Trust, which has over 2 million members (see p. 368).

The Government greatly values the voluntary sector's contribution to society and, as a result, is keen to encourage productive partnerships between the statutory and voluntary sectors. For example, voluntary organisations are important providers of government-supported employment and training services for unemployed people.

'Make a Difference' Initiative

The Voluntary and Community Unit within the Home Office[2] co-ordinates government policy towards the voluntary sector throughout Britain. It also aims to support a

healthy and cost-effective voluntary sector and to promote volunteering throughout the community. The 'Make a Difference' initiative, launched in 1994, brought together the business, voluntary and public sectors to promote volunteering.

Government funding in 1996–97 has included grants of £2.3 million to help existing volunteer bureaux increase their effectiveness, while £2.5 million has been given to complete a network of local volunteer development agencies. These agencies provide a focus for volunteering in localities where there is at present no volunteer bureau.

Funding

Voluntary organisations receive income from several sources, including

- contributions from individuals, businesses and trusts;
- central and local government grants;
- earnings from commercial activities and investments; and
- fees from central and local government for those services which are provided on a contractual basis.

In 1994–95 direct grants to voluntary organisations from government amounted to £957 million.

Charities currently benefit from tax reliefs worth £1,700 million. These consist of about £1,000 million direct tax relief, £200 million VAT relief, and the balance on relief from business rates. Tax changes in recent budgets have helped the voluntary sector secure more funds from industry and individuals. The Gift Aid scheme provides tax relief on single cash donations of at least £250. Under the Payroll Giving scheme, employees can also make tax-free donations to charity from their earnings.

A review of the taxation of charities was announced in July 1997. A consultation paper will be published in spring 1998.

Charities

In England and Wales over 181,800 charities are registered with the Charity Commission, a non-ministerial government department. Their combined income is around £18,000

---

[2] In May 1997 responsibility for the voluntary sector was transferred from the former Department of National Heritage to the Home Office.

million. Over 70 per cent of those registered had a recorded income of under £10,000. The Commission also gives advice to trustees of charities on their administration and checks abuse. Organisations may qualify for charitable status if they are established for exclusively charitable purposes such as the relief of poverty, the advancement of education or religion, or the promotion of certain other purposes of public benefit. These may include good community relations, the prevention of racial discrimination, the protection of health and the promotion of equal opportunity. The Charity Commission also has a statutory responsibility to ensure that charities make effective use of their resources.

Recent legislation has strengthened the Commissioners' power to investigate and supervise charities. For example, new measures to protect charities and donors from bogus fund-raisers came into force in 1995, while a new framework for charity accounts and reports came into force in 1996.

The introduction of the National Lottery (see p. 47) has given charities and voluntary organisations new opportunities to secure substantial new funding for projects across a range of activities. By October 1997 the National Lottery Charities Board, which distributes the portion of the proceeds of the National Lottery allocated to charities, had made over 11,000 grants totalling over £680 million. The Board's aim is to give grants to support organisations which help meet the needs of those in society at greatest disadvantage, and to improve the quality of life in the community.

The Charities Aid Foundation, an independent body, is one of the main organisations aiding the flow of funds to charity from individuals, companies and grant-making trusts.

Umbrella Organisations

The National Council for Voluntary Organisations is one of the main co-ordinating bodies in England, providing close links between voluntary organisations, government departments, local authorities, the European Commission and the private sector; around 1,000 national voluntary organisations are members. It also protects the interests and independence of voluntary agencies, and provides them with advice, information and

Table 6.5: Income of the Top Fund-raising Charities, 1995–96

Charity	Total income	£ million Voluntary income[a]
National Trust	151.0	77.0
Oxfam	129.4	92.3
Barnardo's	96.0	47.3
British Red Cross Society	95.2	38.4
Save the Children Fund	84.4	33.0
Imperial Cancer Research Fund	80.4	70.9
SCOPE (for People with Cerebral Palsy)	79.2	37.2
Salvation Army	74.4	36.3
Cancer Research Campaign	66.2	60.2
British Heart Foundation	64.9	57.2
Royal National Lifeboat Institution	61.1	55.7
Help the Aged	52.4	43.1
National Society for the Prevention of Cruelty to Children	44.8	35.0
Marie Curie Cancer Care	44.4	34.3
Royal National Institute for the Blind	54.2	27.1
Cancer Relief Macmillan Fund	38.2	34.1

Source: Charities Aid Foundation

[a] Includes donations, legacies, covenants and Gift Aid, and charity shop income.

other services. Councils in Scotland, Wales and Northern Ireland perform similar functions. The National Association of Councils for Voluntary Service is another umbrella organisation, which has a membership of over 230 local Councils for Voluntary Service (CVS), covering both urban and rural areas of England. CVS are local voluntary organisations set up and run by local groups to support, promote and develop local voluntary action.

National Lottery

Launched in 1994, the National Lottery has become the biggest lottery in the world. About 95 per cent of adults have participated and nearly 70 per cent regularly buy tickets. Lottery ticket sales amounted to £4,720 million in 1996–97. Tickets or scratchcards are available from almost 35,500 retail outlets.

In February 1997 a new mid-week draw was introduced, supplementing the weekly draw on Saturdays. Ticket sales have subsequently risen by around 30 per cent. Saturday sales are now running at between £60 million and £70 million, while the mid-week draw attracts sales of between £27 million and £30 million. Weekly sales of scratchcards are over £16 million.

Camelot Group plc, a private sector consortium, has the franchise to run the Lottery until 2001. The Lottery is regulated by the Director General of the National Lottery, who heads the Office of the National Lottery ('OFLOT').

Large sums have already been raised for good causes by the Lottery—£3,065 million up to February 1997. By 2001 it is expected to have generated at least £10,000 million for good causes, around £1,000 million more than originally forecast. The proceeds from the Lottery are distributed as follows:

- 50 per cent for prizes;
- 28 per cent for good causes, one of the highest proportions allocated for this purpose by any national lottery;
- 12 per cent for National Lottery duty;
- 5 per cent for retailers' commission; and
- 5 per cent for operating costs and profit.

Awards

Nearly 28,000 projects have received awards since the launch of the Lottery. Awards are distributed to five good causes: sport, charities, the arts, heritage and projects to mark the millennium. Each receives one-fifth of the money generated for good causes. There are a number of large-value schemes, but over half the awards have been for less than £50,000.

Millennium Projects

The Millennium Commission is supporting projects which mark the end of the second millennium and the start of the third. By July 1997 the Commission had awarded £993 million to 111 capital projects. It is also supporting the New Millennium Experience at Greenwich in London (see p. 371), a Millennium Festival in 2000, and a Millennium Awards scheme designed to help individuals— 13 voluntary and other organisations have become partners under the scheme and up to 8,000 individuals are expected to benefit from projects announced so far.

Among the 14 'landmark' projects supported are:

- the Odyssey Project, providing a mixture of education, entertainment and sporting activities in Belfast;
- the Millennium Stadium in Cardiff (see p. 527);
- the Millennium Seed Bank, at the Royal Botanic Gardens (see p. 342);
- a National Space Science Centre, in Leicester; and
- a new Tate Gallery of Modern Art in London (see p. 483).

Planned Changes

In July 1997 the Government issued a White Paper containing its plans to reform the Lottery. A Bill will be introduced into Parliament later in 1997.

A sixth good cause—the New Opportunities Fund—will support spending on initiatives to improve education, health and the environment.

The first three initiatives will involve:

- training and support for Britain's 500,000 teachers and some 10,000 library staff in information and communications technology;
- out-of-school activities, including homework clubs and creative activities; and
- a network of healthy living centres.

The Bill will also provide for the establishment of NESTA—the National Endowment for Science, Technology and the Arts. NESTA, an independent trust, will help talented individuals to develop their full potential in the creative industries, science and technology; help to turn ideas into products or services which are effectively exploited; and contribute to the advance of public education about, and awareness and appreciation of, these subjects. The Government believes that NESTA should have a particular focus on multimedia and other areas where the arts and science and technology meet.

Various measures are proposed to improve the distribution of Lottery funding to good causes, for example, by ensuring a more strategic approach and that money is allocated fairly across all regions of Britain and among different groups in society.

The Government wishes to introduce a new system for operating the Lottery when the current licence expires in 2001. It is inviting proposals for a system based on the objectives of maximising the return to good causes and removing unnecessary profit margins. A new panel will assist the Director General of OFLOT in selecting the Lottery operator.

Leisure Trends

Nearly 16 per cent of total household expenditure went on leisure goods and services in 1996–97. The most common leisure activities are home-based, or social, such as visiting relatives or friends. Television viewing is by far the most popular leisure pastime, and nearly all households have one television set or more. Average viewing time is over 25 hours a week. Around 82 per cent of households now have at least one video recorder, compared with 30 per cent in 1985.

Listening to radio has been increasing, and averages over 10 hours a week. Purchases of compact discs have risen very rapidly, and since 1992 have exceeded the sales of audio cassettes. The proportion of households with a compact disc player has grown considerably, from 15 per cent in 1989 to 59 per cent in 1996–97. Ownership of some other consumer durable goods, such as microwave ovens and home computers, has also been rising significantly.

Other popular pursuits include: reading, do-it-yourself home improvements, gardening and going out for a meal, for a drink or to the cinema. About half of households have a pet. Cats have overtaken dogs to become the most popular type of pet—the latest estimates being 7.2 million and 6.6 million respectively.

Holidays

In 1996, 58 per cent of the adult population took at least one long holiday of four or more nights away from home. The number of long holidays taken by British residents was 54 million, of which 31 million were taken in Britain. The most frequented free attraction was Blackpool Pleasure Beach (Lancashire), with an estimated 7.5 million visitors in 1996. The most popular holiday destinations are the West Country, Scotland, the south of England and Wales.

In 1996 the most visited destinations for overseas holidays of one night or more by British residents were:

- Spain (28 per cent);
- France (9 per cent);
- the United States (8 per cent); and
- Greece (6 per cent).

British residents took 23 million long holidays overseas in 1996, of which 57 per cent involved 'package' arrangements. About 70 per cent of all holidays abroad are taken in Europe, although many people take holidays further afield, for example to the United States, the Far East or Australia. The proportion of adults taking two or more holidays of four or more nights in 1996 was 24 per cent.

Further Reading

Ethnic Minorities (2nd edn). Aspects of Britain series, The Stationery Office, 1997.
Make a Difference: An Outline Volunteering Strategy for the UK. Home Office, 1995.
The People's Lottery. Cm 3709. The Stationery Office, 1997.
Population. Aspects of Britain series, HMSO, 1995.
Social Focus on Families. Office for National Statistics, The Stationery Office, 1997.
Women (2nd edn). Aspects of Britain series, HMSO, 1996.

Annual Reports

Family Spending, Office for National Statistics, The Stationery Office.
Living in Britain: Results from the General Household Survey. The Stationery Office.
Social Trends, Office for National Statistics, The Stationery Office.

7 Government

The system of parliamentary government in Britain is not based on a written constitution, but is the result of gradual evolution over many centuries. The Monarchy is the oldest institution of government, dating back to at least the ninth century. Parliament is one of the oldest representative assemblies in the world, the House of Lords and the House of Commons both having medieval origins. The new Labour administration has held referendums in Scotland and Wales which have confirmed popular demand for devolving power from the Westminster Parliament to a Scottish Parliament and a Welsh Assembly; and a referendum in London on setting up a city-wide authority and directly elected mayor is planned. Other major proposals include incorporating the European Convention on Human Rights into domestic law; increasing the openness of government through a Freedom of Information Act; modernising the procedures of the House of Commons; and reforming the House of Lords.

The Constitution

The British constitution, unlike that of most other countries, is not set out in any single document. Instead it is made up of statute law, common law and conventions. (Conventions are rules and practices which are not legally enforceable but which are regarded as indispensable to the working of government.)

The constitution can be altered by Act of Parliament, or by general agreement, and is thus adaptable to changing political conditions.

The organs of government overlap but can be clearly distinguished:

Parliament is the legislature and the supreme authority. The *executive* consists of: the Government—the Cabinet and other ministers responsible for national policies; government departments and agencies, responsible for national administration; local authorities, responsible for many local services; public corporations, responsible for operating particular nationalised industries; independent bodies responsible for regulating the privatised industries; or other bodies, subject to ministerial control.

The *judiciary* (see chapter 8) determines common law and interprets statutes.

Origins of Government

The origins of government in Britain are to be found in each of its four component parts:

England, Wales, Scotland and Northern Ireland. England was united as a kingdom over a thousand years ago, and Wales became part of the kingdom during the Middle Ages (see p. 27). The thrones of England and Scotland were dynastically united in 1603, and in 1707 legislation passed in the two countries provided for the establishment of a single Parliament of Great Britain with supreme authority both in England and Wales and in Scotland (see p. 21). Ireland had had links with the kingdom of England since the 13th century, and in 1800 the creation of the United Kingdom was completed by a union joining the Irish Parliament to that of Great Britain (see p. 13). In 1922 Southern Ireland (now the Irish Republic) became an entirely separate and self-governing country. The six counties of Northern Ireland had been given their own subordinate Parliament in 1920, and voted to remain within the United Kingdom. The British Parliament at Westminster in London—with an elected chamber comprising members from English, Scottish, Welsh and Northern Ireland constituencies—thus represents people sharing very varied backgrounds and traditions. It has ultimate authority for government and law-making, but administrative arrangements have developed in such a way as to take account of the particular needs of different areas.

Administration of Scottish, Welsh and Northern Ireland Affairs

England and Wales on the one hand and Scotland on the other have different systems of law, a different judiciary, different education systems, different systems of local government and, for most domestic matters, different government departments. Wales has its own language and cultural traditions. In Scotland, departments are grouped under a Secretary of State—a Cabinet minister with a ministerial team—who has responsibility in Scotland for a wide range of policy matters. He is head of The Scottish Office, with headquarters in Edinburgh and an office in London (see p. 536). The distinctive conditions and needs of Scotland and its people are also reflected in separate Scottish legislation on many domestic matters. In the administration of Welsh affairs there is already a considerable measure of devolution under a Secretary of State, who is also a member of the Cabinet, with a ministerial team (for further details see p. 537.) The Secretary of State's department, the Welsh Office, is based in Cardiff with branches throughout Wales and a small ministerial office in London.

The British Government assumed direct responsibility for Northern Ireland from the Northern Ireland Parliament in 1972 (see p. 14), and since then the Secretary of State for Northern Ireland, with a seat in the Cabinet, has been in charge of the Northern Ireland Office. Assisted by a ministerial team, the Secretary of State has overall responsibility for the government of Northern Ireland and is directly responsible for political and constitutional matters, security policy and broad economic questions and other major policy issues.

Proposals for Devolution

Legislation was passed in July 1997 to allow the people of Scotland and Wales to vote in separate referendums (held in September 1997), on proposals to devolve power from Parliament at Westminster to a Scottish Parliament (see p. 22) and a Welsh Assembly (see p. 28). Following the endorsement of the proposals in each referendum, the Government is to introduce legislation before the end of 1997 to implement the devolution settlements.

The Scottish Parliament would have law-making powers, including defined and limited financial powers to vary revenue. It would extend democratic control over the responsibilities currently exercised by the Scottish Office. The Welsh Assembly would provide democratic control over the existing Welsh Office functions. It would have secondary legislative powers and would be able to reform and control the non-departmental public bodies (NDPBs—see p. 74) in Wales. The Scottish and Welsh bodies would each be elected by both a simple majority system and a form of proportional representation.

The responsibilities of the Westminster Parliament would remain unchanged over economic, defence and foreign policy.

Proposed Code of Human Rights

The Government is to publish a White Paper in autumn 1997 on proposals to enact a Code of Rights which would incorporate the European Convention on Human Rights into domestic law. This would enable people in Britain to secure decisions on their human rights from British courts and not just from the European Court of Human Rights in Strasbourg.

At present Britain is virtually alone among the major nations of Western Europe in that there is no direct means for its citizens to assert their Convention rights through their national courts. British courts can only take the Convention into account in certain limited circumstances, and when any breach of the Convention is found by the European Court in Strasbourg, courts in Britain are bound to amend domestic laws and procedures to make good the breach and to prevent a recurrence. In the Government's view, incorporation of the Convention would increase the judges' powers to protect the individual against the abuse of power by the State.

For the first time judges would be given a framework by Parliament within which to interpret the law. Incorporation would make Convention rights accessible in British courts at every level, making them British rights and not just European rights.

The Monarchy

The Monarchy is the oldest institution of government. Queen Elizabeth II is herself directly descended from King Egbert, who united England under his rule in 829. The only interruption in the history of the Monarchy was the republic, which lasted from 1649 to 1660.

Today the Queen is not only Head of State, but also a symbol of national unity. The Queen's title in Britain is: 'Elizabeth the Second, by the Grace of God of the United Kingdom of Great Britain and Northern Ireland and of Her other Realms and Territories Queen, Head of the Commonwealth, Defender of the Faith'.

In the Channel Islands and the Isle of Man the Queen is represented by a Lieutenant-Governor.

The Commonwealth

Although the seat of the Monarchy is in Britain, the Queen is also head of state of a number of Commonwealth states.[1] In each such state the Queen is represented by a Governor-General, appointed by her on the advice of the ministers of the country concerned and completely independent of the British Government.

In British Dependent Territories (see p. 121) the Queen is usually represented by governors, who are responsible to the British Government for the administration of the countries concerned.

Succession

The title to the Crown is derived partly from statute and partly from common law rules of descent. Despite interruptions in the direct line of succession, the hereditary principle upon which it was founded has always been preserved.

Sons of the Sovereign have precedence over daughters in succeeding to the throne. When a daughter succeeds, she becomes Queen Regnant, and has the same powers as a king. The consort of a king takes her husband's rank and style, becoming Queen. The constitution does not give any special rank or privileges to the husband of a Queen Regnant.

Under the Act of Settlement of 1700, only Protestant descendants of Princess Sophia, the Electress of Hanover (a granddaughter of James I of England and VI of Scotland) are eligible to succeed. The order of succession can be altered only by common consent of the countries of the Commonwealth of which the Queen is Sovereign.

Accession

The Sovereign succeeds to the throne as soon as his or her predecessor dies: there is no interregnum. He or she is at once proclaimed at an Accession Council, to which all members

---

[1] The other Commonwealth states of which the Queen is head of state are: Antigua and Barbuda; Australia; Bahamas; Barbados; Belize; Canada; Grenada; Jamaica; New Zealand; Papua New Guinea; St Christopher and Nevis; Saint Lucia; St Vincent and the Grenadines; Solomon Islands and Tuvalu.

The Royal Family from the Reign of Queen Victoria to August 1997

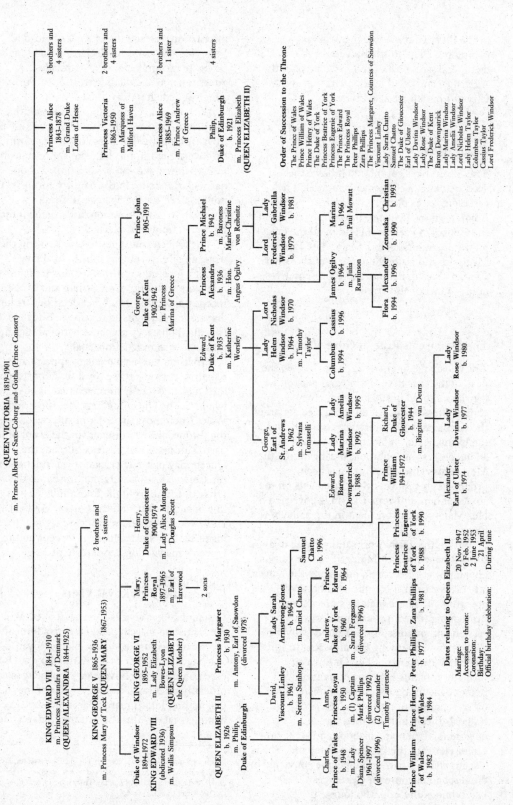

QUEEN VICTORIA 1819–1901
m. Prince Albert of Saxe-Coburg and Gotha (Prince Consort)

KING EDWARD VII 1841–1910
m. Princess Alexandra of Denmark
(QUEEN ALEXANDRA 1844–1925)

KING GEORGE V 1865–1936
m. Princess Mary of Teck (QUEEN MARY 1867–1953)

2 brothers and 3 sisters

Duke of Windsor
1894–1972
KING EDWARD VIII
(abdicated 1936)
m. Wallis Simpson

KING GEORGE VI
1895–1952
m. Lady Elizabeth
Bowes-Lyon
(QUEEN ELIZABETH
the Queen Mother)

Mary,
Princess
Royal
1897–1965
m. Earl of
Harewood

2 sons

Henry,
Duke of Gloucester
1900–1974
m. Lady Alice Montagu
Douglas Scott

George,
Duke of Kent
1902–1942
m. Princess
Marina of Greece

Prince John
1905–1919

QUEEN ELIZABETH II
b. 1926
m. Philip,
Duke of Edinburgh

Princess Margaret
b. 1930
m. Antony, Earl of Snowdon
(divorced 1978)

David,
Viscount Linley
b. 1961
m. Serena Stanhope

Lady Sarah
Armstrong-Jones
b. 1964
m. Daniel Chatto

Samuel
Chatto
b. 1996

Charles,
Prince of Wales
b. 1948
m. Lady
Diana Spencer
1961–1997
(divorced 1996)

Anne,
Princess Royal
b. 1950
m. (1) Captain
Mark Phillips
(divorced 1992)
(2) Commander
Timothy Laurence

Andrew,
Duke of York
b. 1960
m. Sarah Ferguson
(divorced 1996)

Prince Edward
b. 1964

Prince William
of Wales
b. 1982

Prince Henry
of Wales
b. 1984

Peter Phillips
b. 1977

Zara Phillips
b. 1981

Princess Beatrice
of York
b. 1988

Princess Eugenie
of York
b. 1990

Prince
William
1941–1972

Richard,
Duke of
Gloucester
b. 1944
m. Birgitte van Deurs

Alexander,
Earl of Ulster
b. 1974

Lady
Davina Windsor
b. 1977

Lady
Rose Windsor
b. 1980

Edward,
Baron
Downpatrick
b. 1988

Lady
Marina Windsor
b. 1992

Lady
Amelia
Windsor
b. 1995

George, Earl of
St. Andrews
b. 1962
m. Sylvana
Tomaselli

Lady
Helen
Windsor
b. 1964
m. Timothy
Taylor

Lord
Nicholas
Windsor
b. 1970

Columbus
b. 1994

Cassius
b. 1996

Edward,
Duke of Kent
b. 1935
m. Katherine
Worsley

Princess
Alexandra
b. 1936
m. Hon.
Angus Ogilvy

Prince Michael
b. 1942
m. Baroness
Marie-Christine
von Reibnitz

James Ogilvy
b. 1964
m. Julia
Rawlinson

Marina
b. 1966
m. Paul Mowatt

Lord
Frederick
Windsor
b. 1979

Lady
Gabriella
Windsor
b. 1981

Flora
b. 1994

Alexander
b. 1996

Zenouska
b. 1990

Christian
b. 1993

Dates relating to Queen Elizabeth II

Birthday:	20 Nov. 1947
Marriage:	6 Feb. 1952
Accession to throne:	2 June 1953
Coronation:	21 April
Birthday:	During June
Official birthday celebration:	

Order of Succession to the Throne

The Prince of Wales
Prince William of Wales
Prince Henry of Wales
The Duke of York
Princess Beatrice of York
Princess Eugenie of York
The Prince Edward
The Princess Royal
Peter Phillips
Zara Phillips
The Princess Margaret, Countess of Snowdon
Viscount Linley
Lady Sarah Chatto
Samuel Chatto
The Duke of Gloucester
Earl of Ulster
Lady Davina Windsor
Lady Rose Windsor
The Duke of Kent
Baron Downpatrick
Lady Marina Windsor
Lord Nicholas Windsor
Lady Helen Taylor
Columbus Taylor
Cassius Taylor
Lord Frederick Windsor

Princess Alice
1843–1878
m. Grand Duke
Louis of Hesse

3 brothers and
4 sisters

Princess Victoria
1863–1950
m. Marquess of
Milford Haven

2 brothers and
4 sisters

Princess Alice
1885–1969
m. Prince Andrew
of Greece

2 brothers and
1 sister

Philip,
Duke of Edinburgh
b. 1921
m. Princess Elizabeth
(QUEEN ELIZABETH II)

4 sisters

of the Privy Council (see p. 55) are summoned. The Lords Spiritual and Temporal (see p. 58), the Lord Mayor and Aldermen and other leading citizens of the City of London are also invited.

Coronation

The Sovereign's coronation follows the accession after a convenient interval. The ceremony takes place at Westminster Abbey in London, in the presence of representatives of the Houses of Parliament and of all the great public organisations in Britain. The Prime Ministers and leading members of the other Commonwealth nations and representatives of other countries also attend.

The Monarch's Role in Government

The Queen personifies the State. In law, she is head of the executive, an integral part of the legislature, head of the judiciary, the commander-in-chief of all the armed forces of the Crown and the 'supreme governor' of the established Church of England. As a result of a long process of evolution, during which the Monarchy's absolute power has been progressively reduced, the Queen acts on the advice of her ministers. Britain is governed by Her Majesty's Government in the name of the Queen.

Within this framework, and in spite of a trend during the past hundred years towards giving powers directly to ministers, the Queen still takes part in some important acts of government. These include summoning, proroguing (discontinuing until the next session without dissolution) and dissolving Parliament; and giving Royal Assent to Bills passed by Parliament. The Queen also formally appoints many important office holders, including the Prime Minister and other government ministers (see p. 63), judges, officers in the armed forces, governors, diplomats, bishops and some other senior clergy of the Church of England. She is also involved in pardoning people convicted of crimes; and in conferring peerages, knighthoods and other honours.[2] In international affairs the Queen, as Head of State, has the power to declare war and make peace, to recognise foreign states and governments, to conclude treaties and to annex or cede territory.

With rare exceptions (such as appointing the Prime Minister), acts involving the use of 'royal prerogative' powers are now performed by government ministers, who are responsible to Parliament and can be questioned about particular policies. Parliamentary authority is not required for the exercise of these prerogative powers, although Parliament may restrict or abolish such rights.

The Queen continues to play a role in the working of government. She holds Privy Council meetings, gives audiences to her ministers and officials in Britain and overseas, receives accounts of Cabinet decisions, reads dispatches and signs state papers. She must be consulted on every aspect of national life, and must show complete impartiality.

Provision has been made to appoint a regent to perform these royal functions should the Queen be totally incapacitated. The regent would be the Queen's eldest son, the Prince of Wales, then those, in order of succession to the throne, aged 18 or over. In the event of her partial incapacity or absence abroad, the Queen may delegate certain royal functions to the Counsellors of State (her husband, the Duke of Edinburgh, the four adults next in line of succession, and the Queen Mother). However, Counsellors of State may not, for instance, dissolve Parliament (except on the Queen's instructions), or create peers.

Ceremonial and Royal Visits

Ceremonial has always been associated with the British monarchy, and many traditional ceremonies continue to take place. Royal marriages and funerals are marked by public ceremony, and the Sovereign's birthday is officially celebrated in June by Trooping the Colour on Horse Guards Parade. State banquets take place when a foreign monarch

---

[2] Although most honours are conferred by the Queen on the advice of the Prime Minister, a few are granted by her personally—the Order of the Garter, the Order of the Thistle, the Order of Merit and the Royal Victorian Order.

or head of state visits Britain and investitures are held at Buckingham Palace and the Palace of Holyroodhouse in Scotland to bestow honours.

Each year the Queen and other members of the Royal Family visit many parts of Britain. They are also closely involved in the work of many charities. For example, the Prince of Wales is actively involved in The Prince's Trust, set up to encourage small firms and self-employment in inner cities, while the Princess Royal is President of the Save the Children Fund. The Queen pays state visits to foreign governments, accompanied by the Duke of Edinburgh. She also tours the other countries of the Commonwealth. Other members of the Royal Family pay official visits overseas, occasionally representing the Queen.

Royal Income and Expenditure

Until 1760 the Sovereign had to provide for payment of all government expenses, including the salaries of officials and the expenses of the royal palaces and households. These were met from hereditary revenues, mainly income from Crown lands, and income from some other sources granted to the Monarch by Parliament. The income from these sources eventually proved inadequate and in 1760 George III turned over to the Government most of the hereditary revenue. In return he received an annual grant (Civil List), from which he continued to pay royal expenditure of a personal character, the salaries of government officials, the costs of royal palaces, and certain pensions. The last three categories were removed from the Civil List in 1830.

Present Arrangements

Today the expenditure incurred by the Queen in carrying out her public duties is financed from the Civil List and from government departments, which meet the cost of, for example, the Royal Yacht and the aircraft of No 32 (The Royal) Squadron. All such expenditure is approved by Parliament. In 1991 Civil List payments were fixed at

£7.9 million a year for ten years. About three-quarters of the Queen's Civil List provision is required to meet the cost of staff. The Queen's private expenditure as Sovereign is met from the Privy Purse, which is financed mainly from the revenue of the Duchy of Lancaster;[3] her expenditure as a private individual is met from her own personal resources.

Under the Civil List Acts, other members of the Royal Family also receive annual parliamentary allowances to enable them to carry out their public duties. The Prince of Wales, however, receives no such allowance, since as Duke of Cornwall he is entitled to the income of the estate of the Duchy of Cornwall. Each year the Queen refunds the Government for all parliamentary allowances paid to members of the royal family except the Queen Mother and the Duke of Edinburgh.

Since 1993 the Queen has voluntarily paid income tax on all personal income and on that part of the Privy Purse income which is used for private purposes. The Queen also pays tax on any realised capital gains on her private investments and on the private proportion of assets in the Privy Purse. Inheritance tax will not, however, apply to transfers from one sovereign to his or her successor, although any personal bequests other than to the successor will be subject to inheritance tax. In line with these changes the Prince of Wales pays income tax on the income from the Duchy of Cornwall so far as it is used for private purposes.

The Privy Council

The Privy Council was formerly the chief source of executive power in the State; its origins can be traced back to the King's Court, which assisted the Norman monarchs in running the government. As the system of Cabinet government developed in the 18th century, however, much of the role of the Privy Council was assumed by the Cabinet, although the Council retained certain executive functions. Some government

---

[3] The Duchy of Lancaster is an inheritance which, since 1399, has always been enjoyed by the reigning sovereign. It is kept quite apart from his or her other possessions and is separately administered by the Chancellor of the Duchy of Lancaster.

departments originated as committees of the Privy Council.

Nowadays the main function of the Privy Council is to advise the Queen on the approval of Orders in Council, which are made both under prerogative powers, such as Orders approving the grant of Royal Charters of incorporation and under statutory powers. Responsibility for each Order, however, rests with the minister answerable for the policy concerned, regardless of whether he or she is present at the meeting where approval is given.

The Privy Council also advises the Sovereign on the issue of royal proclamations, such as those summoning or dissolving Parliament. The Council's own statutory responsibilities, which are independent of the powers of the Sovereign in Council, include supervising the registration authorities of the medical and allied professions.

Membership of the Council, with the style of 'Right Honourable', is retained for life, except for very occasional removals. It is accorded by the Sovereign on the recommendation of the Prime Minister to people eminent in public life—mainly politicians and judges—in Britain and the Commonwealth realms. Cabinet ministers must be Privy Counsellors and, if not already members, are admitted to membership before taking their oath of office at a meeting of the Council. There are about 470 Privy Counsellors. A full Council is summoned only on the accession of a new Sovereign or when the Sovereign announces his or her intention to marry.

Committees of the Privy Council

There are a number of Privy Council committees. These include prerogative committees, such as those dealing with legislation from the Channel Islands and the Isle of Man, and with applications for charters of incorporation. Committees may also be provided for by statute, such as those for the universities of Oxford and Cambridge and the Scottish universities. Membership of such committees is confined to members of the current administration. The only exceptions are the members of the Judicial Committee

and the members of any committee for which specific provision authorises a wider membership.

Administrative work is carried out in the Privy Council Office under the President of the Council, a Cabinet minister.

The Judicial Committee of the Privy Council is primarily the final court of appeal for British dependent territories and those independent Commonwealth countries which have retained this avenue of appeal after independence. The Committee also hears appeals from the Channel Islands and the Isle of Man, and from the disciplinary and health committees of the medical and allied professions. It has a limited jurisdiction to hear certain ecclesiastical appeals. In 1996 the Judicial Committee heard 85 appeals and 99 petitions for special leave to appeal.

The members of the Judicial Committee include the Lord Chancellor, the Lords of Appeal in Ordinary, other Privy Counsellors who hold or have held high judicial office and certain judges from the Commonwealth.

Parliament

Origins of Parliament

The medieval kings were expected to meet all royal expenses, private and public, out of their own revenue. If extra resources were needed for an emergency, such as a war, the Sovereign would seek to persuade his barons, in the Great Council—a gathering of leading men which met several times a year—to grant aid. During the 13th century several English kings found the private revenues and baronial aids insufficient to meet the expenses of government. They therefore summoned not only the great feudal magnates but also representatives of counties, cities and towns, primarily to get their assent to extraordinary taxation. In this way the Great Council came to include those who were summoned by name (those who, broadly speaking, were to form the House of Lords) and those who were representatives of communities—the commons. The two parts, together with the Sovereign, became known as 'Parliament' (the term originally meant a meeting for parley or discussion).

Over the course of time the commons began to realise the strength of their position. By the middle of the 14th century the formula had appeared which in substance was the same as that used nowadays in voting supplies to the Crown—that is, money to the government—namely, 'by the Commons with the advice of the Lords Spiritual and Temporal'. In 1407 Henry IV pledged that henceforth all money grants should be approved by the House of Commons before being considered by the Lords.

A similar advance was made in the legislative field. Originally the King's legislation needed only the assent of his councillors. Starting with the right of individual commoners to present petitions, the Commons gained the right to submit collective petitions. During the 15th century they gained the right to participate in giving their requests—their 'Bills'—the form of law.

The subsequent development of the power of the House of Commons was built upon these foundations. The constitutional developments of the 17th century led to Parliament securing its position as the supreme legislative authority.

The Powers of Parliament

The three elements which make up Parliament—the Sovereign, the House of Lords and the elected House of Commons—are constituted on different principles. They meet together only on occasions of symbolic significance such as the State opening of Parliament, when the Commons are summoned by the Sovereign to the House of Lords. The agreement of all three elements is normally required for legislation, but that of the Sovereign is given as a matter of course. Parliament can legislate for Britain as a whole, or for any part of the country. It can also legislate for the Channel Islands and the Isle of Man, which are Crown dependencies and not part of Britain. They have local legislatures which make laws on island affairs (see p. 1).

As there are no legal restraints imposed by a written constitution, Parliament may legislate as it pleases, subject to Britain's obligations as a member of the European Union. It can make or change any law, and overturn established conventions or turn them into law. It can even prolong its own life beyond the normal period without consulting the electorate.

In practice, however, Parliament does not assert its supremacy in this way. Its members bear in mind the common law and normally act in accordance with precedent. The House of Commons is directly responsible to the electorate, and in this century the House of Lords has recognised the supremacy of the elected chamber. The system of party government helps to ensure that Parliament legislates with its responsibility to the electorate in mind.

The European Union

As a member of the European Union, Britain recognises the various types of Community legislation and wider policies. It sends 87 elected members to the European Parliament (see chapter 9).

The Functions of Parliament

The main functions of Parliament are:

- to pass laws;
- to provide, by voting for taxation, the means of carrying on the work of government;
- to scrutinise government policy and administration, including proposals for expenditure; and
- to debate the major issues of the day.

In carrying out these functions Parliament helps to bring the relevant facts and issues before the electorate. By custom, Parliament is also informed before important international treaties and agreements are ratified. The making of treaties is, however, a royal prerogative exercised on the advice of the Government and is not subject to parliamentary approval.

The Meeting of Parliament

A Parliament has a maximum duration of five years, but in practice General Elections are usually held before the end of this term. The maximum life has been prolonged by legislation in rare circumstances such as the two world wars. Parliament is dissolved and writs for a General Election are ordered by the Sovereign on the advice of the Prime Minister.

The life of a Parliament is divided into sessions. Each usually lasts for one year—normally beginning and ending in October or November. There are 'adjournments' at night, at weekends, at Christmas, Easter and the late Spring Bank Holiday, and during a long summer break usually starting in late July. The average number of 'sitting' days in a session is about 157 in the House of Commons and about 140 in the House of Lords. At the start of each session the Sovereign's speech to Parliament outlines the Government's policies and proposed legislative programme. Each session is ended by prorogation. Parliament then 'stands prorogued' for about a week until the new session opens. Prorogation brings to an end nearly all parliamentary business: in particular, public Bills which have not been passed by the end of the session are lost.

The House of Lords

The House of Lords consists of the Lords Spiritual and the Lords Temporal. The Lords Spiritual are the Archbishops of Canterbury and York, the Bishops of London, Durham and Winchester, and the 21 next most senior diocesan bishops of the Church of England. The Lords Temporal consist of:

- all hereditary peers of England, Scotland, Great Britain and the United Kingdom (but not peers of Ireland);
- life peers created to assist the House in its judicial duties (Lords of Appeal or 'law lords);[4] and
- all other life peers.

Hereditary peerages carry a right to sit in the House provided holders establish their claim and are aged 21 years or over. However, anyone succeeding to a peerage may, within 12 months of succession, disclaim that peerage for his or her lifetime. Disclaimants lose their right to sit in the House but gain the right to vote and stand as candidates at parliamentary elections. When a disclaimant dies, the peerage passes on down the family in the usual way.

Peerages, both hereditary and life, are created by the Sovereign on the advice of the Prime Minister. They are usually granted in recognition of service in politics or other walks of life or because one of the political parties wishes to have the recipient in the House of Lords. The House also provides a place in Parliament for people who offer useful advice, but do not wish to be involved in party politics.

Peers who attend the House (the average daily attendance is about 380) receive no salary for their parliamentary work, but can claim for expenses incurred in attending the House (for which there are maximum daily rates) and certain travelling expenses.

In August 1997 there were 1,223 members of the House of Lords, including the two archbishops and 24 bishops. The Lords Temporal consisted of 752 hereditary peers who had succeeded to their titles, 10 hereditary peers who had had their titles conferred on them (including the Prince of Wales), and 435 life peers, of whom 26 were 'law lords'. There were 86 women peers.

The total potential membership of the House is reduced by about 60 by a scheme which allows peers who do not wish to attend to apply for leave of absence for the duration of a Parliament. In addition some hereditary peers do not receive a writ of summons entitling them to sit in the House, for example, because they have not established their claim to succeed or because they are minors; there were 74 such peers in August 1997.

Officers of the House of Lords

The House is presided over by the Lord Chancellor, who takes his or her place on the woolsack[5] as ex-officio Speaker of the House.

---

[4] The House of Lords is the final court of appeal for civil cases in Britain and for criminal cases in England, Wales and Northern Ireland.

[5] The woolsack is a seat in the form of a large cushion stuffed with wool from several Commonwealth countries; it is a tradition dating from the medieval period, when wool was the chief source of the country's wealth.

In the Lord Chancellor's absence, his or her place is taken by a deputy. The first of the deputy speakers is the Chairman of Committees, who is appointed at the beginning of each session and normally chairs Committees of the Whole House and some domestic committees.

As Clerk of the House of Lords, the Clerk of the Parliaments is responsible for the records of proceedings of the House of Lords and for the text of Acts of Parliament. He or she is the accounting officer for the House, and is in charge of the administrative staff of the House, known as the Parliament Office. The Gentleman Usher of the Black Rod, usually known as 'Black Rod', is responsible for security, accommodation and services in the House of Lords' part of the Palace of Westminster.

Proposals for Reform

The new Government intends to introduce legislation to end the right of hereditary peers to sit and vote in the House of Lords. This is intended to be the first stage in a process of reform to make the House of Lords more democratic and representative. The legislative powers of the Lords will remain unaltered.

The House of Commons

The House of Commons is elected by universal adult suffrage (see below) and consists of 659 Members of Parliament (MPs). In June 1997 there were 120 women and 9 MPs from ethnic minorities. Of the 659 seats, 529 are for England, 40 for Wales, 72 for Scotland, and 18 for Northern Ireland.

General Elections are held after a Parliament has been dissolved and a new one summoned by the Sovereign. When an MP dies or resigns,[6] or is given a peerage, a by-election takes place. Members are paid an annual salary (from 1 April 1997 to 31 March 1998) of £43,860 and an office costs allowance (from April 1997) of up to £47,568. Other allowances include travel allowances, a

supplement for London members and, for provincial members, subsistence allowances and allowances for second homes. (For ministers' salaries see p. 72.)

Officers of the House of Commons

The chief officer of the House of Commons is the Speaker, elected by MPs to preside over the House. Other officers include the Chairman of Ways and Means and two deputy chairmen, who act as Deputy Speakers. They are elected by the House on the nomination of the Government but are drawn from the Opposition as well as the government party. They, like the Speaker, neither speak nor vote other than in their official capacity. Responsibility for the administration of the House rests with the House of Commons Commission, a statutory body chaired by the Speaker.

Permanent officers (who are not MPs) include the Clerk of the House of Commons, who is the principal adviser to the Speaker on the House's privileges and procedures. The Clerk's other responsibilities relate to the conduct of the business of the House and its committees. The Clerk is also accounting officer for the House. The Serjeant at Arms, who waits upon the Speaker, carries out certain orders of the House. He is also the official housekeeper of the Commons' part of the building, and is responsible for security. Other officers serve the House in the Library, the Department of the Official Report (*Hansard*), the Finance and Administration Department, and the Refreshment Department.

Parliamentary Electoral System

For electoral purposes Britain is divided into constituencies, each of which returns one member to the House of Commons. To ensure that constituency electorates are kept roughly equal, four permanent Parliamentary Boundary Commissions, one each for England, Wales, Scotland and Northern Ireland, keep constituencies under review. They recommend any adjustment of seats that may seem necessary in the light of population

---

[6] An MP who wishes to resign from the House can do so only by applying for an office under the Crown as Crown Steward or Bailiff of the Chiltern Hundreds, or Steward of the Manor of Northstead.

movements or other changes. Reviews are conducted every 8 to 12 years. The recommendations in the Commissions' last general reviews were approved by Parliament in 1995.

Voters

British citizens, together with citizens of other Commonwealth countries and citizens of the Irish Republic resident in Britain, may vote provided they are:

● aged 18 or over;

● included in the annual register of electors for the constituency; and

● not subject to any legal incapacity to vote.

People not entitled to vote include young people under 18, members of the House of Lords, foreign nationals (other than Commonwealth citizens or citizens of the Irish Republic), some patients detained under mental health legislation, sentenced prisoners and people convicted within the previous five years of corrupt or illegal election practices. Members of the armed forces, Crown servants and staff of the British Council employed overseas (together with their wives or husbands if accompanying them) may be registered for an address in the constituency where they would live but for their service. British citizens living abroad may apply to register as electors for a period of up to 20 years after they have left Britain.

Voting Procedures

Each elector may cast one vote, normally in person at a polling station. Electors whose circumstances on polling day are such that they cannot reasonably be expected to vote in person at their local polling station—for example, electors away on holiday—may apply for an absent vote at a particular election. Electors who are physically incapacitated or unable to vote in person because of the nature of their work or because they have moved to a new area may apply for an indefinite absent vote. People entitled to an absent vote may vote by post or by proxy, although postal ballot papers cannot be sent to addresses outside Britain.

Voting is not compulsory; 71.5 per cent of a total electorate of 44.2 million people voted in the General Election in May 1997. The simple majority system of voting is used. Candidates are elected if they have more votes than any of the other candidates (although not necessarily an absolute majority over all other candidates).

The Government which took office in May 1997 proposes to hold a referendum on the voting system for the House of Commons. It plans to appoint an independent commission to recommend a proportional representation alternative to the present first-past-the-post system.

Candidates

British citizens and citizens of other Commonwealth countries, together with citizens of the Irish Republic, may stand for election as MPs provided they are aged 21 or over and are not disqualified. Those disqualified include undischarged bankrupts; people who have been sentenced to more than one year's imprisonment; clergy of the Church of England, Church of Scotland, Church of Ireland and Roman Catholic Church; peers; and holders of certain offices listed in the House of Commons Disqualification Act 1975.

A candidate's nomination for election must be proposed and seconded by two electors registered as voters in the constituency and signed by eight other electors. Candidates do not have to be backed by a political party. A candidate must also deposit £500, which is returned if he or she receives 5 per cent or more of the votes cast.

The maximum sum a candidate may spend on a general election campaign is £4,965 plus 4.2 pence for each elector in a borough constituency, or 5.6 pence for each elector in a county constituency. Higher limits have been set for by-elections in order to reflect the fact that they are often regarded as tests of national opinion in the period between General Elections. The maximum sum is £19,863 plus 16.9 pence for each elector in borough seats, and 22.2 pence for each elector in county seats. A candidate may post an election communication to each elector in the constituency, free of charge. All election expenses, apart from the candidate's personal expenses, are subject to the statutory maximum.

The Political Party System

The party system, which has existed in one form or another since the 18th century, is an essential element in the working of the constitution. The present system depends upon the existence of organised political parties, each of which presents its policies to the electorate for approval. The parties are not registered nor formally recognised in law, but in practice most candidates in elections, and almost all winning candidates, belong to one of the main parties.

For the last 150 years a predominantly two-party system has existed. Since 1945 either the Conservative Party, whose origins go back to the 18th century, or the Labour Party, which emerged in the last decade of the 19th century, has held power. A new party—the Liberal Democrats—was formed in 1988 when the Liberal Party, which traced its origins to the 18th century, merged with the Social Democratic Party, formed in 1981. Other parties include two nationalist parties, Plaid Cymru (founded in Wales in 1925) and the Scottish National Party (founded in 1934).

RESULTS OF 1 MAY 1997 GENERAL ELECTION

Table 7.1: Summary of voting

Party	Total votes	Share of votes	Candidates	MPs elected
Labour	13,516,632	43.2%	639	418
Conservative[a]	9,602,857	30.7%	648	165
Liberal Democrat	5,242,894	16.8%	639	46
Referendum	811,827	2.6%	547	–
Scottish National Party	621,540	2.0%	72	6
Ulster Unionist	258,349	0.8%	16	10
Social Democratic and Labour	190,814	0.6%	18	3
Plaid Cymru (Welsh Nationalist)	161,030	0.5%	40	4
Sinn Fein[b]	126,921	0.4%	17	2
Democratic Unionist	107,348	0.3%	9	2
UK Independence	106,028	0.3%	194	–
Green[c]	63,991	0.2%	95	–
Alliance	62,972	0.2%	17	–
Socialist Labour	52,110	0.2%	64	–
Liberal	44,989	0.1%	54	–
British National	35,833	0.1%	57	–
Natural Law[d]	30,281	0.1%	196	–
Speaker	23,969	0.1%	1	1
ProLife Alliance	18,545	0.1%	53	–
United Kingdom Unionist	12,817	0.0%	1	1
Progressive Unionist	10,934	0.0%	3	–
National Democrat[c]	10,829	0.0%	21	–
Scottish Socialist Alliance	9,740	0.0%	16	–
National Front	2,716	0.0%	6	–
Others	160,631	0.5%	300	1
Total	**31,286,597**	**100.0%**	**3,723**	**659**

Source: House of Commons Library
[a] Includes 8 candidates in Northern Ireland.
[b] The two Sinn Fein members have not taken their seats.
[c] Includes one candidate in Northern Ireland.
[d] Includes 18 candidates in Northern Ireland.
A full breakdown of the results in Northern Ireland is given in chapter 3, Table 1.

Table 7.2 : Overall Turnout

	1992	1997
England	78.0%	71.5%
Wales	79.7%	73.5%
Scotland	75.5%	71.4%
Great Britain	77.9%	71.6%
Northern Ireland	69.8%	67.3%
Britain	77.7%	71.5%

Source : House of Commons Library

Table 7.3: Seats Won by Party in Each Constituent Region of Britain

	Labour	Conservative	Liberal Democrat Party	Scottish National	Plaid Cymru	Other	Total
England	328	165	34	–	–	2	529
Wales	34	–	2	–	4	–	40
Scotland	56	–	10	6	–	–	72
Northern Ireland	–	–	–	–	–	18	18[a]
Britain	418	165	46	6	4	20	659

Source: House of Commons Library
[a] Ulster Unionist 10; Social Democratic & Labour Party 3; Democratic Unionist 2; Sinn Fein 2; United Kingdom Unionist 1.

The General Election of 1 May 1997

The May 1997 general election was notable in a number of ways:

- The Labour Party's 13.5 million votes have been exceeded only in 1951, and the party's share of 43.2 per cent of the vote is its highest since 1966. The 418 seats won are the party's largest number ever, and compare with 393 won in 1945.

- The Conservative Party's 9.6 million votes are its fewest since 1929, and its share of 30.7 per cent of the vote, the lowest since 1832. The 165 seats won are its smallest number since 1906. The Conservatives won no seats in Scotland, Wales or Northern Ireland.

- The Liberal Democrats' 5.2 million votes are fewer than in 1992, as is the party's share of the total vote, but the 46 seats won represents the party's highest number since 1929, when it won 56 as the Liberal Party.

- Turnout at the election was relatively low, at 71.5 per cent—the lowest national level of turnout since 1935 (see Table 7.2).

- A record number of women were elected in 1997. In all 120 women MPs were returned, double the number in 1992. Of the new women MPs, 101 are Labour, 13 Conservative, 3 Liberal Democrat, two SNP and one is the Speaker.

Northern Ireland has a number of parties. They include the Ulster Unionist Party, formed in the early part of this century; the Democratic Unionist Party, founded in 1971 by a group which broke away from the Ulster Unionists; Social Democratic and Labour Party, founded in 1970, and Sinn Fein.[7]

Since 1945 eight General Elections have been won by the Conservative Party and seven by the Labour Party; the great majority of members of the House of Commons have belonged to one of these two parties.

The party which wins most seats (although not necessarily the most votes) at a General Election, or which has the support of a majority of members in the House of Commons, usually forms the Government. By tradition, the leader of the majority party is asked by the Sovereign to form a government. About 100 of its members in the House of Commons and the House of Lords receive ministerial appointments (including appointment to the Cabinet—see p. 72) on the advice of the Prime Minister. The largest minority party becomes the official Opposition, with its own leader and 'shadow cabinet'.

The Party System in Parliament

Leaders of the Government and Opposition sit on the front benches of the Commons with their supporters (the backbenchers) sitting behind them. Similar arrangements for the parties also apply to the House of Lords; however, a significant number of Lords do not wish to be associated with any political party, and sit on the 'cross-benches'.

The effectiveness of the party system in Parliament rests largely on the relationship between the Government and the opposition parties. Depending on the relative strengths of the parties in the House of Commons, the Opposition may seek to overthrow the Government by defeating it in a vote on a 'matter of confidence'. In general, however, its aims are to contribute to the formulation of policy and legislation by constructive criticism; to oppose government proposals it considers objectionable; to seek amendments to Government Bills; and to put forward its own policies in order to improve its chances of winning the next General Election.

The detailed arrangements of government business are settled, under the direction of the Prime Minister and the Leaders of the two Houses, by the Government Chief Whips of each House in consultation with the Opposition Chief Whips. The Chief Whips together constitute the 'usual channels' often referred to when the question of finding time for a particular item of business is discussed. The Leaders of the two Houses are responsible for enabling the Houses to debate matters about which they are concerned.

Parliamentary party control is exercised by the Chief Whips and their assistants, who are chosen within the party. Their duties include keeping members informed of forthcoming parliamentary business, maintaining the party's voting strength by ensuring members attend important debates, and passing on to the party leadership the opinions of backbench members. Party discipline tends to be less strong in the Lords than in the Commons, since Lords have less hope of high office and no need of party support in elections.

The formal title of the Government Chief Whip in the Commons is Parliamentary Secretary to the Treasury. Of the other Government Whips, three are officers of the Royal Household (one of these is Deputy Chief Whip), five hold titular posts as Lords Commissioners of the Treasury and five are Assistant Whips. The Government Whips in the Lords hold offices in the Royal Household; they also act as government spokesmen.

Financial Assistance to Parties

Annual assistance from public funds helps opposition parties carry out parliamentary work at Westminster. In the House of Commons it is limited to parties which had at least two members elected at the previous General Election or one member elected and a minimum of 150,000 votes cast. The amount for the period 1 April 1997 to 31 March 1998 is £3,254 for every seat won at the 1997

---

[7] Sinn Fein is the political wing of the IRA.

General Election, plus £7.04 for every 200 votes. Financial assistance has been provided to the two main opposition parties in the House of Lords since 1 October 1996. For the period 1 April 1997 to 31 March 1998 the Conservative Party will receive £102,600 and the Liberal Democrats £30,780.

The Government intends to introduce legislation to prohibit foreign donations to political parties and to oblige political parties to declare all donations above a minimum figure.

Parliamentary Procedure

Parliamentary procedure is based on custom and precedent, partly codified by each House in its Standing Orders. The system of debate is similar in both Houses. Every subject starts off as a proposal or 'motion' by a member. After debate, in which each member may speak only once, the motion may be withdrawn: if it is not, the Speaker or Chairman 'puts the question' whether to agree with the motion or not. The question may be decided without voting, or by a simple majority vote. The main difference of procedure between the two Houses is that the Speaker or Chairman in the Lords has no powers of order; instead such matters are decided by the general feeling of the House.

In the Commons the Speaker has full authority to enforce the rules of the House and must guard against the abuse of procedure and protect minority rights. The Speaker has discretion on whether to allow a motion to end discussion so that a matter may be put to the vote, and has powers to put a stop to irrelevance and repetition in debate, and to save time in other ways. In cases of grave disorder the Speaker can adjourn or suspend the sitting. The Speaker may order members who have broken the rules of behaviour of the House to leave the Chamber or can initiate their suspension for a period of days.

The Speaker supervises voting in the Commons and announces the final result. In a tied vote the Speaker gives a casting vote, without expressing an opinion on the merits of the question. Voting procedure in the House of Lords is broadly similar, although the Lord Chancellor does not have a casting vote.

Modernisation of the House of Commons

A Select Committee on Modernisation of the House of Commons was set up in June 1997 to consider how the practices and procedures should be modernised. Its First Report on the Legislative Process, issued in July 1997, called for greater flexibility in the way legislation is handled, including pre- and post-legislative scrutiny; proposed that a number of Bills should be programmed on an experimental basis, and suggested that it should be possible in defined circumstances to carry forward Bills from one session to the next. The Committee has also modernised the contents and layout of the Order Paper (the agenda of the House of Commons). It will now look at other issues, including the structure of the parliamentary year, the process for scrutinising European legislative proposals, and the ability of MPs to make the Government accountable for its actions.

Financial Interests

The Commons has a public register of MPs' financial (and some non-financial) interests. Members with a financial interest must declare it when speaking in the House or in Committee and must indicate it when giving notice of a question or motion. In other proceedings of the House or in dealings with other members, ministers or civil servants, MPs must also disclose any relevant financial interest. In 1995 the House agreed that members cannot advocate matters in the House which are related to the source of any personal financial interest.

Also in 1995 the House of Lords passed a Resolution to establish a Register of Lords' Interests, on lines similar to that for MPs. The most recent Register was published in February 1997 and is open to public inspection.

Parliamentary Commissioner for Standards

Following recommendations of the Committee on Standards in Public Life (the Nolan Committee—see p. 76), the post of Parliamentary Commissioner for Standards was created in 1995. The Commissioner, who is independent of government, can advise MPs

Germany, 1990: visiting the families of Service personnel serving in the Gulf.

Nepal, March 1993: Panuati Village. Visiting various Red Cross projects,
including a clinic and dispensary, a new community services centre and a primary school.

Zimbabwe, July 1993: Nemazuva Child Feeding Centre (Red Cross project).

Angola, 1997: highlighting the plight of the innocent victims of anti-personnel landmines.

on matters of standards, and conduct a preliminary investigation into complaints about alleged breaches of the rules. The Commissioner reports to the House of Commons Select Committee on Standards and Privileges.

In a report published by the Select Committee in June 1997,[8] the Commissioner, Sir Gordon Downey, presented his findings on a number of serious allegations of misconduct, including the 'cash for questions' case, in which a number of MPs and former ministers in the previous administration were accused of accepting secret payments in return for providing lobbying services in the House of Commons. The report found that the conduct of five former MPs, three of whom had been ministers, fell below the standards expected of Members of Parliament to varying degrees. It also recommended that the rules governing the registration of election donations should be reviewed.

Public Access to Parliamentary Proceedings

Proceedings of both Houses are normally public. The minutes and speeches (transcribed verbatim in *Hansard*, the official report) are published daily.

The records of the Lords from 1497 and of the Commons from 1547, together with the parliamentary and political papers of a number of former members of both Houses, are available to the public through the House of Lords Record Office.

The proceedings of both Houses of Parliament may be broadcast on television and radio, either live or, more usually, in recorded or edited form. Complete coverage is available on cable television.

The Law-making Process

Statute law consists of Acts of Parliament and delegated legislation made by ministers under powers given to them by Act (see p. 67). While the interpretation of the law undergoes

---

[8] Committee on Standards and Privileges: First Report: *Complaints from Mr Mohamed Al Fayed, The Guardian and Others against 25 Members and Former Members.* HC 30-1, The Stationery Office, 1997.

constant refinement in the courts (see p. 87), changes to statute law are made by Parliament.

Draft laws take the form of parliamentary Bills. Proposals for legislation affecting the powers of particular bodies (such as individual local authorities) or the rights of individuals (such as certain proposals relating to railways, roads and harbours) are known as Private Bills, and are subject to a special form of parliamentary procedure. Bills which change the general law and which constitute the more significant part of the parliamentary legislative process are Public Bills.

Public Bills can be introduced into either House, by a government minister or by an ordinary ('private' or 'backbench') member. Most public Bills that become Acts of Parliament are introduced by a government minister and are known as 'Government Bills'. Bills introduced by other MPs or Lords are known as 'Private Members' Bills'.

The main Bills which constitute the Government's legislative programme are announced in the Queen's Speech at the State Opening of Parliament, which usually takes place in November, and the Bills themselves are introduced into one or other of the Houses over the succeeding weeks.

Before a Government Bill is drafted, there may be consultation with professional bodies, voluntary organisations and other agencies interested in the subject, and with interest and pressure groups which seek to promote specific causes. 'White Papers', which are government statements of policy, often contain proposals for legislative changes; these may be debated in Parliament before a Bill is introduced. From time to time consultation papers, sometimes called 'Green Papers', set out government proposals which are still taking shape and seek comments from the public.

Passage of Public Bills

Public Bills must normally be passed by both Houses. Bills relating mainly to financial matters are almost invariably introduced in the Commons. Under the provisions of the Parliament Acts 1911 and 1949, the powers of the Lords in relation to 'money Bills' are very restricted. The Parliament Acts also provide for a Bill to be passed by the Commons without consent of the Lords in certain (very rare) circumstances.

The process of passing a Public Bill is similar in each House. On presentation the Bill is considered, without debate, to have been read for a first time and is printed. After an interval, which may be between one day and several weeks, a Government Bill will receive its second reading debate, during which the general principles of the Bill are discussed.

If it obtains a second reading in the Commons, a Bill will normally be committed to a standing committee (see p. 67) for detailed examination and amendment. In the Lords, the committee stage usually takes place on the floor of the House, and this procedure may also be followed in the Commons if that House so decides (usually in cases where there is a need to pass the Bill quickly or where it raises matters of constitutional importance). The Commons may also decide to divide the committee stage of a Bill between a standing committee and a committee of the whole House (which is commonly the case with the annual Finance Bill).

The committee stage is followed by the report stage ('consideration') on the floor of the House, during which further amendments may be made. In the Commons, the report stage is usually followed immediately by the third reading debate, where the Bill is reviewed in its final form. In the Lords, a Bill may be further amended at third reading.

After passing its third reading in one House, a Bill is sent to the other House, where it passes through all its stages once more and where it is, more often than not, further amended. Amendments made by the second House must be agreed by the first, or a compromise reached, before a Bill can go for Royal Assent.

In the Commons the House may vote to limit the time available for consideration of a Bill. This is done by passing a 'timetable' motion proposed by the Government, commonly referred to as a 'guillotine'. There are special procedures for Public Bills which consolidate existing legislation or which enact private legislation relating to Scotland.

Royal Assent

When a Bill has passed through all its parliamentary stages, it is sent to the Queen for Royal Assent, after which it is part of the law of the land and known as an Act of Parliament. The Royal Assent has not been refused since 1707. In the 1996–97 session 58 Pubic Bills were enacted. (A list of the main Public Bills receiving Royal Assent since autumn 1996 is given on p. 538.)

Limitations on the Power of the Lords

Most Government Bills introduced and passed in the Lords pass through the Commons without difficulty, but a Lords Bill which was unacceptable to the Commons would not become law. The Lords, on the other hand, do not generally prevent Bills insisted upon by the Commons from becoming law, though they will often amend them and return them for further consideration by the Commons.

By convention, the Lords pass Bills authorising taxation or national expenditure without amendment. Under the Parliament Acts 1911 and 1949, a Bill that deals only with taxation or expenditure must become law within one month of being sent to the Lords, whether or not they agree to it, unless the Commons directs otherwise. If no agreement is reached between the two Houses on a non-financial Commons Bill, the Lords can delay the Bill for a period which, in practice, amounts to at least 13 months. Following this the Bill may be submitted to the Queen for Royal Assent, provided it has been passed a second time by the Commons. The Parliament Acts make one important exception: any Bill to lengthen the life of a Parliament requires the full assent of both Houses.

The limits to the power of the Lords, contained in the Parliament Acts, are based on the belief that nowadays the main legislative function of the non-elected House is to act as a chamber of revision, complementing but not rivalling the elected House.

Private Members' Bills

Early in each session backbench members of the Commons ballot (draw lots) for the opportunity to introduce a Bill on one of the Fridays during the session on which such Bills have precedence over government business. The first 20 members whose names are drawn win this privilege, but it does not guarantee that their Bills will pass into law. Members may also present a Bill on any day without debate, and on most Tuesdays and Wednesdays on which the Commons is sitting there is also an opportunity to seek leave to present a Bill under the 'ten minute rule'. This provides an opportunity for a brief speech by the member proposing the Bill (and by one who opposes it).

Few of these Bills make further progress or receive any debate, but in most sessions some do become law (22 in the 1996–97 session). Recent examples include the Proceeds of Crime (Scotland) Act 1995, the Energy Conservation Act 1996 and the Confiscation of Alcohol (Young Persons) Act 1997. Private Members' Bills do not often call for the expenditure of public money; but if they do they cannot proceed to committee stage unless the Government decides to provide the necessary money. Peers may introduce Private Members' Bills in the House of Lords at any time. A Private Member's Bill passed by either House will not proceed in the other House unless taken up by a member of that House.

Private and Hybrid Bills

Private Bills are promoted by people or organisations outside Parliament (often local authorities) to give them special legal powers. They go through a similar procedure to Public Bills, but most of the work is done in committee, where procedures follow a semi-judicial pattern. Hybrid Bills are Public Bills which may affect private rights, for example, the Channel Tunnel Rail Link Bill which was passed in 1996. As with Private Bills, the passage of Hybrid Bills through Parliament is governed by special procedures which allow those affected to put their case.

Delegated Legislation

In order to reduce unnecessary pressure on parliamentary time, primary legislation often gives ministers or other authorities the power to regulate administrative details by means of secondary or 'delegated' legislation. To minimise any risk that delegating powers to the executive might undermine the authority of Parliament, such powers are normally delegated only to authorities directly accountable to Parliament. Moreover, Acts of Parliament which delegate such powers usually provide for some measure of direct parliamentary control over proposed delegated legislation, by giving Parliament the opportunity to affirm or annul it. Certain Acts also require that organisations affected must be consulted before rules and orders can be made.

A joint committee of both Houses reports on the technical propriety of these 'statutory instruments'. In order to save time on the floor of the House, the Commons uses standing committees to debate the merits of instruments; actual decisions are taken by the House as a whole. The House of Lords has appointed a delegated powers scrutiny committee which examines the appropriateness of the powers to make secondary legislation in Bills.

Parliamentary Committees

Committees of the Whole House

Either House may pass a resolution setting itself up as a Committee of the Whole House to consider Bills in detail after their second reading. This permits unrestricted discussion: the general rule that an MP or Lord may speak only once on each motion does not apply in committee.

Standing Committees

House of Commons standing committees debate and consider Public Bills at the committee stage. The committee considers the Bill clause by clause, and may amend it before reporting it back to the House. Ordinary standing committees do not have names but are referred to simply as Standing Committee A, B, C, and so on; a new set of members is appointed to them to consider each Bill. Each committee has between 16 and 50 members, with a party balance reflecting as far as possible that in the House as a whole. The standing committees include two Scottish standing committees, and the Scottish, Welsh and Northern Ireland Grand Committees.

The Scottish Grand Committee comprises all 72 Scottish MPs (and may be convened anywhere in Scotland as well as at Westminster). It may consider the principle of any Scottish Bills at the second and third reading stages, where such a Bill has been referred to the Committee by the House for that purpose. It also debates other matters concerning Scotland. In addition, its business includes questions tabled for oral answer, ministerial statements and other debates, including those on statutory instruments referred to it.

The Welsh Grand Committee, consisting of all 40 Welsh MPs and up to five others who may be added from time to time, considers Bills referred to it at second reading stage, questions tabled for oral answer, ministerial statements, and other matters relating exclusively to Wales.

The Northern Ireland Grand Committee considers Bills in relation to their principle at the second and third stages, takes oral questions and ministerial statements, and debates matters relating specifically to Northern Ireland. It includes all 18 Northern Ireland MPs and up to 25 others who may be added from time to time.

In addition there is a Standing Committee on Regional Affairs, consisting of all Members sitting for consitituencies in England, plus up to 5 others. It has not met, however, since 1977.

There are also standing committees to debate proposed European legislation, and to scrutinise statutory instruments and draft statutory instruments brought forward by the Government.

In the Lords, various sorts of committees on Bills may be used instead of, or as well as, a Committee of the Whole House. Such committees include Public Bill Committees, Special Public Bill Committees, Grand Committees, Select Committees and Scottish Select Committees.

Select Committees

Select committees are appointed for a particular task, generally one of enquiry,
investigation and scrutiny. They report their conclusions and recommendations to the House as a whole; in many cases their recommendations invite a response from the Government, which is also reported to the House. A select committee may be appointed for a Parliament, or for a session, or for as long as it takes to complete its task. To help Parliament with the control of the executive by examining aspects of public policy, expenditure and administration, 16 committees, established by the House of Commons, examine the work of the main government departments and their associated public bodies. The Foreign Affairs Select Committee, for example, 'shadows' the work of the Foreign & Commonwealth Office. The committees are constituted on a basis which is in approximate proportion to party strength in the House.

Other regular Commons select committees include those on Public Accounts, Standards and Privileges and European Legislation. 'Domestic' select committees also cover the internal workings of Parliament.

To keep the two Houses informed of EU developments, and to enable them to scrutinise and debate Union policies and proposals, there is a select committee in each House, and two Commons standing committees debate specific European legislative proposals. Ministers also make regular statements about EU business.

In their examination of government policies, expenditure and administration, committees may question ministers, civil servants and interested bodies and individuals. Through hearings and published reports, they bring before Parliament and the public an extensive body of fact and informed opinion on many issues, and build up considerable expertise in their subjects of inquiry.

In the House of Lords, besides the Appeal and Appellate Committees in which the bulk of the House's judicial work is transacted, there are two major select committees: on the European Community and on Science and Technology. *Ad hoc* committees may also be set up to consider particular issues (or, sometimes, a particular Bill), and 'domestic' committees—as in the Commons—cover the internal workings of the House.

Joint Committees

Joint committees, with a membership drawn from both Houses, are appointed in each session to deal with Consolidation Bills[9] and statutory instruments (see p. 67). The two Houses may also agree to set up joint select committees on other subjects.

Unofficial Party Committees

The Parliamentary Labour Party comprises all members of the party in both Houses. When the Labour Party is in office, a parliamentary committee, half of whose members are elected and half of whom are government representatives, acts as a channel of communication between the Government and its backbenchers in both Houses. When the party is in opposition, the Parliamentary Labour Party is organised under the direction of an elected parliamentary committee, which acts as the 'shadow cabinet'.

The Conservative and Unionist Members' Committee (the 1922 Committee) consists of the backbench membership of the party in the House of Commons. When the Conservative Party is in office, ministers attend its meetings by invitation and not by right. When the party is in opposition, the whole membership of the party may attend meetings. The then leader appoints a consultative committee, which acts as the party's 'shadow cabinet'.

Other Forms of Parliamentary Control

In addition to the system of scrutiny by select committees, both Houses offer a number of opportunities for the examination of government policy by both the Opposition and the Government's own backbenchers. In the House of Commons, the opportunities include:

1. Question Time, when for 55 minutes on Monday, Tuesday, Wednesday and Thursday, ministers answer MPs' questions. The Prime Minister's Question Time takes place for one half hour every Wednesday when the House is sitting.

Parliamentary questions are one means of seeking information about the Government's intentions. They are also a way of raising grievances brought to MPs' notice by constituents. MPs may also put questions to ministers for written answer; the questions and answers are published in *Hansard*. There are some 50,000 questions every year.

2. Adjournment debates, when MPs use motions for the adjournment of the House to raise constituency cases or matters of public concern. There is a half-hour adjournment period at the end of the business of the day, and opportunities for several adjournment debates on Wednesday mornings. In addition, an MP wishing to discuss a 'specific and important matter that should have urgent consideration' may, at the end of Question Time, seek leave to move the adjournment of the House. On the very few occasions when leave is obtained, the matter is debated for three hours in what is known as an emergency debate, usually on the following day.

3. Early day motions (EDMs) provide a further opportunity for backbench MPs to express their views on particular issues. A number of EDMs are tabled each sitting day; they are very rarely debated but can be useful in gauging the degree of support for the topic by the number of signatures of other MPs which the motion attracts.

4. The 20 Opposition days each session, when the Opposition can choose subjects for debate. Of these days, 17 are at the disposal of the Leader of the Opposition and three at the disposal of the second largest opposition party.

5. Debates on three days in each session on details of proposed government expenditure, chosen by the Liaison Committee (a select committee largely made up of select committee chairmen, which considers general matters relating to the work of select committees).

Procedural opportunities for criticism of the Government also arise during the debate on the Queen's Speech at the beginning of each session; during debates on motions of censure

---

[9] A Consolidation Bill brings together several existing Acts into one, with the aim of simplifying the statutes.

for which the Government provides time; and during debates on the Government's legislative and other proposals.

House of Lords

Similar opportunities for criticism and examination of government policy are provided in the House of Lords at daily Question Time, during debates and by means of questions for written answer.

Control of Finances

The main responsibilities of Parliament, and more particularly of the House of Commons, in overseeing the revenue of the State and public expenditure, are to authorise the raising of taxes and duties, and the various objects of expenditure and the sum to be spent on each. It also has to satisfy itself that the sums granted are spent only for the purposes which Parliament intended. No payment out of the central government's public funds can be made, and no taxation or loans authorised, except by Act of Parliament. However, limited interim payments can be made from the Contingencies Fund.

The Finance Act is the most important of the annual statutes, and authorises the raising of revenue. The legislation is based on the Chancellor of the Exchequer's Budget statement. This includes a review of the public finances of the previous year, and proposals for future expenditure (see p. 157). Scrutiny of public expenditure is carried out by House of Commons select committees (see p. 68).

The Commons' Ability to Force the Government to Resign

The final control is the ability of the House of Commons to force the Government to resign by passing a resolution of 'no confidence'. The Government must also resign if the House rejects a proposal which the Government considers so vital to its policy that it has declared it a 'matter of confidence' or if the House refuses to vote the money required for the public service.

Parliamentary Commissioner for Administration

The Parliamentary Ombudsman—officially known as the Parliamentary Commissioner for Administration—investigates complaints from members of the public (referred through MPs) alleging that they have suffered injustice arising from maladministration. The Ombudsman is independent of government and reports to a Select Committee of the House of Commons. The Ombudsman's jurisdiction covers central government departments and agencies and a large number of non-departmental public bodies. He or she cannot investigate complaints about government policy, the content of legislation or relations with other countries.

In making his investigations, the Commissioner has access to all departmental papers, and has powers to summon those from whom he wishes to take evidence. When an investigation is completed, he sends a report with his findings to the MP who referred the complaint (with a copy report for the complainant). In reports of justified cases, the Ombudsman normally recommends that the department provides redress (which can include a financial remedy for the complainant in appropriate cases). There is no appeal against the Ombudsman's decision. He submits an annual report to Parliament, and also publishes selected cases three times a year.

In 1996 the Ombudsman received a record 1,920 new complaints (an increase of 12.5 per cent over the previous year). He completed 260 investigations; of these he found 246 wholly or partly justified and 14 unjustified. Complaints against the Department of Social Security accounted for over 47 per cent of the total received.

The Parliamentary Ombudsman also monitors the Code of Practice on Access to Official Information (see p. 75).

Parliamentary Privilege

Each House of Parliament has certain rights and immunities to protect it from obstruction in carrying out its duties. The rights apply collectively to each House and to its staff and individually to each member.

For the Commons the Speaker formally claims from the Queen 'their ancient and undoubted rights and privileges' at the beginning of each Parliament. These include freedom of speech; first call on the attendance of its members, who are therefore free from arrest in civil actions and exempt from serving on juries, or being compelled to attend court as witnesses; and the right of access to the Crown, which is a collective privilege of the House. Further privileges include the rights of the House to control its own proceedings (so that it is able, for instance, to exclude 'strangers'[10] if it wishes); to decide upon legal disqualifications for membership and to declare a seat vacant on such grounds; and to punish for breach of its privileges and for contempt. Parliament has the right to punish anybody, inside or outside the House, who commits a breach of privilege—that is, offends against the rights of the House.

The privileges of the House of Lords are broadly similar to those of the House of Commons. The law of privilege is to be examined by a Joint Committee of both Houses of Parliament.

Her Majesty's Government

Her Majesty's Government is the body of ministers responsible for the conduct of national affairs. The Prime Minister is appointed by the Queen, and all other ministers are appointed by the Queen on the recommendation of the Prime Minister. Most ministers are members of the Commons, although the Government is also fully represented by ministers in the Lords. The Lord Chancellor is always a member of the House of Lords.

The composition of governments can vary both in the number of ministers and in the titles of some offices. New ministerial offices may be created, others may be abolished, and functions may be transferred from one minister to another.

Prime Minister

The Prime Minister is also, by tradition, First Lord of the Treasury and Minister for the Civil Service. The Prime Minister's unique position of authority derives from majority support in the House of Commons and from the power to appoint and dismiss ministers. By modern convention, the Prime Minister always sits in the House of Commons.

The Prime Minister presides over the Cabinet (see p. 72), is responsible for the allocation of functions among ministers and informs the Queen at regular meetings of the general business of the Government.

The Prime Minister's other responsibilities include recommending a number of appointments to the Queen. These include: Church of England archbishops, bishops and deans and some 200 other clergy in Crown 'livings'; senior judges, such as the Lord Chief Justice; Privy Counsellors; and Lord-Lieutenants. He or she also recommends certain civil appointments, such as Lord High Commissioner to the General Assembly of the Church of Scotland, Poet Laureate, Constable of the Tower, and some university posts; and appointments to various public boards and institutions, such as the BBC (British Broadcasting Corporation), as well as various royal and statutory commissions. Recommendations are likewise made for the award of many civil honours and distinctions and of Civil List pensions (to people who have achieved eminence in science or the arts and are in financial need). The Prime Minister also selects the trustees of certain national museums and institutions.

The Prime Minister's Office at 10 Downing Street (the official residence in London) has a staff of civil servants who assist the Prime Minister. The Prime Minister may also appoint special advisers to the Office to assist in the formation of policies.

Departmental Ministers

Ministers in charge of government departments are usually in the Cabinet; they are known as 'Secretary of State' or 'Minister', or may have a special title, as in the case of the Chancellor of the Exchequer.

Non-departmental Ministers

The holders of various traditional offices, namely the President of the Council, the

---

[10] All those who are not members or officials of either House.

Chancellor of the Duchy of Lancaster, the Lord Privy Seal, the Paymaster General and, from time to time, Ministers without Portfolio, may have few or no departmental duties. They are thus available to perform any duties the Prime Minister may wish to give them. In the present administration, for example, the President of the Council is Leader of the House of Commons and the Chancellor of the Duchy of Lancaster is Minister of the Public Service.

Lord Chancellor and Law Officers

The Lord Chancellor holds a special position, as both a minister with departmental functions and the head of the judiciary (see p. 88). The four Law Officers of the Crown are: for England and Wales, the Attorney General and the Solicitor General; and for Scotland, the Lord Advocate and the Solicitor General for Scotland.

Ministers of State and Junior Ministers

Ministers of State usually work with ministers in charge of departments. They normally have specific responsibilities, and are sometimes given titles which reflect these functions. More than one may work in a department. A Minister of State may be given a seat in the Cabinet and be paid accordingly.

Junior ministers (generally Parliamentary Under-Secretaries of State or, where the senior minister is not a Secretary of State, simply Parliamentary Secretaries) share in parliamentary and departmental duties. They may also be given responsibility, directly under the departmental minister, for specific aspects of the department's work.

Ministerial Salaries

The salaries of ministers in the House of Commons range from £23,623 a year for junior ministers to £60,000 for Cabinet ministers. In the House of Lords salaries range from £43,632 for junior ministers to £77,693 for Cabinet ministers. The Prime Minister is entitled to a salary of 100,000.[11] The Lord Chancellor receives £140,665.

In addition to their ministerial salaries, ministers in the Commons, including the Prime Minister, receive a full parliamentary salary of £43,860 a year in recognition of their constituency responsibilities and can claim the other allowances which are paid to all MPs.

The Leader of the Opposition in the Commons receives a salary of £55,000 (and in addition, the full parliamentary salary of £43,860); two Opposition whips in the Commons and the Opposition Leader and Chief Whip in the Lords also receive salaries.

The Cabinet

The Cabinet is composed of about 20 ministers (the number can vary) chosen by the Prime Minister and may include departmental and non-departmental ministers.

The functions of the Cabinet are to initiate and decide on policy, the supreme control of government and the co-ordination of government departments. The exercise of these functions is vitally affected by the fact that the Cabinet is a group of party representatives, depending upon majority support in the House of Commons.

Cabinet Meetings

The Cabinet meets in private and its proceedings are confidential. Its members are bound by their oath as Privy Counsellors not to disclose information about its proceedings, although after 30 years Cabinet papers may be made available for inspection in the Public Record Office at Kew, Surrey.

Normally the Cabinet meets for a few hours each week during parliamentary sittings, and less often when Parliament is not sitting. To keep its workload within manageable limits, a great deal of work is carried on through the committee system. This involves referring issues either to a standing Cabinet committee or to an *ad hoc* committee of the ministers directly concerned. The committee then considers the matter in detail and either disposes of it or reports upon it to the Cabinet with recommendations for action.

---

[11] The Prime Minister has declined the full salary to which he is entitled; he draws instead a salary of £58,557. Similarly, Cabinet Ministers have decided to accept salaries of £43,991 (Commons) and £58,876 (Lords) rather than the full entitlement.

There are standing committees dealing with defence and overseas policy, economic affairs, home and social affairs, the environment and local government. Following the election of the new Government in May 1997, two new committees have been set up: on devolution to Scotland and Wales and the English regions; and on constitutional reform policy. Three committees active under the previous administration have been disbanded: those on nuclear defence policy; competitiveness; and on the co-ordination and presentation of government policies.

The membership and terms of reference of all ministerial Cabinet committees are published. Where appropriate, the Secretary of the Cabinet and other senior officials of the Cabinet Office attend meetings of the Cabinet and its committees.

The Cabinet Office

The Cabinet Office is headed by the Secretary of the Cabinet (a civil servant who is also Head of the Home Civil Service) under the direction of the Prime Minister. It comprises the Cabinet Secretariat and the Office of Public Service (OPS).

The Cabinet Secretariat serves ministers collectively in the conduct of Cabinet business, and in the co-ordination of policy at the highest level.

The Chancellor of the Duchy of Lancaster is in charge of the OPS and is a member of the Cabinet. The OPS is responsible for:

- ensuring that Government provides high-quality, efficient and customer-friendly public services at the lowest possible cost to the taxpayer (to be achieved through a refocusing of the Citizen's Charter programme—see p. 75);

- promoting the Government's policies on deregulation;

- promoting greater openness and accountability in government; and

- improving the effectiveness and efficiency of central government, through the creation and review of executive agencies (see p. 78).

The Historical and Records Section is responsible for Official Histories and managing Cabinet Office records.

Ministerial Responsibility

'Ministerial responsibility' refers both to the collective responsibility for government policy and actions which ministers share, and to ministers' individual responsibility for their departments' work.

The doctrine of collective responsibility means that all ministers unanimously support government policy once it has been settled. The policy of departmental ministers must be consistent with the policy of the Government as a whole. Once the Government's policy on a matter has been decided, each minister is expected to support it or resign. On rare occasions, ministers have been allowed free votes in Parliament on government policies involving important issues of principle. In April 1996, for example, free votes were allowed on the length of time that must elapse before a divorce application can be made, and in June 1997 on prohibiting the private ownership of handguns.

The individual responsibility of ministers for the work of their Departments means that they have a duty to Parliament to account, and to be held to account for, the policies, decisions and actions of their Departments. Departmental ministers normally decide all matters within their responsibility. However, on important political matters they usually consult their colleagues collectively, either through the Cabinet or through a Cabinet committee. A decision by a departmental minister binds the Government as a whole.

On assuming office ministers must resign directorships in private and public companies, and must ensure that there is no conflict between their public duties and private interests.

Government Departments

Government departments and their agencies, staffed by politically impartial civil servants, are the main instruments for implementing government policy when Parliament has passed the necessary legislation, and for advising ministers. They often work alongside local authorities, statutory boards, and government-sponsored organisations operating under various degrees of government control.

A change of government does not necessarily affect the number or general functions of government departments, although major changes in policy may be accompanied by organisational changes.

The work of some departments (for instance, the Ministry of Defence) covers Britain as a whole. Other departments, such as the Department of Social Security, cover England, Wales and Scotland, but not Northern Ireland. Others, such as the Department of the Environment, Transport and the Regions are mainly concerned with affairs in England.

The ten Government Offices for the Regions are responsible for administering the main regional programmes of the Departments of Environment, Transport and the Regions, Trade and Industry, and Education and Employment, as well as programmes from the Home Office; they also administer the Single Regeneration Budget (see p. 371).

Some departments which have direct contact with the public throughout the country also have local offices.

Departments are usually headed by ministers. In some departments the head is a permanent official, and ministers with other duties are responsible for them to Parliament. For instance, ministers in the Treasury are responsible for HM Customs and Excise, the Inland Revenue, the Office for National Statistics and a number of other departments, as well as executive agencies such as the Royal Mint. Departments generally receive their funds directly out of money provided by Parliament and are staffed by members of the Civil Service.

The functions of the main government departments and agencies are set out on pp. 530–7.

Non-departmental Public Bodies

Non-departmental public bodies (NDPBs) have a role in the process of national government but are neither government departments nor parts of a department. There are three main kinds: executive bodies, advisory bodies and tribunals. Tribunals are a specialised group of bodies whose functions are essentially quasi-judicial (see p. 111).

The continuing need for each NDPB is regularly reviewed in a continuous programme. When they are no longer needed in their existing form, the bodies are abolished, merged or privatised. The overall number of NDPBs decreased from 1,658 in 1986 to 1,194 in 1996, a reduction of 28 per cent. During the same period the number of staff in executive NDPBs decreased from 146,300 to 107,000—a reduction of 27 per cent.

The new Government proposes to undertake a review of NDPBs with a view to further reducing their numbers and making the remainder more accountable.

Executive Bodies

Executive bodies normally employ their own staff and are responsible for their own budget. They are public organisations whose duties include executive, administrative, regulatory or commercial functions. They are normally set up in statute, and operate within broad policy guidelines set by departmental Ministers but are in varying degrees independent of government in carrying out their day-to-day responsibilities. Examples include the Commission for Racial Equality and the Police Complaints Authority.

Ministerial appointments to executive NDPBs are subject to the Commissioner for Public Appointments' Code of Practice (see p. 76). The Government is considering whether the Commissioner's remit should be extended to cover other groups of public bodies.

Advisory Bodies

Many government departments are assisted by advisory councils or committees which carry out research and collect information, mainly to give ministers access to informed opinion before they come to a decision involving a legislative or executive act. In some cases a minister must consult a standing committee, but advisory bodies are usually set up administratively at the discretion of the minister. Examples include the British Overseas Trade Board and the Farm Animal Welfare Council.

The membership of advisory councils and committees varies according to the nature of the work involved, but often includes representatives of the relevant interests and professions.

For some particularly important issues, Royal Commissions, whose members are chosen for their wide experience, may be appointed. Royal Commissions examine evidence from government departments, interested organisations and individuals, and submit recommendations; some prepare regular reports. One example is the standing Royal Commission on Environmental Pollution, set up in 1970. Inquiries may also be undertaken by departmental committees (which are not classified as advisory NDPBs).

The Lobby

As press adviser to the Prime Minister, the Prime Minister's Press Secretary and other staff in the Prime Minister's Press Office have direct contact with the parliamentary press through regular meetings with the Lobby correspondents. The Lobby correspondents are a group of political correspondents with the special privilege of access to the Lobby of the House of Commons, where they can talk privately to government ministers and other members of the House. The Prime Minister's Press Office is the accepted channel through which information about parliamentary business is passed to the media.

Improving Public Services

The Citizen's Charter

The Citizen's Charter was launched in 1991 as a ten-year programme to raise the standard of public services and make them more responsive to the needs and wishes of their users. The new Government is to consult widely with the general public on plans to transform the existing programme of charters

to deliver what people want from public services.

The Charter sets out a number of key principles which users of public services are entitled to expect. They include requirements for published standards of services and results achieved; comprehensive information on services; consultation with users of services; courteous and helpful service from public servants; effective redress if things go wrong, including well-publicised and easy-to-use complaints procedures; and independent inspectorates and auditing.

The Charter applies to all public services, at both national and local level, and to the privatised utilities. Most major public services have now published separate charters. In many cases separate charters have been published for services in Northern Ireland, Scotland and Wales. (Details of many of the charters can be found in the relevant chapters.)

Implementing the Charter

A Cabinet Minister, the Chancellor of the Duchy of Lancaster, is responsible for the Charter programme; he is supported by the Citizen's Charter Unit within the OPS (see p. 73).

The Charter Mark Award Scheme rewards excellence in delivering public services. Applicants have to demonstrate that they have achieved measurable improvements in the quality of services over the previous two years, and that their customers are satisfied with their services.

In 1996 there were over 15,000 nominations and 323 awards were made. Winners came from all parts of the public sector throughout Britain. They included: Greater Manchester Police; the Science Museum (London); Mater Hospital Trust Maternity Unit (Belfast); Dumfries and Galloway Fire Brigade; and the Welsh Institute of Sport (Cardiff).

Open Government

The Code of Practice on Access to Government Information was introduced in 1994. It continues in force, in slightly modified form. Under the Code, government departments, agencies and executive public bodies that are within the jurisdiction of the Parliamentary Ombudsman should:

- give facts and analysis with major policy decisions;
- make available internal guidelines about dealings with the public;
- give reasons with administrative decisions;
- provide information under the Citizen's Charter about public services; and
- respond to requests providing the information requested unless it is considered exempt from disclosure under specified exemptions.

The Parliamentary Ombudsman (see p. 70) acts as an independent appeals mechanism for those seeking information under the Code who are dissatisfied with the response to their enquiry and with the results of any internal review of the original decision. Complaints to the Parliamentary Ombudsman must be referred through an MP.

A similar Code of Practice on Openness covering all National Health Service (NHS) organisations came into force in 1995. Also in 1995, the Local Authority Associations published a guidance note on openness, which was recommended to member authorities.

Freedom of Information

As part of its programme of constitutional reform, the Government intends to introduce a Freedom of Information Bill. A White Paper setting out the Government's proposals is due towards the end of 1997 and a draft Bill will follow in early 1998.

In the meantime, departments, agencies and other public bodies covered by the Code of Practice have been encouraged to be as open as possible and to make full use of the considerable discretion which the present Code allows to enable a more positive interpretation in individual cases.

Better Government

The new Government intends to publish a White Paper early in 1998 on its programme for 'Better Government'. The Paper will address four key challenges:

- cleaning up politics;
- rooting out waste and inefficiency in public spending and getting results;
- listening to the people and developing services to meet their needs; and
- breaking down institutional barriers and working better together.

Committee on Standards in Public Life

This Committee was set up in 1994, under the chairmanship of Lord Nolan, against a background of increasing public concern about standards in many areas of public life. The Committee was asked to consider standards of conduct and to make recommendations designed to ensure that the highest standards are maintained.

The Committee has produced three reports (see Further Reading). Its first, in 1995, on MPs, ministers and civil servants and national non-departmental public bodies (NDPBs— see p. 74), recommended, among other things, independent elements in the scrutiny of the conduct of MPs (see p. 64), in the acceptance of appointments by ministers when they leave office, and of how ministers make appointments to public bodies. This led to the issue of a code of conduct regulating the behaviour of MPs and the appointment in November 1995 of an independent *Commissioner for Public Appointments*. The Commissioner provides advice and guidance to departments and monitors, regulates and audits their procedures for making appointments to executive NDPBs and NHS bodies, ensuring that they are governed by the overriding principle of appointment on merit. He or she publishes an annual report containing the results of the monitoring of all departments' appointments procedures.

Recommendations in Lord Nolan's first report also led to the revision in 1996 of the rules on the acceptance of appointments outside government by former civil servants. This brought special advisers within the system and enabled the Prime Minister's Advisory Committee on Business

Appointments to announce the reasons for its decisions and to advise a civil servant or minister if the acceptance of a particular appointment is inappropriate.

Building on recommendations in Nolan's first report, the new Government published a consultation paper on the prevention of corruption in June 1997.[12] This proposes creating a new single criminal offence of corruption covering both the public and private sectors, where those found guilty could face up to seven years' imprisonment.

Lord Nolan's latest report, on aspects of conduct in local government, was published in July 1997. It calls for a radical change in the ethical framework within which local government operates. Its recommendations include, among other things, a new statutory criminal offence of misuse of public office. The Government plans to implement the Nolan recommendations fully and to extend them to all public bodies.

The Civil Service

The Civil Service is concerned with the conduct of the whole range of government activities as they affect the community. These range from policy formulation to carrying out the day-to-day duties of public administration.

Civil servants are servants of the Crown. For all practical purposes the Crown in this context means, and is represented by, the Government of the day. In most circumstances the executive powers of the Crown are exercised by, and on the advice of, Her Majesty's ministers, who are in turn answerable to Parliament. The Civil Service as such has no constitutional personality or responsibility separate from that of the Government of the day. The duty of the individual civil servant is first and foremost to the minister of the Crown who is in charge of the Department in which he or she is serving. A change of minister, for whatever reason, does not involve a change of staff. Ministers sometimes appoint special advisers from outside the Civil Service. (There are about 44 such advisers in the present administration.)

The advisers are normally paid from public funds, but their appointments come to an end when the Government's term of office finishes, or when the minister concerned leaves the Government or moves to another appointment.

A new Civil Service code came into force in January 1996. This provides a statement of the constitutional framework within which all civil servants work and the values they are expected to uphold. The Code includes an independent line of appeal to the Civil Service Commissioners on alleged breaches of the Code. The Government intends to give legal force to the Code.

The number of civil servants fell from a peak of 751,000 in 1976 to 476,000 in April 1997, a decrease of 37 per cent and its lowest since 1945. This reflects the Government's policy of controlling the cost of the Civil Service and of improving its efficiency.

About half of all civil servants are engaged in the provision of public services. These include paying sickness benefits and pensions, collecting taxes and contributions, running employment services, staffing prisons, and providing services to industry and agriculture. A further quarter are employed in the Ministry of Defence. The rest are divided between central administrative and policy duties; support services; and largely financially self-supporting services, for instance, those provided by National Savings and the Royal Mint. Four-fifths of civil servants work outside London.

The total also includes members of the Senior Civil Service—around 3,000 of the most senior managers and policy advisers. They are responsible for serving the collective interest of government with a focus and loyalty wider than their own departments and agencies.

Equality of Opportunity

The Government is committed to achieving equality of opportunity for all its staff. In support of this commitment, the Civil Service, which recruits and promotes on the basis of merit, is actively pursuing policies to develop career opportunities for women, ethnic minorities and people with disabilities. In April 1996:

---

[12] *Prevention of Corruption: Consolidation and Amendment of the Prevention of Corruption Acts 1889-1916: A Government Statement.*

- women represented 51 per cent of all non-industrial civil servants—47 per cent of all staff at Executive Officer level (the first management grade) were women and around 17 per cent of women worked in the Senior Civil Service. Nearly 21 per cent of all female non-industrial staff were working part-time.

- 5.5 per cent of non-industrial civil servants were of ethnic minority origin, compared with 4.9 per cent in the economically active population in spring 1996; and

- 2.9 per cent of disabled people were employed in the non-industrial home Civil Service.

Progress is monitored and reported on regularly by the Cabinet Office (OPS).

Central Management

Responsibility for central co-ordination and management of the Civil Service is divided between the Cabinet Office (OPS) and the Treasury. The OPS, which is under the control of the Prime Minister, as Minister for the Civil Service, oversees organisation, senior civil service pay, pensions and allowances, recruitment, retirement and redundancy policy, personnel management and statistics, and the overall efficiency of the Service.

The function of official Head of the Home Civil Service is combined with that of Secretary of the Cabinet.

Executive Agencies: Next Steps Programme

The Next Steps Programme, launched in 1988, aims to deliver government services more efficiently and effectively within available resources for the benefit of taxpayers, customers and staff. This has involved setting up, as far as is practicable, separate units or agencies to perform the executive functions of government. Agencies remain part of the Civil Service, but under the terms of individual framework documents they enjoy greater delegation of financial, pay and personnel matters. Agencies are headed by chief executives who are normally directly accountable to ministers but who are personally responsible for day-to-day operations. The pay of agency chief executives is normally directly related to their agency's performance.

No body carrying out a government function can become an agency until the 'prior options' of abolition, privatisation and contracting out have been considered and ruled out. These 'prior options' are reconsidered when agencies are reviewed, normally after five years of operation.

By July 1997, 138 agencies were in existence, together with 24 Executive Units of Customs and Excise and 24 Executive Offices of the Inland Revenue. At that time over 387,000 civil servants—76 per cent of the total —worked in organisations run on Next Steps lines. At the same time a further 16 agency candidates— employing nearly 7,300 staff—had been identified as suitable for agency status.

The Diplomatic Service

The Diplomatic Service, a separate service of some 5,800 people, provides the staff for the Foreign & Commonwealth Office (see p. 115) and for British diplomatic missions abroad.

The Diplomatic Service has its own grade structure, linked to that of the Home Civil Service. Terms and conditions of service are comparable, but take into account the special demands of the Service, particularly the requirement to serve abroad. Home civil servants, members of the armed forces and individuals from the private sector may also serve in the Foreign & Commonwealth Office and at overseas posts on loan or attachment.

Political and Private Activities

Civil servants are required to perform loyally the duties assigned to them by the Government of the day, whatever its political persuasion. It is essential that ministers and the public should have confidence that the personal views of civil servants do not influence the performance of their official duties, given the role of the Civil Service in serving successive governments formed by different parties.

The aim of the rules which govern political activities by civil servants is to allow them, subject to these fundamental principles, the greatest possible freedom to participate in public affairs consistent with their rights and duties as citizens. The rules are therefore concerned with activities liable to give public expression to political views rather than with privately held beliefs and opinions. The Civil Service is divided into three groups for the purposes of deciding the extent to which individuals may take part in political activities:

- those in the 'politically free' group, consisting of industrial staff and non-office grades, are free to engage in any political activity outside official time, including adoption as a prospective candidate for the British or the European Parliament (although they would have to resign from the Service before giving their consent to nomination);

- those in the 'politically restricted' group, which comprises staff in Grade 7 and above as well as Administration Trainees and Higher Executive Officers (D), may not take part in national political activities but may apply for permission to take part in local political activities; and

- the 'intermediate' group, which comprises all other civil servants, may apply for permission to take part in national or local political activity, apart from candidature for the British or the European Parliament.

Where required, permission is granted to the maximum extent consistent with the Civil Service's reputation for political impartiality and the avoidance of any conflict with official duties. A code of discretion requires moderation and the avoidance of embarrassment to ministers.

Generally, there are no restrictions on the private activities of civil servants, provided that these do not bring discredit on the Civil Service, and that there is no possibility of conflict with official duties. For instance, a civil servant must comply with any departmental instruction on the need to seek authority before taking part in any outside activity which involves official experience.

Security

Each department is responsible for its own internal security. As a general rule the privately held political views of civil servants are not a matter of official concern. However, no one who is, or has been involved in, or associated with, activities threatening national security may be employed on work which is vital to the security of the State. Certain posts are not open to people who fall into this category, or to anyone whose reliability may be in doubt for any other reason.

The Security Commission may investigate breaches of security in the public service and advise on changes in security procedure if asked to do so by the Prime Minister after consultation with the Leader of the Opposition.

Local Government

Although the origins of local government in England can be traced back to Saxon times, the first comprehensive system of local councils was established in the late 19th century. Major reforms to the structure of local government are now being implemented.

Local Authorities' Powers

Local authorities derive their power from legislation. They can act only under powers conferred on them by Acts of Parliament. If these powers are exceeded, the local authority concerned can be challenged in a court of law. Local authorities' functions are far reaching. Some are mandatory, which means that the authority must do what is required by law; others are purely permissive, allowing an authority to provide services if it wishes. In certain services, ministers have powers to secure a degree of uniformity in standards in order to safeguard public health or to protect the rights of individual citizens.

The main link between local authorities and central government in England is the Department of the Environment, Transport and the Regions. However, other departments such as the Department for Education and Employment and the Home Office are also concerned with various local government functions. In the rest of Britain the local authorities deal with the Scottish or Welsh Offices or the Department of the Environment for Northern Ireland, as appropriate.

In June 1997 the Government signed the Council of Europe's Charter of Local Self Government. This lays down standards for protecting and developing the rights of local authorities.

Local Government Reform

A major reform of local government took place in 1974 in England and Wales and in 1975 in Scotland. This created two main tiers of local authority throughout England and Wales: counties and the smaller districts. Local government in London had been reorganised along the same lines in 1965. In Scotland functions were allocated to regions and districts on the mainland; single-tier authorities were introduced for the three Islands areas. In Northern Ireland changes were made in 1973 which replaced the two-tier county council and urban/rural council system with a single-tier district council system.

The Local Government Act 1985 abolished the Greater London Council and the six metropolitan county councils in England. Most of their functions were transferred to the London boroughs and metropolitan district councils respectively in 1986 (see below).

Recent Changes

During the last five years a further restructuring of local government has taken place in non-metropolitan England and in Scotland and Wales. In 1992 the Local Government Commission was established to review the structure, boundaries and electoral arrangements of local government in England and to undertake periodic electoral reviews. So far most of its work has been to review the structure of local government in non-metropolitan England. The reviews considered whether the two-tier structure should be replaced by single-tier ('unitary') authorities in each area; for the most part the Commission recommended the retention of two-tier government, but suggested unitary authorities

for some areas, especially the larger cities. Parliament approved reorganisation in 25 counties, creating a total of 46 unitary councils (see map on p. 7). By April 1997, 27 of these had been established; the last 19 will be in place by April 1998.

In Scotland 29 new unitary councils replaced the previous system of nine regional and 53 district councils in April 1996; the three Islands councils have remained in being. In Wales, 22 unitary authorities replaced the previous eight county councils and 37 district councils, again in April 1996.

Principal Types of Local Authority

Greater London

Greater London is divided into 32 boroughs and the Corporation of the City of London, each with a council responsible for all local government services in its area. Exceptions include London's metropolitan police force, which is responsible to the Home Secretary, and public transport, responsibility for which lies with London Transport (see p. 309).

Proposals for London Government

At present London is the only Western capital without an elected city-wide government. In July 1997 the Government issued a Green Paper[13] on proposals for establishing a directly elected strategic authority and directly elected mayor in London. The strategic authority, which would encompass the 32 London boroughs and the City of London Corporation, would not duplicate the work of the London boroughs, but would take responsibility for London-wide issues such as economic regeneration, planning, policing, transport and environmental protection. The Government plans to introduce legislation to enable a referendum to be held in London to confirm popular demand. A White Paper describing the proposed new authority would be issued before the referendum. Subject to parliamentary approval, the referendum

---

[13] *New Leadership for London: the Government's Proposals for a Greater London Authority.* Cm 3724.

would be held in May 1998, and in the event of a majority in favour of those voting, and parliamentary approval of the necessary legislation, the new mayor and authority would be elected in May 2000.

English Metropolitan Counties

The six metropolitan counties—Tyne and Wear, West Midlands, Merseyside, Greater Manchester, West Yorkshire and South Yorkshire—have 36 district councils, but no county councils. The district councils are responsible for all services apart from those which require a statutory authority over areas wider than the individual boroughs and districts. They are: waste disposal (in certain areas); the fire services, including civil defence; and public transport. These are run by joint authorities composed of elected councillors nominated by the borough or district councils. Local councils also provide many of the members of the police authorities (see p. 92).

English Non-Metropolitan Counties

Outside Greater London and the metropolitan areas, England was, before the recent reforms, divided into counties, sub-divided into districts. All the districts and the non-metropolitan counties and districts had locally elected councils with separate functions. County councils provided large-scale services such as education and social services, while district councils were responsible for the more local ones (see below). These arrangements are broadly continuing in areas where two-tier local government will remain. In areas where the new unitary authorities are being created, both county and district level functions are being brought together.

County councils are responsible for strategic planning, transport planning, highways, traffic regulation, education,[14] consumer protection, refuse disposal, the fire

service, libraries and the personal social services. District councils are responsible for environmental health, housing, decisions on most local planning applications, and refuse collection. Both tiers of local authority have powers to provide facilities such as museums, art galleries and parks; arrangements depend on local agreement. Where unitary authorities are created in non-metropolitan areas, they are generally responsible for both county and district level functions.

In addition to the two-tier local authority system in England, over 8,000 parish councils or meetings provide and manage local facilities such as allotments and village halls, and act as agents for other district council functions. They also provide a forum for discussion of local issues.

Scotland, Wales and Northern Ireland

In Scotland the 32 single-tier councils are responsible for the full range of local government services. In Wales the 22 single-tier councils have similar functions, except that fire services are provided by three combined fire authorities. In addition, about 730 community councils in Wales have functions similar to those of the parish councils in England (see above); in Scotland community councils exist to represent the views of their local communities to local authorities and other public bodies in the area.

In Northern Ireland 26 district councils are responsible for local environmental and certain other services, such as leisure and the arts. Responsibility for planning, roads, water supply and sewerage services is exercised in each district through a divisional office of the Department of the Environment for Northern Ireland. Area boards, responsible to central departments, administer education, public libraries and the health and personal social services locally. Statutory bodies, such as the Northern Ireland Housing Executive and area boards, are responsible to central government departments for administering other major services.

Election of Councils

Local councils consist of elected councillors. In England and Wales each council elects its

---

[14] Under the Education Reform Act 1988, schools have been able to 'opt out' of local education authority control by obtaining grant-maintained status. However legislation is now before Parliament to end the grant maintained schools programme (see p. 437).

presiding officer annually. Some districts have the ceremonial title of borough, or city, both granted by royal authority. In boroughs and cities the presiding officer is normally known as the Mayor. In the City of London and certain other large cities, he or she is known as the Lord Mayor. In Scotland the presiding officer of the district council of each of the four cities—Aberdeen, Dundee, Edinburgh and Glasgow—is called the Lord Provost.

Most councillors are elected for four years. All county councils in England, borough councils in London, and about two-thirds of non-metropolitan district councils are elected in their entirety every four years. In the remaining districts (including all metropolitan districts) one-third of the councillors are elected in each of the three years when county council elections are not held. In Scotland local elections will now be held every three years, with the next elections due in 1999. Each election covers the whole council. In Wales elections for the full councils will continue to be held every fourth year, again with the next due in 1999.

Councillors are paid a basic allowance but may also be entitled to additional allowances and expenses for attending meetings or taking on special responsibilities. Parish and community councillors cannot claim allowances for duties undertaken within their own council areas. In Scotland community councillors are not eligible for any form of allowance.

Voters

Anyone may vote at a local government election in Britain provided he or she is:

- aged 18 years or over;
- a citizen of Britain or of another Commonwealth country, or of the Irish Republic, or a citizen of the European Union;
- not subject to any legal incapacity to vote; and
- on the electoral register.

To qualify for registration a person must be resident in the council area on the qualifying date. In Northern Ireland there are slightly different requirements.

Candidates

Most candidates at local government elections stand as representatives of a national political party, although some stand as independents. Candidates must be British citizens, other Commonwealth citizens or citizens of the European Union, and aged 21 or over. In addition, they must also either:

- be registered as local electors in the area of the relevant local authority; or
- have occupied (as owner or tenant) land or premises in that area during the whole of the preceding 12 months; or
- have had their main place of work in the area throughout this 12-month period; or
- have resided in the area throughout this 12-month period.

No one may be elected to a council of which he or she is an employee, and there are some other disqualifications. All candidates for district council elections in Northern Ireland are required to make a declaration against terrorism.

Electoral Divisions and Procedure

Counties in England are divided into electoral divisions, each returning one councillor. Districts in England and Northern Ireland are divided into wards, returning one councillor or more. In Scotland the new unitary councils are divided into wards and in Wales into electoral divisions; each returns one or more councillors. Parishes (in England) and communities (in Wales) may be divided into wards. Wards return at least one councillor.

The procedure for local government voting in Great Britain is broadly similar to that for parliamentary elections. In Northern Ireland local government elections are held by proportional representation, and electoral wards are grouped into district electoral areas.

The boundaries and electoral arrangements of local authorities in England are kept under review by the Local Government Commission (see p. 80), and in Wales and Scotland by the Local Government Boundary Commissions.

Provision of Local Services

In recent years, there has been a move away from direct service provision, to a greater use of private contractors, and an increase in what is often called the 'enabling' role. Local authorities now carry out many functions in partnership with other organisations, public and private. For example, councils often have nomination rights to housing association properties (see p. 385), so that they are acting not as provider but as 'gatekeeper'. Likewise, under the community care reforms, councils with social services responsibilities draw up care plans for those who need them (see p. 414), but the care is often provided by the private or voluntary sectors funded by the council rather than directly by the local authority itself.

The previous administration introduced legislation in the 1980s aimed at encouraging local authorities to obtain better value for money in the services they provide. It introduced a practice known as compulsory competitive tendering (CCT), under which many services traditionally provided by the council's own staff, such as refuse collection and leisure management, must now be put out to tender and won in open competition.

In a departure from the approach of its predecessor, the Government elected in May 1997 intends to develop a new system to achieve best value in the delivery of local government services. It considers that councils should not be forced to put their services out to tender, but equally it sees no reason why a service should be delivered directly if more efficient means are available elsewhere. It intends to replace CCT with a new duty for local councils to ensure best value for the public and will introduce legislation as soon as the parliamentary timetable allows.

Before replacing CCT, pilot schemes are to be run in some local authority areas to see how a best-value regime would work. Criteria for the pilot schemes will include a requirement for an authority to publish its plans for improving the quality of services, increasing efficiency, and reducing costs to the taxpayer. The criteria will also reflect the Government's view that competition will continue to be an important management tool and test of best value, but that it will not be the only management tool and is not in itself enough to demonstrate that best value is being achieved.

Internal Organisation of Local Authorities

Local authorities have considerable freedom to make arrangements for carrying out their duties. Some decisions are made by the full council; many other matters are delegated to committees composed of members of the council. A council may delegate most functions to a committee or officer, although certain powers are legally reserved to the council as a whole. Parish and community councils in England and Wales are often able to do their work in full session, although they appoint committees from time to time as necessary.

In England and Wales committees generally have to reflect the political composition of the council (although the legislation governing this specifically excludes parish or community councils). In practice, this is often also the case in Scotland, although it is not enforced by legislation. People who are not members of the council may be co-opted onto decision-making committees and can speak and take part in debates; they cannot normally vote. Legislation also prevents senior officers and others in politically sensitive posts from being members of another local authority or undertaking public political activity.

Some of these provisions have not been introduced in Northern Ireland.

Public Access

The public (including the press) are admitted to council, committee and sub-committee meetings, and have access to agendas, reports and minutes of meetings and certain background papers. Local authorities may exclude the public from meetings and withhold these papers only in limited circumstances.

Employees

About 1.4 million people[15] are employed by local authorities in England (the figure for

---

[15] Whole time equivalents.

Scotland is 240,000). These include administrative, professional and technical staff, teachers, fire-fighters, and manual workers, but exclude those in law and order services. Education is the largest service. Councils are individually responsible, within certain national legislative requirements, for deciding the structure of their workforces.

Senior staff appointments are usually made by the elected councillors. More junior appointments are made by heads of departments. Pay and conditions of service are usually a matter for each council, although there are scales recommended by national negotiating machinery between authorities and trade unions, and most authorities follow these.

Local Authority Finance

Local government expenditure accounts for about 25 per cent of public spending. In 1996–97 expenditure by local authorities in Britain was about £75,560 million. Current expenditure amounted to £65,514 million; capital expenditure, net of capital receipts, was £5,920 million; and debt interest £4,115 million. Local government capital expenditure is financed primarily by borrowing within limits set by central government and from capital receipts from the disposal of land and buildings. Local authorities in Great Britain raise revenue through the council tax (see chapter 11), which meets about 20 per cent of their revenue expenditure. Their revenue spending is, however, financed primarily by grants from central government and by the redistribution of revenue from the national non-domestic rate, a property tax levied on businesses and other non-domestic properties.

District councils in Northern Ireland continue to raise revenue through the levying of a domestic rate and business rates.

Financial Safeguards

Local councils' annual accounts must be audited by independent auditors appointed by the Audit Commission in England and Wales, or in Scotland by the Accounts Commission for Scotland. In Northern Ireland this role is exercised by the chief local government auditor, who is appointed by the Department of the Environment for Northern Ireland.

Local Government Complaints System

Local authorities are encouraged to resolve complaints through internal mechanisms, and members of the public will often ask their own councillor for assistance in this. Local authorities must also appoint a monitoring officer, whose duties include ensuring that the local authority acts lawfully in the conduct of its business.

Allegations of local government maladministration leading to injustice may be investigated by statutory independent Commissioners for Local Administration, often known as 'local government ombudsmen'. There are three of these in England, and one each in Wales and Scotland. A report is issued on each complaint fully investigated and, if injustice caused by maladministration is found, the local ombudsman normally proposes a remedy. The council must consider the report and reply to it. In 1996–97 the local government ombudsman for England received 15,322 complaints, less than one per cent fewer than in 1995–96. Of these, 273 led to the issue of a formal report.

An independent review of the local government ombudsman service in England was completed in 1996. This identified ways of providing a better service to the public, and the Commission is taking action to implement improvements.

In Northern Ireland a Commissioner for Complaints deals with complaints alleging injustices suffered as a result of maladministration by district councils and certain other public bodies.

Pressure Groups

Pressure groups are informal organisations which aim to influence Parliament and Government in the way decisions are made and carried out, to the benefit of their members and the causes they support. There is a huge range of groups, covering politics, business, employment, consumer affairs, ethnic minorities, aid to developing countries, foreign relations, education, culture, defence, religion, sport, transport, social welfare, animal welfare and the environment. Some have over a million members, others only a few dozen. Some exert pressure on a number of different issues; others are concerned with a single issue. Some have come to play a recognised role in the way Britain is governed; others seek influence through radical protest. While political parties seek to win political power, pressure groups aim to influence those who are in power, rather than to exercise the responsibility of government and to legislate.

Pressure Groups and Policy

Pressure groups operating at a national level have a number of methods for influencing the way Britain is governed. Action by them may highlight a particular problem, which is then acknowledged by the Government. Groups whose scale of membership indicates that they are broadly representative in their field may then be consulted by a government department, or take part in Whitehall working groups or advisory councils. If the Government considers that legislation is necessary, then proposals are drafted, which are circulated to interested groups for their comments. Legislation is then put before Parliament, and at various times during the passage of a Bill—especially at the committee stage—pressure groups have opportunities to influence its content. If the Act includes delegated legislation (see p. 67), pressure groups may be consulted and have the opportunity to provide information and express their views.

Pressure Groups and Government

The principle of consultation to gain the consent and co-operation of as wide a range of organisations as possible, and ensure the smooth working of laws and regulations, plays an important part in the relationship between government departments and interested groups.

In some instances a department is under legal obligation to consult interested groups. The Government has a duty to consult organised interests, providing the pressure

groups involved have a broad enough membership for them to represent a majority view, and provided that they observe confidentiality about their discussions with the department. Members of pressure groups often have direct expertise, and an awareness of what is practicable, and can give advice and information to civil servants engaged in preparing policy or legislation. In return, the pressure groups have the opportunity to express their opinions directly to the Government. The contacts between civil servants and pressure group representatives may be relatively informal—by letter or telephone—or more formal, through involvement in working parties or by giving evidence to committees of inquiry.

Administration by Pressure Groups

The Government also makes grants to pressure groups which, as well as speaking on behalf of their members or for an issue, provide a service. For example, Relate: National Marriage Guidance has received grants for the advice centres it runs, and government departments make grants to a number of pressure groups for research relating to public policy.

Pressure Groups and Parliament

Lobbying—the practice of approaching MPs or Lords, persuading them to act on behalf of a cause, and enabling them to do so by providing advice and information—is a form of pressure group activity which has substantially increased in recent years.

A common pressure group tactic is to ask members of the public to write to their MP about an issue—for example, the Sunday trading laws, or the plight of political prisoners in particular countries—in order to raise awareness and persuade the MP to support the cause.

Raising Issues in Parliament

Other ways through which pressure groups may exert influence include:

- suggesting to MPs or Lords subjects for Private Members' Bills (see p. 66); many pressure groups have ready-drafted legislation waiting to be sponsored;

● approaching MPs or Lords to ask parliamentary questions as a means of gaining information from the Government and of drawing public attention to an issue;

● suggesting to MPs subjects for Early Day Motions (see p. 69) and suggesting to Lords subjects for debates; and

● orchestrating public petitions as a form of protest against government policy, or to call for action. If the petition is to be presented in Parliament, it must be worded according to Commons or Lords rules, and be presented by an MP or Lord in his or her own House.

Parliamentary Lobbyists

Many pressure groups employ full-time parliamentary workers or liaison officers, whose job is to develop contacts with MPs and Lords sympathetic to their cause, and to brief them when issues affecting the group are raised in Parliament.

There are also public relations and political consultancy firms specialising in lobbying Parliament and Government. Such firms are employed by pressure groups—as well as by British and overseas companies and organisations—to monitor parliamentary business, and to promote their clients' interests where they are affected by legislation and debate.

Further Reading

Committee on Standards in Public Life:

– *First Report: MPs, Ministers and Civil Servants, Executive Non Departmental Public Bodies.* Cm 2850, HMSO, 1995.

– *Second Report: Local Public Spending Bodies.* Cm 3270. The Stationery Office, 1996.

– *Third Report: Standards in Public Life - Standards of Conduct in Local Government in England, Scotland and Wales.* Cm 3702, The Stationery Office, 1997.

The British System of Government (3rd edn). Aspects of Britain series, The Stationery Office, 1996.

The Civil Service. Aspects of Britain series, HMSO, 1995.

Government and the Individual: The Citizen's Means of Redress. Aspects of Britain series, HMSO, 1996.

Honours and Titles (2nd edn). Aspects of Britain series, HMSO, 1996.

Local Government. Aspects of Britain series. HMSO, 1996.

Organisation of Political Parties (2nd edn). Aspects of Britain series, HMSO, 1994.

Parliament (3rd edn). Aspects of Britain series, The Stationery Office, 1996.

Parliamentary Elections (2nd edn). Aspects of Britain series, HMSO, 1995.

Pressure Groups. Aspects of Britain series, HMSO, 1994.

8 Justice and the Law

The Government elected in May 1997 has been carrying out an investigation into the efficiency and effectiveness of the criminal justice system in England and Wales. It plans to introduce legislation to improve the youth justice system and to combat anti-social behaviour and petty criminality in local communities. Plans for fundamental reform of the civil justice and legal aid systems in England and Wales were unveiled in October 1997.

Although Britain is a unitary state, it does not have a single legal system. England and Wales, Scotland, and Northern Ireland have their own systems, with differences in law, organisation and practice (although Northern Ireland's legal system is in many ways similar to that in England and Wales). This situation arises from the different arrangements that existed in the constituent parts of the country when they were united.

Main Branches of Law

The two main branches of the law in Britain are criminal law and civil law: criminal law deals with wrongs affecting the community for which the State may prosecute in the criminal courts, while civil law is about deciding disputes between two parties—individuals or administrative authorities or commercial organisations.

Sources of Law

One of the main sources of law in England and Wales and in Northern Ireland is common

law, which has evolved over centuries from judges' decisions. It forms the basis of the law except when superseded by legislation. The doctrine of legal precedent has also been more strictly applied in Scotland since the end of the 18th century.

Much of the law, particularly that relating to criminal justice, is statute law passed by Parliament. If a court reaches a decision which is contrary to the intentions of Parliament, then Parliament must either accept the decision or pass amending legislation. Some Acts create new law, while others draw together existing law on a given topic. Parliament can repeal a statute and replace it with another.

European Community Law

European Community law, which applies to Britain by virtue of its membership of the European Union (see p. 116), derives from the European Community treaties and the legislation adopted under them. EC legislation has been adopted in most of the fields covered by the Community treaties, including economic and social matters, agriculture and the environment. Where EC law is applicable, it takes precedence over domestic law. It is normally applied by the domestic courts, but the most authoritative rulings are given by the European Court of Justice in Luxembourg (see p. 118).

The new Government proposes to incorporate the main provisions of the 1950 European Convention on Human Rights into domestic law, but without reducing the sovereignty of the British Parliament (see p. 52).

Administration of the Law

GOVERNMENT RESPONSIBILITIES

England and Wales

The *Lord Chancellor* is the head of the judiciary and a senior Cabinet Minister. His administrative responsibility for the Supreme Court (comprising the Court of Appeal, High Court and Crown Court) and the county courts in England and Wales is exercised through the Court Service. He is also responsible for the locally administered magistrates' courts. He advises the Crown on the appointment of most members of the higher judiciary, and he appoints most magistrates. In addition, he is responsible for promoting general reforms of the civil law and for the legal aid schemes.

The *Home Secretary* has overall responsibility for criminal law, the police service, the prison system, the probation and after-care service, and advising the Crown on the exercise of the royal prerogative of mercy.

The *Attorney General* and the *Solicitor General* are the Government's principal legal advisers and represent the Crown in appropriate domestic and international cases. The former is also Attorney General for Northern Ireland. As well as exercising various civil law functions, the Attorney General has final responsibility for enforcing the criminal law. The Solicitor General is the Attorney's deputy.

As head of the Crown Prosecution Service (see p. 96), the *Director of Public Prosecutions* is subject to superintendence by the Attorney

General, as are the Director of the Serious Fraud Office and Director of Public Prosecutions for Northern Ireland.

Scotland

The *Secretary of State for Scotland* is responsible for Scottish criminal law, crime prevention, the police, the penal system and legal aid. He or she is also responsible for substantive civil law. The Secretary of State recommends the appointment of all judges other than the most senior ones, appoints the staff of the High Court of Justiciary and the Court of Session, and is responsible for the administration and staffing of the sheriff courts.

The *Lord Advocate* and the *Solicitor General for Scotland*, both government ministers, are the chief legal advisers to the Government on Scottish questions and the principal representatives of the Crown for the purposes of prosecutions and other litigation in Scotland. The Lord Advocate has ministerial responsibility for the law of evidence (civil and criminal) and for jurisdiction and procedures of the civil courts in Scotland.

Northern Ireland

Court administration is the responsibility of the *Lord Chancellor*, while the Northern Ireland Office, under the *Secretary of State for Northern Ireland*, deals with policy and legislation concerning criminal law, the police and the penal system. The Lord Chancellor has general responsibility for legal aid, advice and assistance.

PERSONNEL OF THE LAW

The law is enforced by judicial officers, ranging from judges in the House of Lords and the superior courts to the stipendiary and lay justices who, together with juries in certain cases, are responsible for deciding disputed cases. It also depends on officers of the court who have general or specialised functions of an administrative, and sometimes of a judicial, nature in the courts to which they are attached. Barristers—or advocates in Scotland—and solicitors represent the interests of parties to a dispute.

Judges are not subject to ministerial direction or control. They are normally appointed from practising barristers and advocates or solicitors.

Lay magistrates in England and Wales, and Scottish district court justices, are trained in order to give them sufficient knowledge of the law, including the rules of evidence, and of the nature and purpose of sentencing. In Northern Ireland members of a lay panel who serve in juvenile courts undertake training courses; resident magistrates are drawn from practising solicitors or barristers.

The legal profession is divided into two branches: barristers—or advocates in Scotland—and solicitors. Barristers and advocates advise on legal problems submitted through solicitors or other recognised professional bodies and present cases in all courts. Solicitors undertake legal business for individual and corporate clients; they can also, after appropriate training and accreditation, present cases in all courts. Although people are free to conduct their own cases, most people prefer to be legally represented, especially in more serious cases.

The Legal Services Ombudsman for England and Wales conducts investigations into the way professional bodies handle complaints against barristers, solicitors and licensed conveyancers. There is a separate Ombudsman for Scotland.

Criminal Justice

Crime Statistics

There are two main measures of the likely scale of crime in Britain—the recording of offences by the police, and periodic surveys among representative samples of crime victims. Recorded crime in England and Wales in 1996 is given in Table 8.1. In 1996–97 the Scottish police recorded 440,687 crimes; of these, 37 per cent were cleared up. In Northern Ireland, of the 68,549 recorded crimes in 1996, 23,103 were cleared up.

While increasing crime has been shown to be an international phenomenon, some categories of recorded crime in England and Wales, and in Scotland, have shown reductions in recent years.

Crime in Britain tends to be concentrated in cities and urban areas. About 92 per cent of offences recorded by the police in 1996 in England and Wales were directed against property; only 7 per cent involved violence. Car crime accounted for about 26 per cent of recorded crimes (and has been the focus for much government crime prevention activity). The demand for, and supply of, illegal drugs has also been a rising factor in the incidence of crime.

While regular crime surveys indicate that many crimes go unrecorded by the police (as not all victims report what has happened to them), they do confirm that the great majority of crimes are against property.

Table 8.1: Notifiable Crimes Recorded by the Police in England and Wales, 1996			
Offence Group	Recorded crimes	Crimes cleared up	Per cent
Violence against the person	239,109	184,416	77
Sexual offences	31,247	23,946	77
Burglary	1,164,364	245,878	21
Robbery	73,957	19,266	26
Theft and handling stolen goods	2,382,956	560,436	24
Fraud and forgery	135,902	67,360	50
Criminal damage[a]	782,559	141,643	18
Other	55,595	53,761	97
Total	4,865,689	1,296,706	27

Source: Home Office
[a] Excludes criminal damage of £20 or under.

Crime Prevention Measures

Crime prevention is an important strand of government criminal justice policy. The Crime Prevention Agency was established within the Home Office in 1996 to initiate, develop and co-ordinate effective crime prevention and reduction initiatives in England and Wales. Its work is overseen by the Crime Prevention Agency Board, bringing together the key bodies involved in promoting crime prevention—the Home Office, the Association of Chief Police Officers, Crime Concern (an independent organisation which encourages local initiatives and business participation in crime prevention), local government authorities, police authorities (see p. 92) and business.

The agency supports the police crime prevention effort through its Crime Prevention College near York, which is the national centre for training police officers in prevention skills. About 800 specialist crime prevention officers are employed in police forces across England and Wales.

There is a Crime Prevention Council in Scotland and a Crime Prevention Panel in Northern Ireland.

Initiatives

The public help the police to deter crime through, particularly, Neighbourhood Watch and Street Watch schemes, in which local people keep a look-out for any suspicious activity in their area and inform the police accordingly. There are many thousands of such schemes across Britain.

The widespread introduction of closed-circuit television (CCTV) surveillance systems is proving very effective in preventing and detecting crime, and in deterring criminals, in high streets, shopping centres, schools, industrial estates and other areas.

Since 1988 the Safer Cities programme has, with substantial government funding, promoted joint crime prevention action by local government, businesses, the police and voluntary agencies in England and Wales. There is a parallel Safer Cities programme in Scotland, and similarly funded projects in Northern Ireland.

The Government intends to introduce legislation to place a new responsibility on police services and local authorities to develop statutory partnerships to help prevent crime and enhance community safety. Local authorities will then be required to set targets for the reduction of crime and disorder in their area.

Helping Victims and Witnesses

Throughout England and Wales there are some 365 victim support schemes, with over 12,000 volunteer visitors, providing practical help and emotional support to victims of crime. The schemes are co-ordinated by a national organisation, Victim Support, which receives government funding. Victim Support runs the Witness Service, which helps victims and other witnesses attending Crown Court centres. Similar victim support schemes operate in Scotland and Northern Ireland.

A Victim's Charter, published in 1996, sets out the standards of service that victims should expect from criminal justice agencies in England and Wales.

In June 1997 the new Government announced a review of the way in which victims and vulnerable witnesses are treated by the criminal justice system. The review will be wide-ranging, from the initial investigation through to the trial and beyond, with the aim of identifying measures to protect those likely to be subject to intimidation and to assist vulnerable witnesses give best evidence in court.

Blameless victims of violent crime in England, Wales and Scotland, including foreign nationals, may be eligible for compensation from public funds under the Criminal Injuries Compensation Scheme. In Northern Ireland there are separate statutory arrangements for compensation for criminal injuries, and for malicious damage to property, including any resulting loss of profits.

Tackling Drug Misuse

The Government's strategy for tackling drug misuse involves:

- international co-operation against production and trafficking;

- law enforcement by police and customs, and maintenance of tight domestic controls and effective deterrents; and

- preventive education, publicity, and community action, and the treatment and rehabilitation of offenders.

> The new Government has appointed an Anti-Drugs Co-ordinator (or 'Drug Czar') to co-ordinate the fight against drugs in Britain. The Drug Czar will report to the newly appointed Cabinet sub-committee on Drug Misuse, and will review the overall direction of government action, support and help co-ordinate the effort of relevant agencies, put forward proposals for a new strategy for England and ensure strategic coherence to the government efforts across Britain and internationally.

In England the drugs strategy for the period 1995–98 seeks to involve the voluntary and private sectors, local authorities, schools, parents, health professionals and criminal justice agencies in a comprehensive programme to reduce supply, demand and misuse of illegal drugs. It aims to take action by vigorous law enforcement, accessible treatment and a new emphasis on education and prevention to:

- increase the safety of communities from drug-related crime;

- reduce the acceptability and availability of drugs to young people; and

- reduce the health risks and other damage related to drug misuse.

Across England 105 Drug Action Teams have been set up to implement the strategy at local level. The teams consist of senior representatives from the key statutory agencies—the police, probation and prison services, customs, and health and local authorities—working with the voluntary sector, local media, parents and young people. Each Drug Action Team receives, on average, annual £33,000 development funding from central government.

Separate strategies are in place for Scotland, Wales and Northern Ireland.

In 1996–97 the European Drug Liaison Officer network of the National Criminal Intelligence Service (NCIS—see p. 93) contributed to the seizure in Britain of drugs with a street value of more than £182 million, and the recovery of property worth over £12 million.

Measures to Combat Terrorism

Most of the powers which the police use to combat terrorism and the offences with which terrorists might be charged are contained in the general criminal law. However, the Prevention of Terrorism (Temporary Provisions) Act 1989, and legislation relating specifically to Northern Ireland (see below), confer some exceptional powers, and create additional offences, in order to combat terrorism.

The special counter-terrorist legislation gives the Secretary of State the power to:

- proscribe any organisation which appears to be concerned with terrorism in Northern Ireland; and

- exclude from all or part of Britain people who are believed to be, or to have been, involved in terrorism connected with the affairs of Northern Ireland.

The police have wider powers of arrest and detention under the Prevention of Terrorism Act than under the general criminal law when dealing with suspected terrorists. They can arrest and detain someone for up to 48 hours (and for a further five days if a Secretary of State approves) on reasonable suspicion of involvement in terrorism. They also have powers to conduct security checks at ports, and special investigative powers for offences relating to the financing of terrorism.

Extended police powers to stop and search pedestrians, to search non-residential premises and unaccompanied goods at ports, to impose cordons, and to restrict parking and remove vehicles were introduced under the Prevention of Terrorism (Additional Powers) Act 1996.

Northern Ireland

Powers similar to those provided in England and Wales under the Prevention of Terrorism

(Additional Powers) Act 1996 have existed for a number of years in Northern Ireland under successive Northern Ireland (Emergency Provisions) Acts, which have a fixed lifespan.

Despite the ceasefires declared by the paramilitary groupings in Northern Ireland in 1994, the previous Government did not think it prudent to remove from the statute book the protection provided by the emergency legislation while illegal weaponry and explosives were still at large.

The Provisional Irish Republican Army reverted to violence, from February 1996, in mainland Britain and in Northern Ireland, but declared a resumption of its ceasefire in July 1997 (see below).

Control of Weapons

Britain has strict legislative controls on firearms. The police license the possession of firearms and have powers to regulate their safekeeping and movement. A ban on the private ownership of machine guns, high-powered self-loading rifles and burst-fire weapons has been extended under new legislation in 1997 to include all handguns.

It is illegal to manufacture, sell or import certain weapons such as knuckledusters and swordsticks. The law relating to knives has recently been strengthened, with higher penalties for carrying a knife in a public place without good reason, new measures against the marketing of knives, and extended stop and search powers for the police.

THE POLICE SERVICE

The Home Secretary and the Scottish and Northern Ireland Secretaries, together with police authorities and chief constables, are responsible for providing an effective and efficient police service in Britain.

Organisation

There are 52 police forces in Britain, mainly organised on a local basis—43 in England and Wales, eight in Scotland and one (the Royal Ulster Constabulary) in Northern Ireland. The Metropolitan Police Service and the City of London force are responsible for policing London. The police service is financed by central and local government.

At the end of March 1997 police strength in England and Wales was about 127,150, of which the Metropolitan Police numbered around 27,000. The establishment of the Royal Ulster Constabulary (RUC) was around 8,500. Police strength in Scotland was about 14,500. With the exception of the RUC, each force has volunteer special constables who perform police duties in their spare time, without pay, acting in support of regular officers. There are currently about 20,000 special constables. In Northern Ireland there is a 5,000-strong reserve force.

Police forces are maintained in England and Wales by local police authorities. In the 41 police areas outside London, police authorities normally have 17 members—nine locally elected councillors, three magistrates and five independent members. A 12-member Metropolitan Police Committee assists the Home Secretary, currently the police authority for the Metropolitan Police. For the City of London Police the authority is a committee of the Corporation of London. Police authorities, in consultation with the chief constables and local community, set local policing objectives, while the Government sets key objectives for the police as a whole. The police authorities in Scotland are composed of elected councillors. In Northern Ireland the Secretary of State appoints the police authority.

Provincial forces are headed by chief constables (appointed by their police authorities with the Secretary of State's approval), who are responsible for the direction and control of their police forces and for the appointment, promotion and discipline of all ranks below assistant chief constable. On matters of efficiency they are generally answerable to their police authorities. In the Metropolitan Police District the commissioner of police is appointed by royal warrant on the recommendation of the Home Secretary.

Police forces are overseen by independent inspectors of constabulary, whose reports to central government are published.

Police officers are not allowed to join a trade union or to go on strike. All ranks, however, have their own staff associations.

Co-ordination of Operations

The National Criminal Intelligence Service (NCIS) has the leading role in collecting and analysing criminal intelligence for use by police forces and other law enforcement agencies in Britain. The NCIS has a headquarters and south-east regional office in London, with five other regional offices in England and an office in Scotland. It acts as co-ordinator for the activities of the Security Service in support of the law enforcement agencies against organised crime, and liaises with the International Criminal Police Organisation (INTERPOL), which promotes international co-operation between police forces. New legislation—the Police Act 1997—provides for the NCIS, currently part of the Home Office, to be put on a statutory footing outside central government.

There are six regional crime squads in England and Wales, and a Scottish Crime Squad, which investigate serious crime occurring across police force boundaries and abroad. The Police Act 1997 contains powers to establish a National Crime Squad in England and Wales. The same legislation also provides for the authorisation of intrusive surveillance operations by the police and HM Customs and Excise to be put on a statutory basis.

Britain has taken a leading role in developing a new European Union police agency (EUROPOL) to provide EU-wide intelligence about serious crime; in 1996, it was the first EU member state to ratify the convention giving EUROPOL legal status. The NCIS provides the channel for communication between Britain and EUROPOL.

Access to Information

The Police Information Technology Organisation (PITO), launched in 1996, is responsible for specifying and procuring the delivery of national information technology systems (such as the Police National Computer) for the police service, and for promoting the National Strategy for Police Information Systems (which develops common information technology applications) at force level. The PITO will become a non-departmental public body (see p. 74) in April 1998.

The Police National Computer provides all police forces in Britain with rapid 24-hour-a-day access to operationally essential information. Phoenix, the Criminal Justice Record Service, gives the police direct on-line access to national records of arrests, cautions, bail decisions and convictions. This is gradually replacing the manual record-keeping service maintained on microfiche by the National Identification Service (NIS). Phoenix will eventually provide information direct to other criminal justice agencies.

Under the Police Act 1997, new arrangements are being made for the disclosure of criminal records information for employment and related purposes in England, Wales and Northern Ireland. In Scotland criminal record checks are undertaken by the Scottish Criminal Records Office (SCRO). The SCRO has an automatic national fingerprint record system; a similar national system in England and Wales (NAFIS) is being implemented from 1997–98.

Forensic Science Service

The Forensic Science Service (FSS) is a Home Office executive agency. It provides scientific support in the investigation of crime and expert evidence to the courts. Its customers include the police, the Crown Prosecution Service, coroners and defence solicitors. In 1996 the FSS merged with the Metropolitan Police Forensic Science Laboratory to form a single agency serving all police forces in England and Wales through six regional laboratories. The FSS operates the national DNA database (see p. 95).

In Scotland forensic science services are provided by forces' own laboratories. Northern Ireland has its own forensic science laboratory.

Powers and Procedures

(For information on police powers relating to the prevention of terrorism, see p. 91.)

England and Wales

Police powers and procedures in criminal investigation and apprehension are defined by legislation and accompanying codes of practice. A police officer is liable to disciplinary proceedings if he or she fails to comply with any provision of the codes, and evidence obtained in breach of the codes may be ruled inadmissible in court. The codes must be readily available for consultation in all police stations.

● *Stop and search*—Police officers have the power to stop and search people and vehicles if there are reasonable grounds for suspecting that they will find stolen goods, offensive weapons or implements that could be used for theft, burglary and other offences. An officer must make a record of the grounds for the search and of anything found, and the person stopped is entitled to a copy of the record. A senior police officer (superintendent or above) who reasonably believes that serious incidents of violence may take place can authorise uniformed officers to stop and search people and vehicles for offensive weapons or dangerous implements. The authorisation must specify the timescale and area in which the powers are to be exercised.

● *Arrest*—The police have various powers to arrest people suspected of having committed an offence. They may arrest on a warrant issued by a court, but can arrest without warrant for arrestable offences. An arrestable offence is one for which the sentence is fixed by law or for which the term of imprisonment is five years or more. This category includes serious arrestable offences such as murder, rape and manslaughter. There is a general power of arrest for all other offences if it is impracticable or inappropriate to proceed by way of summons to appear in court, or if a police officer has reasonable grounds for believing that an arrest is necessary to prevent a suspect from causing injury to someone else or damage to property.

● *Detention and questioning*—A person suspected of an offence must be cautioned before the police can ask any questions about the offence: suspects must be informed that they do not have to say anything, but anything that they do say may be given in evidence in court. The caution also tells suspects that it may be harmful to their defence if they fail to mention something during questioning which they later rely on in court. A caution will also

be given in similar terms when a suspect is charged. A court may draw inferences from a defendant's failure to mention facts when questioned or charged.

The length of time that a suspect is held in police custody before charge is strictly regulated. For arrestable offences this may not exceed 24 hours. A person suspected of committing a serious arrestable offence can be detained for up to 96 hours without charge, but beyond 36 hours only if a warrant is obtained from a magistrates' court. Reviews must be made of a person's detention at regular intervals to check whether the criteria for detention are still satisfied.

Interviews with suspects at police stations must be tape-recorded when the police are investigating indictable offences and in certain other cases. The police are not precluded from taping interviews for other types of offence. Suspects are entitled to a copy of the recording if they are charged or informed that they will be prosecuted.

Someone who thinks that the grounds for his or her detention are unlawful may apply to the High Court for a writ of *habeas corpus* against the person responsible, requiring that person to appear before the court to justify the detention. *Habeas corpus* proceedings take precedence over others.

● *Charging*—Once there is sufficient evidence, the police have to decide whether a detained person should be charged with an offence. If the police institute criminal proceedings against a person, the Crown Prosecution Service (see p. 96) then takes control of the case.

Scotland

The police in Scotland can arrest someone without a warrant if he or she is seen committing a crime or is reasonably suspected of an offence against laws controlling the use of drugs. In other cases the police may seek a warrant to arrest a person suspected of a crime by applying to a Justice of the Peace (JP—see p. 97).

As in England and Wales, Scottish police have powers to enter a building without a warrant if they are pursuing someone who has committed, or attempted to commit, a serious crime. A court can grant the police a search warrant giving them the power to search premises for stated items in connection with a crime. The police may search anyone suspected of carrying an offensive weapon.

Anyone suspected of an imprisonable offence may be detained for questioning by the police without being arrested, but for no more than six hours without being charged. When someone is arrested, they must be charged and cautioned that they need say nothing but that anything that is said may be given in evidence. The case is then referred to the procurator fiscal (see p. 97). Failure to caution a suspect, or unreasonable harshness in questioning by the police, may result in any alleged confession being considered inadmissible in court.

Tape recording of interviews with suspects is common practice.

Northern Ireland

The law in Northern Ireland relating to the powers of the police in the investigation of crime and to evidence in criminal proceedings is very similar to that in force in England and Wales.

DNA Testing

The police may take certain body samples for DNA analysis from people detained or convicted for a recordable offence, and use the samples to search against existing records of convicted offenders or unsolved crimes. A national DNA database, the first of its kind in the world, was introduced in 1995.

Firearms

Police officers in Great Britain do not normally carry firearms. About five per cent of officers are allowed to be issued with firearms, on the authority of a senior officer, where there is a special need. Most forces operate armed response vehicles which can be deployed quickly to contain firearms incidents. In Northern Ireland police officers are issued with firearms for their personal protection.

Police Discipline

A police officer may be prosecuted if suspected of a criminal offence. Officers are also subject to a disciplinary code designed to deter abuse of police powers and maintain public confidence in police impartiality. If found guilty of breaching the code, an officer can be dismissed from the force.

Members of the public can make complaints against police officers if they feel that they have been treated unfairly or improperly. In England and Wales the investigation of such complaints by the force concerned is overseen, or in more serious cases supervised, by the independent Police Complaints Authority. In Scotland complaints against police officers involving allegations of criminal conduct are referred to the procurator fiscal for investigation. The Scottish Inspectorate of Constabulary considers representations from complainants dissatisfied with the way the police have handled their complaints.

In Northern Ireland the Independent Commission for Police Complaints is required to supervise the investigation of complaints regarding death or serious injury and has the power to supervise that of any other complaint.

Community Relations

Within every police authority there are police/community liaison consultative arrangements, drawing in representatives from the police, local councillors and community groups. Efforts are made to develop relations with young people through greater contact with schools.

All police officers should receive training in community and race relations issues. Home Office and police service initiatives aim to ensure that racially motivated crime is treated as a police priority. Forces' responses to racial incidents are monitored by the Inspectorate of Constabulary. Discriminatory behaviour by police officers, towards either other officers or members of the public, is an offence under the police disciplinary code.

Police forces recognise the need to recruit more women and members of the ethnic minorities in order to ensure the police fully represent the community. Each force has an equal opportunities policy.

PROSECUTION AND THE CRIMINAL COURTS

Awaiting Trial

England and Wales

If someone is charged with an offence, he or she may be released on bail to attend a magistrates' court. When bail is not granted by the police, the defendant must be brought before a magistrates' court as soon as possible.

Although all those accused of offences have a general right to bail, magistrates may withhold bail if there are substantial grounds for believing that an accused person would abscond, commit an offence, interfere with witnesses, or otherwise obstruct the course of justice. Recent legislation has removed the presumption in favour of bail for people alleged to have offended while on bail, and also removes the right to bail for someone charged with murder, manslaughter or rape if previously convicted of the same offence.

If bail is refused by the magistrates, the defendant is entitled to apply to the Crown Court or the High Court judge in chambers and must be informed of this right. In certain circumstances the prosecution may appeal to a Crown Court judge against the granting of bail by magistrates.

Scotland

When arrested, an accused person in Scotland may be released by the police to await summons, on an undertaking to appear at court at a specified time, or be held in custody to appear at court on the next working day. Following that appearance, the accused person may be remanded in custody until trial or released by the court on bail. If released on bail, the accused person must undertake to appear at trial when required, not to commit an offence while on bail, and not to interfere with witnesses or obstruct the course of justice. The court may also impose additional conditions on the accused (for example, to keep away from certain people or locations).

There is a right of appeal to the High Court by an accused person against the refusal of bail, or by the prosecutor against the granting of bail, or by either against the conditions imposed.

Bail will not be granted where an accused person is charged with murder, attempted murder, culpable homicide, rape or attempted rape and has a previous conviction for such a crime (in the case of culpable homicide, involving a prison sentence).

Northern Ireland

In Northern Ireland bail may be granted by a resident magistrate except in cases dealt with under emergency provisions, where the decision is made by a judge of the High Court.

Prosecution Arrangements

England and Wales

Once the police have charged a person with a criminal offence, the independent Crown Prosecution Service (CPS) takes control of the case, reviews the evidence and advises the police on whether the case should be continued. A prosecution will proceed only if the prosecutor is satisfied that there is, on the evidence, a realistic prospect of conviction, and if so, that it is in the public interest for the prosecution to proceed.

The CPS is headed by the Director of Public Prosecutions, who is accountable to Parliament through the Attorney General. It is at present divided into 13 geographical areas, each headed by a Chief Crown Prosecutor, and below these there are 98 branches. Every

The new Government is decentralising the structure of the CPS, so that there will be a one-to-one relationship between a police force and its corresponding CPS area, with the aim of making co-operation more effective. By April 1998 the CPS will be divided into 42 new areas—one for each police force outside London, with the Metropolitan Police and City of London Police being served by one CPS area—each having its own Chief Crown Prosecutor.

branch has a number of teams, each of which is responsible for casework from particular police divisions and feeding into particular courts. A fourteenth area—Central Casework—deals with some especially sensitive cases, including terrorist offences and breaches of the Official Secrets Act.

Scotland

The Lord Advocate is responsible for prosecutions in the High Court of Justiciary, sheriff courts and district courts. The High Court of Justiciary will only grant the right to prosecute to a private person in very exceptional cases. The Lord Advocate is advised by the Crown Agent, who is head of the Procurator Fiscal Service and is assisted in the Crown Office by a staff of legally qualified civil servants.

Prosecutions in the High Court of Justiciary are prepared by procurators fiscal and Crown Office officials. They are conducted by the Lord Advocate, the Solicitor General for Scotland (the Lord Advocate's ministerial deputy) and advocate deputes, collectively known as Crown Counsel.

Crimes tried before the sheriff and district courts are prepared and prosecuted by procurators fiscal. The police and other law enforcement agencies investigate crimes and offences and report to the procurator fiscal, who decides whether to prosecute, subject to the directions of Crown Counsel.

Northern Ireland

The Director of Public Prosecutions for Northern Ireland, appointed by the Attorney General, prosecutes all offences tried on indictment and may do so in other (summary) cases. Most summary offences are prosecuted by the police.

Prosecutions for Fraud

The Serious Fraud Office prosecutes the most serious and complex cases of fraud in England, Wales and Northern Ireland. Investigations are conducted by teams of lawyers, accountants, police officers and other specialists. In Scotland the Crown Office Fraud Unit, which is part of the public prosecution service, directs the investigation and preparation for prosecution of serious and complex fraud cases.

Courts

England and Wales

Very serious offences such as murder, manslaughter, rape and robbery can only be tried on indictment in the Crown Court, where all contested trials are presided over by a judge sitting with a jury. Summary offences (the less serious offences and the vast majority of criminal cases) are tried by unpaid lay magistrates or, in a few areas, by a single paid stipendiary magistrate; both sit without a jury.

Offences in a third category, such as theft, the less serious cases of burglary and some assaults, are known as 'either way' offences. They can be tried either by magistrates or by jury in the Crown Court. If magistrates are content to deal with the case, the accused person has the right to choose either trial by magistrates or trial by jury in the Crown Court.

All those charged with offences triable in the Crown Court must first appear before a magistrates' court, which decides whether to commit them to the Crown Court for trial. In committal proceedings a magistrates' court considers only documentary evidence and exhibits submitted by the prosecution, together with representations by both parties, when determining whether there is a case to answer. No witnesses are called to give evidence or be cross-examined.

A magistrates' court usually consists of three lay magistrates, known as Justices of the Peace (JPs), who are advised by a legally qualified clerk or a qualified assistant. There are about 30,000 lay magistrates serving some 400 courts. The few full-time, legally qualified stipendiary magistrates may sit alone and usually preside in courts where the workload is heavy. Magistrates' courts are open to the public and the media.

Most cases involving people under 18 are heard in youth courts. These are specialist magistrates' courts which either sit apart from other courts or are held at a different time.

Restrictions are placed on access by ordinary members of the public.

Where a young person under 18 is charged jointly with someone aged 18 or over, the case may be heard in an ordinary magistrates' court or the Crown Court. If the young person is found guilty, the court may transfer the case to a youth court for sentence.

An independent inspectorate monitors the administration of magistrates' courts in order to assess performance and spread good practice. It does not comment on the judicial decisions of magistrates or their clerks in particular cases.

The Crown Court sits at about 90 venues, in six regional areas called circuits, and is presided over by High Court judges, full-time circuit judges and part-time recorders. The kind of judge chosen to preside over a case depends on its complexity and seriousness.

A Charter for Court Users sets out standards of service in the High Court, Crown Court and county courts in England and Wales, covering areas such as witness and juror care, and correspondence and complaints handling. The Charter does not cover the judiciary. Magistrates' courts are developing their own charters.

Scotland

The High Court of Justiciary tries the most serious crimes and has exclusive jurisdiction in cases involving murder, treason and rape. The sheriff court is concerned with less serious offences and the district court with minor offences.

Criminal cases in Scotland are heard under solemn or summary procedure. In solemn procedure, an accused person's trial takes place before a judge sitting with a jury of 15 people. As in England and Wales, details of the alleged offence are set out in a document called an indictment. In summary procedure the judge sits without a jury.

All cases in the High Court and the more serious ones in sheriff courts are tried by a judge and jury. Summary procedure is used in the less serious cases in the sheriff courts, and in all cases in the district courts. District court judges are lay magistrates. In Glasgow there are also stipendiary magistrates, who are full-time lawyers with the same powers as a sheriff in summary procedure.

Children under 16 who have committed an offence are normally dealt with by children's hearings (see p. 108).

Northern Ireland

Cases involving minor summary offences are heard by magistrates' courts presided over by a full-time, legally qualified resident magistrate. Young offenders under 17 are dealt with by a juvenile court consisting of the resident magistrate and two specially qualified lay members, at least one of whom must be a woman.

The Crown Court deals with criminal trials on indictment. It is served by High Court and county court judges. Contested cases are heard by a judge and jury, although people charged with terrorist-type offences are tried by a judge sitting alone because of the possibility of jurors being intimidated by terrorist organisations.

In non-jury Crown Court trials the onus remains on the prosecution to prove guilt beyond reasonable doubt, and defendants have the right to be represented by a lawyer of their choice. The judge must set out in a written statement the reasons for convicting, and there is an automatic right of appeal against conviction and sentence on points of fact as well as law.

Trial

Criminal trials in Britain have two parties: the prosecution and the defence. The law presumes the innocence of an accused person until guilt has been proved by the prosecution. An accused person has the right to employ a legal adviser and may be granted legal aid from public funds (see p. 112). If remanded in custody, he or she may be visited by a legal adviser to ensure a properly prepared defence.

Pre-Trial Preparation

The Criminal Procedures and Investigations Act 1996 has amended the law in England and Wales on prosecution and defence disclosure of evidence, and introduced other measures relating to pre-trial procedures. Since April 1997, a new statutory scheme (also applicable in Northern Ireland) places limits on what the police and prosecution must disclose to the defence, with protection for sensitive material such as the identity of informants. The defence is required to disclose before the trial the general nature of its case, and the matters on which it takes issue with the prosecution, with its reasons. Defence disclosure is mandatory in the Crown Court.

The 1996 legislation has also:

- created a statutory scheme for pre-trial hearings in the Crown Court in England and Wales, with the aim of ensuring that potentially difficult cases come to court as well prepared as they can be; and

- given judges a new power to make a binding ruling on the admissibility of evidence or other point of law in any case before the start of a trial.

In Scotland, the court in summary cases is required to call an additional hearing (intermediate diet) at some time between the first court appearance and the trial to establish the state of readiness of both the defence and the prosecution. In solemn procedure, once an accused person has had the opportunity of consulting a solicitor, he or she may go before a sheriff for judicial examination, which takes place in private. A record of the examination may be used in evidence at a subsequent trial. Solemn procedure in the sheriff court requires a hearing, like that held in summary cases, to find out whether the case is ready to go to trial. The prosecution in solemn cases must give the defence advance notice of the witnesses it intends to call and of the documents and other items on which it will rely. In summary cases this is usually done as a matter of practice, although there is no obligation on the Crown to do so.

Trial Procedure

Criminal trials normally take place in open court and rules of evidence are rigorously applied. Certain evidence is excluded because it is unduly prejudicial to the defendant, inherently unreliable, or its utterance is against the public interest. If evidence is improperly admitted or excluded a conviction can be quashed on appeal.

During the trial the defendant has the right to hear and cross-examine prosecution witnesses. The defendant can call his or her own witnesses who, if they will not attend voluntarily, may be legally compelled to do so. The defendant can also address the court in person or through a lawyer, the defence having the right to the last speech before the judge sums up. The defendant cannot be questioned without consenting to be sworn as a witness in his or her own defence.

Child Witnesses

Legislation in 1988 tackled the presumption in England and Wales that children were incompetent as witnesses, and introduced the system which allows children to give their evidence at court by means of a closed-circuit television link. Subsequent legislation, which has abolished the presumption, extends the closed-circuit television provisions, forbids the cross-examination of a child directly by the accused, and provides for a video-recorded interview with a child victim or witness to be admissible in court as his or her main evidence. Judges are required to admit the evidence of a child unless he or she is incapable of giving intelligible testimony. The jury must decide what weight should be placed on a child's evidence. These provisions have been replicated in Northern Ireland.

In Scotland live television links installed in a number of criminal courts enable children (and, from August 1997, certain categories of vulnerable adults) to give their evidence without entering the courtroom. Evidence may also be given from behind a screen in the courtroom. In addition, there is provision for a child to give video-recorded evidence before and during the trial. The child who has given evidence in this manner is not subject to cross-examination on that evidence in court.

The Jury

In jury trials the judge decides questions of law, sums up the evidence for the jury, and discharges or sentences the accused. The jury is responsible for deciding questions of fact.

In England, Wales and Northern Ireland the jury verdict may be 'guilty' or 'not guilty', the latter resulting in acquittal. If the jury cannot reach a unanimous decision, the judge may allow a majority verdict provided that, in the normal jury of 12 people, there are no more than two dissenters. In Scotland the jury's verdict may be 'guilty', 'not guilty' or 'not proven'; the accused is acquitted if either of the last two verdicts is given. A Scottish jury consists of 15 people and a verdict of 'guilty' can be reached only if at least eight members are in favour.

If the jury acquits the defendant, the prosecution has no right of appeal and the defendant cannot be tried again for the same offence. However, there is provision for retrial of an acquitted person if the acquittal has been tainted by a subsequent conviction for interfering with, or intimidating, a juror or witness in the proceedings which resulted in the acquittal.

A jury is independent of the judiciary and any attempt to interfere with its members is a criminal offence. Jurors are selected from a pool of potential jurors before the start of a trial. Both the prosecution and the defence may object to particular jurors. People between the ages of 18 and 70 (65 in Scotland) whose names appear on the electoral register are, with certain exceptions, liable for jury service and their names are chosen at random. Ineligible people include judges and people who have been members of the legal profession or the police, prison or probation services within the previous ten years. Those convicted of certain offences within the previous ten years cannot serve on a jury. Anyone who has received a prison sentence of five years or more is disqualified for life. People on bail are also ineligible.

Sentencing

If a person is convicted, the court decides on the most appropriate sentence, taking into account the facts of the offence, the circumstances of the offender, any previous convictions or sentences and any statutory limits on sentencing. The defence lawyer may make a speech in mitigation.

Courts in England and Wales must obtain a 'pre-sentence' report from the probation service on offenders under the age of 18 in cases involving an offence triable either way before passing a custodial or more complex community sentence. In most other circumstances, such reports are discretionary. In Scottish cases a court must obtain a social enquiry report before imposing a custodial sentence if the accused is under 21 or has not previously served a custodial sentence. A report is also required before making a probation or community service order (see p. 102), or in cases involving people subject to supervision.

Courts may take into account, when deciding the appropriate sentence, the fact that an accused person pleaded guilty, and the timing and circumstances in which the plea was made.

Confiscation of Criminal Proceeds

Courts in Britain have wide powers to order the confiscation of profits made by drug traffickers and other criminals. These were first introduced in 1986, in relation to the proceeds of drug trafficking, and have since been strengthened and extended to the proceeds of other serious crimes. The amount owing under a confiscation order is liable to forfeiture even when the offender has served a term of imprisonment in default for failing to pay the order. Britain co-operates with a number of countries in freezing and confiscating the proceeds of serious crime.

There are heavy penalties for those who launder money gained from any sort of serious crime.[1]

Appeals

England and Wales

A person convicted by a magistrates' court may appeal to the Crown Court against the sentence if he or she has pleaded guilty. An appeal may be made against both conviction and sentence, or sentence alone, if a 'not guilty' plea has been made. The High Court

---

[1] Money-laundering is the process by which illegally obtained money or other property—from drugs or arms trafficking, terrorist activities or other serious crimes—is given the appearance of having originated from a legitimate source.

hears appeals on points of law and procedure, by either prosecution or defence, in cases originally dealt with by magistrates. If convicted by the Crown Court, a defendant may seek leave to appeal to the Court of Appeal (Criminal Division) against both the conviction and the sentence imposed. The House of Lords is the final appeal court, but will only consider cases that involve a point of law of general public importance and where leave to appeal is granted.

The Attorney General may seek a ruling of the Court of Appeal on a point of law which has been material in a case where a person is tried on indictment. The Court has power to refer the point to the House of Lords if necessary. The ruling will constitute a binding precedent, but an acquittal in the original case is not affected.

The Attorney General can apply for leave to refer to the Court of Appeal a sentence which, in his or her view, appears unduly lenient. This power covers offences triable on indictment and certain offences triable either way (where sentence has been passed in the Crown Court). Such triable either way offences are indecent assault, making threats to kill, and cruelty to, or neglect of, a child. The Attorney General's power also covers certain types of serious or complex fraud. The Court of Appeal may, if it decides to quash the original sentence, impose in its place any sentence which the original sentencing court had the power to impose.

The Criminal Cases Review Commission, established in January 1997, operates in England and Wales and in Northern Ireland. This body, independent of both Government and the courts, examines possible miscarriages of justice in cases tried on indictment or summarily and decides whether to refer them to the courts on the grounds of sentence and conviction. It directs and supervises investigations undertaken on its behalf and approves the appointment of investigating officers. Referral of a case requires some new argument or evidence not previously raised at the trial or on appeal.

The final decision on any case referred rests with the respective Courts of Appeal in England and Wales and Northern Ireland (if the case was tried originally on indictment) or with the Crown Court following a referral in a summary case.

The Court of Appeal will allow any appeal where it considers the conviction unsafe and will dismiss it in any other case.

Scotland

All appeal cases are dealt with by the High Court of Justiciary. In both solemn and summary procedure, a convicted person may appeal against conviction, or sentence, or both. The Court may authorise a retrial if it sets aside a conviction. There is no further appeal to the House of Lords. In summary proceedings the prosecutor may appeal on a point of law against acquittal or sentence. The Lord Advocate may seek the opinion of the High Court on a point of law in a case where a person tried on indictment is acquitted. The acquittal in the original case is not affected. The Crown has a right of appeal against lenient sentences in both solemn and summary procedure.

Legislation passed in 1995 introduced a requirement for leave to appeal. This involves a single judge assessing whether there are arguable grounds for an appeal. The legislation also reduced the number of High Court judges required to consider appeals against sentence only from three to two.

A person convicted on indictment may petition the Secretary of State to refer the case to the High Court on the ground that a miscarriage of justice has occurred. If the case is referred, then it will be dealt with as though it were a normal appeal.

Northern Ireland

In Northern Ireland, appeals from magistrates' courts against conviction or sentence are heard by the county court. An appeal on a point of law alone can be heard by the Northern Ireland Court of Appeal, which also hears appeals from the Crown Court against conviction and/or sentence. Procedures for a further appeal to the House of Lords are similar to those in England and Wales.

A person convicted of a terrorist offence in a non-jury court has an automatic right of appeal against conviction and/or sentence.

The new Criminal Cases Review Commission operates in Northern Ireland as well as in England and Wales.

Coroners' Courts

In England and Wales the coroner (usually a senior lawyer or doctor) must hold an inquest if the deceased died a violent or unnatural death, a sudden death where the cause is unknown, or in prison or in other specified circumstances. In Northern Ireland in such circumstances the coroner investigates the matter to decide whether an inquest is necessary. The coroner's court establishes how, when and where the deceased died. A coroner may sit alone or, in certain circumstances, with a jury.

In Scotland the local procurator fiscal inquires privately into all sudden and suspicious deaths and may report the findings to the Crown Office. When appropriate a fatal accident inquiry may be held before the sheriff; this is mandatory in cases of death resulting from industrial accidents and of deaths in custody.

TREATMENT OF OFFENDERS

Non-custodial Sentences

A range of non–custodial sentences is available to the courts (see also Young Offenders—p. 107). These include:

Fines

About 75 per cent of offenders are punished with a fine. There is no limit to the fine which the Crown Court (and High Court of Justiciary and the sheriff court in Scotland under solemn procedure) may impose on indictment. The maximum fine that can be imposed by a magistrates' court in England and Wales (and a sheriff court in Scotland under summary procedure) is £5,000. When fixing the amount of a fine, courts are required to reflect the seriousness of the offence and to take into account the financial circumstances of the offender.

Probation

The locally organised probation service in England and Wales supervises offenders in the community under direct court orders and after release from custody. It also provides offenders in custody with help and advice.

A court probation order requires offenders to maintain regular contact with their probation officer, who is expected to supervise them and confront them with the consequences of their offence. Probation is intended as a punishment, although the time spent by offenders under supervision in the community offers an opportunity for constructive work to reduce the likelihood of reoffending. A probation order can last from six months to three years; an offender who fails to comply with any of the requirements of the order can be brought before the court again. The probation service also administers some supervision orders and supervises those subject to community service orders and those released from prison on parole.

HM Inspectorate of Probation monitors the work of the voluntary and private sectors with the probation service, in addition to its inspection and advisory duties.

In Scotland local authority social work departments supervise offenders on probation, community service and other community disposals, and offenders subject to supervision on release from custody.

In Northern Ireland the probation service is administered by the government-funded Probation Board, whose membership is representative of the community.

Community Service

In England and Wales offenders aged 16 or over convicted of imprisonable offences may be given community service orders. The court may order between 40 and 240 hours' unpaid service to be completed within 12 months. Examples of work done include decorating the houses of elderly or disabled people and building adventure playgrounds for children. From January 1998, community service orders for periods of between 20 and 100 hours for fine defaulters and persistent petty offenders will be piloted.

In Scotland the minimum number of hours for which a community service order can be made is 80 and the maximum, in higher courts, is 300.

Combination Order

A court may impose an order which combines probation and community service elements on an offender aged 16 or over who has been convicted of an imprisonable offence. The probation element may be of one to three years' duration, the community service element of between 40 to 100 hours.

Electronic Monitoring

The use of curfew orders with electronic monitoring was introduced in 1995 in three trial areas in England and Wales for offenders aged 16 and over. Offenders sentenced to the order are required to remain at a place or places specified by the court for between two and 12 hours a day for up to six months. The Crime (Sentences) Act 1997 contains provisions to extend courts' powers to impose a curfew order, monitored by electronic tagging, to offenders aged 10 to 15. In July 1997 the new Government announced that the current trials would be extended to other areas, and that there would be pilot projects for tagging those on bail, fine defaulters, persistent petty offenders and juveniles.

In Scotland the Crime and Punishment (Scotland) Act 1997 includes provision for the introduction of a restriction of liberty order, enabling the courts to curtail an offender's movements for up to 12 hours a day for 12 months using electronic monitoring. The new Government has announced that it intends to set up pilot schemes in selected courts. Scottish legislation does not provide for the 'tagging' of offenders aged under 16.

Supervised Attendance Order

In Scotland supervised attendance order schemes operate in a number of areas, and will be available to all Scottish courts in 1998. These provide an alternative to imprisonment for fine default, and incorporate aspects of work and training. Their use as an alternative in the first instance to fines for young offenders is being piloted in selected areas.

Compensation

The courts may order an offender to pay compensation for personal injury, loss or damage resulting from an offence. Compensation takes precedence over fines.

Other Measures

A court in England and Wales may discharge a person either absolutely or conditionally if it believes that it is not necessary to inflict punishment. If conditionally discharged, the offender remains liable to punishment for the offence if convicted of another offence within a period specified by the court (not more than three years).

Courts may also require an offender to keep the peace and/or be of good behaviour. If this requirement is not complied with, the offender is liable to forfeit a sum of money. Similar powers are available to courts in Northern Ireland.

Courts have the power to defer sentence, so as to enable the court, in subsequent dealings with the offender, to consider his or her conduct or any changes in circumstances.

The police have discretion whether to charge an offender or formally to caution him or her. Cautioning is a form of warning and no court action is taken. The new Government proposes to end the practice of repeat cautions, replacing them with a single final warning. Cautioning is not available in Scotland.

Custody

A custodial sentence is the most severe penalty available to the courts. A court must explain to the offender why it is passing a custodial sentence, and the length of the sentence must reflect the seriousness of the offence. There is a mandatory sentence of life imprisonment for murder throughout Britain. Life imprisonment is the maximum penalty for a number of serious offences such as robbery, rape, arson and manslaughter. Since October 1997 the courts in England and Wales have been required to impose automatic life sentences on those convicted for a second time of a serious violent or sexual offence.

England and Wales

A magistrates' court cannot impose a term of more than six months' imprisonment for an individual offence tried summarily. It can impose consecutive sentences for 'either way' offences, subject to an overall maximum of 12 months' imprisonment. If an offence carries a higher maximum penalty, the court may commit the offender for sentence at the Crown Court. The Crown Court may impose a custodial sentence for any term up to life, depending on the seriousness of the offence and the maximum penalty available.

If a court decides that an offence is sufficiently serious to justify an immediate custodial sentence of not more than two years, the sentence may be suspended for a period of at least one year and not more than two years if exceptional circumstances justify the suspension. If the offender commits another imprisonable offence during the period of suspension, the court may order the suspended sentence to be served as well as any punishment imposed for the second offence. When passing a suspended sentence, the court must consider whether it would also be appropriate to impose a fine or make a compensation order. The court may also order the offender to be supervised by a probation officer if the suspended sentence is for more than six months.

Northern Ireland

In Northern Ireland the position is generally the same as for England and Wales. A magistrates' court, however, cannot commit an offender for sentencing at the Crown Court if it has tried the case.

Scotland

In Scottish trials on indictment the High Court of Justiciary may impose a sentence of imprisonment for any term up to life, and the sheriff court any term up to three years. The sheriff court may send any person to the High Court for sentence if the court considers its powers are insufficient. In summary cases the sheriff or stipendiary magistrate may normally impose up to three months' imprisonment or six months for some repeated offences. The district court can impose a maximum term of imprisonment of 60 days.

The Crime and Punishment (Scotland) Act 1997 includes provision for increases in the sentencing powers of the sheriff and district courts; implementation of this is under consideration by the new Government.

Prisons

The Prison Service in England and Wales, the Scottish Prison Service and the Northern Ireland Prison Service are all executive agencies. Government ministers remain accountable for policy, while agencies' chief executives (the Director General in the case of England and Wales) are responsible for the delivery of services.

Prisoners are housed in accommodation ranging from open prisons to high security establishments. In England, Wales and Scotland sentenced prisoners are classified into different risk-level groups for security purposes. Women prisoners are held in separate prisons or in separate accommodation in mixed prisons. There are no open prisons in Northern Ireland, where the majority of offenders are serving sentences for terrorist offences. People awaiting trial in custody have certain rights and privileges not granted to convicted prisoners. Where possible, they are separated from prisoners who have been convicted and sentenced.

There are currently 133 prison establishments in England and Wales and 22 in Scotland. Thirty-seven establishments in England and Wales hold prisoners under the age of 21 (22 of which are dedicated to such offenders only) and five cater for them in Scotland. Northern Ireland has three prisons and one young offenders' centre.

In 1996 the average prison population was 55,280 in England and Wales, 5,900 in Scotland and 1,640 in Northern Ireland. The prison population in Great Britain fell in the late 1980s and early 1990s, but has been growing since 1993. In Northern Ireland it has fallen by 17 per cent since 1987.

Although many prisons were built in the 19th century, there has been a refurbishment and prison-building programme over recent years. All prisoners in England and Wales now have access to sanitation 24 hours a day, as do an increasing proportion (two-thirds) in Scotland.

Private Sector Involvement

The Home Secretary has the power to contract out the management of prisons in England and Wales to the private sector, as well as escort and guarding functions. Four prisons (which remain part of the Prison Service) are currently managed by private contractors. Three prisons being built under the Private Finance Initiative (PFI—see chapter 11, p. 160) in Merseyside, Nottinghamshire and south Wales are expected to be in operation in 1998–99. In Scotland a new prison near Kilmarnock is also to be built under the PFI.

Early Release of Prisoners

At present, prisoners in England and Wales sentenced to less than four years are released once they have served half of their sentence. Long-term prisoners (those sentenced to four years or more) become eligible to be considered for early release once they have served half of their sentence; if not found suitable for parole they are released automatically at the two-thirds point. The Parole Board has the final decision on the early release of prisoners sentenced (after 1 October 1992) to four years or more, but less than seven years. In other cases the Board makes a recommendation to the Home Secretary about a prisoner's suitability for parole. All prisoners sentenced to a year or more are released on licence to be supervised until the three-quarters point of the sentence. If ordered by the sentencing court, sex offenders may be supervised to the end of the sentence. If convicted of another offence punishable with imprisonment and committed before the end of the original sentence, a released prisoner may be required by the court to serve all or part of the original sentence outstanding at the time the fresh offence was committed.

In Scotland similar arrangements apply except that the Parole Board has the power to release prisoners from halfway through their sentence if they are serving between four and ten years. Those serving 10 years or more may only be released with the consent of the Secretary of State. All prisoners sentenced to four years or more are supervised from release until the end of their sentence.

In Northern Ireland prisoners serving a sentence of more than five days are eligible for remission of half their sentence. Those convicted of terrorist offences are eligible for release at the halfway point in their sentence but remain under licence (until the two-thirds point) and may be subject to recall during that period. If convicted of another terrorist offence before the expiry of the original sentence, the prisoner must complete that sentence before serving any term for the second offence.

Life Sentence Prisoners

People serving life sentences for the murder of police or prison officers, terrorist murders, murder by firearms in the course of robbery and the sexual or sadistic murder of children are normally detained for at least 20 years.

The release on licence of prisoners serving mandatory life sentences for murder may only be authorised by the Home Secretary on the recommendation of the Parole Board and after consultation with the judiciary. A similar policy applies in Scotland.

The Home Secretary is required to release prisoners serving life sentences for offences other than murder after an initial period set by the trial judge if so directed by the Parole Board. The Board has to be satisfied that the protection of the public does not require their further confinement. Similar procedures apply in Scotland, and under the Crime and Punishment (Scotland) Act 1997 they will extend to those serving life sentences for murder committed while under the age of 18.

On release, life sentence prisoners remain on licence for the rest of their lives and are subject to recall if their behaviour suggests that they might again be a danger to the public.

In Northern Ireland the Secretary of State reviews life sentence cases on the recommendation of an internal review body.

Repatriation

Sentenced prisoners who are nationals of countries which have ratified the Council of Europe Convention on the Transfer of Sentenced Persons, or similar international arrangements, may apply to be returned to their own country to serve the rest of their sentence there.

Independent Oversight of the Prison System

Every prison and young offender institution in England and Wales has a board of visitors. Board members are volunteers drawn from the local community and appointed by the Home Secretary. They are independent of the prison and the Prison Service, visit the prison often, hear any complaints by prisoners and concerns of staff, and report as necessary to the Home Secretary. In Scotland, the visiting committees to prisons are appointed by local authorities; those to young offender institutions are appointed by the Secretary of State for Scotland.

Independent Prisons Inspectorates report to the respective Secretaries of State on the treatment of prisoners and prison conditions. Each establishment is visited about once in every three years. The Inspectorates submit annual reports to Parliament.

In England and Wales prisoners who fail to get satisfaction from the Prison Service's internal request and complaints system may complain to the Prisons Ombudsman. The Ombudsman is independent of the Prison Service and investigates complaints from individual prisoners over decisions relating to them which have been taken by Prison Service staff, or other people working in prisons.

In Scotland, prisoners who exhaust the internal grievance procedure may make application to the Scottish Prisons Complaints Commission, which is independent of the Scottish Prison Service.

Prison Industries

Prison industries aim to give inmates work experience which will help them when released and to secure a return which will reduce the cost of the prison system. The main industries are clothing and textile manufacture, engineering, woodwork, laundering and horticulture. A few prisoners are employed outside prison, some in community service projects.

Prison Education

Education is compulsory for young people in custody below school leaving age; otherwise it is voluntary. There are many facilities available for prisoners to gain vocational qualifications, and some prisoners study for public examinations, including those of the Open University (see p. 453).

Physical education is compulsory for young offenders, but otherwise voluntary. Practically all prisons have physical education facilities. Opportunities are given for inmates to obtain sporting proficiency awards. Inmates also compete against teams from the local community.

Healthcare

The Health Care Service for Prisoners is responsible for the physical and mental healthcare of all those in prison custody in England and Wales. A Health Advisory Committee provides independent medical advice to government ministers and the Prison Service's Director General and Director of Health Care. Its overall objective is to ensure that prisoners have access to the same range and quality of services as do the general public from the National Health Service (NHS).

In Scotland general medical services are provided mainly by visiting general practitioners (GPs—see chapter 24). Psychiatric services are bought in from local health boards responsible for the NHS. Psychological services are provided partly in-house.

Privileges and Discipline

Prisoners may write and receive letters and be visited by relatives and friends, and those in all establishments in England, Wales and Scotland may make telephone calls. Privileges include a personal radio; books, periodicals and newspapers; watching television; and the opportunity to buy goods from the prison shop with money earned in prison. Depending on the facilities available, prisoners may be granted the further privileges of dining and recreation with other inmates.

Under the national framework for incentives and earned privileges now in force in all prisons in England and Wales, inmates are required to earn privileges above a minimum by good behaviour and performance, and can lose them if they fail to maintain acceptable standards.

Offences against prison discipline are dealt with by prison governors, who act as adjudicators. Measures to counter drug misuse in prisons include mandatory drug testing.

Preparation for Release

The Prison Services have a duty to prepare prisoners for release. Planning for safe release starts at the beginning of an offender's sentence and ties in with the training, education and work experience provided. It aims to help prisoners reintegrate into society and to cope with life without reoffending. Risk assessment and confronting offending behaviour are essential elements of this process.

Prisoners may be released on temporary licence for short periods but they are subject to a rigorous risk assessment and are released only for precisely defined and specific activities which cannot be provided in prison establishments.

The Pre-Release Employment Scheme in England and Wales and the Training for Freedom Scheme in Scotland enable selected long-term prisoners to spend some time before release in certain units or prisons in order to help them readapt to society and renew ties with their families. Prisoners in such units work in paid employment in the community and return to the unit each evening.

In Northern Ireland prisoners serving fixed sentences may have short periods of pre-release home leave in their final period of sentence. Fortnightly weekend home leave for life sentence prisoners who have been recommended for release was introduced in 1996.

Aftercare

Professional support is given to offenders after release. All young offenders and all prisoners in England and Wales sentenced to 12 months' imprisonment and over are supervised on release by the probation service, or, in the case of certain young offenders, by local authority social services departments.

In Scotland supervision on release is provided by local authority social work services.

Young Offenders

England and Wales

Criminal proceedings cannot be brought against children below the age of 10. Offenders aged 10 to 17 years fall within the jurisdiction of youth courts.

Existing non-custodial penalties for young offenders include fines and compensation orders (which the parents of offenders may be ordered to pay), supervision orders and attendance centre orders; 16- and 17-year-olds may also be given the same probation, community service and curfew sentences as older offenders.

Under a supervision order, which can remain in force for up to three years, a young offender would normally live at home under the supervision of a social worker or a probation officer. The order may contain a number of conditions including the requirement for an offender to live in local authority accommodation and/or participate in specified activities at specified times.

A young offender found guilty of an imprisonable offence can be ordered by the courts to an attendance centre, as can an offender who refuses to comply with another order (for example, breach of a probation order). The maximum number of hours of attendance is 36 (or 24 if the offender is aged under 16) spread over a period; the minimum is 12 hours. The order aims to encourage offenders to make more constructive use of their leisure time.

Custodial sentences are available to the courts where no other alternative is considered to be appropriate. The main custodial sentence for offenders aged 15 and over is detention in a young offender institution.

Offenders aged 10 to 14 may also be detained if convicted of murder, manslaughter, or other serious offences for which an adult can be jailed for 14 years or more (including rape, arson and robbery). Post-release supervision is carried out by a probation officer or local authority social worker.

The Criminal Justice and Public Order Act 1994 makes provision for five secure training centres to accommodate persistent offenders aged between 12 and 14. Secure training orders, imposed by the court, will mean a period of detention in a centre followed by a period of supervision, and will be available for young offenders who have committed three or more imprisonable offences and have failed to respond to punishment in the community. The first secure training centre will be opened in April 1998.

Scotland

Criminal proceedings may be brought against any child aged 8 years or over, but the instructions of the Lord Advocate are necessary before anyone under 16 years of age is prosecuted.

Most children under 16 who have committed an offence or are considered to be in need of care and protection may be brought before a children's panel. The panel, consisting of three lay people, determines in an informal setting whether compulsory measures of care are required and, if so, the form they should take. An official known as the reporter decides whether a child should come before a hearing. If the grounds for referral are not accepted by the child or parent, the case goes to the sheriff for proof. If the sheriff finds the grounds established, he or she remits the case to the reporter to arrange a hearing. The sheriff also decides appeals against a hearing's decision.

Young people aged between 16 and 21 serve custodial sentences in young offender institutions. Remission of part of the sentence for good behaviour, release on parole and supervision on release are available.

Northern Ireland

Those aged between 10 and 16 who are charged with a criminal offence are normally brought before a juvenile court. If found guilty of an offence punishable in the case of an adult by imprisonment, the court may order the offender to be placed in care, under supervision or on probation. The offender may also be required to attend a day attendance centre, be sent to a training school or committed to residence in a remand home. Non-custodial options are the same as in England and Wales.

Offenders aged between 16 and 24 who receive custodial sentences of less than four years' detention serve them in a young offenders' centre.

Government Proposals on Youth Justice

In response to the problem of youth crime,[2] the new Government intends to introduce legislation to improve the youth justice system and curb disorder in local communities. A White Paper is to be published later in 1997. The proposed legislation will include:

- a fast track system to halve the time it takes from arrest to sentence for persistent young offenders, and to streamline the youth court system;

- a single final warning to replace repeat cautions;

- new Youth Offender Teams to plan and supervise intervention programmes which will follow a final warning, and new and revised community sentences aimed at changing young offenders' behaviour;

- giving courts new sentencing powers, which will help both offenders and their parents face up to their responsibilities; and

- a Youth Justice Board to monitor the operation of the youth justice system in England and Wales, to promote good practice and to draw up standards for work with young offenders.

---

[2] Almost four in ten offenders found guilty of, or cautioned for , an indictable offence in England and Wales in 1995 were aged 14 to 20 years old. According to police figures, the peak age for offending for males in England and Wales was 18 in 1995; almost 9 per cent of 18-year-old males were found guilty of, or cautioned for, an indictable offence in that year. For females, rates of offending were lower, and the peak age was younger—at 14.

The Government has set up a Task Force on Youth Justice to advise Home Office ministers on government proposals for the development of youth justice policies, and to follow up action agreed by a new interdepartmental Ministerial Group on Youth Justice.

Civil Justice

The Civil Law

England, Wales and Northern Ireland

The main subdivisions of civil law are:

- *family law*, which includes the laws governing marriage, divorce, and the welfare of children;
- the *law of property* (including intellectual property), which governs ownership and rights of enjoyment, the creation and administration of trusts, and the disposal of property on death;
- the *law of contract*, which regulates, for instance, the sale of goods, loans, partnerships, insurance and guarantees; and
- the *law of torts*, which deals with non-contractual wrongful acts suffered by one person at the hands of another.

Civil law also encompasses administrative law (concerned with the powers of the State), industrial law (relating to employment), Admiralty (maritime) law, ecclesiastical law and service (military) law.

Scotland

In Scotland, civil law comprises public law and private law. Public law deals with the regulation and control of political and administrative power within the State; it concerns the activities of Parliament, the courts, central and local government, and public authorities, and their relationships with individual citizens. Private law—family law, the law of contract, law of property, law of delict (concerning civil wrongs for which the wrongdoer must pay compensation), and

mercantile law (regulating trade, companies and bankruptcy)—deals with the rights and obligations of citizens among themselves.

CIVIL COURTS

England and Wales

Civil cases are heard in county courts and the High Court. Magistrates' courts have a concurrent jurisdiction with the county courts and the High Court in cases relating to children.

The jurisdiction of the 240 county courts covers:

- actions founded upon contract and tort;
- trust and mortgage cases;
- actions for the recovery of land;
- cases involving disputes between landlords and tenants;
- complaints about race and sex discrimination;
- Admiralty cases (maritime questions and offences) and patent cases; and
- divorce cases and other family matters.

Specialised work (patent cases, for example) is concentrated in certain designated courts. For small claims (up to the value of £3,000), there are special arbitration facilities and simplified procedures.

The High Court, which is divided into three divisions, deals with the more complicated civil cases. Its jurisdiction covers mainly civil and some criminal cases; it also deals with appeals from tribunals (see p. 111) and from magistrates' courts in both civil and criminal matters. The three divisions are:

- the Family Division, which is concerned with family law, including adoption and divorce;
- the Chancery Division, which deals with corporate and personal insolvency; disputes in the running of companies, between landlords and tenants and in intellectual property matters; and the interpretation of trusts and contested wills; and
- the Queen's Bench Division, which has a wide and varied jurisdiction, including contract and tort cases. It also deals with

applications for judicial review. Maritime law and commercial law are the responsibility of the Division's Admiralty and commercial courts.

In the event of overlapping jurisdiction between the High Court and the county courts, cases of exceptional importance, complexity or financial substance are reserved or transferred for trial in the High Court.

Appeals

Appeals in family cases which have been heard by magistrates' courts go to the Family Division of the High Court. Appeals from the High Court and county courts are heard in the Court of Appeal (Civil Division), and may go on to the House of Lords (the final national court of appeal in civil and criminal cases).

The Law Lords deal with cases submitted to the House of Lords. They are professional judges who have been given life peerages (see chapter 7, p. 58). A group of five judges usually deals with cases. The Lord Chancellor is President of the House in its judicial capacity.

Scotland

The civil courts in Scotland are the Court of Session (the supreme central court, subject only to the House of Lords) and the sheriff court (the principal local court), which have the same jurisdiction over most civil litigation. However, cases with a value of less than £1,500 are dealt with only by the sheriff court. Appeals from the sheriff court may be made to the sheriff principal or directly to the Court of Session.

The Court of Session sits in Edinburgh, and in general has jurisdiction to deal with all kinds of action. It is divided into the Outer House (a court of first instance) and the Inner House (mainly an appeal court). Appeals to the Inner House may be made from the Outer House and from the sheriff court. From the Inner House an appeal may go to the House of Lords.

Northern Ireland

Civil cases up to a limited and specified monetary value are dealt with in county courts. The magistrates' courts in Northern Ireland also deal with certain limited classes of civil case. The superior civil law court is the High Court of Justice, from which an appeal may be made to the Court of Appeal. The House of Lords is the final civil appeal court. Appeals from county courts are dealt with by the High Court or the Court of Appeal.

Civil Proceedings

England and Wales

Actions in the High Court are usually begun by a writ served by the plaintiff (the aggrieved party) on the defendant, stating the nature of the claim. Before the case is tried, documents (pleadings) setting out the scope of the dispute are filed with the court; the pleadings are also served on the parties to the case. County court proceedings are initiated by a summons, usually served on the defendant by the court. Child care cases are initiated by an application in the magistrates' courts.

The High Court and the county courts can order pre-trial exchange of witness statements, and may impose penalties in costs on parties who unreasonably refuse to admit facts or to disclose documents before trial.

Civil proceedings, as a private matter, can usually be abandoned or ended by settlement between the parties at any time. Actions brought to court are usually tried without a jury, except in defamation, false imprisonment or malicious prosecution cases or where fraud is alleged, when either party may apply for trial by jury. The jury decides questions of fact and determines the damages to be paid to the injured party; majority verdicts may be accepted. The Court of Appeal can increase or reduce damages awarded by a jury if it considers them inadequate or excessive.

Most judgments are for sums of money and may be enforced, in cases of non-payment, by seizure of the debtor's goods or by a court order requiring an employer to make periodic payments to the court by deduction from the debtor's earnings. Other court remedies may include an injunction restraining someone from performing an unlawful act. Refusal to obey a court order may result in a fine or imprisonment for contempt of court.

Normally the court orders the costs of an action to be paid by the party losing it.

In civil cases heard by a magistrates' court, the court issues a summons to the defendant setting out details of the complaint and the date on which it will be heard. Parties and witnesses give their evidence at the court hearing. Family proceedings are normally heard by not more than three lay justices, including both men and women. Members of the public are not allowed to be present. The court may make orders concerning residence, contact and supervision of children, and in some cases maintenance payments for spouses and children.

Proposed Reforms for England and Wales

Following on from the recommendations of a government-commissioned report into reducing the cost, delay and complexity of civil litigation in England and Wales (the *Woolf Report*, published in 1996—see p. 114), the Government announced its plans in October 1997 for reform of the civil justice system.

Adopting the *Woolf Report's* proposals for more hands-on management of cases by judges, the Government intends to oversee the creation of two new routes through civil justice—a fast-track and a multi-track procedure—to replace the present complexities. It is proposed that the fast-track procedure should be accompanied by an associated fixed-costs regime.

Regarding civil legal fees, a consultation paper is inviting discussion on the principles which should underlie a new fee structure.

In the longer term, the Government is proposing the creation of a Community Legal Service, the main aim of which would be to help people decide if their problem is really a legal one and, if it is not, to guide them to the appropriate source of advice and information.

Other recommendations of the *Woolf Report* are being implemented under the terms of the Civil Procedure Act, which came into force in April 1997. The legislation provides for:

- a unified Civil Procedure Rule Committee, replacing the Supreme Court and County Court Rule Committees, with the power to make rules of court for all civil, non-matrimonial litigation; and

- the establishment of a Civil Justice Council, an advisory body to keep the civil justice system under review and make proposals for research.

Scotland

Proceedings in the Court of Session or ordinary actions in the sheriff court are initiated by serving the defender with a summons or, in sheriff court cases, an initial writ. A defender who intends to contest the action must inform the court; if he or she fails to do so, the court normally grants a decree in absence in favour of the pursuer. Where a case is contested, both parties must prepare written pleadings. Time is allowed for either party to adjust their pleadings in the light of what the other has said. At the end of this period a hearing will normally be arranged.

In cases involving sums between £750 and £1,500 in the sheriff court, a statement of claim is incorporated in the initial writ. The procedure is designed to enable most actions to be settled without the parties having to appear in court. Normally they, or their representatives, need appear only when an action is defended.

Tribunals

Tribunals exercise judicial functions separate from the courts and are intended to be more accessible, less formal and less expensive. They are normally set up under statutory powers, which also govern their constitution, functions and procedure. Tribunals often consist of lay people, but they are generally chaired by a legally qualified person.

Some tribunals settle disputes between private citizens. Industrial tribunals, for example, have a major role in employment disputes. Others, such as those concerned with social security, resolve claims by private citizens against public authorities. A further group, including tax tribunals, decide disputed claims by public authorities against private citizens. Tribunals usually consist of an uneven number of people so that a majority decision can be reached.

In the case of some tribunals a two-tier system operates, with an initial right of appeal to a lower tribunal and a further right of appeal, usually on a point of law, to a higher one, and in some cases to the Court of Appeal. Appeals from single-tier tribunals can usually be made only on a point of law to the High Court in England and Wales, to the Court of Session in Scotland, and to the Court of Appeal in Northern Ireland.

The independent Council on Tribunals exercises general supervision over many tribunals. A Scottish Committee of the Council exercises the same function in Scotland.

Legal Aid

A person who needs legal advice, assistance or representation may be able to get help with legal costs from the legal aid scheme. People who qualify for help may have all their legal costs paid for, or may be asked to make a contribution towards them, depending on their means and, in civil cases, the outcome of the case.

Legal Advice and Assistance

Legal advice is available under the Legal Advice and Assistance ('Green Form') Scheme in England and Wales. People whose income and capital are within certain limits are entitled to free advice from a solicitor on most legal matters. The scheme provides initially for up to three hours' work for matrimonial cases where a petition is drafted, and two hours for other work. Similar schemes operate in Northern Ireland and Scotland.

Legal Aid in Civil Proceedings

At present civil legal aid may be available for most civil proceedings to those who satisfy the financial eligibility conditions and have reasonable grounds for taking, defending or being a party to proceedings. It may be refused if it is considered unreasonable that an applicant should receive it in the particular circumstances. Legal aid is available on a non-means, non-merits tested or means-tested-only basis to certain categories of applicant in certain specified proceedings regarding

children. In England and Wales payments to lawyers are made through the Legal Aid Fund, administered by the Legal Aid Board. Scotland has a separate Legal Aid Fund, administered by the Scottish Legal Aid Board. In Northern Ireland legal aid is administered by the Law Society for Northern Ireland.

An assisted person has some protection against orders for costs being made against him or her, and in certain limited circumstances the successful unassisted opponent of a legally aided party may recover his or her costs from the Legal Aid Board. Where the assisted person recovers or preserves money or property in the proceedings, the Legal Aid Fund will usually have a first charge on that money or property to recover money spent on the assisted person's behalf (the 'statutory charge').

Legal Aid in Criminal Proceedings

England, Wales and Northern Ireland

In criminal proceedings in England, Wales and Northern Ireland legal aid may be granted by the court if it appears to be in the interests of justice and if a defendant is considered to require financial assistance. A contribution towards the costs may be payable.

The Legal Aid Board makes arrangements for duty solicitors to assist unrepresented defendants in the magistrates' courts. Solicitors are also available, on a 24-hour basis, to give advice and assistance to those being questioned by the police. The services of a solicitor at a police station and of the duty solicitor at court are not means-tested and are free.

Where legal aid is granted for criminal cases in Northern Ireland it is free. There is a voluntary duty solicitor scheme at the main magistrates' court in Belfast.

Scotland

A duty solicitor is available to represent people in custody on their first appearance in the sheriff courts and the district courts without enquiry into the person's means. In other cases, a person seeking legal aid in summary criminal proceedings must apply to the

Scottish Legal Aid Board, which must be satisfied that the costs of the case cannot be met by the applicant without undue hardship, and that it is in the interests of justice that legal aid is awarded.

In solemn proceedings the court decides on the availability of legal aid and must be satisfied that the accused cannot meet the costs of the defence without undue financial hardship. Where legal aid is granted to the accused in criminal proceedings, he or she is not required to pay any contribution towards expenses.

Administrative Reform

England and Wales

In October 1997, in the light of rapidly increasing legal aid expenditure (up from £682 million in 1990–91 to £1,477 million six years later), the Government announced plans for reform of the legal aid system in England and Wales. The changes include contracting for legal services, in both criminal and civil cases, with contracts specifying in advance what services are being bought, and at exactly what prices. The aim is to ensure that resources are targeted at those who need them, to stop cases going on too long, to trim costs and to cut waste and duplication. It is also intended that, in determining which cases should be assisted from the legal aid fund, the merits test should stipulate a 75 per cent likelihood of success.

The Government is also consulting on the maximum possible extension of conditional fee agreements (where the risk of bringing a case is shared between litigants and their lawyers) to all civil proceedings, other than family cases, from April 1998.

Subject to consultations, the reforms are expected to exclude most claims for money or damages from legal aid, so that taking forward a civil case will depend on whether or not it has the merit to persuade a lawyer to handle it on a 'no win, no fee' basis.

Scotland

In July 1997 the new Government announced the implementation of the criminal legal assistance provisions in the Crime and Punishment (Scotland) Act 1997. From October 1997:

- the Scottish Legal Aid Board (SLAB) assumes increased enforcement powers; and
- the Secretary of State may prescribe fixed payments to solicitors for providing criminal legal assistance.

From October 1998:

- all solicitors providing legal aid must register with the SLAB and conform to the Board's code of practice; and
- a pilot scheme for a public solicitor employed by the SLAB will be introduced to test alternative ways of providing publicly funded legal representation;

The 1997 Act does not apply to civil legal aid.

Free Representation Units

The Bar Council, the barristers' professional body, supports a Free Representation Unit for clients at a variety of tribunals for which legal aid is not available. Most of the representation by the London unit is carried out by Bar students supported and advised by full-time case workers. Elsewhere, barristers do such work through regional units. A special Bar unit, based in London, was formed in 1996 through which more senior barristers provide representation in cases which might otherwise not be heard.

Law Centres

In some urban areas law centres provide free legal advice and representation. They may employ a salaried lawyer and many have community workers. Much of their time is devoted to housing, employment, social security and immigration problems. Although there is a restriction on cases they will accept, most law centres will give preliminary advice.

Advice at minimal or no cost may be available in Citizens Advice Bureaux, consumer and housing advice centres and in specialist advice centres run by voluntary organisations.

Further Reading

Access to Justice—Final Report, the Rt Hon the Lord Woolf. HMSO, 1996.

Britain's Legal Systems (2nd edn). Aspects of Britain series, HMSO, 1996.

Departmental Report of The Lord Chancellor's and Law Officers' Departments: The Government's Expenditure Plans 1997–98 to 1999–2000. Cm 3609. The Stationery Office, 1997.

Home Office Annual Report 1997: The Government's Expenditure Plans 1997–98 to 1999–2000. Cm 3608. The Stationery Office, 1997.

Report of the Royal Commission on Criminal Justice. HMSO, 1993.

Striking the Balance: the Future of Legal Aid in England and Wales. Cm 3305. HMSO, 1996.

9 Overseas Relations

In addition to furthering its national interests, Britain wants to contribute to a strong world community, promoting security, prosperity, quality of life and mutual respect. The main aims of the new Government's foreign policy are to:

- make Britain a leading player in a Europe of independent nation states;
- strengthen the Commonwealth;
- secure more effective international action to preserve world peace and combat world poverty;
- increase respect and goodwill for Britain among the peoples of the world by drawing on the assets of the British Council and the BBC World Service; and
- strengthen Britain's relationships in all regions of the world.

ADMINISTRATION OF FOREIGN POLICY

Foreign & Commonwealth Office

The Foreign & Commonwealth Office (FCO) is in charge of overall foreign policy and is headed by the Foreign Secretary, who is assisted by four ministers without Cabinet rank. The FCO's Permanent Under-Secretary of State is a civil servant who heads the Diplomatic Service and provides advice to the Foreign Secretary.

Britain maintains a worldwide presence through 222 diplomatic missions and has diplomatic or consular relations with 189 countries.

Of the 5,800 FCO staff, some 2,400 serve overseas, of whom 121 are seconded from other government departments and other public and private organisations. British diplomatic missions also employ some 7,600 locally engaged staff. Staff overseas deal with political, commercial and economic work; entry clearance to Britain and consular work; aid administration; and information and other activities, such as culture, science and technology.

The FCO's only executive agency, Wilton Park International Conference Centre (at Wiston House in West Sussex), contributes to the solution of international problems by organising conferences in Britain, attended by politicians, business people, academics and other professionals from all over the world.

Other Departments

Several other government departments are closely involved with foreign policy issues. The newly created Department for International Development administers Britain's bilateral aid programme (see p. 136). The Ministry of Defence maintains military liaison with Britain's NATO and other allies, in addition to controlling and administering the armed·forces (see p. 149). The Department of Trade and Industry (DTI) has an important influence on international trade policy and commercial relations with other countries, including European Union (EU) member states. The FCO and DTI work hand in hand on export and inward investment promotion and have recently established a joint forum to consider how to improve British export promotion initiatives. HM Treasury is involved in British international economic policy and is responsible for Britain's relations with the World Bank and other international financial institutions.

When other departments are involved, the FCO decides policy in consultation with them. The FCO co-ordinates British EU policy through the Cabinet Office European Secretariat.

The British Council is responsible for Britain's cultural relations with other countries (see p. 140).

INTERNATIONAL ORGANISATIONS

Britain belongs to about 80 international organisations. Membership of the following bodies is of particular importance.

United Nations

Britain is a founder member of the United Nations (UN) and one of the five permanent members of the Security Council, along with China, France, Russia and the United States. In 1996 it was the fifth largest contributor to the UN regular budget. It is also a significant contributor to UN peacekeeping operations (see p. 128). Britain is fully committed to the purposes and principles of the UN Charter, including the maintenance of international peace and security, the development of friendly relations among nations, the achievement of international co-operation on economic, social, cultural and humanitarian issues and the protection of human rights and fundamental freedoms.

European Union

Britain is a member of the European Union (EU), which comprises the European Community (EC) and intergovernmental co-operation on foreign and security policy, and on justice and home affairs. The EU has 15 democratic nations as members; they are Austria, Belgium, Britain, Denmark, Finland, France, Germany, Greece, the Irish Republic, Italy, Luxembourg, the Netherlands, Portugal, Spain and Sweden. As one of the five most populous countries, Britain provides two of the 20 members of the European Commission, which puts forward legislative proposals, executes the decisions taken by the Council of the European Union and ensures that EC rules are correctly observed. Britain is represented at every meeting of the Council, which is the main decision-making body. Each Council consists of government ministers from the 15 member states, representing national interests in the subjects under discussion, for example, trade, agriculture or transport. When a member state has the Presidency of the Union (for a period of six months), its ministers are responsible for chairing meetings of the Council. Britain assumes the Presidency in January 1998. The Committee of Permanent Representatives, consisting of member states' ambassadors to the EU, prepares the work of the Council. European Community policies are implemented by various forms of Community legislation.

The European Council, which meets at least twice a year, comprises the heads of state or government and their foreign ministers and the President of the Commission, usually accompanied by a fellow Commissioner.

There are 626 members of the directly elected European Parliament, which is

The European Union

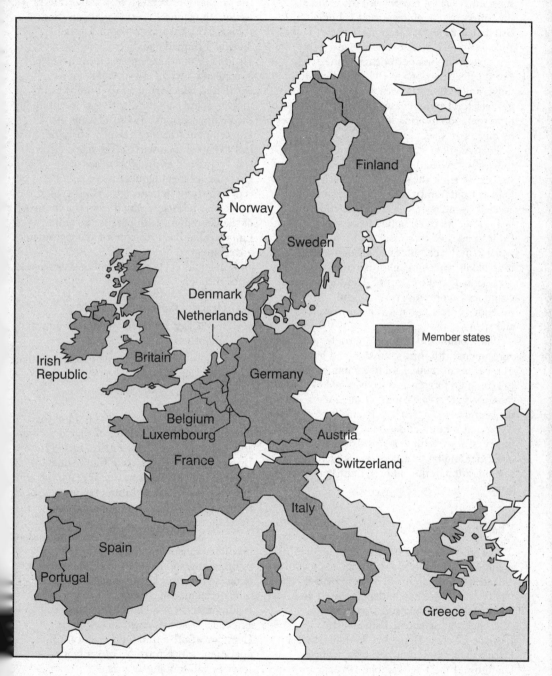

consulted about major decisions and has substantial shared power with the Council of the European Union over the EC budget. Britain has 87 seats. Elections to the Parliament take place every five years, the most recent having been held in June 1994. For the next elections in 1999, the British Government has proposed the adoption of a new electoral system based on proportional representation to bring it in line with the other member states.

Each member state provides one of the judges to serve in the European Court of Justice, which is the supreme authority in the field of Community law. Its rulings must be applied by member states, and sanctions can be imposed on those failing to do so. The Court is assisted by a Court of First Instance, which handles certain cases brought by individuals and companies. Britain is also represented on the Court of Auditors, which examines Community revenue and expenditure to see that it is legally received and spent.

The Community enters into trade agreements with third countries and has a number of substantial aid programmes. Under the common foreign and security policy, member states issue common statements and declarations and agree legally binding common positions and joint actions on foreign policy issues. Member states also co-operate on justice and home affairs issues such as asylum, immigration and the fight against crime.

The Commonwealth

There are 54 members of the Commonwealth, including Britain. It is a voluntary association of states, nearly all of which were British territories but are now independent. The members are Antigua and Barbuda, Australia, the Bahamas, Bangladesh, Barbados, Belize, Botswana, Britain, Brunei Darussalam, Cameroon, Canada, Cyprus, Dominica, Fiji, The Gambia, Ghana, Grenada, Guyana, India, Jamaica, Kenya, Kiribati, Lesotho, Malawi, Malaysia, Maldives, Malta, Mauritius, Mozambique, Namibia, Nauru, New Zealand, Nigeria (suspended), Pakistan, Papua New Guinea,

St Kitts and Nevis, St Lucia, St Vincent and the Grenadines, Samoa, Seychelles, Sierra Leone, Singapore, Solomon Islands, South Africa, Sri Lanka, Swaziland, Tanzania, Tonga, Trinidad and Tobago, Tuvalu, Uganda, Vanuatu, Zambia and Zimbabwe. Nauru and Tuvalu are special members, entitled to take part in all Commonwealth meetings and activities, with the exception of the biennial Commonwealth Heads of Government Meetings. South Africa rejoined in 1994 after an absence of 33 years. Nigeria was suspended at the 1995 heads of government meeting because of political repression and human rights abuses. Sierra Leone has been suspended from the councils of the Commonwealth because its military junta has not been recognised as a legitimate government.

Consultation between member states takes place through:

- Heads of Government Meetings;
- specialised conferences of other ministers and officials;
- diplomatic representatives known as high commissioners; and
- non-governmental organisations.

The Queen is recognised as head of the Commonwealth and is head of state in Britain and 15 other member countries. In 1997 Britain hosted the Heads of Government Meeting for the first time in 20 years; the Meeting took place in Edinburgh and its main theme was trade, investment and development.

The Commonwealth Secretariat in London promotes consultation, disseminates information, and helps the host government to organise Heads of Government Meetings, ministerial meetings and other conferences. It administers co-operative programmes agreed at these meetings, including the Commonwealth Fund for Technical Co-operation, which provides consultancy services and training awards to Commonwealth developing countries.

Membership of the Commonwealth enables Britain to play a responsible part alongside other nations in aiding the democratisation and progress of the developing world.

The Commonwealth

ARCTIC OCEAN

NORTH PACIFIC OCEAN

NORTH ATLANTIC OCEAN

SOUTH ATLANTIC OCEAN

SOUTH PACIFIC OCEAN

NORTH PACIFIC OCEAN

INDIAN OCEAN

BAFFIN BAY

HUDSON BAY

GULF OF CALIFORNIA

GULF OF MEXICO

CARIBBEAN SEA

CANADA

Bermuda

Turks & Caicos Is
British Virgin Is
Anguilla
ANTIGUA & BARBUDA
DOMINICA
ST LUCIA
BARBADOS
GRENADA
TRINIDAD & TOBAGO

BAHAMAS
Cayman Is
BELIZE
JAMAICA
ST CHRISTOPHER & NEVIS
Montserrat
ST VINCENT & THE GRENADINES

GUYANA

Christmas Island
Cook Islands
Oeno I
Henderson I
Pitcairn I
Ducie I

Falkland Is
S. Georgia
S. Orkney Is
S. Sandwich Is
S. Shetland Is
British Antarctic Territory

BRITAIN
BAY OF BISCAY
Gibraltar
MALTA
MEDITERRANEAN SEA
CYPRUS
BLACK SEA
NORTH SEA
RED SEA
THE GULF
CASPIAN SEA
ARABIAN SEA

SIERRA LEONE
THE GAMBIA
GHANA
NIGERIA
Ascension I
St Helena
Tristan da Cunha

UGANDA
KENYA
TANZANIA
Zanzibar
ZAMBIA
MALAWI
ZIMBABWE
MOZAMBIQUE
NAMIBIA
BOTSWANA
SWAZILAND
LESOTHO
SOUTH AFRICA

PAKISTAN
INDIA
BANGLADESH
BAY OF BENGAL
SRI LANKA
Nicobar Is
Andaman Is
MALDIVES
Mahé
SEYCHELLES
British Indian Ocean Territory
MAURITIUS

SEA OF JAPAN
PHILIPPINE SEA
SOUTH CHINA SEA
BRUNEI
MALAYSIA
Sabah
Sarawak
SINGAPORE

PAPUA NEW GUINEA
CORAL SEA
AUSTRALIA
Tasmania

NAURU
KIRIBATI
SOLOMON IS
TUVALU
Tokelau
WESTERN SAMOA
VANUATU
Niue
FIJI
TONGA

SOUTH PACIFIC OCEAN

NEW ZEALAND

Australian Antarctic Territory

Ross Dependency

North Atlantic Treaty Organisation (NATO)

Membership of NATO is central to British defence policy (see p. 143). Its core functions are to:

- provide a foundation of security in the North Atlantic area, linking European security with that of North America;
- deter aggression and defend member states against it; and
- act as the primary forum for consultation among Allies on security and defence issues.

Each of the 16 member states (Belgium, Britain, Canada, Denmark, France, Germany, Greece, Iceland, Italy, Luxembourg, the Netherlands, Norway, Portugal, Spain, Turkey and the United States) has a permanent representative at NATO headquarters in Brussels. The main decision-taking body is the North Atlantic Council. It meets at least twice a year at foreign minister level, and weekly at the level of permanent representatives. Defence ministers also meet at least twice a year.

Western European Union

Britain is a member of the Western European Union (WEU), which is the main forum for co-operation and consultation on defence issues for NATO's European members. The WEU's other full members are Belgium, France, Germany, Greece, Italy, Luxembourg, the Netherlands, Portugal and Spain. Iceland, Norway and Turkey are associate members; Austria, Denmark, Finland, the Irish Republic and Sweden are observers. 'Associate partnership' has been extended to ten Central European and Baltic states.

The Group of Seven/Eight

Britain is part of the Group of Seven (G7) leading industrialised countries. The other members are Canada, France, Germany, Italy, Japan and the United States. The G7 is an informal group with no secretariat. Its Presidency rotates each year among the members, the key meeting being an annual summit of heads of government. Originally formed in 1975 to discuss economic issues, the G7 agenda now includes a wide range of issues such as international crime, terrorism, nuclear safety, the environment, UN reform and development assistance.

Russia has participated in these political discussions since 1994 (thereby constituting the G8). In 1998 Britain will host the G7/8 summit in Birmingham.

Organisation for Security and Co-operation in Europe (OSCE)

Britain is a signatory to the 1975 Helsinki Final Act, which established a framework for co-operation between states participating in the Conference on Security and Co-operation in Europe (CSCE), respect for human rights and economic matters. Britain also signed the 1990 Paris Charter, committing its signatories to democracy, human rights and market economies. In 1994 the CSCE was retitled the Organisation for Security and Co-operation in Europe, reflecting its transition from a conference to a more formalised institution. It has a Secretariat in Vienna, where Britain has a permanent delegation. Day-to-day business is conducted in the Permanent Council. A Prague office organises occasional meetings of senior officials.

The OSCE has 54 participating states, including every country in Europe, the states of the former Soviet Union, and the United States and Canada. The Federal Republic of Yugoslavia was suspended in 1992. All states participate on an equal basis, and decisions are taken by consensus.

The main areas of OSCE work are:

- early warning of potential conflict through preventive diplomacy missions and the work of the OSCE High Commissioner on National Minorities;
- observing elections and providing advice on human rights, democracy and law through the OSCE Office for Democratic Institutions and Human Rights in Warsaw (see p. 135); and
- promoting security through arms control and military confidence-building.

The OSCE has been given responsibility under the Dayton Peace Agreement for preparation of elections, monitoring human rights and arms control in Bosnia and Herzegovina (see p. 128).

Council of Europe

Britain is a founding member of the Council of Europe, which is open to any European state accepting parliamentary democracy and the protection of fundamental human rights and freedoms. The 40 member states co-operate on culture, education, sport, health, anti-crime policy, measures against drug trafficking, youth affairs and the improvement of the environment. The Council adopted its European Convention on Human Rights in 1950 (see p. 134).

Other International Bodies

Britain belongs to many other international bodies, and was a founder member of the International Monetary Fund (IMF) and the World Bank. The IMF regulates the international financial system and provides credit for member countries facing balance-of-payments difficulties. The World Bank provides loans to finance economic and social projects in developing countries.

In addition, Britain, along with 27 other industrialised countries, is part of the Organisation for Economic Co-operation and Development (OECD), which promotes economic growth, support for less developed countries and worldwide trade expansion.

Other organisations to which Britain belongs or extends support include the regional development banks in Africa, the Caribbean, Latin America and Asia, and the European Bank for Reconstruction and Development.

BRITAIN'S DEPENDENT TERRITORIES

Britain's Dependent Territories have a combined population of some 200,000. Most territories have considerable self-government, with their own legislatures. Governors appointed by the Queen are responsible for external affairs, internal security (including the police) and the public service. Certain responsibilities are delegated to locally elected representatives, but the ultimate responsibility for all government affairs rests with the Foreign Secretary. The British Indian Ocean Territory, the British Antarctic Territory, and South Georgia and the South Sandwich Islands have commissioners, not governors. Britain seeks to provide the territories with security and political stability, ensure efficient and honest government, and help them achieve economic and social development on a par with neighbouring countries.

The territories are: Anguilla; Bermuda (where, in a referendum in 1995, voters rejected decisively the principle of independence from Britain); British Antarctic Territory; British Indian Ocean Territory; British Virgin Islands; Cayman Islands; Falkland Islands; Gibraltar; Montserrat; Pitcairn, Ducie, Henderson and Oeno; St Helena and St Helena Dependencies (Ascension and Tristan da Cunha); South Georgia and the South Sandwich Islands; and Turks and Caicos Islands.

British policy is to help the inhabitants of the Dependent Territories to take independence if they want it and where it is practicable, and to do so in accordance with treaty obligations. The reasonable needs of the Dependent Territories are a first call on the British aid programme.

The Falkland Islands

The Falkland Islands are the subject of a territorial claim by Argentina, but the inhabitants wish to remain under British sovereignty. The British Government does not accept the Argentine claim and is committed to defending the Islanders' right to live under a government of their own choice. This right of self-determination is set out in the 1985 Falkland Islands Constitution.

In 1982 Argentina invaded and occupied the Islands, but its forces were expelled by British troops following Argentina's failure to abide by UN resolutions requesting its forces to withdraw. Britain and Argentina, while sticking to their respective positions on sovereignty, maintain diplomatic relations and continue to discuss their common interests in the South Atlantic region, such as fisheries conservation and the exploitation of oil reserves. A Joint Declaration on co-operation over offshore activities was signed in 1995, enabling the Falkland Islands to launch an oil licensing round.

Gibraltar

Spain ceded Gibraltar to Britain in perpetuity by the 1713 Treaty of Utrecht. Spain has long sought the return of Gibraltar. However, Britain is firmly committed to the principle, set out in the preamble to the 1969 Gibraltar Constitution, that it will never enter into arrangements under which the people of Gibraltar would pass under the sovereignty of another state against their freely and democratically expressed wishes.

Gibraltar has an elected House of Assembly and, under the 1969 Constitution, responsibility for a wide range of 'defined domestic matters' is devolved to the elected local ministers.

Gibraltar is within the European Union, as part of the United Kingdom member state, although it is outside the common customs system and does not participate in the Common Agricultural or Fisheries Policies or the EU's value added tax arrangements. The people of Gibraltar have been declared United Kingdom nationals for EU purposes.

Caribbean Dependent Territories

The Dependent Territories Regional Secretariat in Barbados administers aspects of British government policy towards the Caribbean territories (Anguilla, the British Virgin Islands, the Cayman Islands, Montserrat, and the Turks and Caicos Islands). Jointly agreed country policy plans for each territory receiving British aid have been introduced or are under discussion.

In London an FCO minister chairs the Ministerial Group for the Caribbean Dependent Territories, which is drawn from a number of government departments and agencies. It meets two or three times a year.

Policy initiatives by the Group are supported by the Good Government Fund which, among other objectives, pays for British personnel on loan to local governments to help them fight drug trafficking and other criminal activity. Assistance is also given to local disaster response teams. In addition, the Group monitors a programme of action designed to improve regulation of the offshore finance sector and anti-money-laundering measures.

The Territories At A Glance

Anguilla

Area: 96 sq km (37 sq miles).
Population: 10,300 (1995).
Economy: tourism, construction, offshore banking, fishing and farming.
History: British territory since 1650.
Government: Governor with Executive Council and elected House of Assembly.

Bermuda

Area: 53.3 sq km (20.6 sq miles).
Population: 63,000 (1994).
Economy: tourism, insurance, business services.
History: first British settlers in 1609–1612. Government passed to Crown in 1684.
Government: Governor, appointed Senate and elected House of Assembly.

British Antarctic Territory

Area: 1,709,400 sq km (666,000 sq miles).
Population: no permanent inhabitants. There are two British Antarctic Survey stations with 50 people in winter and 150 in summer. Scientists from other Antarctic Treaty powers bring the total to 1,000 in winter and 2,500 in summer.
History: the Antarctic Peninsula was discovered in 1820, and in 1832 was taken over by Britain. Britain is one of 43 signatories to the 1961 Antarctic Treaty, which says that the area should be used for peaceful purposes only.
Administration: administered by FCO commissioner and FCO administrator.

British Indian Ocean Territory

Area: 54,400 sq km (21,000 sq miles) of ocean.
Land area: the Chagos Archipelago with no permanent inhabitants.
Economy: territory used for defence purposes by Britain and United States; 1,700 military personnel plus 1,500 civilians (1995).
History: archipelago ceded to Britain by France under 1814 Treaty of Paris.
Government: archipelago administered from London by a British commissioner.

British Virgin Islands

Area: 153 sq km (59 sq miles).
Population: 16,100 (1995).
Economy: tourism and financial services.
History: discovered in 1493 by Columbus and annexed by Britain in 1672.
Government: Governor, Executive Council and elected Legislative Council.

Cayman Islands

Area: 259 sq km (100 sq miles).
Population: 33,600 (1995).
Economy: tourism and financial services.
History: 1670 Treaty of Madrid recognised Britain's claim to islands.
Government: Governor, Executive Council, elected Legislative Council, ministerial system.

Falkland Islands

Area: 12,173 sq km (4,700 sq miles).
Population: 2,231 (1996), plus British garrison.
Economy: fishing and sheep farming.
History: discovered in 1690 by British seafarer. Since 1832 they have been under British occupation and administration.
Government: Governor, Executive Council and elected Legislative Council.

Gibraltar

Area: 6.5 sq km (2.5 sq miles).
Population: 27,170 (1995).
Economy: financial services, tourism, conferences.

History: ceded to Britain in 1713 by Treaty of Utrecht.
Government: Governor, elected House of Assembly, ministerial system.

Montserrat

Area: 102 sq km (32 sq miles).
Population: 11,000 (before recent volcanic eruptions began—see p. 140).
Economy: agriculture and fishing.
History: colonised by English and Irish settlers in 1632.
Government: Governor, Executive Council and elected Legislative Council.

Pitcairn Islands

Area: 33.5 sq km (13.7 sq miles).
Population: 58 (1996).
Economy: fishing, agriculture and postage stamp sales.
History: occupied by mutineers from the British ship *Bounty* in 1790 and became British settlement in 1887.
Government: administered by an Island Council (half members elected), presided over by Island Magistrate, with a commissioner linking Council and the Governor.

St Helena

Area: 122 sq km (47 sq miles).
Population: 5,660 (1987).
Economy: fishing and agriculture.
History: taken over in 1661 by British East India Company.
Government: Governor, Executive Council and elected Legislative Council.

Ascension Island (St Helena Dependency)

Area: 88 sq km (34 sq miles).
Population: 1,110 (1993).
Economy: communications and military base.
History: British garrison dates from Napoleon's exile on St Helena after 1815.
Government: Governor of St Helena with local administration.

Tristan da Cunha (St Helena Dependency)

Area: 98 sq km (38 sq miles).
Population: 290 (1996).
Economy: fishing industry.
History: occupied by British garrison in 1816.
Government: Governor of St Helena with local administration and elected Island Council.

South Georgia and South Sandwich Islands

No permanent inhabitants. First landings by Captain Cook in 1775. Small British military detachment on South Georgia, plus British Antarctic Survey all-year research station on Bird Island. Administered by civil commissioner based in Falkland Islands.

Turks and Caicos Islands

Area: about 500 sq km (193 sq miles).
Population: 14,800 indigenous people plus around 7,000 expatriates and illegal immigrants (1990).
Economy: tourism, financial services, agriculture and fishing.
History: planters from USA loyal to Britain settled islands in late 18th century.
Government: Governor, Executive Council and a majority elected Legislative Assembly.

EUROPEAN UNION POLICY

The new British Government is pledged to play a constructive part in the European Union. Its priorities are the completion of the single market in financial services, EU enlargement to include Cyprus and the democratic nations in Central and Eastern Europe, reform of the Common Agricultural Policy and a more effective Common Foreign and Security Policy. It also believes that substantial progress can be made by member states through a common approach to transport and environment issues. In particular, the Government wants the EU to become much more relevant to its inhabitants, for example, by taking effective action to cut high rates of unemployment. In the national interest Britain will retain its veto on issues such as frontier controls, taxation, social security, defence decisions, the EU budget and changes in the EU treaties.

Background

The Union had its origins in the post-Second World War resolve by Western European nations, particularly France and Germany, to prevent wars breaking out again between themselves. The 1957 Rome Treaty, which established the European Community, defined its aims as the harmonious development of economic activities, a continuous and balanced economic expansion and an accelerated rise in the standard of living. These objectives were to be achieved by the creation of a common internal market, including the elimination of customs duties between member states, free movement of goods, people, services and capital, and the elimination of distortions in competition within this market. These objectives were reaffirmed by the 1986 Single European Act, which agreed measures to complete the internal market (see p. 125).

Maastricht Treaty

The 1992 Maastricht Treaty amended the Rome Treaty and made other new commitments, including moves towards economic and monetary union. It established the EU, which comprises the European Community, intergovernmental arrangements for a common foreign and security policy (see p. 127) and increased co-operation on interior/justice policy issues. The Maastricht Treaty also codified the principle of subsidiarity, under which action should be taken at European level only if its objectives cannot be achieved by member states acting alone and can be better achieved by the Community. Under an agreement reached in 1992, a subsidiarity test is applied to all European Commission proposals for action. In addition, the Treaty introduced the concept of European Union citizenship as a supplement to national citizenship.

Economic and Monetary Union

The Maastricht Treaty provided for progress towards economic and monetary union (EMU) in three stages: the first, completion of the single market, was largely achieved at the end of 1993. The second stage, which began on 1 January 1994, includes the establishment of a European Monetary Institute with a largely advisory and consultative role. Although the Institute is preparing for stage 3, monetary policy remains a national responsibility. Member states co-ordinate economic policies in the context of agreed non-binding policy guidelines. The British Government is participating in stage 2.

The third stage is a single currency for EU member states. Under the Treaty this is envisaged by 1 January 1999, although member states will have to satisfy certain convergence criteria on inflation rates, government deficit levels, currency fluctuation margins and interest rates.

The Government believes that British membership of the single currency would, in principle, benefit both Britain and Europe, provided that there were clear advantages for business and industry. It has stated, however, that it would not be in Britain's economic interests to join the single currency in 1999, and that a decision to do so during the current Parliament is not realistic, since sustainable economic convergence with other member states will not be achieved by 2002. Nevertheless, the Government has pledged that it will make intensive preparations during the current Parliament, so that Britain is in a position to join the single currency after 2002, if such a decision is approved by Parliament and by the British people in a referendum.

Amsterdam Treaty

Following on from the Maastricht Treaty, an intergovernmental conference (IGC) was convened by EU heads of government in March 1996 to consider further treaty amendments. The result of these negotiations was the draft treaty agreed in Amsterdam in May 1997 and signed by member states in October. Among the main points are:

- the outlawing of discrimination on the basis of gender, race, religion, sexual orientation and age;
- more co-ordination by member states of measures designed to cut unemployment;

- the reintegration of the social chapter (see p. 127) in the Treaty, following Britain's decision to sign and support the chapter;
- new mechanisms to improve the co-ordination and effectiveness of the Common Foreign and Security Policy (CFSP—see p. 127);
- arrangements for improved co-operation between the EU and Western European Union on the defence aspects of the CFSP;
- simplification of the European Parliament's procedures by increasing its powers of co-decision with the Council of Ministers; and
- a binding protocol on subsidiarity.

During the Amsterdam discussions, Britain succeeded in obtaining legal security for its border controls, thereby ensuring that policies on immigration, asylum and visas are made in Britain and not Brussels.

Treaty Ratification

Any amendments to the Treaties can only be agreed unanimously and must then be ratified by each member state according to its own constitutional procedures. In Britain Treaty ratifications have to be approved by Parliament before they can enter into force.

The Community Budget

The Community's revenue consists of:

- levies on agricultural imports;
- customs duties;
- the proceeds of a notional rate of value added tax of up to 1.4 per cent on a standard 'basket' of goods and services; and
- contributions from member states based on gross national product (GNP).

Britain has an annual rebate worth some £2,000 million because, without it, the British net contribution would be far greater than that justified by its share of Community GNP.

Single Market

The single market, providing for the free movement of people, goods, services and capital, is largely complete in legislative terms. It covers, among other benefits, the removal of customs barriers, the liberalisation of capital movements, the opening of public procurement markets and the mutual recognition of professional qualifications. It is not fully operative, especially in the area of financial services, where Britain is seeking to make progress.

Under the European Economic Area (EEA) Agreement, which entered into force in January 1994, most of the EU single market measures have been extended to Iceland, Norway and Liechtenstein.

Transport, Energy and Telecommunications

The concept of a common transport policy was laid down in the Treaty of Rome. Liberalisation measures relating to civil aviation, shipping, and road haulage and passenger services are described in chapter 19.

The EU is working towards the completion of trans-European networks in the fields of transport, energy and telecommunications. The aim is to improve the interconnection and interoperability of national networks. One of the main transport projects endorsed by the European Council is the planned construction of a new rail link between London and the Channel Tunnel (see p. 313).

Trade

Britain is the world's fifth largest trading nation. EEA member states comprise the world's largest trading bloc, accounting for about 40 per cent of all trade. The British Government favours an open world trading system, on which EU member states depend for future economic growth and jobs.

Under the Rome Treaty, the European Commission speaks on behalf of Britain and the other member states in international trade negotiations. The Commission negotiates on a mandate agreed by the Council. For further information on trade, see chapter 12.

The Environment

EU member states are at the forefront of many international measures on environmental issues, such as air quality standards and the depletion of the ozone layer. For further information, see chapter 21.

Agriculture and Fisheries

The Common Agricultural Policy (CAP) is designed to secure food supplies and to stabilise markets. It has also, however, created overproduction and unwanted food surpluses, placing a burden on the Community's budget. The Common Fisheries Policy is concerned with the conservation and management of fishery resources. The operation of these policies, and Britain's advocacy of CAP reform, are described in chapter 18.

Regional and Infrastructure Development

There are a number of Structural Funds designed to:

- promote economic development in underdeveloped regions;
- regenerate regions affected by industrial decline;
- combat long-term unemployment and facilitate the entry of young people into the labour market;
- help workers adapt to industrial changes and to advances in production systems;
- speed up the adjustment of production, processing and marketing structures in agriculture; and
- promote development in rural areas.

Infrastructure projects and industrial investments are financed by the European Regional Development Fund. The European Social Fund supports training and employment measures for the unemployed and young people. The Guidance Section of the European Agricultural Guidance and Guarantee Fund supports agricultural restructuring and some rural development measures. The Financial Instrument of Fisheries Guidance helps to modernise the fishing industry. A Cohesion Fund, set up under the Maastricht Treaty, is designed to reduce disparities between levels of development in the poorer and richer member states.

Other initiatives assist the development of new economic activities in regions affected by the restructuring of traditional industries, such as steel, coal and shipbuilding.

The European Investment Bank, a non-profit-making institution, lends at competitive interest rates to public and private capital investment projects.

Employment and Social Affairs

In May 1997 the Government announced that it would end Britain's opt-out from the Maastricht Treaty's social chapter (extending Community social policy and qualified majority voting into new areas of social affairs). Two measures so far adopted under the chapter deal with European works councils and parental leave, both of which are designed to promote good working conditions. By ending the opt-out, the Government wants to play a full part in negotiations on such social matters by ensuring that the chapter promotes labour flexibility and employability.

Under the Amsterdam Treaty it has been agreed that the European Investment Bank should be more closely involved in measures to cut unemployment.

Research and Development

Research collaboration among member states is promoted primarily through a series of framework programmes defining priorities and setting out the overall level of funding. The Government actively encourages British companies and organisations to participate in collaborative research and development (R & D) with European partners (see p. 326).

The Fourth Framework Programme, adopted in April 1994, focuses on generic and precompetitive research which is of use to a number of industries. It covers information and communications technologies, industrial technologies, the environment, life sciences and technology, energy, transport and socio-economic research. The programme also provides for international co-operation, dissemination of research, and training and mobility of researchers.

Negotiations are currently taking place on the Fifth Framework Programme which is likely to be adopted during the latter part of 1998.

Common Foreign and Security Policy

The common foreign and security policy (CFSP), established by the Maastricht Treaty, is intergovernmental, decisions being taken unanimously. Common policies have been agreed on issues such as the delivery of humanitarian aid to Bosnia, assistance to the Middle East peace process (including the appointment of an EU special envoy), efforts to restore stability to the Great Lakes region of Africa and measures to encourage transition to democracy and respect for human rights in Burma, Cuba, Nigeria and Zaire. Efforts have also been made to combat the indiscriminate use of anti-personnel landmines.

In Britain's view, one of the main weaknesses of the CFSP has been the practical implementation of policy initiatives. During the negotiations on the Amsterdam Treaty, Britain successfully pressed for new mechanisms to make the policy more effective. The Amsterdam Treaty will introduce several key changes, including:

- the appointment, unanimously by the Council, of a High Representative to assist with the formulation, preparation and presentation of CFSP policy decisions; and

- the establishment of a policy planning and early warning unit in the Council Secretariat to sharpen the preparation and focus of common foreign policy decisions.

Furthermore, decisions implementing common strategies will be by qualified majority voting in the Council, although a member state will be able to prevent a vote being taken for 'important and stated reasons of national policy'. If this occurs, the matter may be referred to the European Council for decision by unanimity. Provision for 'constructive abstention' allows a member state to abstain and stand aside from an EU decision/action when its interests are not engaged; this does not affect the right to veto.

The EU continues to look to the Western European Union to handle defence issues under the CFSP. The Amsterdam Treaty provides for the 'progressive framing of a common defence policy', in which the Western European Union would support the EU. The WEU also provides the EU with access to an operational military capacity. The Treaty recognises that NATO provides common defence for Britain and its allies.

INTERNATIONAL PEACE AND SECURITY

The United Nations is the principal body responsible for the maintenance of international peace and security. Britain is active in looking for ways of strengthening the capacity of the UN and other international organisations to predict and prevent conflicts before they arise.

Britain and UN Peacekeeping

Several British officers are currently serving in the UN's Department of Peacekeeping Operations and are performing operational, financial and other specialist functions. Britain pays an assessed share of the costs of UN peacekeeping (nearly 7 per cent of the total), contributing about £54 million in 1996.

Cyprus

Britain has a contingent of more than 400 troops in the UN Force in Cyprus, which was established in 1964 to help prevent the recurrence of fighting on the island between Greek and Turkish Cypriots. Since the serious hostilities of 1974, when Turkish forces occupied the northern part of the island, the Force has been responsible for monitoring the ceasefire and control of a buffer zone between the two communities. Both Britain and the United States have appointed special representatives to Cyprus to support a UN-led effort to promote a settlement between Greek and Turkish Cypriots.

Iraq/Kuwait

In 1991 Security Council Resolution 687 established a demilitarised zone extending 10 km into Iraq and 5 km into Kuwait to deter violations of the boundary and to observe hostile or potentially hostile actions. Britain, with the other permanent members of the Security Council, contributes 11 personnel to the UN Iraq/Kuwait observer mission (UNIKOM).

Georgia

Britain contributes eight military personnel to the UN Observer Mission in Georgia, which was established in 1993. Its mandate includes monitoring a ceasefire between Georgian government troops and rebels in the Georgian region of Abkhazia.

Bosnia and Herzegovina

Britain supports the establishment of a peaceful, multi-ethnic and democratic Bosnia and Herzegovina, and is playing a central role in the implementation of the Dayton Peace Agreement, which was signed in Paris in December 1995. Some 5,000 British troops are participating in the NATO-led Stabilisation Force (SFOR), which comprises around 30,000 troops from NATO nations and other contributing countries, including Russia and a number of other Partnership for Peace members (see p. 129).

The main task of the force is to ensure continuing compliance with the military aspects of the Dayton Agreement, which includes monitoring the ceasefire, separating rival armed forces and inspecting weapon sites. As a secondary task, SFOR provides selective support to the main organisations responsible for the civil aspects of the Agreement (for example, holding elections), including the Office of the High Representative, the UN International Police Task Force, the UN High Commissioner for Refugees, and the OSCE. Although the military requirements of the Dayton Agreement have largely been met, many of the civil aspects are yet to be fully implemented.

Britain attaches high priority to assisting the international criminal tribunal in The Hague, which was set up to try those indicted for war crimes in the former Yugoslavia. Although governments in the region are

It took 97 days, they travelled over 30,000 miles and, on 15 August 1997, grandmother Jennifer Murray, accompanied by co-pilot Quentin Smith, returned to Britain as the first woman to have piloted a helicopter around the world. During their trip they raised substantial funds for Save the Children.

Right: arriving in Hong Kong, where they took part in a fly-past to mark the handover celebrations (June 1997).

Below: visiting a Save the Children project in Delhi, India (May 1997).

The *Endeavour*, a faithful copy in iron, oak and sailcloth of the ship James Cook captained during his exploration of Australasia in the 18th century, sails home into Whitby harbour, Yorkshire, on 9 May 1997. The ship had an international crew of young trainees, and visited Mauritius, South Africa and Madeira on its way from Australia.

Three members of the Barry Amateur Radio Society mark the centenary of Guglielmo Marconi's first ever wireless transmission across water in 1897. Dressed in Victorian attire, and using a replica of Marconi's original equipment, they re-created this historic event by sending his exact message again, in Morse, from the Island of Flat Holm in the Bristol Channel to Lavernock Point, Vale of Glamorgan.

Despite appalling weather conditions,
the last team of the all-women McVitie's Penguin Polar Relay
successfully reached the Geographic North Pole on 27 May 1997, exactly on schedule.
Polar explorer and managing director of The Polar Travel Company, Pen Hadow,
his wife Mary Nicholson and Caroline Hamilton raised the necessary funds, trained the teams and
organised the complex logistics to enable 20 'ordinary' women from all walks of life to create polar history.

responsible for arresting indictees and handing them over to the tribunal, in most cases they have failed to do so. In addition to supporting the tribunal through the provision of staff, information and forensic science expertise, Britain has provided funds to establish a second courtroom in The Hague.

CENTRAL AND EASTERN EUROPE AND CENTRAL ASIA

Since the disintegration of the Warsaw Pact and the formation of democratically elected governments in Central and Eastern Europe and Central Asia, the European security situation has been transformed. In 1990 NATO Allies and former Warsaw Pact states formed the North Atlantic Co-operation Council to foster understanding. In May 1997 the Council's foreign ministers agreed to establish a new form of political consultation called the Euro-Atlantic Partnership Council.

In 1994 a NATO summit meeting invited the non-NATO states in Central and Eastern Europe and Central Asia to join a Partnership for Peace in order to:

- develop a practical working relationship; and

- enlist the Partners' assistance in peacekeeping operations and guide their armed forces towards compatibility with those of NATO countries.

The Partnership for Peace, which now includes 27 countries, has grown rapidly into a formidable and varied programme of military and political co-operation. In May 1997 NATO foreign ministers agreed to increase the scope of Partnership activities. Partners will remain free to determine their own level of co-operation with NATO, and will have the opportunity to plan and train with NATO for the most demanding military operations.

In July 1997 a NATO summit invited the Czech Republic, Hungary and Poland to negotiate accession to NATO. The summit expressed the hope that they would be members by 1999 and pledged the Alliance's continuing openness to further new members.

In May 1997 a Founding Act was signed in Paris between NATO member states and Russia, the aim of which is to establish a strong and lasting partnership. One of the main provisions is the creation of a Permanent Joint Council which would give neither side a veto over the other's activities but will enable Russia to be associated with, and involved in, the main decisions on European security; it will also provide a framework for greater security and defence co-operation.

NATO and Ukraine signed a Charter for a Distinctive Partnership in May 1997 providing for expanded co-operation and consultation.

Economic Help

Britain and other Western countries are taking action to help deal with the vast economic problems following the fall of Communism, and to promote the development of market economies. The IMF and World Bank, with Britain's active support, provide advice and finance to nearly all countries in the region, while the European Bank for Reconstruction and Development channels Western investment. The European Community's PHARE scheme is assisting Central European countries in the process of reform and the development of infrastructure. Countries of the former Soviet Union and Mongolia receive help through a parallel programme (TACIS), which concentrates on financial services, transport, energy (including nuclear safety) and humanitarian needs. Britain's Export Credit Guarantee Department provides insurance cover for exporters to a number of these countries.

Know How Fund

The Know How Fund is Britain's programme of bilateral technical assistance to the countries of Central and Eastern Europe and Central Asia. It aims to support their transition to pluralist democracy and a market economy by providing British skills and by encouraging British investment in the region. Britain spends about £85 million a year on the programme.

Europe (Association) Agreements

The European Union has strengthened relations with Bulgaria, the Czech Republic,

Estonia, Hungary, Latvia, Lithuania, Poland, Romania, Slovakia and Slovenia by signing Europe (Association) Agreements with them. The agreements envisage accession to the European Union when these countries are able to assume the obligations of membership.

The EU has signed partnership and co-operation agreements with Russia, Ukraine, Moldova, Kazakhstan, Kyrgyzstan, Belarus, Georgia, Armenia, Azerbaijan and Uzbekistan. A Trade and Co-operation Agreement is in force with Albania. The purpose of all these agreements is to reduce trade barriers, develop wide-ranging co-operation and increase political dialogue at all levels.

OTHER REGIONS

The Middle East

Middle East Peace Process

Britain supported the breakthrough in the Middle East peace process in 1993, when Israel and the Palestine Liberation Organisation (PLO) agreed to mutual recognition and signed a Declaration of Principles on interim self-government for the Palestinians in Israeli-held territories occupied in 1967. The first stage of the Declaration was implemented in May 1994, when the Palestinians adopted self-government in the Gaza Strip and the Jericho area. In October 1994 a peace treaty between Israel and Jordan was formally signed. Britain continues to encourage peace negotiations between Israel, Syria and Lebanon.

A further advance was achieved in September 1995, when Israel and the PLO reached an Interim Agreement providing for a phased Israeli troop withdrawal from occupied Palestinian areas of the West Bank and for elections to a new Palestinian Council with legislative and executive powers. Britain took part in the EU-co-ordinated international observation of the Palestinian elections in January 1996.

Progress has been less smooth in recent months, in part because of delays in implementing the Interim Agreement, the continued expansion of Israeli settlements in the occupied territories and terrorist bomb attacks in Israel and Jerusalem. EU member states continue to support the peace process and have appealed to all parties in the region to avoid and prevent actions which might destroy prospects for a lasting peace and prejudice further negotiations. The British Government has proposed that it and the other EU states should become leading partners in attempts to reactivate the process so as to ensure security for the Israelis and take full account of the wishes and aspirations of the Palestinian people.

Britain has given £87 million over three years in aid to the Palestinians and the peace process through bilateral and multilateral channels. Programmes support Palestinian administration, police training, the Palestinian Monetary Authority, legal structures and the judiciary, water management and healthcare.

The Gulf Conflict

As a permanent member of the UN Security Council, Britain strongly condemned Iraq's invasion of Kuwait in August 1990 and supported all the Council's resolutions designed to force Iraqi withdrawal and restore international legality. Because of Iraq's failure to withdraw, its forces were expelled in February 1991 by an international coalition led by the United States, Britain, France and Saudi Arabia, acting under a UN mandate.

UN Security Council Resolution 661 imposed sanctions on Iraq on 6 August 1990. Resolution 687, adopted on 3 April 1991, formalised the ceasefire in the Gulf War and stipulated conditions for Iraqi acceptance, including measures to prevent the development of weapons of mass destruction, recognition of the border with Kuwait and the payment of compensation to those who suffered as a result of the invasion of Kuwait. The resolution, supported by Britain, modified sanctions on Iraq; these remain in force until the Security Council is satisfied that Iraq is fully in compliance with all relevant Security Council resolutions.

As part of the agreement ending hostilities, the Security Council authorised the creation of a Special Commission (UNSCOM) to supervise the elimination of Iraq's weapons of mass destruction. Britain has provided considerable support to UNSCOM and the International Atomic Energy Authority in the form of personnel, equipment and information since the first inspection in 1991.

In April 1995 Britain co-sponsored Resolution 986, which was renewed in June 1997 by Resolution 1111, allowing Iraq to sell oil worth US$1 billion every 90 days in exchange for humanitarian goods. Although implementation has been delayed on several occasions because of the actions of the Iraqi regime, goods supplied under these resolutions are now beginning to arrive in Iraq. Britain has also provided £94 million in humanitarian aid to Iraq since 1992.

Southern Africa

Since the abolition of apartheid and the election of President Mandela's government in 1994, South Africa's relations with Britain have broadened into new areas, ranging from development assistance to military advice, and from sporting links to scientific co-operation. There has also been a steady flow of state and ministerial visits to and from South Africa.

In addition to recent aid packages, Britain is supporting South Africa's development through trade and investment and through official export credit guarantees. Britain is the second highest exporter to South Africa and its largest foreign investor. Nine of the top twenty foreign employers in South Africa are British. There is a British investment promotion scheme designed to encourage more small and medium-sized businesses to invest in the region. South Africa also has a significant investment in Britain.

Asia-Pacific Region

Britain maintains close relations with Japan, China, the Republic of Korea, many South East Asian countries, Australia and New Zealand. It has defence links with some countries in the region, including the loan of a garrison to Brunei.

In South Asia the Indo-British Partnership initiative, established in 1993, has strengthened commercial relations between Britain and India. Bilateral trade has doubled in four years and Britain is India's second

largest new investor. In Pakistan, Britain is the largest foreign investor, with bilateral trade up by almost 50 per cent in the last five years.

The Queen and the Duke of Edinburgh paid a State Visit to India and Pakistan in October 1997 as part of these countries' 50th anniversary of independence celebrations. A number of other high-profile events to mark the anniversary took place in Britain and South Asia. Highlights included, in India, the largest exhibition of British Museum treasures ever mounted overseas and the Indo-British Partnership's biggest trade fair to date. In Pakistan the 'Traditions of Respect' exhibition celebrated the cultural links between Britain and Islam.

Britain has stepped up political dialogue with countries in the region and has developed British commercial activity through more trade and investment and the setting up of business councils, joint commissions or industrial co-operation agreements. In addition Britain is taking advantage of increased opportunities for English language teaching, co-operation in science and technology, and educational exchanges.

Britain has welcomed the Asia-Europe Meeting (ASEM) process inaugurated in Bangkok in March 1996. ASEM is intended to balance existing transatlantic and transpacific relationships and foster closer economic and political ties between EU countries and Brunei, China, Indonesia, Japan, the Republic of Korea, Malaysia, Singapore, the Philippines, Thailand and Vietnam. In April 1998 Britain will host the second Europe-Asia summit, and will work for enhanced dialogue and measures of co-operation, particularly on trade and investment.

Hong Kong

At the end of June 1997 the British dependent territory of Hong Kong was returned to Chinese sovereignty under the provisions of the 1984 Sino-British Joint Declaration, which contains guarantees about Hong Kong's way of life for the next fifty years. Hong Kong's return to China was necessary because of the expiry of the 99-year lease under which the vast majority of the territory was transferred by China to Britain under the 1898 Peking Convention.

As set out in the Joint Declaration, Hong Kong is a Special Administrative Region (SAR) of China. Apart from the fields of foreign affairs and defence, the Hong Kong SAR enjoys a high degree of autonomy, maintaining its own government. Its capitalist economy and freedoms, including its social systems, will remain intact for at least the next fifty years. The Sino-British Liaison group will remain in existence until 2000 to discuss matters relating to the implementation of the Joint Declaration. A major area of disagreement has been China's decision to replace the Legislative Council elected in 1995 with an appointed provisional legislature. The SAR government has announced that elections will be held for a new legislature in May 1998.

Britain is represented in Hong Kong by its largest consulate-general in the world. As a co-signatory of the Joint Declaration, Britain will continue to have strong responsibilities towards Hong Kong and the 3.5 million British passport holders living there. In addition, Hong Kong is Britain's second largest export market in Asia.

The Americas

Links between Britain, the United States and Canada are uniquely close, all three countries sharing a common commitment to democracy and free enterprise. The British Government believes that this transatlantic relationship remains essential to guarantee the security and prosperity of Europe and North America. All three countries meet at the negotiating table in almost all the major international organisations.

Britain and the US co-operate especially closely on nuclear, defence and intelligence matters. As founding members of NATO, Britain and the US are deeply involved in Western defence arrangements (see p. 143) and, as permanent members of the UN Security Council, work closely together on major international issues.

There are also important economic links. Britain is the largest foreign investor in the US; about 1 million jobs have been created in the US by British investment worth £82,500 million. Over 40 per cent of US investment in Europe comes to Britain. The US and EU markets account for more than 50 per cent of world trade and 75 per cent of all overseas investment.

Strong links are also maintained with Canada, with whom Britain shares membership of the Commonwealth, NATO and other key international organisations. Britain is the second largest foreign investor in Canada and its third largest trading partner. Strongly supported by Britain, Canada recently reached agreement with the EU on a framework for co-operation on a wide range of issues.

Important British connections with Latin America date from the participation of British volunteers in the wars of independence in the early 19th century. Britain has welcomed the fact that democratically elected governments are now the norm in the region; this, together with the trend towards freer market economies, has enabled Britain to strengthen its relations with Latin American governments. As a result of the free market economic policies and economic growth of the last few years, British investment has increased, making it the largest investor in the region after the United States.

ARMS CONTROL

Because of the global reach of modern weapons, Britain has a clear national interest in preventing proliferation of weapons of mass destruction and promoting international control.

Weapons of Mass Destruction

Nuclear Weapons

The main instrument for controlling nuclear weapons is the 1968 Nuclear Non-Proliferation Treaty (NPT). Britain took an active part in negotiating the Treaty and more recently in securing its indefinite extension in 1995. It will also fully participate in the preparatory meetings leading up to the next NPT Review Conference.

Britain played an important role in negotiations on the recently agreed Nuclear Test Ban Treaty, which it signed in September 1996. It is contributing about 6 per cent of the budget of the Preparatory

Commission of the Comprehensive Test Ban Treaty Organisation, responsible for verifying the Treaty through on-site inspections.

Britain has also made reductions in its nuclear forces. The new Government is committed to the goal of the global elimination of nuclear weapons and is determined to press for multilateral negotiations towards mutual, balanced and verifiable reductions in such weapons. During the current strategic defence review, which is foreign-policy led, the Government will be considering how best to implement these commitments (see chapter 10).

Biological Weapons

Britain is playing a leading part in promoting the 1972 Biological Weapons Convention, which provides for a worldwide ban on such weapons. Unfortunately, it has no effective verification mechanism. Britain is currently leading international efforts to formulate such measures for inclusion in a Protocol to the Convention. These include mandatory declarations of key facilities and challenge inspections to address concerns about possible non-compliance.

Chemical Weapons

The 1993 Chemical Weapons Convention, which entered into force in April 1997, provides for a worldwide ban on chemical weapons. The Organisation for the Prohibition of Chemical Weapons is responsible for verification. During the negotiations Britain made major contributions to drawing up extensive and effective verification provisions. All the necessary British legislation is in place to license the production, possession and use of the most toxic chemicals and to implement the Convention's trade controls. Some 100 countries have ratified the Convention.

Conventional Weapons

Britain and its NATO Allies have ratified a number of agreements which enhance security and stability in Europe. Britain is committed to work with its Allies and other European countries to develop and improve these agreements in the light of the changing security environment.

The main agreements are:

- the 1990 Conventional Armed Forces in Europe (CFE) Treaty, which reduces and limits the numbers of five categories of heavy weapons in the 30 countries of NATO and the former Warsaw Pact, and includes an intrusive verification regime. The CFE Treaty is widely regarded as the linchpin of European security; over 50,000 heavy weapons have been destroyed by the treaty signatories.

- the Vienna Document, developed under the auspices of the OSCE, which is a binding agreement by 54 states on the promotion of stability and openness on military matters in Europe; it contains a wide range of confidence and security building measures, including verification arrangements.

- the 1992 Open Skies Treaty, which, when it enters into force, will provide for the overflight and photography of the entire territory of the 27 participating states to monitor their military capabilities and activities. The treaty will

Landmines

In May 1997 the new Government announced an immediate moratorium on the operational use of anti-personnel landmines. This will become a ban by 2005 or earlier if an effective international treaty enters into force. The Government also announced that it will introduce a ban on the manufacture, import and transfer of anti-personnel landmines. In addition, Britain is taking part in negotiations in Ottawa (the 'Ottawa Process') through which nearly 100 countries are seeking to draw up an international treaty to ban the production, stockpiling, export and use of mines. Since 1991 Britain has committed more than £31 million, in close co-operation with international and non-governmental organisations, to humanitarian demining activities.

enter into force when ratified by Russia, Belarus and Ukraine.

In 1991 Britain was instrumental in establishing the UN Register of Conventional Arms, which came into effect in 1992. The aim of the Register is to introduce greater transparency in international transfers of conventional arms and to help identify excessive arms build-up in any one country or region. The new British Government has pledged to strengthen the Register by encouraging greater disclosure of information on arms exports and arms transfers by all countries.

Export Controls

In addition to efforts to control weapons of mass destruction and conventional arms, it is also necessary to control the export of conventional arms and so-called dual-use goods. The latter may have a quite legitimate civilian use but could also have a military application. Britain participates actively in all the major international export control regimes.

In July 1997 the British Government issued new criteria for a responsible arms trade, whereby export licences will not be granted if there is a clearly identifiable risk that weapons might be used for internal repression or international aggression. At the same time it banned the export of certain equipment for which there is clear evidence that it has been used for torture or other abuses; it also declared its commitment to preventing British companies from manufacturing, selling or procuring such equipment and to pressing for a global ban. An annual report to Parliament on strategic export controls and their application is to be produced.

The Government supports the introduction of a European Union Code of Conduct setting high common standards to govern arms exports from all EU countries.

HUMAN RIGHTS

Universal respect for human rights is an obligation under the UN Charter, reinforced by human rights law in the form of UN and regional human rights treaties. Expressions of concern about human rights do not, therefore, constitute interference in the internal affairs of another state. The new Government has announced that it will publish an annual report on its work in promoting human rights abroad and has stated that the protection and promotion of human rights are at the centre of its foreign policy.

The Universal Declaration of Human Rights was adopted by the UN General Assembly in 1948. Since this is not a legally binding document, the General Assembly adopted two international covenants in 1966, placing legal obligations on those states ratifying or acceding to them. The covenants came into force in 1976, Britain ratifying both in the same year. One covenant deals with economic, social and cultural rights and the other with civil and political rights. States which are parties to the covenants undertake to submit periodic reports detailing compliance with their terms. Each covenant has a UN treaty monitoring committee which examines these reports. Britain recognises the competence of these committees to receive and consider state-to-state complaints. Other international conventions to which Britain is a party include those on:

- the elimination of racial discrimination;
- the elimination of all forms of discrimination against women;
- the rights of the child;
- torture and other cruel, inhuman or degrading treatment or punishment;
- the prevention of genocide;
- the abolition of slavery; and
- the status of refugees.

Council of Europe

Britain is bound by the Council of Europe's Convention for the Protection of Human Rights and Fundamental Freedoms, which covers:

- the right to life, liberty and a fair trial;
- the right to marry and have a family;
- freedom of thought, conscience and religion;

- freedom of expression, including freedom of the press;

- freedom of peaceful assembly and association;

- the right to have a sentence reviewed by a higher tribunal; and

- the prohibition of torture and inhuman or degrading treatment.

Complaints about violations of the Convention are made to the European Commission of Human Rights in Strasbourg. Although one state may lodge a complaint against another, most complaints are brought against states by individuals or groups. The Commission decides whether cases are admissible and, if so, examines the matter with the parties with a view to achieving a settlement. If this fails, the Commission or the state concerned can refer the case to the European Court of Human Rights, which rules on whether the Convention has been breached. Britain has signed and ratified the 11th Protocol to the Convention, which replaces the existing Commission and Court with a full-time Court.

The new Government has announced that it will incorporate the main provisions of the Council of Europe Convention into British law, thereby ensuring swifter adjudication of any complaints by British citizens about alleged violations of the Convention by any British public authority (see p. 52).

Organisation for Security and Co-operation in Europe

The OSCE's human rights body, the Office for Democratic Institutions and Human Rights (in Warsaw), is responsible for furthering human rights, democracy and the rule of law. It provides a forum for meetings and expert seminars to discuss the implementation of commitments in the area of human rights. The Office shares and exchanges information on the building of democratic institutions and the holding of elections in participating states. It also co-ordinates the monitoring of elections and provides expertise and training on constitutional and legal matters.

British observers formed part of the OSCE mission sent to Albania in 1997 to monitor a general election.

Westminster Foundation for Democracy

The Westminster Foundation for Democracy, an independent non-departmental public body established in 1992, provides assistance in building and strengthening pluralist democratic institutions overseas. It receives an annual grant from the FCO and raises funds through donations from other organisations. The three main political parties (see p. 61) have representation on the Foundation's Board of Governors; these are appointed by the Foreign Secretary after consultations with the parties. There is also a representative from one of the smaller political parties and non-party figures drawn from business, trade unions, the academic world, the media and other non-government sectors.

The British Government has no right of veto over the projects which the Board chooses to support. The FCO provides a non-voting member of the Board to act as a channel of communications and provide factual advice when required.

Efforts are being concentrated on Central and Eastern Europe, Russia and Central Asia, and Anglophone Africa. The Foundation also gives sympathetic consideration to worthwhile projects in other parts of the world.

INTERNATIONAL CRIME

Britain and the other members of the European Union have agreed not to export arms or other military equipment to countries clearly implicated in supporting terrorist activity, and to take steps to prevent such material being diverted for terrorist purposes. It is EU policy that no concessions should be made to terrorists or their sponsors, and that there should be solidarity among member states in the prevention of terrorism.

Britain participates actively in international forums on co-operation against the illegal drugs trade, maintains a substantial programme of overseas assistance in this field and stations drug liaison officers in a number of countries in order to work with the host authorities in the fight against drug trafficking. Britain is one of the main contributors to the UN International Drug Control Programme, providing £2.5 million in 1996–97. In 1995, a British-French initiative to combat drug trafficking in the Caribbean secured support from the EU, and has since been extended to Latin America. Both countries are also looking at a similar programme in Central Asia.

EU member states have agreed to set up a European Police Office (EUROPOL) in order to support investigations and operations conducted by national law enforcement agencies into serious and organised international crime such as illegal drug trafficking. EUROPOL powers and duties are set out in the EUROPOL Convention currently subject to ratification by EU member states.

EU member states also belong to the International Criminal Police Organisation (INTERPOL). British liaison with INTERPOL is provided by the National Criminal Intelligence Service (see p. 93).

Co-operation between the governments of EU member states on justice and home affairs takes place under the provisions of the Maastricht Treaty (see p. 124). A number of conventions have been agreed under these arrangements, including those on EUROPOL, extradition and the protection of the EU's financial interests.

Britain plays a leading role in supporting international and regional initiatives to counter money-laundering.

DEVELOPMENT CO-OPERATION

In 1995–96 Britain's overseas aid programme (the sixth largest in the world) amounted to £2,610 million. Of this, 87 per cent went to developing countries and 11 per cent to countries in transition in Central and Eastern Europe and the former Soviet Union. (The rest comprises mainly administrative costs.) About 53 per cent was given directly to individual countries and the remainder channelled through international bodies, such as the European Union, the United Nations and the World Bank group of institutions. In addition, over £280 million was invested in developing countries by the Commonwealth Development Corporation in 1995–96 (see below). Some of the aid budget goes to programmes administered by the British Council (see p. 140) and by non-governmental organisations such as Oxfam and Save the Children Fund.

Under the new Government, Britain's aid programme is being concentrated on improved access for poor people to essential health and basic education services and on finding ways to increase the incomes of smallholder farmers and the urban poor. An overall policy review of the programme has been conducted in order to ensure that the aid effort is focused on eliminating poverty and helping the human development of the poorest people, as well as supporting the process of transition in Central and Eastern Europe and Central Asia in a way that ensures that the benefits are spread throughout society. The Government has stressed Britain's commitment to reaching the United Nations target of donor countries providing 0.7 per cent of their gross national product on aid programmes for poor countries.

Britain has welcomed a report by the OECD's Development Assistance Committee which proposes that the number of people living in extreme poverty should be halved by 2015. The report proposes universal primary education in all countries, progress towards equality for women and improvements in healthcare and mortality rates. Britain also supports the conclusion of the UN human development report for 1997 that the elimination of poverty is both affordable and achievable.

Britain believes that, in addition to aid programmes, development policies must be concerned with issues like trade, debt and agriculture. Otherwise the aid programme can merely lessen the impact of other policies which can create impoverishment, for example trade barriers by rich countries to imports from developing countries.

Economic Management and the Private Sector

Britain has worked closely with developing countries to promote sound economic management and sensibly regulated market economies. It believes that governments and markets must work together to ensure viable development and that neither the public nor private sector has complete answers acting in isolation from the other.

Under the aid programme, British experts have been helping countries design and implement changes to their economies, for example, tax reform, civil service reform and management of the financial sector. Aid is also used to support imports of essential goods and pay for important public services.

Britain is also encouraging the creation of co-operatives in order to manage a communal resource, share risk or increase the power of individuals in the market. In its view co-operatives represent a useful middle way between centralised state control and the free market by balancing profit-seeking with social goals. Discussions have been held with the International Co-operative Alliance to see how the British aid programme can learn from experience in other countries.

The Commonwealth Development Corporation (CDC) encourages private sector investment in developing countries. It provides loans, equity funds and management services for financially viable investments in agriculture, fisheries, minerals, industry, transport, communications and housing. By the end of 1996 it had invested £1,560 million in 393 enterprises in 54 countries. The Government is to sell a majority of its stake in the CDC, with all the proceeds going to the British aid programme.

Britain wants to see more private investment in the poorest countries while recognising that they will continue to depend on substantial resource transfers from richer countries in order to generate sustainable development.

Ethical Trading

Following expressions of concern among many British consumers about the working conditions of people in developing countries, the Department for International Development is working with consumer, investor and producer groups to see whether international codes for ethical trading can be achieved. All the major supermarket chains in Britain are involved in these discussions.

Good Government

Assistance for good government has been a major priority for the British aid programme on the grounds that successful development will be impossible without it. In 1995–96 there were 167 new projects designed to help promote democracy, human rights and the rule of law. British assistance has included:

- support for civil service and local government reform;
- electoral assistance;
- reform of the police and judiciary;
- projects to control corruption; and
- advice on the promotion and protection of human rights.

Debt Relief

Britain has cancelled debts owed to it in aid loans by over 30 of the poorest countries. It has also initiated a number of schemes for debt relief, including the present rescheduling arrangements agreed by western creditor governments (the Paris Club) in 1995. These terms will shortly make possible up to 80 per cent relief on the eligible debt of the poorest, most indebted countries that have a good record of economic reform. Britain is pressing the leading international financial institutions, such as the World Bank and the International Monetary Fund, to provide increased debt relief for the poorest, most indebted countries. When granting debt relief Britain wants to ensure that such relief contributes to economic development and lasting poverty reduction.

Education

British aid to education has focused on primary and tertiary education, concentrating on key areas such as:

- curriculum development;
- teacher education;
- examination reform;

- the development of learning materials, including books;
- the planning, financing and administration of education; and
- the provision of school buildings and equipment.

Over 5 million primary school children have learnt to read and write in South Africa, Namibia and Botswana as a result of the Molteno project, supported by Britain since 1980. Children are first taught to read and write in their own languages and then go on to learn English. Another British-aided project has assisted the government of Malawi, in consultation with parents, to provide primary schools in locations where they are most needed. In 1997 Britain announced that it would provide £41 million to assist the government of India to implement a seven-year district primary education programme in West Bengal.

In 1995–96 some 9,000 students and trainees from developing countries, mainly postgraduates, received British support to study and train in Britain under technical co-operation training arrangements and three scholarship schemes—the Commonwealth Scholarship and Fellowship Plan, the British Chevening Scholarships (see p. 455) and the Shared Scholarships Scheme. Part of Britain's grant aid to South Africa provides bursaries and loans to 1,000 university and technical students from disadvantaged communities studying science, engineering, commerce and medicine.

Health

Britain aims to help countries obtain the best possible use of limited resources by improving the effectiveness and coverage of health services, in particular by increasing access to essential healthcare for women and children. Six per cent of bilateral aid is spent on health and population activities.

Through its 'Children by Choice, Not Chance' policy, Britain has sought to ensure that more people receive good-quality family planning services and to enable women to go through pregnancy and childbirth more safely. At the 1994 Cairo conference, Britain pledged

itself to make commitments of £100 million in the next two years: the pledge was exceeded, and 112 projects worth over £184 mllion were approved in 1994 and 1995.

The British aid programme has also focused on the reduction of suffering from communicable diseases, especially tuberculosis, malaria and HIV/AIDS. In 1995 Britain was the largest bilateral donor to the World Health Organisation's anti-tuberculosis programme. Britain has also strongly supported the establishment of the new joint UN programme on HIV/AIDS.

Britain has been funding a strong programme of research and development—about £9 million annually—in four priority health areas:

- healthcare management and health sector reform;
- reproductive health;
- communicable diseases; and
- healthcare in unstable living environments.

Promoting Opportunities for Women

In the last few years Britain has made considerable progress in supporting the advancement of women in the aid programme. In 1995–96 over 11 per cent of bilateral aid was targeted at improving women's as well as men's needs, since making women and men more equal will improve the quality of life for people in poorer countries.

At the Fourth World Conference on Women in Peking in 1995 the governments of 189 countries committed themselves to the long-term goal of gender equality. Projects designed to help women and girls gain greater access to education, health and incomes will continue to play a key role in the British aid programme.

The Environment

Protection and sustainable management of the environment are key aims of the British aid programme. In 1995–96 Britain committed over £153 million bilaterally to support 182 projects aimed at protecting the environment, promoting cleaner technologies or supporting sustainable agriculture. Britain has also ratified a UN Convention aimed at combating desertification in Africa and mitigating its effects.

The Global Environment Facility (GEF) is a trust fund of over US$2,000 million which helps developing countries and countries with economies in transition to meet the incremental costs of protecting the world's environment in four main areas:

- climate change;
- biodiversity;
- pollution of international waters; and
- protection of the ozone layer (for countries in transition only).

Britain is the Fund's fifth largest donor and is committed to a further substantial replenishment to the GEF later in 1997.

Climate Change

Britain signed the Convention on Climate Change at the 1992 Earth Summit and ratified it in the following year. During the recent special UN General Assembly discussions on progress made since Rio, Britain expressed strong concern at the failure of the international community, especially the richer countries, to implement fully the commitments agreed in 1992.

In 1995–96 Britain committed £32 million for development projects designed to promote energy efficiency and assist developing countries to reduce pollution from greenhouse gas emissions.

Ozone Depletion

The Montreal Protocol's Multilateral Fund helps developing countries to meet some of the extra costs of phasing out ozone-depleting substances. By the end of 1996, Britain had committed £27 million to the Fund.

Biodiversity

The Rio Biodiversity Convention, which Britain signed in June 1992 and ratified a year later, requires countries to take action to halt the loss of animal and plant species and preserve genetic resources, and to produce plans for conserving them.

Britain is helping countries to fulfil their obligations under the Convention through its contributions to the GEF, the British bilateral aid programme, and the Darwin Initiative for the Survival of Species, which was launched at the Earth Summit in 1992. Since 1994 Britain has committed £81 million to projects promoting biodiversity.

Forestry

Britain is supporting about 251 forestry projects in 74 countries at a total cost of over £174 million. The aim is to help developing countries utilise their forests sustainably and to reduce the rate of deforestation. When sustainably managed, forests can be an invaluable resource for communities in developing countries and represent a major habitat for biological diversity. Forests are also important for the world's climate, since trees absorb carbon dioxide, a gas which contributes to global warming.

Natural Resources

Britain has spent some £145 million a year on helping developing countries to promote sustainable and efficient management of their renewable resources in agriculture, forestry and fisheries. This involves working directly with communities as well as helping governments to formulate and implement appropriate policies. Examples of British natural resources programmes have included:

- helping Botswana develop better rangelands and wildlife management systems;
- working through the non-governmental organisation CARE to help farmers in Bangladesh farm fish in their rice fields; and
- developing sustainable land-use systems in the buffer zones around national parks and protected areas in Bolivia.

Britain also spends around £32 million a year on technology development and research in agriculture, forestry, livestock and fisheries.

Britain is a founder member of, and contributor to, the Consultative Group on International Agricultural Research. The Group's research helps to increase the supply of staple foods, preserve plant genetic resources and strengthen science in developing countries.

Emergency Relief

The Department for International Development's Disaster Unit co-ordinates Britain's provision of humanitarian aid, such as financial grants, tents, blankets and medical supplies, or staff with needed skills. The unit works closely with the International Red Cross and Red Crescent, the European Union and voluntary agencies. It also mounts its own response to emergencies overseas.

In 1995–96 Britain spent some £271 million on emergencies, 22 per cent of which was channelled through non–governmental organisations.

Following a devastating volcanic eruption on Montserrat, a British Dependent Territory (see p. 123), in June 1997, Britain's emergency response included the provision of transport and communications, fuel and food supplies, and funds to help build emergency shelter and maintain hospital services.

CULTURAL RELATIONS

The British Council is Britain's principal agency for cultural relations overseas. Its purpose is to promote a wider knowledge of Britain and the English language and to encourage cultural, scientific, technological and educational co-operation between Britain and other countries. The Council:

● helps people to study, train or make professional contacts in Britain;

● enables British specialists to teach, advise or establish joint projects abroad;

● teaches English and promotes its use;

● provides library and information services;

● promotes scientific and technical training, research collaboration and exchanges; and

● makes British arts and literature more widely known.

The Council works in 228 towns and cities in 109 countries. It runs 209 libraries and information centres which have about 450,000 members borrowing some 10 million books, videos and tapes each year. The Council funds over 9,000 scientific visits and some 1,300 research links. Additionally, it administers over 450,000 British professional and academic examinations each year. The Council is financed partly by a grant from the Foreign & Commonwealth Office. The training and education programmes organised by the Council as part of the British aid programme are another important aspect of the organisation's work, for which it receives funding from the Department for International Development. One-third of its income comes from other earnings such as, for example, fees earned from administration of examinations or from English language teaching.

Educational Exchanges

The British Council recruits teachers for work overseas, organises short overseas visits by British experts, encourages cultural exchange visits, and organises academic interchange between British universities and colleges and those in other countries.

The British aid programme has helped fund certain Council programmes, such as:

● recruitment of staff for overseas universities;

● secondment of staff from British higher education establishments; and

● organisation of short-term teaching and advisory visits.

The Council's Central Bureau for Educational Visits and Exchanges focuses on education for international understanding through partnerships between educational establishments, curriculum-related exchange programmes, and workshops and conferences related to professional international experience. Information is also provided on work, study and travel opportunities worldwide. The Bureau is government-funded and is the national agency in Britain for many European Union education and training programmes.

United Nations Educational, Scientific and Cultural Organisation (UNESCO)

In July 1997, after a 12-year absence, Britain officially rejoined UNESCO, a UN specialised agency which promotes collaboration between nations through education, science, culture and communication.

The Arts

The British Council initiates or supports more than 2,000 events each year with its international partners in the fields of the performing arts, film and television, visual arts, literature and design. These activities include British participation in major international festivals and biennials, tours and exhibitions, special showcases of British work for international promoters, and a programme of professional exchanges, including residencies, workshops and seminars. The emphasis is on contemporary creation, highlighting excellence and innovation as well as Britain's strong cultural diversity.

Further Reading

Departmental Report 1997: The Government's Expenditure Plans 1997–98 to 1999–2000. Foreign & Commonwealth Office, including Overseas Development Administration. Cm 3603. The Stationery Office, 1997.

British Council Annual Report.

British Overseas Aid Annual Review.

European Union. Aspects of Britain series, HMSO, 1994.

Human Rights (2nd edn). Aspects of Britain series, HMSO, 1995.

Britain and Development Aid. Aspects of Britain series, HMSO, 1995.

10 Defence

Britain's defence policy supports its wider security policy, which is to maintain the country's freedom and territorial integrity, and that of its Dependent Territories, as well as its ability to pursue its legitimate interests at home and abroad. As a member of NATO (the North Atlantic Treaty Organisation), Britain makes a significant contribution to maintaining stability throughout Europe. The Government has initiated a Strategic Defence Review of Britain's security interests and requirements to ensure that its defence capabilities are matched to changing international circumstances.

INTRODUCTION

In the immediate aftermath of the Cold War, defence policy remained focused on the need to protect Britain, through NATO, from any reversal in the reforms being put in place in Russia. The extent and pace of these reforms has now made such a posture inappropriate. However, Britain's security and way of life remain vulnerable to other risks and challenges—including aggressive nationalism, religious extremism or ethnic rivalry, state-sponsored terrorism, organised crime, and the proliferation of weapons of mass destruction —and its defence policy must adapt accordingly.

Defence policy is under examination as part of the Strategic Defence Review announced by the Government in May 1997. The Review, which is foreign-policy-led, will identify Britain's interests and commitments, and then decide how the armed forces should

be structured, equipped and deployed to meet them. The aim is to complete the Review in 1998.

The main policy principles underlying the Review are:

- the continued reliance on the collective defence provided through NATO as the basis of Britain's security;

- the maintenance of strong conventional forces;

- the maintenance of a national nuclear deterrent until Britain is satisfied with verifiable progress towards the goal of global elimination of nuclear weapons, at which point the Government will ensure that Britain's nuclear weapons are included in multilateral negotiations; and

- a commitment to a strong defence industry, which is a strategic part of Britain's industrial base as well as its defence effort.

Britain is determined to contribute to wider international peace and security through NATO and the Western European Union (WEU—see p. 120), and through other international organisations such as the United Nations (UN—see p. 116) and the Organisation for Security and Co-operation in Europe (OSCE—see p. 120). The Strategic Defence Review will not affect Britain's place as a permanent member of the UN Security Council.

To achieve its policy objectives, Britain requires forces with a high degree of military effectiveness, at sufficient readiness and with a clear sense of purpose, for combat operations, conflict prevention, crisis management and humanitarian activities. These forces must therefore be flexible and able to undertake the full spectrum of military tasks.

NORTH ATLANTIC TREATY ORGANISATION

NATO remains essential to the future of Britain—a founder member of the Alliance— and Europe. It was established in 1949, and is the only forum binding North America to European defence arrangements. It currently has 16 members. Most of Britain's forces are assigned to NATO.

Adaptation of NATO

As part of its continuous post-Cold War evolution, NATO has pursued a number of important initiatives, including the Partnership for Peace, the enlargement of NATO, the development of close ties with Russia and Ukraine, the development of a stronger European defence identity, and the creation of the Combined Joint Task Force concept as part of a new command structure.

Partnership for Peace and the Euro-Atlantic Partnership Council

In June 1997 NATO established the Euro-Atlantic Partnership Council to provide an overarching framework for co-operation with Partner countries in the Partnership for Peace. The Partnership for Peace seeks to deepen co-operative political and military ties between NATO and the countries of central and eastern Europe and of central Asia. It also promotes better co-operation between military forces engaged in multinational operations such as peacekeeping, humanitarian relief and other crisis management missions. NATO currently has 27 Partner countries, including Russia, almost all the central and eastern European states, Sweden, Finland, Austria, Malta and most of the central Asian and Trans-Caucasian states of the former Soviet Union.

Outreach

In addition to its work with NATO on the Partnership for Peace, Britain conducts a wide variety of bilateral defence activities through its Outreach initiative, which now extends to 20 countries; in 1997 over 1,000 individual activities took place. The focus and scope for the programme complements and helps to underpin Partnership for Peace.

Outreach also covers civilian areas of interest to a rather greater extent than Partnership for Peace, ranging from English language training to military logistics techniques and environmental management.

Relationships with Russia and Ukraine

NATO attaches great importance to building up its relationships with Russia and Ukraine. In May 1997 it signed with Russia the NATO/Russia Founding Act, which provides for an unprecedented level of consultation and co-operation between NATO and Russia over a wide range of security issues of mutual interest, including the possibility of joint crisis management operations under UN or OSCE auspices. Similarly, NATO and Ukraine have signed a Charter which underlines NATO's recognition of Ukraine's role in European security and provides a platform for increased co-operation.

NATO Enlargement

Following a study into the principles guiding enlargement and their implication, NATO agreed to intensify discussions with Partner members interested in joining the Alliance. At the 1997 Madrid Summit, NATO invited the Czech Republic, Hungary and Poland to begin talks with a view to their becoming members in 1999. This expansion is the largest in NATO's history. The Madrid Summit also agreed that NATO would review the process of enlargement at a further summit in 1999, and would maintain dialogue with other countries interested in membership.

Combined Joint Task Force

The Combined Joint Task Force concept is being developed to enhance NATO's ability to command and control multinational and multiservice forces, deployed at short notice, which can conduct a wide range of operations, including peacekeeping, under the auspices of the UN and OSCE. It will also make possible participation by non-NATO nations in operations (as is already happening in Bosnia—see p. 128), and, by enabling the conduct of such operations to be led by the WEU, will contribute to the development of the European Security and Defence Identity within NATO.

European Security and Defence Identity

Under the European Security and Defence Identity, NATO assets and capabilities will be available for WEU operations. The Alliance is building this concept on solid military principles, supported by appropriate military planning; the aim is to permit the creation of coherent and effective forces that can operate under the political control and strategic direction of the WEU.

BRITISH DEFENCE POLICY

British defence policy is designed to support its security policy. It guides the contribution of its armed forces to defence and security goals, and shapes its force structures and capabilities.

The aim of Britain's defence policy is:

- to deter any threats to, and, if necessary, defend the freedom and territorial

integrity of Britain and its Dependent Territories, including the provision of support as necessary for the civil authorities in countering terrorism;

- to contribute to the promotion of Britain's wider security interests, including the protection of freedom, democratic institutions and free trade; and

- thus to promote peace and help maximise Britain's international prestige and influence.

In 1997 a new planning framework that will support the formulation of Britain's defence policy was developed, based on the likely missions in which the armed forces might expect to be engaged. These missions will be revised where necessary in the light of the findings of the Strategic Defence Review, but are currently:

- security of Britain and its citizens in peacetime, including military aid to the civil authorities;

- security of Britain's Dependent Territories;

- defence support to wider British interests, which involves the provision of forces to conduct military assistance and training, and other activities to promote British influence and standing at home and abroad;

- support of international order and humanitarian principles;

- responding to a regional conflict outside NATO (but not an attack on NATO or one of its members) which could adversely affect European security, or which could pose a serious threat to British interests elsewhere or to international security; and

- responding to a NATO regional crisis in which an ally is attacked; or a strategic attack on NATO.

Military tasks are allocated against these missions, and provide the components for more detailed planning. This is the mechanism by which forces are matched to policy, and by which capabilities, commitments and resources are kept in balance.

Britain and its Dependencies

The armed forces continue to have day-to-day responsibility for safeguarding Britain's territory, airspace and territorial waters. They also provide for the security and reinforcement, as necessary, of the Dependent Territories and, when required, support for the civil authorities in Britain and the Dependent Territories.

Maritime Defence

The Royal Navy ensures the integrity of British territorial waters and the protection of British rights and interests in the surrounding seas. The maintenance of a 24-hour, year-round presence in British waters provides considerable reassurance to merchant ships and other mariners. The Royal Air Force (RAF) also contributes to maritime requirements, for instance through the Nimrod MR2 force, which provides air surveillance of surface vessels and submarines.

Land Defence

Army units committed to the defence of Britain, its Dependent Territories and the Sovereign Bases in Cyprus include 21 Regular Infantry battalions and seven Home Service battalions. Tasks include contributing to the security of national and NATO nuclear forces, military support to the machinery of government in war, military aid to the civil power throughout Britain and its Dependent Territories, maintaining the security of the Dependent Territories, and State ceremonial and public duties.

Air Defence

Air defence of Britain and the surrounding seas is maintained by a system of layered defences. Continuous radar cover is provided by the Improved United Kingdom Air Defence Ground Environment (IUKADGE), supplemented by the NATO Airborne Early Warning Force, to which the RAF contributes six E-3D aircraft. The RAF also provides six squadrons of all-weather Tornado F3 air defence aircraft, supported by tanker aircraft and, in wartime, an additional F3 squadron.

Royal Navy air defence destroyers can be also linked to the IUKADGE, providing radar and electronic warfare coverage and surface-to-air missiles. Ground-launched Rapier missiles defend the main RAF bases. Naval aircraft also contribute to British air defence.

Overseas Garrisons

Britain maintains garrisons in Gibraltar, the Sovereign Base Areas of Cyprus and the Falkland Islands. In addition, Gibraltar provides headquarters and communications facilities for NATO in the western Mediterranean, while Cyprus acts as a base for operations in the Middle East and North Africa. The garrison on the Falkand Islands, which has been in place since 1982, guarantees the Islands' security.

Northern Ireland

The armed forces provide support to the Royal Ulster Constabulary (RUC) in maintaining law and order and countering terrorism. Up to18 major units are assigned to the infantry role in Northern Ireland, including six Home Service battalions of the Royal Irish Regiment. The number of those major units deployed to the Province at any one time is dependent on the prevailing security situation. The Royal Navy patrols territorial waters around Northern Ireland and its inland waterways in order, among other things, to deter and intercept the movement of terrorist weapons. The Royal Marines provide troops to meet Navy and Army commitments, while the RAF provides elements of the RAF Regiment and Chinook, Wessex and Puma helicopters.

Other Tasks

Other tasks include the provision of:

- military assistance to civil ministries, including assistance to maintain the essentials of life in the community and carrying out work of national importance, providing fishery protection duties, and helping in the fight against drugs;

- military aid to the civil community, including during emergencies; and

- military search and rescue.

Britain and its Allies

The foundation of Britain's defence is provided through its membership of NATO.

Maritime Forces

Most Royal Navy ships are committed to NATO. Permanent contributions are made to NATO's standing naval forces in the Atlantic, the English Channel and the Mediterranean. The main components of the Fleet are:

- three aircraft carriers operating Sea Harrier aircraft and Sea King anti-submarine helicopters;

- 35 destroyers and frigates;

- 12 nuclear-powered attack submarines; and

- amphibious forces, including two assault ships and a new helicopter carrier due to enter service in 1998.

For information on Britain's independent nuclear deterrent see p. 147.

Land Forces

The multinational Allied Command Europe Rapid Reaction Corps (ARRC) is the key land component of NATO's Rapid Reaction Forces. Britain is the 'framework nation' for the Corps. Capable of deploying up to four NATO divisions, the ARRC is commanded by a British general, and some 55,000 British regular troops are assigned to it. This includes Britain's contribution of some 60 per cent of the headquarters staff and Corps level combat support and combat service support units. Britain also provides two of the ten divisions available to the Corps—an armoured division of three armoured brigades stationed in Germany, and a mechanised division of two mechanised brigades and an airborne brigade based in Britain. An air-mobile brigade, assigned to one of the Corps' two multinational divisions, is also located in Britain.

Air Forces

The RAF makes a major contribution to NATO's Immediate and Rapid Reaction Forces. Around 100 fixed-wing aircraft and 40 helicopters are allocated to them. Tornado F3 and Rapier surface-to-air missiles form part of the Supreme Allied Commander Europe's Immediate Reaction Force; while Harrier and Tornado GR1 and GR1a aircraft provide offensive support and tactical reconnaissance for the Rapid Reaction Force. Chinook and Puma helicopters provide troop airlift facilities for the ARRC or other deployed land forces. Tornado F3, Tornado GR1b and Nimrod aircraft provide air defence, attack and anti-submarine capabilities for NATO's Maritime Reaction Forces.

Modified RAF Tornado GR1 aircraft (designated GR1b), equipped with the Sea Eagle missile, have the task of maritime attack. The RAF will continue to provide Nimrod maritime patrol aircraft and search and rescue helicopters.

Four Tornado GR1 strike/attack squadrons and two Harrier offensive support squadrons are stationed in Germany at RAF Bruggen and RAF Laarbruch. It is planned that RAF Laarbruch will close in 1999 and, subject to consultation, RAF Bruggen will close in 2002; the aircraft squadrons currently based there will be withdrawn to existing bases in Britain. Meanwhile these aircraft and personnel, alongside the continuing and significant Army presence in Germany, are a visible sign of Britain's commitment to the defence of Europe.

Other Forces

Britain contributes to NATO's Maritime Augmentation Forces. These are held at the lowest state of readiness and in peacetime comprise ships mainly in routine refit or maintenance. It also contributes special forces to support reaction and main defence force deployments for surveillance, reconnaissance, offensive action and military assistance operations. Troops held for national defence could also be allocated to NATO. The United Kingdom Amphibious Force, together with its Dutch counterpart, is assigned to the Supreme

Allied Commander Atlantic for the reinforcement of Norway and could be deployed by the Supreme Allied Commander Europe, for example, with the ARRC. The Force is also a candidate for a range of WEU operations. RAF fighter, maritime patrol and transport aircraft will also be available for WEU operations.

Wider Security Interests

Military tasks to promote Britain's wider security interests may be undertaken unilaterally or multilaterally with support from NATO or directly for UN or OSCE operations.

United Nations Operations

Britain remains committed to UN operations. Contingents are currently deployed in Cyprus, where Britain is the largest UN contributor, and Iraq/Kuwait, where RAF Tornado GR1s, supported by VC10 tanker aircraft, are policing the no–fly zones (see p. 128).

Other Operational Deployments

Royal Navy ships of the Armilla Patrol continue to provide reassurance and assistance to entitled merchant shipping in the Gulf area and regularly participate in maritime exercises with navies of Gulf states and Gulf war coalition allies. The Patrol also conducts interception and boarding operations to ensure that ships do not breach UN sanctions against Iraq (see p. 130).

The number of operations against trafficking in illicit drugs has increased in recent years, especially in the Caribbean, where the West Indies Guardship and other Royal Navy ships work closely with the authorities of the United States, the Dependent Territories and the Regional Security System to combat drug trafficking. Although primary responsibility for this work rests with other government departments, the armed forces assist where they can do so without detriment to the performance of their other military tasks.

British troops remain ready to participate in operations or potential operations throughout the world. In the past three years in Africa alone, British troops have taken part in UN and multinational forces in evacuation operations in Rwanda, Somalia, Angola, Liberia, the former Zaire and Sierra Leone.

British Garrisons

A British garrison is maintained in Brunei, South-East Asia, at the request of the Brunei Government. A British military presence is maintained in Belize, Central America, in the form of a jungle training support unit.

Military Assistance

During 1996–97, some 3,793 students from 140 countries attended military training courses in Britain. On 1 June 1997, about 450 British service personnel were on loan, secondment, or short-term training teams.

NUCLEAR FORCES

Britain will retain the Trident submarine force to provide a minimum, but credible, nuclear deterrent. The nuclear deterrent forces provide the ultimate guarantee of national security and make an importance contribution to NATO's policy of war prevention.

The Government is committed to the goal of global elimination of nuclear weapons. Its objective is to maintain strong defences to counter the security challenges of the post-Cold War world and to develop the stability in which multilateral, balanced and verifiable disarmament can become a sustainable reality.

Britain's strategic and sub-strategic nuclear capability is currently provided by Tornado aircraft equipped with the WE177 free-fall nuclear bomb and three Vanguard class ballistic missile submarines. The fourth submarine will be ready to enter service around the turn of the century. This four-boat Trident fleet will ensure that continuous deterrent patrols can be maintained throughout the lifetime of the force.

The WE177 bombs are being withdrawn from service, a process to be completed by March 1998, when the sub-strategic role will be wholly undertaken by Trident.

DEFENCE EQUIPMENT PROGRAMMES

Modern equipment is essential if one of the key aims of Britain's force restructuring programme is to be achieved, namely that of increasing the flexibility and mobility of the armed forces. The outcome of a Defence Costs Study has enabled the front line (and its essential operational support) to be preserved and a number of important improvements in the armed forces to be introduced.

Current and planned front-line improvements for the *Royal Navy* equipment programme include:

- the introduction of the fourth Trident submarine and the rest of the missiles;
- the building of a second batch of Trafalgar class submarines (to be named the Astute class) to enter service early next century, with a capability to carry conventionally armed cruise missiles;
- a substantially modernised destroyer and frigate fleet, including the introduction of a new air defence frigate developed collaboratively with France and Italy;
- a follow-on batch of seven Sandown class single role minehunters;
- the introduction of a new helicopter carrier, planned to enter service in 1998, to enhance Britain's amphibious forces;
- 18 new Sea Harrier F/A2 aircraft ; and
- the building of replacements for the assault ships *Fearless* and *Intrepid*.

The *Army* front line is being enhanced by:

- the introduction of an all-Challenger 2 tank fleet (386 in all);
- Westland Apache attack helicopters to replace the Lynx in the anti-armour role;
- improved Rapier and new Starstreak missiles to improve air defence;
- a medium-range anti-tank missile;
- bridging equipment to increase the Army's mobility and flexibility; and
- a new generation of combat radios.

Improvements for the *RAF* include:

- the Eurofighter from the beginning of the

next century, to replace Tornado F3 and Jaguar aircraft;

- the upgrading of the Jaguar GR1a (to GR3), Tornado GR1 (to GR4), and Tornado F3 aircraft;
- orders for 21 new Nimrod MRA4 maritime patrol aircraft;
- orders for new air-launched anti-armour and stand-off missiles; and
- orders for further EH101 and Chinook support helicopters and the introduction of Hercules C130J aircraft from 1998.

Finally, the armed forces are to be equipped with a new electronic question and answer system, to improve their ability to distinguish between friendly and potentially hostile forces.

THE ARMED FORCES

Personnel

In 1997 the strength of the armed forces was around 112,700 in the Army, about 57,000 in the RAF and about 46,000 in the Royal Navy. Regular reserves totalled 258,000 and volunteer reserves 63,300. Civilian staff numbers are planned to fall from 123,200 (in April 1997) to 112,800 (99,500 British-based and 13,300 locally engaged) by 2002.

Commissioned Ranks

Commissions, either by promotion from the ranks or by direct entry based on educational and other qualifications, are granted for short, medium and long terms. All three Services have schemes for school, university and college sponsorships.

Commissioned ranks receive initial training at the Britannia Royal Naval College, Dartmouth; the Royal Military Academy, Sandhurst; or the Royal Air Force College, Cranwell. This is followed by specialist training, which may include degree courses at service establishments or universities.

Courses for higher training for officers are provided at a new Joint Services Command and Staff College, established in January 1997. This followed a Defence Costs Study proposal that such courses, formerly offered by single-service colleges, should be subsumed into a tri-service course that would reinforce the joint approach to the tactical and operational levels of conflict. The new college is at present operating from a number of sites, mainly Bracknell, until a permanent base is ready at Shrivenham in 1999.

Non-commissioned Ranks

Engagements for non-commissioned ranks in the Army and the RAF range from six months to 22 years; they can be for a maximum of 37 years in the Royal Navy (22 years in the Royal Marines). There is a wide choice of engagement length and terms of service. Subject to a minimum period of service, entrants may leave at any time, giving 18 months' notice (12 months for certain engagements). Discharge may also be granted on compassionate or medical grounds.

In addition to their basic training, non-commissioned personnel receive supplementary specialist training throughout their careers. Study for educational qualifications is encouraged and service trade and technical training lead to nationally recognised qualifications.

A new Army Foundation College will open in September 1998, initially for some 600 students. Offering a 42-week course combining military training and the opportunity to acquire national qualifications, it is intended to attract high-quality recruits who will go on to fill senior posts in front-line roles. Its funding through the Private Finance Initiative is being investigated (see p. 160).

Reserve Forces

Reserve forces are a central component of Britain's armed forces. They include members who become reservists following a period of regular service (regular reserve); and volunteers who train in their spare time. Volunteer reserve forces include the Royal Naval Reserve, the Royal Marines Reserve, the Territorial Army and the Royal Auxiliary Air Force. Reserves are available to support regular forces, either as units or as individuals, in times of tension or war. In particular,

reserves can provide skills and units not available or required in peacetime. Reserves are also a valuable link between the services and the civil community. The Reserve Forces Act 1996 allows more flexible use of the reserves in roles such as peacekeeping, humanitarian and disaster relief operations.

Gulf War Syndrome
In July 1997, the Government announced a new £2.5 million research programme into the possible adverse health effects of the combination of vaccines and tablets given to British troops in the Gulf War in 1990–91 to protect them against the threat of biological and chemical warfare. This research is in response to the illnesses suffered by a number of Gulf veterans who served in the war against Iraq (see p. 130).

ADMINISTRATION

The Defence Budget

The defence spending plans announced in November 1996 were £21,822 million, £22,276 million and £22,832 million for 1997–98, 1998–99 and 1999–2000 respectively. The new Government is only committed to these plans for the first two years. Under these plans, defence spending will fall by 16 per cent in real terms between 1992–93 and 1997–98 and will amount to 2.6 per cent of gross domestic product (from 2.9 per cent in 1996–97). The current average for NATO countries is 2.3 per cent.

Defence Management

The Ministry of Defence is not only a Department of State, but also incorporates the highest military headquarters of the armed forces. A unified Central Staff made up of military officers and civilians is responsible for defence policy, resource allocation and equipment requirements, direction of operations at the highest level, and management policy for the armed forces and the Ministry of Defence.

The Procurement Executive is responsible for the development and acquisition of weapon systems. The day-to-day activities of the armed forces are managed through operational, personnel and logistics commands outside London.

The Chief of Staff of the Defence Staff is the professional head of the armed forces and under him each Service's Chief of Staff is responsible for the fighting effectiveness, efficiency and morale of his Service. They and other senior officers and officials at the head of the department's main functions form the Ministry of Defence's corporate board, chaired by the head of the department, the Permanent Under-Secretary. The Secretary of State chairs the Defence Council and is responsible to Parliament for the formulation and conduct of defence policy, and the provision of the means to implement it.

Since 1991, military and civilian managers have been given ever greater authority and responsibility for fulfilling their objectives through the most efficient use of the resources allocated to them. The aim is to concentrate resources on front-line capability, and minimise the costs of essential support. Many functions are now embodied in defence agencies, each of which has a chief executive who is accountable for its performance against objectives and targets agreed by ministers. The department has also exposed over 150 support activities to private sector competition, with significant annual savings, and is seeking, through the Private Finance Initiative, to transfer the risk and capital cost of certain projects to the private sector.

Defence Procurement

About 40 per cent of the defence budget is spent on military equipment, including the procurement of spares and associated costs. When assessing options, a systematic approach is taken to defence industrial factors and particular consideration is given not just to the initial procurement costs of a project, but also to those necessary to support it throughout its service life. Competition for contracts takes place wherever possible and, in general, is open to prime and sub-contractors from overseas. Britain also seeks to promote market liberalisation for defence equipment worldwide.

International Procurement Collaboration

International collaboration provides an effective way of developing complex and costly new-generation weapon systems at a time of increasing production costs and reduced defence budgets. Britain favours such co-operation as a means of producing top-quality products on a value-for-money basis, and plays an active role in NATO's Conference of National Armaments Directors, which promotes equipment collaboration between NATO nations. It is also a member of the WEU's Western European Armaments Group, which is the main European forum for the discussion of armaments matters.

Current collaborative programmes include:

- development of the Eurofighter (with Germany, Italy and Spain);
- anti-tank guided weapons (with Belgium, France, Germany and the Netherlands);
- a new air defence frigate (with France and Italy);
- the Multiple Launch Rocket System (with the United States, Germany, France and Italy);
- the EH101 helicopter (with Italy);
- anti-air missiles (with France and Italy);
- a multi-role armoured vehicle (with France and Germany); and
- a request for proposals for a Future Large Aircraft (with Germany, France, Italy, Spain and Turkey).

Further Reading

Britain, NATO and European Security. Aspects of Britain series. HMSO, 1994.

The Government's Expenditure Plans 1997–98 to 1999–2000. Departmental Report by the Ministry of Defence. The Stationery Office, 1996.

11 Economy

Following the recession of 1990–92, the British economy has experienced continuous growth combined with low inflation; total output is currently 13 per cent above the previous peak reached in 1990, although, within this overall figure, manufacturing output is only just under 5 per cent higher. Major contributions to growth have come from exports and consumer spending. Notwithstanding this, long-term problems have left Britain with lower income per head than other G7 countries. The Government's economic policies are directed towards the achievement of high and sustainable levels of growth and employment within a dynamic market economy, enabling everyone to share in higher living standards and greater job opportunities.

THE ECONOMY

The value of all goods and services produced in the economy is measured by gross domestic product (GDP). In 1996 GDP at current factor cost (the cost of the goods and services before adding taxes and subtracting subsidies) totalled £642,916 million. Between 1986 and 1996 the index of GDP at constant factor cost increased by 24 per cent.

Values for some of the main economic indicators in selected years since 1986 are shown in Table 11.1. Table 11.2 shows output and employment in 1995 and 1996, and Table 11.3 compares GDP by industry in 1986 and 1996.

Output

During the past 25 years, Britain has experienced slower growth of output and productivity than any other member of the G7 group of major industrialised countries, and GDP per head remains below that of other G7 countries. Economic stability has been adversely affected by two of the deepest and longest recessions since 1945, the latest starting in 1990. After two years of continuous decline, output began to rise in 1992. Following an increase in GDP of 4.5 per cent in 1994, economic growth slowed to 2.8 per cent in 1995 and 2.5 per cent in 1996. In the second quarter of 1997 GDP was 3.5 per cent higher than a year earlier. The Government expects the economy to grow by 3.25 per cent in 1997 and 2.5 per cent in 1998. Consumer spending is forecast to increase by 4.5 per cent in 1997 and 4 per cent in 1998.

Recent decades have generally seen the fastest growth in the services sector (see chapter 16), which now accounts for around two-thirds of GDP, compared with about a

Table 11.1: Economic Indicators

	1986	1991	1996
Gross domestic product[a]	488,122	540,308	601,720
Exports[a]	114,047	132,252	179,805
Imports[a]	113,255	140,598	184,671
Consumers' expenditure[a]	295,622	340,037	376,648
Gross domestic fixed capital formation[a]	83,685	97,403	104,090
Percentage increase in Retail Prices Index	3.3	5.9	2.4
Workforce in employment (000s)	24,719	26,313	25,819
Percentage of workforce unemployed	11.1	8.0	7.5

Sources: *United Kingdom National Accounts 1997 Edition*; *Economic Trends*; *Labour Market Trends*
[a] £ million at 1990 market prices.

Table 11.2: Output and Employment (Indices: 1990 = 100)

	Output		Employment[a]	
	Index 1995	Index 1996	Index 1995	Index 1996
Agriculture, hunting, forestry and fishing	97.1	95.4	85.2	86.9
Production industries	106.7	107.9	82.7	83.5
of which: Electricity, gas and water	116.3	123.6 }	58.5	59.0
Mining and quarrying	138.7	143.3 }		
Manufacturing	102.5	102.8	84.7	85.7
Construction	90.0	91.1	73.3	70.9
Services	108.9	112.6	101.6	103.7
GDP	**106.9**	**109.5**		
Employees in employment			95.7	97.3

Sources: *United Kingdom National Accounts 1997 Edition*; *Labour Market Trends*
[a] Employment figures relate to Great Britain and cover employees in employment at June on a seasonally adjusted basis.

half in 1950. Manufacturing (see chapter 15) now contributes less than a quarter of GDP, compared with over a third in 1950. During the 1990s, services industries' output has been on an upward trend, with only a minor drop in output during 1991 and 1992, reaching a record level in 1996. In the second quarter of 1997, services' output was 4.3 per cent higher than a year earlier. Manufacturing growth resumed slowly in 1992–93, and in 1994 output rose by 4.7 per cent, falling back to 1.7 per cent in 1995 and 0.3 per cent in 1996.

Oil and gas production has had a major impact on the British economy since substantial production of gas started in the late 1960s and oil began to be produced in significant quantities in 1976. Gas production has been increasing each year since 1989, while oil production has also been rising

recently, with a new record output in 1995. Oil and gas output was up by 7 per cent in 1996, and in the three months to August 1997 there was growth of 3.6 per cent compared with the same period a year earlier. The extraction of oil and gas accounted for 2.5 per cent of GDP in 1996, while net exports of crude oil and petroleum products contributed a positive £4,300 million to the current account.

Investment and Profitability

Britain invested a smaller share of GDP than any other G7 country in the last full international economic cycle, between 1982 and 1993. Following growth of around 4 per cent a year in the 1980s, investment in Britain declined during the recession of the early

Table 11.3: Gross Domestic Product by Industry[a]

	1986		1996	
	£ million	per cent	£ million	per cent
Agriculture, hunting, forestry and fishing	6,680	2.0	11,790	1.8
Mining and quarrying, including oil and gas extraction	13,533	4.1	18,068	2.8
Manufacturing	81,252	24.8	137,006	21.3
Electricity, gas and water supply	9,407	2.9	13,606	2.1
Construction	19,916	6.1	33,746	5.2
Wholesale and retail trade, repairs, hotels and restaurants	45,617	13.9	93,091	14.5
Transport, storage and communications	27,247	8.3	54,056	8.4
Finance, real estate and business activities	33,197	10.1	73,464	11.4
Rent	23,848	7.3	63,850	9.9
Public administration, defence and social security	22,604	6.9	38,244	5.9
Education, health and social work	31,645	9.6	81,876	12.7
Other services	13,326	4.1	24,713	3.8
GDP at factor cost	**328,272**	**100.0**	**642,916**	**100.0**

Source: *United Kingdom National Accounts 1997 Edition*
[a] Before provision for depreciation but after deducting stock appreciation. Differences between totals and the sums of their component parts are due to rounding. GDP for 1996 includes statistical discrepancy (−£595 million).

1990s. However, in 1996 investment increased by 1.8 per cent and during the second quarter of 1997 it was 2.4 per cent higher than a year earlier, with a stronger rise in manufacturing investment. The Government expects investment in the economy to rise by 5 per cent in 1997 and 6 per cent in 1998; business investment is forecast to grow by 9.25 per cent in 1997 and 6.25 per cent in the following year.

Between 1980 and 1996 the private sector's share of fixed capital investment increased from 73 to 86 per cent, due in part to privatisation (see p. 186). In the same period, there was a rise in the share of investment undertaken by the services sector and a fall in that carried out by manufacturing. Table 11.4 shows investment by business sector.

The rate of return on capital employed in non-oil industrial and commercial companies in Britain increased in the 1980s to the highest levels for 20 years. It then fell back, but since 1992 there has been a recovery. In 1996, net profitability of industrial and commercial companies reached 10.1 per cent, up from 9.5 per cent a year earlier, although the rise for

non-oil industrial and commercial companies was smaller—from 9.0 to 9.2 per cent. These latest profitability figures are approaching the peak levels of the 1980s.

Inward Investment

Britain is recognised as a prime location for inward direct investment and over 8,000 overseas companies are currently operating in Britain, including some 4,500 from the United States, over 1,000 from Germany and more than 250 from Japan (see p. 210). In recent years, Britain has received the greatest share of inward investment into the European Union, including about 40 per cent of Japanese and US investment. It is second only to the United States as a destination for international direct investment.

Income and Expenditure

Table 11.5 shows the categories of total final expenditure in 1996. Consumers' expenditure accounted for 49 per cent of total final

Table 11.4: Gross Domestic Fixed Capital Formation (Investment) by Sector 1996

	£ million at market prices	£ million at 1990 prices	Index at 1990 prices (1990 = 100)
Agriculture, hunting, forestry and fishing	1,126	977	71.4
Mining and quarrying, including oil and gas extraction	4,623	4,415	93.9
Manufacturing	15,388	12,442	87.5
Electricity, gas and water supply	4,567	4,021	84.8
Construction	1,165	986	102.2
Services	61,012	57,176	102.3
Dwellings	22,538	19,909	92.9
Transfer costs	4,204	4,164	97.9
Whole economy	**114,623**	**104,090**	**96.8**

Source: *United Kingdom National Accounts 1997 Edition*

Table 11.5: Total Final Expenditure in 1996 at Market Prices

	£ million	per cent
Consumers' expenditure	473,509	49.1
General government final consumption	155,732	16.2
Gross domestic fixed capital formation	114,623	11.9
Value of physical increase in stocks and work in progress	2,917	0.3
Total domestic expenditure	746,781	77.5
Exports of goods and services	217,147	22.5
Total final expenditure	**963,928**	**100.0**

Source: *United Kingdom National Accounts 1997 Edition*

expenditure, and exports of goods and services for 22.5 per cent.

Personal disposable income consists of personal incomes after deductions—mainly taxation and social security contributions. Between 1986 and 1996 it rose by 32 per cent in real terms to £427,690 million at 1990 prices (£537,677 million at current prices). The increase in 1996 was 3.7 per cent in real terms. Consumers' expenditure rose by 3.5 per cent in real terms in 1996.

In 1996, 88 per cent of post-tax personal income was spent and 12 per cent saved. Table 11.6 shows the pattern of consumers' expenditure in 1986 and 1996. Declining proportions are being spent on food and alcoholic drink, tobacco, clothing and footwear, and fuel and power. Over the longer term, as incomes rise, people tend to spend increasing proportions on services. Spending on leisure pursuits and tourism, health and financial services have all shown significant growth in recent years. Housing, food, alcoholic drink, tobacco, clothing and footwear, and fuel and power together accounted for 44 per cent of the total in 1996.

The ratio of saving to personal disposable income declined substantially during the 1980s, to 6.2 per cent in 1988. However, it rose strongly to reach 12 per cent in 1992, and has subsequently remained above 10 per cent.

The proportion of total personal pre-tax income accounted for by income from employment was nearly 60 per cent in 1996. Self-employment accounted for 10 per cent of personal pre-tax income, and social security benefits and other current grants from government for 15 per cent.

Table 11.6: Consumers' Expenditure in 1986 and 1996 at Market Prices

	1986	1996	
	per cent	per cent	£ million
Food (household expenditure)	13.5	11.0	52,024
Alcoholic drink	6.8	5.9	28,015
Tobacco	3.1	2.5	11,812
Clothing and footwear	6.9	5.8	27,434
Housing	15.1	15.8	74,690
Fuel and power	4.5	3.4	16,074
Household goods and services	6.6	6.3	29,945
Transport and communications	17.2	17.2	81,470
Recreation, entertainment and education	9.2	10.5	49,711
Other goods and services	15.6	19.6	92,874
Other items[a]	1.6	2.0	9,460
Total	**100.0**	**100.0**	**473,509**

Source: *United Kingdom National Accounts 1997 Edition*
[a] Household expenditure overseas plus final expenditure by private non-profit-making bodies, minus expenditure by foreign tourists in Britain.
Note: Differences between totals and the sums of their component parts are due to rounding.

With the recent unprecedented conversion by a number of major building societies to banks and the flotation of a leading insurance company (see chapter 16), many of their members received shares in the new concerns in 1997. The total value of these 'windfalls' has been estimated at around £35,000 million. Responses to a MORI survey suggest that, while the majority of these windfalls have been saved, people intending to spend the proceeds of their windfalls were planning expenditure in areas such as home improvements, holidays, cars and household goods.

Inflation

Since 1971 inflation, as measured by the Retail Prices Index (RPI, which records the price of goods and services purchased by households in Britain and is often referred to as 'headline' inflation), has ranged from a rise of 26.9 per cent in August 1975 to one of only 1.2 per cent in June 1993. In general, inflation has been at a much lower level in the 1990s. The annual rate was 3.6 per cent in September 1997. The RPI excluding mortgage interest payments, a measure of 'underlying' inflation, was 2.7 per cent in September 1997. Underlying inflation has now been below 4 per cent for five years. The Government's forecast for underlying inflation is 2.5 per cent at the end of 1997, rising slightly in 1998 and then falling back to around 2.5 per cent by the middle of 1999.

Labour Market

Unemployment has fallen in recent years, but on the International Labour Organisation measure is still around 2 million in Great Britain (see chapter 12). Unemployment increased during the early 1990s, reaching nearly 3 million in winter 1992–93, 10.6 per cent of the workforce. Since then it has dropped by over 900,000, to its lowest level for seven years. Following an increase of about 3.3 million between 1983 and 1990, employment fell by nearly 1.5 million in the early 1990s. With economic recovery, employment levels have stabilised at an earlier stage than in previous cycles and are now rising gradually. In spite of large falls recently in unemployment, the growth of average earnings remains steady, at around 4.5 per cent a year.

Overseas Trade

Britain has an open economy in which international trade plays a key role (see chapter 14). The share of GDP accounted for by exports of goods and services was 29 per cent in 1996. Income from direct overseas investments accounted for around 29 per cent of all Britain's investment income in 1996.

Membership of the European Union has had a major impact on Britain's pattern of trade. Between 1972—the year before Britain became a member—and 1996 the share of its exports of goods going to other EU members rose from 40 per cent to 57 per cent. Imports have followed a similar trend.

Since 1983 Britain has had a deficit on its trade in goods. In 1996 it stood at £12,598 million, over £1,000 million higher than in 1995. Nevertheless, visible exports have been performing strongly, reflecting a sharp recovery in world trade and despite a stronger pound in 1997. Substantial earnings from trade in services and from overseas investments, which have continued to reach record levels, kept the balance of payments current account in surplus between 1980 and 1985. However, it has been in deficit since then, although in 1996 it was close to balance, with the deficit down to £435 million, compared with £3,672 million in 1995. The Government expects the current account deficit to increase to £6,000 million in 1997 and to £9,000 million in 1998.

ECONOMIC STRATEGY

The Government is implementing a comprehensive set of economic policies designed to improve the underlying rate of growth and employment, by creating economic stability based on low inflation and prudent government borrowing, and by improving the environment for long-term investment in industry, education and training. The Welfare State is being modernised in order to help people back into employment (see p. 421). The Government has launched a comprehensive spending review (see p. 160) to ensure that spending is in line with its own priorities and is targeted efficiently and effectively. It is reviewing the tax system to make sure that it is demonstrably fair to all (see p. 162). The Government is working with business to

improve the competitiveness of companies through raising investment in infrastructure, science and technology, and in education and skills training. It believes that economic development must take place in a way that is consistent with high standards of environmental protection.

HM Treasury is the government department with prime responsibility for the formulation and conduct of economic policy, which it carries out in conjunction with other government departments, such as Trade and Industry; Education and Employment; and the Environment, Transport and the Regions. Responsibility for the objectives of monetary policy rests with the Chancellor of the Exchequer. To ensure that interest rate decisions are taken in the long-term interests of the economy, the Government has given operational responsibility for setting interest rates to the Bank of England (the central bank, see p. 235).

ECONOMIC POLICY

Action is being taken by the Government to bring about price stability and sound public finances, which will underpin a strengthened economy. Price stability is seen as a precondition for high and sustainable levels of growth and employment. The new monetary framework is designed to secure permanently low inflation, which will help to generate greater business confidence. Under the new monetary arrangements, the Government sets the inflation target, and the Bank of England takes operational decisions on interest rates to meet the target. Without prejudice to the price stability objective, the Bank supports the Government's economic policy, including its objectives for growth and employment. The Government has set the inflation target for underlying inflation (see p. 155) at 2.5 per cent. Although short-term interest rates have been raised in pursuit of the Government's inflation target, the reforms giving the Bank of England operational responsibility for setting interest rates should lead to lower interest rates in the long run. Long-term interest rates and inflation expectations have fallen since the new monetary arrangements were announced.

Fiscal policy is guided by two overriding principles: over the economic cycle, the Government will only borrow to invest, not to fund current expenditure; and will hold public debt as a proportion of national income at a stable and prudent level. These rules require public borrowing to be kept under firm control, and mean that current taxpayers pay for current spending. The Government is seeking to increase public trust in fiscal policy by conducting it in a more open and transparent way (see below).

The main objective of the July 1997 Budget was to put the public finances on a sound long-term footing. The budget deficit reduction plan was introduced to ensure the Government meets its fiscal objectives and to reverse the rising burden of public debt. Budget measures to encourage long-term investment included cuts in corporation tax (see p. 162), reinvigorating the Private Finance Initiative (see p. 160) and releasing local authority capital receipts for reinvestment (see p. 381). Other measures were introduced to encourage more balanced growth (see p. 162).

THE BUDGET

The Budget is the Government's main economic statement of the year. In a major speech to Parliament, the Chancellor of the Exchequer reviews the nation's economic performance and describes the Government's economic objectives and the policies it intends to follow to help achieve them. The Budget statement also includes details of the taxes the Government proposes to finance the coming year's public spending.

Until March 1993, the Budget was usually held in the spring and focused mainly on economic policy and taxation, with the initial announcement of the Government's new public spending plans taking place in November in an Autumn Statement. From November 1993 to November 1996, there was a unified Budget which included announcements on both tax and spending. Following the May 1997 General Election, the new Government's first Budget was in July 1997. The next Budget is planned to be in spring 1998.

The Government is seeking greater openness in the area of public finance, and has announced action in two areas:

- In May 1997 it asked the National Audit Office (NAO—see p. 161) to review some key assumptions in the public finance forecasts. The NAO's report was published before the July Budget. The NAO will have a continuing role in auditing the public finances in future Budgets.

- The Government plans to publish a consultative paper several months ahead of each Budget, spelling out the state of the economy, the progress made towards the Government's economic objectives and the forecast for the following year; and encouraging a wide-ranging debate about the policy action necessary to ensure that the objectives are achieved. The first such paper will be published in November 1997.

Public Finance Strategy

General government expenditure (GGE) is the total public expenditure by central and local government. An alternative measure used is GGE (X) (see Table 11.7), which excludes privatisation proceeds, spending financed out of the proceeds of the National Lottery, and interest and dividend receipts. GGE(X) is expected to be around £315,300 million in 1997–98 .

The Government's view is that sound public finances are essential for economic stability. In the July 1997 Budget it announced a five-year plan aimed at reducing the structural budget deficit (see above). This is supported by a comprehensive spending review of government expenditure (see p. 160).

The Public Sector Borrowing Requirement (PSBR) rose rapidly during the early 1990s, but since then it has fallen and in 1996–97 amounted to £22,700 million, 3 per cent of GDP. The PSBR is expected to fall significantly over the period to 1998–99, primarily as a result of tight control of public spending.

Table 11.7: Public Expenditure Plans

| | £ thousand million | | |
| | 1996–97 | 1997–98 | 1998–99 |
	Outturn	Forecast	
Control Total	260.4	266.4	273.6
Welfare-to-Work spending	–	0.2	1.2
Local authority spending under the Capital Receipts Initiative	–	0.2	0.7
Cyclical social security	14.3	13.7	14.0
Central government debt interest	22.3	24.6	24.4
Accounting adjustments [a]	11.4	10.1	10.7
General government expenditure (X)	308.4	315.3	324.7
Privatisation proceeds	–4.4	–2.0	–
Lottery-financed spending and interest and dividend receipts	5.1	6.2	6.6
General government expenditure	309.0	319.4	331.3

Source: *Financial Statement and Budget Report July 1997*
[a] A number of adjustments are needed to relate the Government's forecast for public expenditure to the broader concepts of general government expenditure.
Note: Differences between totals and the sums of their component parts are due to rounding.

Table 11.8: Projected Public Expenditure, Receipts and Borrowing Requirement

| | £ thousand million | | |
| | 1996–97 | 1997–98 | 1998–99 |
	Outturn	Forecast	
General government expenditure	309.0	319.4	331.3
of which: Control Total	260.4	266.4	273.6
General government receipts	286.3	308.3	327.2
of which: income tax	69.5	76.5	83.7
corporation tax	27.7	30.1	32.0
VAT	46.7	50.0	52.5
fuel, alcohol and tobacco duties	30.6	33.4	35.4
social security contributions	47.4	49.5	52.0
Public sector borrowing requirement (PSBR)	22.7	10.9	4.0
PSBR[a] as percentage of GDP	3	1.75	0.75

Source: *Financial Statement and Budget Report July 1997*
[a] Excluding windfall tax and associated spending.

Government Receipts and Expenditure 1997–98

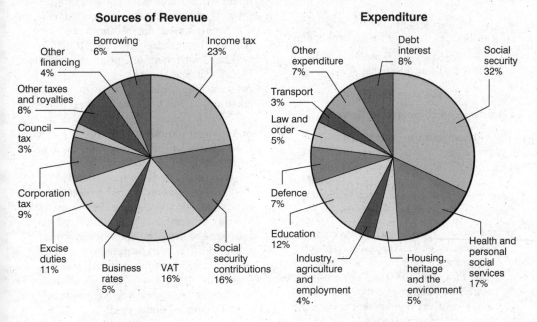

Sources of Revenue

Borrowing 6%
Income tax 23%
Other financing 4%
Other taxes and royalties 8%
Council tax 3%
Corporation tax 9%
Excise duties 11%
Business rates 5%
VAT 16%
Social security contributions 16%

Expenditure

Debt interest 8%
Social security 32%
Other expenditure 7%
Transport 3%
Law and order 5%
Defence 7%
Education 12%
Industry, agriculture and employment 4%
Housing, heritage and the environment 5%
Health and personal social services 17%

Note: As a result of rounding and omission of minor items, percentages do not necessarily add up to 100.

Source: HM Treasury

MAIN PROGRAMMES AND PRIORITIES

The diagram above shows the main categories of expenditure, together with the main sources of revenue.

The government departments with the largest spending programmes are:

- the Department of Social Security (with planned expenditure of £79,800 million in 1997–98, excluding 'cyclical' social security);

- the Department of the Environment, Transport and the Regions (£44,100 million, of which nearly £31,400 million is on local government);

- the Department of Health (£34,900 million); and

- the Ministry of Defence (£21,100 million).

Local authorities spend about £76,000 million a year, around a quarter of public expenditure. The main categories of expenditure are education, law and order, personal social services, housing and other environmental services, and roads and transport.

July 1997 Budget Measures

The centrepiece of the new Government's first Budget is a Welfare-to-Work programme, which is being financed by a windfall tax on the excess profits of the privatised utilities (see p. 162). The programme contains measures to tackle youth and long-term unemployment (see p. 173), low levels of employment among lone parents and rising spending on social security (see p. 424). Its cost of £5,200 million includes £3,150 million to help young people and £350 million for the long-term unemployed, and £1,300 million for capital investment in school infrastructure and technology. The Capital Receipts Initiative is releasing £900 million to local authorities over the next two years to boost investment in housing (see p. 381).

The Government has announced the allocation of extra resources for its priority areas of education and health in 1998–99 from the Reserve:

- an extra £1,000 million for local authorities to spend on education; and
- an additional £1,200 million for the National Health Service.

Comprehensive Spending Review

The Government has instituted a comprehensive review of government spending, under which departments are examining all aspects of central and local government expenditure. Lasting about a year, the review will operate at two levels:

- separate departmental reviews are examining objectives and all aspects of expenditure with a view to setting new plans for 1999–2000 and beyond—there are also a number of cross-departmental reviews of key policies that cover more than one department; and
- there will be an examination of the overall allocation of resources, leading to a complete set of new departmental spending plans from 1999–2000 onwards.

In addition, departments are reviewing the allocation of expenditure within their budgets for 1997–98 and 1998–99 to reflect the Government's priorities.

Private Finance and Public-Private Partnerships

The Private Finance Initiative (PFI), launched in 1992, aims to bring the private sector more directly into the provision of public services. The public sector specifies the service or infrastructure needed, and private sector companies compete to provide these requirements. By April 1997 some £7,000 million of projects had been agreed. The largest single PFI project is the £3,000 million Channel Tunnel Rail Link (see p. 313). Other schemes include a number of 'design, build, finance and operate' road projects (see p. 305); the Croydon Tramlink (see p. 313); three new prisons (see p. 105); a new National Insurance records system; and a 'smart card' system for the Benefits Agency. 'Challenge funding', under which funding for public sector capital projects is allocated on a competitive basis, has also been adopted, notably for urban regeneration schemes (see p. 372).

The Government sees productive Public-Private Partnerships as a key factor in the delivery of high-quality public services. It has taken steps to make the PFI process more effective, for example, by abandoning the requirement for universal testing of projects. It accepted all 29 of the recommendations of a review of the PFI process, including the establishment of a taskforce within HM Treasury to combine central project and policy expertise, to confirm the commercial viability of significant projects and to provide assistance to departments on these projects. Legislation has been introduced to tackle problems which were holding up major hospital projects, and in July 1997 plans for 14 new hospital schemes, worth £1,300 million, were announced under the PFI.

CONTROL OF PUBLIC EXPENDITURE

Public Expenditure Survey

Departmental spending decisions are based on allocating available resources within agreed ceilings for aggregate spending, with an emphasis on obtaining maximum value for money. Usually, the process of deciding individual departmental allocations within the overall target takes place each autumn in the Public Expenditure Survey, but the 1997 Survey is not taking place as a result of the decision to conduct the comprehensive spending review. In the July 1997 Budget the Government announced that it would stick to the expenditure ceilings set in the 1996 Budget for 1997–98 and 1998–99.

Estimates

Requests for funds for the coming financial year for each government department are presented to Parliament by HM Treasury. The aim is to present these Main Supply Estimates before the end of March. Parliamentary authorisation is given by the passage of the annual Appropriation Act. Individual departmental reports on planned spending are usually published just prior to presentation of the Estimates. Supplementary Estimates may be presented to Parliament during the course of the year to reflect any necessary changes to the original Main Estimate.

In each parliamentary session, up to three 'Estimates days' are available for debates on the Supply Estimates, following scrutiny by select committees of the House of Commons. If any Supply Estimate is overspent, the excess will appear in the department's appropriation accounts and will be reported on to the Public Accounts Committee (see below) by the Comptroller and Auditor General. Subject to this report, the necessary provision is sought in an Excess Vote.

Cash Limits

The Government establishes cash limits on just over 60 per cent of Supply expenditure—expenditure financed out of money voted by Parliament in the Supply Estimates. The imposition of cash limits indicates that the Government intends to avoid extra provision for programmes even in the event of unexpected increases in costs. In such circumstances the Government will seek to re-order priorities or take offsetting action so that the cash limit is not exceeded, or a corresponding reduction will be made in another cash limit.

Expenditure not subject to a cash limit mainly finances demand-led services like some Department of Social Security benefits. In such cases, once policy and rates of payment are determined, expenditure depends on factors beyond the direct control of government—such as the number of eligible recipients and demographic factors. However, the Government still seeks to offset or minimise any non–cash-limited increases, in some cases by a reduction in cash-limited expenditure.

Changes in Government Accounting Procedures

Cash-based government accounts are being replaced by more commercial 'resource accounting' and budgeting methods, a process initially adopted in executive agencies and the National Health Service. Resource accounting took effect for most departments in April 1997 and will be extended to other departments in April 1998.

The new system is designed to bring improved efficiency and focus more on departmental objectives and outputs in terms of resources used rather than the money available for spending. Full information about the assets and liabilities of departments will become available from the resource accounts for 1998–99 onwards. All departments are compiling an asset register, to ensure the efficient use of government assets.

Examination and Audit of Public Expenditure

Examination of public expenditure is carried out by select committees of the House of Commons. These study in detail the activities of particular government departments and cross-examine ministers and officials.

The Public Accounts Committee considers the accounts of government departments, executive agencies and other public sector bodies, and reports by the Comptroller and Auditor General on departments and their use of resources. It submits reports to Parliament.

Audit of the Government's spending is exercised through the functions of the Comptroller and Auditor General, the head of the National Audit Office. The NAO's responsibilities include certifying the accounts of all government departments and executive agencies and those of a wide range of other public sector bodies; scrutinising the economy, efficiency and effectiveness of their operations; examining revenue accounts and inventories; and reporting the results of these examinations to Parliament.

MAIN SOURCES OF REVENUE

The main sources of revenue are:
● taxes on income (together with profits), which include personal income tax, corporation tax and petroleum revenue tax;

- taxes on capital, which include inheritance tax, capital gains tax, council tax and non-domestic rates;

- taxes on expenditure, which include VAT (value added tax) and customs and excise duties; and

- National Insurance contributions, which give entitlement to a range of benefits, including the Retirement Pension and Jobseeker's Allowance (see chapter 25).

Taxation Policy

The Government intends to develop a tax system that reflects, and is underpinned by, the following key principles:

- encouraging employment opportunities and work incentives for everyone;

- promoting savings and long-term investment;

- fairness; and

- a system which is seen to be fair.

Tax Measures in the 1997 Budget

The main tax changes in the Budget in July 1997 were:

- a windfall tax (see below) to provide the finance for the new Welfare-to-Work programme (see p. 173);

- measures to encourage long-term investment, including cuts in the main rate of corporation tax from 33 to 31 per cent and in the rate for small businesses from 23 to 21 per cent, both taking effect from April 1997, and abolition of payments of tax credits to pension schemes and British companies;

- measures for moving towards a fairer tax system—a reduction in the rate of VAT on fuel and power from 8 to 5 per cent, from September 1997, which will be financed by the abolition of tax relief on premiums for private medical insurance for those aged over 60 and a package of measures to tackle tax avoidance;

- measures to protect the environment and health; and

- measures to promote economic stability—a reduction in mortgage interest tax relief from 15 to 10 per cent, and an increase in the rate of stamp duty on transfers of property above £250,000.

Windfall Tax

The windfall tax is a one-off tax on the excess profits of the privatised utilities, payable in two instalments, in December 1997 and December 1998. The tax will apply to companies privatised by flotation and regulated by statute. It will be charged at a rate of 23 per cent on the difference between a company's value at flotation and the value calculated by reference to profits over a period of up to four years following privatisation.

The tax is expected to yield £5,200 million:

- around £2,100 million from the electricity sector;

- £1,650 million from the water industry; and

- £1,450 million from other companies: BAA, the successor companies to British Gas (BG and Centrica), BT and Railtrack.

Encouraging Long-term Investment

Changes to corporate taxation are designed to create a climate for long-term investment, and the cuts in the rates of corporation tax will enhance Britain's position as having the lowest corporate tax rate of a major industrialised country. Abolishing payment of tax credits to pension schemes and British companies is intended to remove a major distortion in the tax system. Other shareholders will generally not be affected by changes to tax credits until April 1999 when the rate of tax credits will halve to 10 per cent and tax credits will normally no longer be payable to other shareholders with no tax liability.

The change in April 1999 is designed to fit in with the introduction of the 'individual savings account' (ISA). This will extend the principles of TESSAs (Tax Exempt Special Savings Accounts) and PEPs (Personal Equity Plans) (see p. 244) to encourage people, through tax reliefs, to raise the level of their long-term savings. It will have a particular emphasis on encouraging those on low incomes to save.

Protecting the Environment and Health

The Government places a high priority on the use of the tax system to deliver its environmental objectives (see chapter 21). In line with these objectives, it is introducing higher duties on road fuel and tobacco:

- road fuel duties will now rise by 6 per cent a year in real terms; and
- tobacco duties will go up by at least 5 per cent a year in real terms.

From 1998 a lower level of vehicle excise duty will be applied to lorries and buses meeting low emission standards. The Government is also considering the case for environmental taxes on the extraction of aggregates and other quarrying (which will be examined in conjunction with an assessment of the landfill tax—see p. 166) and on water pollution.

Tax and Benefit Reform

In May 1997 the Government established a taskforce to consider streamlining and modernising the tax and benefit system in order to help increase employment opportunities and work incentives, reduce poverty and welfare dependency, and strengthen community and family life.

Tax Policy Reviews

A number of tax policy reviews are in progress, including reviews of:

- North Sea taxation;
- capital gains taxation;
- taxation on charities;
- anti-avoidance—leakage and avoidance of direct taxes; and
- alcohol and tobacco duties.

Collection of Taxes and Duties

The Inland Revenue assesses and collects taxes on income, profits and capital, and stamp duty. HM Customs and Excise collects the most important taxes on expenditure (VAT and most duties). Vehicle excise duty is the responsibility of the Department of the Environment, Transport and the Regions. National Insurance contributions are the responsibility of the Department of Social Security, although they are mainly collected by the Inland Revenue. The main local taxes—council tax and non-domestic rates (see p. 167)—are collected by local authorities.

Taxes on Income

Income Tax

Taxes on individual incomes are generally progressive in that larger incomes are subject to a greater amount of tax. Income tax is imposed for the year of assessment beginning on 6 April. The tax rates and bands for 1996–97 and 1997–98 are shown in Table 11.9 and apply to total income, including earned and investment income. The Government has announced that it will not raise the basic and upper rates of income tax—23 and 40 per cent respectively—in the current Parliament. It has also announced its long-term objective of introducing a lower starting rate of tax of 10 per cent. Of nearly 26 million income taxpayers, around 7.2 million are expected to pay only lower rate tax in 1997–98, about 16.2 million will be basic rate taxpayers and 2.2 million will be in the higher rate tax band.

Allowances and reliefs reduce an individual's income tax liability, and the main allowances are shown in Table 11.9. All taxpayers are entitled to a personal allowance against income from all sources. In addition, there is a married couple's allowance, which may be allocated to either partner, or they may receive half each. Wives have the right to receive half the allowance. Tax relief for some allowances, including the married couple's allowance, is restricted to 15 per cent.

Among the most important reliefs is that for mortgage interest payments on borrowing for house purchase up to a limit of £30,000. Relief, which is limited to 15 per cent (10 per cent from April 1998), is usually given 'at source', that is, repayments which the borrower makes to the lender are reduced to take account of tax relief and the tax refund is passed directly by the tax authorities to the

Table 11.9: Tax Bands and Allowances £

	1996–97	1997–98
Income tax allowances:		
Personal allowance	3,765	4,045
Married couple's allowance, additional personal allowance and widow's bereavement allowance[a]	1,790	1,830
Allowances for those aged 65–74:		
personal allowance	4,910	5,220
married couple's allowance[a]	3,115	3,185
Allowances for those aged 75 and over:		
personal allowance	5,090	5,400
married couple's allowance[a]	3,155	3,225
Income limit for age-related allowances	15,200	• 15,600
Blind person's allowance	1,250	1,280
Bands of taxable income:		
Lower rate of 20 per cent	0–3,900	0–4,100
Basic rate[b]	3,901–25,500	4,101–26,100
Higher rate of 40 per cent	over 25,500	over 26,100

Source: HM Treasury

[a] Tax relief for these allowances is restricted to 15 per cent. The additional personal allowance may be claimed by a taxpayer who is single, separated, divorced or widowed and who has a child at home.

[b] Basic rate is 24 per cent for 1996–97 and 23 per cent for 1997–98.

lender rather than to the individual borrower. Employees' contributions to their pension schemes also qualify for tax relief.

In general, income tax is charged on all income which originates in Britain—although some forms of income are exempt, such as child benefit—and on all income arising abroad of people resident in Britain. Britain has entered into agreements with many countries to provide relief from double taxation; where such agreements are not in force, unilateral relief is often allowed. British residents working abroad for the whole year may benefit from 100 per cent tax relief.

Most wage and salary earners pay their income tax under a Pay-As-You-Earn (PAYE) system whereby tax is deducted and accounted for to the Inland Revenue by the employer, in a way which enables most employees to pay the correct amount of tax during the year.

A new self-assessment system for collecting personal taxation has been introduced. The first 'new style' tax returns were sent out in April 1997 to around 8 million people who regularly complete a tax return—primarily higher-rate taxpayers, the self-employed and those receiving investment income

(particularly where this is paid without tax being deducted). Taxpayers are now able to calculate their own tax liability, although they can choose to have the calculations done by the Inland Revenue. There is a new legal requirement to keep records of income and capital gains from all sources.

Corporation Tax

The rates of company tax in Britain are lower than in most other industrialised countries. Companies pay corporation tax on their income and capital gains after deduction of certain allowances and reliefs. A company which distributes profits to its shareholders is required to pay advance corporation tax (ACT) on these distributions to the Inland Revenue. ACT is set against the company's liability to corporation tax, subject to a limit. Shareholders (except pension schemes and companies) resident in Britain receiving distributions from British-resident companies are treated as having some or all of their liability to income tax satisfied for such income.

The main rate of corporation tax is 31 per cent, with a reduced rate of 21 per cent for small companies (those with profits below £300,000 in a year). Relief is allowed for companies with profits between £300,000 and £1.5 million, so that the company's overall rate is between the main rate and the small companies' rate. Some capital expenditure may qualify for relief in the form of capital allowances. Examples include expenditure on machinery and plant, industrial buildings, agricultural buildings and scientific research. Expenditure on machinery or plant by small or medium-sized businesses qualifies for a first-year allowance, normally of 50 per cent if expenditure is incurred in the year to July 1998.

Petroleum Revenue Tax

Petroleum revenue tax (PRT), deductible in computing profits for corporation tax, is charged on profits from the production—as opposed, for example, to the refining—of oil and gas in Britain and on its Continental Shelf under licence from the Department of Trade and Industry. Each licensee of an oilfield or gasfield is charged at a rate of 50 per cent on the profits from that field after deduction of certain allowances and reliefs. New fields given consent for development on or after 16 March 1993 and gas from certain fields sold under contracts negotiated before 1975 are not liable to PRT.

Taxes on Capital

Taxes on capital include capital gains tax (CGT) and inheritance tax. A review of CGT is in progress, partly with the aim of examining the case for measures to encourage long-term holding of assets. It is expected to be completed in time for any changes to be announced in the 1998 Budget.

Capital Gains Tax

Capital gains tax is payable by individuals and trusts on gains realised from the disposal of assets. It is payable on the amount by which total chargeable gains for a year exceed the exempt amount (£6,500 for individuals and £3,250 for trusts in 1997–98). For individuals, CGT is calculated at income tax rates, as if the amount were additional taxable income, while there are special rates for trusts. Only gains arising since 1982 are subject to tax. Indexation relief is given to take account of the effects of inflation. Gains on some types of asset are exempt from CGT. These include the principal private residence, government securities, certain corporate bonds, and gains on shares and corporate bonds owned under PEPs.

For companies capital gains are charged to corporation tax, although there is no annual exempt amount.

Inheritance Tax

Inheritance tax is essentially charged on estates at the time of death and on gifts made within seven years of death; most other lifetime transfers are not taxed. There are several important exemptions. Generally, transfers between spouses are exempt, and gifts and bequests to British charities, major political parties and heritage bodies are also normally exempt. In general, business assets and farmland are exempt from inheritance tax, so that most family businesses can be passed on without a tax charge.

Tax is charged at a single rate of 40 per cent above a threshold, currently £215,000. Only about 2 per cent of estates a year become liable for an inheritance tax bill.

Taxes on Expenditure

Value Added Tax

VAT is a broadly based expenditure tax, with a standard rate of 17.5 per cent and a reduced rate of 5 per cent on domestic fuel and power. It is collected at each stage in the production and distribution of goods and services by taxable persons. The final tax is payable by the consumer.

The annual level of turnover above which traders must register for VAT is £48,000 (£49,000 from December 1997). Certain goods and services are relieved from VAT, either by being charged at a zero rate or by being exempt.

● Under zero rating, a taxable person does not charge tax to a customer but reclaims any input tax paid to suppliers. Among the main categories where zero-rating applies are goods exported to other countries; most food; water and sewerage for non-business use; domestic and international passenger transport; books, newspapers and periodicals; construction of new residential buildings; young children's clothing and footwear; drugs and medicines supplied on prescription; specified aids for handicapped people; and certain supplies by or to charities.

- For exempt goods or services, a taxable person does not charge any output tax but is not entitled to reclaim the input tax. The main categories where exemption applies are many supplies of land and buildings; insurance and other financial services; postal services; betting; gaming (with certain important exceptions); lotteries; much education and training; and health and welfare.

Customs Duties

Customs duties are chargeable on goods from outside the EU in accordance with its Common Customs Tariff. Goods can move freely across internal EU frontiers without making customs entries at importation or stopping for routine fiscal checks. For commercial consignments, excise duty and VAT are charged in the member state of destination, at the rate in force in that state.

Excise Duties

Mineral oils used as road fuel are subject to higher rates of duty than those used for other purposes, although there are reduced rates to encourage the use of more environmentally friendly fuels, such as unleaded petrol, ultra low sulphur diesel, and gas used as road fuel. Kerosene not used as road fuel, most lubricating oils and oils used for certain industrial, horticultural and marine uses are free of duty. Fuel substitutes are taxed at the same rate as the corresponding mineral oil. There are duties on spirits, beer, wine, made-wine (wine with added constituents, such as fruit juice), cider and perry, charged according

to alcoholic strength and volume. Spirits used for scientific, medical, research and industrial processes are generally free of duty. Cigarette duty is charged partly as a cash amount per cigarette and partly as a percentage of retail price. Duty on other tobacco products is based on weight.

Duties are charged on off-course betting, pool betting, gaming in casinos, bingo and amusement machines. Rates vary with the particular form of gambling. Duty is levied either as a percentage of gross or net stakes or, in the case of amusement machines, as a fixed amount per machine according to the cost of playing and the prize level. On the National Lottery (see pp. 47–8) there is a 12 per cent duty on gross stakes, but no tax on winnings.

Annual vehicle excise duty (VED) on a privately owned motor car, light van or taxi with fewer than nine seats will rise by £5 to £150 for licences taken out after 15 November 1997. The duty on goods vehicles is levied on the basis of gross weight and, if over 12 tonnes, according to the number of axles; it is designed to ensure that such vehicles at least cover their share of the full costs of road use through the tax paid (VED and fuel duty). Duty on taxis and buses varies according to seating capacity, and duty on motorcycles according to engine capacity. Privately owned vehicles over 25 years old—cars, taxis, motorcycles and non-commercial vehicles— are exempt from VED. A review of VED is in progress in connection with the development of the Government's integrated transport policy (see p. 304).

Other taxes include:

- insurance premium tax chargeable at 4 per cent on all types of taxable insurance risk in Britain (unless specifically exempted) or at 17.5 per cent on certain premiums charged in relation to the sale or hire of relevant goods and services;

- air passenger duty of £5 for flights to internal destinations and to those in the European Economic Area and £10 elsewhere (£10 and £20 respectively from 1 November 1997); and

- a landfill tax of £2 a tonne on inactive waste (such as bricks) which does not

decay or contaminate land, and £7 a
tonne on other waste.

Stamp Duty

Certain kinds of transfer are subject to stamp
duty. Transfers of shares attract duty at 0.5
per cent of the cost, while certain instruments,
such as declarations of trust, have small fixed
duties of 50p or £1. Transfers by gift and
transfers to charities are exempt. The July
1997 Budget raised the rate of stamp duty on
the transfers of property (except shares) over
£250,000, in order to encourage stability in
the housing market. Duty is now payable at 1
per cent of the total price above £60,000, 1.5
per cent for property above £250,000 and 2
per cent for property where the price exceeds
£500,000.

Other Revenue

National Insurance Contributions

There are five classes of National Insurance
contribution:

- Class 1—paid by employees and their
  employers;
- Class 1A—paid by employers on the cash
  equivalent of the benefit of cars and fuel
  provided to their employees for private
  use;
- Class 2—paid by the self-employed;
- Class 3—paid voluntarily for pension
  purposes; and
- Class 4—paid by self-employed people
  on their taxable profits between £7,010
  and £24,180 a year (in addition to their
  Class 2 contribution).

Details of the rates of contribution are
given in chapter 25 on pp. 423–4.

Local Authority Revenue

Local authorities in Great Britain have four
main sources of revenue income: grants from
central government; council tax; non-domestic
rates (sometimes known as business rates); and
sales, fees and charges. About 80 per cent of
expenditure (excluding sales, fees and charges)
is financed by government grants and
redistributed non-domestic rates.

Non-domestic rates are a tax on the
occupiers of non-domestic property. The
rateable value of property is assessed by
reference to annual rents and reviewed every
five years. The non-domestic rate is set
nationally by central government and collected
by local authorities. It is paid into a national
pool and redistributed to local authorities in
proportion to their population.

Domestic property in Great Britain is
generally subject to the council tax. Each
dwelling is allocated to one of eight valuation
bands, based on its capital value (the amount it
might have sold for on the open market) in
April 1991. Discounts are available for
dwellings with fewer than two resident adults,
and those on low incomes may receive council
tax benefit of up to 100 per cent of the tax bill
(see p. 432).

In Northern Ireland, rates—local domestic
property taxes based on the value of the
property—are collected by local authorities.

GOVERNMENT FINANCIAL OPERATIONS

Debt Management

The Government funds its borrowing
requirement by selling debt to the private
sector. There has been a steady increase in
government debt during the 1990s, and in
1996–97 net public sector debt was £350,000
million, 45 per cent of GDP, as against 27 per
cent in 1990–91. From 1997–98 the burden of
debt is expected to fall as government
borrowing declines substantially.

The funding requirement for 1997–98 is
forecast to be about £28,100 million, of which
National Savings products (see p. 240) are
assumed to contribute about £3,000 million,
with gilt-edged stock contributing the balance.

Gilt-edged Stock

The major debt instrument, government
bonds, is known as gilt-edged stock ('gilts') as
there is no risk of default. Gilts are marketable
and widely traded; holdings of gilts total over

> Among the criteria for participating in the single currency under the Maastricht Treaty (see p. 125) are reference values for a government's financial deficit and its debt. Britain expects to meet both these criteria in 1997, with the general government financial deficit forecast to be 2 per cent of GDP, compared with the reference value of 3 per cent, while the gross public sector debt ratio (which is expected to have peaked at nearly 55 per cent of GDP in 1996–97) is forecast to be below the Maastricht level of 60 per cent.

£270,000 million. Pension funds and life insurance companies have the largest holdings. The Government publishes an annual debt management report which sets out the framework for issuing gilts in the coming year. Gilts are currently sold by the Bank of England on the Government's behalf. Under the proposed reforms of the Bank (see p. 235), this role will be transferred to the Treasury in 1998.

Gilt issues are primarily by auction (broadly monthly), supplemented by ad hoc 'tap' sales. Gilts include 'conventionals', which pay fixed rates of interest and redemption sums; index-linked stocks, on which principal and interest are linked to movements in the Retail Prices Index; and floating-rate gilts, with payments linked to short-term interest rates. A series of changes has been implemented to increase the efficiency and liquidity of the gilts market, so enhancing the overall efficiency of Britain's financial system. Among these was a new open sale and repurchase ('repo') market in gilts, launched in 1996, while a market for gilt 'strips' will start in December 1997.

Bills

Sterling Treasury bills are sold at a weekly tender; the majority have a maturity of three months. These are used to manage the money markets and meet the weekly cash needs of the Government, rather than to meet its annual borrowing needs. The Government also issues bills denominated in European Currency Units (ECUs).[1] The proceeds are added to the official foreign exchange reserves rather than being used to finance public expenditure.

---

[1] The ECU is a composite currency consisting of specified amounts of each EU currency.

Further Reading

Debt Management Report, annual report, HM Treasury.

Financial Statement and Budget Report, annual report, The Stationery Office.

United Kingdom National Accounts, annual report, The Stationery Office.

12 Employment

The labour market in Britain has undergone major changes in recent years, notably with more women in the workforce, increased levels of part-time working and the continuing move towards employment in service industries. Over three-quarters of employees now work in the service sector, compared with less than one-fifth in manufacturing. With the growth in economic activity, unemployment has fallen since the end of 1992, although it remains above the long-term average. The Government's policy is focusing on the need for a skilled, trained and adaptable labour force and flexible labour market, supported by minimum standards of fairness and decency. Health and safety at work has improved, with fatalities from accidents at work at a historically low level.

PATTERNS OF EMPLOYMENT

There were 28.8 million people classed as economically active in Britain in spring 1997. The number in employment totalled 26.8 million (see Table 12.1), of whom 23.1 million (12.1 million men and 11 million women) were classed as employees. Employment is growing again following a decline during the recession of the early 1990s, but remains below the pre-recession peak in spring 1990. Since winter 1992–93 (the most recent employment trough) employment in Great Britain has grown by almost 1.2 million.

Two main long-term trends have been the growing number of women in the workforce and the move from full-time to part-time jobs (see charts on p. 171):

- Women now comprise 44 per cent of all those in employment in Britain, and a higher proportion of employees (47 per cent) than of the self-employed (25 per cent).

- Since 1987 part-time employment in Great Britain has risen by 24 per cent, to over 6.5 million in summer 1997: nearly 5.3 million women and almost 1.3 million men. About 45 per cent of women were working part-time, compared with 9 per cent of men.

About 1.2 million people in Great Britain in spring 1997 had two or more jobs, while around 1.8 million were engaged in temporary jobs. The main reason for people working in temporary jobs is that they cannot find a permanent one, although a significant number prefer a temporary job. Temporary workers included 861,000 on fixed-period contracts, 332,000 on casual work and 227,000 doing temporary work for an employment agency.

There has been considerable interest in Britain recently in labour market statistics. In May 1997, the Office for National Statistics (ONS) initiated wide public consultation on how these statistics should be presented in future. The consultation revealed that most people supported ONS's plans:

- to provide a more coherent and rounded picture of the labour market by publishing statistics in an integrated format;
- to give greater prominence to data from the Labour Force Survey (LFS), whose estimate of those unemployed is in line with the International Labour Organisation's definition; and
- in addition to unemployment data, to provide statistics on those who are not unemployed as such, but are economically inactive and would like a job.

Contracting out by firms of specialist and non-core functions has increased. 'Teleworking'—people working from home using information technology—is also becoming more widespread, for example, in journalism, consultancy and computer programming.

Over 3.3 million people are self-employed in Britain, 7 per cent more than in 1987 but below the peak level in 1990. Agriculture and fishing, and construction have the highest proportions of self-employed people, while relatively few of those engaged in manufacturing and public administration are self-employed. Around 17 per cent of men and 7 per cent of women in employment are self-employed.

Occupational Changes

There has been a gradual move away from manual to non-manual occupations, which are now held by 61 per cent of people in employment in Great Britain. Over half of non-manual workers are women. Self-employment is highest in craft and related occupations (28 per cent of self-employed in Great Britain in spring 1997), followed by managers and administrators (24 per cent).

Employment by Sector

As in other industrialised countries, there has been a marked shift in jobs from manufacturing to service industries (see Table 12.2). In the last 40 years the proportion of employees in employment engaged in service industries has more than doubled, to 76 per cent. In June 1997 there were 16.8 million employees in the service sector in Great Britain, about 2.3 million more than in 1987 (see Table 12.3). Business activities, distribution, hotels and restaurants, education, medical services and social work experienced significant increases. Some new services, such as call centres, have developed. Not all services have grown, with employment having fallen in areas such as the Civil Service, defence and retail banking.

Table 12.1: Employment in Britain				*Thousands, seasonally adjusted, spring*	
	1987[a]	1992	1995	1996	1997
Employees	21,355	22,077	22,251	22,619	23,065
Self-employed	3,058	3,227	3,361	3,294	3,348
Work-related government-supported training programmes[a]	509	377	284	248	219
Unpaid family workers	n.a.	181	140	127	118
Employment	**24,930**	**25,862**	**26,036**	**26,288**	**26,751**

Source: Office for National Statistics: Labour Force Survey
[a] Not seasonally adjusted.
n.a. = not available.

Full- and Part-time Employment in Great Britain, Seasonally Adjusted

Full-time

Men

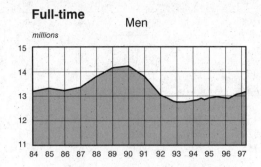

Women

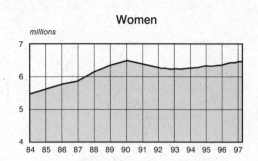

Part-time

Men

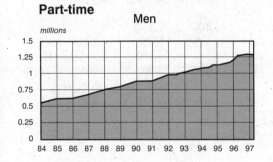

Women

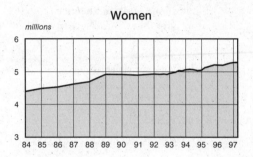

Note: Data are for spring quarters only for 1984–91 and are for every quarter for 1992 onwards. Data from spring 1992 contain unpaid family workers.

Source: *Labour Market Trends*

Table 12.2: Employees by Main Sector in Britain (at June)

	1992	1995	1996	1997
Thousands				
Service industries	16,199	16,606	16,939	17,263
Manufacturing industries	4,096	4,026	4,068	4,111
Mining, energy and water supply	344	240	241	251
Other industries	1,265	1,115	1,093	1,166
Per cent of employees				
Service industries	74.0	75.5	75.8	75.7
Manufacturing industries	18.7	18.3	18.2	18.0
Mining, energy and water supply	1.6	1.1	1.1	1.1
Other industries	5.8	5.1	4.9	5.1

Source: Office for National Statistics: employees in employment series

Table 12.3: Employees in Employment in Services in Great Britain

Thousands: seasonally adjusted, June

	1987	1992	1995	1996	1997
Wholesale and retail trade, and repairs	3,291	3,521	3,631	3,688	3,845
Hotels and restaurants	993	1,174	1,204	1,240	1,249
Transport and storage	832	887	856	843	827
Postal services and telecommunications	436	446	423	431	473
Financial services	920	991	985	957	1,018
Real estate	165	205	260	265	284
Renting, research, computer and other business activities	1,846	2,158	2,348	2,556	2,617
Public administration, defence and compulsory social security	1,436	1,406	1,347	1,338	1,308
Education	1,680	1,774	1,781	1,786	1,777
Health activities	1,332	1,513	1,519	1,490	1,504
Social work activities	767	846	903	961	973
Other community, social and personal activities	852	894	928	958	956
All services	**14,549**	**15,808**	**16,184**	**16,515**	**16,830**

Source: Office for National Statistics: employees in employment series

Most other sectors—manufacturing, construction, agriculture, and mining, energy and water supply—have experienced lower levels of employment. Traditional manufacturing industries, such as steel and shipbuilding, have recorded particularly large falls in employment, while employment in mining, energy and water supply has fallen by 38 per cent in the 1990s. By 1997 manufacturing accounted for 18 per cent of employees in employment, compared with 42 per cent in 1955. In June 1997 employment in the main manufacturing sectors in Great Britain included:

- 712,000 employees in non-metallic mineral products, metal and metal products;
- 493,000 in electrical and optical equipment;
- 461,000 in paper, pulp, printing, publishing and recording media;
- 430,000 in food products, beverages and tobacco; and
- 361,000 in clothing, textiles, leather and leather products.

Unemployment

Unemployment in Britain has fallen considerably since the peak at the end of 1992, and is now lower than in many other European countries. However, it remains above the levels which prevailed during the post-war years up to the end of the 1970s. The level of unemployment in summer 1997 was just under 2 million in Great Britain, according to the International Labour Organisation (ILO) definition of unemployment, measured by the LFS. There were 1.6 million people claiming Jobseeker's Allowance in Britain in June 1997.

Although there is a significant difference, both measures show a downward trend in unemployment. ILO unemployment has declined in all regions—in summer 1997 it ranged from 5.1 per cent in the South East (outside London) to 10.4 per cent in Merseyside. However, over 690,000 people in Great Britain in summer 1997 had been unemployed for more than a year, and the unemployment rate for those under 25 is almost double the overall rate of unemployment. In addition, the LFS identified around 2.5 million people classed as economically inactive who say that they would like a job.

LABOUR MARKET POLICY

There are four key aspects to the Government's labour market policies: the Welfare-to-Work programme, education and training, a national minimum wage and its employability initiative.

Welfare-to-Work

The Government's Welfare-to-Work programme is a series of measures designed to tackle youth and long-term unemployment, promote employability and develop skills, and move people from welfare into jobs. The programme is being funded by a windfall tax on the excess profits of the privatised utilities (see p. 162). Some £5,200 million will be invested in the programme, in a number of 'New Deals' including:

- £3,150 million for young people;
- £350 million for the long-term unemployed;
- £200 million for lone parents;
- £1,300 million for schools; and
- £200 million for people with disabilities.

Young Unemployed

From January 1998 in 13 'pathfinder' areas and from April 1998 nationally, the New Deal for young people will help those under 25 who have been unemployed for more than six months through four options:

- a job attracting a wage subsidy of £60 a week, payable to employers for up to six months;
- a work placement with a voluntary organisation;
- a six-month work placement with a new Environmental Task Force; and
- for those without basic qualifications, a place on a full-time education and training course, which might last for up to one year.

All the options will include an element of training. For each young person the programme will start with a 'Gateway' period of careers advice and intensive help with looking for work, and with training in the skills needed for the world of work. The programme is expected to help around 250,000 people.

Long-term Unemployed

The New Deal for the long-term unemployed will start in June 1998 when employers will receive a subsidy of £75 a week for six months if they employ anyone who has been unemployed for two years or longer.

Other Groups

The New Deal for Lone Parents will provide job search help, advice and training for lone parents whose youngest child is aged over five, and will be accompanied by measures to increase the supply of, and help with, childcare. In addition, the Government is developing proposals to help those who are disabled or on incapacity benefit who want training or work.

Education and Training

The Government has described education and training as its top priorities. It considers that they are central to ensuring that Britain meets the requirements of the rapidly changing world economy, and that the workforce has the necessary skills to adapt to the new opportunities. Its measures on education (see chapter 26) and on training are designed to help achieve high and stable levels of economic growth and employment.

Government proposals to improve training and to increase participation in training by both individuals and employers will be contained in a White Paper to be issued in autumn 1997.

Young People

The Government plans to ensure that all young people will have access to high-quality education and training. It intends to replace Youth Training (see p. 176) with a new programme, Target 2000. Young people will have two routes after 16: one based on school and college education, and a work-based route covering apprenticeship and training. In addition, under the Welfare-to-Work programme (see above) all young unemployed people will be guaranteed education and training opportunities, while those with poor basic skills will have the option of participating in full-time study on an approved course.

Lifelong Learning

To encourage individuals to invest in training and so maintain and enhance their skills, the Government is planning a number of measures, including Individual Learning Accounts and a new University for Industry (see chapter 26, p. 454).

Minimum Wage

The Government plans to introduce legislation for a statutory national minimum wage; all other modern industrialised countries have some form of comprehensive minimum wage-fixing machinery. The minimum wage is intended to remove the worst excesses of exploitation of low-paid workers and ensure greater fairness in the workplace. Sectors likely to be affected include those, such as retailing, catering and hairdressing, where there used to be wages councils setting statutory minimum pay.

An independent Low Pay Commission will recommend to the Government the level at which the national minimum wage might initially be set. Before making its recommendation, the Commission will undertake a wide-ranging consultation exercise, and take evidence on the issues surrounding the introduction of the national minimum wage. The Government will then set the level of the minimum wage, taking into account the prevailing economic circumstances.

Employability Initiative and Other International Aspects

The Government has announced that Britain will now play a full part in the direction of social affairs in Europe. Accordingly, it has ended Britain's opt-out from the European Union (EU) Agreement on Social Policy (the social chapter—see p. 127). Two measures have so far been adopted under the social chapter: directives on European works councils (see p. 182) and parental leave. Detailed arrangements for applying these two measures to Britain have still to be agreed, but the Government has undertaken to implement both directives within two years.

'Employability' will be an important theme when Britain holds the EU's presidency in the first half of 1998. In October 1997 the Chancellor of the Exchequer launched a British employment action plan to tackle British and European employment problems. The plan is part of the 'Getting Europe Back to Work' initiative and calls on the EU to focus its efforts in five broad areas:

- promoting economic growth and stability;
- investing in human capital;
- helping people from welfare into work;
- improving the workings of markets; and
- through these and other actions, creating a fair and inclusive society.

The Chancellor will also host a special G8 conference in Britain in 1998 when employability will be a key subject.

TRAINING, EDUCATION AND ENTERPRISE

According to the Labour Force Survey in spring 1997, nearly 3.2 million people received job-related training in the previous four weeks, 14 per cent of employees of working age. Training is highest for young workers, especially those between 16 and 24. Around 84 per cent of medium and large establishments provide off-the-job training for their employees.

Current government-supported training programmes are described in this section; a number of these are being reviewed.

National Training Organisations

A new network of National Training Organisations (NTOs) is gradually replacing industry training organisations, 'lead bodies' and occupational standards councils. The NTOs act as the focal point for training matters in their particular sector of industry, commerce or public service. Their role is to ensure that the skills needs of their sectors are being met and that occupational standards are being established and maintained for key occupations. There are 37 NTOs, covering sectors employing about 63 per cent of the workforce.

Training and Enterprise Councils

There are 79 Training and Enterprise Councils (TECs) in England and Wales. These are independent companies with employer-led boards. Their objective is to foster local economic development and stimulate employer investment in skills—in particular through the Investors in People standard (see below)—within their area. Their special focus is to strengthen the skills base and assist local training and enterprise programmes which are funded by the Government. They are also lead partners in many of the projects funded through the Single Regeneration Budget (see p. 371).

TECs are developing a new system of training inspection, to be introduced in April 1998, for publicly funded training qualifications, such as Modern Apprenticeships (see p. 176). They will also have an important role in the delivery of the New Deals for the unemployed (see p. 173).

TECs are accountable to the Government through their contracts. The Government Offices for the Regions are responsible for managing and overseeing the overall government contract with TECs.

Local Enterprise Companies

A separate network of 22 Local Enterprise Companies (LECs) exists in Scotland. These have wider-ranging responsibilities than the TECs, covering economic development and environmental improvement. LECs are also responsible for the delivery of the Government's national training programmes in Scotland but, unlike TECs, have no responsibility for work-related further

education. They run under contract to two non-departmental public bodies: Scottish Enterprise and Highlands and Islands Enterprise (see p. 197).

National Targets for Education and Training

The National Targets for Education and Training were launched by the Confederation of British Industry in 1991 and are supported by the Government and many national and local organisations, including NTOs, TECs and LECs, and other major education, training and employer bodies. The Targets aim to improve Britain's international competitiveness by raising standards and attainment levels in education and training.

The Targets, which relate to the end of the year 2000, cover both young people and the workforce as a whole. (For further details, see chapter 26, p. 450).

Investors in People

The Investors in People standard, introduced in 1991, provides a framework for employers to support their investment in people. It helps companies to improve their performance by linking the training and development of all employees directly to the achievement of business objectives. TECs and LECs provide advice and information to help organisations to work towards the standard.

Over 28,000 organisations, employing some 30 per cent of the workforce, have made a commitment to work towards the Investors in People standard. By mid-1997 more than 7,150 organisations had achieved the standard. Reported benefits include increased productivity, higher profits, lower rates of sickness and absenteeism, and improved morale. The Government is committed to making Investors in People the general standard across all British employers. It is looking particularly to see many more small businesses work towards the standard.

Training for Work

The Training for Work programme is designed to help unemployed and disadvantaged adults to find jobs through training and work experience. The programme is open to those aged 18 to 63 who have been unemployed for six months or longer, although some groups with special needs can join earlier. Training is carried out by training providers under contract with the local TEC or LEC. Each new trainee receives an individually adapted package of training and/or structured work activities.

National Training Awards

The National Training Awards are an annual competition designed to promote good training practice by example, rewarding those who have carried out exceptionally effective training. The competition was revised in 1997 to concentrate more on training by employers. In 1997, 92 awards were presented to national winners, who were selected from about 880 entrants.

Career Development Loans

Career development loans are available to help people to pay for vocational education or training in Great Britain. Loans of between £200 and £8,000 are provided through four major banks, and interest payments on the loans during training and for one month after training are funded by the Department for Education and Employment. The loans help to pay for courses lasting up to two years. More than 87,000 people have borrowed over £266 million through the programme since 1988 to pay for training.

Small Firms Training

The Small Firms Training Loans programme helps firms with 50 or fewer employees to meet a range of training-related expenses, including training consultancy. Loans of between £500 and £125,000 are available through seven major banks, and repayments can be deferred for up to 12 months.

Skills for Small Businesses is designed to help companies by training selected key workers—one per company—who then pass on their knowledge and expertise to other employees. Over 13,000 firms have participated in the programme since its launch in April 1995.

Improving the Training Market

The Improving the Training Market programme covers a range of activities funded by the Department for Education and Employment aimed at improving the quality, impact and cost-effectiveness of vocational education and training. Priority is being given to encouraging investment by individuals in learning, and supporting the implementation of new qualifications.

Training for Young People

The objectives of the two main youth programmes—Modern Apprenticeships and Youth Training—are to:

- provide participants with training leading to vocational qualifications at National Vocational Qualification/Scottish Vocational Qualification (NVQ/SVQ) levels 2 and 3 or above and with the broad-based skills necessary to become flexible and self-reliant employees; and
- meet the skill needs of the national and local economies.

The delivery of training is arranged through TECs and LECs. In Scotland, training for young people is arranged through the Skillseekers scheme.

Youth Training is due to be replaced by a new programme, Target 2000 (see p. 174). Meanwhile, new National Traineeships for training to NVQ levels 1 and 2, which will draw on the best features of the current arrangements, were phased in from September 1997 and will play an important part in Target 2000. They will offer a broad and flexible learning programme, including the key skills of communication, numeracy and information technology.

Modern Apprenticeships, which became fully operational in 1995, are designed to increase significantly the number of young people trained to technician, supervisory and equivalent levels. More than 100,000 young people have begun Modern Apprenticeships, which are in operation in over 70 industry sectors. Evaluation studies have found that Modern Apprenticeships are of high quality, are very popular and have met the expectations of both employers and young people.

Northern Ireland

The Training and Employment Agency, an executive agency within the Department of Economic Development, has primary responsibility for training and employment services. It aims to assist economic development and help people to find work through training and employment services delivered on the basis of equality of opportunity.

The Agency has encouraged the formation of a sector training council in each of the main sectors to advise on employers' training needs and develop sectoral training strategies. In addition, the Agency supports company training through its Company Development Programme and encourages management development by providing training programmes and seminars.

Northern Ireland has its own range of training and employment programmes for people seeking work. Its Jobskills programme is designed to raise skill levels—and is linked to the attainment of NVQs—and to enhance the employment prospects of school-leavers and unemployed adults. About 15,000 places are available in 1997–98. In order to combat the relatively high level of long-term unemployment in Northern Ireland, the Agency is spending £28.5 million in 1997–98 on its Action for Community Employment Scheme, a pilot Community Work Programme and on Enterprise Ulster (a statutory organisation which provides employment, training and work experience for adults, especially those aged 18 to 25 who have been unemployed for over three months). The Agency is reviewing its programmes in the light of the Welfare-to-Work programme.

RECRUITMENT AND JOB-FINDING

There are a variety of ways in which people find jobs. According to the Labour Force Survey in spring 1996, the main methods were:

- replying to advertisements in the national, local and specialist press (33 per cent), with a further 10 per cent answering other advertisements;
- visiting a Jobcentre or employment agency office (29 per cent);
- personal contacts (12 per cent); and
- direct approaches to employers (10 per cent).

About 16 per cent of employees changed jobs in 1996, according to a survey by the Confederation of British Industry. Turnover was higher for part-time workers (25 per cent) than for full-time workers (12 per cent). By industry sector, turnover was highest in retailing and wholesaling (39 per cent) and lowest in local government and manufacturing (7 per cent). Most people left their job voluntarily, although 22 per cent of full-time employees left because of redundancy.

Government Employment Services

The Government provides a range of services to jobseekers through the Employment Service, an executive agency of the Department for Education and Employment. These include:

- a network of local offices, at which people can find details of job opportunities;
- advice and guidance so that people can find the best route back into employment, for example, by training; and
- a range of special programmes.

The Employment Service has about 1,030 Jobcentres and a budget of £1,188 million for 1997–98. In 1996–97 it placed 1.7 million unemployed people into jobs and conducted some 7.3 million advisory interviews to help people find appropriate work or places on employment and training programmes.

Advisory Services

Through the main Jobcentre services, unemployed people have access to vacancies, employment advice and training opportunities. Employment Service advisers see all jobseekers when a claim is made for Jobseeker's Allowance (see p. 427) to assess their eligibility and to provide advice about jobs, training and self-employment opportunities. To receive the allowance, each unemployed person has to complete a Jobseeker's Agreement, which includes details of availability for work and the steps that he or she has agreed to take to find work. Unemployed people are required to attend a Restart advisory interview every six months, when an adviser reviews with the jobseeker his or her situation and, if appropriate, revises the Jobseeker's Agreement.

The Employment Service will be responsible for delivering the New Deal programmes for the young and long-term unemployed (see p. 173). It currently runs a variety of programmes. Among those for the long-term unemployed are:

- '1-2-1', a programme offering 180,000 opportunities in 1997–98, which is designed to provide intensive help with looking for jobs for those who have been unemployed for over a year;

- Jobplan, which provides guidance and other support to enable those unemployed for a year to assess their skills, qualities and training needs, and to act as an introduction to future job and training options;

- Jobclubs, where participants are given training and advice in job-hunting skills and have access to facilities to help an intensive job search;

- Restart courses, designed to rebuild self-confidence and motivation, and including help with job-hunting skills; and

- Project Work, which is aimed at people who have been unemployed for two years or more and who are aged between 18 and 50. It offers an intensive period of help in finding a job, followed by a period of practical work experience of benefit to the local community.

Help for People with Disabilities

Most disabled people assisted by the Employment Service are helped through its mainstream services, and have priority access to the main programmes for unemployed people. Services for people with disabilities who need more specialist help to get or keep a job are available through Disability Employment Advisers based in Jobcentres. The advisers are members of local integrated specialist teams—Placing Assessment and Counselling Teams.

These services include:

- the Access to Work programme, which helps people with disabilities to overcome barriers to employment; and

- the Supported Employment Programme, which supports jobs for over 22,000 people with severe disabilities. The programme helps people who are able to undertake meaningful employment, but who cannot obtain or retain jobs in open employment because of the severity of their disability and who have a limited productivity.

Employment Agencies

There are many private employment agencies, including several large firms with many branches. The total value of the market has been estimated at about £8,000 million a year.

The law governing employment agencies is less restrictive than in many other EU countries. However, agencies must comply with legislation which seeks to protect agency users, both workers and hirers, by creating a framework of minimum standards. The Department of Trade and Industry is responsible for investigating complaints.

TERMS AND CONDITIONS OF EMPLOYMENT

Employment Rights

Employment protection legislation provides a number of safeguards for employees. For example, most employees have a right to a written statement setting out details of the main conditions, including pay, hours of work and holidays. Employees with at least two years of continuous employment with their employer are entitled to lump-sum redundancy payments if their jobs cease to exist, and their employers cannot offer suitable alternative work. Where employers are insolvent, redundancy payments are met directly from the National Insurance fund.

Minimum periods of notice when employment is to be terminated are laid down for both employers and employees. Most employees who believe they have been unfairly dismissed have the right to complain to an industrial tribunal (see below), subject to the general qualifying period of two years' continuous service. If the complaint is upheld, the tribunal may make an order for re-employment or award compensation.

All pregnant employees have the right to 14 weeks' statutory maternity leave with their non-wage contractual benefits maintained, and protection against dismissal because of pregnancy.

Under the Disability Discrimination Act 1995, disabled people have the right not to be discriminated against in employment. Employers with 20 or more employees have a duty not to discriminate against disabled employees or applicants. A Code of Practice gives guidance to employers on the Act's requirements.

Legislation forbids any employment of children under 13 years of age, and employment in any industrial undertaking of children who have not reached the statutory minimum school-leaving age, with some exceptions for family undertakings. Some minor changes are planned to bring the law into line with the EC Directive on the Protection of Young People at Work. A permitted list of occupations would be set for those aged 13, and children would be required to have a period free from work during school holidays.

Equal Opportunities

The Race Relations Act 1976 makes it generally unlawful to discriminate on grounds of colour, race, nationality (including citizenship) or ethnic or national origin, in employment, training and related matters. The Department for Education and Employment's Race Relations Employment Advisory Service promotes those government policies aimed at combating racial discrimination in employment and at ensuring fair treatment and equality of opportunity in employment. Advisers provide employers with practical help in developing and implementing effective equal opportunity strategies.

The Sex Discrimination Act 1975, as amended, makes it generally unlawful in Great Britain to discriminate on grounds of sex or marital status when recruiting, training, promoting, dismissing or retiring staff. The Equal Pay Act 1970 makes it generally unlawful to discriminate between men and women in pay and other terms and conditions of employment. The Act was significantly extended in 1984 to meet EU requirements by providing for equal pay for work of equal value.

Practical advice to employers and others on the best arrangements for implementing equal opportunities policies in Great Britain is given in codes of practice from the Commission for Racial Equality and from the Equal Opportunities Commission (see p. 44). The Government is encouraging voluntary action by employers to increase the employment opportunities for women and supports the 'Opportunity 2000' campaign (see p. 43).

Similar legislation to that in Great Britain on equal pay and sex discrimination applies in Northern Ireland, and legislation on race relations was introduced in August 1997. Discrimination in employment on grounds of religious belief or political opinion is unlawful. The Fair Employment Commission (see p. 17) has the task of promoting equality of opportunity and investigating employment practices, with powers to issue legally enforceable directions. The Government is considering a report on employment equality by the Standing Advisory Commission on Human Rights (SACHR), issued in June 1997. The report has proposed changes to policies and procedures in education, training and other areas (see p. 17).

Industrial Tribunals

Industrial tribunals in Great Britain have jurisdiction over complaints on a range of employment rights, including unfair dismissal, redundancy pay, equal pay, and sex and race discrimination. They received 89,000 applications in 1996–97 and the number of cases continues to grow steadily.

The Government is supporting a Private Peer's Bill, now before Parliament, which would streamline industrial tribunal procedures and introduce new voluntary procedures to resolve disputes on employment rights. Industrial tribunals would be renamed employment tribunals to reflect their new role. An important aspect of the Bill concerns alternative means of resolving disputes, in particular provision to allow those involved in unfair dismissal disputes to opt for a binding arbitration scheme run by ACAS (see p. 184) which would be cheaper and less formal than going through tribunal procedures.

Northern Ireland has a separate tribunal system. Reform of tribunals there will take into account the SACHR's review and its recommendations on tribunals.

Earnings

According to the official New Earnings Survey, the average weekly earnings, unaffected by absence and including overtime payments, in Great Britain in April 1997 of full-time employees on adult rates were £368. Earnings were higher for non-manual employees (£407) than for manual employees (£293), with managerial and professional groups the highest paid. The sectors with the highest average weekly earnings are financial services (£494) and mining and quarrying (£474), while the sectors with the lowest earnings are hotels and restaurants, the manufacture of textiles and textile products, agriculture, hunting and forestry, and the retail trade.

Overtime and other additional payments are particularly important for manual employees, for whom such additional payments represented over one-fifth of earnings. About 50 per cent of manual employees and 19 per cent of non-manual employees received overtime payments.

In the year to August 1997 the underlying average increase in earnings in Great Britain was about 4.5 per cent, compared with a rise of 3.5 per cent in the Retail Prices Index.

Fringe Benefits

A variety of fringe benefits are used by employers to provide additional rewards to their employees, including schemes to encourage employee financial participation in their companies, pension schemes, private medical insurance, subsidised meals, company cars and childcare schemes.

Many employees are covered by pension schemes provided by their employers. Such benefits are more usual among clerical and professional employees than among manual workers. About 11 million people in Britain are active members of occupational pension schemes.

Company cars are provided for employees in a wide variety of circumstances. Around 1.7 million people have a company car available for private use and about half of these receive fuel for private motoring in their car.

Profit-related pay (PRP) schemes, which link part of pay to changes in a business's profits, have become more extensive. By the end of March 1997, some 14,500 PRP schemes were registered with the Inland Revenue, covering around 4.1 million people. Many companies have adopted employee share schemes, where employees receive free shares or options to buy shares at a discount from their employer without paying income tax.

Hours of Work

Most full-time employees have a basic working week of between 34 and 40 hours, and work a five-day week. When overtime is taken into account, average weekly hours worked by full-time employees on adult rates in Great Britain in April 1997 were 41.8 for men and 37.6 for women. More men than women work overtime, and those in manual occupations generally work more overtime than employees in non-manual jobs.

Both male and female full-time employees tend to work more hours than in other EU countries. Hours worked tend to be longest in agriculture, construction and transport and communications, and shortest in most service industries.

The Government intends to press ahead to implement the European Community (EC) directive on working time. The directive will apply to most sectors, with some exceptions, such as in the transport and offshore oil sectors. Legislation will set limits on maximum weekly working hours, place restrictions on night-time working, and create entitlements to minimum rest periods and paid annual leave.

Flexible working patterns are becoming more widespread, and are now followed by around one-fifth of employees. The most common aspect is flexible working hours, which were worked by 13 per cent of female and 9 per cent of male full-time employees in spring 1996.

Holidays with Pay

Holiday entitlements have generally been determined by negotiation. In spring 1996 the average paid holiday entitlement for full-time workers was just under five weeks. However, some employees, such as part-time and temporary employees, may have much less holiday entitlement. Under the EC's directive on working time, there will be provision for three weeks' paid holiday a year, rising to four weeks in 1999.

INDUSTRIAL RELATIONS

The structure of industrial relations in Britain has been established mainly on a voluntary basis. The system is based chiefly on the organisation of employees and employers into trade unions and employers' associations, and on freely conducted negotiations at all levels.

Trends in Bargaining and Pay

Some 8.1 million employees (37 per cent of employees) in Great Britain in 1996 were in workplaces covered by collective bargaining. Public sector employees are more likely than those in the private sector to be covered by collective bargaining, which is generally more prevalent in large establishments. Collective bargaining mainly concerns pay and working conditions, although there have been a number of examples of agreements covering job security and minimum employment standards.

The general trend, though, is for more negotiation to be conducted at a local level, although many large firms retain a degree of central control over the bargaining process. Industry-wide agreements in the private sector are often supplemented by local agreements in companies or factories (plant bargaining). Most medium and large employers make some use of performance-related pay systems such as profit-related pay and payment by results. Performance-related pay has also become much more widespread in the public sector.

Recently negotiated agreements have often featured greater flexibility in working practices, the adoption of integrated wage structures for manual and non-manual workers in 'single status' deals, and more emphasis on multiskilling and teamworking.

A new pay agreement for local government became effective in April 1997, covering some 1.3 million workers. It is thought to be the largest of its type in Britain. The agreement introduces equal status for manual and non-manual workers by the year 2000, establishes a minimum wage for the lowest paid workers, and provides for the same rights for part-time and temporary staff as for full-time employees.

Employee Involvement

The Government believes that the best companies recognise their employees as partners in the enterprise. Employers use a variety of methods of involving their employees in the running of the organisations in which they work. These methods include employee bulletins and reports, quality circles, suggestion schemes and attitude surveys as well as works councils and other forms of information and consultation mechanisms.

One of the EC measures which will eventually come into force in Britain following the acceptance of the social chapter is the

European Works Councils Directive, which will require firms with 1,000 or more employees and which operate in two or more member states to establish European-level information and consultation procedures. A number of the largest British-based multinational companies, such as Barclays Bank and ICI, have already set up European Works Councils, including their British workforce.

Trade Unions

Trade unions have members in nearly all occupations. They are widely recognised by employers in the public sector and in large firms and establishments. As well as negotiating pay and other terms and conditions of employment with employers, they provide benefits and services such as educational facilities, financial services, legal advice and aid in work-related cases. In recent years many unions have extended their range of services for members.

In 1996 there were 7.2 million trade union members in Great Britain, 20 per cent fewer than in 1989. During this period the proportion of employees who are union members fell from 39 to 31 per cent. The decline in membership was particularly noticeable where it has traditionally been high—among male employees, manual workers and those in production industries. Union membership is now at a similar level among manual and non-manual employees, having fallen much less in the latter group. It is now only slightly higher for men (33 per cent) than for women (29 per cent).

Rail transport has the highest proportion of union members, around 75 per cent of employees. Among female workers, banks and building societies have the highest level (56 per cent). Sectors with relatively few union members include agriculture, forestry and fishing, hotels and restaurants, and wholesaling.

Unison, with about 1.4 million members, is the biggest union in Britain, accounting for 17 per cent of all union members. Three other unions have over 500,000 members:

- the Transport and General Workers Union (with 897,000 members);

- GMB (740,000)—a general union with members in a range of public and private sector industries; and

- the Amalgamated Engineering and Electrical Union (726,000).

The number of unions has declined by around a third in the last 20 years, mainly as a result of mergers. At the end of 1996 there were 245 trade unions on the list maintained by the Certification Officer, who, among other duties, is responsible for certifying the independence of trade unions. To be eligible for entry on the list a trade union must show that it consists wholly or mainly of workers and that its principal purposes include the regulation of relations between workers and employers or between workers and employers' associations. A further 20 unions were known to the Certification Officer.

Trades Union Congress

In Britain the national body of the trade union movement is the Trades Union Congress (TUC), founded in 1868. Its affiliated membership comprises 74 trade unions, which together represent some 6.8 million people.

The TUC's objectives are to promote the interests of its affiliated organisations and to improve the economic and social conditions of working people. It deals with all general questions concerning trade unions, and provides a forum in which affiliated unions can collectively determine policy. There are six TUC regional councils for England and a Wales Trades Union Council. The annual Congress meets in September to discuss matters of concern to trade unionists. A General Council represents the TUC between annual meetings.

The TUC plays an active part in international trade union activity, through its affiliation to the International Confederation of Free Trade Unions and the European Trade Union Confederation. It also nominates the British workers' delegation to the annual International Labour Conference.

Scotland and Northern Ireland

Trade unions in Scotland also have their own national central body, the Scottish Trades

Union Congress, to which British unions usually affiliate their Scottish branches. Nearly all trade unions in Northern Ireland are represented by the Northern Ireland Committee of the Irish Congress of Trade Unions (ICTU). Most trade unionists in Northern Ireland are members of unions affiliated to the ICTU, while the majority also belong to unions based in Great Britain which are affiliated to the TUC. The Northern Ireland Committee of the ICTU enjoys a high degree of autonomy.

Legal Requirements

The Government's view is that there should be a suitable balance in industrial relations law, with minimum standards for the individual at work. It intends to retain the framework established by the previous Government. However, it plans to make a number of changes to the law. The main change will be a new right for a trade union to be recognised where a majority of the workforce vote in a ballot for representation by the union. Before introducing any changes, interested parties will be fully consulted.

Union Membership and Non-membership Rights

All individuals have the right under the law not to be dismissed or refused employment (or the services of an employment agency) because of membership or non-membership of a trade union. Individuals who believe that they have been dismissed or refused employment on such grounds may complain to an industrial tribunal. Employees who are union members also have the right not to have union membership subscriptions deducted from their pay without their authorisation.

The Conduct of Union Affairs

A trade union must elect every member of its governing body, its general secretary and its president. Elections must be held at least every five years and be carried out by a secret postal ballot under independent scrutiny.

A trade union may establish a political fund if it wishes to use its money for what the law

defines as 'political objects'. If a union wishes to set up a political fund, its members must first agree in a secret ballot a resolution adopting those political objectives as an aim of the union. The union must also ballot its members every ten years to maintain the fund. Union members have a statutory right to opt out of contributing to a political fund.

Union members have the right to inspect their union's accounting records and obtain an annual statement about its financial affairs.

Industrial Action

For a union to have the benefit of statutory immunity when organising industrial action, the action must be wholly or mainly in contemplation or furtherance of a trade dispute between workers and their own employer. Various other requirements must be met. For example, industrial action must not involve workers who have no dispute with their own employer (so-called 'secondary' action) or involve unlawful forms of picketing. Before calling for industrial action, a trade union must first obtain the support of its members in a secret postal ballot and must notify employers of its intention to conduct such a ballot.

Industrial Disputes

The number of days lost as a result of industrial action in 1994 and 1995 (see Table 12.4) were the lowest annual figures since records began in 1891. Disputes increased in 1996, reflecting increased strike rates in the transport, storage and communications sector, and in the education and public administration sectors. However, the number of days lost (1.3 million) remained below the levels in the 1970s and 1980s.

Employers' Organisations

Many employers in Britain are members of employers' organisations, some of which are wholly concerned with labour matters, although others are also trade associations concerned with commercial matters in general. With the move away from national pay bargaining, many employers' associations are tending to concentrate on areas such as supplying

Table 12.4: Industrial Disputes, 1986–96

	Working days lost (thousands)	Working days lost per 1,000 employees[a]	Workers involved (thousands)	Number of stoppages
1986	1,920	90	720	1,074
1991	761	34	176	369
1992	528	24	148	253
1993	649	30	385	211
1994	278	13	107	205
1995	415	19	174	235
1996	1,303	59	364	244

Source: Office for National Statistics.

[a] Based on the mid-year (June) estimates of employees in employment.

information for bargaining purposes and dealing with specialist issues. As with some of the larger trade unions, a number of employers' associations are increasingly concerned with legislation and other issues relating to Europe.

Employers' organisations are usually established on an industry basis rather than a product basis, for example, the Engineering Employers' Federation. A few are purely local in character or deal with a section of an industry or, for example, with small businesses; most are national and are concerned with the whole of an industry. In some of the main industries there are local or regional organisations combined into national federations. At the end of 1996, 110 listed and 115 unlisted employers' associations were known to the Certification Officer.

Most national organisations belong to the Confederation of British Industry (see p. 188), which represents directly or indirectly some 250,000 businesses.

Advisory, Conciliation and Arbitration Service

The Advisory, Conciliation and Arbitration Service (ACAS) is an independent statutory body with a general duty of promoting the improvement of industrial relations. ACAS aims to operate through the voluntary co-operation of employers, employees and, where appropriate, their representatives. Its main functions are collective conciliation, provision of arbitration and mediation facilities, advisory mediation services for preventing disputes and improving industrial relations through the

joint involvement of employers and employees, and the provision of a public enquiry service. ACAS also conciliates in disputes on individual employment rights.

In 1996 ACAS:

● received over 1,300 requests for collective conciliation, of which nearly half related to pay or other terms and conditions of employment, and handled 117 arbitration cases;

● received 100,400 individual conciliation cases, 10 per cent more than in 1995; and

● answered over 446,000 calls on employment-related matters through its public enquiry points.

In Northern Ireland the Labour Relations Agency, an independent statutory body, provides services similar to those provided by ACAS in Great Britain.

HEALTH AND SAFETY AT WORK

Health and safety standards in Britain are among the best in the world. There has been long-term decline in injuries to employees, reflecting improvements in safety, together with a change in industrial structure away from the traditional heavy industries, which tend to have higher risks. In 1995–96 the number of deaths for employees and the self-employed from accidents at work was 256, which represented a fatal accident rate of 1.0 per 100,000 workers. About 18 million working days a year are lost as a result of work-related injuries and 13 million from work-related illnesses.

The principal legislation is the Health and Safety at Work etc. Act 1974. It imposes general duties on everyone concerned with work activities, including employers, the self-employed, employees, and manufacturers and suppliers of materials for use at work. Associated Acts and regulations deal with particular hazards and types of work. Employers with five or more staff must prepare a written statement of their health and safety policy and bring it to the attention of their staff.

The Control of Substances Hazardous to Health Regulations 1988 (which were revised in 1994) constitute one of the most important sets of regulations made under the 1974 Act. They replaced a range of outdated legislation by a comprehensive and systematic approach to the control of exposure to virtually all substances hazardous to health.

Health and Safety Commission

The Health and Safety Commission (HSC) has responsibility for developing policy on health and safety at work in Great Britain, including proposals for new or revised regulations and approved codes of practice.

The HSC has advisory committees covering subjects such as toxic substances, genetic modification and the safety of nuclear installations. There are also several industry advisory committees, each covering a specific sector of industry.

Health and Safety Executive

The Health and Safety Executive (HSE) is the primary instrument for carrying out the HSC's policies and has day-to-day responsibility for enforcing health and safety law, except where other bodies, such as local authorities, are responsible. Its field services and inspections are carried out by the Field Operations Directorate. This incorporates the Factory, Agricultural and Quarries inspectorates, together with the regional staff of the Employment Medical Advisory Service and the Regional Specialist Groups, which provide technical support to the inspectorates.

The HSE's Directorate of Science and Technology provides technical advice on industrial health and safety matters. The Health and Safety Laboratory provides scientific and medical support and testing services, and carries out research.

In premises such as offices, shops, warehouses, restaurants and hotels, health and safety legislation is enforced by inspectors appointed by local authorities, working under guidance from the HSE. Some other official bodies work under agency agreement with the HSE.

Northern Ireland

The general requirements of the Northern Ireland health and safety legislation are broadly similar to those for Great Britain. They are enforced mainly by the Department of Economic Development and the Department of Agriculture through their health and safety inspectorates, although the district councils have an enforcement role similar to that of local authorities in Great Britain. There is a Health and Safety Agency, roughly corresponding to the HSC but without its policy-making powers, and an Employment Medical Advisory Service.

Further Reading

Employment. Aspects of Britain series, HMSO, 1994.
Labour Market Trends. Office for National Statistics. Monthly.

Annual Reports
Advisory, Conciliation and Arbitration Service. ACAS.
Certification Officer. Certification Office for Trade Unions and Employers' Associations.
Health and Safety Commission. HSC.

13 Industry

The health of British industry is vital to the wealth of the nation. The Government's key objective for business is to provide a stable economic environment, to encourage investment and enterprise, and to broaden the industrial base. In 1997 it launched an initiative on competitiveness, and is planning to introduce a new Competition Bill.

STRUCTURE AND ORGANISATION OF INDUSTRY

Private sector enterprises now account for by far the greater part of activity in the agricultural, manufacturing, construction, distributive, financial and other service sectors. Some 50 major public sector businesses, including gas, electricity supply, coal and telecommunications, have been privatised since 1979.

In some sectors, a small number of large companies and their subsidiaries are responsible for a substantial proportion of total production, for instance in the chemical, motor vehicle and aerospace industries. About 250 British industrial companies each have an annual turnover of over £500 million; 16 are among the top 25 European companies in terms of profitability. Among the biggest British-owned companies are BP, ICI, Glaxo Wellcome, British Aerospace, BT and GEC. Small firms with fewer than 100 staff provide over 50 per cent of the private sector workforce. Industries with the fastest growth rates in recent years are in the services sector, particularly finance, property, and professional and business services.

Legal Framework

All British companies are registered with the Registrar of Companies. Companies with a place of business or branch in Britain, but which are incorporated overseas, are also required to register. Legislation deals with capital structure, rights and duties of directors and members, and the preparation and filing of accounts (see p. 187). Most corporate businesses are 'limited liability' companies. The liability of members of a limited company is restricted to contributing an amount related to their shareholding (or to their guarantee where companies are limited by guarantee). In the case of unincorporated businesses, such as sole proprietorships or partnerships, individuals are personally liable for any business debts, except where a member of a partnership is a limited liability company or a limited member of a limited partnership. However, proposals for making limited liability partnerships available to regulated professions are being reviewed.

Companies may be either public or private. A company must satisfy certain conditions before it can become a public limited company (plc). It must:

- be limited by shares or guarantee and have a share capital;

- state in its memorandum of association that it is to be a public limited company;

- meet specified minimum capital requirements; and

- have as the suffix to its name the words 'public limited company' or 'plc'.

All other British companies are private companies and are generally prohibited from offering their shares to the public.

Industrial Financing

Over half of companies' funds for investment and other purposes is generated internally. Banks are the chief external source of finance, but companies have increasingly turned to equity finance. The main forms of short-term finance in the private sector are bank overdrafts, trade credit and factoring (making cash available to a company in exchange for debts owing to it).

Types of medium- and long-term finance include bank loans, mortgaging of property and the issue of shares and other securities to the public through the London Stock Exchange. The leasing of equipment may also be regarded as a form of finance. Other sources of funding for industry include government, the European Union (EU) and specialist financial institutions, such as financing and leasing, factoring, and venture capital companies.

Venture Capital

Venture capital provides long term equity capital for unquoted companies which are starting up or expanding as well as those undergoing management buy-outs and buy-ins. It is available principally from venture capital firms. The British Venture Capital Association has 101 full members, which represent virtually every major source of venture capital in Britain. During 1996, £3,239 million was invested by British venture capital companies in 1,200 businesses; of this, over £2,800 million was invested in Britain. Some 49 per cent of venture capital deals were

in expansion-stage companies; 74 per cent of the total amount was invested in management buy-outs and buy-ins.

'Business angels' (private investors) are an increasingly important source of smaller amounts of early-stage venture capital. The Enterprise Investment Scheme (EIS) and Venture Capital Trusts (VCTs) seek to encourage individuals to invest in smaller unlisted trading companies in return for various tax reliefs. Introduced in 1994 and 1995 respectively, the EIS and VCTs are designed to help smaller early-stage and expanding firms. The EIS allows business angels to take a position on the board of the investee company. VCTs are similar to an investment trust and are quoted on the Stock Exchange; they are more suited to less active investors.

Taxation

The rates of corporation tax were reduced in the July 1997 Budget (see p. 162) in order to promote greater long-term investment and reduce the tax burden on smaller companies. The main rate of corporation tax was lowered from 33 to 31 per cent, and for small firms (those with annual profits of less than £300,000) the rate was brought down from 23 to 21 per cent. For companies with profits of between £300,000 and £1.5 million, the overall corporation tax rate is between the main rate and the rate for small firms. Expenditure on business plant and machinery, industrial building, and scientific research qualifies for annual allowances against profit for tax purposes.

Company Law

Laws relating to companies are designed to meet the need for proper regulation of business, to maintain open markets and to create safeguards for those wishing to invest in companies or do business with them. They take account of EC (European Community) directives on company law, and on company and group accounts and their auditing.

The Stock Exchange requires firms to state whether they are complying with a Code of Best Practice, recommended in 1992 by the

Cadbury Committee Report on the management of companies, and give reasons for areas of non-compliance. Shareholders, including institutional shareholders, are encouraged by the Government to play a more active role in overseeing management. Insider dealing in shares is a criminal offence and inspectors may be appointed to investigate possible occurrences of it. A licensing procedure helps guarantee the professional competence, integrity and independence of people acting as trustees of bankrupt individuals, or as liquidators, receivers or administrators of insolvent companies.

Industrial Associations

The Confederation of British Industry (CBI) is the largest employers' organisation in Britain, representing about 250,000 companies. Most national employers' organisations, trade associations, and some chambers of commerce are also members. The CBI aims to ensure that the Government, national and international institutions and the general public understand the needs, intentions and problems of business. It campaigns to lessen the administrative and regulatory burdens on business, tackle handicaps on competition, and improve the performance of companies. It offers members a forum, a lobby and a range of advisory services. The CBI also conducts surveys of activity in manufacturing, distribution, financial services, the regions, property, innovation, and pay and productivity. It has 13 regional offices and an office in Brussels. The CBI is the British member of the Union of Industrial and Employers' Confederations of Europe.

Chambers of commerce represent business views to the Government at national and local levels. They promote local economic development, for example, through regeneration projects, tourism, inward investment promotion and business services, including overseas trade missions, exhibitions and training conferences. The Association of British Chambers of Commerce, representing about 100,000 businesses, provides commercial and export-related services and publishes business surveys. The Institute of

Directors (IOD) has 27,400 members in Britain, many of whom are from small businesses. It provides business advisory services on matters affecting company directors, such as corporate management, insolvency and career counselling, and represents the interests of members to authorities in Britain and the EU.

The Federation of Small Businesses is the main organisation representing the interests of the self-employed and small firms. The Federation advances the cause of more than 90,000 small businesses, raises public awareness of its members' issues, and supplies information on subjects such as employment, environment, Europe, finance and taxation.

Trade associations represent companies producing or selling a particular product or group of products. They exist to supply common services, regulate trading practices and represent their members in dealings with government departments.

Nationalised Industries

The remaining major nationalised industries are the Post Office, London Transport, and the Civil Aviation Authority. Managing boards are appointed by ministers, who have power to give general directions but are not engaged in day-to-day management. Managing boards and staffs of nationalised industries are not civil servants.

The nationalised industries are required to act as commercial enterprises and are expected to conform to specific guidelines. These involve:

- clear government objectives;
- regular corporate plans and performance reviews;
- agreed principles relating to investment and pricing;
- financial and performance targets;
- external financing limits; and
- systematic monitoring.

The Government is reviewing the future status of London Transport and the Civil Aviation Authority, and options for granting the Post Office greater commercial freedom.

GOVERNMENT POLICY

The Department of Trade and Industry (DTI) is the department mainly responsible for the Government's relations with industry and commerce. Specific areas of responsibility which are dealt with in this chapter include company law, small firms, competition policy and consumer affairs, intellectual property, regional industrial development and inward investment. The Department of the Environment, Transport and the Regions oversees provision of regional industrial aid through the Government Offices for the Regions (see p. 6). The Scottish, Welsh and Northern Ireland Offices are responsible for industrial policies in their areas. Export promotion, and technology and innovation, which are also part of the DTI's remit, are dealt with in chapters 14 and 20 respectively. The DTI's duties regarding industrial relations are covered in chapter 12.

DTI Aims

The DTI seeks to work in partnership with businesses and the scientific community to achieve excellence in science and to support the endeavours of business to become as competitive as possible, so expanding the country's wealth, and providing employment.

On its side of the partnership, the DTI aims to:

- promote open and competitive markets at home and abroad;
- encourage the development of a skilled and flexible labour market founded on the principle of social partnership;
- encourage investment, the pursuit of quality and good management practice;
- provide support for small and medium-sized firms;
- foster economic growth and competitiveness in the regions;
- strengthen support for British business abroad;
- give consumers a fair deal;
- maintain and enforce an effective framework for commercial activity while removing unnecessary burdens on business;

- help business take full advantage of technological developments and follow sound environmental policies; and
- maximise the contribution of science, engineering and technology to sustainable growth and quality of life.

EU Single Market

Britain, as a member of the EU, has firmly supported the development of the single market. The Government considers that the single market (see p. 125) is beneficial to the economies of all member states of the EU, and that removal of trade barriers will lead to reduced business costs and greater competition and efficiency. It is committed to making progress on issues that would lead to the completion of the single market, including removing remaining barriers to investment, opening up government procurement, making competition policy more streamlined and reducing bureaucracy.

Specific advantages of the single market include:

- wider consumer choice;
- removal of barriers to trade through mutual recognition of standards and harmonisation;
- the right to trade financial services throughout the EU on the basis of a single authorisation 'passport' (see p. 235);
- mutual recognition of professional and vocational qualifications; and
- a reduction in export business bureaucracy.

Competitiveness

Maintaining and helping to improve the competitiveness of business are the centre of the Government's approach to economic and industrial policy. It believes that a competitive Britain is the only way to deliver wealth and prosperity, as well as employment. The Government's priority is to work in close partnership with industry.

To further this partnership, therefore, the Government launched in 1997 an initiative—

Competitiveness UK: our partnership with business. A number of measures have already been announced, including:

- the establishment of an Advisory Group on Competitiveness, comprising prominent business people and other key partners, to offer practical and informed advice on issues affecting British competitiveness;

- an audit of industry's competitiveness setting out how Britain compares with its overseas competitors across a range of competitiveness indicators;

- the establishment of working parties of business people to offer detailed advice on such issues as innovation, investment and exports, which will be taken into account in government proposals to be presented in a White Paper during 1998;

- plans to establish a University for Industry, designed to provide opportunities for adults to improve their skills (see p. 194);

- measures designed to improve vocational preparation and training for young people, including the unemployed (see chapter 12);

- a review of government support to smaller firms, including measures to strengthen the quality of Business Link services (see p. 195); and

- plans to establish Regional Development Agencies (see p. 371).

Regulation

The Government considers that, while bad regulation is a burden on business, especially small firms, good regulation is of value both for public and consumer protection and for carrying out the functions of government. Under a new *Work for Better Regulation* programme, regulatory policy will focus on ensuring regulations are necessary, fair to all parties, properly costed, practical to enforce and straightforward to comply with. The programme will involve:

- greater consultation with business and the public and the establishment of a new

taskforce, half of whose members will represent small firms, to oversee the consultation process;

- proper published assessment of the cost and benefits of proposed regulations, especially for consumers and the environment;

- clear and accessible information and advice on necessary regulations from a unified service, open to business and other interested groups such as the elderly and the voluntary sector; and

- promoting better-quality regulations in Europe.

In addition, a review of regulatory policy is being undertaken with the object of ensuring that necessary regulation provides a framework which helps business and encourages innovation, investment and growth.

Independent regulatory bodies exist for the privatised utilities—telecommunications, electricity, gas, water and so on—with powers and duties to promote competition and the interests of consumers. These usually include considering all complaints and representations about the companies' services. Each privatised utility operates under a pricing policy set by the regulator, which often limits annual price increases to significantly less than the rate of inflation.

An interdepartmental review of utility regulation was announced in June 1997. The review will concentrate on gas, electricity, telecommunications and water, although it will also consider whether there are lessons to be learned from other regulatory experiences.

Competition Policy and Markets

The Government considers that competition is essential to the efficient working of markets as it encourages enterprise and efficiency and widens choice, so providing for consumers greater value for money and quality. The overall aim of competition policy is to encourage and enhance the competitive process. The law provides several ways in which market situations can be examined and, if necessary, altered.

Responsibility for competition policy lies with the President of the Board of Trade (the ministerial head of the DTI). Competition law is administered by the Director General of Fair Trading, the Monopolies and Mergers Commission (MMC) and the Restrictive Practices Court. The principal legislation comprises:

- the Fair Trading Act 1973 and the Competition Act 1980, which deal with mergers and monopolies, and anti-competitive practices respectively;

- the Restrictive Trade Practices Act 1976, which regulates agreements between people or companies that could limit their freedom to operate independently; and

- the Resale Prices Act 1976, covering attempts to impose minimum prices at which goods can be sold.

The Government intends to introduce a Competition Bill, which will be based closely on EC competition rules. Its aim is to reform competition in a way which is both effective in addressing anti-competitive practices and avoids unnecessary burdens on business. It plans to achieve this aim by prohibiting anti-competitive agreements and the abuse of market power. Only those businesses which are involved in anti-competitive agreements, cartels and similar practices will be affected by the first prohibition, compared with the present situation where businesses are required to notify, often innocuous, agreements, to the Office of Fair Trading. The new legislation will replace the Restrictive Trade Practices legislation of 1976 and 1977, the Resale Prices Act 1976 and certain provisions of the Competition Act 1980. The second prohibition covering abuse of a dominant position strengthens the existing regime operated under the Fair Trading Act.

Monopolies

A simple monopoly is defined as a situation where a company or group of companies supplies or purchases 25 per cent or more of a particular product or service in Britain, or a defined part of Britain. A complex monopoly is a situation where a number of companies or groups together have 25 per cent or more of the market and behave in a way that adversely affects competition.

The Director General of Fair Trading may enquire into possible abuse of a monopoly position. If an investigation shows that a monopoly situation exists, the Director General can refer the matter to the MMC for further investigation. The MMC consists of a wide range of specialists, including businessmen and women, lawyers, economists and trade unionists. If the MMC finds that a monopoly situation operates, or may be expected to operate, against the public interest, the President of the Board of Trade can take steps to remedy the matter. This is usually in the form of a request to the Director General to negotiate appropriate undertakings.

Mergers

Broadly, a merger situation qualifies for investigation if it involves the acquisition of gross assets worth £70 million or more, or the creation or enhancement of a 25 per cent share of the supply of goods or services of any description in Britain or a substantial part of it.

Qualifying mergers are considered by the Director General of Fair Trading, who then advises the President of the Board of Trade. There is a voluntary procedure for pre-notification of proposed mergers which offers prompt clearance of straightforward cases. The majority of mergers are not found to operate against the public interest and are not prohibited. However, if there are reasonable grounds for believing that a merger could have a detrimental effect, the Director General can advise the President of the Board of Trade to refer it to the MMC. Alternatively, the Director General may be asked to obtain suitable undertakings from the companies involved to remedy the adverse effects identified. The President of the Board of Trade may accept undertakings by the parties concerned to dispose of assets or to behave in a certain way in order to eliminate the need for a full investigation by the MMC.

If a merger or proposed merger is referred and the MMC finds that it could be expected to operate against the public interest, the President of the Board of Trade can prohibit it or allow it subject to certain conditions being met. Where the merger has already taken place, action can be taken to reverse it. There are special provisions for newspaper and water company mergers.

Certain mergers with an EC dimension, assessed by reference to turnover, come under the exclusive jurisdiction of the European Commission. The Commission can ban mergers if it concludes that they create or strengthen a dominant position which would significantly impede effective competition within the EU or a substantial part of it; alternatively, it may negotiate undertakings to correct the adverse effect.

Anti-competitive Practices

The Director General of Fair Trading can investigate the conduct of any business which may restrict, distort or prevent competition concerning the supply or acquisition of goods and/or services. If a practice is found to be anti-competitive, undertakings may be sought from the business responsible for the conduct. In the event of a suitable undertaking not being given, the matter may be referred to the MMC. In the case of an adverse finding by the MMC, the President of the Board of Trade has powers to take remedial action. Broadly, businesses are exempt from investigation if they have a turnover of less than £10 million, or have less than 25 per cent of a relevant market in Britain.

Restrictive Trade Practices

The Restrictive Trade Practices Act requires, with some exceptions, that particulars of business agreements containing certain anti-competitive restrictions have to be notified to the Director General of Fair Trading for registration. The most serious restrictions are those fixing prices or dividing markets. Unless the restrictions in an agreement are insignificant, the Director General must refer it to the Restrictive Practices Court. Where the Court finds the restrictions to be against

the public interest, it will make an order prohibiting them, or may accept undertakings given in lieu of an order.

Resale Price Maintenance

It is in general unlawful for manufacturers or suppliers to stipulate to dealers or retailers a minimum resale price. It is also unlawful for suppliers to seek to impose minimum resale prices by withholding supplies of goods or by discriminating against price-cutting dealers in other ways. There is, however, the possibility of exemption for particular classes of goods by the Restrictive Practices Court on public interest grounds. These exemptions remain in force until it can be shown by the Director General of Fair Trading, or third parties, to the Court's satisfaction that there has been a material change in circumstances from the time the exemptions were first granted. One exemption is now in force in respect of certain pharmaceuticals, but is being reviewed by the Office of Fair Trading; another, the Net Book Agreement, was made unlawful by the Restrictive Practices Court in March 1997.

Consumer Protection

The Government aims to maintain and develop a clear and fair regulatory framework which gives confidence to consumers and contributes to the competitiveness of business. It works closely with outside bodies which have expert knowledge of consumer issues to develop policies and legislation.

Existing legislation covers the sale and supply of goods and services. The Sale of Goods Act 1979 (as amended in 1994) ensures that consumers are entitled to receive goods which fit their description and are of satisfactory quality. The Trade Descriptions Act 1968 prohibits misdescriptions of goods, services, accommodation and facilities. This Act enables regulations to be made requiring information or instructions relating to goods to be marked on or to accompany the goods or to be included in advertisements. False or misleading indications about prices of goods are covered by the Consumer Protection Act 1987 which also makes it a criminal offence to supply unsafe consumer products. A range of

INTERIORS

Plas Mawr (in Conwy, north Wales) is the best-preserved Elizabethan town-house in Britain,
and is famous for the quality and quantity of its plasterwork decoration.
It was built by Robert Wynn in the 16th century.

Ulster Carpet Mills (in Portadown, Northern Ireland) began as a small concern in 1938 and has been expanding steadily ever since. Pictured below is one of their designs in the Swaminarayan mandir in Neasden, London, the first traditional Hindu mandir of stone to be constructed in Europe. It was opened by His Holiness Pramukh Swami Maharaj in 1995.

'Some of the People', contained within a floor-to-ceiling glass box, was commissioned
to celebrate the 100th anniversary of Glasgow's Underground system.
The artist, David Mach, took photographs of six passengers, enlarged them
to larger-than-life size and glued them on top of 3,000 postcards
arranged to give the impression of a moving figure.

The reconstruction of Shakespeare's Globe Theatre opened in London in 1997. The Centre comprises an international Theatre Company, Globe Education (exploring Shakespeare's scripts with students of all ages), and an exhibition devoted to Shakespeare and his contemporaries.

Henry V was one of the plays in the opening season, and some performances, as with Shakespeare's own company, were without intervals.

public safety information for consumers is made available by the DTI. The marking and accuracy of quantities are regulated by weights and measures legislation. Another law provides for the control of medical products, and certain other substances and articles, through a system of licences and certificates.

The Director General of Fair Trading promotes good trading practices and acts against malpractice. Under the Fair Trading Act, the Director General can recommend legislative or other changes to stop practices adversely affecting consumers' economic interests; encourage trade associations to develop codes of practice promoting consumers' interests; and disseminate consumer information and guidance. The Director General can also take assurances as to future conduct from traders who persistently breach the law to the detriment of consumers. The Unfair Terms in Consumer Contracts Regulations empower the Director General to act against traders using unfair contract terms.

The Consumer Credit Act 1974 is intended to protect consumers in their dealings with credit businesses. Businesses connected with the consumer credit or hire industry or which supply ancillary credit services—for example, credit brokers, debt collectors, debt counsellors and credit reference agencies—require a consumer credit licence. The Director General is responsible for administering the licensing system, including revoking licences of those unfit to hold them. He or she also has powers to take court action to prevent the publication of misleading advertisements, and to prohibit unfit people from carrying out estate agency work.

The EU's consumer programme covers activities such as health and safety, protection of the consumer's economic interests, promotion of consumer education and strengthening the representation of consumers. The views of British consumer organisations on EU matters are represented by the Consumers in Europe Group (UK). British consumer bodies also have a voice on the European consumer 'watchdog' body, the Bureau Européen des Unions de Consommateurs.

Consumer Advice and Information

Advice and information on consumer matters are given by Citizens Advice Bureaux, trading standards and consumer protection departments of local authorities (in Northern Ireland the Department of Economic Development) and, in some areas, by specialist consumer advice centres.

The National Consumer Council (and associated councils for Scotland and Wales), which receives government finance, presents the consumer's view to government, industry and others. The General Consumer Council for Northern Ireland has wide-ranging duties in consumer affairs in general.

Consumer bodies for privatised utilities investigate questions of concern to the consumer (see p. 190). Some trade associations in industry and commerce have established codes of practice. In addition, several private organisations work to further consumer interests. The largest is the Consumers' Association, funded by the subscriptions of its 700,000 or so members and publisher of *Which?* magazine.

Design, Quality and Standards

A wider and more effective use of design can make a significant contribution to improving competitiveness. The application of good design is paramount in the creation of innovative products, processes and services. The DTI supports the benefits of good design through the independent Design Council. As advocate for design at the national level, the Council undertakes research into design issues, develops design tools for use by industry and publicises the results. A separate design service offers support for industry through Business Links in England (and equivalent bodies in Scotland and Wales), with financial support from the DTI (see p. 195).

Quality is vital throughout the stages of the business cycle—design, production, marketing and delivery to customers. Accreditation is a key method of improving quality and competitiveness. Through its support for consultancy projects, the Government assists small and medium-sized firms to learn about and apply quality management techniques based on a national standard—EN ISO 9000—meeting international requirements. In order to increase customer confidence, companies are encouraged to obtain assessment and certification to this standard. The competence and performance of organisations undertaking such certification are officially accredited by the United Kingdom Accreditation Service. Companies certified by accredited bodies are permitted to use the national 'crown and tick' accreditation mark.

The DTI is responsible for policy relating to the National Measurement System. This provides, through several DTI-funded agencies, many of the physical measurement standards and associated calibration facilities necessary so that measurements in Britain are made on a common basis and to the required accuracy (see p. 332).

British Standards Institution

The British Standards Institution (BSI) is the national standards body and is the British member of the European and international standards organisations. It works with industry, consumers and government to produce standards relevant to the needs of the market and suitable for public purchasing and regulatory purposes. Government support for the BSI is directed particularly towards European and international standards, which account for over 90 per cent of its work. Harmonised standards contribute to removing technical barriers to trade in the EU. The Kitemark is the BSI's registered product certification trade mark.

Awards

The Queen's Awards for Export, Technological and Environmental Achievement recognise outstanding performance in their respective fields. Awarded annually, they are valid for five years and are granted by the Queen on the advice of the Prime Minister, who is assisted by an Advisory Committee consisting of senior representatives from business, trade unions and government departments. Any self-contained 'industrial unit' in Britain with at

least two employees is eligible to apply so long as it meets the scheme's criteria. Other awards include the Export Award for Smaller Businesses (for firms employing fewer than 200 people) and the MacRobert Award for engineering made by the Fellowship of Engineering for technological innovation.

Industrial and Intellectual Property

The Government supports innovation by providing systems which enable the originators of inventions and industrial designs and the proprietors of trade marks to protect their rights. These matters, along with copyright in literary, artistic and musical works, are the responsibility of the DTI's Patent Office, which includes the Designs Registry and the Trade Marks Registry. The Patent Office is also involved with the international harmonisation of rules and procedures and with modernising and simplifying intellectual property law. Patent protection is available under the European Patent Convention and the Patent Co-operation Treaty; trade mark registration is available through a Community Trade Mark. Rights may be established in other countries by virtue of separate conventions on industrial property, literary and artistic work, and music and broadcasting.

Education and Training

Business can only compete successfully in rapidly changing world markets by employing a flexible, highly skilled and highly qualified workforce. The Government is committed to increasing investment in education and training (see chapters 12 and 26), and is also planning to establish a University for Industry through a public/private partnership. This will:

● help adults improve their skills and realise their potential;

● improve the quality and accessibility of learning opportunities by applying new technology; and

● supply small businesses with trained personnel and consultancy and other services.

Recent measures to raise standards in education and training include:

- improved careers information, education and guidance for young people;
- a strengthening of academic and vocational qualifications;
- modern apprenticeships;
- initiatives to help firms develop and implement training plans;
- making training loans available to smaller firms; and
- a competition open to small firms for the best co-ordinated training projects.

Training and Enterprise Councils and Local Enterprise Companies

Training schemes are available through a network of 79 business-led Training and Enterprise Councils (TECs) in England and Wales and 22 local enterprise companies (LECs) in Scotland, run by Scottish Enterprise and Highlands and Islands Enterprise (see p. 197).

TECs and LECs are independent companies managed by boards of directors, the majority of whom are drawn from private sector business. They provide training, vocational education and enterprise programmes on behalf of the Government and encourage employers to develop the potential of all their employees through, for instance, attainment of the Investors in People standard (see p. 175). In addition, they offer advisory and training services to businesses, including schemes to enhance the expertise of managers. In Scotland, LECs supply the full range of services offered by the enterprise bodies—support and advice to businesses, environmental renewal, training programmes for young and long-term unemployed people and encouragement to businesses to invest in management and skills. TECs and LECs also have a key role in regeneration and economic development activities locally.

Management Education and Development

Management education is available at most universities and colleges of higher and further education. Regional management centres have been established in England and Wales by associations of these colleges, and there are several similar organisations in Scotland. Universities run full-time postgraduate programmes at business schools, such as those of London, Manchester, Durham, Warwick and Strathclyde universities.

The British Institute of Management encourages excellence in management. Other bodies are concerned with standards and training in specialised branches of management. The employer-led Management Charter Initiative (MCI) is the operating arm of the National Forum for Management Education and Development and the leading industrial body for management standards.

Business Support Services

Government business support services comprise a number of different schemes delivered via a variety of mechanisms. These schemes are intended to support a range of objectives, including improved business performance, employment creation, increased exports and environmental improvements. Some schemes provide grants, but the main emphasis is on the provision of advice and guidance, with the aim of improving the underlying capabilities of firms. Since the main customers for business support services are small and medium-sized enterprises, local delivery is preferred wherever possible. In many cases, the Government's role is simply to provide a framework within which business people can share expertise and help one another.

The main mechanism for delivering services in England is a network of 300 Business Links, which bring together in a single point of access organisations supporting enterprise, such as TECs, chambers of commerce, local authorities and enterprise agencies. Business Links are local, commercial partnerships, in which larger firms can make contacts and expertise available to smaller firms. Over 500 personal business advisers offer small firms a full complement of consultancy and other services, calling on about 150 specialist counsellors for export development, design, and innovation and technology. In addition, regional staff from three government departments (Trade and Industry, Education and Employment, and

Environment, Transport and the Regions), seconded to Business Links, provide advice and guidance especially on government support.

Examples of the sorts of services provided are help in using modern technologies, such as the Internet, World Wide Web and e-mail; and a regional supply network, designed to help both purchasers find competitive suppliers and suppliers exploit new markets. Best management practice activities are also promoted, such as:

- the national UK Benchmark Index, which allows small firms to compare their performance with other local companies, in order to identify their strengths and weaknesses;

- a CD-ROM-based package of presentation material to enable Business Links to highlight management best practice; and

- a company visit programme which enables companies to see world-class practices at first hand.

To give greater discretion to the Business Links and their partner organisations in the design and delivery of services to businesses, central DTI programmes have been reduced and the funding channels simplified, with support being brought together into one local competitiveness budget. In addition, a new government/private sector funding scheme, Local Challenge, has been set up in England, which makes finance available to the most effective partnership projects. A separate DTI-managed national Sector Challenge with similar funding has also been introduced for projects in specific sectors of industry, with priority being given to small and medium-sized enterprises.

In Scotland, Business Shops are run by local partnerships between LECs, local authorities and business support organisations; trained advisers supply information and direct enquiries to the business support services of local partners. Similar arrangements have been set up in Wales through Business Connect, which has a network of business support centres. In Northern Ireland small firms are helped by the Local Enterprise Development Unit's network of regional offices, which provide co-ordinated advice and support.

Consultancy

Business Links are responsible for supplying a flexible consultancy and diagnostic service, which gives assessments of smaller firms' strengths and weaknesses and draws up plans for their future development. A parallel service is available in Scotland through Business Shops in lowland Scotland and Business Information Source in the Highlands and Islands area. Small and medium-sized companies can also use a consultancy brokerage service to assist them in selecting consultants.

Small Firms Schemes

Financial help is available for small and medium-sized firms to undertake innovation activities under the new SMART scheme (see p. 330). Other government assistance on offer to smaller businesses includes:

- the Small Firms Loan Guarantee Scheme, which helps businesses with viable proposals to obtain finance where conventional loans are unavailable as a result of a lack of financial security or previous performance; the scheme gives banks and other financial institutions a government guarantee on a certain percentage of the loan in return for a premium payment; about 6,490 loans valued at £255 million were guaranteed in 1996–97;

- a programme to encourage small and medium-sized firms to make better use of new information technology; and

- an initiative allowing small firms to develop key workers' training skills in-house.

Regional Industrial Development

Regional policy is designed to encourage investment in economic development and regeneration in all areas of Britain. Where additional help is needed, it is focused on the Assisted Areas (Development Areas and

Intermediate Areas), which cover around 35 per cent of Britain's working population. The promotion of inward investment is a key element in the Government's regional policy (see p. 198).

The main instrument of DTI support to industry in the Assisted Areas is Regional Selective Assistance (RSA), which is designed to:

- help create and safeguard jobs;
- help attract international investment;
- improve regional and local competitiveness; and
- help areas adversely affected by the impact of economic change.

In 1996–97, each £1 million RSA grant attracted £11 million of capital investment and directly created or safeguarded an average of 245 jobs.

England

English Partnerships promotes job creation, inward investment and environmental improvement through reclamation and development of vacant, derelict, under-used or contaminated land and buildings (see p. 372). The Rural Development Commission advises the Government on economic and social development in the countryside, promotes jobs and supports essential services. The Commission's resources are concentrated in areas of greatest need, known as Rural Development Areas, covering about 35 per cent of the area of England (see p. 374). The Government intends to establish Regional Development Agencies and a strategic authority for London, which will assist in improving regional competitiveness, promoting inward investment, helping small businesses, and co-ordinating economic development (see p. 371). Due to come into operation in April 1999, the Agencies will work with the Government Offices for the Regions, chambers of commerce, TECs and other bodies involved in economic development.

Scotland

Scottish Enterprise and Highlands and Islands Enterprise manage government and EU support to industry and commerce, in lowland and highland Scotland respectively, operating mainly through the network of LECs (see p. 175). The two bodies have a broad range of duties, including:

- promoting industrial efficiency and competitiveness;
- attracting inward investment and encouraging exports;
- giving financial and management support to new businesses and helping existing ones to expand;
- improving the environment by reclaiming derelict and contaminated land; and
- increasing job opportunities and skills.

A Scottish Enterprise-initiated Scottish Equity Partnership fund is designed to improve access to finance for smaller companies. Involving both Scottish Enterprise and private investors, the fund provides venture and development capital for start-ups, early-stage investments, management buy-outs/buy-ins and mature businesses seeking to expand.

Wales

The purposes of the Welsh Development Agency (WDA—see p. 31) are to further the economic development, promote industrial efficiency and improve the environment of Wales. In conjunction with the private sector, it provides affordable, high-quality sites and premises for existing businesses and inward investors. It encourages private sector investments (through its Welsh Property Venture), as well as investment from outside Wales. The WDA's land reclamation programme is the largest and most sustained landscape improvement project in Europe. Its Business Development division focuses on developing stronger regional clusters (such as supply and services chains), increasing standards and efficiency, and helping Welsh companies to exploit new technology.

The Land Authority for Wales is a public body with a fundamental role in economic regeneration. It works with the private and public sectors, making available land for urban development, employment and affordable housing (see p. 375). The Development Board for Rural Wales promotes the economic and social well-being of rural mid-Wales. It concentrates investment in market towns, especially those in the west, in order to help stimulate business confidence and prosperity. Priority is also being given to activities in smaller communities.

Northern Ireland

Industrial development policy in Northern Ireland is the responsibility of the Department of Economic Development (see p. 535) and is implemented through various agencies:

- the Industrial Development Board, which deals with overseas companies considering Northern Ireland as an investment location, as well as the development of local companies with more than 50 employees;

- the Local Enterprise Development Unit, which promotes enterprise and the development of small businesses;

- the Industrial Research and Technology Unit, providing advice and assistance on research and development, innovation and technology transfer; and

- the Training and Employment Agency (see p. 177), which helps with in-company training and management development.

A variety of schemes are on offer to help companies with marketing, exporting, product development and design, improving productivity and quality, training, and research and development. A full range of assistance is available to those companies able to demonstrate development potential and the prospect of long-term competitive growth. This assistance includes capital grants, loans and share capital investment.

Inward Investment

Inward investment is increasingly important to the economy, with around £154,000 million currently invested from overseas; in 1996 alone, some £21,000 million of inward direct investment came to Britain.

Britain is second only to the United States as the destination for international direct investment, which helps to develop and modernise the industrial base by introducing new products and processes, as well as bringing in management expertise. It also provides new jobs and boosts output, exports and tax revenues.

Britain is the EU's major location for inward investment from North America and the Asia Pacific region, attracting about 40 per cent of investment from these areas. For the prospective inward investor Britain's strengths include its membership of the single European market, a flexible and adaptable workforce, good labour relations, low corporate and personal taxation, a respected legal system, and the English language.

A growing proportion of inward investment has been through expansion or reinvestment by existing investors. The DTI's Invest in Britain Bureau (IBB) and its regional partners give high priority to supporting these, to ensure that they are aware of the advantages of remaining and expanding in Britain. Overall policy and co-ordination of overseas promotion of inward investment are the responsibility of the IBB, which represents Britain as a whole. It is supported in Britain by several territorial and regional bodies, and overseas it operates through British Embassies, High Commissions and Consulates-General.

Similar advice and assistance to that provided in England by regional development organisations (to be replaced by the Regional Development Agencies in 1999) is available through:

- Locate in Scotland, operated jointly by the Scottish Office and Scottish Enterprise;

- the Welsh Office Industry and Training Department and the Welsh Development Agency's International Division; and

- the Industrial Development Board in Northern Ireland.

European Union Regional Policy and Aid

The EU seeks to reduce disparities between the different regions of the Union. The principal responsibility for helping poorer areas remains with national authorities, but the EU complements schemes by awarding grants and loans from various sources, including the European Regional Development Fund (ERDF).

EU Structural Funds, especially the ERDF, play an important role in regional development. Three areas—Northern Ireland, the Highlands and Islands, and Merseyside—are eligible for assistance under 'Objective 1', which aims to promote the development of regions lagging behind; they are receiving around £1,900 million of EU funding over the period 1997–99. The ERDF also provides finance for areas of industrial decline and for rural development. Structural Funds are also available to help areas previously dependent on the coal, steel, textile, fishing and defence industries and to create employment and secure jobs through training.

The European Investment Bank (see p. 127) offers loans for public and private capital investment schemes. Assisted projects typically include improvements to and building of infrastructure projects; construction of trans-European transport links; support for business and tourism development; and capital investment in industry, such as factory construction.

Further Reading

Trade and Industry: The Government's Expenditure Plans 1997–98 to 1999–2000. Cm 3605, The Stationery Office, 1997.

Government and Industry. Aspects of Britain series, HMSO, 1995.

Competitiveness UK: our partnership with business. DTI, 1997.

14 Overseas Trade

Overseas trade has been of vital importance to the British economy for hundreds of years. With only about 1 per cent of the world's population, Britain is the fifth largest trading nation, accounting for around 5 per cent of world trade in goods and services. As a member of the European Union (EU), it is part of the world's largest established trading group, responsible for 40 per cent of world exports. In 1996 Britain had its lowest deficit on the current account of the balance of trade since 1985. The surplus on trade in services was the highest recorded. The deficit on trade in goods, however, has grown slightly since 1994, although it is falling as a percentage of total trade.

The Government wants to see an enlarged and more effective EU, and will work towards breaking down remaining barriers to competition in the single European market. With a higher degree of inward and outward investment than any other leading economy, relative to gross domestic product (GDP), Britain is taking advantage of increasing global free trade. It will encourage the World Trade Organisation (WTO) to take further action to reduce non-tariff barriers and to open up world financial markets.

Britain exports more per head than the United States and Japan. Its overseas sales of goods and services are equivalent to about a quarter of GDP. Re-exporting plays a prominent role in trade. Receipts from trade in services and investment income make up about half of its total overseas earnings, and Britain consistently runs large surpluses on these accounts. It is the world's second biggest overseas investor and the leading destination for inward direct investment into the EU. British investors have more overseas direct investments than foreign firms have in Britain.[1] The financial services sector plays a key role in both services and investment income, achieving net overseas earnings of £6,400 million on services and £9,700 million from overseas investments in 1996.

World trade is set to grow by 5 to 10 per cent a year in the next ten years, due in part to the successful conclusion of the Uruguay Round of negotiations under the General Agreement on Tariffs and Trade (GATT) in 1993. This led to the creation in 1995 of the

---

[1] Overseas direct investment consists of investment in branches, subsidiaries and associated companies, giving the investor a significant influence over the operations of the company. The other main type of overseas investment is known as portfolio investment; it consists of investment in the securities of overseas-registered companies and governments and does not entitle the investor to any significant influence over company operations (see Table 14.8).

Table 14.1: Overseas Trade 1994–96

	1994	1995	1996
Value (£ million)[a]			
EXPORTS			
Goods	134,664	153,077	166,340
Oil	8,494	8,801	10,327
Other goods	126,170	144,276	156,013
Services	41,938	46,598	50,807
Goods and services	**176,602**	**199,675**	**217,147**
IMPORTS			
Goods	145,793	164,659	178,938
Oil	4,591	4,472	5,448
Other goods	141,202	160,187	173,490
Services	37,162	39,721	43,665
Goods and services	**182,955**	**204,380**	**222,603**
Volume indices (1990 = 100)			
EXPORTS			
Goods			
All goods	118.4	127.8	136.3
Non-oil goods	116.6	126.7	136.2
Services	113.2	121.7	130.8
Goods and services	**117.2**	**126.3**	**135.0**
IMPORTS			
Goods			
All goods	109.4	114.3	124.1
Non-oil goods	110.3	115.9	126.2
Services	113.6	117.0	126.5
Goods and services	**110.2**	**114.8**	**124.5**
Price indices (1990 = 100)			
EXPORTS			
All goods	118.6	126.4	128.4
Non-oil goods	121.6	129.7	130.7
IMPORTS			
All goods	116.1	127.7	128.3
Non-oil goods	117.8	129.6	129.3
TERMS OF TRADE[b]			
All goods	102.2	99.0	100.1
Non-oil goods	103.2	100.1	101.1

Source: *United Kingdom Balance of Payments 1997 Edition*
[a] Balance-of-payments basis.
[b] Export price index as a percentage of import price index.

Geographical Distribution of Trade in Goods 1996

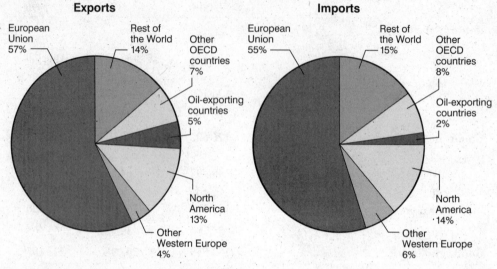

Source: *United Kingdom Balance of Payments 1997 Edition*

Table 14.2: Sector Analysis of Trade in Goods 1996[a]			£ million
	Exports	Imports	Balance
Food, beverages and tobacco	11,296	16,644	−5,348
Basic materials	2,804	6,528	−3,724
Oil	10,327	5,448	4,879
Other mineral fuels and lubricants	654	1,173	−519
Semi-manufactured goods	45,317	46,576	−1,259
Finished manufactured goods	93,985	100,805	−6,820
Commodities and transactions not classified according to kind	1,957	1,764	193
Total	**166,340**	**178,938**	**−12,598**

Source: *United Kingdom Balance of Payments 1997 Edition*
[a] Balance-of-payments basis

World Trade Organisation, of which Britain was a founder member.

TRADE IN GOODS

In 1996 Britain's exports of goods were valued at about £166,340 million and imports at £178,938 million on a balance of payments basis (see Table 14.1). Between 1995 and 1996 the volume of exports of goods rose by 7 per cent and their value by 9 per cent. Over the same period, imports grew by 9 per cent in terms of both volume and value.

Commodity Composition

Britain traditionally used to be an exporter of manufactured goods and an importer of food and basic materials. In 1970 manufactures accounted for 84 per cent of its exports; this fell to around 66 per cent by the mid-1980s as North Sea oil exports increased their share. The proportion of manufactures in exports has since risen, to 84 per cent in 1996 (see Table 14.2). Britain has not, however, had a surplus on manufactures since 1982. Machinery and transport equipment account for about 44 per cent of exports and 42 per

Table 14.3: Commodity Composition of Trade in Goods 1996[a]   £ million

	Exports	Imports
Food and live animals	7,002	14,613
Beverages and tobacco	4,387	2,927
Crude materials	2,621	6,306
of which: Wood, lumber and cork	47	1,271
Pulp and waste paper	57	702
Textile fibres	629	687
Metal ores	665	1,617
Fuels	11,030	7,060
Petroleum and petroleum products	10,370	5,750
Coal, gas and electricity	656	1,309
Animal and vegetable oils and fats	208	724
Chemicals	22,360	18,540
of which: Organic chemicals	5,214	4,857
Inorganic chemicals	1,217	1,283
Plastics	3,329	4,418
Manufactures classified chiefly by material	23,287	29,222
of which: Wood and cork manufactures	224	1,111
Paper and paperboard manufactures	2,340	5,056
Textile manufactures	3,472	5,180
Iron and steel	4,124	3,610
Non-ferrous metals	2,708	3,837
Metal manufactures	3,373	3,557
Machinery and transport equipment	74,141	77,778
Mechanical machinery	20,789	16,868
Electrical machinery	33,369	36,461
Road vehicles	14,528	20,745
Other transport equipment	5,461	3,709
Miscellaneous manufactures	21,077	25,540
of which: Clothing and footwear	3,929	8,024
Scientific and photographic	6,671	6,183
Other commodities and transactions	1,940	1,612
Total	**168,041**	**184,305**

Source: *Monthly Digest of Statistics*
[a] On an overseas-trade-statistics basis, seasonally adjusted. This differs from a balance-of-payments basis in that, for imports, it includes the cost of insurance and freight, and, for both exports and imports, includes returned goods.

cent of imports (see Table 14.3). Aerospace, chemicals and electronics have become increasingly significant export sectors, while textiles have declined in relative importance. Britain is Europe's biggest exporter of computers, television sets and microchips; many of the firms involved are large multinationals from the Far East and the United States.

Since the mid-1970s North Sea oil has made a substantial contribution to Britain's overseas trade in terms of both exports and import substitution. In 1996 exports of fuels in volume terms were nearly six times their 1975 level, while imports were around three-fifths of the 1975 figure. The share of fuels in exports was 7 per cent in 1996, while the import share had fallen from 17 per cent in

1975 to 4 per cent by 1996. In 1996 the surplus on trade in oil amounted to nearly £4,300 million on a balance of payments basis.

Imported manufactures have taken a greater share of the domestic market in recent decades. Between 1970 and 1996 the share of finished manufactures in total imports rose from 25 to 56 per cent, while the share of basic materials fell from 15 to 4 per cent. The percentage of food, beverages and tobacco in total imports has been dropping since the 1950s, down to 9 per cent in 1996, as a result both of the extent to which food demand has been met from domestic agriculture and of the decline in the proportion of total expenditure on food.

Geographical Distribution

Britain's overseas trade is mainly with other developed countries. Other countries in the Organisation for Economic Co-operation and Development (OECD) took 82 per cent of Britain's exports in 1996 and supplied 83 per cent of imports. In 1972, the year before Britain joined the European Community (as the EU was then known), 43 per cent of its trade in goods was with the other 14 countries which presently make up the EU. The proportion rose to 56 per cent in 1996. Western Europe as a whole took 62 per cent of British exports in 1996. In 1996 EU countries accounted for eight of Britain's top ten export markets and seven of the ten leading suppliers of goods to Britain (see Table 14.4). In 1990 Germany overtook the United States to become Britain's biggest overseas market for goods; Germany is also Britain's largest single supplier. In 1996 it took 12 per cent of Britain's exports and supplied nearly 15 per cent of its imports.

There have been a number of other changes in the pattern of Britain's overseas trade in recent years. Exports to Japan, which is presently Britain's tenth largest export market, rose by 13 per cent by value in 1996,

Table 14.4: Trade in Goods—Main Markets and Suppliers 1996[a]

	Value (£ million)	Share (per cent)
Main markets		
Germany	20,752	12.3
United States	19,831	11.8
France	17,119	10.2
Netherlands	13,481	8.0
Irish Republic	8,669	5.2
Belgium/Luxembourg	8,548	5.1
Italy	8,048	4.8
Spain	6,737	4.0
Sweden	4,432	2.6
Japan	4,265	2.5
Main suppliers		
Germany	27,202	14.8
United States	22,812	12.4
France	17,719	9.6
Netherlands	12,418	6.7
Japan	8,994	4.9
Italy	8,783	4.8
Belgium/Luxembourg	8,625	4.7
Irish Republic	7,222	3.9
Switzerland	5,411	2.9
Spain	5,043	2.7

Source: *Monthly Digest of Statistics*
[a] On an overseas-trade-statistics basis, seasonally adjusted.

Table: 14.5: Britain's Trade in Services 1996 — £ million

	Credits	Debits	Balance
Private sector and public corporations	**50,390**	**40,871**	**9,519**
Sea transport	4,698	5,203	−505
Civil aviation	6,313	7,038	−725
Travel	12,790	16,685	−3,895
Financial services (net credits)	6,397	−	14,644
Other business services	20,192	11,945 }	
General government	**417**	**2,794**	**−2,377**
Total	**50,807**	**43,665**	**7,142**

Source: *United Kingdom Balance of Payments 1997 Edition*

Table 14.6: Investment Income and Transfers 1996 — £ million

	Credits	Debits	Balance
Investment income	**96,071**	**86,419**	**9,652**
General government	1,569	4,352	−2,783
Private sector and public corporations	94,501	82,067	12,434
Transfers	**6,950**	**11,581**	**−4,631**
General government	4,390	9,323	−4,933
Private sector	2,560	2,258	302
Total	**103,021**	**98,000**	**5,021**

Source: *United Kingdom Balance of Payments 1997 Edition*

while Japan is Britain's fifth largest supplier, accounting for 5 per cent of imports. There were substantial increases in Britain's exports to a number of other markets in Asia in 1996, including Thailand (up by 17 per cent), South Korea (by 13 per cent) and Hong Kong (by 10 per cent), while exports to Saudi Arabia rose by 51 per cent.

OTHER TRANSACTIONS

Other transactions fall into three main groups: internationally tradeable services; investment income on external assets; and non-commercial transfers (chiefly between governments, between the British Government and EU organisations, and between private individuals).

Services range from banking, insurance and stockbroking, tourism, and shipping and aviation to specialist services such as engineering consultancy, computer programming and training. Financial services make a major contribution to overseas earnings: net overseas receipts from services rendered were £6,397

million in 1996. Earnings from trade in services as a whole rose by 9 per cent in 1996 to £50,807 million (see Table 14.5). There was an overall surplus on services of £7,142 million, compared with £6,877 million in 1995.

Earnings on investment income increased by 5 per cent to £96,071 million in 1996, while debits rose by 4 per cent to £86,419 million (see Table 14.6). The surplus on investment income was £9,652 million. Within this, there were surpluses on earnings from direct investment of £12,889 million and from portfolio investment of £3,854 million, although these were partly offset by a deficit on bank borrowing and lending. Transfers have almost always been in deficit, amounting to £4,631 million in 1996—with a deficit on government transfers of £4,933 million and a surplus on private sector transfers of £302 million.

COMMERCIAL POLICY

Government policy seeks to promote an open multilateral trading system and the further liberalisation of world trade. To this end, Britain has taken a leading part in the activities of such organisations as the WTO, the International Monetary Fund (IMF) and the OECD, as well as the EU.

European Union

The single European market 'opened for business' in 1993, with the essential legislation in place for the free movement of goods, services, people and capital within the EU. There has been:

- abolition of exchange controls;
- ending of routine customs clearance of commercial goods at national frontiers within the EU;
- creation of common technical standards;
- introduction of the right to trade financial services throughout the EU on the basis of a single home authorisation 'passport' (see p. 235); and
- deregulation of airlines, with no preferential treatment for national flag carriers.

Efforts are now being made to enhance the effectiveness of the single market through the European Commission's Single Market Action Plan. Among the issues on which the plan focuses are enforcement; simplification; liberalisation of financial services, telecommunications and energy markets; opening up of public procurement; and mutual recognition of national arrangements for testing and certification of goods where there are no EC rules. The Department of Trade and Industry's (DTI's) Action Single Market team helps companies that encounter illegal barriers to trade to overcome them and also pursues complaints about illegal state aids. The British Government supports efforts to extend the single market to those countries of Central and Eastern Europe which are applying for EU membership.

World Trade Organisation

The eighth GATT round—the Uruguay Round—was launched in 1986 and successfully concluded in 1993. It was the biggest ever multilateral trade negotiation and established the World Trade Organisation (WTO) as successor to the GATT at the beginning of 1995. There are currently 130 WTO members, and over 30 countries are negotiating their accession.

The WTO incorporates the GATT, which covers trade in goods and agreements in a number of other areas, including agriculture, services, textiles, intellectual property, subsidies, technical barriers to trade, and trade-related investment measures. A new binding dispute settlement procedure was also agreed, ensuring that the WTO rules are applied and enforced.

Overall tariff reductions achieved during the Uruguay Round amount to about 40 per cent across all countries. Members also agreed not to raise tariffs again on 95 per cent of world trade. The Information Technology Agreement signed in March 1997 will result in the phasing out of tariffs on information technology products by 2000; this could ultimately mean gains for Britain of £1,900 million a year. In February 1997 a substantial liberalisation package was concluded in telecommunications services, with 69 countries (representing over 91 per cent of the world telecommunications market) guaranteeing access to their markets. Britain supports all the WTO's agreements, its dispute settlement system and moves to reduce both tariff and non-tariff barriers that still remain through the multilateral system; a particular priority is to conclude negotiations to further liberalise trade in financial services by the end of 1997.

The first WTO Ministerial Conference, held in Singapore in December 1996, reaffirmed the primacy of the multilateral system and confirmed the commitment by all WTO members to implementing in full the Uruguay Round agreements. New work on government procurement, trade facilitation, trade and competition, and trade and investment was agreed.

Britain's priorities for the WTO's work programme include:

- further tariff reductions;
- improved respect for intellectual property rights;

- liberalising public procurement rules;
- removing technical barriers to trade;
- simplification of trade procedures for imports and exports;
- simplification and harmonisation of preferential rules of origin; and
- tighter disciplines on state subsidies.

Bilateral Relations

Britain places great importance on developing strong relations with third countries, in particular through the EU. One example of this is the Asia-Europe Meeting (ASEM), an inter-regional forum set up in 1996, which Britain sees as providing opportunities to encourage further efforts towards trade liberalisation among ASEM's 25 member countries, including the newly industrialising countries in Asia. Britain will be hosting the second ASEM Summit in London in April 1998. Relations with the United States are enhanced through the EU-US Action Plan, which encourages co-operation on a number of issues, including trade.

Special Trading Arrangements

The multilateral trading system provides the foundation for the EU's common commercial policy. However, the EU has preferential trading arrangements with a number of countries. These fall into three main categories:

- Those that prepare countries in Central and Eastern Europe for possible EU membership. Europe Agreements have been signed between the EU and Poland, Hungary, the Czech Republic, Slovakia, Bulgaria, Romania, Slovenia, Estonia, Latvia and Lithuania. They are designed to facilitate closer political and economic ties and the eventual liberalisation of trade with a view to these countries becoming full members of the EU. Interim Agreements are in place with Slovenia and the three Baltic states until their Europe Agreements are ratified. A trade and economic co-operation agreement has also been made with Albania.

- Those that provide an economic dimension to wider agreements with neighbouring countries. The EU has association and co-operation agreements with virtually all non-member countries with a Mediterranean coastline, plus Jordan. These provide preferential access to EU markets on a reciprocal basis.

- Those that provide an economic dimension to its assistance to former dependent territories. Trade relations with these countries (known as ACP countries—African, Caribbean and Pacific) are governed by the Lomé Convention, which gives them tariff-free access, subject to certain safeguards, to the EU for industrial and agricultural products. The EU also operates a Generalised System of Preferences (GSP), which is available to nearly all developing countries. This applies to industrial products, including textiles and certain (mainly processed) agricultural products.

Partnership and co-operation (non-preferential agreements) have been concluded with ten states of the former Soviet Union. Non-preferential co-operation agreements have also been made with countries in South Asia and Latin America, as well as with the People's Republic of China, the Association of South East Asian Nations, the Andean Pact, and the Organisation of Central American States.

CONTROLS ON TRADE

With the completion of the single European market, all routine internal border controls and requirements were removed for trade in EU goods between the members of the EU. This has substantially cut travel times and costs; for example, freight journey times by road from Britain to Italy have been reduced by up to 24 hours.

Import Controls

Following the completion of the single European market, all national quantitative restrictions have been abolished. However, some EU-wide quotas have been imposed on a small range of non-textile and clothing products from the People's Republic of China, while EU imports of some steel products from Russia, the Ukraine and Kazakhstan are also restricted. Quantitative restrictions on textiles and clothing stem from the Multi-Fibre Arrangement (MFA), under which there is a series of bilateral agreements. Some quotas are also maintained for imports from non-WTO countries. The MFA restrictions will be eliminated by 2005 as part of the WTO agreement.

Imports from certain countries remain subject to sanctions or embargo agreed by, for example, the United Nations. Imports of certain other goods from all countries are prohibited or restricted to protect human, animal or plant life and health. These include firearms and ammunition; nuclear materials; certain drugs; explosives; endangered wildlife and derived products; and certain agricultural, horticultural and food products.

Export Controls

The great majority of British exports are not subject to any government control. Controls on certain strategic goods are, though, imposed for a variety of reasons, including foreign policy and non-proliferation concerns, the need to comply with international treaty commitments, the operation of sanctions and national security. The scope of export controls is limited to what is necessary to meet these concerns. Most controls apply on a worldwide basis, although certain sanctions and embargoes are applied against specific countries as a result of agreement by members of bodies such as the United Nations.

There are controls relating to the export of conventional military goods, arms, ammunition and related materials as well as dual-use industrial goods that can be used for civil and military purposes. Most dual-use industrial goods are allowed to move within the EU without an export licence. Britain works with the other members of the Wassenaar Arrangement to promote transparency and greater responsibility in the transfer of conventional weapons and dual-use goods and technologies. Two lists of goods are in place. Lists of controls on certain dual-use

related goods are also agreed by members of the Australia Group, the Nuclear Suppliers Group and the Missile Technology Control Regime; Britain is a member of all three. The aim of these groups is to help prevent the spread of chemical, biological and nuclear weapons and missile systems for their delivery. In July 1997 the British Government issued new criteria for a responsible arms trade (see p. 134).

SERVICES FOR EXPORTERS

The Government provides a wide range of advice and practical support to meet the needs of exporters. This support is designed to help businesses, especially small and medium-sized enterprises, through all stages of the exporting process.

Export Promotion Services

The DTI and the FCO provide support through the joint Overseas Trade Services (OTS) operation. OTS has a network of some 2,000 staff worldwide to help British businesses compete successfully throughout the world. In 1997–98 over £200 million is being spent on support for exporters.

The network comprises country help desks, whose staff include export promoters seconded from industry, and other teams providing export information services in the DTI's headquarters in London; the commercial sections at more than 200 FCO diplomatic posts overseas; over 70 Business Links throughout England (see p. 195); Scottish Trade International; Welsh Office Overseas Trade Services; and the Industrial Development Board for Northern Ireland. Services include export intelligence, market information, help in researching potential markets and finding partners, and support for firms participating in trade fairs and missions. The Oil, gas and petrochemicals Supplies Office (OSO—see p. 264) provides information on oil and gas markets and projects around the world.

For companies based in England local Business Links are usually the first point of contact for firms requiring OTS services. International trade teams at the Business Link can offer specialist help from their export development counsellors and from seconded DTI export staff. Elsewhere in Britain access is via the export sections in the relevant home country department.

The Government's trade promotion policy is guided by advice from businessmen and women who serve on the British Overseas Trade Board. Its Area Advisory Groups, consisting of business people with expert knowledge of trade with particular world markets, provide advice on the world's main trading areas. The Overseas Project Board advises on major project business overseas, and the Small Firms Committee gives guidance on matters relating to small businesses.

British Invisibles

British Invisibles is an organisation which promotes the international activities of financial institutions and business services. Its role is to suggest and, where possible, implement measures for boosting such earnings in Britain and abroad. It also seeks to increase awareness of London as an international financial centre and of the role of the service sector in the British economy.

Export Insurance

ECGD (Export Credits Guarantee Department) is a government department responsible to the President of the Board of Trade, the minister heading the DTI. It helps British firms overcome many of the risks of selling and investing overseas. ECGD supports British exporters of capital goods and services usually sold on medium- and long-term credit by:

- guaranteeing exporters and financing banks against the risk of non-payment by overseas buyers/borrowers;

- giving interest rate support to British banks, allowing overseas borrowers access to funds at fixed, often favourable, rates of interest; and

- providing reinsurance to private sector insurance companies covering British exports sold on short-term credit.

In order to encourage investment in less developed countries, ECGD also insures investment earnings against the main political risks, such as war, expropriation and restrictions on repatriation of profits.

ECGD has cover available for over 125 markets worldwide. The Asia-Pacific region is currently its largest source of new business.

BALANCE OF PAYMENTS

The balance of payments statistics record transactions between residents of Britain and non-residents. The transactions are classified into two groups: current account, and transactions in Britain's external assets and liabilities, sometimes known as the capital account. The current account records trade in goods and services, including finance, tourism and transport; transactions in investment income; and transfers. Capital transactions include inward and outward investment, overseas transactions by banks in Britain, external borrowing and lending by residents in Britain, and drawings on and accruals to the official reserves.

Britain has no exchange controls; residents are free to acquire foreign currency for any purpose, including direct and portfolio investment overseas. There are also no controls on the lending of sterling abroad, and non-residents can acquire sterling for any purpose. Gold may be freely bought and sold. Exchange controls were abolished in 1979, and Britain meets in full its obligations on capital movements under an OECD code and under EC directives.

Britain's balance of payments current account has been in deficit since 1986, although the deficit recorded in 1996 was the lowest since 1985, at £435 million (see Table 14.7), representing less than 1 per cent of GDP. Since 1983 Britain has had a deficit on trade in goods, and this amounted to £12,598 million in 1996. However, it has almost always run large surpluses on trade in services and investment income. In 1996 the surplus on services rose by £265 million and that on investment income by £1,732 million, while the deficit on transfers fell by £2,256 million.

Table 14.7: Britain's Balance of Payments 1992–96 £ million

	1992	1993	1994	1995	1996
Current account					
Trade in goods and services	–8,154	–7,944	–6,353	–4,705	–5,456
Investment income	3,124	2,595	9,667	7,920	9,652
Transfers balance	–5,102	–4,946	–4,969	–6,887	–4,631
Current balance	–10,133	–10,295	–1,655	–3,672	–435
Transactions in assets and liabilities					
British external assets	–81,600	–157,248	–34,865	–118,844	–219,293
British external liabilities	86,586	169,075	31,491	120,524	217,095
Balancing item	5,147	–1,532	5,029	1,992	2,633

Source: *United Kingdom Balance of Payments 1997 Edition*
Note: Differences between totals and the sums of their component parts are due to rounding.

Table 14.8: Summary of Transactions in External Assets[a] and Liabilities[b] 1994-96
£ million

	1994	1995	1996
Overseas direct investment in Britain	6,087	14,325	20,758
Overseas portfolio investment in Britain	32,928	19,453	27,701
British direct investment overseas	–21,982	–27,927	–28,560
British portfolio investment overseas	18,448	–38,115	–60,691
Borrowing from overseas	–8,024	85,008	169,428
Deposits and lending overseas	–29,667	–52,365	–129,898
Official reserves[a]	–1,045	200	509
Other external liabilities of general government	500	1,738	–792
Other external assets of central government	–619	–637	–653
Total	–3,374	1,680	–2,198

Source: *United Kingdom Balance of Payments 1997 Edition*
[a] Increase –/decrease +
[b] Increase +/decrease –
Note: Differences between totals and the sums of their component parts are due to rounding.

Inward and Outward Investment

The Government welcomes both outward and inward investment. Outward investment helps to develop markets for British exports while providing earnings in the form of investment income. Inward investment is promoted by the Invest in Britain Bureau (IBB), which reports jointly to the DTI and the FCO—see p. 198. This investment is seen as a means of introducing new technology, products and management styles; creating or safeguarding employment; and increasing exports (around 90 per cent of inward investors export from their British base) or substituting imports.

The IBB was notified of 483 new inward investment projects from 26 countries in 1996-97, which are expected to create or safeguard 94,000 jobs. Inward investment is playing an increasingly important role in Britain's economy, with overseas firms providing 19 per cent of all manufacturing jobs, 26 per cent of net output, 30 per cent of manufacturing investment and about 40 per cent of manufacturing exports. At present, Britain has over 40 per cent of US and Japanese and over 50 per cent of South Korean and Taiwanese investment in the EU. Inward investment has benefited a range of industries, including telecommunications and the information sector, electronics, medical equipment, pharmaceuticals, financial services, food and drink, and the automotive industry. The single European market and relatively low taxation are among the most frequently quoted reasons for locating in Britain.

At the end of 1996 the stock of inward direct investment (investment in branches, subsidiaries and associated companies which gives the investor an effective role in their management) was around £154,000 million. The stock of direct investment overseas by British residents was £214,600 million at the end of 1996. The stock of overseas portfolio investment in Britain amounted to nearly £351,000 million at the end of 1996, while the stock of British portfolio investment overseas was £517,000 million. An analysis of transactions in Britain's external assets and liabilities for 1994–96 is given in Table 14.8. Britain's identified external assets at the end of 1996 exceeded liabilities by nearly £5,000 million.

At the end of 1995, 86 per cent of outward direct investment was in developed countries, with 40 per cent in the United States and 37 per cent in the EU. Investment from developed countries accounted for over 97 per cent of overseas direct investment in Britain: 68 per cent originated in the United States and 30 per cent in the EU.

Further Reading

Overseas Trade. Aspects of Britain series, HMSO, 1994.

United Kingdom Balance of Payments 1997 Edition. Office for National Statistics, The Stationery Office, 1997.

Trade and Industry. The Government's Expenditure Plans 1996–1998 to 1999–2000. The Stationery Office, 1997.

15 Manufacturing and Construction

Britain became the world's first industrialised country in the mid-19th century. Wealth was based on manufacturing iron and steel, heavy machinery and cotton textiles, and on coalmining, shipbuilding and trade. Manufacturing continues to play an important role in the modern economy. Britain excels in high-technology industries such as chemicals, plastics, pharmaceuticals, electronics, motor vehicles and components, aerospace, offshore equipment, and paper and printing, where British companies are among the world's largest and most successful. Britain's construction industry has made its mark around the world and continues to be involved in some of the most prestigious international building projects.

Introduction

Manufacturing accounted for about 21 per cent of gross domestic product (GDP) in 1996 and for 18 per cent of employment. More than four-fifths of visible exports consisted of manufactured or semi-manufactured goods. Almost all manufacturing is carried out by private sector businesses. Overseas companies are responsible for one-third of manufacturing investment in Britain, nearly one-fifth of manufacturing employment, a quarter of net output and two-fifths of exports.

The recession in the early 1990s led to a serious decline in manufacturing output, but it began to rise again in 1993 and by 1996 was 2.8 per cent above the 1990 level (see Table 15.2). Employment in manufacturing in 1996 was 4.1 million. Total capital investment was £15,388 million.

The construction industry contributes around 5 per cent of GDP and provides employment for some 800,000 people. Following a period of marked decline as recession affected the industry in the early 1990s, output has picked up slightly since 1993 while remaining some way below pre-recession levels. Total domestic fixed capital investment was £1,165 million in 1996, 42 per cent higher than the figure for the previous year.

Sectors of Manufacturing

Relative sizes of enterprises and the main sectors are shown in Tables 15.1 and 15.2. Table 15.3 indicates output and investment. A more detailed description of some of the main sectors is given below.

Food and Drink

Britain has a comprehensive food and drink manufacturing industry, which has accounted for a growing proportion of total domestic food supply since the 1940s; it achieved export sales of £10,100 million in 1996. One of the country's biggest manufacturing industries in terms of output, it employs approximately

Table 15.1: Manufacturing and Construction—Size of Businesses by Turnover and Employment

Annual turnover (£ '000)	Number of businesses 1996	Employment size	Number of businesses 1996
1–49	26,845	1–9	110,415
50–99	26,150	10–19	19,605
100–249	34,110	20–49	13,825
250–499	21,995	50–99	5,020
500–999	17,230	100–199	3,260
1,000–1,999	11,800	200–499	2,095
2,000–4,999	9,260	500–999	690
5,000–9,999	3,870	1,000+	475
10,000+	4,900		
Total	**156,155**	**Total**	**155,385**

Source: *Size Analysis of United Kingdom Business. Business Monitor PA 1003*

Table 15.2: Indices of Manufacturing Output (1990=100)

1992 Standard Industrial Classification Category	Share of output 1990 (weight per 1,000)	1994	1995	1996
Food and beverages	29	104.2	106.2	107.3
Tobacco products	2	107.5	102.8	106.9
Textiles and leather products	14	91.9	90.1	89.2
Wood and wood products	4	97.0	91.2	89.4
Pulp, paper products, printing and publishing	26	102.2	102.5	101.1
Solid and nuclear fuels, oil refining	7	115.9	131.2	117.0
Chemicals and man-made fibres	24	114.0	116.9	119.3
Rubber and plastics products	10	111.1	114.5	113.3
Other non-metallic mineral products	9	93.9	92.3	88.7
Basic metals and metal products	27	87.5	89.0	88.9
Machinery and equipment	21	90.4	90.9	89.4
Electrical and optical equipment	27	115.5	121.6	124.8
Transport equipment	27	92.5	92.0	95.5
Other manufacturing	6	91.0	89.6	91.1
Total	**232**	**100.8**	**102.5**	**102.8**

Source: *United Kingdom National Accounts 1997 Edition*

430,000 people in over 8,200 enterprises, most of which are small to medium-sized companies. The greatest concentration of firms is to be found in the production of bread, cakes and fresh pastry goods, followed by those engaged in processing and preserving fruit and vegetables. The south east of England provides the greatest number of food-based jobs (15 per cent of the total); other areas with large numbers of such jobs are Yorkshire and Humberside and north-west England. Scotch whisky production gives Scotland the highest concentration of employment in the drinks manufacturing industry (27 per cent of the total), with large numbers of jobs in economically deprived

Table 15.3: Output and Investment in Manufacturing

1992 Standard Industrial Classification Category	Gross output (£ million) 1996	Gross domestic fixed capital formation (£ million) 1996
Food and beverages	15,998	2,073
Tobacco products	1,624	72
Textiles and leather products	7,186	481
Wood and wood products	1,513	260
Pulp, paper products, printing and publishing	16,214	1,448
Solid and nuclear fuels, oil refining	3,033	568
Chemicals and man-made fibres	15,819	2,323
Rubber and plastics products	6,551	1,049
Other non-metallic mineral products	4,931	715
Basic metals and metal products	15,199	1,164
Machinery and equipment	12,196	1,072
Electrical and optical equipment	18,270	1,982
Transport equipment	13,914	1,897
Other manufacturing	4,559	284
Total	**137,005**	**15,388**

Source: *United Kingdom National Accounts 1997 Edition*

rural areas; south-east England has the second highest concentration (19 per cent) of drinks-related jobs.

In the last few years, productivity has increased and the food and drink manufacturing industry has undergone restructuring, partly in order to take advantage of the single European market. By far the biggest export category is alcoholic drinks, which account for nearly a third of the value of total food and drink sales overseas. The Scotch whisky industry is one of Britain's top export earners, with overseas sales worth £2,300 million in 1996. Export performance in the food and non-alcoholic beverages sectors is strongest in the areas of milk and cream, biscuits, chocolate and sugar confectionery, tea processing, farm animal feeds and pet food.

Among the biggest companies involved in food manufacturing and processing are Unilever, Northern Foods, Unigate, Hillsdown Holdings, Tate and Lyle, Cadbury Schweppes, Associated British Foods, and United Biscuits. Guinness, Grand Metropolitan and Allied Domecq are three of the world's top four alcoholic drinks companies. Alongside these large concerns, there is a thriving specialist food and drink sector made up of hundreds of small firms supplying high-quality 'niche' products, often to small retail outlets, such as delicatessens.

Frozen foods and chilled convenience foods, such as frozen potato products and ready-prepared meals, salads and pasta, together with yogurts, desserts and 'instant snacks', have formed some of the fastest-growing sectors of the food market in recent years. The range of ready-cooked meals is expanding rapidly, and includes international cuisine. Companies have introduced many new low-fat and fat-free items, ranging from dairy products to complete prepared meals, in order to meet growing consumer health concerns. There has also been a rise in sales of vegetarian foods (both natural vegetable dishes and vegetable-based substitutes of meat products, where soya plays an ever bigger role). Genetically modified foods and drinks with improved consistency of quality and, allegedly, taste are being gradually introduced onto the market, although public acceptance of them is far from certain.

Around 40 per cent of liquid milk in Britain is distributed through a doorstep delivery system employing about 22,500 people; the proportion is, however, declining. Household milk consumption per head—1.85 litres (3.25 pints) a week—is among the highest in the world. Consumption of skimmed and semi-skimmed milk continues to rise as people seek to reduce the fat content in their diet. Milk for manufacturing purposes goes principally into butter, cheese, condensed milk, dried whole and skimmed milk powder, cream and other products such as yogurt. The British dairy industry accounts for around two-thirds of butter and cheese supplies to the domestic market and achieves significant sales in overseas markets.

More than three-quarters of bread is produced in large bakeries. A steady growth in the varieties available, greater awareness of the nutritional value of bread and the growth of the sandwich market have helped stabilise consumption in the last few years. Sales of ready-made sandwiches are now worth an estimated £2,000 million a year. Exports of biscuits were valued at £287 million in 1996 and those of chocolate and sugar confectionery at £567 million.

There are 92 Scotch whisky distilleries in Scotland, producing either malt whisky or grain whisky. The raw material of the former is malt (that is, malted barley) and the latter other grain mixed with malt. Most Scotch whisky consumed is a blend of malt and grain whisky. Examples of well-known brands of such blended Scotch whisky are J & B, Johnnie Walker, Chivas Regal, Famous Grouse, Bell's and Teacher's. Some 13,000 people work in the industry and a further 55,000 are employed in associated sectors such as supplying ingredients and materials. Almost 90 per cent of Scotch whisky production is exported, the European Union (EU) taking 36 per cent, the United States 12 per cent and Japan 4 per cent by volume. Gin and vodka production are also an important part of the spirits industry. Internationally popular brands of liqueur made by British firms include Bailey's Irish Cream and Drambuie, made to an old Scottish recipe.

The brewing industry has four major national brewery groups—Scottish Courage, Bass, Whitbread and Carlsberg-Tetley—and about 480 regional and local brewers of beer. British malt, which is made almost entirely from home-grown barley, is used by brewers throughout the world. Demand for traditional cask-conditioned ales ('real ale') remains steady, while lager now accounts for over half of all beer sales. In recent years there has been a shift towards stronger bottled beers, a significant proportion of which are imported. Cider is made primarily in south-west England, Gloucestershire, Herefordshire and Worcestershire.

Some 410 vineyards and 120 wineries, mainly in southern England, produce an average of 1.8 million litres of wine a year, most of which is white. Quality has steadily improved through the use of new technologies and winemaking techniques.

The soft drinks industry, which had a turnover of £6,500 million in 1996, produces carbonated drinks, concentrates, fruit juices, and natural mineral and bottled waters. A highly competitive industry, it is one of the fastest-growing sectors of the grocery trade, introducing many innovative products each year.

Tobacco

The British tobacco industry manufactures nearly all cigarettes and tobacco goods sold in Britain. Almost all domestic output is provided by three major manufacturers (Imperial Tobacco, Gallaher and Carreras Rothmans). The industry specialises in the production of high-quality cigarettes made from flue-cured tobacco, and achieves significant export sales—£1,200 million in 1996. Europe, the Middle East and Africa are important markets.

Textiles, Clothing and Footwear

Textiles, clothing and footwear make a substantial contribution to the British economy in terms of employment, exports and annual turnover. They benefit greatly from the creative talents of British fashion designers, many of whom have worldwide reputations. Imports from low-cost nations have restrained recent production and employment; nonetheless, together with leather industries, textiles, clothing and footwear employ around 360,000 people. The international Multi-Fibre Arrangement

(MFA—see p. 208) allows a measure of restraint on imports into the EU from low-cost countries; however, the MFA is being phased out over ten years to the year 2005. Increased investment in new machinery and greater attention to design, training and marketing have helped to raise competitiveness. New technologies, largely designed to improve response times and give greater flexibility in production, are being used throughout the industries.

For textiles, there is a high degree of regional concentration, particularly in the East Midlands, north-west England, West Yorkshire, Scotland and Northern Ireland. The clothing industry is scattered throughout Britain, with significant concentrations in north-east England, the East Midlands, south-east England and Scotland. The principal products are spun yarns, woven and knitted fabrics, apparel, industrial and household textiles, and carpets based chiefly on wool, cotton and synthetic fibres. Exports of textiles, clothing and footwear totalled about £6,900 million in 1996.

The textile and clothing industries have around 14,000 firms, comprising a few substantial multi-process companies and two of the world's major groups—Coats Viyella and Courtaulds Textiles—as well as a large number of small and medium-sized firms. Britain's wool textile industry is one of the most important in the world. West Yorkshire is the main producing area, but Scotland is also famous as a specialist originator of high-quality yarns and tweeds. Raw wool is scoured and cleaned in Britain in preparation for woollen and worsted spinning and weaving. (Worsted is fine wool fabric often used for making suits.) British mills also process rare fibres such as cashmere and angora. Low-cost competition has cut progressively into British markets for cotton and allied products. Production includes yarn and fabrics of cotton, synthetic fibres and cotton-synthetic mixes, with large-scale dyeing and printing of cotton and synthetic fibre fabric. The linen industry is centred in Northern Ireland. The high quality and variety of design make Britain one of the world's leading producers of woven carpets. Over half the value of carpet and rug output

is made up of tufted carpets. Woven carpets, mainly Axminster, account for most of the remaining sales. There is a higher wool content in woven types, although in these, too, considerable use is being made of synthetic fibres.

Industrial textiles account for an increasing proportion of textile industry output, covering such items as conveyor belting and geotextiles used in civil engineering. Many of these are non-woven. Synthetic polypropylene yarn is used in the manufacture of carpet backing and ropes, and woven into fabrics for a wide range of applications in the packaging, upholstery, building and motor vehicle industries. The British silk industry employs around 4,000 people and produces goods valued at over £170 million each year.

The clothing industry, with about 8,000 companies, is more labour-intensive than textiles. While a broad range of clothing is imported from Europe and Asia, British industry supplies about one-half of domestic demand. Exports have risen since the British fashion designer industry regained prominence during the 1980s, and traditional design and high-quality production enable branded clothing companies such as Daks Simpson and Jaeger to compete successfully overseas. The hosiery and knitwear industry comprises about 1,000 companies, mainly in the East Midlands and Scotland. The 500 footwear manufacturers, with around 22,000 employees, are predominantly found in Northamptonshire, Leicestershire and Lancashire; they include C. & J. Clark, Church and R. Griggs (makers of the 'Doc Martens' range). Exports of British footwear exceeded £500 million in 1996.

Paper, Printing and Publishing

There are 97 paper and board mills in Britain, employing 23,000 people. Among the largest British groups are Shotton, St Regis and Bridgewater. Production has been concentrated in large-scale units to enable the industry to compete more effectively within the single European market. Between 1986 and 1996 output increased by almost two-thirds. Over half the industry is made up of forestry product companies from Scandinavia, North America, Australia and elsewhere. There has been a significant trend towards waste-based packaging grades. Usage of recycled waste paper is increasing and research is helping to extend it. In 1996 the total amount of waste paper used in British newspapers accounted for three-quarters of newsprint produced. Waste paper provides over half of the industry's fibrous raw materials.

Employment in the paper products, printing and publishing industries is 440,000. Much printing and publishing employment and output is in firms based in south-east England. Mergers have led to the formation of large groups in newspaper, magazine and book publishing. The British book-publishing industry is a major exporter: in 1996 it published 101,500 new titles, a 6.8 per cent rise on 1995; British publishers' sales within Britain were worth £1,949 million and their exports £1,143 million. Security printers (of, for example, banknotes and postage stamps) are also important exporters, the major company being De La Rue.

Chemicals and Related Products

The chemicals industry, which is the fifth largest in the world, accounts for almost one-tenth of Britain's manufacturing output, making it the country's fourth largest manufacturing sector. It provides direct employment for about 250,000 people working in 3,900 enterprises. About a half of all the industry's employment is divided between south-east England (especially strong in pharmaceuticals) and the north west of England (basic chemical production). Basic industrial chemicals and pharmaceuticals are the biggest sectors. Products of the chemicals industry underpin almost all other industrial processes and output. Sectors include petrochemicals derived from hydrocarbon feedstock resources; suppliers to other manufacturing industries, such as specialised organic chemicals for pharmaceuticals; and suppliers of consumer products such as paints, soaps and detergents.

The industry's largest markets are plastics processing, packaging, agriculture, the National Health Service, and the clothing and textiles industries. It is at the forefront of modern technology, spending about 8 per cent of total sales on research and development (R & D). Around two-thirds of its output is exported, making it British manufacturing's greatest single export earner. Exports in 1996 were worth around £23,000 million, the strongest sectors being organic chemicals, plastics and synthetic rubbers, pharmaceuticals, soaps and detergents, and man-made fibres. Imports, mainly consisting of plastics, pharmaceuticals, photographic chemical materials and perfumes, were valued at £18.8 million. Productivity has increased sharply over the past ten years.

Traditionally, Britain has been a major producer of basic industrial chemicals, for example basic organic and inorganic chemicals, plastics and fertilisers, which together comprise around a third of output. The most rapid growth in recent years has, however, been in pharmaceuticals. The most important bulk products are ethylene, propylene and benzene. Britain is one of the world's biggest producers of specialised organic chemicals.

Much inorganic chemical production consists of relatively simple bulk chemicals, such as sulphuric acid and metallic and non-metallic oxides, serving as basic materials for industry. Speciality chemicals include pharmaceutical ingredients, essential oils and flavourings, adhesives and sealants, and explosives, including those used for car safety airbags. Investment in environmentally safe products and processes, for example substitutes for chlorofluorocarbons (CFCs), is increasing.

Many major chemical companies in Britain are multinationals; several are subsidiaries of overseas companies and others are specialist manufacturers of pharmaceuticals, such as Glaxo Wellcome (see p. 218). Imperial Chemical Industries (ICI), one of the world's biggest chemicals groups, manufactures industrial chemicals, paints, materials and explosives. In May 1997, ICI announced its intention to restructure its operations, which involved buying Unilever's specialised chemicals division and selling its own industrial chemicals businesses. BOC, the industrial gases group, is Britain's second largest chemicals company. Zeneca, formerly part of ICI, produces pharmaceuticals, agrochemicals and seeds, and speciality chemicals. Laporte is Britain's biggest speciality chemicals firm.

Teesside, which has been particularly successful in attracting investment from some of the leading domestic and overseas chemical firms, now rivals Rotterdam as Europe's largest petrochemicals zone. Grangemouth in Scotland is also an important petrochemicals zone. BP and Shell, along with several other large oil and gas companies, are major producers of petrochemicals.

The agrochemicals sector invests heavily in R & D. Notable discoveries include diquat and paraquat herbicides, pyrethroid insecticides, systemic fungicides and aphicides, genetically engineered microbial pesticides and methods of encouraging natural parasites to eradicate common pests in horticulture.

Exports of soap and detergent preparations in 1996 were valued at £673 million. This sector is dominated by Lever Brothers (part of Unilever) and Procter and Gamble.

Plastics

About 183,800 people are employed by 5,940 firms involved in the plastics industry. Regions with the highest concentrations of employment are south-east England, the West Midlands and the north west of England. Total turnover of the industry was about £12,000 million in 1996, with exports reaching £3,300 million. Plastics have a plethora of applications in the packaging, building, electrical and electronic, automotive, medical, furniture and clothing industries. Britain's plastic processing industry continues to be a world leader in material specification and design, with new processes allowing stronger plastics to replace other materials or spread into new applications.

Paints

Sales of paint, varnishes and similar coatings were worth £2,300 million in 1996. ICI is the world's largest paint manufacturer. Among its products are new ranges of non-drip and quick-drying paints, and paints needing only one top coat. Its best-known consumer product is the 'Dulux' paint range. Two of the more significant innovations have been solid emulsion paint and a temporary water-based finish which can be removed easily by chemical treatment, for vehicle bodies and road markings.

Pharmaceuticals

The British pharmaceutical industry is the world's third biggest exporter of medicines, accounting for around 10 per cent of the world market. It manufactures the complete range of medicinal products—human and veterinary medicines, medical dressings and dental materials. In recent times, the largest growth has been in medicines that act on the respiratory system, followed by cardiovascular, muscular and skeletal, anti-infective and alimentary tract remedies. Pharmaceutical exports in 1996 reached a record £5,700 million. The main overseas markets are Western Europe and North America, with Japan an expanding market.

Over 400 pharmaceutical manufacturers and research organisations operate in Britain, including several British and US parent multinationals which dominate production (the biggest 21 firms account for 70 per cent of production and employment). The three largest are the British-owned group Glaxo Wellcome; Zeneca, also British-owned and the world's second biggest manufacturer of cancer therapies; and SmithKline Beecham, manufacturer of four of the world's best-selling antibiotics. A growing trend is the production of generic medicines—versions of branded medicines whose patents have expired. They are mostly unbranded and cheaper than the branded originals. More than 50 per cent of prescriptions dispensed by pharmacists are for generic medicines.

Some 75,000 people work in the industry, of whom more than a quarter are engaged in R & D; another 250,000 are employed in related sectors. The industry, which is largely based in the south east and north west of England, invested around £2,000 million in R & D in 1996. This sum amounts to about one-fifth of British industry's R & D. Progress in devising vaccines over the last few decades has helped to reduce dramatically the impact of infectious diseases such as polio, whooping cough, mumps and measles. British firms discovered and developed five of the world's 20 best-selling medicines, including Glaxo Wellcome's ulcer treatment Zantac, in recent years the world's best-selling medicine, SmithKline Beecham's ulcer treatment Tagamet, and Zeneca's beta-blocker Tenormin, for treating high blood pressure. Other major developments pioneered in Britain are semi-synthetic penicillins and cephalosporins, both powerful antibiotics, and new treatments for asthma, arthritis, migraine and coronary heart disease.

Among Zeneca's products are Zestril (for combating high blood pressure), Zoladex (a prostate cancer therapy) and Diprivan (an anaesthetic). SmithKline Beecham developed Augmentin, used to treat a range of infections that have become resistant to other antibiotics. It is one of the world's biggest manufacturers of vaccines. Glaxo Wellcome's drug Zidovudine (AZT) is one of the most widely used anti-viral agents for the treatment of HIV infection. Zofran, also produced by Glaxo Wellcome and one of the company's most successful new medicines, is an anti-nausea drug for countering the unpleasant side- • effects of cancer treatments. British companies lead in the development of molecular graphics. These contribute to the design of new and improved medicines through a computer-aided technique for analysing the structures of complicated organic molecules.

Biotechnology

It is estimated that world markets for biotechnology products could exceed £70,000 million by the year 2000. With one-third of Europe's biotechnology firms (around 220 in total), the British biotechnology industry is second only to that of the United States, employing over 10,000 people and achieving yearly sales of £700 million. As well as Zeneca, Glaxo Wellcome and SmithKline Beecham, around 40 smaller independent firms, including British Biotech, Celltech, Scotia, Chiroscience and Biocompatibles, contribute to the industry. The most

important sectors include chemicals, pharmaceuticals, food, agriculture, diagnostics and environmental clean-up. The industry is heavily dependent on Britain's universities' considerable expertise in biotechnology.

Biotechnology has improved the specificity of pharmaceuticals through greater understanding of disease at the molecular level. It has enabled companies to manufacture products using genetic modification. British Biotech is developing an anti-cancer drug, Marimastat, which can be taken orally and is claimed to have few serious adverse side-effects. Among other major advances in the development of drugs are human insulin and interferons, genetically engineered vaccines, antibiotics produced by fermentation, and alternative bactericidal drugs based on Nisin, a food preservative made in Britain.

A second generation of vaccines based on recombinant DNA technology includes SmithKline Beecham's Engerix-B vaccine against hepatitis. Therapies based on correcting the function of defective genes are under development. Diseases being targeted include those where a single defective gene needs correcting, such as in cystic fibrosis, and those where there are genetic and environmental components, like cardiovascular disease.

Agricultural products include infection-resistant crops; Zeneca is a world leader in plant breeding, having brought onto the market a genetically modified tomato paste. Biotechnology is providing new tools for the selection and design of microbes and enzymes in food production. Diagnostic devices for the medical, food, and product hygiene industries are another strong sector.

Specialist goods from Britain's small and medium-sized biotechnology firms comprise, among other items, medical diagnostics and microbial pesticides. Medical diagnostics products are used to diagnose diseases, identify different blood types and can be employed in the treatment of a range of conditions, including cancer.

Important R & D activities include gene therapy, combinatorial chemistry, regulation of the cell cycle, and the development of transgenic animals as sources of organs and as bioreactors.

Synthetic Fibres

Synthetic fibres are supplied to the textiles, clothing and footwear industries. The main types of synthetic fibre are still those first developed in the 1940s: regenerated cellulosic fibres such as viscose, and the major synthetic fibres like nylon polyamide, polyester and acrylics. Extensive research continues to produce a wide variety of innovative products; antistatic and flame-retardant fibres are examples. More specialist products include the aramids (with very high thermal stability and strength), elastanes (giving very high stretch and recovery) and melded fabrics (produced without the need for knitting or weaving).

Courtaulds, one of Britain's biggest chemical companies, was responsible for developing the first new artificial fibre for decades, Tencel, a solvent-spun, biodegradable fibre. It is twice as strong as cotton while being soft enough to be used by designers of luxury garments.

Mineral and Metal Products

In total these industries employ up to 700,000 people. From total crude steel output of 18 million tonnes, British producers delivered 17.5 million tonnes of finished steel in 1996, of which 50 per cent was exported. Over the past ten years annual steel industry exports have increased by 44 per cent—to £3,700 million in 1996, creating a favourable balance of trade in steel products of £2,300 million. Metals can be recycled many times over: every year the British metals recycling industry processes around 2 million tonnes of scrap metal and 8 million tonnes of 'end of life' items.

The major areas of steel production are in south Wales and northern England, with substantial processing in the Midlands and Yorkshire. Major restructuring in the steel industry took place during the 1980s and early 1990s. Productivity and efficiency have improved and the industry is now one of the most competitive in Europe.

British Steel is the fourth largest steel producer in the world, employing 50,000 people worldwide (41,000 in Britain) and producing 85 per cent of Britain's crude steel in 1996. The company's output is based on semi-finished steel, strip mill products, plate, heavy sections, bars, wire rod and tubes. These are used principally in the construction, automotive, engineering, transport, metal goods, packaging and energy industries. British Steel is Europe's biggest producer of engineering steels— specialist grades used to make components for the automotive and aerospace industries. It owns 51 per cent of Avesta Sheffield, one of Europe's leading stainless steel producers.

Other important steel producers in Britain include Caparo, Allied Steel and Wire, Co-Steel Sheerness and the Glynwed Group. Products manufactured by these companies include reinforcing bars for the construction industry, wire rod, hot rolled and cold finished bars, and other special steels for the aerospace and offshore oil and gas industries.

Several multinational companies, including Alcan, Norsk Hydro, Kaiser, MIM and Quexco, have plants in Britain producing non-ferrous metals. The aluminium industry, which has raised its productivity and competitiveness significantly in recent years, supplies customers in the aerospace, transport, automotive and construction industries. Other important non-ferrous metal sectors are copper, used for heat exchangers, boilers, tubing and electrical gear; lead for lead acid batteries and roofing; zinc for galvanising to protect steel; nickel, used principally as an alloying element to make stainless steel and high temperature turbine alloys; and titanium for high-strength, low-weight aerospace applications.

Construction Materials and Products

A vast range of products is used in the construction process, from structural steel, glass and bricks to tiles and bathroom fittings. Some 60 per cent of buildings of two or more floors constructed today in Britain are based on steel. Materials are estimated to make up around 40 per cent of the value of construction output, some £22,000 million a year. In 1996 exports amounted to approximately £4,000 million. The industry comprises some 20,000 firms employing 400,000 people.

Most crushed rock, sand and gravel quarried by the aggregates industry is used in construction. The brick industry, one of

Britain's oldest, is regarded as the world's most technically advanced. Portland cement, a 19th-century British innovation, is the most widely used chemical compound in the world. Glass-reinforced cement composites for the construction industry were invented in Britain in the early 1970s and are made under licence in over 40 countries. Blue Circle, Britain's largest producer of cement, and Rugby, the third largest, are planning new plants, on a wide scale, in south-east England and the Midlands respectively.

Britain is a world leader in the manufacture of glass used in windows, doors and cladding. Flat glass is manufactured through the float glass process, which was developed by Pilkington Brothers and is licensed to glassmakers throughout the world. Pilkington has also produced an energy-saving window glass, which reflects room heat without impairing visibility. The manufacture and supply of windows and doors are carried out by a large number of other companies operating in one of three product sectors—timber, metal (aluminium and steel) and UPVC.

Ceramics

The ceramics industry manufactures domestic pottery, as well as durables such as sanitaryware, tiles and clay pipes for the building trade. Domestic tableware production includes fine china, earthenware and stoneware. Tableware is produced predominantly in Stoke-on-Trent. Britain is the world's leading manufacturer and exporter of fine bone china: Waterford, Wedgwood, Spode and Royal Doulton are among the more famous names.

Research is being conducted into ceramics for use in housebuilding and diesel and jet engines (see p. 228). Important industrial ceramics invented in Britain include some forms of silicon carbide and sialons, which can withstand ultra-high temperatures.

China Clay

Britain is the world's second biggest exporter of china clay (kaolin), three-quarters of which is used in paper-making, and 2 million tonnes of which were sold overseas in 1996. The main company is ECC International, part of the English China Clays Group.

Mechanical Engineering

The mechanical engineering sector has about 29,000 firms employing some 560,000 people. In 1996 exports totalled nearly £21,000 million. Output includes pressure vessels, heat exchangers and storage tanks for chemical and oil-refining plant; steam-raising boilers (including those for power stations); nuclear reactors; water and sewage treatment plant; and fabricated steelwork for bridges, buildings and industrial installations.

Machine-building is an area in which British firms excel, especially construction and earth-moving equipment, wheeled tractors, internal combustion engines, textile machinery, medical equipment, fork-lift trucks, pumps and compressors. Britain is one of the world's major producers of tractors (almost a third of tractors produced in Europe are manufactured in Britain), which make up a large proportion of the country's total output of agricultural equipment. Among leading tractor manufacturers are Massey Ferguson, Case, New Holland and JCB. Widely used technical innovations include computer-controlled tractors, a highly efficient pesticide sprayer and combined mower/conditioners that reduce the drying time for grass. Much new machinery is designed for use in a variety of conditions to meet the needs of overseas farmers.

Britain is a leading producer of machine tools. Almost all are purchased by the engineering, aerospace, automotive and metal goods industries. The machine tools sector has made a good recovery after a substantial downturn in the early 1990s, with exports doing especially well. Turnover of machine tools was valued at over £870 million in 1996, 35 per cent more than in 1995; exports account for almost two-thirds of turnover. British manufacturers have made technological advances in probes, sensors, co-ordinate measuring devices, laser melting and the installation of flexible manufacturing systems. Computer numerical-controlled machines account for an increasing proportion of output. Of the top six machine tool companies in Britain, five are foreign-owned; the 600 Group is the biggest British company.

Most sales of textile machinery are to export markets. British innovations include computerised colour matching and weave simulation, friction spinning, high-speed computer-controlled knitting machines and electronic jacquard attachments for weaving looms. Britain also produces world-leading printing machinery and ceramic processing equipment, and other types of production machinery.

Britain's mining and tunnelling equipment industry leads in the production of coal-cutting and road-heading (shearing) equipment, hydraulic roof supports, conveying equipment, flameproof transformers, switchgear, and subsurface transport equipment and control systems. JCB, Britain's biggest construction equipment manufacturer, is the world's leading maker of backhoe loaders and telescopic handlers.

The mechanical lifting and handling equipment industry makes cranes and transporters, lifting devices, escalators, conveyors, powered industrial trucks and air bridges, as well as electronically controlled and automatic handling systems. Britain is also a major producer of industrial engines, pumps, valves and compressors, and of pneumatic and hydraulic equipment. Companies such as Babcock manufacture steam generators and other heavy equipment for power plants. Despite an overall decline in the castings industry, some foundries have invested in new melting, moulding and quality control equipment.

Electrical, Electronic and Instrument Engineering

The electrical engineering industry manufactures a broad range of goods: power plant, cable, transformers and switchgear, lighting, electrical installation products, and heating, ventilating and air conditioning equipment. The British-French group GEC Alsthom is one of only a handful of firms in the world which can supply the major components for a complete power station project and the transformers and switchgear needed in transmission and distribution of electricity. Rolls-Royce Industrial Power Group uses highly efficient aero-derivative gas turbines in smaller applications. Britain is a world leader in the manufacture of generating sets. In the cables sector, BICC and Pirelli produce high-voltage transmission cables and optical fibre cables for telecommunications. TLG (formerly Thorn Lighting Group) is Britain's largest manufacturer of lighting products.

The domestic electrical appliance sector manufactures 'white' goods (washing machines, refrigerators, dishwashers and so on), vacuum cleaners, small domestic electrical appliances and domestic gas appliances. It employs about 28,000 people. Household brand names include Hotpoint, Creda, Candy/Hoover and Electrolux. Among innovative products in the last few years is the dual cyclone vacuum cleaner manufactured by Dyson, which is now the leading upright vacuum cleaner manufacturer in Britain. The commercial heating, ventilation, air-conditioning and refrigeration sector is served to a great extent by small and medium-sized firms, although several large multinational companies have sites in Britain.

Eleven of the world's leading electronics firms have manufacturing plants in Britain, and inward investment has become extremely important. Chunghwa, Fujitsu, Motorola, NEC, Seagate and Siemens are among major overseas conglomerates to make substantial outlays in Britain in the last few years. In 1996 South Korea's Hyundai and LG groups announced investments in Britain totalling more than £4,000 million; the latter will employ over 6,000 people at Europe's largest inward investment project in Newport, south Wales, manufacturing semiconductors and wide-screen television sets and components. Several leading Japanese consumer electronics firms, among them Sony and Panasonic, are establishing major manufacturing bases in Britain, with south Wales attracting a large share of the funds.

Britain has the fifth largest electronics industry in the world, with an annual turnover of about £22,000 million. Products include computers, telecommunications equipment and a wide range of components, including semiconductors. The major electronic consumer goods produced are television sets and high-fidelity audio and video equipment. British manufacturers have a worldwide reputation for high-quality goods aimed at the upper end of the market.

Scotland's electronics industry ('Silicon Glen') directly employs about 40,000 people. It produces 13 per cent of Europe's semiconductors, about 35 per cent of its personal computers, about 45 per cent of its computer workstations and some 50 per cent of its automated cash dispensers. Japanese, US and other overseas companies located in the area include Compaq, Digital, Hughes, IBM, Motorola, National Semiconductor and NEC.

Computers

This sector produces an extensive range of systems, central processors and peripheral equipment, from large computers for bulk data-processing and scientific work to mini- and microcomputers for control and automation systems, and for home, educational and office use. In 1996 exports of computers and other information processing equipment amounted to over £11,000 million. For information on software, see chapter 16, pp. 247–8.

Britain's biggest computer manufacturer is the largely Japanese-owned ICL. Other companies, such as Psion (a pioneer of the 'palmtop' computer), have concentrated on developing new lines for specialised markets. These include palmtop hand-held, pocket-sized computers, increasingly used by company sales forces, and notebook and pen computers.

British firms and research organisations have been involved in the development and application of the family of 'three-five' semiconductor materials, such as gallium arsenide; these are used in a number of devices and in the production of faster-working computers. Major advances are being made by British firms and academic institutions in the

field of 'virtual reality', a three-dimensional computer simulation technique with a host of industrial and other applications. It is being used to design buildings and a range of products, including cars, pharmaceuticals and machine tools.

Telecommunications

Britain has over 150 telecommunications companies, including major multinationals, as well as 2,500 call centres (central customer service points), meeting the growing demand for equipment and services (see pp. 321–3). There has been rapid expansion in the market for cordless and mobile telephones in the last decade or so. Residential customers are beginning to make greater use of what have been primarily business communication services, such as faxes, modems and videotext.

The domestic telecommunications market is worth some £3,200 million annually in equipment. The equipment industry, which has about 28,000 employees, is dominated by large inward investors. It is at the forefront in developing software-controlled digital public switching. Britain's main telecommunications products are switching and transmission equipment, telephones and terminals. GPT is Britain's foremost telecommunications manufacturer; its range includes PBXs (private branch exchanges), transmission systems and videoconferencing equipment. There has been major investment in Britain in digital exchanges—BT has invested over £20,000 million since the mid-1980s in replacing electro-mechanical exchanges with digital exchanges, which now account for four-fifths of the network.

Transmission equipment and cables for telecommunications and information networks include submarine and high-specification data-carrying cables. BT has led in the development of optical fibre communications systems. It paved the way for simpler and cheaper optical cables by laying the first non-repeatered cable over 100 km (62 miles) long, and by devising the first all-optical repeater. Britain also has a world lead in the transmission of computerised data along telephone lines for reproduction on television screens.

Another sector of the industry manufactures radio communications equipment, radar, radio and sonar navigational aids for ships and aircraft, thermal imaging systems, alarms and signalling equipment, public broadcasting equipment and other capital goods. Radar was invented in Britain and British firms are still in the forefront of technological advances. Racal Avionics' X-band radar for aircraft ground movement control is in use at airports in several overseas countries. Solid-state secondary surveillance radar, manufactured by Cossor Electronics, is being supplied to 50 overseas civil aviation operators. Cable and Wireless's submarine cable-laying robot 'CIRRUS', which can work at depths of up to 1 km (3,280 ft), is controlled entirely by a computer on its mother ship.

Medical Equipment

The high demand for advanced medical equipment in Britain stems from its comprehensive health care system and numerous clinical research and testing facilities undertaking research in the chemical, biological, physical and molecular sciences. Important contributions have been made by Britain's scientists and engineers to basic R & D in endoscopy, CT (computerised tomography) scanning, magnetic resonance imaging (pioneered in Britain), ultrasonic imaging, CADiagnosis and renal analysis.

Against this background, the industry—in total more than 1,000 firms—continues its tradition of developing and manufacturing a large range of medical equipment for domestic and overseas health sectors. It is especially strong in the fields of electronic measurement and test equipment, analytical instruments, and process control equipment. Companies such as GEC and Oxford Instruments produce, among other things, ultrasound scanners, electromyography systems and patient monitoring systems for intensive and coronary care and other uses. Other well-known British-owned companies include BTR, Smith and Nephew, Vickers and Smiths Industries. Over half of medium to large companies have a US or other overseas parent and these account for over two-fifths of total output.

Other Electronic Equipment

A variety of electronic measurement and test equipment is made in Britain, as well as analytical instruments, process control equipment, and numerical control and indication materials for use in machine tools. The instrument engineering industry makes measuring, photographic, cinematographic and reprographic items; watches, clocks and other timing devices; and medical and surgical instruments. Overseas sales of scientific and photographic equipment were worth almost £6,671 million in 1996.

Materials

New and improved materials, and the ability to process and fabricate them more efficiently into components, finished products and systems, are vital to manufacturing industry. Britain devotes a substantial proportion of its R & D resources to developing these materials and processes. Materials can be classified into two main types: structural—which include steels, non-ferrous alloys, engineering ceramics, reinforced plastics, wood and concrete; and functional—for exploiting the electronic make-up and properties of such things as conductors, semiconductors, magnets and sensors. Materials are a key element in medical engineering, and much R & D work is being done in biomaterials, biomechanics, implantable devices and cellular/tissue engineering, for example.

Britain is at the leading edge of materials science and technology. It is a prime manufacturer in the areas of high temperature materials, weight-saving technologies, superconductivity, offshore supplies and materials processing. It excels in the areas of engineering ceramics and ceramic composites, surface coatings, high temperature metals, polymers, elastomers, polymer composites, and metal matrix composites. Through the development of new materials and improvement of conventional ones, important advances have been made in leading industrial sectors such as aerospace, defence, telecommunications, power generation, offshore oil and gas structures, medical equipment, construction and packaging. As with traditional materials, the key properties most often sought in a new one are fatigue strength, stress/strain relationships, corrosion resistance, and processability.

The aerospace industry has pioneered various developments. Rolls-Royce is testing ceramic and metal matrix composite materials at high temperatures and aims to increase their usage in aero-engines, improving the performance of components while reducing engine weight. Fibre-reinforced polymer composites, increasingly used in aerospace structures, possess high specific strength and stiffness. Structural health monitoring of these components may in the near future depend on the use of 'smart' materials, in the form of sensors (using optical fibres, for instance) to be incorporated during manufacture into the aircraft structure to produce a 'sensitive skin'. Smart materials could also be used in bridges; they would indicate when and where repairs were needed.

Biomaterials are being used in implant and medical devices. HAPEX, a composite ceramic with similar properties to the human skeleton, has been developed at London University. An artificial hip made from HAPEX could last 25 years, compared with 15 years for existing artificial metal hips.

Automotive Industry

Around 750,000 jobs are dependent on the automotive industry, including 310,000 engaged in vehicle and component production and manufacturing activities. There are 22 car and ten truck and van manufacturers, and 7,000 components manufacturers. Car output is dominated by seven overseas groups, accounting for 99 per cent of the total: Rover (a subsidiary of BMW), Ford (including Jaguar), Vauxhall, Peugeot-Talbot, Honda, Nissan and Toyota. The remainder is in the hands of smaller, specialist producers such as Rolls-Royce, whose cars are renowned for their quality and durability. Rover's model range includes the highly successful Land Rover four-wheel drive vehicles and a full range of family cars.

Capital investment continues on a large scale, including nearly £2,600 million by Ford between 1996 and 2000 and around £500

million a year by Rover as well as a £400 million investment in a new engine factory. Since their arrival in the mid-1980s, Nissan, Toyota and Honda have invested nearly £4,000 million and by 1998 all three will be producing two models in Britain. A period of major change has accompanied the arrival of the three Japanese car manufacturers. Their management approach, high productivity, quality, workforce commitment and co-operative partnerships have had a positive effect on established car and component manufacturers alike.

New car registrations increased by 4 per cent in 1996 to 2.025 million, the third highest total on record and the first time since 1990 that they have exceeded 2 million. Car production, at 1.7 million, was at the highest level since 1973, owing in large part to a strong export performance. A total of 908,000 passenger cars were exported in 1996, more than twice as many as in 1990. Exports of road vehicles and their components in 1996 were valued at £18,000 million, some 21 per cent up on 1995.

Volvo is the biggest builder of buses in Britain; in autumn 1996 it announced orders for over 500 double-deck buses for operators in Hong Kong and Singapore. In spring 1997, Dennis Specialist Vehicles received orders for 421 double-deck buses from Hong Kong bus operators. Britain's first purpose-built bus to be powered by liquefied petroleum gas is being developed by Northern Counties.

The motor components industry has enjoyed strong growth in recent times—both in the British-owned sector and from international investment—and is ranked as one of Britain's major industries. It includes British companies with worldwide operations, such as LucasVarity, GKN and T&N, as well as several of the world's top-selling firms—including Bosch and Valeo. Altogether, there are now 28 German, 35 Japanese, 22 US and 15 French companies established in Britain. Two-thirds of the components used in British-built Japanese cars are manufactured in Britain.

LucasVarity, which includes Varity Perkins, is Britain's largest automotive systems supplier and one of the world's top ten automotive suppliers. It specialises in

The motor sport industry employs 50,000 people full-time and 100,000 part-time in Britain, and has annual sales of £1,300 million, of which 60 per cent are export sales. About 700 firms are involved exclusively in the industry. Six of the 11 Formula 1 car makers are based in Britain, taking advantage of the country's engineering expertise in the design and construction of racing chassis and engines. Cosworth, a Vickers subsidiary, is the producer of the most successful engine in Grand Prix motoring history.

braking, diesel, and electrical and electronic components. GKN is a world leader in the design and manufacture of automotive driveline systems; it is the world's foremost producer of constant velocity joints linking engines to wheels. T&N supplies customers all over the world with bearings, friction materials and piston and engine products.

Ford's engine plant at Bridgend in south Wales turns out over 500,000 Zetec engines a year for export to Ford plants around Europe. At its nearby Swansea factory, the company produces 10 million components annually, including camshafts, crankshafts and disc brakes.

Shipbuilding and Marine Engineering

In 1996 the merchant shipbuilding industry had a turnover of £200 million and provided employment for some 4,000 people in nine yards. Order books of British merchant shipbuilders for new building were estimated to be worth £370 million at the end of March 1997. Merchant shiprepairers, with some 4,000 employees, had a turnover of £300 million in 1996. Including warship building, repair and refit, the sector employs 26,000 people. The marine equipment industry is a major contributor to the shipbuilding industry, with equipment installed in a ship's hull accounting for about 50 per cent of its total cost. In 1995 some 130 firms had a turnover of £825 million. In total, there are around 800 firms offering a complete range of products, from sophisticated navigational systems to diving equipment, about 70 per cent of which is exported.

More than two decades of oil and gas exploitation in the North Sea have generated a major offshore industry (see p. 264). Shipbuilders and fabricators build floating production units and semi-submersible units for drilling, production and emergency/maintenance support; drill ships; jack-up rigs; modules; and offshore loading systems. UIE Scotland, Highlands Fabricators, John Brown and McDermott Scotland are among the larger manufacturers and designers. In 1996 Harland and Wolff of Belfast was awarded a £70 million contract by BP to build the hull for the world's largest newly constructed floating oil production vessel. Several thousand firms supply other products needed by the offshore industry—such as diving equipment and helicopters—as well as services, including consultancy, design, project management and R & D. Their experience of North Sea projects has enabled them to establish themselves in oil and gas markets throughout the world.

Railway Equipment

A number of companies based in Britain manufacture locomotives, rolling stock, signalling and other equipment for domestic and overseas railway operators. The newly privatised passenger train operators have announced plans for major investments in new trains in the next few years. In addition, Railtrack plans to invest £10,000 million in track, signalling and other rail infrastructure equipment (see p. 311). Adtranz and GEC Alsthom have secured orders in Britain worth respectively £360 million and £190 million in 1996–97.

Aerospace and Defence

Britain's aerospace industry, the biggest in Europe, is one of only three in the world with a complete capability across the whole spectrum of aerospace. The leading companies are British Aerospace (BAe), Rolls-Royce and GEC-Marconi, all of which are among Britain's top five exporters. Just under 93,000 people are directly employed in the aerospace industry, with a further 140,000 working in related sectors. The Society of British Aerospace Companies represents the interests of 350 aerospace firms. Total sales of the industry amounted to over £13,000 million in 1996, with exports contributing nearly £10,000 million. Aircraft and parts account for about two-fifths of overseas sales, with engines and parts, missiles and aerospace equipment (including satellite equipment) making up the rest.

The industry's activities cover designing and constructing airframes, aero-engines, guided weapons, simulators and space satellites, materials, flight controls including 'fly-by-wire' and 'fly-by-light' equipment (see p. 228), avionics and complex components, with their associated services. In order to improve fuel economy, engine and airframe manufacturers use lighter materials such as titanium and carbon-fibre composites (see p. 225), combined with advanced avionics and improved aerodynamic techniques.

Britain is the second largest defence supplier after the United States. The aerospace industry has improved efficiency and competitiveness to cope with reductions in defence orders following the end of the Cold War. British-based firms achieved a record share of the world market for defence supplies in 1996, with exports estimated at £4,700 million. An increase in the amount of collaborative development of civil and military aircraft and engines, as well as aviation equipment and satellites, is leading to significant savings on the costs of long-term programmes. The four-nation Eurofighter programme (see p. 148), involving British Aerospace, Rolls-Royce and 200 other British defence firms, is expected to support up to 14,000 jobs in Britain at the peak of production early next century.

Civil Aircraft

British Aerospace (BAe) produces both civil and military aircraft, as well as guided weapons and aircraft components. It has a 20 per cent share of the European consortium Airbus Industrie, with responsibility for designing and manufacturing the wings for the whole family of Airbus airliners, from the short- to medium-

haul A320 series (the first civil airliner to use fly-by-wire controls—see p. 228) to the large long-range four-engined A340. In 1996 Airbus signed firm orders for 326 new aircraft worth a total of US$23,600 million from 31 customers around the world, giving it a 40 per cent market share for airliners with more than 100 seats. With Aerospatiale of France and Italy's Alenia, BAe has formed a regional aircraft alliance which jointly markets turboprops and jet aircraft with between 29 and 115 seats; these include BAe's Avro RJ family of regional 'quiet jet' airliners.

The Canadian-owned Short Brothers of Belfast, with 9,000 employees, is engaged in the design and production of major civil aircraft sub-assemblies, advanced engine nacelles and components for aerospace manufacturers as well as the provision of aviation support services. It is a leading supplier to Boeing and McDonnell Douglas among others. Shorts is a partner in manufacturing the 50-seat Canadair Regional Jet airliner (it will also contribute airframe parts for the new 70-seat version); the Learjet 45, a small business jet aircraft; and the Bombardier Global Express long-range business jet.

Slingsby Aviation produces several versions of the T67 Firefly two-seater training and acrobatic aircraft for customers around the world. The United States Air Force has chosen the T67 as its new basic trainer and 113 aircraft are being built. Slingsby also designs and makes composite components for the aviation and other industries. Pilatus Britten-Norman manufactures the Islander light utility aircraft, which has had sales in over 100 countries.

Military Aircraft and Missiles

British Aerospace is one of the world's top defence companies, with more than four-fifths of its military production exported in 1996. Among its military aircraft is the Harrier, a vertical/short take-off and landing (V/STOL) military combat aircraft. BAe produces the Hawk fast-jet trainer; the company has signed a £1,000 million contract for the sale of 40 Hawks to Australia. It has also created, with McDonnell Douglas, the Goshawk T45 carrier jet trainer.

The Tornado combat aircraft is built by a company set up jointly by BAe, Alenia and Daimler-Benz Aerospace. A £5,000 million order for 48 Tornado bombers for Saudi Arabia, confirmed in 1993, made it one of Britain's biggest ever export deals. Together with Alenia, Daimler-Benz and Aerospatiale, BAe has formed a new company, a military subsidiary of Airbus Industrie, to manage the Future Large Aircraft military transport programme.

BAe is a major supplier of tactical guided weapon systems for use on land, at sea and in the air, having merged its missile business with that of France's Matra Corporation to form Europe's largest guided weapons concern. Shorts Missile Systems Ltd (SMS) is a joint venture between Shorts and Thomson-CSF of France in the area of very short-range air defence systems.

GEC-Marconi has an annual turnover of £3,500 million, and employs a total of 29,000 people in Britain and overseas. The company is prime contractor for the PHOENIX unmanned aerial vehicle project. Due to enter service with the British Army in 1998, PHOENIX will provide reconnaissance and target acquisition support to artillery systems.

Helicopters

GKN-Westland Helicopters manufactures the Sea King, Lynx and Apache military helicopters, and, in partnership with Agusta of Italy, the multi-role EH101 medium-lift helicopter at its Somerset facilities. Over 1,000 Westland helicopters are in service in 19 countries. Orders currently being fulfilled include ones for the Royal Navy (for the EH101), Royal Air Force (EH101 and Sea King) and the British Army (Apache), and customers from Brazil (Lynx), Norway (Sea King) and Italy (EH101). Major Sea King upgrading programmes are being undertaken for Australia, Belgium and Norway.

Aero-engines

Rolls-Royce is one of the world's three prime manufacturers of aero-engines, with a turnover in 1996 of nearly £3,000 million for its aerospace division. The Group's commercial aero-engine company makes engines for airliners and regional, executive and corporate jets. Over 50,000 Rolls-Royce engines are in service with more than 300 airlines in over 100 countries. More than 80 per cent of Boeing 757 operators have selected RB211-535 engines. The company's latest large engine, the Trent, powers the new generation of wide-body twin-engined airliners, such as Boeing's 777 and the Airbus A330. Rolls-Royce is a partner in the five-nation International Aero Engine consortium, which manufactures the low-emission V2500 aero-engine, now in service on the Airbus A320 and A321 as well as the McDonnell Douglas MD90. It is also in partnership with BMW, producing engines for large corporate jets and regional aircraft.

Rolls-Royce produces military engines for both fixed-wing aircraft and helicopters, and is a partner in the EJ200 engine project for the Eurofighter. It also owns the Allison Engine Company of the United States—a world leader in helicopter and large turboprop engines.

Aviation Equipment

Around one-third of the aerospace industry is devoted to designing and manufacturing aviation equipment. British firms have made significant technological advances. Manufacturers like Dowty, GEC-Marconi, Lucas, Smiths Industries, Racal, Normalair-Garrett and BAe provide equipment and systems for engines and aircraft propellers, navigation and landing systems, engine and flight controls, environmental controls and oxygen breathing and regulation systems, electrical generation, mechanical and hydraulic power systems, cabin furnishings, flight-deck controls and information displays. GEC-Marconi is the world's largest manufacturer of head-up displays (HUDs).

British firms have made important advances in developing ejection seats, firefighting equipment and flight simulators, as well as fly-by-wire and fly-by-light technology, where control surfaces on the wings and elsewhere are moved by means of automatic electronic signalling and fibre optics respectively, rather than by mechanical means. GEC-Marconi supplies the fly-by-wire system for the Boeing

777. Britain's aerospace companies provide radar and air traffic control equipment and ground power supplies to airports and airlines worldwide.

Space Equipment and Services

Over 400 companies employing almost 6,500 people are engaged in industrial space activities (see pp. 334–5). With growth of more than 10 per cent a year in the last decade, annual turnover of this sector is now around £800 million. The British National Space Centre (BNSC) is a partnership comprising government departments concerned with civil space. Through its participation in the European Space Agency, the BNSC has enabled British-based companies to participate in many leading space projects covering telecommunications, satellite navigation, Earth observation, space science and astronomy. Britain is Europe's biggest user of space.

The industry is strong in the development and manufacture of civil and military communications satellites and associated Earth stations and ground infrastructure equipment. In the field of Earth observation, it plays a major role in manufacturing platforms, space radar and meteorological satellite hardware, and in the exploitation of space data imaging products.

The largest British space company is Matra Marconi Space UK, which, together with its French partner, is one of the world's major space companies. It has become the leading provider of direct broadcast television satellites, acting as prime contractor for Eutelsat's Hot Bird satellites, SES' Astra 2B, ST-1 for Singapore and Taiwan, and Intelsat's K-TV satellite. Other activities include design and manufacture of the SKYNET 4 and NATO IV military communications satellites. It is also developing a new telecommunications spacecraft 'bus'—Eurostar 3000—which will be able to deliver direct-to-home broadcasting services. It is involved in nearly all of Europe's space science projects, including the SOHO scientific satellite launched in 1995 to study the Sun, as well as in Earth observation missions, having responsibility for the ENVISAT spacecraft and space radar systems.

Other firms, such as EEV, Sira, Pilkington, Com Dev, ERA and AEA Technology, supply satellite subsystems, and IGG is Europe's leading procurer and tester of space qualified components. British companies such as Surrey Satellite Technology and Space Innovations are leaders in the field of micro and mini satellites, which provide relatively quick and cheap access to space. Major suppliers of satellite ground stations include Anite, EOS, Logica, Science Systems and Vega. Companies operating in the field of remote sensing applications—the development of information products from satellite data—include the National Remote Sensing Centre, Remote Sensing Applications Consultants and Nigel Press Associates.

Construction

Annual output of the construction industry is around £55,000 million. Most construction work is done by private firms, the majority of which employ fewer than 25 people. While only 87 out of a total of nearly 165,000 firms employ more than 600 people directly, these companies undertake 15 per cent of all construction in Britain. Some larger firms own quarries and factories for materials manufacture, and sophisticated plant. Several undertake responsibility for all stages of projects from design to final construction.

Efficiency and productivity in construction have benefited from greater off-site fabrication of standardised components and from techniques such as computer-aided design, computerised stock ordering and job costing, electronic load safety measures for cranes, and distance measuring equipment.

Building Regulations

Building regulations issued by the Department of the Environment, Transport and the Regions prescribe minimum standards of construction in England and Wales. Administered and enforced by local government, the regulations apply to new building, the installation or replacement of fittings, alterations and extensions to existing buildings, and certain changes of use of existing buildings. Similar controls apply in Scotland and Northern Ireland. An alternative to local authority building control involves private certification of compliance with building regulations. The British Standards Institution is providing much of Britain's contribution to the drafting of European standards, which are increasingly replacing national construction standards.

Research and Advisory Services

The Building Research Establishment, sold by the Government to the Foundation for the Built Environment in March 1997, provides advice and research services to government and industry on the design, construction and performance of buildings, together with the health and safety of people in and around buildings. Its areas of expertise include prevention and control of fires and protection of the environment. It supports the development of European codes and standards, and has links with a variety of international organisations. Other research associations, as well as major construction and materials firms, universities and colleges and the British Board of Agrément, also carry out research and provide advisory services for government and industry. The Building Centre supplies exhibition and information services on materials, products, techniques and building services.

Project Procurement, Management and Financing

The most common basis of procurement for construction projects is a lump-sum contract with provision for variation. The largest projects are often carried out under the direction of construction managers or management contractors. Clients generally employ architects, project managers or civil engineers to advise on the feasibility of projects, draw up plans, and inspect and supervise the construction work.

Private and public sector projects are managed in a variety of ways. Most clients invite construction firms to bid for work by competitive tender, having used the design services of a consultant. The successful contractor will then undertake on-site work with a number of specialist sub-contractors. Alternative methods of contracting are becoming more common: for example, contracts

might include subsequent provision of building maintenance or a comprehensive 'design-and-build' service, where a single company accepts responsibility for every stage of a project.

Under the Government's Private Finance Initiative/Public-Private Partnerships (see p. 160), following competitive bidding, private sector companies construct large-scale public infrastructure projects. The initiative is providing a substantial boost to the construction industry. Among current projects are the Heathrow Express line and the £200 million Lewisham extension to London's Docklands Light Railway (see pp. 312–3). The Channel Tunnel Rail Link (CTRL) and the Thameslink 2000 railway will also be built by the private sector. The CTRL will be a 110-km (68-mile) high-speed railway costing about £3,000 million; the Thameslink 2000 scheme will extend services between north and south London through the City. The Government has also signed contracts for several DBFO (Design, Build, Finance and Operate) road schemes (£700 million) and three prisons (£200 million).

Housing

During 1996 construction of some 172,800 dwellings was started in Great Britain. Starts by private sector concerns were 143,500, by housing associations 28,800 and in the public sector 600. Around 179,000 dwellings were completed: 146,700 by the private sector, 31,500 by housing associations and 800 by the public sector. The total value of new housing orders was £6,500 million.

Major Construction Projects in Britain

The most important recent construction project is the Channel Tunnel, the largest single civil engineering project ever undertaken in Europe (see p. 312). Completed in 1993, its estimated cost was £10,000 million. Building work was carried out by a consortium of ten French and British contractors working together as Transmanche Link (TML). The tunnel is nearly 50 km (31 miles) long and is 70 m (230 ft) below sea level at its deepest. Associated projects included new international stations at Waterloo in London and Ashford (Kent), and an international terminal at Folkestone.

Other major building projects in hand or recently completed are the London Underground Jubilee Line extension, the M74 in Scotland, the extensive development in London's Docklands, and the Sizewell B nuclear power station in Suffolk. Both Stansted and Manchester airports have been substantially redeveloped. There has also been large-scale redevelopment of sports stadiums, including: Twickenham (near London) and Murrayfield (Edinburgh) rugby grounds; Wembley football stadium; a new rugby stadium in Cardiff; and new football stadiums for Middlesbrough and Sunderland football clubs. Major redevelopment work is taking place at the Wimbledon lawn tennis complex.

Overseas Contracting and Consultancy

British companies are engaged in major undertakings throughout the world and have been in the forefront of management contracting and of 'design and construct' operations. They are increasingly engaged in developing privately financed projects. Contractors and consultants undertake the supervision and all or part of the construction of a project. Consultants are engaged in the planning, design and supervision of construction enterprises. British companies have a reputation for integrity and independence.

British contractors are active in over 100 countries. In 1996 they won new international business valued at £4,800 million. North America remains the most valuable market, accounting for two-fifths of all new contracts. Important international contracts won in 1996–97 include:

- a suspension bridge across the Yangtse River in China, which will be the fourth longest bridge in the world;
- the Harare international airport terminal;

- the new arrivals building at New York's JFK international airport;
- Ashgabat Airport in Turkmenistan;
- a hospital in Hong Kong;
- elevated road/rail systems in Bangkok;
- stations and other buildings for the Kuala Lumpur light rail transit;
- a new metro project in Copenhagen; and
- a television complex in Cairo.

British engineering consultants are engaged in projects in 140 countries. In 1996 members of the Association of Consulting Engineers were engaged in new programmes overseas with a total value of £46,000 million. The capital value of projects under way at the end of 1996 was £108,000 million, 32 per cent up on the previous year. British consulting engineers had estimated gross earnings in 1996 of nearly £900 million from overseas commissions, an increase of 20 per cent over 1995. The three largest categories of work covered roads, bridges and tunnels; land planning and development; and structural-commercial projects. The most important markets were the Far East (accounting for one-half of current and new work), Africa, India and the Middle East; Eastern Europe is an increasingly important market, providing new work valued at £6,000 million in 1996, compared with £1,500 million in 1995. Major new international projects include:

- airports in Hong Kong and South Korea;
- railways in Singapore and Hong Kong;
- a chemical plant in Nigeria;
- hydro-electric plants in Mozambique and Pakistan;
- a thermal power station in Pakistan;
- water works in Nigeria;
- land planning and development in China;
- a water treatment project in Shanghai; and
- the Cairo waste water project.

Further Reading

Aerospace Industry. Aspects of Britain series, HMSO, 1993.
Overseas Trade. Aspects of Britain series, HMSO, 1994.
Telecommunications. Aspects of Britain series, HMSO, 1994.

16 Finance and Other Service Industries

Britain remains a world leader in the provision of financial and business services, which make a substantial contribution to its balance of payments. As well as finance, the service industries include business services, retailing and tourism. They contribute about 63 per cent of gross domestic product and 75 per cent of employment. The number of employees in services rose from over 13 million in 1983 to nearly 17.3 million by June 1997. Several of the largest building societies have recently become banks.

The Government has announced plans to strengthen and simplify the system of financial regulation. Reforms are also under way at the Bank of England, the most radical in its 300-year history.

As a result of rising real incomes, consumer spending on financial, personal and leisure services has increased considerably. Travel, hotel and restaurant services in Britain are among those to have benefited from the rapid growth in tourism over recent years. Indeed, by the year 2000, tourism is expected to be the world's biggest industry, and Britain is one of the world's leading tourist destinations. The industry is one of Britain's largest, employing about 7 per cent of the workforce. Another important growth area is business services, which covers areas such as exhibition and conference facilities, computing services, market research, management consultancy, and advertising and public relations.

Financial Services

Historically the heart of the financial services industry in Britain has been located in the 'Square Mile' in the City of London, and this remains broadly the case. Other financial centres are Edinburgh (the sixth largest in Europe, in terms of institutional equity funds managed), Manchester, Cardiff, Liverpool, Leeds and Glasgow.

The City is one of the world's three leading financial centres, along with Tokyo and New York, and by far the biggest in Europe. An important feature is the size of its international activities. It is noted for having:

● more overseas banks than any other financial centre;

- one of the world's largest international insurance markets;
- the biggest market in the world for trading foreign equities, accounting for 60 per cent of global turnover;
- by far the world's biggest foreign exchange market, actively trading the largest range of currencies and handling 30 per cent of worldwide dealing;
- the world's second largest fund management centre, with £1,681,000 million of institutional equity holdings in 1996;
- Europe's leading financial futures and options market;
- the world's largest centre for issuance of international bonds, with 60 per cent of this market and 75 per cent of secondary trading;
- important markets for transactions in commodities; and
- a full range of ancillary and support services—legal, accountancy and management consultancy—which contribute to London's strength as a financial centre.

British financial institutions' net overseas earnings were a record £22,700 million in 1996, 9 per cent higher than in 1995.

DEVELOPMENT OF FINANCIAL SERVICES

The markets for financial and related services have grown and diversified greatly during the last 25 years. Major events during this period include the abolition of exchange controls in 1979, the 'Big Bang' in 1986 (see p. 245) and legislation allowing building societies and friendly societies to diversify their activities.

Traditional distinctions between financial institutions have been eroded, so that single firms now supply a broader range of services, in both domestic and international markets. In the British market recent developments have included:

- intense competition between financial institutions in providing services to personal customers;

- rapid growth in the use of debit and credit cards (see p. 239);
- greater use of telephone-based services, for example in insurance, home banking and mortgages; and
- new financial products, such as tax-free TESSAs (Tax Exempt Special Savings Accounts, which allow tax-free saving with a bank or building society of up to £9,000 over five years), PEPs (Personal Equity Plans, see p. 244) and PEP-backed mortgages.

A significant feature of 1997 has been the conversion of several of the biggest building societies into banks (see p. 237). They have changed from mutual societies, owned by their members, into private sector companies owned by their shareholders and quoted on the London Stock Exchange. Many members of the societies concerned have received shares in the new companies, and this has led to a substantial increase in the number of shareholders. Building society flotations, together with the flotation of the Norwich Union insurance company (which has also abandoned its mutual status), are estimated to have created 'windfall gains' of over £35,000 million for their former members.

SUPERVISION

Current System

HM Treasury is the government department with principal responsibility for oversight of the financial services sector. In particular, it is responsible for legislation covering the regulation of banks, building societies, friendly societies, credit unions and investment business. It also oversees the Bank of England and the new Financial Services Authority (FSA), which succeeded the Securities and Investments Board in October 1997 under the changes to the regulatory framework (see below).

The Department of Trade and Industry (DTI) is responsible for company law and insolvency matters. Its duties include prudential supervision of insurance undertakings, handling of European Community (EC) directives, and consideration of general issues affecting the insurance industry. It also has powers to investigate 'insider dealing'—securities trading carried out on the basis of privileged access to relevant information.

Regulation of Investment Business

Under the Financial Services Act 1986, those dealing in, arranging deals in, managing or advising on investments, operating collective investment schemes or providing safe custody services require authorisation and are subject to rules on the conduct of business. The FSA is responsible for recognising a number of 'front-line' regulators: self-regulating organisations (SROs) and recognised professional bodies (RPBs). Most investment businesses are authorised by virtue of membership of one of these. The SROs are:

- the Investment Management Regulatory Organisation (IMRO), which regulates about 1,100 fund management firms;

- the Securities and Futures Authority (SFA), which has about 1,300 members, including member firms of the London Stock Exchange, as well as futures brokers and dealers, and eurobond dealers; and

- the Personal Investment Authority (PIA), which regulates some 4,000 firms, including independent financial advisers, which advise on or market retail investment products (such as life insurance, personal pensions and unit trusts) or act for private investors in relation to such products.

The FSA also supervises the six recognised investment exchanges in Britain (such as the London Stock Exchange), and is responsible for recognising and supervising the clearing houses, which organise the settlement of transactions on these exchanges.

The Investors Compensation Scheme can make payments of up to £48,000 to private investors if a firm regulated by an SRO or by the FSA is unable to meet its investment business liabilities. Since 1988, the scheme has helped customers of about 300 firms, and paid out £117 million to over 10,000 investors.

Banking Supervision

The Bank of England has statutory responsibility for the supervision of banks in Britain within the framework of the Banking Act 1987 and legislation implementing EC directives. The Bank carries out its responsibilities with the aim of strengthening, but not guaranteeing, the protection of bank depositors and thereby increasing confidence in the banking system as a whole. Banks are required to meet minimum standards on the integrity and competence of directors and management, the adequacy of capital and of cash flow, and the appropriateness of systems and controls to deal with the risks experienced by banks.

If a bank fails to meet the criteria, its activities may be restricted, or it may be closed. If a bank fails, there is a limited amount of protection available to small depositors, financed by levies on the banking system.

The Bank of England also has formal responsibility for supervising firms in the wholesale markets for sterling, foreign exchange and bullion, and monitors links between the various financial markets.

Proposed New Regulatory Framework

The Government believes that the current arrangements for financial services regulation need modernising and strengthening in keeping with the rapid change in the structure of financial markets, to deliver more effective and efficient supervision. It has decided to bring the regulation of banking, securities and insurance together under a single regulator, enabling the regulatory system to cope better with Britain's increasingly integrated financial markets. It has therefore announced a number of major changes:

- responsibility for banking supervision will be transferred to the FSA, probably in spring 1998;

- the FSA will oversee all the financial markets and acquire the functions of the

SFA, IMRO, the PIA and the DTI's insurance responsibilities; and

- the current system of self-regulation in investment services will be replaced by a fully statutory system designed to put the public interest first and restore confidence in the regulatory system.

A draft Regulatory Reform Bill will be published in 1998, with a view to having the new regulatory system fully operational by about the end of 1999.

International Agreements

HM Treasury represents Britain in negotiating and ensuring the implementation of relevant EC directives on the financial services sector, co-ordinating as necessary with the Bank of England, the FSA and other bodies. The main purpose of such directives is to provide a framework to allow banking, investment and insurance firms to operate throughout the European Economic Area (EEA) on the basis of their home state authorisation.

Britain plays a major role in encouraging international regulatory co-operation in the G7 and other intergovernmental fora and, at the technical level, in the Bank for International Settlements, the Basle Committee on Banking Supervision, the International Organisation of Securities Commissions and the International Association of Insurance Supervisors. Appropriate cross-border information-sharing arrangements are significant in the success of such co-operation, and the regulatory bodies play a key role in these arrangements. Britain is also at the forefront of action to encourage international liberalisation in financial services, having played a leading role in negotiating the General Agreement on Trade in Services, part of the World Trade Organisation series of agreements (see p. 206). It is also involved in negotiations within the OECD, which aim to reach by April 1998 a new Multilateral Agreement on Investment that will provide for high standards of liberalisation and investment protection.

BANK OF ENGLAND

The Bank of England was established in 1694 by Act of Parliament and Royal Charter as a corporate body. Its capital stock was acquired by the Government in 1946. As Britain's central bank, its overriding objective is to maintain a stable and efficient monetary and financial framework for the effective operation of the economy. In pursuing this goal, it has three main purposes:

- maintaining the integrity and value of the currency;
- maintaining the stability of the financial system; and
- seeking to ensure the effectiveness of the financial services sector.

Changes affecting the role of the Bank and its accountability were announced by the Government in May 1997.

New Monetary Policy Framework

Under the new framework for monetary policy (see p. 156), the Bank of England has acquired operational responsibility for setting interest rates. The Bank's monetary policy objective is to deliver price stability, as defined by the target set by the Government, by setting short-term interest rates. Decisions on interest rate changes are made by the Bank's newly established Monetary Policy Committee and implemented through the Bank's operations in the financial markets. These arrangements are operating on an interim basis until the required legislation to set up the new framework and provide for greater accountability is enacted, probably in the first half of 1998.

Other Changes

The Bank is currently responsible for banking supervision (see p. 234), but its role would be transferred to the FSA after enactment of the Bank of England Bill. Its role as the Government's agent for debt management, and its oversight of the gilts market (see p. 167) would be transferred to the Treasury.

The Bill will also provide for reforms to the Court of the Bank of England, which will be responsible for reviewing the performance of the Bank, including the Monetary Policy Committee. The Government plans that the non-executive members of the Court will be representative of the whole of Britain; they will be widely drawn from industry, commerce and finance.

In addition, some changes are being made to the Bank's role in the foreign exchange markets. The Government remains responsible for determining exchange rate policy, while the Bank will continue to act as the Treasury's agent in managing the Government's reserves of gold and foreign exchange and its foreign currency borrowing. Under the Bank of England Bill, the Bank will have its own pool of foreign exchange reserves which it may use to intervene in support of its monetary policy objective. It will continue to undertake foreign exchange transactions on behalf of its customers.

Other Functions

The Bank provides banking services to its customers, principally the Government, the banking system and other central banks. It plays a key role in payment and settlement systems, and has sole right in England and Wales to issue banknotes, which are backed by government and other securities. The profit from the note issue is paid directly to the Government. Three Scottish and four Northern Ireland banks may also issue notes, but these have to be fully backed by Bank of England notes.

The Bank of England plays an active role in ensuring that the City maintains its position as a leading international financial centre, and that it provides appropriate financial services. It carries out this role by monitoring the structure and operation of City markets and the performance of City firms. The Bank promotes collective initiatives where the interests of the financial institutions differ. It is playing a full part in the technical preparations for economic and monetary union within the EU (see p. 124).

BANKING SERVICES

The main financial institutions offering banking services are banks and building societies. However, the distinction between them is becoming less, as both types of institution diversify their services.

A distinction can still be made between 'retail' and 'wholesale' banking:

- Retail banking is primarily for personal customers and small businesses. Its main services are deposit and withdrawal facilities, personal and business lending, and money transmission.

- Wholesale business involves taking larger deposits, deploying funds in money-market instruments (see p. 245), and making corporate loans and investments. Nearly all banks in Britain engage in some wholesale activities and some, such as the merchant banks and overseas banks operating in Britain, centre their business on them. Many dealings are conducted on the inter-bank market, between banks themselves.

Other businesses, particularly insurance companies and supermarkets, are entering the banking field. Among insurance companies now offering banking services are Prudential, Standard Life, and Legal & General. Three of the large supermarket chains—Tesco, J. Sainsbury and Safeway—also offer banking services, run in conjunction with major banks. For example, Sainsbury's Bank, a joint venture with the Bank of Scotland launched in spring 1997, has some 500,000 customers and deposits of £1,000 million.

In 1997 there were 361 institutions authorised under the Banking Act 1987, including clearing banks, investment banks, branches of overseas banks from outside the EEA, and banking subsidiaries of banking and non-banking institutions from Britain and overseas. A further 105 branches of banks from other EEA countries were entitled to accept deposits in Britain. Of the total of 516 institutions permitted to take deposits in Britain, over 300 were members of the British Bankers' Association, the principal representative body for banks operating in Britain.

Retail Banks and Banking Groups

Retail banks now offer many more services than just the traditional banking services of current accounts, deposit accounts and loan arrangements. Credit and debit cards are widely available through banks, as are mortgages, insurance, investment products—including TESSAs, PEPs, pensions and unit trusts—and share-dealing services. Most major British banks are complex financial groups, which own finance houses, leasing and factoring companies, merchant banks, securities dealers, insurance companies and unit trust companies, and most also have overseas subsidiaries or branches.

Six banks are in Britain's top 20 companies, in terms of market capitalisation: Lloyds TSB, HSBC (including its subsidiary Midland), Barclays, Halifax, National Westminster and Abbey National (the first building society to convert to a bank, in 1989).

The banking sector has been transformed during 1997 with five top-ten building societies becoming, or being taken over by, banks: Halifax, Woolwich, Alliance & Leicester, Bristol & West (which was acquired by the Bank of Ireland) and Northern Rock. Halifax plc, Britain's biggest mortgage lender, is by far the largest of the new banks. On its flotation in June 1997 it had nearly 8 million shareholders. Among the reasons given for converting were to facilitate expansion and offer a wider range of financial services. Banks now account for some 70 per cent of mortgage loans (see p. 382), double the level prevailing before the changes.

Other major banks are the Bank of Scotland and the Royal Bank of Scotland. Among the smaller retail banks are the Co-operative Bank and two banks owned by National Australia Bank: the Clydesdale Bank and the Yorkshire Bank. Northern Ireland is served by branch networks of four major banking groups: Northern Bank, Ulster Bank, First Trust Bank and Bank of Ireland.

Competition among the banks and other financial institutions is intense, especially in the markets for personal savings, consumer credit and mortgages. The banks have taken steps to increase efficiency and control costs by, for example, providing new services and extending opening hours. However, the network of bank branches has fallen, in part because of the move to telephone and computer banking (see p. 240), and staff levels have declined, especially through centralising 'back-office' operations and reducing head office and support functions. Profitability has risen, reflecting, among other things, the strengthening of the economy, cost savings and lower bad debts; in 1996 profits of the eight large British banks totalled £10,640 million. Total liabilities/assets of banks in Britain amounted to over £2,181,800 million at the end of June 1997.

Merchant Banks

The traditional role of merchant banks was to accept, or guarantee, commercial bills, and to sponsor (underwrite) capital issues on behalf of their customers. Today they undertake a much wider range of investment banking activities. They have important roles in equity and debt markets and in the provision of advice and financial services to industrial companies, especially where mergers, takeovers and other forms of corporate reorganisation are involved. Management of investment holdings, including trusts, pensions and other funds, is another important function. As with retail banks, there has been a process of consolidation, and several British-owned merchant banks have been acquired by overseas banks.

Overseas Banks

London is a major centre for international banking; in 1996 more international banking business took place in Britain than in any other market in the world. Banks from many countries have subsidiaries, branches or representative offices in London. France has the greatest number—50—followed by Japan, the United States and Italy. Like the major British banks, these overseas banks offer a comprehensive banking service in many parts of the world, and engage in financing trade not only between Britain and other countries but also between third-party countries.

British-based Overseas Banks

A small number of banks have their head offices in Britain, but operate mainly abroad, often specialising in particular regions. Standard Chartered, which is represented in Asia, Africa and the Middle East, is the major example of this type of bank. It has a network of around 500 offices in nearly 50 countries.

Building Societies

Building societies are mutual institutions, owned by their savers and borrowers, which specialise in housing finance and retail deposit-taking services. They are the second main source of housing finance in Britain. They make long-term mortgage loans against the security of property—usually private dwellings purchased for owner-occupation. Competition between lenders for business intensified in the first half of the 1990s when house prices fell and fewer people moved house, and remains intense despite an improving housing market since 1995. Remortgaging, whereby a borrower changes lender or switches to a different mortgage from the same lender, has become much more prevalent. Societies are extending their banking services, for example by providing current account facilities, such as cheque books and automated teller machines (ATMs).

Structure

During 1997 the sector was transformed as a result of the decision by five of the biggest societies to abandon their mutual status and become banks (see p. 237). Members of all these societies voted for conversion by large majorities; qualifying members were usually eligible for cash or shares in the new bank. As a result, the level of assets in the building society sector has fallen by over half since the end of 1996, when it was around £300,000 million. There has also been a process of mergers between building societies, the latest being between the Portman and the Greenwich in July 1997. There are now 71 authorised building societies, of which 70 are members of the Building Societies Association.

The largest building society is now the Nationwide, with group assets of £37,600 million. Other large societies are Bradford & Bingley, Britannia and Yorkshire.

Diversification

The Building Societies Act 1986 enabled societies to diversify into a wider range of financial and housing-related services, and established the Building Societies Commission to carry out the prudential supervision of building societies. Since then, further steps have been taken to relax restrictions on their commercial activities. The Building Societies Act 1997 established a new, more 'permissive' regime whereby, with a few exceptions, societies could undertake a wider variety of activities, enabling them to respond quickly to developments in the financial services and housing markets. The chief requirements for societies are that:

- at least 75 per cent of lending has to be on the security of housing; and
- a minimum of 50 per cent of funds has to be in the form of shares held by individual members.

The Act also contained provisions to increase the accountability of societies to members, and strengthened the supervisory powers of the Building Societies Commission.

Friendly Societies

Friendly societies have traditionally been unincorporated societies of individuals, offering their members a limited range of financial and insurance services, particularly provision for retirement and against loss of income through sickness or unemployment. The Friendly Societies Act 1992 enabled friendly societies to incorporate, take on new powers and provide a broader range of financial services through subsidiaries. It also established the Friendly Societies Commission to administer a system of regulation and to promote the financial stability of societies. Nearly 120 friendly societies are authorised to accept new business.

Payment Systems

Apart from credit and debit card arrangements, the main payment systems are run by three separate companies operating under an umbrella organisation, the

Table 16.1: Transaction Trends

	1986	1991	1994	1995	million 1996
Payments for goods, services and financial transfers:					
Cheque payments	3,117	3,403	3,016	2,903	2,838
Paper credit transfers	465	479	414	405	419
Automated payments	1,081	1,848	2,198	2,402	2,613
Credit card purchases	415	661	765	850	965
Debit card purchases	–	359	808	1,004	1,270
Store card and other purchases	63	84	150	169	188
Total payments and transfers	**5,141**	**6,834**	**7,351**	**7,733**	**8,293**
Cash withdrawals at ATMs and counters	1,154	1,796	2,061	2,153	2,248
Post Office Order Book payments	864	866	841	900	958
Cash payments over £1 (estimated)	14,700	15,300	14,200	14,200	14,200
Total transactions[a]	**21,900**	**24,800**	**24,500**	**25,000**	**25,700**

Source: APACS

[a] Figures rounded, so that the totals do not exactly add up to the sums of the component parts.

Association for Payment Clearing Services (APACS). One system covers bulk paper clearings—cheques and credit transfers. A second deals with high-value clearings for same-day settlement, namely the nationwide electronic transfer service, Clearing House Automated Payment System (CHAPS). A third covers bulk electronic clearing for standing orders and direct debits. Membership of each company is open to any bank, building society or other financial institution meeting criteria for appropriate supervision and volume of transactions; 22 banks and building societies are members of one or more clearing companies.

Trends in Financial Transactions

There have been major changes in the nature of financial transactions in recent years. Plastic cards, which first started to appear in 1966, have become much more widespread, with 97 million in circulation in Britain; 83 per cent of adults have one or more cards. Cash, though, continues to be the most popular form of

payment in terms of the volume of transactions—about two-thirds of payments above £1 are made in cash. The use of cheques has been declining during the 1990s (see Table 16.1), as cards have increased in popularity.

The installation of ATMs has greatly improved consumers' access to cash, particularly outside bank opening hours. The number of ATMs has more than doubled in the last ten years, to 22,100 in 1996. All the major retail banks and building societies participate in nationwide networks of ATMs. There were 1,600 million cash withdrawals from ATMs in 1996, the average withdrawal being £50.

Plastic Cards

The main types of plastic card are cheque guarantee cards, debit cards, credit cards, charge cards and cash cards. Individual cards frequently cover more than one use, such as a cheque guarantee and cash card.

Cheque guarantee cards entitle holders to cheque-cashing facilities in participating institutions, and guarantee retailers that transactions up to the specified guarantee limit—typically £50 or £100—will be honoured. Eurocheques supported by a eurocheque card are available from major banks and may be used to obtain cash or make payments throughout the EU and in a few other overseas countries; cheques are made out in the currency of the country in which they are being used.

Most credit cards are affiliated to one of the major international organisations, Visa and MasterCard. At the end of 1996, there were 33 million credit cards issued by banks and building societies in use in Britain: 20 million Visa cards and 13 million MasterCards. Barclays is by far the largest issuer, with over 9 million. There are a growing number of 'affinity' cards, where the card is linked to an organisation such as a charity or trade union. Charge cards are similar to credit cards, but are designed to be paid off in full each month; they are usually available only to those with relatively high incomes or assets. Several major retailers issue store cards for use within their own outlets.

The use of debit cards has increased rapidly since their introduction in 1987. Some 62 per cent of adults in Britain hold a debit card, and nearly 33 million have been issued. Payments are deducted directly from the purchaser's current account. There are three debit card schemes in operation: Switch, Visa Delta and Visa Electron.

Electronic Banking

Many banks and building societies offer home banking services, whereby customers use a telephone to obtain account information, make transfers and pay bills. Some banks and building societies offer a home banking service for customers via a personal computer. Other innovations include banking services over the Internet and self-service kiosks containing ATMs and video links to banks' central facilities. The most recent development is the trial in a number of locations of Mondex, a new type of electronic card, which is 'charged' with money from the card holder's bank account. These cards can be used to purchase goods or services at participating retailers through electronic tills.

National Savings

National Savings, an executive agency of the Chancellor of the Exchequer, is a source of finance for government borrowing and aims to encourage saving by offering personal savers a range of investments. Certain National Savings products provide tax-free returns. In May 1997 the total amount invested in National Savings was £62,000 million. Sales of National Savings products totalled £13,354 million in 1996-97. After allowing for repayments, the net contribution to government funding was £4,804 million. The largest contributions were made by Pensioners Bonds and Premium Bonds, with net additions to funding of £2,480 million and £1,710 million respectively.

Other important products include:

- Savings Certificates, which pay either a fixed rate of interest alone or a lower fixed rate of interest combined with index-linking (rising in line with the Retail Prices Index);

- Income and Capital Bonds;

- Children's Bonus Bonds, designed to accumulate capital sums for those under 21;

- Ordinary and Investment Accounts, where deposits and withdrawals can be made at post offices throughout Britain; and

- FIRST Option Bonds, which offer a guaranteed rate of interest fixed for one year.

INSURANCE

London is the world's leading centre for insurance and international reinsurance. It handles an estimated 20 per cent of the general insurance business placed on the international market. EC directives to create a single European market in insurance came into force in 1994. As well as the British companies and the Lloyd's market (see below), many overseas firms are represented, with which British companies have formed close relationships. Authorised insurance companies are supervised by the DTI under the Insurance Companies Act 1982.

Main Types of Insurance

There are two broad categories of insurance: long-term life insurance, where contracts may be for periods of many years; and general insurance, including accident and short-term health insurance, where contracts are for a year or less.

Long-term Insurance

As well as providing life cover, life insurance is a vehicle for saving and investment because premiums are invested in securities and other assets. About 65 per cent of households have life assurance cover. Total long-term insurance assets under management by companies in 1996 were £600,000 million on behalf of their worldwide operations. Long-term insurance is handled by around 220 companies.

General Insurance

General insurance business is undertaken by insurance companies and by underwriters at Lloyd's. It includes fire, accident, general liability, motor, marine, aviation and transport risks. Total worldwide premium income of members of the Association of British Insurers (ABI) in 1996 was £35,000 million, of which £22,000 million was earned in Britain.

Structure of the Industry

At the end of 1996, over 800 companies were authorised to carry on one or more classes of insurance business in Britain. Around 450 companies belong to the ABI.

The industry includes both public limited companies and mutual institutions—companies owned by their policyholders. Among the largest insurance companies are Commercial Union, Prudential, General Accident, Royal & Sun Alliance, and Norwich Union.

Lloyd's

Lloyd's, the origins of which go back to the 17th century, is an incorporated society of private insurers in London. It is not a

As with banks and building societies, the insurance industry is undergoing a series of major changes, affecting both the services supplied and the structure of the industry. In June 1997, Norwich Union ceased to be a mutual institution when it floated on the London Stock Exchange; it is now the third largest publicly quoted insurance company. Its 2.9 million members received shares in the flotation. Another mutual insurer, Scottish Amicable, has been taken over by the Prudential.

company but a market for insurance administered by the Council of Lloyd's and Lloyd's Regulatory and Market Boards.

The premium income of the market in 1996 was approximately £8,000 million. For 1997 the market has a total capacity of £10,300 million, which is provided by around 10,000 members who are underwriting through 164 syndicates. Each syndicate is managed by an underwriting agent responsible for appointing a professional underwriter to accept insurance risks and manage claims on behalf of the members of the syndicate. With the exception of motor insurance business, insurance may only be placed through the 201 Lloyd's-registered broking companies, which negotiate with Lloyd's syndicates on behalf of the insured. Reinsurance constitutes a large part of Lloyd's business—more than 6 per cent of the world's reinsurance is placed at Lloyd's. Around one-third of Lloyd's current business is in its traditional marine market, and Lloyd's also has a significant share of the British motor insurance market, insuring about 15 per cent of British motorists. Lloyd's is also a major insurer of aviation and satellite risks, and underwrites in all other areas of insurance.

During the late 1980s and early 1990s, Lloyd's suffered severe losses, partly caused by a series of natural disasters and claims arising from asbestosis and pollution. The Council of Lloyd's took action to reconstruct the market, securing an injection of new capital from interested parties, and reinsuring the liabilities arising from 1992 and previous underwriting years into a new company, Equitas.

The market has returned to profitability, and is continuing to develop following its reconstruction. An increasing share of capacity is being provided by corporate members with limited liability rather than the traditional individual 'Names'—wealthy individuals who accept insurance risks for their own profit or loss, with unlimited liability. Lloyd's is strengthening the financial requirements on all members in order to increase the security of the market and enhance the confidence of policyholders.

Institute of London Underwriters

The Institute of London Underwriters, formed in 1884 as a trade association for marine underwriters, provides a market where member insurance companies transact marine, energy, commercial transport and aviation business. It issues combined policies in its own name on risks underwritten by member companies. Gross premium income processed by the Institute for its member companies in 1996 was £1,500 million. About half of the 55 member companies are branches or subsidiaries of overseas companies.

Insurance Brokers and Other Intermediaries

Insurance brokers, who act on behalf of the insured, are a valuable part of the company market and play an essential role in the Lloyd's market. Smaller brokers mainly deal with the general public or specialise in a particular type of commercial insurance. Medium to large brokers almost exclusively handle commercial insurance, with the biggest dealing in risks worldwide. Some brokers specialise in reinsurance business. Registration and regulation of individuals and firms practising as insurance brokers are conducted by the Insurance Brokers Registration Council, under a statutory regime of professional standards which is obligatory for those who use the title 'insurance broker'. Some 15,800 individuals are registered with the Council, the majority of whom are employed by about 2,200 limited companies. Nearly 2,000 individuals carry on business in their own right, trading as sole proprietor, or in partnership.

All intermediaries who advise on, or arrange, life insurance falling within the scope of the Financial Services Act 1986 are subject to regulation under the Act, mainly through the Personal Investment Authority (see p. 234), on their conduct of business.

Other independent intermediaries may also arrange insurance, but are not allowed to use the title 'insurance broker'. There are about 6,000 independent intermediaries operating under the ABI's code of practice.

INVESTMENT

Britain has a great deal of expertise in fund management, which involves managing funds on behalf of investors, or advising investors how best to invest their funds. The main types of investment fund include pension schemes, life assurance, unit trusts, investment trusts and new open-ended investment companies (oeics).

An analysis of the fund management industry identified assets totalling more than £1,800,000 million at the end of 1995 (see Table 16.2), of which over a quarter were managed on behalf of overseas clients. The industry is estimated to contribute £2,700 million a year to GDP and to generate £425 million in overseas earnings. London is the second largest fund management centre in the world after Tokyo.

Pension Funds

Over 11 million people belong to occupational pension schemes and more than 5 million to personal pension schemes. Most occupational pension schemes pay benefits related to final salary, although a growing number are on a 'money purchase' basis where benefits depend on the size of the accrued funds. Benefits are normally funded in advance by employer and employee contributions, which are held and invested by trustees on behalf of beneficiaries. Pension funds are major investors in securities markets, holding around 30 per cent of securities listed on the London Stock Exchange. Total British pension fund net

Table 16.2: Funds under Management in Britain			£'000 million
	British clients December 1995	Overseas clients March 1996	Total
Pension funds	519	232	751
Insurance	556	68	625
Unit trusts	111	36	147
Investment trusts	45	3	48
Other	0	163	163
less unit trusts held by other funds	*-53*	*0*	*-53*
Total institutional funds	**1,179**	**502**	**1,681**
Private clients	136	28	163
TOTAL	1,314	530	1,844

Source: British Invisibles
Note: Differences between totals and the sums of their component parts are due to rounding.

assets were worth about £566,000 million at the end of 1996.

Unit Trusts

Around 1,700 authorised unit trusts (open-ended collective funds) pool investors' money, and divide funds into units of equal size, enabling people with relatively small amounts to benefit from diversified and managed portfolios. The industry has grown rapidly during the last decade, and in the five years to 1997 total funds under management more than doubled, to £163,000 million. Some are general funds, investing in a wide variety of British or international securities, and there are also many specialist trusts.

Over 40 unit trust management groups have total fund values of more than £1,000 million. The largest is Schroder Unit Trusts Ltd, which manages 34 funds, with a total fund value of £14,180 million in August 1997. Unit trust management groups are represented by the Association of Unit Trusts and Investment Funds.

Open-ended Investment Companies

A new type of scheme—open-ended investment companies—has become available in 1997. Oeics are similar to unit trusts, but an investor in an oeic buys shares rather than units in the company. The new schemes should

enable British companies to compete on an equal footing with similar schemes operating elsewhere in the EU. The first oeic was launched by Global Asset Management in May 1997. Several unit trust management groups are looking at oeics with a view to converting and rationalising some of their funds.

Investment Trusts

Investment trust companies, which also offer the opportunity to diversify risk on a relatively small lump-sum investment or through regular savings, are listed on the London Stock Exchange and their shares are traded in the usual way. They must invest mostly in securities, and the trusts themselves are exempt from tax on gains realised within the funds. Assets are purchased mainly out of shareholders' funds, although investment trusts are also allowed to borrow money for investment. There were 322 members of the Association of Investment Trust Companies in June 1997, with £58,400 million of assets under management. The three largest trusts are the venture capital company 3i Group, Foreign & Colonial Investment Trust, and Alliance Trust.

Share Ownership

Prior to 1997, about 10 million adults—22 per cent of the adult population in Great Britain—held shares. Privatisation (see p.

186), employee share schemes (see p. 180), Personal Equity Plans and, more recently, building society flotations have been among the factors increasing share ownership. The number of investment clubs—groups of individuals, usually around 15 to 20 people, who regularly invest in shares—has grown to around 1,600.

During 1997 share ownership rose considerably as a result of the demutualisation of five building societies and the Norwich Union insurance company (see pp. 237 and 241). About 16 million members received shares, many having shares in more than one institution. Although around one-quarter of the new shareholders in the three largest building society flotations—the Halifax, Woolwich, and Alliance & Leicester—elected to sell their shares immediately, most have retained their shares.

Personal Equity Plans

Personal Equity Plans (PEPs) allow tax-free investment in shares, including investment trust companies, in unit trusts, and in certain corporate bonds (except those issued by financial services companies), preference shares and 'convertibles' (bonds or preference shares which can eventually be converted into a company's ordinary shares). Up to £6,000 in a single tax year may be invested in a general PEP and up to £3,000 in a single company PEP. Dividends and capital gains on assets held in a PEP are exempt from income tax and capital gains tax, and withdrawals from PEPs are normally tax free.

Since their introduction in 1987, nearly £42,000 million had been invested in over 12 million PEPs by April 1997. PEPs are likely to be absorbed within the new individual savings accounts, which are expected to start in 1999. The Government is developing plans for these new accounts, which will extend the principles of TESSAs (see p. 233) and PEPs, and encourage long-term savings, especially among those on low incomes.

SPECIAL FINANCING INSTITUTIONS

Several specialised institutions offer finance and support to personal and corporate sector borrowers. Among public sector agencies are Scottish Enterprise, Highlands and Islands Enterprise, the Welsh Development Agency, the Industrial Development Board for Northern Ireland (see pp. 197–8) and ECGD (see p. 209). The main private sector institutions are described below.

Finance and Leasing Companies

The Finance and Leasing Association represents the interests of firms offering motor finance, consumer credit, and business finance and leasing. Its 106 full members undertook new business worth £50,000 million in 1996.

Credit Unions

Credit unions—non-profit-making savings and loans bodies—are less widespread in Britain than in some other countries. However, they have grown rapidly during the 1990s, and there are now more than 700, with total assets of over £300 million.

Factoring Companies

Factoring comprises a range of financial services allowing companies to obtain finance in exchange for outstanding invoices not yet paid. During the 1990s the factoring and discounting industry has been growing at over 20 per cent a year. The industry provides working capital to more than 19,000 businesses a year. Member companies of the Factors & Discounters Association handled business worth £40,400 million in 1996.

Venture Capital Companies

The British venture capital industry is the largest and most developed in Europe. Venture capital companies offer medium- and long-term equity financing for new and developing businesses, management buy-outs and buy-ins, and company rescues. The British Venture Capital Association has 101 full members, which account for 95 per cent annual venture capital investment in Britain. Worldwide investment by British venture capital firms rose by 28 per cent in 1996 to a record £3,239 million, of which £2,806 million was invested in Britain; investments were made in 1,200 businesses.

FINANCIAL MARKETS

The City of London's financial markets include the London Stock Exchange, the foreign exchange market, the financial futures and options market, eurobond and eurocurrency markets, Lloyd's insurance market (see p. 241), and bullion and commodity markets. The securities markets are supervised jointly by the Treasury, the Bank of England, FSA and the London Stock Exchange, among others (see p. 234).

London Stock Exchange

The London Stock Exchange plays a vital role in maintaining London's position as a major financial centre. It is one of the top three global exchanges. The Exchange is based in London, and there are regional representatives in Belfast, Birmingham, Glasgow, Leeds and Manchester. As a result of a set of legal reforms implemented in 1986 known as the 'Big Bang', the Exchange has changed considerably over recent years. The most fundamental change has been the move away from the traditional market floor to screen based trading.

At the end of 1996, 2,171 British and 533 international companies were listed on the main market, with a market capitalisation of £1,011,700 million and £2,388,300 million respectively. Turnover rose to record levels in 1996: £741,600 million for British equities and £1,039,200 million for international equities.

The market is now undergoing a period of change considered the most significant since the 'Big Bang'. The Exchange introduced an electronic order book in October 1997. This is a new trading service, through which share transactions between buyers and sellers are matched automatically, rather than being passed through market-making firms under the current 'quote-driven' system. Initially, it is limited to the most liquid stocks—the top 100 shares.

AIM, the Alternative Investment Market, was established by the London Stock Exchange in 1995, for small, young and growing companies wishing to raise capital and increase their profile. By August 1997 over 290 companies, with a total capitalisation exceeding £5,000 million, had joined AIM and had raised more than £1,000 million. Tradepoint, a computer-based, order-driven share dealing system in competition with the London Stock Exchange, also started operation in 1995.

In April 1997 CREST, a new computerised settlement system for shares and other securities developed by a project team from the Bank of England, took over the settlement of all securities traded in Britain. This is expected to increase efficiency and lower the cost by eliminating much of the paperflow. CREST is owned and operated by CRESTCo, a private sector consortium representing a wide spread of City interests.

The gilts market (see p. 167) allows the Government to raise money by issuing gilt-edged stock. The London Stock Exchange offers a secondary or trading market where investors can buy or sell gilts. Turnover in the market rose by 26 per cent in 1996 to a record £1,983,000 million.

Money Markets

The London money markets comprise the interbank deposit markets plus a range of other instruments, usually short term in maturity. Banks are the major participants in these markets.

Euromarkets

Euromarkets operate for currencies lent or invested outside their domestic marketplace, particularly as a means of financing international trade and investment. Transactions can thus be carried out in eurodollars, eurodeutschemarks, euroyen and so on. London is at the heart of the euromarkets and houses most of the leading international banks and securities firms. Distinctions between markets have been breaking down and euromarkets form a major part of the wider international money and capital markets. Participants include multinational trading corporations, financial companies, governments, and international organisations like the World Bank and the European Investment Bank.

The euro-securities markets have grown considerably in recent years because the instruments traded on them—eurobonds, euro-medium-term notes (EMTNs), euro-commercial paper and so on—are seen as flexible alternatives to bank loans. There is a growing market in ECU-denominated deposits, securities and eurobonds.

Foreign Exchange Market

London is the world's biggest centre for foreign exchange trading, accounting for about 30 per cent of global net daily turnover in foreign exchange. Average daily turnover in London amounted to about £294,000 million in 1995.

The foreign exchange market consists of telephone and electronic links between the participants, which include banks, other financial institutions and several foreign exchange broking firms acting as intermediaries. It provides those engaged in international trade and investment with foreign currencies for their transactions. The banks are in close contact with financial centres abroad and are able to quote buying and selling rates for both immediate ('spot') and forward transactions in a variety of currencies and maturities. The forward market enables traders and dealers who, at a given date in the future, wish to receive or make a specific foreign currency payment, to contract in advance to sell or buy the foreign currency involved for sterling at a fixed exchange rate.

Derivatives

Financial derivatives are contracts to buy or sell, at a future date, financial instruments such as equities, bonds or money-market instruments. Their use has grown rapidly, especially among companies and investment institutions, and instruments have become more complex, as advances have been made in information technology. Derivatives offer a

means of protection against changes in prices, exchange rates and interest rates. They include:

- futures—agreements to buy or sell financial instruments or physical commodities at a future date;
- options—the right to buy or sell financial instruments or physical commodities for a stated period at a predetermined price; and
- 'over-the-counter' products, including swaps—a foreign exchange swap can convert a money-market instrument in one currency into a money-market instrument in another.

Financial Futures and Options

Commodity and financial futures and options are traded at the London International Financial Futures and Options Exchange (LIFFE), the largest futures and options exchange in Europe. There are over 220 member firms, including many of the world's leading financial institutions. Its trading floor in the City contains one of the world's most modern 'open outcry' trading facilities, with members executing their business through a system of hand signals and shouting on the trading floor.

Business on LIFFE reached a new annual record in 1996, when 168 million futures and options contracts were traded, 27 per cent higher than in 1995. In the first half of 1997 business grew further, and over 100 million contracts were traded—an average daily volume of around 814,000. LIFFE is continuing to strengthen its links with other exchanges; in May 1997 it joined with the Chicago Board of Trade (the world's largest futures exchange) in a link covering trading of the world's two biggest debt contracts. In 1996 LIFFE merged with the London Commodity Exchange, where trading includes contracts in coffee, cocoa, sugar, grain, potatoes and the dry freight index.

London Bullion Market

London is the hub of the international bullion market. Around 60 banks and other financial trading companies participate in the London gold and silver markets, which trade by telephone or other electronic means. Members of the London Bullion Market Association meet twice daily to establish a London fixing price for gold—a reference point for worldwide dealings. The silver fixing is held once a day. Although much interest centres on the fixings, active dealing takes place throughout the day.

Commodity, Shipping and Freight Markets

Britain is a major international centre for commodities trading and the home of many related international trade organisations. The London Metal Exchange is the primary base metals market in the world, trading contracts in aluminium, aluminium alloy, copper, lead, nickel, tin and zinc. The International Petroleum Exchange is Europe's only energy futures exchange. The Baltic Exchange, which finds ships for cargoes and cargoes for ships throughout the world, is the world's leading international shipping market.

Other Services

BUSINESS SERVICES

Exhibition and Conference Centres

Britain is one of the world's three leading countries for international conferences—the others being the United States and France. London and Paris are the two most popular conference cities. A large number of other towns and cities in Britain—including several traditional seaside holiday resorts wishing to diversify and take advantage of the growing business tourism market—have facilities for conferences and exhibitions.

Among the most modern purpose-built conference and exhibition centres are the International Conference Centre in Birmingham; the Queen Elizabeth II and Olympia Conference Centres, both in London; and Cardiff International Arena, a 5,000-seat multi-purpose facility. In Scotland, Edinburgh, Glasgow and Aberdeen have major exhibition and conference centres. The

£29 million Belfast Waterfront Hall opened in 1997. Brighton (East Sussex), Harrogate (North Yorkshire), Bournemouth (Dorset), Birmingham, Manchester, Nottingham and Torquay (Devon) all have exhibition and conference centres. Other important exhibition facilities are situated in London at the Barbican, Earls Court, Alexandra Palace and Wembley Arena.

Many of the larger sites belong to a marketing group, Conventions Great Britain.

Computing Services

The computing services industry comprises businesses engaged in software development; production of packaged software; consultancy; information technology 'outsourcing'; processing services; and the provision of complete computer systems. It also includes companies that provide information technology (IT) education and training; independent maintenance; support, contingency planning and recruitment; and contract staff. The turnover of companies in the Computing Services & Software Association, which represents about 80 per cent of the industry in Britain, totalled £11,000 million in 1996.

British firms and universities have established strong reputations in software R & D. A number of international IT conglomerates have set up R & D operations in Britain—among them are Hitachi, IBM, Nortel, Philips and Sharp. US software company Computer Associates has announced plans to build a new £100 million European headquarters at Datchet, near Heathrow Airport. Microsoft intends to make a major R & D investment at Cambridge (see p. 340). Academic expertise is particularly evident in such areas as artificial intelligence, neural networks, formal programming for safety critical systems, and parallel programming systems. Software firms have developed strengths in sector-specific applications, including systems for retailing, banking, finance and accounting, medical and dental industries, and the travel and entertainment industries. The market leader in Britain for 'point-of-sale' systems is ICL. Specialist 'niche' markets in which Britain's software producers are active include artificial intelligence, scientific and engineering software, especially computer-aided design, mathematical software, geographical information systems, and data visualisation packages. Firms specialise in devising multimedia software. Distance learning, 'virtual reality' and computer animation all benefit from a large pool of creative talent. British-based companies are achieving outstanding sales in the United States. All-Voice Computing is a market leader in devising software for voice-activated word-processing.

One of the biggest users of software is the telecommunications industry. The major telecommunications operators and several specialist companies are active in this sector. The provision of almost all new telecommunications services is dependent on software; switching and transmission, for example, are primarily digital and controlled by software. Teleshopping, video-on-demand, payphones and answering services are also now software-based.

Market Research

The market research profession in Britain has developed strongly in the past decade or so, and now accounts for 10 per cent of worldwide market research spending. It has a wide range of domestic and overseas clients, including government bodies.

Management Consultancy

Britain's 27,000 management consultants supply technical assistance and advice to business and government clients. Typically, consultants identify and investigate problems and opportunities, recommend appropriate action and help to implement recommendations. Many British-based consultancies operate internationally; the most recent trend has been for the biggest firms to set up offices in Eastern Europe and the Pacific Rim. The 31 member firms of the Management Consultancies Association are among the largest in the industry and account for more than half of management consultancy work. They range from Andersen Consulting

and CMG Management, with a strong technical bias, to Coopers & Lybrand and PA Consulting group, which specialise in market/industry sectors. In 1996 member firms earned over £1,400 million in Britain and £236 million overseas.

Advertising and Public Relations

Britain is a major centre for creative advertising, and multinational corporations often use advertising created in Britain for marketing their products globally. British agencies have strong foreign links through overseas ownership and associate networks.

Spending on advertising in 1996 amounted to £11,900 million, up 9 per cent on the previous year. The press accounted for 54 per cent of the total, television for 28 per cent, direct mail for 12 per cent, and posters, transport, commercial radio and cinema for the rest. The largest advertising expenditure is on food, household durables, cosmetics, office equipment, motor vehicles and financial services. Among the biggest spenders in 1996 were BT, Dixons, McDonalds, Tesco, J. Sainsbury, the National Lottery (see p. 47) and the major car manufacturers. British television advertising receives many international awards.

Campaigns are planned by around 2,000 advertising agencies. In addition to their creative, production and media buying roles, some agencies offer integrated marketing services, such as consumer research (see above) and public relations. Many have sponsorship departments, which arrange for businesses to sponsor products and events, including artistic, sporting and charitable events. In return for financial or other support, the sponsoring company is associated with a worthy product or event, thereby raising its profile with consumers. Leading agencies include Abbott Mead Vickers BBDO, J. Walter Thompson, Leo Burnett, and Ogilvy and Mather Advertising.

Government advertising campaigns—on crime prevention, health promotion, armed services recruitment and so on—are often organised by the Central Office of Information, an executive agency of the Government (see p. 535), which is able to secure substantial discounts because of its centralised buying power.

Britain's public relations industry has grown rapidly over the past ten years and is now the most developed in Europe.

DISTRIBUTION AND SALES

The distribution of goods, including food and drink, to their point of sale by road, rail, air and sea is a major economic activity. The large wholesalers and retailers operate, either directly or through contractors, extensive distribution networks.

Wholesaling

In 1994 there were 117,800 businesses, with a workforce of 800,000 and a turnover of £296,900 million (see Table 16.3), engaged in wholesaling and dealing in Great Britain.

In the food and drink trade almost all large retailers have their own buying and central distribution operations. Many small wholesalers and independent grocery retailers belong to voluntary 'symbol' groups (for example, Spar, Landmark and Londis), which operate under a corporate fascia and provide access to central purchasing facilities and co-ordinated promotions. This has helped smaller retailers to remain relatively competitive; many local 'corner shops' and village stores would not otherwise be able to stay in business. Booker, Batleys and Bestways are the major 'cash and carry' wholesalers. London's wholesale markets play a significant part in the distribution of fresh foodstuffs. New Covent Garden is the main market for fruit and vegetables, Smithfield for meat and Billingsgate for fish.

The Co-operative Wholesale Society (CWS) is the principal supplier of goods and services to the Co-operative Movement and was a founder member of the Co-operative Retail Trading Group. Formed in 1993 to act as a central marketing, buying and distribution partnership for retail co-operative societies, the Group now accounts for around 65 per cent of Co-op food trade. The CWS is also the largest co-operative retailer in Europe, with 684 stores located in Scotland, Northern Ireland, the east and south Midlands, and south-east and north-east England. Retail co-operative societies are voluntary organisations controlled by their members, membership being open to anyone paying a small deposit on a minimum share. Throughout the Co-operative Movement, which comprises 49 independent societies, there are nearly 2,500 stores.

Retailing

In 1994 there were 196,600 retail businesses, with 290,000 outlets, employing 2.4 million

Table 16.3: Wholesale Trade in Great Britain 1994

	Number of businesses	Turnover (£ million)[a]
Food and drink	15,754	52,539
Petroleum products	938	37,871
Clothing, furs, textiles and footwear	9,813	11,142
Coal and oil merchants	2,681	2,948
Builders' merchants	3,989	9,415
Agricultural supplies and livestock dealing	2,812	8,183
Industrial materials	5,527	26,827
Scrap and waste products	3,084	2,062
Industrial and agricultural machinery	8,663	25,806
Operational leasing	2,239	2,582
Other goods	62,271	117,520
Total wholesaling and dealing	**117,771**	**296,896**

Source: *Business Monitor SDA26, Wholesaling, 1996*
[a] Excludes value added tax (VAT).

Table 16.4: Retail Trade in Great Britain 1994

	Number of businesses	Number of outlets	Number of people engaged ('000s)	Turnover[a] (£ million)
Non-specialised stores	21,146	36,910	917	69,014
Specialised stores	175,417	253,086	1,462	87,635
of which:				
Food, drinks or tobacco	45,971	59,814	270	13,103
Pharmaceuticals, cosmetics and toilet articles	7,275	12,529	88	5,860
Businesses having:				
1 outlet	173,113	173,113	708	35,328
2–9 outlets	22,212	51,575	270	15,401
10–99 outlets	1,096	18,840	301	20,412
100 or more outlets	141	46,466	1,100	85,508
of which:				
All businesses selling food, drinks or tobacco	66,575	92,600	1,020	70,906
Total retail trade	**196,563**	**289,996**	**2,379**	**156,649**

Source: *Business Monitor SDA25, Retailing, 1996*
[a] Includes value added tax (VAT).

people in Great Britain (see Table 16.4). These range from national supermarket and other retail chains to independent corner grocery shops, hardware stores, chemists, newsagents and a host of other types of retailer. During recent years the large multiple retailers have grown considerably, tending to reduce numbers of stores but increase outlet size and diversify product ranges. Some, such as Marks & Spencer, J. Sainsbury and Tesco, have acquired other retailers and made franchise arrangements abroad. Small independent retail businesses and co-operative societies have been in decline for some time. Sunday trading laws have been relaxed to allow retailers to open for specified periods on Sundays; smaller retailers are permitted to open for longer hours on Sundays than the larger supermarkets and department stores, to help their competitive position. The four main supermarket chains are experimenting with 24–hour opening on selected days.

The biggest supermarket groups are Tesco, J. Sainsbury, Safeway and Asda. Other large food retailers include Marks & Spencer, Morrisons, Iceland, Somerfield, Waitrose and Kwik Save (the leading discount food retailer

in Britain). Several overseas discount food retailers, such as Aldi of Germany and Denmark's Netto, have recently entered the British market. Alcoholic drinks are sold mainly in specialist 'off licences' and supermarkets, which have roughly equal sales. The principal off–licence chains are Cellar Five, Oddbins, Threshers and Victoria Wine.

The leading mixed retail chains are found in high streets nationwide. Among them are Marks & Spencer (selling clothing and food and drink in the main), Boots (pharmaceuticals and cosmetic goods), F. W. Woolworth (a variety of products, from clothing to kitchenware), W. H. Smith (newspapers, books and stationery), Argos (a very large range of products that are ordered in the stores from a catalogue and may be taken away by customers), Dixons (consumer electronics), John Menzies (newspapers, books and stationery), Burton Group (clothing) and John Lewis and Debenhams (a wide variety of products, including furniture, clothing and electrical goods) .

Several chains of DIY (Do-It-Yourself) stores and superstores cater for people carrying out their own repairs and improvements on their homes and gardens; they stock a broad range of tools, decorating and building materials, kitchen and bathroom fittings, garden products and so on. The three biggest are B&Q, Homebase and Do It All.

Vehicle, Vehicle Parts and Petrol Retailing

In 1997, 550,000 people were employed in Great Britain in retailing motor vehicles and parts, and in petrol stations. Many businesses selling new vehicles are franchised by the motor manufacturers. Vehicle components are available for sale at garages which undertake servicing and repair work and also at retail chains like Halfords and independent retailers. Drive-in fitting centres sell tyres, exhaust systems, batteries, clutches and other vehicle parts; the largest chains include Kwik-Fit and ATS.

Many petrol stations are owned by oil companies. The three companies with the highest number of outlets are Shell, Esso and BP. Unleaded petrol accounts for about 70 per cent of petrol sold. The vast majority of petrol stations are self-service. The number of petrol stations has been reduced by about a half in the last decade or so as owners focus on larger sites that can accommodate the broad range of retail services, including food, that are now commonly available at petrol stations. About one-fifth of petrol sold in Britain comes from supermarket forecourts.

Mail Order

All kinds of goods and services can be purchased through mail order catalogues from such firms as Great Universal Stores, Littlewoods, Freeman's, Grattan and Empire. The largest selling items are clothing, footwear, furniture, household textiles and domestic electrical appliances.

Shopping Facilities

Britain has a wide choice of shopping facilities. Government policy is to encourage a balanced mixture of facilities that will satisfy the needs of all consumers, whether they have access to a car or not, and enable businesses of all sizes and types to prosper.

The pre-recorded video retail market has shown exceptional growth since the mid-1980s, when it was virtually non-existent: in 1996 total sales reached over £800 million, 8 per cent more than in 1995. The video version of *Independence Day*, one of Hollywood's most successful feature films in recent years, has sold more than 1 million copies in Britain.

The Government is intensifying efforts to help revitalise shopping and other facilities in town centres. One of the most significant trends in retailing has been the spread of superstores, many of which have been built away from urban centres in recent years. Social, economic and environmental considerations have led government planning authorities to try to limit large-scale new retail developments, especially those outside urban centres, which could undermine the viability of existing town centres and further encroach on the countryside and encourage greater car use. All new retail development requires planning permission from the local government planning authority. These authorities must consult central government before granting permission for developments of 20,000 sq m (215,000 sq ft) or more. Encouraged by the Government, the main multiple grocery companies are turning their attention back to town centres, redeveloping existing stores and building smaller outlets. Examples include Tesco's 'Metro' format and J. Sainsbury's 'Central' stores.

Regional out-of-town shopping centres are located on sites offering good road access and ample parking facilities. One of the first was the Metro Centre at Gateshead in north-east England, which is currently the largest of its kind in Europe. Other major centres include Merry Hill at Dudley in the West Midlands, Meadowhall in Sheffield and the Lakeside Centre at Thurrock in Essex. The Trafford Centre, now being built on the outskirts of Manchester and due to open in 1998, will contain 280 shops, 25 restaurants and a leisure complex. Another new shopping and leisure centre is being built at Bluewater Park near Dartford, Kent; when this is completed, it will be the biggest shopping centre in Europe. About half of total food sales are accounted for by superstores away from town centres, compared with a fifth at the beginning of the 1980s.

Retailers of non-food goods, such as DIY products, toys, furniture and electrical appliances, sportswear, and office and computer products, have also built outlets away from urban centres. There is a continuing trend towards grouping retail warehouses into retail parks, often with food and other facilities, although planning controls are now limiting new approvals for such parks.

Other Trends

The large multiple groups tend to sell a much greater number of goods and services than previously. For example, large food retailers are increasing their range of foods. Greater emphasis has also been placed on selling own-label goods (which now account for up to one-half of sales) and environmentally friendly products (including organic produce) and household products and clothing. Many sell fresh food, such as meat, fish, vegetables and, in some cases, bread baked on the premises. In-store pharmacies, post offices and dry-cleaners are now a feature of large supermarkets, which have in recent times also begun selling books, magazines, newspapers, pre-recorded video cassettes (see p. 251) and recorded music. 'Stores within stores' are common; for example, sportswear and sports goods retailers are to be found in several of the big mixed retail department stores, while Laura Ashley, the furnishings and fabrics retailer, has facilities in Homebase (a DIY chain owned by J. Sainsbury). The major supermarket chains have their own petrol stations at some of their bigger outlets (see p. 251).

Several large retailers now offer personal finance facilities for customers in an attempt to encourage sales, particularly of high-value goods. 'Loyalty' cards have also been introduced by supermarket and other retail groups, giving regular customers cash discounts related to the size of their purchases.

Information Technology

Information technology is central to distribution and retailing. Computers monitor stock levels and record sales figures through electronic point-of-sale (EPOS) systems. EPOS systems read a bar-code printed on the retail product that holds price and product information and can be used to generate orders for stock replenishment as well as totalling up bills and providing a receipt for customers. Techniques such as 'just-in-time' ordering, in which produce arrives at the store at the last possible moment before sale, have become widespread as a result. Leading retailers have set up electronic data interchange (EDI) systems; these enable their computers to communicate with those of their suppliers, and transmit orders and invoices electronically, so reducing errors and saving time.

EFTPOS (electronic funds transfer at point of sale) systems allow customers to pay for purchases using debit cards which automatically transfer funds from their bank account. Several major EFTPOS schemes are in operation and the number of terminals is growing rapidly. 'Superscan' technology—which involves customers using an electronic scanning device to work out their own bills, thus avoiding the need to queue at a check-out—is undergoing trials in a number of supermarkets. Electronic home shopping, using a television and telephone, and 'online' shopping, where personal computers are linked to databases, are also being introduced. Tesco and J. Sainsbury are among those testing supermarket shopping using the Internet.

Franchising

Nearly 500 franchisers operate in Britain, with 26,000 outlets. Franchising is a business in which a company owning the rights to a particular form of trading licenses them to franchisees, usually by means of an initial payment with continuing royalties. The main areas are cleaning services, film processing, print shops, hairdressing and cosmetics, fitness centres, courier delivery, car rental, engine tuning and servicing, and fast food retailing. Familiar high street names include McDonalds, Body Shop (environmentally friendly cosmetics and other products) and Kall Kwik (fast printing).

Rental Services

A broad range of rental services, many franchised, are on offer throughout Britain. These include hire of cars and other vehicles, televisions and video cassette recorders, household appliances such as washing machines and tumble dryers, tools and heavy decorating equipment (ladders, floor sanders and so on) and video films and computer games. Retailing of many types of service is dominated by chains, though independent operators are still to be found in most fields.

Auction Houses

Britain attracts buyers and sellers from around the world and has a long tradition of expertise and innovation in auctioneering. Its chief auction houses are active in the international auction markets for works of art, trading on their acknowledged expertise. The two leading houses, Sotheby's and Christie's, are established worldwide. The former handled sales valued at £1,017 million in 1996, while Christie's sales amounted to £1,016 million. Phillips and Bonhams are also prominent auctioneers.

HOTELS, HOLIDAY CENTRES, CATERING AND PUBLIC HOUSES

The hotel and catering trades, which include public houses (pubs), wine bars and other licensed bars, employ 1.3 million people in Britain. The largest hotel business is Forte Hotels, now owned by Granada Group, with 326 hotels in Britain. At the other end of the scale, numerous guest houses and hotels (many individually owned) have fewer than 20 rooms. Holiday centres, including holiday camps with full board, self-catering centres and caravan parks, are run by Butlins, Holiday Club, Center Parcs, Warner Holidays and Pontin's.

Britain's 100,000 restaurants offer cuisine from virtually every country in the world; they cater for the whole spread of income groups and several of the highest quality ones have international reputations. Chinese, Indian, Thai, Italian, French and Greek restaurants are among the most popular. 'Fast food' restaurants, an area where franchising plays a significant role, are widespread. They specialise in selling hamburgers, chicken, pizza and a variety of other foods (some specialising in foreign cuisine—Greek kebabs, for instance), to be eaten on the premises or taken away. The most well-known nationwide chains include McDonalds (hamburgers), Burger King (hamburgers), KFC (chicken), Pizza Hut and Pizza Express. Traditional fish and chip shops are another main provider of cooked take-away food. Sandwich bars are common in towns and cities, typically in areas with high concentrations of office workers. In 1996 sandwiches accounted for 30 per cent of the fast food market, hamburgers 24 per cent, fish and chips 17 per cent, pizzas 13 per cent, ethnic food (Chinese, Indian, Greek, Mexican and so on) 10 per cent and chicken 5 per cent.

About 50,000 pubs sell beer, wines, soft drinks and spirits to adults for consumption on the premises, and most also serve hot and cold food. Many pubs are owned by the large brewing companies, which either provide managers to run them or offer tenancy agreements; these pubs tend to sell just their own brands of beer, although some also offer 'guest' beers. Others, called 'free houses', are independently owned and managed and frequently serve a variety of beers. Wine bars are normally smaller than pubs and tend to specialise in wine and food; they more closely resemble bars in other parts of Europe.

Pubs and bars are permitted by law to open from 11.00 to 23.00 from Monday to Saturday (on Sunday they may open between 12.00 and 22.30). The introduction of liquor licences for cafe-style premises allows children under 14 to accompany adults to selected places where alcoholic drinks are served.

TOURISM, TRAVEL AND LEISURE

Tourism is one of the key growth sectors, contributing £38,000 million annually to the economy (equivalent to over 5 per cent of GDP). In the region of 1.8 million people are employed in tourism and related activities; of these, around 200,000 are self-employed. Over 200,000 businesses, mainly independent small ones—hotels and guest houses, restaurants, holiday homes, caravan and camping parks and so on—are responsible for providing the bulk of tourism services; about 8 per cent of small businesses are engaged in tourism.

Although its share of world tourism earnings fell in the ten years to 1994, it began to rise again in 1995—reaching 5 per cent in 1996. While more than 50 per cent of overseas tourists spend all or almost all of their visit in London, others venture further afield to see the many attractions in the English regions as well as Scotland, Wales and Northern Ireland. The Channel Tunnel has improved access to many of Britain's tourist attractions. It is one of the reasons France has become the country sending the largest number of overseas tourists to Britain.

Domestic tourism was worth around £14,000 million in 1996 (see p. 48). Of British residents opting to take their main holiday in Britain, 38 per cent choose a traditional seaside destination, such as Blackpool (Lancashire), Bournemouth (Dorset), Great Yarmouth (Norfolk) and resorts in Devon and Cornwall. Short holiday breaks (one to three nights), valued at £2,600 million in 1996, make up an increasingly significant part of the market.

Britain's historic towns and cities and its scenic rural and coastal areas continue to have great appeal for British and overseas tourists alike. There is a growing interest in heritage, arts and culture; attractions include museums, art galleries, historic buildings and monuments, and theatres, as well as shopping, sports and business facilities. Domestic and foreign tourists play an increasingly important role in supporting Britain's national heritage and creative arts, in addition to the large financial contribution they make to hotels, restaurants, cafes and bars, and public transport. Business travel is accounting for a growing share of the tourism market; it includes attendance at conferences, exhibitions, trade fairs and other business sites. Activity holidays—based on walking, canoeing, mountain climbing, or artistic activities, for example—are becoming more popular. The Youth Hostel Association operates a comprehensive network of hostels offering young people and families a range of affordable facilities, including self-catering.

> The number of overseas visitors coming to Britain has more than doubled in the last 20 years. In 1996 a record 25.3 million—over 7 per cent more than in 1995—spent almost £12,400 million. An estimated 67 per cent were from Western Europe and 15 per cent from North America. Business travel accounts for about £3,500 million, 27 per cent of all overseas tourism revenue.

'Theme parks' attract more than 15 million visitors a year. Alton Towers (Staffordshire), Chessington World of Adventures and Thorpe Park (both in Surrey) are three of the biggest; 2.7 million people visited Alton Towers in 1996–97, the largest number of visitors for any paid-for tourist attraction (see Table 2.3, p. 11). Legoland near Windsor in Berkshire is the newest theme park. As well as spectacular 'white knuckle' rides and attractions and overhead cable cars and railways, some parks also feature displays of domesticated and wild animals.

Most British holiday-makers wishing to go overseas buy 'package holidays' from travel agencies, where the cost covers both transport and accommodation. The most popular package holiday destinations are Spain, France and Greece. Long-haul holidays to places like the United States, the Caribbean and Australia have gained in popularity as air fares have come down. Winter skiing holidays to resorts in Austria, France, Italy and Switzerland and other countries inside and outside Europe continue to attract large numbers of Britons.

Around 80 per cent of travel agencies are members of the Association of British Travel Agents (ABTA). Although most are small businesses, a few large firms, such as Lunn Poly and Thomas Cook, have hundreds of branches. Some 630 tour operators are members of ABTA; about half are both retail agents and tour operators. ABTA operates financial protection schemes to safeguard its members' customers and maintains codes of conduct drawn up with the Office of Fair Trading (see p. 191). It also offers a free consumer affairs service to help resolve complaints against members and a low-cost independent arbitration scheme for members' customers. The British Incoming Tour Operators' Association is the leading body representing tour operators engaged in incoming tourism to Britain.

Tourism Promotion

The Department for Culture, Media and Sport is responsible for tourism in England, and the Scottish, Welsh, and Northern Ireland Offices have responsibility for tourism in their respective countries. The government-supported British Tourist Authority (BTA) promotes Britain overseas as a tourist destination through 43 offices in 37 countries and encourages the development of tourist facilities in Britain to meet the needs of overseas visitors. The tourist boards for England, Scotland, Wales and Northern Ireland, which also receive government finance, support domestic tourism and work with the BTA to promote Britain overseas.

The Government is working with the tourism industry to raise standards of accommodation and service, and to address certain key issues facing the industry. These include the industry's communications strategy; improving visitor attractions; boosting business tourism; encouraging best practice for the development of workforce skills; and government-industry communication.

The BTA and the national tourist boards inform and advise the Government on issues of concern to the industry. They also help businesses and other organisations to plan by researching and publicising trends affecting the industry. The national tourist boards work closely with regional tourist boards, on which local government and business interests are represented. There are over 800 local Tourist Information Centres in Britain.

Accommodation classification and quality grading schemes are operated by the national tourist boards, including the Crown scheme for hotels, guest houses, inns, bed and breakfast and farmhouse holiday accommodation. A new Lodge category has been introduced for purpose-built accommodation alongside motorways and other major roads. Common standards are applied throughout Britain, and all participating establishments are inspected every year. By 2000 a new harmonised accommodation rating scheme using internationally recognised star symbols will be adopted in England by the English Tourist Board and the motoring organisations—the AA and the RAC.

Eight tourism projects, principally concentrating on staff training and developing key tourism sectors, were awarded a total of £2.5 million under the Government's Sector Challenge initiative (see p. 196) in May 1997.

Further Reading

Financial Services. Aspects of Britain series, HMSO, 1995.

17 Energy and Natural Resources

Britain is self-sufficient in energy in net terms. In 1996 the energy industries accounted for 5 per cent of gross domestic product (GDP), 7 per cent of total investment and 7 per cent of all expenditure on research and development. Energy production directly employs 150,000 people—3.5 per cent of industrial employment. In 1996 it produced a trade surplus in fuels of £4,300 million.

In 1996 combined oil and gas production again achieved a new high, up 7 per cent on 1995. A record number of development wells were drilled. Competition is well advanced in the gas and electricity supply industries and has recently been extended to over 2 million residential gas consumers in England, with about 20 per cent switching from British Gas. The Government has issued a plan for a more closely regulated water industry in England and Wales.

Energy Resources

Britain has large reserves of fossil fuels and a more varied and balanced energy supply than many other countries. It is far less dependent on imports than its EU partners, and was one of only five OECD countries which produced more energy than it consumed in 1995.[1] The mix of primary fuels (oil, gas, nuclear power and coal) consumed in Britain has become increasingly diverse in recent years, mainly as a result of a decline in coal use and the growing use of gas. Coal still supplied a

significant proportion of the country's primary energy needs: 44 per cent of electricity production by the major generators in 1996, while nuclear power provided 30 per cent and oil and gas 25 per cent. In the second quarter of 1997, nuclear power overtook coal as the main fuel used.

In the early 1970s, energy imports accounted for over 50 per cent of Britain's primary energy consumption, as recently discovered oil and gas reserves were still being developed. By 1981, Britain had become a net exporter of energy, as oil and gas production came on stream. Following the Piper Alpha accident in the North Sea in 1987, oil production fell and Britain again became a net

---

[1] The others were Norway (exceptional in producing more than seven times as much energy as it consumes), Australia, Mexico and Canada.

Edward Wadsworth:
'Floats and Afloat' (1928).

John Hawkesworth: 'The Keep, Dover Castle' (1950).

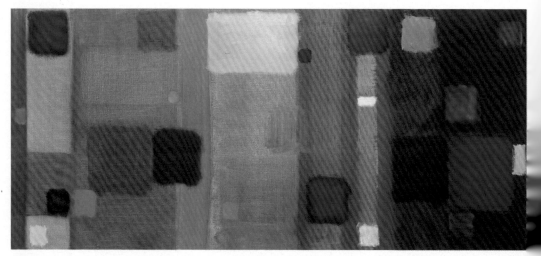

Patrick Heron: 'Horizontal Painting with Soft Black Squares' (1959).

John Lavery: 'Lady on a Safety Tricycle' (1885).

Richard Platt: 'Coronation Decoration, Calverley Grove, London N19' (1953).

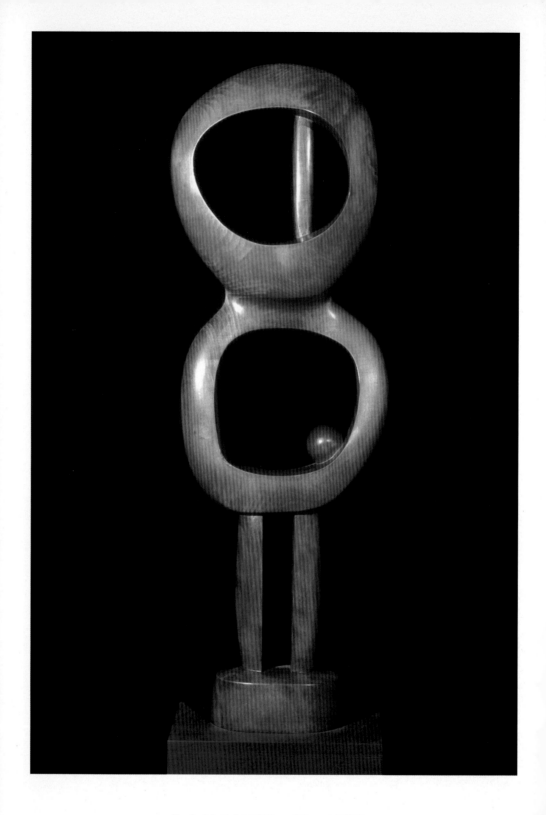

Frederick E. McWilliam: 'Figure' (1937).

Olwen Jones: 'Downstairs' (c.1974).

Stephen Tomlin:
'Giles Lytton Strachey (1880-1932)
Critic and Biographer'
(c.1928-30).

Ronald Moody:
'The Priest' (1939).

Osmund Caine: 'The Grand Union Canal: Brentford Lock' (1954).

John Ridgewell: 'Landscape IV' (1961).

importer until 1993. In 1996 it exported 116.2 million tonnes of oil equivalent, and imported 78.2 million tonnes, generating an energy trade surplus of £4,300 million, some £600 million higher than in 1995. Energy represents 6.5 per cent of British exports and 4 per cent of imports.

ENERGY POLICY

The Government's energy policy is to ensure secure, diverse and sustainable supplies at competitive prices. It believes that this is best achieved by competition between suppliers in open markets. The Government considers that in the long run a balance needs to be achieved between the demands of economic growth and the necessity of reducing the impact of energy-related emissions on the environment. All this is as true for other countries as it is for Britain.

By 1998 all British gas and electricity markets will be opened up to full competition. The independent regulators (see pp. 266 and 269) were put in place at privatisation and have a duty to encourage the development of competition and protect the interests of consumers, by administering price controls and enforcing standards of service in remaining areas of monopoly. While supply monopoly is receding as competition advances, there will always be areas of natural monopoly in the transmission/distribution networks—the pipes and wires.

International Developments

The EU imports about 50 per cent of its energy needs. Its White Paper published in 1995 sought to adapt energy policy to the challenges the EU faces, taking account of the rapid development of markets and what is likely to happen on the international stage. It also aimed to ensure further integration of the EU internal energy market, based on the principle of openness and competitiveness. Energy and environmental objectives were to be made more compatible, and member states persuaded to make energy choices in accordance with EU objectives. Wherever possible, the full cost of energy production

and consumption was to be established openly and reflected in prices. Another priority was to undertake research and development (R & D) into new, cleaner and more efficient energy technologies. The R & D framework programme has an R & D component, JOULE (see p. 259), and a demonstration component, THERMIE. They focus, among other things, on energy security, environmental protection and a close relation between R & D and the energy markets.

The EU undertakes international technical assistance programmes and co-financing in the energy sector. For example, the ALURE programme, in co-operation with the countries of Latin America, encourages optimum use of energy sources in the region. The EU also collaborates with specialist international organisations, such as the International Energy Agency (IEA), in particular for crisis measures, such as the obligation on member states to maintain a minimum crude-oil and petroleum product stock or to reduce consumption in times of shortage.

An EC directive establishing the internal market in electricity came into force in February 1997. Most member states must implement it within two years; it requires them to introduce competition in generation and phase in competition in supply. They have to open 23 per cent of their market to competition, rising to 28 per cent after three years and 30 per cent after six.

Discussions of the rules concerning the internal market in gas are nearing completion.

The Energy Charter treaty, signed in 1994 but not formally ratified, is being provisionally applied. It creates a legal framework for energy investment and trade with the countries of Central and Eastern Europe and of the former Soviet Union, and helps them to set up open and non-discriminatory energy markets.

ENERGY CONSUMPTION

In 1996 energy consumption in Britain was only 9 per cent higher than in 1970, despite a 69 per cent increase in GDP; however, taking account of temperature correction—which shows what the annual consumption might have been if the average temperature during the year had been the same as the average for

Table 17.1: Inland Energy Consumption (in terms of primary sources)[a]						
					Million tonnes oil equivalent	
	1986	1992	1993	1994	1995	1996
Oil	72.3	78.3	78.9	78.0	76.2	78.6
Coal	70.0	63.6	55.6	52.2	49.9	46.7
Natural Gas	52.7	54.5	62.5	64.8	70.1	82.4
Nuclear Energy	15.4	18.5	21.5	21.2	21.4	22.1
Hydro-electric power[b]	0.4	0.5	0.4	0.5	0.5	0.3
Net imports of electricity	0.4	1.4	1.4	1.5	1.4	1.4
Total	211.2	216.8	220.3	218.1	219.5	231.6

Source: Department of Trade and Industry
[a] Adjustments in the figures for recent years are the result of methodological review.
[b] Excludes pumped storage. Includes generation at wind stations from 1988.
Note: Differences between totals and the sums of their component parts are due to rounding.

the years 1961–90—consumption has risen for the last four years in succession. Energy consumption by final users in 1996 amounted to 160.8 million tonnes of oil equivalent[2] on an 'energy supplied' basis, of which transport consumed 33 per cent, industrial users 23 per cent, residential users 30 per cent, and commerce, agriculture and public services 14 per cent.

Primary energy consumption grew by 6 per cent in 1996, the largest increase for over 30 years. The year was colder than normal, however, and 1995 had been warmer. Final energy consumption (including petroleum products and secondary electricity, for example) also increased, by 7 per cent over 1995: residential consumption was up 13 per cent; industrial consumption up 4 per cent; services up 6 per cent; and transport up 4 per cent.

ENERGY EFFICIENCY

In 1996 energy consumption in Britain's housing, offices and industrial buildings was worth about £22,985 million. The Environmental and Energy Management Directorate (EEMD) of the Department of the Environment, Transport and the Regions (DETR) estimates that at least 20 per cent could be saved through investment in cost-effective energy efficiency measures. Such

[2] 1 tonne of oil equivalent = 41.868 gigajoules.

improvements offer a means of reducing carbon dioxide (CO_2) emissions. The EEMD encourages investment in these improvements through various programmes (see below). Its budget for 1997–98 is £160 million.

The Energy Saving Trust is an independent organisation which aims to stimulate investment in energy efficiency and is developing pilot schemes in the drive to change the way consumers and providers think about energy and its efficient use. The Trust's government funding for the three years to 1999–2000 is £71.5 million.

Every new home in England and Wales is now required to hold the Standard Assessment Procedure (SAP) for home energy rating, which demonstrates energy efficiency and impact on the environment. Similar standards will apply in Scotland from early 1998. Retailers have to display energy efficiency standard labels on refrigerators, freezers, washing machines and tumble dryers.

Environmental and Energy Management Schemes

The Energy Efficiency Best Practice programme, run by the Energy Technology Support Unit for the DETR, prepares and promotes authoritative information, with the help of guides and case studies, on energy efficiency techniques and technologies in industry and buildings. As a result of the programme, over £500 million a year of energy savings have been made so far and over 3 million tonnes of CO_2 emissions have been avoided.

The Home Energy Efficiency Scheme (HEES) is the Government's main domestic energy efficiency programme in Great Britain. It offers grants for loft insulation, tank and pipe lagging, draught-proofing, and energy advice. Over 2 million homes have been insulated since the scheme started in 1991, and more than £350 million awarded in grants.

HEES grants (average £160; maximum £315) are available to householders who receive income-related benefit; disability allowances; or are aged 60 or more. Provision for 1997–98 is £75 million. Households getting grants can save about £45 in fuel costs a year. Claimants with benefits or disability allowances only contribute towards the cost of the work if it is above maximum grant. Those who qualify through age alone have to contribute 75 per cent of the cost up to maximum grant value.

Under the Small Company Environmental and Energy Management Assistance Scheme (SCEEMAS), government grants subsidise 40-50 per cent of the cost of consultancy help to guide manufacturing companies through the EU Eco-Management and Audit Scheme (see p. 346) in Britain. The grant applies to firms with fewer than 250 employees, and an annual turnover of less than £32 million.

The EU SAVE II programme (Specific Actions for Vigorous Energy Efficiency), adopted in December 1996, aims to stimulate energy efficiency in industry and in the home through funding of studies during 1996–2000. Some 18 million ECUs have been allocated from the EU budget to SAVE II for 1997. The EU normally provides up to 50 per cent of the project costs.

ENERGY AND THE ENVIRONMENT

There is increasing awareness in Britain of the environmental implications of the production and use of energy. Although demand for electricity has increased by an average of 2 per cent a year since 1985 and generation is up by 16 per cent, CO_2 emissions are falling (by 7 per cent since 1990), largely because of changes in the use of fuels for electricity generation.

Through SAVE and JOULE-THERMIE (see above), the EU aims to develop a culture of energy-saving behaviour and rational energy consumption. These programmes play a role in developing high energy efficiency and new technologies for exploiting fossil fuels, nuclear energy or renewable energy.

Climate Change

Britain's second assessment report on climate change, published in February 1997, encourages cost-effective measures to reduce greenhouse gas emissions—especially CO_2 and methane—and confirms that Britain is likely to exceed its commitment to return emissions of CO_2 and other greenhouse gases to 1990 levels by 2000 (see chapter 21). The Government has proposed a domestic target of a 20 per cent reduction in CO_2 below 1990 levels by 2010.

The EU, with only 6 per cent of world population, is responsible for about 16 per cent of global energy-related CO_2 emissions. The negotiating position at the Climate Change Conference at Kyoto is for a 15 per cent reduction in greenhouse gas emissions below 1990 levels by 2010, with at least half this being achieved by 2005. Within the EU, a burden-sharing arrangement has been agreed for the first 10 per cent of this, with Britain's share being a 10 per cent reduction. Some member states' emissions will be allowed to rise to permit them to secure further economic growth. A steady increase in EU energy demand is likely despite the assumption of a fall in energy intensity[3] of 1.3 per cent in 1995–2005, and 1.6 per cent in 2005–2010. A problem arising from climate change will be to try to decouple economic growth and energy demand growth, which have hitherto tended to march in step.

---

[3]Energy intensity is defined as energy consumption per unit of activity—not the same as energy efficiency because it is affected by changes in the pattern of activity within a sector as well as by genuine efficiency changes. For most sectors, however, changes in intensity will owe much to changes in efficiency and can serve as a reasonable proxy for them.

Table 17.2: Oil Statistics					Million tonnes	
	1986	1992	1993	1994	1995	1996
Oil Production						
land	0.4	4.0	3.7	4.6	5.1	5.3
offshore	127.2	85.2	90.2	114.4	116.7	116.5
Refinery output	72.9	85.8	89.6	86.6	86.1	89.9
Deliveries	69.8	75.5	75.8	75.0	73.7	75.4
Exports						
Crude, NGL, feedstock	83.0	57.6	64.4	82.4	84.6	80.6
refined petroleum	14.8	20.3	23.0	22.2	21.6	23.7
Imports						
Crude, NGL, feedstock	35.6	57.7	61.7	53.1	48.7	50.1
refined petroleum	13.1	10.6	10.1	10.4	9.9	9.2

Source: Department of Trade and Industry

OIL AND GAS EXPLORATION AND PRODUCTION

For centuries small quantities of oil have been produced in mainland Britain, though by the early 1960s this amounted to only 150,000 tonnes a year, about 0.3 per cent of refinery output. Britain was almost wholly dependent for its oil supplies on imports. The first notable offshore discovery of oil (Arbroath field) in the United Kingdom Continental Shelf (UKCS) was made in 1969 and the first oil brought ashore, from the Argyll field, in 1975. In 1996, output of crude oil and natural gas liquids (NGLs) in Britain averaged 2.78 million barrels (about 355,700 tonnes) a day, making Britain the world's ninth largest producer.

Structure of the Industry

The Government grants licences to private sector companies to explore and exploit oil and gas resources (see below). Its main sources of revenue from oil and gas activities are Petroleum Revenue Tax (see p. 161), levied on all fields approved between 1975 and March 1993; Corporation Tax, charged on the profits of oil and gas companies—the only tax on profits of fields approved after March 1993; and royalty, which applies only to fields approved before April 1982 and is paid at 12.5 per cent of the landed value of the petroleum.

Licensing

Holders of government licences explore for and produce oil and gas from specific offshore or onshore areas. In addition to awarding licences, the Government must approve all proposed wells and field development plans. Since 1964, 17 offshore licensing rounds have been held, and by the end of 1996, 6,221 wells had been, or were being, drilled in the UKCS: 1,950 exploration wells, 1,171 appraisal wells and 3,100 development wells. The 275 blocks, in 68 tranches, offered in the 17th round covered more remote areas than hitherto, such as the Rockall Trough and west of the Hebrides, which have previously seen little exploration or have been thought unexplorable. Licences are subject to conditions to protect other marine interests, including care of the environment.

Production and Reserves

There were 173 offshore fields in production at the end of March 1997—88 oil, 77 gas and 8 condensate (a lighter form of oil). Production started at 16 new offshore oilfields during 1996–97, and a total of 18 new development projects were approved during 1996. Offshore these comprised 13 oilfields and two gasfields; onshore, two gas and one oil. In addition, approval for 12 incremental offshore developments (further developments to existing fields) was granted.

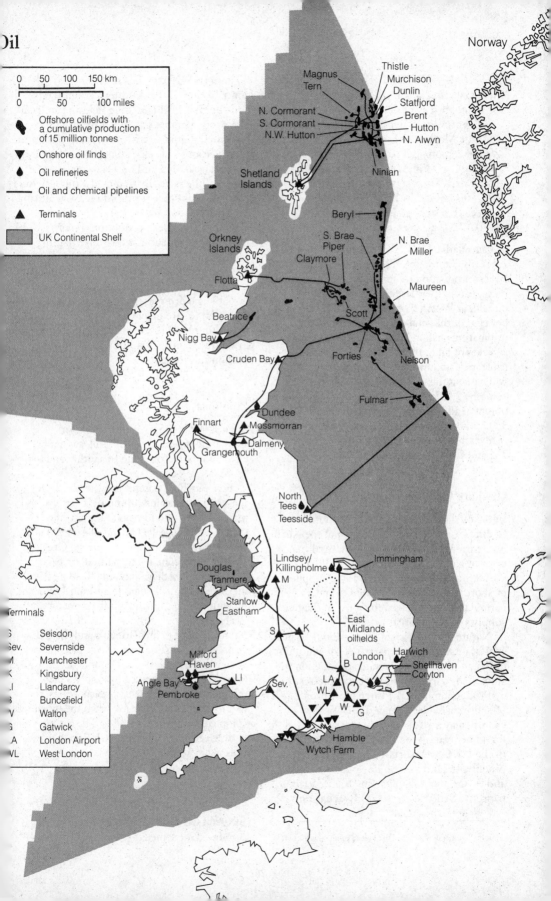

Oil

Norway

Scale
0 50 100 150 km
0 50 100 miles

Offshore oilfields with a cumulative production of 15 million tonnes

▼ Onshore oil finds

🛢 Oil refineries

— Oil and chemical pipelines

▲ Terminals

UK Continental Shelf

Magnus
Tern
Thistle
Murchison
Dunlin
Statfjord
N. Cormorant
S. Cormorant
N.W. Hutton
Brent
Hutton
N. Alwyn
Ninian

Shetland Islands

Beryl

Orkney Islands

S. Brae
Piper
Claymore
N. Brae
Miller

Flotta

Maureen

Beatrice

Nigg Bay
Scott

Cruden Bay
Forties
Nelson

Fulmar

Dundee
Mossmorran
Finnart
Dalmeny
Grangemouth

North Tees
Teesside

Lindsey/
Killingholme
Immingham
M

Douglas
Tranmere
Stanlow
Eastham
S   K
East Midlands oilfields

Milford Haven
LI
Sev.
London
B
Harwich
Shellhaven
Coryton

Angle Bay
Pembroke
LA
WL
W   G

Hamble
Wytch Farm

Terminals

S	Seisdon
Sev.	Severnside
M	Manchester
K	Kingsbury
LI	Llandarcy
B	Buncefield
W	Walton
G	Gatwick
LA	London Airport
WL	West London

Schiehallion, 130 km (80 miles) west of Shetland, discovered in 1993, is the second field approved for development in the Atlantic Margin of the UKCS. With estimated potential recoverable reserves of 56.7 million tonnes, it is significantly larger than the first, the nearby Foinaven field, discovered in 1990, which is expected to start production in 1997.

Cumulative UKCS oil production to date is 2,047 million tonnes. The fields with the largest production totals are Forties, Brent, Ninian and Piper. Britain's largest onshore oilfield, at Wytch Farm (Dorset), produces 90 per cent of the total crude oils and NGLs originating onshore. Remaining recoverable reserves of oil in the 'proven' plus 'probable' categories amount to 3,400 million tonnes, while maximum possible remaining reserves could be 2,025 million tonnes. In addition, potential additional reserves range from 130 to 350 million tonnes and undiscovered recoverable reserves are calculated at between 285 and 2,700 million tonnes.

Offshore Gas

Initial offshore exploration concentrated on finding gas in the Southern Basin of the North Sea. After the first commercial natural gas discovery in the West Sole field in 1965 and the start of its exploitation in 1967, supplies of offshore natural gas grew rapidly, and by 1977 natural gas had replaced town gas in the public supply system in Great Britain.

Natural gas now accounts for about 30 per cent of total inland primary fuel consumption in Britain. In 1996 indigenous production amounted to 89,840 million cubic metres.

Production from the three most prolific offshore gasfields, Leman, Indefatigable (South) and the Hewett area, has accounted for 43 per cent of the total gas produced so far in the UKCS. Associated gas,[4] delivered by pipeline to land via the Far North Liquids and Associated Gas System (FLAGS) and from the Scottish Area Gas Evacuation

System (SAGE), makes additional contributions. The Southern Basin fields and the South Morecambe field in the Irish Sea produce more gas in winter to satisfy increased demand, with the North Sean and South Sean fields also augmenting supplies to meet peak demand on very cold days in winter. The partially depleted Rough field is used as a gas store for rapid recovery during peak winter periods.

Cumulative gas production to date is 1.14 million million cubic metres. Remaining recoverable gas reserves already discovered are estimated at between 760,000 million and 1.96 million million cubic metres. If possible gas from existing discoveries and potential future discoveries are added, the remaining total reserves are estimated to be in the range of 1.29 million million to 3.8 million million cubic metres.

Pipelines

Some 8,500 km (5,312 miles) of major submarine pipeline transport oil, gas and condensate from one field to another and to shore.

Five pipeline terminals on the North Sea coast bring gas ashore to supply a national and regional high- and low-pressure pipeline system some 267,300 km (167,060 miles) long, which transports natural gas around Great Britain. A pipeline taking natural gas from Scotland to Northern Ireland (40.4 km; 25 miles) carried its first gas in autumn 1996. The pipeline under construction from Bacton to Zeebrugge in Belgium will provide an interconnector to link Britain's and the EU gas grids. Some Britain/Europe contracts have already been signed—for example, Centrica (see p. 265) is contracted to supply 3,000 million cubic metres over a seven-year period to Thyssengas of Germany when the pipeline is completed at the end of 1998. The gas pipeline between Scotland and the Irish Republic was finished in 1996.

Economic and Industrial Aspects

In 1996 UKCS oil and gas production accounted for some 2.5 per cent of Britain's

---

[4]Mainly methane, produced and used on oil production platforms.

Gas

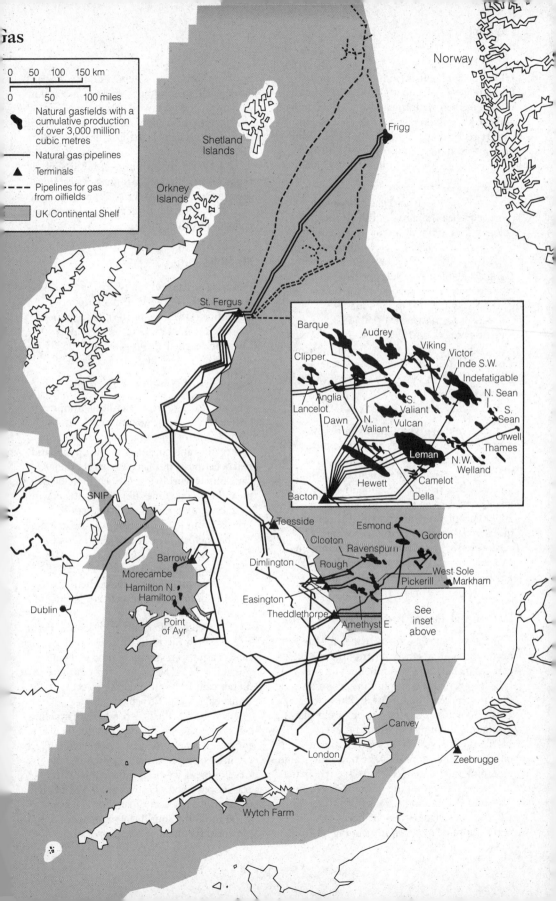

Legend:

0 50 100 150 km
0 50 100 miles

- Natural gasfields with a cumulative production of over 3,000 million cubic metres
- Natural gas pipelines
- ▲ Terminals
- Pipelines for gas from oilfields
- UK Continental Shelf

Norway

Shetland Islands

Orkney Islands

Frigg

St. Fergus

SNIP

Dublin

Barrow
Morecambe
Hamilton N.
Hamilton
Point of Ayr

Teesside

Dimlington

Easington
Theddlethorpe

Esmond
Gordon
Clooton
Ravenspurn
Rough
West Sole
Pickerill
Markham
Amethyst E.

See inset above

Canvey

London

Zeebrugge

Wytch Farm

Inset:

Barque
Audrey
Viking
Victor
Clipper
Inde S.W.
Indefatigable
N. Sean
Anglia
S. Valiant
S. Sean
Lancelot
Dawn
N. Valiant
Vulcan
Orwell
Thames
Leman
N.W. Welland
Hewett
Camelot
Bacton
Della

GDP. Total revenues from the sale of oil (including NGLs) and gas produced from the UKCS in 1996 are estimated at £12,600 million and £5,300 million respectively. Taxes and royalty receipts attributable to UKCS oil and gas came to about £3,600 million in 1996–97, compared with £2,350 million in 1995–96.

Since 1965, the oil and gas production industry has generated trading profits of some £191,000 million, of which nearly £69,000 million has been reinvested in the industry, £83,000 million paid in taxation, and £39,000 million left for disposal by the companies. Total income of the oil and gas sector was £21,000 million in 1996. Proceeds from the sale of oil in 1996 were up 20 per cent on 1995; those from the sale of gas were up 28 per cent. Total value of oil and gas produced onshore was about £490 million in 1996, compared with £440 million in 1995.

Gross capital investment from British sources in the oil and gas extraction industry rose by 3.5 per cent to £4,400 million in 1996. This represented about 18 per cent of total British industrial investment and 4 per cent of gross domestic capital investment. Some 30,000 people were employed by the offshore industry in September 1996, of whom 93 per cent were British nationals. In addition, oil and gas provide employment for about 331,000 people in support industries.

Decommissioning and the Environment

The Petroleum Act 1987 provides for the decommissioning of redundant offshore oil and gas installations and pipelines on the UKCS. Owners have to submit proposals to the Government for approval. The Government is committed to ensuring that the decommissioning programme for every installation meets Britain's international obligations and represents the best practicable environmental option (BPEO). It participates in discussions within the framework of the Oslo and Paris Commissions to consider whether any changes may be necessary to the regime applied to decommissioning in northern European waters. The Brent Spar storage and loading buoy remains moored in Erfjord in Norway, while Shell considers alternatives for its disposal. Any solution will be judged against the BPEO for deep-sea disposal.

In 1996 the total volume of UKCS oil reported as spilt, at 127 tonnes, was at its second lowest level since 1982, with no spill over 20 tonnes; 92 per cent of reports were for spills of less than 1 tonne.

Offshore Safety

Offshore health and safety are the responsibility of the Health and Safety Executive (HSE; see p. 185). Government funding for the HSE's Offshore Safety Division reached £19 million in 1996–97.

Suppliers of Goods and Services

The Oil, gas and petrochemicals Supplies Office (OSO) is the government arm responsible for encouraging British contractors and suppliers in the oil, gas and petrochemicals industry to market their capabilities worldwide. OSO also helps British oil and gas companies develop contacts with overseas governments. It also organises briefing courses for British overseas missions and has helped fund the British industry's Cost Reduction in the New Era initiative (CRINE), relaunched in 1997 as CRINE Network, which aims to make the British offshore industry as competitive as any in the world by 2000.

IEA forecasts attribute most of the recent rise in North Sea output to new medium-size fields coming on stream, a process made possible by CRINE, which has cut more than 30 per cent from oil and gas project costs by improving competitiveness.

Demand for floating production systems has grown quickly and has provided contracts for the offshore industry. Converted tankers are used to exploit smaller oilfields, whose development would not be viable with traditional fixed platforms. An AMEC-led consortium has secured a contract worth £300 million to build the main processing platform for the new Shell-operated

Shearwater oilfield in the North Sea. Yards at Wallsend (Tyne and Wear), Hartlepool and Middlesbrough (Cleveland) have shares in the work. Lewis Offshore at Stornoway (Outer Hebrides) is among Scottish firms working on platforms for the Elgin and Franklin oilfields, both Elf projects.

DOWNSTREAM OIL

Oil Consumption

Deliveries of petroleum products for inland consumption (excluding refinery consumption) in 1996 included 22.4 million tonnes of petrol for motors, 14.4 million tonnes of DERV (diesel-engined road vehicles) fuel, 8 million tonnes of aviation turbine fuel, 7.6 million tonnes of gas oil (distilled from petroleum) and 6.9 million tonnes of fuel oils (blends of heavy petroleum).

Oil Refineries

In 1996, Britain's 15 refineries processed 96.7 million tonnes of crude and process oils, 4 per cent up on 1995. About 80 per cent of output by weight is in the form of lighter, higher-value products, such as gasoline, DERV and jet kerosine. Britain is much more geared towards petrol production than its European counterparts—about a third of the barrel of crude, compared to a European average of just over a fifth.

Trade

In 1996, Britain exported 23.7 million tonnes of refined petroleum products, worth £2,735 million. Virtually all exports went to Britain's partners in the EU and the IEA, the largest markets being France and Germany, and the United States.

British exports of gas were 33 per cent higher in 1996 than in 1995. Some 1,400 million cubic metres of UKCS gas were exported, mainly to the Netherlands, from the British share of the Markham transboundary field. About 1,700 million cubic metres were imported from Norway. Norwegian imports were 2.1 per cent of total supplies in 1996, compared with 2.5 per cent in 1995.

GAS SUPPLY INDUSTRY

Structure of the Industry

The original regime put in place by the Gas Act 1986 envisaged that British Gas would retain a monopoly of supply to tariff customers (those taking less than 25,000 therms a year), while above this threshold, in the contract market, new entrants would be allowed to compete. This has been difficult to enforce; and the Government eventually instructed British Gas to separate its gas supply and transportation activities. The Gas Act 1995, which set the framework for a fully competitive gas market, does not allow a holder of a public gas transporter's licence to hold licences for supply or shipping.[5] In February 1997, British Gas demerged into two entirely separate companies. The supply business is now part of the holding company Centrica plc, while the pipeline and storage businesses, most exploration and production, and R & D have been retained within British Gas plc, renamed BG plc.

The national and regional gas pipeline network is owned by Transco, part of BG plc. A Network Code sets the legal and contractual framework for the rights and responsibilities of Transco and users of its transportation and storage network.

Competition

During 1994–97, competition has developed significantly, with some 70 suppliers having captured about 70 per cent of the overall industrial and commercial market (for customers using more than 2,500 therms a year). In the firm contract market (above 25,000 therms), 80 per cent of gas is now supplied by independents; within the 2,500–25,000 therm market, the comparable figure is 57 per cent; and in the interruptible market,[6] competitors to

---

[5] Suppliers sell piped gas to consumers; public gas transporters (PGTs) operate the pipeline system through which such gas will normally be delivered; shippers arrange with PGTs for appropriate amounts of gas to go through the pipeline system.

[6] Subject to a four-hour notice period Transco may interrupt supplies to various customers, principally because of network capacity constraints or high demand. The Network Code allows Transco to make supply/demand interruptions when demand exceeds 85 per cent of peak day demand.

British Gas Trading (Centrica's supply business) deliver some 65 per cent.

The opening of the domestic market in south-west and south-east England, covering some 2.2 million consumers, has involved 14 new supply companies, including several regional electricity companies (for example, SWEB, NORWEB and Eastern Electricity), and the oil companies Amerada Hess and Total. By August 1997, 21 per cent of consumers in both regions had switched from British Gas to new suppliers. Gas market competition was extended to northern England and Scotland from November 1997, and will be extended to the rest of England and Wales during 1998.

Only companies which have been granted a supplier's licence are allowed to sell gas. The licence carries various conditions, which include providing gas to anyone in the licence area who requests it and is connected to the mains gas supply. Suppliers must offer customers a range of payment options; they are able to set their own charges, but have to publish their prices and other terms so that customers can make an informed choice. BG Transco retains responsibility for dealing with gas leaks and emergencies.

The Director General of Gas Supply, who heads Ofgas, the industry regulator, has powers to control gas prices and to set and enforce standards of performance, and oversees the development of competition.

Consumption

Gas consumption, at an estimated 943.6 terawatt[7] hours (TWh) in 1996, was up 16 per cent on 1995, with gas supplied for electricity generation (amounting to 186.9 TWh) up 31 per cent. Sales to industry (191.3 TWh) were 10 per cent up on 1995; to the commercial sector (122.3 TWh) 9 per cent up. Domestic sales (375.8 TWh) were 15 per cent up. There has been a steady fall in gas prices since 1982. In 1995 they were the lowest among the European G7 countries. Between 1986 and 1996 average industrial gas prices fell by 63 per cent in real terms; domestic prices were

reduced by 20 per cent (including VAT). In Great Britain a typical household's annual gas bill fell in real terms from £400 in 1986 to £320 in 1996.

COAL

The nationalised coal industry was privatised in 1994. The main mining operators are RJB Mining plc (in England and Wales); Mining (Scotland) Ltd; Celtic Energy Ltd; and Tower (a care-and-maintenance pit at Hirwaun in Rhondda, Cynon and Taff, sold to a 'buy-out' team of former employees). RJB Mining and Celtic Energy, together with the Scottish Coal Company Ltd, are the main opencast operators. At the end of 1996, there were 27 major deep mines in operation (with about 12,500 workers), which had been transferred into private ownership from the nationalised industry; another 34 (with about 4,800 workers), which were already in private ownership; and 91 opencast sites. Opencast accounts for most of the relatively low sulphur coal mined in Scotland and south Wales, which contributes towards improving the quality and cost of English coal supplies.

Market for Coal

In 1996 inland consumption of coal was 7 per cent down on the 1995 figure, at 71.4 million tonnes, of which 76.9 per cent was used by the electricity generators, 12.4 per cent by coke ovens, 1.3 per cent by other fuel producers, 5 per cent by industry and 3.8 per cent by domestic consumers. Exports were 988,000 tonnes, while imports amounted to 17.8 million tonnes—mainly of steam coal for electricity generation and coking coal. Total production from British deep mines fell from 35.1 million tonnes in 1995 to 32.2 million tonnes in 1996. Total opencast output stayed at about 16 million tonnes.

Although the British coal industry now has the lowest production costs of any in the EU, and is the only one not in receipt of a government subsidy, it faces a number of significant challenges: in particular, the expiry of its contracts with the main electricity generators in 1998, which is likely to lead to

---

[7] 1 TW = 1,000 gigawatts. 1 GW = 1,000 megawatts (MW). 1 MW = 1,000 kilowatts (kW).

increased use of cheaper imported coal; and the constraints on coal use imposed by tougher environmental standards, which currently help to make gas firing the first choice of most generators for new plant.

Coal Research

The DTI is involved in a collaborative clean coal technology R & D programme, with industry, universities and overseas organisations. The programme has funded 240 projects with a total value of £250 million, of which the DTI has contributed £50 million.

Coal Authority

The Coal Authority, which took over the management of Britain's unworked coal reserves from British Coal in 1994, licenses coal-mining; holds, manages and disposes of interests in unworked coal and coal mines; provides information about mining plans and geological data; and deals with subsidence damage claims arising from former coal-mining.

ELECTRICITY

England and Wales

There are 33 generating companies in England and Wales, of which the principal ones are National Power, PowerGen, Eastern Group, British Energy, and Magnox Electric. They sell electricity to suppliers through a marketing mechanism known as the 'Pool'. The National Grid (NGC) owns and operates the transmission system, and is responsible for calling up generation plant to meet demand.

To ensure a smooth transition to a competitive market, the Government holds special shares in National Power and PowerGen, which limit individual shareholdings to 15 per cent; it also holds a special share in the NGC, which until its flotation in 1995 was owned by the regional electricity companies (RECs). Magnox plc remains wholly publicly owned.

Distribution—transfer of electricity from the national grid to consumers via local networks—is carried out by the 12 RECs in England and Wales. Supply covers the purchase of electricity from generators and its sale to customers. Until 1998, RECs have a monopoly of all franchise sales (to consumers taking 100 kWh a year or less) in their regions, known as 'first-tier' supply. Above 100 kWh, the market is already open to competition, and consumers may have contracts with a 'second-tier' supplier, who could be one of the generators, an REC from a different region, or an independent supplier. This market accounted for almost half the electricity supplied in Britain in 1996–97. Since the expiry of the Government's special shares in the English and Welsh RECs in 1995, there have been take-overs and mergers; ownership of 11 of the 12 RECs has changed, with some being bought by overseas companies, especially from the United States. There has also been a trend towards the creation of multi-utilities, some of which, such as the merger of NorthWest Water and NORWEB, provide the opportunity for creating common services. British electricity companies are also investing overseas. National Power, for example, shares ownership in, and in some cases maintains, power stations in Australia, China, Pakistan, Portugal and the United States; it has invested about £900 million in 7,500 MW of capacity.

Scotland

ScottishPower plc and Scottish Hydro Electric plc are vertically integrated companies which generate, transmit, distribute and supply electricity within their respective franchise areas. They are also contracted to buy all the output from Scottish Nuclear Ltd, now part of British Energy plc, until 2005. There are about 5,500 customers in the Scottish competitive market (comprising those with a maximum demand of 100 kWh or more), which accounts for about 40 per cent of all electricity consumed. Only 9 per cent of this market is met by second-tier suppliers, mainly by Scottish companies securing customers from each other's area.

Northern Ireland

Three private companies, Nigen, Premier Power and Coolkeeragh Power, generate

Electricity

Orkney Islands

Shetland Islands

Dounreay ◆

Fasnakyle ★

▲ Foyers

Peterhead ■

0 20 40 60 80 100 120 km

0   20   40   60   80 miles

□ Conventional power stations
(220 MW and over)
under construction

■ Conventional power stations
(220 MW and over)

★ CCGT power stations
(200 MW and over)

● Nuclear power stations

◆ Power-producing reactors
of the UKAEA or BNFL

★ Hydro-electric power stations
(over 45 MW capacity)

▲ Pumped storage schemes

Errochty ★

Rannoch ★

Cruachan ▲   ★ Clunie

Lochay ★

Sloy ★

Kincardine ■
■ Longannet
Cockenzie ■   Torness ●

● Hunterston B

Coolkeeragh ■

Ballylumford ■
Kilroot ■

Chapelcross ◆
★ Galloway

Blyth A ■
Blyth B ■

Hartlepool ●

Calder Hall ◆
Roosecote ■   ★
★ Heysham II ●●
Heysham I

Teesside ★

Drax ■

Ferrybridge C ■
Eggborough ■   Killingholme
Keadby ★   Brigg ★   PowerGen
Cottam ■   West ★   Killingholme
Deeside ★ Fiddler's   Cottam TDC ★   Burton   Stallingborough
Wylfa ●   Ferry ★   High Marnham ■
Dinorwig ▲   Connah's   Spondon ★
Quay ★   Ratcliffe-on-Soar ■
Ffestiniog ▲   Corby ■   Sutton Bridge ★
Rugeley B ■   ★   King's Lynn
Willington B ■   ★ Peterborough
Rheidol ★   Drakelow   Little Barford ■   Sizewel●
C   ★   Sizewel●
Ironbridge ■   Rye House ★
Barking ★   Bradwell ●
Pembroke ■   Didcot B ■   Kingsnorth
Aberthaw ■   Didcot A ■ ★   Tilbury ■   Grain
Barry ★   Oldbury ●   Littlebrook ■   Medway ★
□ ★ Seabank
Hinkley Point A ●●   Hinkley Point B   Dungeness A ●
Dungeness B ●

electricity from four power stations. They are obliged to sell it to Northern Ireland Electricity (NIE), which has a monopoly of transmission and distribution, and a right to supply. Supply to all customers is open to competition, but the small scale and isolation of the system has so far made it difficult for competition to develop. The largest power station, Ballylumford, has been converted from oil to gas firing and accounts for almost half Northern Ireland's generating capacity (2,243 MW). In 1996 the Director General of Electricity Supply for Northern Ireland (DGES)(NI) assumed responsibility for the natural gas industry and a new combined regulatory authority, OFREG (Office for the Regulation of Electricity and Gas), was established.

Associated Functions

Regulation of the industry in Great Britain is primarily the responsibility of the Office of Electricity Regulation, headed by the DGES, whose duties include the promotion of competition and protection of consumer interests. The DGES is project co-ordinator for full electricity market liberalisation in Great Britain from 1998. The Electricity Association is the principal trade association for the electricity industry. It carries out service and co-ordinating functions for the major companies engaged in transmission, distribution, supply and generation in Britain. It has also a number of overseas members.

Consumption

In 1996 sales of electricity through the distribution system in Britain amounted to 298.9 TWh. Domestic users took 36 per cent of the total, industry 31 per cent, and commercial and other users the remainder. Bitter winter weather pushed up electricity demand in Britain—to a peak of 56.8 GW on one day in January 1997. By comparison, the maximum demand during August 1997 was 31.5 GW.

In 1995–96 the average industrial electricity price was lower in real terms than for any year since 1970. The average price for domestic electricity in 1996 was 2.5 per cent lower than

in 1990. In 1996 an annual electricity bill for a typical household in Britain was £297. British domestic electricity prices in 1996 were the third lowest within the G7 and the fourth lowest within the EU.

Generation

The shares of generating capacity during 1995–97 are shown in Table 17.3.

Non-nuclear power stations owned by Britain's main power producers consumed 54.3 million tonnes of oil equivalent in 1996, of which coal accounted for 60 per cent, natural gas 30 per cent and oil 6 per cent. Other power producers (who mostly use gas), and an increasing number of small autogenerators (who produce power for their own use), have equal access with the major generators to the grid transmission and local distribution systems.

Flue gas desulphurisation (FGD) equipment, to control acid emissions, is fitted at two of Britain's largest coal-fired power stations: Ratcliffe-on-Soar (Nottinghamshire) and Drax (North Yorkshire). A ten-year programme to control emissions of oxides of nitrogen (NO_x) through the installation of low-NO_x burners at 12 major power stations in England and Wales is in progress. ScottishPower has fitted low-NO_x burners at Longannet and Cockenzie.

Table 17.3: Shares of Generating Capacity in England and Wales		
	Winter 1995–96	Winter 1996–97
National Power	35.3	26.5
PowerGen	27.5	25.9
Eastern Group	0.7	10.9
Nuclear Electric	17.2	–
Magnox Electric	–	5.0
British Energy	–	12.0
Pumped Storage	3.7	3.4
Interconnectors	5.6	5.2
Others	10.1	11.1
Total	**100.0**	**100.0**
Total (GW)	57.2	61.4

Source: Department of Trade and Industry

Table 17.4: Generation by and Capacity of Power Stations Owned by the Major Power Producers in Britain

	Electricity generated (GWh)			Per cent 1996	Output capacity (MW)
	1986	1991	1996[a]		
Nuclear plant	54,005	66,329	91,040	28	12,528
Other conventional steam plant	221,426	229,190	160,565	50	38,286
Gas turbines and oil engines	509	3,501	226	–	1,637
Pumped storage plant	2,221	1,523	1,556	–	2,788
Natural flow hydro–electric plant	4,098	3,777	2,801	1	1,313
CCGTs	–	–	65,880	20	12,112
Renewables other than hydro	–	–	1,087	–	70
Total	282,258	301,176	323,155	100	68,734
Electricity supplied (net)[a]	261,160	280,649	304,659	–	–

Source: Department of Trade and Industry

[a] Electricity generated less electricity used at power stations (both electricity used on works and that used for pumping at pumped-storage stations).

Note: Differences between totals and the sums of their component parts are due to rounding.

Combined Cycle Gas Turbines (CCGT)

In 1996, CCGT stations accounted for over 20 per cent of the electricity generated by major power producers, compared with 8 per cent in 1993. This increase has been balanced by a fall in coal- and oil-fired generation. Conversion of two units at Didcot coal-fired power station in Oxfordshire enables gas to be burned as an alternative fuel.

CCGT technology continues to improve. CCGT stations, using natural gas, offer cheap generation, and give out almost no sulphur dioxide and some 55 per cent less CO_2 than coal-fired plant per unit of electricity. In England and Wales, 20 such stations (with a total declared net capacity of 12.23 GW) are generating electricity. About 2.2 GW of CCGT capacity is under construction; there are planning consents for a further 12 GW. Between winter 1995–96 and spring 1997 National Power and PowerGen closed or suspended 1.5 GW of oil-fired capacity.

Combined Heat and Power

Combined Heat and Power (CHP) plants are designed to produce both electricity and usable heat. They can be up to three times more efficient than conventional electricity generation, because they retain and utilise the heat produced in the generating process, rather than discarding it, as conventional generation does. This also benefits the environment by reducing emissions of greenhouse gases. CHP is now also used for cooling and chilling.

CHP can be fuelled by a variety of energy sources. It offers particular benefits in applications where there is a regular need for heat as well as electricity—hospitals, leisure centres, housing developments—and can be provided on a local scale. During 1991–96 the capacity of CHP plants in Britain rose by 54 per cent, and in 1996 CHP provided 3,560 MW, 5 per cent of all Britain's electricity generating capacity, on 1,330 sites; the government target is 5,000 MW by the year 2000. CHP accounts for nearly 10 per cent of electricity produced in the EU, while the Netherlands, Denmark and Finland each use CHP to generate over 30 per cent of their total electricity needs.

Trade

The NGC and Electricité de France run a 2,000-MW cross-Channel cable link, providing for transmission of electricity between the two countries. The link has generally been used to supply 'baseload' power—which needs to be generated and available round the clock—from France to England. Imports met about 0.6 per cent of Britain's electricity needs in 1996.

Scotland has a peak winter demand of under 6 GW. It therefore has an over-capacity (see p. 267) which is used to supply England and Wales through transmission lines linking the Scottish and English grid systems. This interconnector's capacity is now 1,870 MW, with plans to increase it to 2,200 MW. NIE and ScottishPower have signed an agreement for a 60-km (37.5-mile) long 250 MW undersea interconnector. Under the agreement, ScottishPower has agreed to supply NIE with electricity, at England and Wales Pool-related prices, for at least 15 years from the date of commissioning of the interconnector.

Nuclear Power

Nuclear power in Britain is not at present considered economically competitive with fossil fuels, particularly gas, for new electricity generation. However, nuclear power station construction since the 1970s in many Western countries has resulted in a stock of nuclear capacity. Their output substantially reduces the use of fossil fuels which would otherwise be needed for generation—in Britain by between 24 and 29 per cent in 1996. Such an amount would cause emissions of up to 20.5 million tonnes of CO_2.

The privatised nuclear industry in Britain consists of British Energy plc, and its two subsidiaries: Nuclear Electric Ltd, which operates the pressurised water reactor (PWR) and five advanced gas-cooled reactors (AGRs) in England and Wales; and Scottish Nuclear Ltd, which operates the two AGRs in Scotland. Nuclear Electric's reactors have an aggregate capacity of 7,200 MW and in 1996–97 an output of 49.4 TWh, equivalent to about 17 per cent of current sales demand in England and Wales. Scottish Nuclear operates two AGR stations with an aggregate capacity of about 2,400 MW and output of 17.6 TWh in 1996, about 52 per cent of Scottish electricity sales. In 1996–97, 46 per cent of electricity generated in Scotland was produced

by these two stations. Scotland's electricity needs are also met from using hydro, coal and gas resources, which have a total output capacity of approximately 9,300 MW. Scottish Nuclear sells 74.9 per cent of its output to ScottishPower and the rest to Hydro-Electric.

The six Magnox power stations remaining in public ownership are operated by Magnox Electric plc, which is decommissioning three more stations that have already closed. A segregated fund was established on the privatisation of British Energy, with a £228 million initial endowment from the nuclear companies, to cover the eventual cost of decommissioning its reactors. British Energy is contributing £16 million a year.

That part of the fossil fuel levy (see p. 272) attributable to British Energy ceased in 1996. As a result, the levy rate fell from 10 to 2.2 per cent in April 1997. It will continue to cover British Nuclear Fuels (BNFL) and renewables, and (for the present) some small residual payments to Magnox Electric. Separate arrangements apply in Scotland.

British Nuclear Fuels (BNFL)

In 1996 the British nuclear industry achieved record exports of £600 million, including over £500 million of exports of nuclear fuel products and services, mostly from BNFL. BNFL is Britain's primary provider of nuclear fuel cycle services, from fuel manufacture and transportation to recycling used nuclear fuel and associated waste management and decommissioning. The HSE's Nuclear Installations Inspectorate (NII) recently granted a 'consent to operate' at the thermal oxide reprocessing plant (THORP) at Sellafield (Cumbria). THORP already has advance reprocessing orders worth £12,000 million, two-thirds of which come from overseas. The Sellafield Mixed Oxide Fuel plant, due to become operational in 1998, has been designed to fabricate mixed oxide fuel with depleted, natural or recycled uranium and plutonium, recovered from used nuclear fuel reprocessed in THORP. A subsidiary company, BNFL Inc., has won contracts with United States Department of the Environment sites and commercial clients for the cleaning and recycling of contaminated metals for re-use.

United Kingdom Atomic Energy Authority

UKAEA's main function is to maintain and decommission safely and cost-effectively its redundant nuclear facilities used for Britain's nuclear R & D programme. UKAEA owns the sites at Dounreay (Caithness), Culham and Harwell (Oxfordshire), Windscale (Cumbria) and Winfrith (Dorset), and is also responsible for Britain's fusion programme (see below).

AEA Technology

AEA Technology plc was that part of the UKAEA which provided commercial science and engineering services to the worldwide nuclear industry and to the oil and gas, transport and pharmaceutical industries; it also provides environmental services. It was privatised in 1996.

Nuclear Research

Nuclear fusion in Britain is funded by the DTI and Euratom (75 per cent and 25 per cent respectively). The Government plans to spend £14.6 million in 1997–98 on fusion research, of which the main focus is magnetic confinement, based at Culham, where Britain's own nuclear fusion research is carried out. However, Britain is also a partner in the experimental EU JET (Joint European Torus) project, also at Culham. The EU has agreed to extend JET to the end of 1999. As a follow-up to JET, the experimental ITER (International Thermonuclear Experimental Reactor) has entered its detailed project phase; the objective is to show the scientific and technological feasibility of power production from fusion energy for peaceful purposes.

Nuclear Safety

Responsibility for ensuring the safety of nuclear installations falls to nuclear operators and is assured through a system of regulatory control enforced by the nuclear industry's independent regulator, the NII.

The international Convention on Nuclear Safety came into force in October 1996. So far, 42 countries, including Britain, have ratified it. Before April 1999, each country will produce a national report describing the progress it has made in meeting the nuclear safety obligations set out in the Convention.

Britain's main contribution to the international effort to improve safety in Central and Eastern Europe and in the former Soviet Union is channelled through the EU PHARE and TACIS nuclear safety programmes. An agreement between the G7 countries and Ukraine on the closure of the Chernobyl nuclear plant by 2000 involves some US $500 million in grants and US $1,800 million in projected investments by international financial institutions, including 2,400 million ECUs in loans from Euratom— which co-ordinates and develops the EU's nuclear industries.

NEW AND RENEWABLE SOURCES OF ENERGY

Renewables help to provide greater security and diversity of supply, using indigenous resources. They are also relatively benign environmentally: wind, for example, produces no emissions, although turbines can be visually and aurally intrusive.

New and renewable sources, which include biofuels, large- and small-scale hydro, wind power and solar power, accounted for 2 per cent of all electricity generating capacity in Britain in 1996; natural flow hydro schemes provided about three-quarters of this total. Capacity for renewables generation other than hydro is four times the level in 1990. However, renewables provided only about 1.25 per cent of the electricity available in Britain in 1996. The Government is reviewing renewables to assess the feasibility of producing 10 per cent of Britain's electricity demand from renewable sources by 2010.

The EU view on energy supply is that a doubling of its renewables share by 2010 (from the current 6 to 12 per cent) could be an ambitious but realistic objective.

The non-fossil fuel obligation (NFFO) requires each public electricity supplier (PES) to reserve some capacity for a certain amount of electricity to be generated from non-fossil sources. PESs must then buy renewables-sourced power at a premium price, above the market price for conventionally generated

Renewable Sources Used to Generate Electricity and Heat 1996

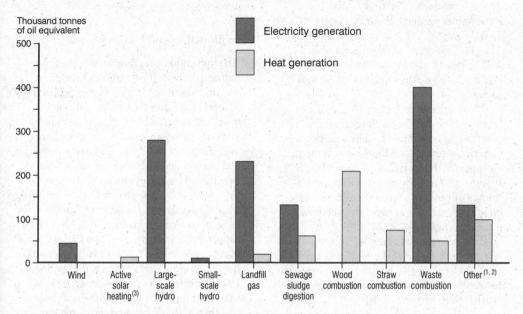

(1) Includes farm waste digestion and poultry litter combustion and waste tyre combustion.

(2) Includes industrial and hospital waste combustion and farm waste combustion.

(3) Excludes all passive use of solar energy.

Source : DTI

electricity, and are reimbursed the difference through the fossil fuel levy, which is paid by all electricity consumers through their bills; some £94 million was paid in 1995-96 under the NFFO arrangements for renewables. (In Scotland the term Scottish Renewables Obligation is used.)

Four Renewables Orders have been made for England and Wales and two each for Scotland and Northern Ireland. At the end of March 1997, 338 projects contracted in England and Wales under NFFO-1-3 had a declared net capacity of 1,251 MW. The fourth, announced in March 1997, was for

The world renewables market is worth about £30,000 million. Britain's share has risen to over £100 million a year. British renewables companies include BP Solar, which has won 8 per cent of the world photovoltaics market. Recent export successes include: European Gas Turbines—sale of more than £2 million-worth of 5 MW turbines for biomass gasification in Sweden; Aerolaminates—more than £7 million of orders for wind turbine blades; and Thermomax—more than £250,000 for solar heating components for Singapore airport.

The British wind industry employs about 1,300 people. The largest single wind farm in Europe, at Carno (Powys), opened in 1996. Developed by National Wind Power Ltd at a cost of £26 million, its 56 600 kW turbines will generate up to 33 MW, enough to meet the average electricity needs of 25,000 homes.

Britain's first community-owned wind turbine has been commissioned as part of the Harlock Hill wind cluster in Cumbria. About 650 small investors, belonging to BayWind co-operative, raised the £620,000 needed to buy the turbine.

195 projects with a possible 843 MW capacity being developed. The first Scottish Renewables Order was for 30 contracts with 76 MW capacity; the second, announced in March 1997, was for 26 projects with 112 MW capacity. The two Northern Ireland Orders involve 30 projects with 32 MW capacity.

Thetford power station (Norfolk), to be on line by 1998, will be the largest single NFFO project commissioned to date and the biggest electricity-producing biomass scheme in Europe. With a capacity of 38.5 MW, its cost is some £69 million and it will burn 400,000 tonnes of poultry litter a year to generate enough electricity to meet the needs of 40,000 homes.

British organisations play an active part in EU programmes. Of the 51 JOULE projects chosen after the EU had invited proposals for renewable R & D schemes, 24 involved British participants.

Non-energy Minerals

Output of non-energy minerals in 1995 totalled just over 336 million tonnes, valued at £2,193

million. The total number of employees in the extractive industry was some 29,900.

Exploration and Development

An exploration programme was started in autumn 1996 in the Crediton Trough in Devon, where the British Geological Survey's Mineral Reconnaissance Programme has indicated the presence of gold. Exploration for gold and development of mines continues in Northern Ireland, at the Cavanacaw openpit, and at the Cononish underground mine in Scotland. It was announced in August 1997 that the South Crofty tin mine in Cornwall, the only remaining tin mine in Britain, is to close, thus bringing to an end 2,500 years of tin production in Britain. The Boulby potash mine in north-east England is Britain's most important non-energy mineral operation. In 1997 the mine obtained planning permission to extend underground mining operations; together with offshore reserves this will further the life of the mine by some 25 years.

Trade and Production

The largest non-energy mineral imports are metals (ores, concentrates and scrap—valued at

Table 17.5: Production of Some of the Main Non-energy Minerals			*million tonnes*
	1986	1990	1996
Sand and gravel	112.0	124.0	96.0
Silica sand	4.1	4.1	4.3
Igneous rock	41.0	57.4	49.0
Limestone and dolomite	100.5	123.3	97.0
Chalk[a]	12.5	13.1	10.0
Sandstone	14.0	18.0	17.0
Gypsum	3.4	3.1	2.0
Salt, including salt in brine	6.9	6.4	6.6
Common clay and shale	17.6[a]	16.2	13.0
China clay	2.9	3.0	2.3[b]
Ball clay	0.6	0.8	0.9
Fireclay[a]	0.9	0.9	0.7
Iron ore	0.3	0.0	1.2
Potash	0.7	0.8	1.0
Fluorspar	0.1	0.1	0.1
Fuller's earth	0.2	0.2	0.1

Source: *British Geological Survey, United Kingdom Minerals Yearbook*
[a] Great Britain only.
[b] Moisture-free basis.

Some Minerals Produced in Britain

Orkney Islands

Shetland Islands

talc

talc

0 20 40 60 80 100 120 km

0   20   40   60   80 miles

● Major metallic and industrial mineral workings

▲ Mineral deposits (unworked)

marble

silica sand

▲ barytes

▲ gold

barytes

silica sand

silica sand

fluorspar, lead

NORTHERN PENNINE OREFIELD

gypsum

barytes

salt

potash/salt

gold ▲

▲ salt

silica sand

SOUTHERN PENNINE OREFIELD

zinc, copper, lead, silver ▲

silica sand

salt

fluorspar, barytes, lead

salt

gypsum

gold

CHESHIRE SALTFIELD

gypsum

gypsum

silica sand

silica sand

fuller's earth

fuller's earth

silica sand

fuller's earth

fuller's earth ▲

fuller's earth

silica sand

fuller's earth

gypsum

ball clay

ball clay

ball clay

china clay

china clay

china clay ▲

tungsten, tin

tin

£1,500 million in 1995), refined non-ferrous metals (£3,800 million) and non-metallic mineral products (£4,000 million, of which rough diamonds account for £2,500 million). Britain is virtually self-sufficient in construction minerals, and produces and exports several industrial minerals, notably china clay, ball clay, potash and salt. China clay is the largest export—£200 million in 1995.

In terms of value, production of limestone and dolomite was about £618 million in 1995, sand and gravel £491 million, clays £309 million (with china clay valued at £230 million), igneous rock £244 million, salt £188 million, sandstone £94 million, potash £84 million, silica sands £58 million, chalk £45 million, gypsum and anhydrite £20 million, tin £7 million and fluorspar £6 million.

Water

About 75 per cent of Britain's water supplies are obtained from mountain lakes, reservoirs and river intakes; and about 25 per cent from water stored underground. Summer 1995 to spring 1997 in England and Wales was the driest two-year period for over 200 years. Some 360 mm less rain fell than normal, equivalent to four months' winter rainfall. Prolonged drought threatens rivers, streams, wetlands and wildlife. Underground water levels, stored in layers of porous rock, are at a record low in many places. Of 33 major rivers in England, only one is not at risk, with some less than a third of average depth. The Environment Agency, which is responsible for protecting water resources, has warned that increasingly dry weather may become long-term as a result of climate change. Heavy rain in June 1997 did not alleviate the drought because summer rain either evaporates or is taken by vegetation before it can replenish water underground, although it reduces the demand for garden sprinklers. Leakage in supply pipes is a serious problem.

By contrast, Scotland has a relative abundance of unpolluted water from upland sources and is in a position to export it. Northern Ireland also has plentiful supplies for domestic use and for industry.

Water put into the public supply system (including industrial and other uses) in England and Wales averaged 17,571 megalitres (Ml) a day in 1995–96, of which average domestic daily consumption per household was about 178.5 litres. An average of 2,322 Ml a day was supplied in Scotland in 1995–96. In Northern Ireland the figure was 703 Ml a day.

Some 55,970 Ml a day were abstracted in England and Wales in 1995, of which public water supplies accounted for 17,346 Ml a day. The electricity supply industry took 25,805 Ml a day; fish farming, cress growing and amenity ponds 4,268 Ml a day; and agriculture 103 Ml a day, with spray irrigation accounting for a further 352 Ml a day.

Fluoridation of water supplies began in the early 1960s after trials which showed improvement in the condition of children's teeth. The Water Industry Act 1991 and the Water (Fluoridation) Act 1985 empower water undertakers in England, Wales and Northern Ireland, and the water authorities in Scotland, to implement a fluoridation scheme at the request of a health authority or board. Before submitting their proposals, the health authority or board must engage in a publicity and consultation process. Those that do add fluoride have to ensure that the concentration is maintained at 1 milligram of fluoride for every litre supplied. There are no current fluoridation schemes in Scotland.

England and Wales

To prevent future shortages, to get across its view that water is a precious resource and to encourage the public to save it, the Government announced a ten-point plan in May 1997, which the water companies have agreed to follow:

- the Director of Water Services to set mandatory targets for total leakage and enforce a substantial reduction in leakage over the next five years;

- provision of free leakage detection and repair service for customer-owned household supply pipes;

- water companies to be under a statutory duty to conserve water in carrying out their functions;

- water companies to promote efficient use of water by customers, for example, by water-saving fittings and appliances, free water-efficiency audits and water-efficient gardening;

- consideration for the role which the Government's Environmental Task Force can play in improving efficiency of water use;

- new water regulations to include significantly tighter requirements for water efficiency; and promotion of water efficiency in industry and agriculture, including use of best practice programmes;

- review of water charging system and metering policy (see below);

- all water companies which have not already done so to agree with the Director General of Water Services amendments to their licences already accepted by other companies, requiring compensation payments to customers affected by drought-related restrictions; compensation payments also recommended to customers who have been exposed to potentially harmful contamination;

- publication at local level of clear details of performance in meeting targets for leakage reduction, water supply and drinking water quality, together with information on investment in the water service and resulting benefits to the environment; and

- the Government to review the water abstraction licensing system and arrangements for bulk transfer of water—to ensure that the environment is given due weight in decisions on use of water; and each water company to agree a detailed, publicly available drought contingency plan with the Environment Agency.

The Director General of Water Services, who heads the industry's regulatory body, Ofwat, is to set each water company mandatory leakage targets for 1998–99 and intends to set them annually. The current targets involve a reduction of leakages by 680 Ml a day and maximum wastage of between 10 and 15 per cent.

Water Companies

Ten water and sewerage companies in England and Wales have statutory responsibilities for water supply, its quality and sufficiency, and for sewerage and sewage treatment. The supply-only companies, of which there were 29 in the private sector in 1989, now, after various mergers, number 18. They supply water to nearly a quarter of the population.

In June 1997 the Government launched a review of the water-charging system. It is looking at charges for both measured and unmeasured systems, the future use of the old rateable value of a property (a system abolished in 1991) to determine charges in the latter, and debt recovery arrangements. After 31 March 2000 companies must not base their charges on rateable values. Over 75 per cent of commercial and industrial customers pay for water and sewerage services on the basis of their metered consumption. Twelve companies install domestic meters without cost to the consumer; it is estimated that one in ten households will have a meter by the end of 1997. The Government, however, while in favour of selective metering to cover large and more affluent households, opposes compulsory metering for essential household use and considers that no one should be deprived of water because of inability to pay for it.

Of the nearly 3 million tests of drinking water carried out by water companies in 1996, 99.7 per cent complied with both EU and national water quality standards (compared with 99.5 per cent in 1995). The Drinking Water Inspectorate of the DETR, which checks that the companies supply wholesome water, carried out inspections to ensure that they complied with the Water Quality Regulations.

Ensuring Supplies

Water company investment for 1996–97 has increased by 16 per cent, largely in the repair of leakages. The industry is under growing pressure to try innovative techniques to increase supplies while reducing bills. All the companies offer a free leak-repair service for

The water supply companies in England and Wales provide almost 4.6 million households with water—about 11 million people. All water supplied to homes is treated to drinking water standards: 1 per cent of total water provided by the companies is used for drinking; 2 per cent for cooking; 49 per cent for the bathroom; 3 per cent is used in the garden. Demand for water is rising by about 2 per cent a year. A bath costs approximately 4.5 pence; a shower 2 pence; and a glass of water 0.02 pence. Total turnover of the 18 water supply companies is about £620 million a year.

A garden sprinkler uses the same amount of water in an hour as a typical family of four uses in two days.

customers' supply pipes. Some have adopted water-saving measures, which include free plumbing help in fitting devices to cisterns, checking overflow efficiency and replacing faulty washers.

Anglian Water, with the lowest rainfall rates in England (600 mm a year on average), has a low leakage rate, which it expects to cut to less than 10 per cent by 2000. It is replacing its Victorian lead pipework with polyethylene. Thames Water, with a leakage rate of 38.6 per cent in 1997, has been ordered by Ofwat to produce quarterly leakage returns. Wessex Water, the smallest of the water and sewerage companies, is to test a technique which involves pumping surplus water into a natural underground reservoir for recovery at times of need. This scheme could supply the company, which produces 434 Ml a day, with an additional 20 Ml a day. Companies in southern and eastern England are considering desalination projects, even though such schemes have hitherto been thought uneconomic. The Folkestone and Dover company (Kent), which has some of the most serious shortages in Britain, has found that metering reduces consumption by 10 per cent, and by 15–20 per cent at peak times. A report for the Drinking Water Inspectorate in 1997 says that there is no reason why greater use should not be made of greywater (recycled

from wash basins, showers and baths) to flush lavatories and thus cut domestic consumption by up to a third.

The statutory duties and powers of the Environment Agency include regulation of the water environment. Its responsibilities extend to all rivers, lakes, reservoirs, estuaries, coastal waters and groundwater. Its consent is needed for the abstraction of water and the discharge of effluent.

Scotland

Since 1996, responsibility for the provision of all water and sewerage services has rested with three public water authorities—the North, West and East of Scotland Water Authorities. The Scottish Water and Sewerage Customers Council protects and represents all their customers. It also approves the water authorities' charging schemes and codes of practice, and is financed by an annual levy on the authorities.

Charges for water supply depend on the type of consumer: domestic consumers pay water charges based on their council tax band (see p. 167) or metered charges, and non-domestic consumers pay non-domestic water rates, or metered charges. For sewerage services, domestic consumers pay a sewerage charge based on their council tax band, and non-domestic consumers pay non-domestic sewerage rates, and, where appropriate, trade effluent charges for the licensed discharge of industrial wastewater. Charges and rates are decided by each water authority and must be approved by the Customers Council. Local authority funding is available to reduce the charges set for domestic sewerage.

The Government is committed to returning the Scottish water industry to local democratic control. A review is in progress.

The Scottish Environment Protection Agency has statutory responsibility for water pollution control.

Northern Ireland

The Department of the Environment for Northern Ireland is responsible for public water supply and sewerage throughout

Northern Ireland. It is also responsible for the conservation and cleanliness of water resources and, with the Department of Agriculture, prepares, if necessary, water management programmes for any area. A domestic water charge is contained in local rates, while agriculture, commerce and industry pay metered charges.

Overseas Contracts

British water companies are winning contracts to upgrade and manage distribution and sewerage networks overseas. Anglian Water, for example, has been instrumental in helping to reduce shortages in Buenos Aires. Thames Water is in a partnership to manage supplies in Adelaide. It is also the major partner in a group which has signed a 25-year agreement, with capital investment of about £160 million in the first five years, to manage and improve the water supply to half the city of Jakarta. North West Water and Severn Trent have been working since 1994 on reforming the water-supply system in Mexico City: making a census, installing meters, creating an infrastructure for paying bills, repairing pipes and reducing leakages. In 1996, Severn Trent started work on a World Bank-sponsored management contract (initially for three to five years) for the water and wastewater system in Trinidad and Tobago.

Further Reading

Digest of Environmental Statistics, No 19, 1997. Department of the Environment, Transport and the Regions. The Stationery Office.

Digest of United Kingdom Energy Statistics 1997. Department of Trade and Industry. The Stationery Office.

The Energy Dimension of Climate Change. Commission of the European Communities. Brussels, 14 May 1997.

The Energy Report 1: Shaping Change (1997). Department of Trade and Industry. The Stationery Office.

The Energy Report 2: Oil and Gas Resources of the United Kingdom (1997). Department of Trade and Industry. The Stationery Office.

An Overall View of Energy Policy and Actions. Commission of the European Communities. Brussels, 23 April 1997.

United Kingdom Minerals Yearbook 1996. British Geological Survey. The Stationery Office.

18 Agriculture, the Fishing Industry & Forestry

The BSE crisis dominated British agriculture in 1996 and 1997. The Government's top priority was to protect public and animal health. Measures were also taken to help the industry adjust and to restore consumer confidence. The Government's next priority is the lifting of the EU worldwide ban on the export of British beef and beef products. Because of the BSE crisis, home-fed production of beef for human consumption fell by 29 per cent between 1995 and 1996, as the carcasses of about 1.4 million cattle (in the year from May 1996 to May 1997) and over 570,000 calves (in the year from April 1996 to April 1997) were removed from the food chain. The Government is committed to establishing an independent Food Standards Agency—to promote the safety and quality of food throughout the chain from production to consumption. Britain has secured agreement among EU members to pay full regard to animal welfare in developing policies on agriculture, transport, the internal market and research.

Some £36.4 million has been spent on decommissioning fishing boats during 1993–96 to meet Britain's fishing fleet reduction targets.

Agriculture

Agriculture plays a key role in European Union (EU) policy. It accounts for the largest proportion of EU legislation and about half of expenditure under the budget. Modernisation of farming within the EU has reduced the proportion of the labour force working in agriculture from almost 20 per cent in the early 1960s to about 5 per cent today. Agriculture accounts for less than 2 per cent of EU gross domestic product (GDP). The share of both agricultural imports and exports as a proportion of total EU trade is about 11 per cent.

In 1996 British agriculture employed 2 per cent (529,000 people) of the total workforce. The agricultural contribution to GDP was £8,888 million in 1996, 1.4 per cent of the total. Food, feed and beverages accounted for 9.6 per cent of Britain's imports by value. Self-sufficiency in food and feed fell in 1996: from 58.4 to 53.4 per cent of all food and feed, and from 75.1 to 69.4 per cent of indigenous-type food and feed. This was mainly owing to lower levels of both output and exports of beef, and higher levels of imports of meat and meat preparations other than beef. Britain is a major agricultural exporter of livestock, food products, agrochemicals and agricultural machinery.

Land Use in Britain

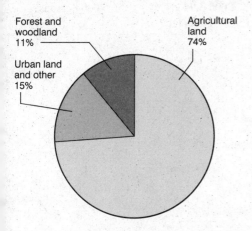

Forest and woodland 11%

Agricultural land 74%

Urban land and other 15%

The Government's pre-election manifesto identified the special needs of people who live and work in rural areas. The Government supports the principle of sustainable development for the countryside and recognises the need for a prosperous rural economy with protection for the environment.

Land Use

In 1996, 11.4 million hectares (28.2 million acres) were under crops and grass. A further 5.7 million hectares (14 million acres) were used for rough grazing, most of it in hilly areas. Soils vary from the thin poor ones of highland Britain to the rich fertile soils of low-lying areas, such as the fenlands of eastern England. The climate is generally temperate, though rainfall distribution over Britain is uneven. The South East receives only about 600 mm (24 inches) a year, compared with over 1,500 mm (59 inches) in parts of west Scotland, Cumbria and Wales.

Farming

In 1996 there were some 234,300 farm holdings in Britain (excluding minor holdings too small to be surveyed on a regular basis), with an average area of 72.6 hectares (179.4 acres), again excluding minor holdings. About two-thirds of all agricultural land is owner-occupied. Some 44 per cent of holdings are smaller than 8 European size units (ESU).[1]

Labour productivity (in terms of gross product per worker) increased by about 23 per

Agricultural Land Use 1996

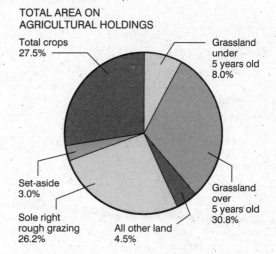

TOTAL AREA ON AGRICULTURAL HOLDINGS

Total crops 27.5%

Grassland under 5 years old 8.0%

Set-aside 3.0%

Grassland over 5 years old 30.8%

Sole right rough grazing 26.2%

All other land 4.5%

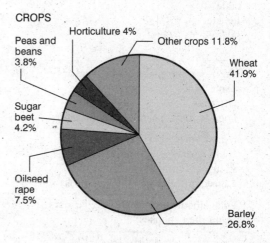

CROPS

Horticulture 4%

Peas and beans 3.8%

Other crops 11.8%

Wheat 41.9%

Sugar beet 4.2%

Oilseed rape 7.5%

Barley 26.8%

cent during 1985–96. Total income from farming (that of farmers, partners, directors and their spouses, and family workers, see Table 18.1) was estimated at £4,889 million in 1996, 5.4 per cent less (at current prices) than in 1995. In real terms this measure of income is about 38 per cent more than the average for 1984–86. High world prices for some basic commodities, including cereals, and the increasing value of EU payments to farmers in respect of, for example, setting land aside have contributed to this growth.

---

[1] ESUs measure the financial potential of the holding in terms of the margins which might be expected from stock and crops: 8 ESU is judged the minimum for full-time holdings.

Table 18.1: Labour Force in Agriculture

	'000 persons 1985–87 average	'000 persons 1996
Workers		
Regular whole time		
hired: male	103	69
female	10	10
family: male	31	20
female	5	3
Total	149	102
Regular part-time		
hired: male	19	19
female	22	17
family: male	14	14
female	7	7
Total	62	57
Seasonal or casual		
male	57	56
female	38	26
salaried managers[a]	8	8
Total workers	315	248
Farmers, partners and directors		
whole-time	197	166
part-time	93	114
Total farmers, partners and directors	290	281
Total farmers, partners, directors and workers	604	529
Spouses of farmers, partners and directors (engaged in farm work)	77	75
Total labour force (including farmers and their spouses)[b]	681	603

Source: *Agriculture in the United Kingdom 1996*
[a] This figure relates to Great Britain only.
[b] Figures exclude schoolchildren and most trainees.
Note: Differences between totals and the sums of their components are due to rounding.

At the end of 1995 the industry's gross capital stock, valued at 1990 prices, amounted to £33,480 million, of which buildings and works made up just under two-thirds. The level of capital stock is now estimated to be 1 per cent below the 1985–87 average.

PRODUCTION

Home production of the principal foods is shown in Table 18.2 as a percentage by weight of total supplies. Total new supply is home production plus imports less exports.

Livestock

Over half of full-time farms are devoted mainly to dairy farming or to beef cattle and sheep. Most of the animals are reared in the hill and moorland areas of Scotland, Wales, Northern Ireland and northern and south-western England. Among world-famous British livestock are the Hereford and Aberdeen Angus beef breeds, the Jersey, Guernsey and Ayrshire dairy breeds, Large White pigs and a number of sheep breeds. Livestock totals are given in Table 18.3.

Table 18.2: British Production as a Percentage of Total New Supplies

Food Product	1985–87 average	1996 (provisional)
Beef and veal	97	86
Eggs	97	96
Milk for human consumption (as liquid)	100	100
Cheese	66	69
Butter	74	67
Sugar (as refined)	57	60
Wheat	116	121
Potatoes	91	90

Source: MAFF

Table 18.3: Livestock and Livestock Products

	1985–87 average	1994	1995	1996 (provisional)
Cattle and calves ('000 head)	12,559	11,834	11,733	11,913
Sheep and lambs ('000 head)	37,149	43,295	42,771	41,530
Pigs ('000 head)	7,917	7,797	7,534	7,496
Poultry ('000 head)[a]	120,796	130,027	130,939	n.a.
Milk (million litres)	15,289	14,222	13,932	13,932
Hen eggs (million dozen)[b]	855	792	792	790
Beef and veal ('000 tonnes)	1,105	943	996	708
Mutton and lamb ('000 tonnes)	309	391	401	374
Pork ('000 tonnes)	755	848	808	810
Bacon and ham ('000 tonnes)	202	191	197	197
Poultry meat ('000 tonnes)	942	1,358	1,394	1,455

Source: MAFF
[a] Includes ducks, geese and turkeys. Figures for turkeys are for England and Wales only.
[b] For human consumption only; does not include eggs for hatching.
n.a.: not available.

Cattle and Sheep

Cattle and sheep constitute about 37 per cent of the value of Britain's gross agricultural output. Dairy production is the largest part of the sector, followed by cattle and calves, and then fat sheep and lambs. Most dairy cattle in Britain are bred by artificial insemination. In 1996 the average size of dairy herds was 67 (excluding minor holdings), while the average yield of milk for each dairy cow was 5,570 litres (1,225 gallons). Average household consumption of liquid (including low-fat) milk per head in 1996 was 1,848 millilitres (3.25 pints) a week.

More than half of home-fed beef production originates from the national dairy herd, in which the Holstein Friesian breed predominates. The remainder derives from suckler herds producing high-quality beef calves, mostly in the hills and uplands. The traditional British beef breeds (see above) and, increasingly, imported breeds such as Charolais, Limousin, Simmental and Belgian Blue, are used for beef production. The size of the beef-breeding herd expanded by 37 per cent during 1987–96, while the dairy herd decreased by 17 per cent.

In spring 1996 the announcement of a possible link between Bovine Spongiform Encephalopathy (BSE) in cattle and Creutzfeldt–Jakob disease (CJD) in humans led to a significant loss of consumer confidence in British beef. Clean cattle (beef animals bred for human consumption) prices fell considerably during the spring and early summer, but partially recovered later in the year. Average consumption for 1996 was 15–20 per cent below the 1995 level and average clean cattle prices were 14 per cent below the 1995 levels. Government aid for beef producers was worth over £265 million in 1996–97 (see p. 290).

Britain has more than 60 native sheep breeds and many cross-bred varieties. The size of the British breeding flock remained almost unchanged in 1996, though production of sheepmeat was an estimated 7 per cent lower, reflecting a general EU trend. The average realised return for sheepmeat in Britain was about 20 per cent higher than in 1995. This can be attributed to a consumer switch from beef as a result of the BSE crisis.

The Integrated Administration and Control System (IACS), an EU-wide anti-fraud measure, requires farmers to submit an annual application giving field-by-field details of their farmed land. This serves as a basis for administrative and on-farm checks on their entitlement to aid under area-based Common Agricultural Policy (CAP) schemes. The IACS includes systems for uniquely identifying farmers' fields and animals. Details of farmers' IACS applications and the results of checks are stored in a computerised database.

Pigs

Pig production is particularly important in East Anglia and Yorkshire. About 22 per cent of holdings with breeding sows account for 83 per cent of the national breeding herd, which comprises some 744,000 sows. Britain exports to such destinations as Germany, Italy, France, Japan and Korea. However, bacon is imported from Denmark, the Netherlands and the Irish Republic. British companies supply about 8 per cent of the genetically improved pigs and sows bought by the world's pig farmers.

Poultry

The total bird population in 1996 was about 131 million: 76.6 million chickens and other table fowls; 32 million birds in the laying flock; 7.5 million fowls for breeding; 12.5 million turkeys (England and Wales only); 2.5 million ducks; and 142,000 geese.

Poultry production in 1996 was 1.45 million tonnes, a 4 per cent increase on 1995. Broiler production, at 1.08 million tonnes, was 58,000 tonnes above the level for 1995. Broilers from the 9 per cent of holdings with over 100,000 table birds account for well over half of the total flock. Hen egg production, for all uses, went up from 887 million dozen in 1995 to 889 million dozen in 1996.

Animal Welfare

Animal welfare continues to attract high levels of public interest. A comprehensive framework of legislation, supported by codes of practice, lays down standards that must apply on the farm, during transport, at markets and at slaughter.

At EU level Britain secured agreement at the Amsterdam intergovernmental conference in 1997 to a protocol to the Treaty of Rome. This recognises that animals are sentient beings and places on EU institutions a formal obligation to pay full regard to animal welfare when developing policies on agriculture, transport, the internal market and research.

Britain was a prime mover in achieving an EU-wide ban on close confinement veal crates (prohibited in Britain since 1990) from 2006. Britain also pressed the European Commission to complete its overdue review of the directive on the welfare of laying hens. Review of the directive on the welfare of pigs is also in hand.

The Government is keen to ensure that welfare requirements are properly enforced. During 1997 it ordered a major review of enforcement procedures relating to the welfare of live animal exports. New rules for Great Britain, implementing EU legislation on the welfare of animals in transport, came into force in 1997. They set down the maximum journey and rest times for different species. Under them, ministers have powers to disqualify transporters who persistently break welfare regulations. All staff working in long-distance transport must have demonstrated their competence in handling animals during transit. Britain has led efforts to ensure that the highest possible welfare standards are applied to the transport of live animals within the EU.

Table 18.4: Main Crops

	1985–87 average	1994	1995	1996 (provisional)
Wheat				
Area ('000 hectares)	1,964	1,811	1,859	1,976
Production ('000 tonnes)	12,632	13,314	14,310	16,041
Yield (tonnes per hectare)	6.43	7.35	7.70	8.12
Barley				
Area	1,905	1,106	1,192	1,267
Production	9,661	5,945	6,833	7,765
Yield	5.07	5.37	5.73	6.13
Oats				
Area	110	109	112	96
Production	524	597	617	594
Yield	4.78	5.50	5.52	6.19
Potatoes				
Area	182	164	171	177
Production	6,663	6,531	6,396	7,020
Yield	36.60	39.90	37.40	40.70
Oilseed rape				
Area	327	496	439	429
Production	1,062	1,253	1,235	1,453
Yield	3.22	2.53	2.81	3.39
Sugar beet				
Area	204	195	196	199
Production	7,942	8,720	8,431	9,555
Yield	39.37	44.71	43.02	48.00

Source: *Agriculture in the United Kingdom 1996* and *Agricultural Census, June 1996*

In 1996 the Farm Animal Welfare Council published advice on the welfare of pigs kept out of doors, of farmed fish and of laying hens.

Crops

The farms devoted primarily to arable crops are found mainly in eastern and central-southern England and eastern Scotland. The main crops are shown in Table 18.4. In Britain in 1996 the area planted to cereals totalled 3.4 million hectares (8.4 million acres), an increase of 6 per cent on 1995, largely as a result of a further reduction in the set-aside rate (see p. 289), with a 9 per cent rise in output. Higher market prices in the first half of 1996 contributed to an increase in the overall value of output of 4 per cent (£121 million).

Large-scale potato and vegetable cultivation takes place on the fertile soils throughout Britain, often with irrigation. Principal areas are the peat and silt fens of Cambridgeshire, Lincolnshire and Norfolk; the sandy loams of Norfolk, Suffolk, West Midlands, Nottinghamshire, South Yorkshire and Lincolnshire; the peat soils of South Lancashire; and the alluvial silts by the river Humber. Early potatoes are produced in Shropshire, Pembrokeshire, Cornwall, Devon, Essex, Suffolk, Kent, Cheshire and south-west Scotland. Production of high-grade seed potatoes is confined to Scotland, Northern Ireland and the Welsh borders.

Sugar from home-grown sugar beet provides about 50 per cent of home needs, most of the remainder being refined from raw cane sugar imported under the Lomé Convention (see p. 207).

Horticulture

In 1996 the land utilised for horticulture (excluding potatoes and peas for harvesting dry) was about 189,000 hectares (467,000 acres). Vegetables grown in the open accounted for 70 per cent of this, orchards for 15 per cent, soft fruit for 6 per cent and ornamentals (including hardy nursery stock, bulbs and flowers grown in the open) for 7 per cent. More than one vegetable crop may be taken from the same area of land in a year, so that the estimated area actually cropped for horticulture in 1996 was 237,700 hectares (587,400 acres).

Mushrooms, carrots and lettuces are the single most valuable horticultural crops, with farm gate values of £166 million, £117 million and £92 million respectively in 1996.

Field vegetables account for 55 per cent of the value of horticultural output and are widely grown throughout the country. Some are raised in blocks of compressed peat or loose-filled cells, a technique which reduces root damage and allows plants to establish themselves more reliably and evenly.

Glasshouses are used for growing tomatoes, cucumbers, sweet peppers, lettuces, flowers, pot plants and nursery stock. Widespread use is made of automatic control of heating and ventilation, and semi-automatic control of watering. Low-cost plastic tunnels extend the season for certain crops previously grown in the open.

Modifications to the EU regime for fresh fruit and vegetables have enabled British growers to apply for about £20 million of EU funding for 1997–98, to help them to adapt production more effectively to meet the needs of the market; to improve product quality, handling, marketing and value; and to encourage environmentally sound practice and waste management techniques. Similar recent changes in the EU flowers and plants regime provide about £675,000 of promotional funding to be spent in Britain.

Alternative Crops

The Alternative Crops Unit of the Ministry of Agriculture, Fisheries and Food (MAFF),

spending just over £1 million on R & D in 1997–98, encourages development of alternative crops where they promise to become economically viable. These include short-rotation coppice for renewable energy, oilseeds for industry, flax and hemp for paper, automotive and other uses, and speciality crops such as evening primrose for pharmaceuticals.

FOOD SAFETY

EU food law harmonisation covers food safety, fair trading and informative labelling. For example, a beef-labelling scheme was agreed in March 1997, to provide information on fresh and frozen beef (including mince) which may be confirmed through improved traceability systems.

Britain identifies food safety risks through food surveys, investigations and research, the results of which are published. Food law enforcement falls mainly to local authorities. Expert independent advisory committees, such as the Spongiform Encephalopathy Advisory Committee, the Advisory Committee on the Microbiological Safety of Food and the Food Advisory Committee, provide systematic assessments of risk.

The Government is committed to ensuring the highest standards of meat hygiene in Britain's abattoirs and is determined that the interests of the consumer should come first. The Meat Hygiene Service, an executive agency of MAFF with responsibility for meat inspection in licensed plants, is pursuing initiatives to improve hygiene, together with the State Veterinary Service (SVS).

Following the concern about BSE (see p. 283), government measures to eliminate any danger from potentially infected material included the prohibition of all cattle over 30 months old from entering the human food chain and stringent controls on slaughterhouses, especially those on the handling and disposal of specified bovine materials (SBMs). These are the parts of the carcass which are considered likely to be BSE infective. The SBM Order 1997 further tightened controls and introduced provisions to cover cosmetic, pharmaceutical and medical products.

In its campaign to promote consumer confidence, the Government plans to transfer primary responsibility for food safety from MAFF to an independent Food Standards Agency. A White Paper and legislation are to set guidelines as soon as possible. Among the Agency's priorities would be the safety of meat from the farm to the abattoir, the butcher and the plate.

The EU Novel Foods regulation, which stipulates approval for all such foods before they are marketed, came into effect in May 1997. It contains labelling provisions, including one to label foods if they contain genetically modified organisms, which apply also to existing EU food labelling legislation.

EXPORTS

Provisional data for 1996 suggest that the value of exports related to agriculture (food, feed and drink), at £10,100 million, was 1 per cent up on 1995. The main markets in 1996 were France (£1,500 million—down 4 per cent), the Irish Republic (£1,110 million—up 10 per cent), Germany (£760 million—up 10 per cent) and Spain (£630 million—down 12 per cent). Severely curtailed beef exports aside, the French market showed a 12 per cent increase on 1995. Other key markets were the United States (£630 million) and Japan (£270 million).

Cereals (both unmilled and processed) and cereal dried products are the largest category of British food exports, worth £1,600 million in 1996. Exports also include specialities such as dairy products, fresh salmon, biscuits, cakes and pastries, jams and conserves, soft drinks, and tea, coffee, cocoa and chocolate. Animal feed is also significant, exports rising from £380 million in 1995 to £400 million in 1996.

In March 1996 the EU imposed an immediate worldwide ban on all British beef and beef products (but not milk and milk derivatives). As a result, worldwide exports of beef fell by 77 per cent and the value of such exports fell from £590 million in 1995 to £140 million in 1996.

Export promotion for food and drink is headed by Food from Britain, an organisation

Exports of Scotch whisky in 1996 were steady, at £2,300 million. Those of beer, at £240 million, were up £66 million worldwide. There was a 14 per cent increase in ice cream sales abroad, from £44 million in 1995 to £50 million in 1996. An export record for unmilled wheat saw a rise of 29 per cent (worth £100 million) to about 3.9 million tonnes worldwide. The 20 per cent growth in the exports of cereals and cereal dried products represented a £270 million increase on 1995.

funded by MAFF (£5.3 million in 1996–97) and industry (£6.2 million). For all other agricultural products, services, machinery, and processing equipment, MAFF co-ordinates export promotion, participates in trade fairs and arranges ministerial visits to other countries. Its presence at overseas trade fairs during 1996 attracted over 850 serious enquiries for British agricultural products. Exports of agricultural machinery and equipment in 1996 were worth £1,300 million.

The annual Royal Agricultural Show, held (early July) at Stoneleigh in Warwickshire, enables visitors to see the latest techniques and improvements in British agriculture. Some 175,000 visitors attended in 1997, of whom 10 per cent were from overseas. Other major agricultural events include the Royal Smithfield Show, held every other year in London, which exhibits agricultural machinery, livestock and carcasses; the Royal Highland Show (June) in Edinburgh; the Royal Welsh Show (late July) in Builth Wells; and the Royal Ulster Agricultural Show in Belfast.

The Horticultural Export Bureau (HEB) was created in 1996 with the support of government funds to seek and develop export opportunities for fresh produce from Great Britain. Backed, through subscriptions, by most of the major marketing organisations, the HEB provides its members with market information and general export advice; develops contacts with international buyers and conveys their needs to members; and undertakes international promotion of the industry.

MARKETING

The Marketing Development Scheme (MDS) encourages the agri-food industry to develop and implement new marketing initiatives. In 1996, 87 awards worth some £4.2 million were made in England; 14, worth £1.1 million, in Scotland; 22, worth about £590,000, in Wales; and 14, worth some £670,000, in Northern Ireland. The scheme closed in England in 1996 (though it remains open in the rest of Britain), to be replaced by a new inter-departmental initiative administered by the Department of Trade and Industry. The DTI's Sector Challenge provides a single source of funds for competitive ventures from various sectors of the economy. In the first round of the Challenge, 28 projects from the agri-food industries secured grants worth around £5.7 million over three years. These cover such topics as developing business skills, technology transfer and export promotion. The Government is conducting a public consultation on the experience of the first round of the Challenge, the conclusions from which will inform a decision on the future of the scheme. It is also contributing £4.5 million over three years, through the MDS, towards a campaign to restore confidence in, and rebuild markets for, the Scottish beef industry. The Government spent some £13 million in 1996–97 on research in support of the competitiveness of the horticultural industry.

Deregulation of milk and potato marketing in Britain in 1996–97 has accorded with government wishes to remove unnecessary burdens which impede business, inhibit innovation and damage competitiveness. The Milk Development Council (MDC) collects a levy on all milk produced and sold by all farmers in Great Britain, to be spent on R & D and other projects to help the milk sector.

The British Wool Marketing Board retains its statutory powers to collect and sell Britain's wool clip (45.6 million kilograms in 1996) on behalf of 82,302 registered producers.

Co-operatives and other farmers' businesses handle much of the marketing of agricultural and horticultural produce, such as grain, fruit and vegetables. These had a turnover of some £7,100 million in 1996.

ROLE OF THE GOVERNMENT

Four government departments have joint responsibility for agriculture and fisheries matters: MAFF; the Scottish Office Agriculture, Environment and Fisheries Department (SOAEFD); the Welsh Office; and the Department of Agriculture for Northern Ireland. MAFF's regional administrative structure in England consists of nine Regional Service Centres (RSCs). Their work relates to payments under domestic and EU schemes, licensing and various other services provided to farmers and growers.

The ten MAFF Inspectorates (such as the Sea Fisheries Inspectorate and the Plant Health and Seeds Inspectorate) enforce quality and health standards in animals, fish, and crops.

Common Agricultural Policy (CAP)

The original aims of the CAP in 1962 were to increase productivity and efficiency, to ensure a fair standard of living for producers, to stabilise markets and to guarantee supplies to consumers at reasonable prices. The main mechanisms for achieving this were a combination of support prices, import duties and market intervention. When prices of main commodities fell below certain agreed levels, intervention authorities (in Britain the Intervention Board executive agency) bought the goods and stored them for later resale. Intervention stocks were exported or disposed of within the EU, where this could be done without disrupting internal markets. The market support system not only raised food prices for consumers but encouraged surplus production. (Production rose by 2 per cent a year between 1973 and 1988.) Exports, either from the market or from intervention stocks, attracted export refunds (or an export tax) to fill the gap between EU and world prices.

The reforms of 1992 moved the CAP away from supporting price levels, and intervention arrangements were made less attractive. Farmers now receive most of their financial support in the form of direct payments from the Exchequer under various arable and livestock schemes (see pp. 291–4) and much less now comes from the consumer through increased food prices. Conditions, in the form

Public Expenditure under the CAP by the Intervention Board and the Agricultural Departments

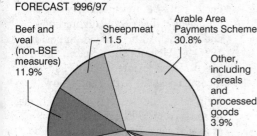

FORECAST 1996/97

Beef and veal (non-BSE measures) 11.9%

Sheepmeat 11.5

Arable Area Payments Scheme 30.8%

Other, including cereals and processed goods 3.9%

Beef and veal (BSE measures) 33.4%

Sugar 3.0%

Milk products 5.5%

of quotas at producer level or obligations to 'set-aside' land, are placed on those who receive these payments, in order to control production. The Government funds expenditure in Britain on CAP measures and later claims reimbursement from the EU. Britain contributes to this reimbursement through payments to the EU budget, to which it is a net contributor.

All CAP support prices and direct subsidy payments are set in European Currency Units (ECUs) and are then converted into the currencies of the member states at special rates of exchange, so–called 'green rates'. These green rates are kept broadly in line with market rates in accordance with agreed rules. The strengthening of sterling from mid–1996, which coincided with a weakening of the Deutschmark and other EU currencies, resulted in a series of revaluations of the British green rate, the first such since August 1993. These revaluations ended the trend in 1994–95 of green rate devaluations and consequent increases in CAP payments and amounts. Nevertheless, the sterling green rate remained 9.4 per cent more generous in June 1997 than in January 1992.

Nearly all the EU's expenditure on agricultural support is channelled through the European Agricultural Guidance and Guarantee Fund (EAGGF). The Fund's guarantee section (with a budget of £29,730 million in 1997) finances market support arrangements, including direct payments made under the CAP, while the guidance section (budget of £2,731 million in 1997) provides funds for structural reform—for example, hill livestock compensatory allowances (HLCAs; see pp. 291–2) and payments to assist certain farmers to change to alternative enterprises.

In addition, Europe Agreements have been concluded in respect of most agricultural products to boost trade with, and to help the economies of, Central European countries while they prepare for accession to the EU. But EU farm exports to Central Europe have increased far more than the other way round, contrary to the original intention. Trade concessions are to be built into the Agreements and the GATT Uruguay Round conclusions (see p. 291) will be taken into account, to ensure that Central Europe's access to the EU market is fairly arranged.

BSE: Government Response

The announcement in March 1996 of a possible link between BSE and a new variant of CJD caused an immediate EU worldwide ban on exports of British beef and beef products (see pp. 283–4).

The Florence Agreement of June 1996 provided a mechanism for resumption of exports, subject to certain conditions being satisfied and the opinion of various EU scientific committees and of the Commission. The agreement set down five preconditions before exports could be resumed, and Britain considered that it had fulfilled these by February 1997. The agreement also set out five steps for the resumption of exports. On the first step, Britain's initial proposals for the export of beef and beef products from herds certified as having no association with BSE (Export Certified Herds Scheme) were criticised by the EU Scientific Veterinary Committee in June 1997. However, in July the Government put forward a revised Export Certified Herds Scheme and is currently discussing a new proposal for an export scheme for beef from animals born after a specified date. A series of government and EU measures have been taken to combat BSE and to support the beef industry (at a total estimated cost of £1,370 million to British public funds), as follows:

Protection of Public and Animal Health

- Continued ban on specified material from bovine animals, and, from September 1996, on the heads of sheep and goats. The latter controls were applied against the theoretical possibility of BSE in sheep: there is no evidence that BSE is present in the British flock. In July 1997 the EU adopted decision 97/534, which will apply from 1 January 1998 an EU-wide prohibition on the use for any purpose of skulls, including brain and eyes, tonsils and spinal cord of cattle, sheep and goats over 12 months old and the spleens of all sheep and goats.

- Over Thirty Months Scheme (OTMS), given effect by Commission regulation 96/716. This excludes all animals over 30 months old from the human and animal food chains and is based on a system of approved abattoirs and collection centres. It had resulted in the slaughter of 1.7 million animals by August 1997.

- Removal of mammalian meat and bonemeal (MBM) from the livestock feed chain, a ban on MBM as fertiliser on agricultural land, a Feed Recall Scheme to remove residual MBM stocks, and legal penalties for holding MBM on premises where animal feed is handled.

- Selective cull of cattle born between 1 July 1989 and 30 June 1993.

Support for Industry

- Calf Processing Aid Scheme (CPAS), which takes calves out of production early, preventing further overproduction of animals which would have no market.

- The Government ensures that reasonable quantities of beef are being accepted into intervention.

- Additional supplements under the Suckler Cow and Beef Special Premium schemes (see below).

- Short-term emergency aid, to be phased out in 1997–98, to the slaughtering and rendering industries. Slaughterhouses and cutting plants received support in 1996–97. Help for the rendering industry was based on maintenance of renderers' income levels for MBM and tallow.

- Help under the Beef Assurance Scheme, introduced in 1996, for those mainly grass-fed specialist beef herds with no history of BSE, and considered to be at very low risk of having a case of BSE in the future, in which the cattle mature slowly and are slaughtered over the age of 30 months. By the end of August 1997, 72 herds were registered under the scheme.

- Cattle Passport Scheme (see p. 295).

Research

MAFF spent £6.8 million in 1996–97 on research into BSE and related diseases, bringing the total to over £30 million since the start of the epidemic in 1986. A further allocation of £12.6 million has been made for research in 1997–98. The programme will continue at or around this level for at least the next three years.

EU Funding

Payments under the CPAS (£53.8 million in 1996–97 and provisionally £62.3 million in 1997–98) are wholly EU-funded; those under the OTMS (£863 million in 1996–97 and provisionally £348.6 million in 1997–98) are partly EU-funded. (Britain meets the costs of slaughtering and destruction of carcasses, £131 million [excluding VAT] in 1996–97, under the OTMS.) In addition, the EU has provided support through intervention buying of beef, as well as supplements to, and increases in the advances of, EU premium payments to beef producers (see below).

The EU agreed two aid packages for the beef sector. Under the first, £110 million was

Table 18.5: Rates of Hill Livestock Compensatory Allowances 1997

	Severely disadvantaged LFA	Disadvantaged LFA
Breeding cows	£97.50	£69.75
Hardy breed ewes	£5.75	£2.65
Other ewes	£3.00	£2.65

Source: MAFF

made available to Britain, of which £81 million was distributed in the form of a top-up of the suckler cow and beef special premiums. The Government decided to use the remaining £29 million to fund a beef marketing payments scheme (BMPS), under which payments worth £66.78 a head were made on adult cattle sold for human consumption between 20 March and 30 June 1996. A further £29 million of national funds were made available to allow the BMPS to be extended to cover cattle slaughtered between 1 July and 30 September (£55 a head) and between 1 October and 9 November (£34 a head).

The second aid package provided some £52 million to Britain, most of which (£49.5 million) was distributed in top-up payments under the 1996 Suckler Cow Premium Scheme and in payments to the owners of Northern Ireland herds which have had cases of BSE. The remainder was spent on promoting the beef industry and on a small-scale aid scheme for veal producers.

CAP Expenditure on Livestock in Britain

Beef Special Premium is paid on male bovine animals in certain age ranges. In 1996 payments worth £93.11 were made for first premium animals (aged at least 10 months and under 23 months) and second premium animals (23 months and over). A single premium for bulls aged between 10 and 23 months was introduced in 1997, with a higher payment rate than for steers—which continue to attract two payments. Supplement granted in 1996 (to help producers who suffered through disruption of the beef market) was worth £19.70 a head. Estimated expenditure in respect of the 1997 scheme, including extensification premium, is £140 million for England and £261 million for Britain as a whole.

Suckler Cow Premium is paid on suckler cows rearing beef calves. In 1996, premium was worth £124.12 a head, with supplements of £23.13 and, separately, £30 to help offset the effects of market disruption. Estimated expenditure in respect of the 1997 scheme, including extensification premium, is £98 million for England and £201 million for Britain.

Two levels of extensification premium are paid under the Beef Special Premium and the Suckler Cow Premium schemes. A supplement of about £29 an animal is paid if the producer has a stocking density of less than 1.4 livestock units (LU) a hectare of forage area or £42 an animal if the stocking density is less than 1 LU a hectare of forage area.

EU beef intervention schemes came to about £156 million in 1996–97. Intervention coverage accounted for more than half of Britain's saleable production. For the EU as a whole the ceiling for beef intervention was increased to 555,000 tonnes. About 44,000 tonnes (carcass weight) of beef were accepted for purchase into intervention in Britain during 1996–97.

Sheep Annual Premium. Producers received a payment of £13.66 an eligible ewe under the 1996 Sheep Annual Premium Scheme. A supplement of £5.38 per eligible ewe was paid to Less Favoured Area (LFA) producers. Total payments in Britain in 1996–97 were £453.9 million, with a total quota of 19.64 million units (8.6 million in England; 4.3 million in Scotland).[2]

Agricultural Trade Liberalisation

The GATT Uruguay Round of world trade negotiations, concluded in 1993, marked an important step forward for agricultural

---

[2] Payments are limited to the number of quota units held by each producer.

liberalisation. For the first time the key elements of import protection, domestic support and subsidised exports were subjected to a framework of specific disciplines designed to reduce distortions in world agricultural trade. In preparation for implementing the new regime the EU made major changes in its cereals, oilseeds and livestock support arrangements designed to make them more competitive.

Negotiations to liberalise agricultural trade further will start in 2000. These will put pressure on the CAP to bring exports into line with world market levels. The outcome would mean further liberalisation through lower protection, a weakening of domestic support arrangements, which distort production and trade, and yet stricter disciplines on the use of export subsidies.

Price Guarantees, Grants and Subsidies

Expenditure in Britain in 1996–97 under the CAP and by the agriculture and other departments (including funding for special areas) on conservation measures was estimated at £4,142 million and £271.5 million respectively.

In LFAs, where land quality is poor, farmers benefit from higher rates of HLCAs. These are headage payments on breeding cattle and sheep, and their purpose is to support the continuation of livestock farming in hills and uplands, thus conserving the countryside and encouraging people to remain in the LFAs.

In 1997 producers in the LFA (United Kingdom)[3] received direct livestock subsidy payments of £650 million, of which £162 million came from HLCAs (see Table 18.5). An additional £60 million was made available to upland cattle farmers in Britain through the HLCA scheme to compensate for a downturn in LFA incomes.

Smallholdings and Crofts

In England and Wales county councils let smallholdings to experienced people who want to farm on their own account. Councils may lend working capital to them. At 31 March 1995 there were approximately 4,700 smallholdings in England and 840 in Wales. Land settlement in Scotland has been carried out by the Government, which still owns and maintains 105,069 hectares (259,520 acres) of land settlement estates, comprising 1,412 crofts and holdings.

In northern Scotland—Highland, parts of Argyll and Bute, Western Isles, Orkney and Shetland—much of the land is tenanted by crofters (smallholders), who enjoy the statutory protection provided by crofting legislation and can benefit from government agriculture and livestock improvement schemes. Most crofters are part-time agriculturalists, using croft income to supplement income from other activities. The Crofters Commission has a statutory duty to promote their interests and to keep all crofting matters under review. The Transfer of Crofting Estates (Scotland) Act 1997 allows the Government to transfer some of its own crofting land to trusts set up by resident crofters, with the aim of giving them more responsibility for their own affairs.

Agricultural Landlords and Tenants

About one-third of agricultural land in England and Wales is rented. The Agricultural Tenancies Act 1995 provides a simplified legal framework for new tenancies entered into on or after 1 September 1995, known as farm business tenancies (FBTs). In the first Annual Survey of Tenanted Land, carried out in October 1996, 559 FBT agreements were recorded in the sample representing over 11 per cent of all types of agreement. Landowners benefit from full relief from inheritance tax on FBTs.

In Scotland about 40 per cent of farmland is rented, partly reflecting the relatively large areas of land in crofting tenure, including common grazings.

Most farms in Northern Ireland are owner occupied, but the conacre system allows occupiers not wishing to farm all their land to let it annually to others. Conacre land—about one-fifth of agricultural land—is used mainly for grazing.

---

[3] Designation of LFA status is decided by the EU. The case for LFAs in Britain was submitted to the EU as covering all of Britain.

Agriculture and Protection of the Countryside

Britain's agri-environment programme, under EU agri-environment regulation 2078/92, provides voluntary incentive schemes to encourage environmentally beneficial farming practices. The Government normally evaluates and reviews the schemes every five years.

Environmentally Sensitive Areas (ESAs)

The ESA scheme (see Table 18.6) remains Britain's largest environmental scheme. Farmers within designated areas receive annual payments for carrying out practices which benefit nature conservation, the landscape and preservation of historic features.

Participation in the scheme is voluntary. Farmers enter into 10-year agreements with the relevant agriculture department. An agreement specifies the agricultural management practices they will carry out. Each ESA has varying tiers of such practices, from basic care and maintenance to more extensive forms of management and environmental restoration. Details also vary, but participants may not convert grassland to arable and are subject to restrictions on fertiliser and chemical usage.

Most ESAs also restrict or control the numbers of stock on the land as well as the timing of cultivation. The annual payments (between £6 and £415 a hectare, depending on the needs of each tier) are designed to compensate for reduced profitability because of these less intensive production methods, and for the further work some management

practices need. Additional payments are made for specific items, such as hedgerows and stone wall renewal, habitat creation, and for allowing public access to suitable farmland.

After public consultation, several new tiers and options were introduced into the first five English ESAs, including, in February 1997: enhancement of herb-rich pastures in the Pennine Dales; creation of fens in the Norfolk Broads to increase biodiversity and improve important habitats; and encouragement of winter stubbles, to attract farmland birds, in the South Downs and West Penwith. The areas of four of these ESAs were also extended. Proposals for the development of 11 of the other English ESAs have been issued for further consultation.

Countryside Stewardship

Countryside Stewardship is the main government incentive scheme in England for the wider English countryside outside the ESAs. It offers payments to farmers and landowners to improve the natural heritage and biodiversity, under 10-year agreements. It targets chalk and limestone grassland, lowland heath, waterside land, coast, uplands, historic landscapes, old orchards, countryside around towns, field boundaries (such as walls, ditches and hedgerows), old meadows and pastures, and uncropped margins in arable fields. MAFF signed 1,105 agreements with farmers in England in 1996, building up the total to 6,225, covering 107,000 hectares (264,400 acres). By 1998–99 total payments to farmers will have risen to over £20 million, including £0.5 million under a pilot scheme for arable land to be introduced as part of Countryside Stewardship.

Table 18.6: ESAs at 31 March 1997					
	Number of ESAs	Farmers with agreements	Land designated	Areas covered by agreements	Payments to farmers in 1996–97 (£'000)
			000 hectares /('000 acres)		
England	22	8,291	1,149 (2,839)	437 (1,080)	27,592
Wales	6	1,757	429 (1,060)	130 (321)	3,456
Scotland	10	1,331	1,439 (3,556)	441 (1,090)	3,767
Northern Ireland	5	3,451	222 (549)	118 (292)	4,219

Source: MAFF, Welsh Office, The Scottish Office, Northern Ireland Office

Organic Aid Schemes

Four such schemes cover England, Northern Ireland, Scotland and Wales. These offer support for the conversion of land to organic production methods. Land thus entered attracts payments for five years from the start of conversion. Payments are on a reducing scale starting at up to £70 a hectare. An additional £30 a hectare is payable on the first 5 hectares entered into a scheme.

From June 1996 the Organic Conversion Information Service has operated in England and from October in Wales. This provides free Helpline information and advisory visits to prospective organic farmers.

By the end of March 1997, 5,482 hectares (13,540 acres) had been entered into conversion in England. The scheme in Scotland has seen 19,062 hectares (47,102 acres) put into conversion. Total expenditure under the schemes in Britain is about £520,300 in 1996–97—£400,000 in England and £88,247 in Scotland. There is also a programme of R & D worth about £1 million, and support is given for the UK Register of Organic Food Standards, which is charged with overseeing standards of such food production. There were 784 registered organic holdings in Britain in June 1995, although in 1997 organic farming still only accounted for 0.3 per cent of the total.

Other Schemes

Other schemes within Britain's agri-environment programme include:

- Nitrate Sensitive Areas;
- Nitrate Vulnerable Zones (see p. 351);
- Arable Area Payments Scheme;
- Farm Woodland Premium Scheme;
- British Habitat Schemes;
- Tir Cymen Scheme (in Wales);
- Moorland Schemes; and
- Countryside Access Scheme.

In Scotland, the Habitat, Moorland and Access schemes became part of the Scottish Countryside Premium Scheme from March 1997.

The Rural Economy and EU Structural Funds

Eleven areas in Great Britain (including South West England, the English Northern Uplands, 70 per cent of the landmass of Wales, and Dumfries and Galloway) have been designated eligible to receive funds under Objective 5b of the EU Structural Funds. Objective 5b aims to promote the economic development of rural areas by supporting the provision of business advice, infrastructure development, diversification, marketing local and regional products, and measures to enhance and conserve the environment. Areas must have a high share of agricultural employment in total employment, a low level of agricultural income and a low population density.

The EU has allocated £376 million to the six Objective 5b programmes in England for the six years 1994–99. Of this, some £112 million is to come from the Government and the EAGGF specifically to assist the agricultural sector.

Northern Ireland, the Highlands and Islands of Scotland and Merseyside qualify for assistance under Objective 1 of the EU Structural Funds, which aims to help those regions whose economic development lags behind the EU average. Some £33 million was spent on measures funded under Objective 1 in Northern Ireland in 1996–97.

Linked to Objective 5b is the LEADER II initiative, designed to help small-scale, innovative measures of benefit to local areas. The EU has allocated over £20 million to England and over £16 million to Scotland for LEADER II measures. With matching national public funds, almost £7 million is available to give direct support to agriculture.

Agricultural Training

ATB-Landbase Limited provides Industry Training Organisation (see p. 174) and other services for agriculture and commercial horticulture, under contract to MAFF. The contract for the three years 1997–2000 is worth £1.5 million and complements funding provided by the Department for Education and Employment, including work on the development of national standards. ATB-

Landbase also receives funding under the Sector Challenge (see p. 196). Two projects, worth a total of £1.9 million over three years, involve support for the training infrastructure and the provision of information on training and business development. MAFF also contributes to the educational activities of the National Federation of Young Farmers' Clubs. The agricultural colleges and other independent organisations also provide training.

Professional, Scientific and Technical Services

In England and Wales ADAS, formerly an executive agency of MAFF and the Welsh Office, provides professional, business, scientific and technical services in the agriculture, food and drink, and environmental markets. Consultancy is on a fee-paying basis. ADAS was privatised in 1997, the sale being to a management buy-out team; it did not include ADAS farms, which are leased to the new owners. A new Farming and Rural Conservancy Agency carries out statutory work no longer undertaken by ADAS. The Government pays for free initial advice on conservation and the prevention of pollution. In England this advice is provided through ADAS and, in the case of conservation, also through the Farming and Wildlife Advisory Group. Similar services in Scotland come from the SOAEFD through the Scottish Agricultural College. In Northern Ireland they are available from the Department of Agriculture's agriculture and science services.

CONTROL OF DISEASES AND PESTS

Farm Animals

Britain enforces controls on imports of live animals and genetic material, including checks on all individual consignments originating from outside the EU and frequent checks on those from other EU member states at destination points. Measures can be taken to prevent the importation of diseased animals and genetic material from regions or countries affected by disease. Veterinary checks also include unannounced periods of surveillance at ports.

The number of confirmed cases of BSE in Britain is falling by about 40 per cent each year. Scientists at the University of Oxford predict that there will be about 7,000 more cases before the disease falls to very low levels in 2001.

Compulsory cattle passports were introduced in Great Britain from 1 July 1996. All cattle, born here or imported after that date, must have a valid passport. It is an offence for animals born or imported after 30 June 1996 to be without one. (Up to the end of August 1997, 3.3 million passports had been issued.) The Cattle Passport Order 1996 prohibits the movement of such cattle on or off holdings. Failure to obtain a cattle passport may result in a fine of up to £5,000 and the animal's ineligibility for slaughter for human consumption. The passport records eartag number, sex, breed, date of birth, dam identification number and name and address of original keeper. The information is recorded in the agriculture department's cattle passport system database. When the animal is moved off the farm, the keeper must enter the movement details on the passport and record them in the farm register. The Government aims to establish a computer-based system to register all cattle and their movements. It will hold identification details and record movements from birth to death, including those through markets and to abattoirs, of all cattle born in or imported into Great Britain, after the system becomes operational. This will be as soon as possible in 1998, well ahead of the EU deadline of 31 December 1999. In Northern Ireland, the Department of Agriculture has operated such a system since 1990, detailing the registration and movements of 1.6 million cattle.

The Government has commissioned further research from the Institute of Occupational Medicine into the effects of organophosphorus sheep dips on users' health. The project is costing £500,000 and the results are due in 1999.

Professional advice and action on the statutory control of animal disease and the welfare of farm livestock are the responsibility of the SVS. It is supported by the Veterinary Laboratories Agency (VLA), a primary supplier of specialist veterinary advice to

MAFF, which also offers its services to the private sector on a commercial basis. A similar service is provided in Scotland by the Scottish Agricultural College and in Northern Ireland by the Department of Agriculture's Veterinary Science Laboratories.

Rabies

Dogs, cats and certain other mammals are subject to import licence and six months' quarantine. Commercially traded dogs and cats from other EU countries which satisfy strict conditions are allowed entry without quarantine. There are severe penalties for breaking the law. No cases of rabies outside quarantine have occurred in Northern Ireland since 1923 and in Britain as a whole since 1970, except for an isolated incident with a bat in 1996. The requirement for imported animals to be quarantined is under review.

Fish

Controls to prevent the introduction and spread of serious diseases of fish and shellfish include restrictions on live fish imports and on the deposit of shellfish on the seabed, and movement restrictions on sites where outbreaks of notifiable diseases have been confirmed.

Plants

The agriculture departments apply statutory controls to implement the EU plant health regime, designed to prevent the introduction or spread of particularly harmful plant pests and disease. They also provide non–statutory services, including certification of exports to third countries and schemes for maintaining the health status of plant propagating material in Britain.

Pesticides

British legislation comprehensively controls pesticides so as to protect the health of humans, creatures and plants, safeguard the environment, and secure safe, efficient and humane methods of pest control. These arrangements are being extended into the wider EU arrangements which are being progressively brought into effect. The Pesticides Safety Directorate, an executive agency of MAFF, is responsible for the evaluation and approval of agricultural pesticides in Great Britain. It also provides policy advice to MAFF in respect of the safety and effectiveness of pesticides and monitors their usage.

Veterinary Medicinal Products

The Veterinary Medicines Directorate is responsible to agriculture and health ministers for ensuring that authorised veterinary medicines meet standards of safety, quality and efficacy. Users of medicines, the health and welfare of treated animals, safety of consumers of food from treated animals, and the environment are all matters of concern. The independent scientific Veterinary Products Committee advises the Government.

The Fishing Industry

In 1996 the fishing industry provided about 54 per cent by quantity of total British fish supplies. Household consumption of fish in Britain, at 470,000 tonnes, showed an increase of over 7 per cent since 1995. Over the past two years there has been a substantial increase in the consumption of fresh and frozen fish, fish products and shellfish.

Fisheries departments are responsible for the administration of legislation, in partnership with the European Commission, concerning the fishing industry, including fish and shellfish farming.

The Sea Fish Industry Authority (SFIA) is an industry financed body. It undertakes R & D, provides training and encourages quality awareness. In 1996 the SFIA paid, on behalf of fisheries departments, almost £1 million in vessel safety grants involving some 319 projects, thus helping owners with work necessary to obtain an official safety certificate.

Fish Caught

In 1996 demersal fish (caught on or near the bottom of the sea) accounted for 46 per cent by weight of total landings by British fishing vessels, pelagic fish (caught near the surface) for 39 per cent and shellfish for 16 per cent. Landings of all types of fish (excluding salmon and trout) by British fishing vessels in Britain totalled 635,000 tonnes compared with 725,600 tonnes in 1995. Cod and haddock represented 22 and 16 per cent respectively of the total value of demersal and pelagic fish landed, while anglerfish (15 per cent), whiting (6 per cent), and plaice and mackerel (5 per cent each) were the other most important sources of earnings to the industry. The quayside value of landings of all sea fish, including shellfish, by British vessels in 1996 was £491 million.

Total allowable catches (TACs) for 1997 (see below) produced British quotas of 485,000 tonnes (expressed as cod equivalent), compared with 547,000 tonnes in 1995 and 512,000 tonnes in 1996. British vessels also have access to stocks where no allocation is made between EU member states.

The Fishing Fleet

Given the continuing pressure on fish stocks, the Government considers that effective fisheries management and enforcement are essential to the future viability of the fishing industry. All British vessels fishing for profit must be licensed by the fisheries departments. To help conserve stocks and contain the size of the fleet only replacement licences are issued. Quotas are allocated annually to groups of fishermen, mainly the producer organisations, in proportion to their catches over the previous three years. In 1996, 31 out of 78 quotas were fished to within 95–105 per cent of allocation; the number of quotas overfished by more than 5 per cent was six. National and EU regulations are enforced through aerial and marine surveillance and by shore-based Sea Fisheries Inspectorates, which also collect information on fishing activity. There were 66 prosecutions for Scotland alone resulting from infringements committed in 1996 and in earlier years.

Under the EU's Multi-Annual Guidance Programme all member states have been set targets for reducing their fleets. Britain aims to achieve this objective through substantial cuts in the fishing fleet and limits on the time vessels spend at sea. Some 8.2 per cent of tonnage has been removed in four tendering rounds: 4,755 gross registered tonnes (GRT) in 1993, 5,270 GRT in 1994, 4,206 GRT in 1995, and 3,381 GRT in 1996, at a cost of £36.4 million. At the end of 1995 the British fleet consisted of 9,174 registered vessels, including 448 deep-sea vessels longer than 24.4 m (80 ft).

Fish Farming and Shellfish Production

Production of salmon and trout in Britain has grown from less than 1,000 tonnes in the early 1970s to 83,121 tonnes of salmon in Scotland and 4,635 tonnes (Scotland) of trout in 1996. Scotland produces the largest amount of farmed salmon (with a first-sale value of £220 million) in the EU. Shellfish farming concentrates on molluscs such as oysters, mussels, clams and scallops, producing an estimated 1,390 tonnes (Scotland) a year.

The fish and shellfish farming industries, predominantly in the Highlands and Islands of Scotland, were estimated to have a combined wholesale turnover of some £227 million in 1996.

Production in Great Britain is based on 1,154 businesses operating from 1,628 sites and employing more than 3,000 people.

Fishery Limits

British fishery limits extend to 200 miles or the median line (broadly halfway between the British coast and the opposing coastline of another coastal state), measured from baselines on or near the coast of Britain.

Common Fisheries Policy (CFP)

For the EU as a whole, catching capacity exceeds available fish. The EU's CFP system for the conservation and management of fishing resources sets TACs each year in order to conserve stocks. TACs are then allocated as quotas between member states on a fixed percentage basis, taking account of traditional fishing patterns. In December 1996, the EU cut quotas for a number of stocks, including

Table 18.7: Imports and Exports of Fish			*tonnes*
	1994	1995 provisional	1996 provisional
Imports			
Salt-water and shellfish	417,858	437,555	476,556
Freshwater fish	39,783	47,134	56,613
Fish meals	247,721	239,187	242,834
Fish oils	138,368	129,292	86,181
Exports and re-exports			
Salt-water fish and fish products	340,726	328,628	276,124
Freshwater fish	31,436	33,492	34,241
Fish meals	17,039	25,969	19,112
Fish oils	12,121	15,581	6,787

Sources: MAFF, The Scottish Office, Northern Ireland Office

North Sea cod, in view of the pressure on them. In April 1997, the EU agreed to cut fishing effort by up to 30 per cent over five years.

British vessels have exclusive rights to fish within 6 miles of the British coast. Certain other EU member states have historic rights in British waters between 6 and 12 miles. British vessels have similar rights in other member states' 6 to 12 mile belts, subject to transitional arrangements for the newer member states. Between 12 and 200 miles EU vessels may fish wherever they have been allocated a share of the EU's TAC against agreed EU quotas, and/or an 'effort allocation' in the case of western waters. Non-EU countries' vessels may fish in these waters if they negotiate reciprocal fisheries agreements. Currently the only countries are Norway and the Faroes.

Technical conservation measures supplement TAC and effort controls. They include minimum mesh sizes for nets and net configuration restrictions, minimum landing sizes and closed areas designed mainly to protect young fish.

Each member state is responsible for enforcement of CFP rules on its own fishermen and those of other member states in its own waters. EU inspectors monitor compliance.

Measures to control fishing by all member states in western waters took effect in 1996. Spanish and Portuguese fishing vessels are excluded from the North Sea, the Irish Sea and the Bristol Channel.

Quota Hoppers

About 10 per cent of Britain's quota stocks are taken by British registered fishing vessels which are partly or wholly foreign-owned. There are an estimated 160 such vessels, accounting for some 25 per cent of the tonnage of Britain's offshore fleet. Although overseas investment in the British fleet is permissible under the Maastricht Treaty, the Commission confirmed to the Government in 1997 that there are steps which Britain may take to ensure that vessels maintain a real economic link with its coastal areas dependent on fishing and related industries. Such measures are expected to operate from 1998, after consultation with the fishing industry.

The Government insists on fisheries enforcement both to conserve fish stocks and to safeguard the long-term interests of the industry. It has also obtained a commitment from the Commission to examine the operation of EU control arrangements and to present a report, with proposals, to the EU before the end of 1997.

Grant Schemes

The fishing industry in England, Wales and Scotland has benefited from some £96 million in EU fisheries grants over the three years 1994–95 to 1996–97. Among grant schemes which provide aid are:

- Vessel Safety Grant Schemes—EU and national schemes available towards the costs of equipment necessary for a vessel to obtain a safety certificate; .
- an EU scheme to improve facilities for fishermen at fishing ports;
- Aquaculture and Development of Enclosed Seawater Areas—an EU scheme, at present operating only in Scotland, for investments in fish farming and protection of enclosed coastal waters;
- the PESCA scheme—an EU scheme to assist the restructuring of the fisheries sector and to encourage the diversification of economic activities in areas dependent on fishing; and
- an EU scheme for decommissioning fishing vessels.

All the EU grants are backed by contributions from the Government or other public authorities.

Fisheries Agreements

CFP provisions are supplemented by a number of fisheries agreements between the EU and third countries, the most important for Britain being the agreements with Norway, Greenland and the Faroe Islands. EU catch quotas have also been established around Spitsbergen (Svalbard).

Fish and Shellfish Hygiene

Community legislation sets minimum hygiene standards for the production and marketing of fish and shellfish. All commercial shellfish beds producing live bivalve molluscs are monitored for microbial contamination. Shellfishharvesting areas are then classified according to EU criteria. Samples of seawater and shellfish flesh are tested for the presence of biotoxins and chemical contaminants.

Salmon and Freshwater Fisheries

Salmon and sea-trout are fished commercially in inshore waters and estuaries around the British coast. Eels and elvers are also taken commercially in both estuaries and fresh water. Angling for salmon and sea-trout (game fishing) and for freshwater species (coarse fishing) is popular throughout Britain. There is no public right to fish in freshwater lakes and non-tidal rivers in Great Britain. Those wishing to fish such waters must first obtain permission from the owner of the fishing rights and, in England and Wales, a licence from the Environment Agency. In Scotland salmon fisheries are managed locally by District Salmon Fishery Boards. In Northern Ireland fishing for freshwater species is licensed by the Fisheries Conservancy Board for Northern Ireland and the Foyle Fisheries Commission in their respective areas, and 65 public angling waters, including salmon, trout and coarse fisheries, are accessible to Department of Agriculture permit holders.

Fisheries and the Aquatic Environment

The Centre for Environment, Fisheries and Aquaculture Science (CEFAS), from April 1997 a government agency, is the new name for the MAFF fisheries and aquatic environment research laboratories, formerly known as the Directorate of Fisheries Research. It provides research, assessment and advice on marine and freshwater fisheries science and management, aquaculture, fish and shellfish hygiene, disease control and diagnostics, environmental research and monitoring, and environmental impacts, to MAFF and to other customers worldwide. MAFF also commissions research work from other bodies, such as the Natural Environment Research Council (NERC), the SFIA and a number of universities. CEFAS has two seagoing research vessels.

In Scotland, Fisheries Research Service, based in Aberdeen, monitors marine and freshwater resources.

The Department of Agriculture for Northern Ireland laboratories undertake research on marine and freshwater fisheries and their environments, aquaculture and oceanography.

Research

Departmental funding of R & D in agriculture, fisheries and food in 1997–98 includes funding by MAFF (£126 million), the SOAEFD (£47 million), and the Department of Agriculture for Northern Ireland (£7.5 million).

MAFF supports an intake of about 70 postgraduate students each year at an annual cost of almost £1.7 million. The scheme is intended to fund research relevant to the Ministry's overall aims and strategy, and to further the education of future agriculturalists, economists and food scientists.

Agriculture and Food

MAFF's nutrition research programme has shown, for example, that increased consumption of mono-unsaturated fatty acids, such as those found in olive oil, can decrease blood cholesterol levels by 10 per cent without the need for a reduction in overall fat intake. Meanwhile, investment in technologies in key British wheat crops has resulted in various promising transformation systems for wheat, which may lead to improved quality characteristics and pest and disease resistance. MAFF is to participate in a £5 million LINK programme, aimed at promoting sustainable production of cereals and other arable crops; it will contribute up to £2.5 million over five years—funds which will be matched by industry sponsors.

Research Bodies

The Biotechnology and Biological Sciences Research Council (BBSRC; see p. 339) supports research in biotechnology and biological sciences related to food and agriculture. The NERC is responsible for research on the environment, including some agricultural aspects. Research institutes sponsored by these councils receive income from work commissioned by MAFF, by industry and by other bodies.

ADAS carries out R & D, through regional centres and on clients' premises, for MAFF and for other bodies. There are research centres across England and Wales. MAFF receives scientific expertise and technical support from its other agencies, the VLA and the Central Science Laboratory, commissioning research from them as well as through open competition. Horticulture Research International, a non-departmental public body, transfers the results of its R & D to the British horticulture industry and the wider public.

The five Scottish Agricultural and Biological Research Institutes, funded by the SOAEFD, cover areas of research relevant to the conditions of northern Britain. The SOAEFD also funds agricultural research, education and advisory services at the Scottish Agricultural College, which operates from three centres. In Northern Ireland the Department of Agriculture conducts publicly funded basic and strategic research in specialist divisions and conducts applied research contracted by external customers. It also funds and provides facilities and teaching for the Queen's University of Belfast and the Agricultural Research Institute of Northern Ireland.

Forestry

Woodland covers an estimated 2.4 million hectares (6 million acres) in Britain: about 8 per cent of England, 15 per cent of Scotland, 12 per cent of Wales and 6 per cent of Northern Ireland. This is over 10 per cent of the total land area and well below the 25 per cent average for the whole of Europe.

Britain's forestry programme protects forest resources and conserves woodland as a home for wildlife and for public recreation. It also promotes the market for home-grown timber. The aim is to double the area of tree cover in England and increase woodlands in Wales by 50 per cent by the middle of the next century. Continued forestry expansion in Scotland is also a commitment.

The area of productive forest in Great Britain is 2.2 million hectares (5.5 million acres), 36 per cent of which is managed by the Forestry Commission. The rate of new planting (including natural regeneration) in 1996–97 was 461 hectares (1,139 acres) by the Commission and 15,971 hectares (39,464 acres) by other woodland owners, with the help of grants from the Commission, mainly in Scotland. In 1996–97, 9,198 hectares

(22,728 acres) of broadleaved trees were planted, a practice encouraged on suitable sites.

The forest area has more than doubled since 1919. During 1987–96, 207,388 hectares (512,476 acres) of new woodland were created. Forestry and primary wood processing employ about 35,000 people. Britain's woodlands produced 8.72 million cubic metres (308 million cubic feet) of timber in 1996—15 per cent of total consumption. Provision has been made for new planting in Great Britain amounting to 63,500 hectares (156,900 acres) in the three years 1997–98 to 1999–2000, comprising 62,800 hectares (155,185 acres) by the private sector and 700 hectares (1,730 acres) by Forest Enterprise.

The volume of timber harvested on Commission lands in 1996–97 was estimated at 4.7 million cubic metres (165 million cubic feet).

The Commission's Woodland Grant Scheme pays grants to help create new woodlands and forests, and regenerate existing ones. Under the scheme a Management Grant is available for work in woods of special conservation and landscape value or where the public are welcome. Two new challenge funds started in 1996: the first to bring undermanaged or low value woodlands back into better care; the second to enhance the diversity of wildlife in Cairngorms semi-natural woodlands, Argyll and Bute oak woods, and Welsh upland oak woods, and to improve conditions for butterflies in English coppice woodlands. EU co-financing of grants will amount to about £31 million over 1997–98 to 1999–2000.

Annual payments to compensate farmers for agricultural income foregone are also available under the Farm Woodland Premium Scheme (see p. 294).

The Forestry Commission and Forestry Policy

The Forestry Commission, established in 1919, is the government department responsible for forestry in Great Britain. With over a million hectares of land (2.7 million acres), it is Britain's largest land manager and the biggest single provider of countryside recreation. The Commissioners advise on forestry matters and are responsible to the Secretary of State for Scotland, the Minister of Agriculture, Fisheries and Food, and the Secretary of State for Wales.

Within the Commission, the Forestry Authority provides grants to private woodland owners for tree planting and woodland management, controls tree felling, and sets standards for the forestry industry as a whole. Forest Enterprise, a Next Steps agency of the Commission, develops and manages the Commission's forests and forestry estate, supplying timber and opportunities for recreation, and enhancing nature conservation and the forest environment. The Forestry Commission Research Agency came into being in April 1997.

The Commission is financed partly by the Government and partly by receipts from sales of timber and other produce, and from rents. Its grant in aid for 1996–97 was £64 million; for 1997–98, £63 million. Provision will decrease and £10 million will be deducted each year for reimbursements for EU co-financing of private woodlands grants. Timber receipts are also expected to grow as production rises.

The Commission continues to sell forestry land, at the rate of 1 per cent a year of its total estate over a 10-year period. During 1989–97 some 81,000 hectares (200,000 acres) were sold. There are safeguards for protecting continued public access to former Commission woodland after sale to private owners.

Native Scots pine woodlands in the Scottish Highlands are recognised as a Class 1 habitat in the EU Habitats Directive, requiring positive management action for restoration. The Forestry Commission disburses grants to support this objective.

Forestry Initiatives

The Forestry Commission continues to promote forestry close to centres of population. 'Locational Supplements' have been introduced, at £600 a hectare and on a three-year basis, to provide an incentive for the planting of new woodlands in priority areas—in the 12 Community Forests and the

National Forest in England, the Central Scotland Forest and the Aman Gwendraeth and North-East Wales initiatives.

The Millennium Commission (see p. 47) has so far awarded £11.7 million to the Millennium Forest for Scotland and £6.5 million to the Woodland Trust's 'Woods on Your Doorstep' programme to support and advise on the creation of new community woodlands in Britain.

The Forestry Authority works closely with the Forestry Commission's research division and plant health branch to monitor forest health and to prevent the entry of pests and pathogens into Britain through imported timber. Meanwhile, efforts to conserve the red squirrel continue. Research suggests that some pine or larch trees in otherwise pure spruce crops can make a positive difference to red squirrel populations.

Forestry in Northern Ireland

Woodland and forest cover about 81,000 hectares (200,000 acres) of Northern Ireland. State-owned forest constitutes 61,000 hectares (150,700 acres).

The Department of Agriculture for Northern Ireland is responsible for forestry through its Forest Service. It administers grant aid for private planting and spent £15 million during 1993-96 supporting private and state forestry. Additional supplements are available where the land is coming out of agriculture or provides recreation. Annual timber production is about 250,000 cubic metres (8.8 million cubic feet), 90 per cent from state forests. Receipts from sales of timber totalled £6 million in 1996–97. Forestry and timber processing employ 1,100 people.

Further Reading

Agriculture in the United Kingdom 1996, MAFF. The Stationery Office.

Annual Report and Accounts 1995–96, Forestry Commission. The Stationery Office.

Departmental Report, Ministry of Agriculture, Fisheries and Food and the Intervention Board, 1997.

United Kingdom Sea Fisheries Statistics 1996, MAFF.

Agricultural Policies in OECD Countries: Monitoring and Evaluation 1997, Organisation for Economic Co-operation and Development.

19 Transport and Communications

Passenger travel within Britain and to overseas countries is continuing to rise. The Government's main focus of attention has switched to developing an integrated transport policy, covering all aspects of public and private transport, and placing greater emphasis on environmental considerations. It is designed to make better use of the existing facilities and infrastructure, with a higher priority envisaged for public transport. Britain has one of the most open telecommunications markets in the world, and telecommunications services are developing rapidly.

Transport

Travel Trends

Passenger travel, in terms of passenger-kilometres, has risen substantially in recent decades, but during the 1990s the pattern has fluctuated, with travel declining in the early 1990s. Nevertheless, over the ten years to 1996 travel grew by 27 per cent. Travel by car and van rose by 33 per cent and air travel also grew substantially. However, travel by bus and coach and by motorcycle has fallen. Rail travel rose in the second half of the 1980s but declined in the early 1990s, although it recovered in 1995 and 1996.

Travel by car is by far the most popular mode of passenger travel (see Table 19.1). Car and van travel accounts for 86 per cent of passenger mileage within Great Britain, buses and coaches for 6 per cent, rail 5 per cent and air 1 per cent. Most freight is carried by road, which accounts for 81 per cent of goods by tonnage and 66 per cent in terms of tonne-kilometres.[1]

Car ownership has grown substantially. In all, 69 per cent of households in Great Britain owned one or more cars in 1996; 21 per cent owned two or more cars. At the end of 1996 there were 26.3 million vehicles licensed for use on the roads of Great Britain, including 22.2 million cars (of which 2.3 million were company-owned); 2 million light goods vehicles; 555,000 other goods vehicles; 739,000 motorcycles, scooters and mopeds; and 158,000 buses and coaches (including minibuses for private use).

---

[1] A tonne-kilometre is equivalent to 1 tonne transported for 1 kilometre.

Table 19.1: Passenger Transport in Great Britain by Mode

Thousand million kilometres

	1976	1986	1991	1994	1995	1996
Buses and coaches	58	47	44	44	44	44
Cars, vans and taxis	348	465	582	595	606	620
Motorcycles, mopeds and scooters	7	8	6	4	4	4
Pedal cycles	5	5	5	5	5	4
All road	418	525	638	647	658	672
Rail[a]	33	37	38	35	37	38
Air[b]	2	4	5	5	6	6
All modes[c]	453	566	681	688	701	717

Source: *Transport Statistics Great Britain*
[a] Financial years from 1986 onwards.
[b] Excludes air taxi services, private flying and passengers paying less than 25 per cent of the full fare. Includes Northern Ireland and the Channel Islands.
[c] Excluding travel by water within Great Britain.
Note: Differences between totals and the sums of their component parts are due to rounding.

Integrated Transport Policy

The Government is committed to developing an integrated transport policy to tackle congestion and pollution, and to serve Britain's needs for a strong economy, a sustainable environment and an inclusive society. It believes that integrating decisions in a broad range of policy areas, including transport and land-use planning, will be important in developing this policy. In June 1997, it merged the Department of the Environment with the Department of Transport to form the Department of the Environment, Transport and the Regions (DETR).

The Government is conducting a fundamental review of transport policy, and in August 1997 published a wide-ranging consultation document. The review will cover issues involving all modes of transport, both passenger and freight, and will also incorporate the review of the road programme (see p. 305)

A White Paper will be published in spring 1998 which will set out the Government's transport strategy for Britain for both the long and the short term. Separate White Papers or policy statements will be published addressing the specific issues and circumstances in Scotland, Wales and Northern Ireland.

ROADS

The total road network in Great Britain in 1996 was 368,800 kilometres (229,200 miles). Trunk motorways[2] accounted for 3,181 kilometres (1,977 miles) of this, less than 1 per cent, and other trunk roads for over 12,350 kilometres (7,680 miles), or 3.4 per cent. However, motorways carry 16 per cent of all traffic, and trunk roads another 16 per cent. Combined, they carry over half of all goods vehicle traffic in Great Britain. In Northern Ireland the road network is over 24,000 kilometres (15,000 miles), of which 112 kilometres (70 miles) are motorways.

Motor traffic in Great Britain in 1996 rose by 2.7 per cent to an estimated 442,500 million vehicle-kilometres (see Table 19.2). Traffic on motorways has been growing particularly quickly, rising by 81 per cent between 1986 and 1996 to 73,700 million vehicle-kilometres, reflecting increases in motorway length as well as traffic flow.

Management

Responsibility for trunk roads, including most motorways, rests in England with the

---

[2] That is, those motorways that are the direct responsibility of central government rather than of the local authority.

Table 19.2: Motor Vehicle Traffic in Great Britain

Thousand million vehicle-kilometres

	1986	1991	1994	1995	1996
Motorways	40.8	61.0	66.7	70.9	73.7
Trunk roads	55.7	69.4	69.8	70.4	72.6
Principal roads	102.9	127.0	130.1	131.2	134.1
Minor roads	125.9	154.2	155.9	158.4	161.9
All roads	**325.3**	**411.6**	**422.6**	**430.9**	**442.5**

Source: *Transport Statistics Great Britain*
Note: Differences between totals and the sums of their component parts are due to rounding.

Secretary of State for the Environment, Transport and the Regions, in Scotland with the Secretary of State for Scotland and in Wales with the Secretary of State for Wales. Central government meets most of the costs of construction and maintenance. The Highways Agency, an executive agency of the DETR, is responsible for building, improving and maintaining motorways and trunk roads in England. Its total budget is £1,685 million in 1997–98. In Northern Ireland the Roads Service, an agency of the Department of the Environment for Northern Ireland, is responsible for the construction, improvement and maintenance of all public roads. The main highway authorities for non-trunk roads in England are the county councils, the metropolitan district councils, the new unitary authorities (see pp. 80–1) and the London borough councils. In Wales and Scotland, the highway authorities are the unitary authorities.

Private sector finance has been playing a greater role in roads under 'Design, Build, Finance and Operate' (DBFO) contracts. Under these schemes, the private sector provides the funding for construction and maintenance, and currently receives government payments linked to usage and performance. There are eight DBFO projects in operation. Among other schemes in which the private sector has been involved, with tolls payable by users, are a bridge between the mainland of Scotland and Skye, and the second crossing of the River Severn. One of the inputs to the review of transport policy will be analysis of the trials of electronic tolling equipment recently conducted at the Transport Research Laboratory.

Road Programme

In summer 1997, 22 motorway and trunk road schemes were under construction in England and 142 further schemes were in preparation. A major review of the road programme was announced in June 1997 and is expected to be completed in spring 1998. The objective is to determine the role of roads in the Government's integrated transport policy, and to establish a new investment programme for the motorway and trunk road network. Among the issues being examined are:

- the environmental impact of roads;
- whether steps should be taken to manage demand for travel by road;
- the extent to which other modes of transport should be encouraged;
- the role of technology and improved driver information systems; and
- the impact of investment in roads on regional development.

Meanwhile, preparatory work on new schemes has mostly been suspended.

Support for local authority road schemes is increasingly approved on a package basis, under which local authorities submit bids covering all transport modes based on a comprehensive transport strategy. For 1997–98 the DETR has approved 65 package bids totalling £79 million. A total of £195 million of government grant is available to support local authority spending on transport in England in 1997–98.

Road communications in Wales have benefited from the second Severn Bridge, which opened in 1996, the completion of the M4 motorway and improvements to the A55 and A465 roads. The A55 is now a dual carriageway across the Welsh mainland, and extension of the dual carriageway to Holyhead on Anglesey is expected to be completed in 2001. The Welsh Office's trunk road and transport grant programme (including support for local authority schemes) for 1997–98 will cost over £167 million.

Planned expenditure on roads and transport in Scotland is £282 million in 1997–98. The main priorities within the trunk road programme are the upgrading to motorway standard of the Glasgow to Carlisle route, and the completion of the motorway network in central Scotland. These routes provide important links for commerce and industry to the south and to mainland Europe. There are also a series of 'route action plans' designed to make significant improvements to safety and journey times on specific major routes.

In Northern Ireland the emphasis is on improving key strategic routes, constructing more bypasses, and improving roads in the Belfast area. Planned expenditure in 1997-98 on roads by the Roads Service is £151 million.

Driver Information

With the growth in traffic, the provision of information to drivers about road conditions has become of greater importance. A new driver information system has been introduced on motorways and trunk roads between London, Birmingham and Nottingham, with over 70 variable message signs at major intersections providing information about accidents and delays, and advice about alternative routes with less congestion. A pilot scheme was introduced in 1995 on the south-west quadrant of the M25 London orbital motorway, which is one of the busiest sections of motorway in Europe. Signals mounted over each lane introduce mandatory speed limits as traffic volumes increase, and before the flow of traffic is interrupted. The results from the pilot scheme indicate better driver behaviour and conditions, and a reduction in accidents.

The Highways Agency is proposing a series of regional traffic control centres for monitoring traffic conditions and advising motorists of delays on the motorway and trunk road network. They will supplement 32 local police control offices in England and provide control over a wider area. A new traffic control centre in south Wales was inaugurated in August 1997.

There are also privately operated driver information services, which supply subscribers with information on congestion. In-car systems, such as Trafficmaster, now cover motorways and many trunk roads in Britain.

Licensing and Standards

The Driver and Vehicle Licensing Agency (DVLA) maintains official records of drivers and vehicles in Great Britain. At the end of 1996, it held records on 35 million drivers and 26 million licensed vehicles. Records for Northern Ireland are maintained by Driver and Vehicle Licensing Northern Ireland.

Minimum ages for driving are:

- 16 for riders of mopeds, drivers of small tractors, and disabled people receiving a mobility allowance;
- 17 for drivers of cars and other passenger vehicles with nine or fewer seats (including that of the driver), motorcycles and goods vehicles not over 3.5 tonnes permissible maximum weight;
- 18 for goods vehicles weighing over 3.5, but not over 7.5, tonnes; and
- 21 for passenger vehicles with more than nine seats and goods vehicles over 7.5 tonnes.

Changes in the arrangements for driver licensing and testing took place in 1996–97. New drivers of motor vehicles must now pass both the practical driving test and a new separate written theory test in order to acquire a full driving licence. The Driving Standards Agency is the national driver testing authority in Great Britain. It also supervises professional driving instructors and the compulsory basic training scheme for learner motorcyclists.

Before most new cars and goods vehicles are allowed on the roads, they must meet safety and environmental requirements, based primarily on standards drawn up by the European Union (EU). The Vehicle Certification Agency is responsible for ensuring these requirements are met through a process known as 'type approval'. It also provides a service to manufacturers wishing to obtain international vehicle system and component type approval in Great Britain.

The Vehicle Inspectorate is responsible for ensuring the roadworthiness of vehicles. It does this through the annual testing of vehicles, including heavy goods vehicles, light goods vehicles, public service vehicles, cars and motorcycles. It also uses roadside and other enforcement checks to ensure that drivers and vehicle operators comply with legislation.

In Northern Ireland the Driver and Vehicle Testing Agency (DVTA) is responsible for testing drivers and vehicles under statutory schemes broadly similar to those in Great Britain. Private cars four or more years old are tested at DVTA centres.

Road Safety

Although Great Britain has one of the highest densities of road traffic in the world, it has a good record on road safety, with the lowest road accident death rate for adults in the EU. In 1996, 3,598 deaths occurred in road accidents in Great Britain, the lowest annual figure since records began in 1926. Serious injuries, at 44,500, were also down on the previous year and represented the lowest level since 1948. However, there has recently been a rise in the number of slight injuries, to 272,200 in 1996.

Since 1981–85 total casualties have fallen by 1 per cent, to 320,300, in a period when traffic has increased by 50 per cent. Several factors, such as developments in vehicle safety standards, improvements in roads, and the introduction of legislation on seat-belt wearing, have contributed to the long-term decline in deaths and serious casualties.

Among road safety measures priority is given to reducing casualties among vulnerable road-users (children, pedestrians, cyclists, motorcyclists and elderly people), particularly in urban areas, where about 75 per cent of road accidents occur. Action includes measures to

combat speeding, improvements in highway design, better protection for vehicle occupants and encouraging the use of cycle helmets. Some £60 million has been allocated for spending on local road safety schemes in England in 1997–98. Gloucester has been chosen in a competition as the site of the first 'Safe Town' initiative. It is receiving £5 million over five years to implement a co-ordinated package of road safety measures.

> Traffic-calming measures, such as road humps, have been introduced in many towns and cities to improve both safety and the environment. Local authorities can introduce 20 mph (32 km/h) zones with traffic-calming features, with central government consent, and over 300 have been authorised. Monitoring has shown that these zones can reduce accident casualties substantially; for example, child pedestrian and cyclist casualties have fallen by 67 per cent.

Traffic in Towns

Traffic management schemes are used in many urban areas to reduce congestion, create a better environment and improve road safety. They include bus lanes, facilities for pedestrians and cyclists, and traffic-calming measures.

A 505-km (315-mile) network of priority 'red routes' for better traffic flow is being introduced in London. Marked by special signs and red lines at the kerb, these routes are subject to special stopping controls and other traffic management measures, strictly enforced with penalties higher than elsewhere. The network is expected to be fully operational by the year 2000.

Many towns have shopping precincts designed for the convenience of pedestrians, from which motor vehicles are excluded for all or part of the day. Controls over on-street parking are enforced through excess charges and fixed penalty fines, supported by powers to clamp or remove vehicles.

Travel to Work

Commuting is the most important single purpose for travel, in terms of distance travelled. Many commuting journeys by car are into city centres or other urban areas. The Government is encouraging employers to find ways of reducing the impact on traffic congestion and on the environment of their employees' travel patterns, especially their commuting journeys. It is supporting companies, such as Boots and BAA, which have developed company travel plans to encourage fewer staff to travel to work by car and more to use other modes such as public transport, cycling or walking, or to use car-sharing arrangements.

Cycling and Walking

A National Cycling Strategy, launched in 1996, is encouraging greater use of cycles and aims to double the number of cycling journeys by 2002. The National Cycling Forum is co-ordinating its implementation. Local authorities are being encouraged to give greater priority to cycling and to improve conditions for cyclists by, for example, providing designated cycle routes. Under the Cycle Challenge Project, around 60 projects have been promoted, many of which are designed to make cycling to work easier. The Government is also supporting the National Cycle Network now being developed which is intended to open up new opportunities for commuter, tourist and recreational cycling. The Millennium Commission is providing significant financial support for the network, which aims to create some 6,500 miles (10,400 kilometres) of routes for cyclists by 2005. A Walking Steering Group within the DETR is developing a strategy to promote walking as a mode of transport.

ROAD HAULAGE

Road haulage traffic by heavy goods vehicles amounted to 147,000 million tonne-kilometres in Great Britain in 1996, 2 per cent more than in 1995. There has been a move towards larger and more efficient vehicles carrying heavier loads—over 80 per cent of the traffic, in terms of tonne-kilometres, is now carried by vehicles of over 25 tonnes gross weight. Journey lengths are increasing, with the average haul

now being 90 kilometres (56 miles), 32 per cent longer than in 1980. Hauliers licensed to transport other firms' goods account for 74 per cent of freight carried in terms of tonne-kilometres.

There are about 14,600 holders of an operator's licence, and 109,300 large goods vehicles. Nearly 90 per cent of operators have fleets of five or fewer vehicles. The biggest in Great Britain are NFC plc, P & O Industrial Services Division, Ocean Group plc and Tibbet & Britten Group plc.

Licensing and Other Controls

In general, those operating goods vehicles or trailer combinations over 3.5 tonnes gross weight require a goods vehicle operator's licence. Licences are divided into restricted licences for own-account operators carrying goods connected with their own business, and standard licences for hauliers operating for hire or reward. Proof of professional competence, financial standing and good repute is needed to obtain a standard licence. In Northern Ireland own-account operators do not require a licence, although this is under consideration.

EC regulations prescribe maximum limits on driving times and minimum requirements for breaks and rest periods for most drivers of heavy goods vehicles over 3.5 tonnes. Drivers' activities are monitored automatically by a tachograph—a recording device in the cab.

Lorry Weights

The current general maximum lorry weight in Britain is 38 tonnes for goods vehicles with five or more axles. However, it is 44 tonnes for certain six-axle vehicles engaged in combined road/rail operations, as an incentive to encourage rail freight. A review of the general maximum weight has been undertaken.

International Road Haulage

International road haulage has grown rapidly and in 1996 about 1.64 million road goods vehicles were ferried to mainland Europe, of which 531,000 were powered vehicles registered in Britain. In 1996 British vehicles carried 15.1 million tonnes internationally, and about 95 per cent of this traffic was with the European Union. The largest commodity group carried is agricultural produce and foodstuffs, which accounted for 31 per cent of inward tonnage and 23 per cent of outward tonnage in 1996.

International road haulage within the EU is fully liberalised. 'Cabotage' (the operation of domestic road haulage within a member state by a non-resident) will be fully liberalised in 1998. Haulage elsewhere takes place under bilateral agreements.

ROAD PASSENGER SERVICES

Buses

Usage of local bus services has shown a long-term decline. In 1995–96 some 4,383 million passenger journeys were made on local bus services in Great Britain, 22 per cent fewer than in 1985-86. This has contrasted with an increase in local bus services in terms of bus mileage operated since the industry was deregulated in 1985.

The Government is conducting a review of all aspects of bus services, with the aim of stimulating greater use of buses as a way of reducing congestion and pollution. The review is examining the scope for more effective use of bus priority measures (see below), better arrangements for passenger information and ticketing, and regulatory and other measures to improve the quality of bus services. For example, the Government is supporting the concept of partnerships between local authorities and bus operators as part of the development of an integrated transport system.

Operators

Almost all bus services in Great Britain are provided by private sector bus operators, apart from 17 bus companies run by local authorities. London Transport (LT), a statutory corporation, is responsible for providing public transport in London. It oversees about 700 bus routes run by private sector companies under contract.

A series of mergers and takeovers has taken place, so that there are now five main groups

There has been renewed interest in reviving local public transport services. As well as several tram or light rail developments (see pp. 313–14), trials of 'guided buses', whereby buses follow guide wires under the road or overhead, are taking place in Leeds and Ipswich.

operating bus services: Cowie Group, FirstBus, Go-Ahead Group, National Express and Stagecoach. These are now substantial undertakings—for example, FirstBus has over 20 separate bus operations, with a fleet of 8,800 buses and more than 22,000 staff. All the main groups except Cowie Group are involved in running rail services (see p. 311), while some of the companies have expanded into bus services in other countries.

Services

Most local bus services are provided commercially, with 85 per cent of bus mileage outside London operated on a commercial basis. Local authorities may subsidise services which are not commercially viable but are considered to be socially necessary. Outside London, operators may provide services without restriction. Local bus services have to be registered with the relevant traffic commissioner. Controls may be imposed on the number of vehicles operating if this would cause congestion or danger to other road users.

Bus priority measures, such as bus lanes and traffic light priority signalling, are being increasingly adopted in order to make bus services quicker and more reliable. They form an important element in many local authorities' package bids (see p. 305) to the DETR. In London the DETR and local authorities are developing an 800-km (500-mile) bus priority network covering all heavily used bus routes in London. The network is receiving support of £9 million in 1997–98.

Northern Ireland

In Northern Ireland subsidiaries of the publicly owned Northern Ireland Transport

Holding Company supply almost all road passenger services. Citybus Ltd operates services in Belfast, and Ulsterbus Ltd runs most of the services in the rest of Northern Ireland. These companies have about 270 and 1,220 vehicles, handling respectively 24 million and 54 million passenger journeys a year. There are also over 90 small privately owned undertakings, often operating fewer than five vehicles.

Coaches

In Britain long-distance coach services are provided by private sector companies. The biggest operator, National Express, has a national network of routes. It carried some 14 million passengers on its coach services in Britain in 1996. Coaches and minibuses carrying three or more children now have to be fitted with seatbelts on all seats. Agreement has been reached within the EU on fitting seatbelts to new coaches and minibuses. The EC directive takes effect over a four-year period to October 2001.

While all regular, and some shuttle, overseas coach services still require authorisation or permission from the authorities of the countries to or through which they travel, most tourist services within the EU have been liberalised. Operators no longer need prior permission to run either holiday shuttle services, where accommodation is included as part of the package, or occasional coach tours to, from or within another member state.

Taxis

There are about 52,000 licensed taxis in England and Wales, mainly in urban areas; London has around 18,700. In London and several other major cities, taxis must be purpose-built to conform to strict requirements and new ones must be able to carry people in wheelchairs. In many urban districts, drivers must have passed a test of their knowledge of the area. At present, a local authority outside London can only limit the number of licensed taxis if it is satisfied that there is no unfulfilled demand for taxis in its area. Private hire vehicles with drivers ('minicabs') may be booked only through the operator and not hired on the street. In most areas outside London, private hire vehicles are licensed; there are about 56,000 in England and Wales outside London. It is estimated that at least 40,000 minicabs operate in London. A licensing system for minicabs in London is planned. There are about 4,000 licensed taxis in Northern Ireland. Licences are issued by the Department of the Environment for Northern Ireland on a broadly similar basis to that in Great Britain.

RAILWAYS

Railways were pioneered in Britain: the Stockton and Darlington Railway, opened in 1825, was the first public passenger railway in the world to be worked by steam power. The main railway services in Great Britain are now provided by private sector companies. Privatisation, involving the sale of around 100 railway operations run by the former British Rail, was completed in 1997. The main system now involves:

- Railtrack, which is responsible for operating all track and infrastructure;
- three rolling stock companies, which lease locomotives and passenger carriages;
- 25 train operating companies, which run passenger rail services under franchise;
- four freight service providers;
- seven infrastructure maintenance companies; and
- six track renewal companies.

Rail Regulation

There are two main bodies involved in overseeing rail services:

- the Office of Passenger Rail Franchising (OPRAF), headed by the Franchising Director; and
- the Office of the Rail Regulator.

OPRAF is responsible for negotiating, awarding and monitoring the franchises for operating rail services. Each franchise agreement specifies provisions governing the contractual level of passenger services to be provided by the operator. The Passenger Service Requirement sets out, for each route, the minimum service level which operators are required to meet covering, among other things, the frequency of trains, stations served, first and last trains, and the provision of sufficient peak train capacity.

The Government is continuing to support socially necessary rail passenger services through grants paid to franchisees and these are administered by OPRAF. Support for passenger rail services in 1996–97 amounted to £1,843 million. In general, the franchise arrangements provide for gradually reducing subsidies to the franchisees.

The functions of the Office of the Rail Regulator include licensing the new railway operators, dealing with agreements governing access by operators to track and stations, and promoting and protecting rail users' interests. It sponsors a network of statutory rail users' consultative committees which represent the interests of passengers.

Railtrack

Railtrack owns and manages the rail infrastructure in Great Britain, including railway track, signalling, bridges, tunnels, stations and depots. Its assets include 32,000 kilometres (20,000 miles) of track, providing a route network of over 16,000 kilometres (10,000 miles), 40,000 bridges, tunnels and viaducts, 2,500 stations and connections to over 1,000 freight terminals. Apart from 14 major stations operated directly by the company, nearly all stations and depots are leased to the train operating companies. Turnover in 1996–97 totalled £2,437 million, of which 94 per cent represented payments by passenger and freight train operators for access to the rail network.

Railtrack is planning to spend over £10,000 million on renewing and maintaining the rail network in the period from 1995 to 2001. Major projects include:

- £1,350 million on the West Coast Main Line route modernisation programme to

Following privatisation, a number of rail services have improved, but problems have arisen in some areas as a result of cancelled trains, trains with fewer carriages and consequent passenger overcrowding, and difficulties over ticketing arrangements. The Government believes that the powers available to the rail regulators may be inadequate. It is therefore seeking to improve public accountability of the railway system and to strengthen rail regulation. This would be achieved through the creation of a Strategic Rail Authority. The Government is undertaking a wide-ranging review of rail regulation to determine, among other things, how the new Authority would operate.

enable better services to be provided between London, the West Midlands, the North West and western Scotland, and a further £150 million to accommodate new high-speed tilting trains planned by Virgin, the train operator on this route (see below); and

- £580 million on Thameslink 2000, which will significantly improve the capacity of north-south services through London.

Passenger Services

The passenger network (see map facing inside back cover) comprises a fast inter-city network, linking the main centres of Great Britain; local stopping services; and commuter services in and around the large conurbations, especially London and south-east England. Some 776 million passenger journeys were made on the rail network in 1996–97. About 30 per cent of route-mileage is electrified.

Passenger services (other than Eurostar services) are run under franchise by 25 train operating companies. Franchises range from large-scale operations covering a wide area (such as the West Coast Main Line) to the smallest franchise, covering services on the Isle of Wight. A variety of operators have obtained franchises. Bus and coach operator National Express has the largest number of franchises—five. Other main operators

> The Heathrow Express rail link will start on a limited basis in autumn 1997 and be fully operational in June 1998. Under the £440 million project, run by BAA, trains will operate between Heathrow Airport and Paddington, while a service from Heathrow to St Pancras is due to start in 1999.

include Connex (which is French-owned and has two franchises running commuter services in the South East), Virgin, Prism and Stagecoach. The companies hire their rolling stock from the three rolling stock companies: Angel Train Contracts, Eversholt Leasing and Porterbrook Leasing (now a subsidiary of Stagecoach).

Most franchises last seven years, but some are for 15 years on condition that the franchisee provides new rolling stock. For example, National Express is to introduce completely new rolling stock on its Gatwick Express service from London (Victoria) to Gatwick Airport by 1999. The train operating companies have agreed to invest an estimated £1,500 million in new and refurbished trains. Several orders have recently been placed for new trains, including a £200 million order for 44 trains for the London, Tilbury and Southend service. Virgin Rail Group is planning to introduce a fleet of 40 high-speed tilting trains on the West Coast Main Line for delivery from 2001 onwards, and is to order new high-speed diesel trains for its cross-country routes.

Freight

Over 80 per cent of rail freight traffic by volume is of bulk commodities, mainly coal, coke, iron and steel, building materials and petroleum. The largest operator is English, Welsh & Scottish Railway (EWS). Since it acquired most of British Rail's freight businesses in 1995–96, EWS has won new traffic to rail, serving sites which have not had rail freight for many years. Freightliner operates container services between major ports and inland terminals. New freight

operators have had rights of open access to the rail network since 1994.

Government grants are available to encourage companies to move goods by rail or water rather than road. Since 1975 over 200 grants have been made, and it is estimated that some 3 million lorry journeys a year have been removed from the roads. The DETR budget for such grants in 1997–98 is about £30 million.

Northern Ireland

In Northern Ireland, the Northern Ireland Railways Company Ltd, a subsidiary of the Northern Ireland Transport Holding Company, operates the railway service on about 336 kilometres (211 miles) of track and handled over 6 million passenger journeys in 1996–97. The Belfast to Dublin service is being upgraded with new rolling stock, and an improved service was introduced in 1997.

Channel Tunnel

The Channel Tunnel, the largest civil engineering project in Europe to be financed by the private sector, was opened to traffic in 1994. The project, which is estimated to have cost about £10,000 million, was undertaken by Eurotunnel, a British-French group, under a 65-year operating concession from the British and French governments.

Eurotunnel Services

Eurotunnel operates shuttle trains through twin one-way rail tunnels between the terminals near Folkestone and Calais, with the journey taking about 35 minutes. These trains provide a drive-on, drive-off service, with separate shuttle trains for passenger and freight vehicles. Eurotunnel runs passenger shuttle services every 15 minutes and freight shuttle services every 20 minutes at peak periods. The service has taken about 40 per cent of the market for tourist vehicles making the crossing between Kent and northern France. Services were disrupted following a fire on a freight shuttle train in November 1996, but by June 1997 had been fully restored.

Eurostar Passenger Services

Up to 28 Eurostar high-speed train services run daily in each direction through the Channel Tunnel between London (Waterloo) and Paris or Brussels, taking less than 3 hours and 3 hours 10 minutes respectively. The London–Brussels journey will be cut to 2 hours 40 minutes when a new high-speed line in Belgium is opened; this is expected in early 1998. Eurostar services are operated by Eurostar (UK) Ltd—owned by London & Continental Railways (LCR)—French Railways and Belgian Railways. Passenger numbers are growing rapidly—nearly 5 million passengers travelled on Eurostar in 1996.

LCR is responsible for the design and construction of the £3,000 million Channel Tunnel Rail Link, a 108-km (67-mile) high-speed railway between London and the Channel Tunnel. Its London terminal will be at St Pancras, with intermediate stations at Stratford in east London, and Ebbsfleet and Ashford in Kent. Construction is expected to begin in 1998 and to be completed in 2003. When the new line is in operation, journey times for the London–Paris and London–Brussels services will be cut to 2 hours 20 minutes and 2 hours respectively.

Channel Tunnel Rail Freight

EWS is expected to acquire British Rail's Channel Tunnel freight business, Railfreight Distribution (RfD), later in 1997. RfD operates over 150 trains a week between Britain and the continent of Europe. It serves terminals at Willesden (London), Wakefield, Manchester, Mossend (near Glasgow), Daventry (Northamptonshire) and Hams Hall (Birmingham), and several terminals for automotive traffic. All these terminal facilities allow freight to be transferred easily between road and rail.

Other Railways in London

London Underground Ltd (LUL), a subsidiary of LT, operates services on 391 kilometres (242 miles) of railway, of which about 171 kilometres (106 miles) are underground. The system, the oldest in the world, has 267 stations, with 477 trains running in the peak period. About 772 million passenger journeys were made on London Underground trains in 1996–97.

The main investment project in the Underground is the extension of the Jubilee Line to Stratford (east London) via Docklands and the north Greenwich peninsula. London Underground aims to open the extension in September 1998. Other projects include a Private Finance Initiative project (see p. 160) for 106 new trains for the Northern Line, the first of which is due to enter service in autumn 1997. Nevertheless, cutbacks in investment have led to problems in maintaining the system. The Government is now looking at a range of public-private partnerships with the aim of bringing in substantial investment to modernise the Underground.

The Docklands Light Railway (DLR), a 22-km (14-mile) system with 28 stations, connects Docklands with the City of London, Beckton and Stratford. The railway is operated by Docklands Railway Management Ltd, owned jointly by Serco Group plc and a team of DLR managers, under a seven-year franchise from April 1997. The company will also operate an extension of the DLR under the River Thames to Greenwich and Lewisham, which is due to open in 1999–2000.

Construction has begun on the Croydon Tramlink, a 28-km (18-mile) light rail network which will connect Croydon with Wimbledon, Beckenham and New Addington and run partly along existing and disused railway track and partly along or beside roads. It is a joint project between LT and a private sector consortium, Tramtrack Croydon Ltd, which will build, operate and maintain the network. The project will cost £200 million, of which the DETR is providing a grant of £125 million, and is expected to open in late 1999.

Other Railways

The Glasgow Underground, a heavy rapid transit system, operates on a 10-km (6-mile) loop in central Glasgow. There has been growing interest in recent years in the development of light rail systems or the reintroduction of trams—traditional trams still operate in Blackpool and Llandudno. The

Tyne and Wear Metro is a 59-km (37-mile) light rail system connecting Newcastle upon Tyne with Gateshead, North and South Shields, Heworth and Jarrow. The Greater Manchester Metrolink connects Altrincham and Bury with Manchester city centre on a 31-km (19-mile) route. Various extensions to the Metrolink are planned, including a £144 million link to Manchester Airport. The South Yorkshire Supertram, a 29-km (18-mile) system, connects Meadowhall, Hillsborough and Halfway to Sheffield City Centre.

Construction work has started on Midland Metro Line One in Birmingham, which is expected to commence operation in summer 1998. Other approved schemes include the Leeds Supertram and the Greater Nottingham Light Rapid Transit.

Over 100 other passenger-carrying railways, many concerned with the preservation of steam locomotives, are to be found throughout Great Britain. Most are operated on a voluntary basis and provide limited services for tourists and railway enthusiasts. They generally run on former branch lines, but there are also several narrow-gauge lines, mainly in north Wales.

INLAND WATERWAYS

Inland waterways are popular for leisure and recreation and make a valuable contribution to the quality of Britain's environment. They also play a significant role in land drainage and water supply, and some are used for carrying freight. The greatest amounts of seagoing freight are carried on the Rivers Thames, Forth, Humber and Mersey and the Manchester Ship Canal. The most important waterways for internal traffic are the Thames, the Aire and Calder Navigation, the Mersey and the Manchester Ship Canal.

British Waterways is responsible for 3,200 kilometres (2,000 miles) of waterways in Great Britain, making up the greater part of the canal system. The majority of its waterways are primarily for leisure use, but about 620 kilometres (385 miles) are maintained as commercial waterways. In 1996–97 British Waterways' revenue amounted to £98.7 million, including a government grant of £51.8 million to maintain its waterways to statutory standards.

SHIPPING

The British merchant fleet has declined considerably in recent years. During 1996 the number of British-owned merchant trading ships of 100 gross tonnes or more fell from 675 to 638. Their total tonnage was 11.6 million deadweight tonnes. Among the ships were 155 vessels totalling 5.5 million deadweight tonnes used as oil, chemical or gas carriers and 450 vessels totalling 6.0 million deadweight tonnes employed as dry-bulk carriers, container ships or other types of cargo ship. In all, 73 per cent of British-owned vessels are registered in Britain or British Dependent Territories such as Bermuda.

The Government is considering, in consultation with shipping interests, ways of reviving the sector and developing its economic potential. Britain plays a significant role in the formulation of shipping policy within the EU. All international services and most cabotage services within the EU have been liberalised. Full cabotage liberalisation will be achieved over the next ten years. Work is progressing on a European programme to improve maritime safety and prevent pollution.

Cargo Services

Seaborne trade amounted to 354 million tonnes in 1996, with a value of £260,900 million (see Table 19.3). About 95 per cent by weight (75 per cent by value) of Britain's foreign trade is carried by sea. Tanker cargo accounted for 40 per cent of this trade by weight, but only 5 per cent by value.

Nearly all scheduled cargo-liner services from Britain are containerised. British tonnage serving these trades is dominated by a relatively small number of private sector companies. P & O has recently merged its container interests with those of Nedlloyd of the Netherlands to form the world's largest container operator. In deep-sea trades, shipping companies usually operate in conjunction with other companies on the same routes in organisations known as

Table 19.3: Britain's International Seaborne Trade by Weight and Value[a]

	1986	1991	1994	1995	1996
Weight (million tonnes)					
Dry bulk cargo	72.0	79.7	84.7	87.6	89.8
Other dry cargo	70.9	86.8	110.0	113.9	113.5
Tanker cargo	155.5	134.8	156.7	154.4	151.0
All cargo	**298.4**	**301.4**	**351.5**	**355.8**	**354.3**
Value (£'000 million)					
Dry bulk cargo	6.6	6.9	7.4	8.5	8.5
Other dry cargo	102.4	149.9	195.7	223.7	236.2
Tanker cargo	12.9	12.4	13.3	13.9	16.2
All cargo	**121.9**	**169.2**	**216.4**	**246.1**	**260.9**

Source: *Transport Statistics Great Britain*
[a] Exports (including re-exports) plus imports.
Note: Differences between totals and the sums of their component parts are due to rounding.

'conferences'. The object of these groupings is to ensure regular and efficient services with stable freight rates, to the benefit of both shipper and shipowner. Besides the carriage of freight by liner and bulk services between Britain and the rest of Europe, many roll-on roll-off services carry cars, passengers and commercial vehicles.

Passenger Services

In 1996, 35 million international sea passenger movements took place between Britain and the rest of the world, compared with about 105 million international air passenger movements. Almost all passengers who arrived at or departed from British ports travelled to or from the continent of Europe or the Irish Republic. In 1996 about 233,000 people embarked on, or landed from, pleasure cruises at British ports. Traffic from southern and south-eastern ports accounts for a substantial proportion of traffic to the continent of Europe.

The main British operators are Stena Sealink Line, P & O European Ferries and Hoverspeed, although not all their vessels are under the British flag. P & O and Stena have announced their intention to merge their services on the short-sea cross-Channel routes. Services are provided by roll-on roll-off ferries, hovercraft, hydrofoils and high-speed catamarans. There has been a trend towards using larger vessels, including new large high-speed vessels, as the ferry companies have faced growing competition from the Channel Tunnel.

Domestic passenger and freight ferry services also run to many of the offshore islands, such as the Isle of Wight, the Orkney and Shetland islands, and the islands off the west coast of Scotland.

Maritime Safety

The DETR currently has two executive agencies concerned with maritime safety and the prevention of marine pollution—the Coastguard Agency and the Marine Safety Agency (MSA)—which are to be merged into a single agency from April 1998. The Coastguard Agency is responsible for HM Coastguard and the Marine Pollution Control Unit (see pp. 351–2). The MSA is responsible for marine safety and the prevention of pollution from ships. It carries out inspections on British and foreign ships using British ports to ensure that they comply with international safety, pollution prevention and operational standards. In 1996–97, 157 overseas-registered ships were detained by the MSA in British ports.

HM Coastguard co-ordinates civil maritime search and rescue operations around the coastline of Britain. In a maritime emergency the coastguard calls on and co-ordinates facilities, such as:

- HM Coastguard helicopters and cliff rescue companies;

- lifeboats of the Royal National Lifeboat Institution (a voluntary body);

- aircraft, helicopters and ships from the armed forces; and

- merchant shipping and commercial aircraft.

Search and rescue incidents handled by HM Coastguard have grown considerably in recent years. In 1996 it co-ordinated action in nearly 11,300 incidents (including cliff rescues), in which over 19,200 people were helped.

Some locations around Britain are hazardous for shipping. Measures are taken to reduce the risk of collision, including the separation of ships into internationally agreed shipping lanes. For example, there is a traffic separation scheme in the Dover Strait, one of the world's busiest seaways. It is monitored by radar from the Channel Navigation Information Service near Dover.

Since the loss of the *Herald of Free Enterprise* in 1987, Britain has played a key role in securing safety improvements for roll-on roll-off ferries. Following the *Estonia* disaster in the Baltic Sea in 1995, Britain helped to conclude the Stockholm Agreement, which sets higher standards for the survivability of roll-on roll-off ferries within north-western Europe and the Baltic, with a phased timetable for implementation. Britain was the first country to sign the Agreement, and regulations applying it to roll-on roll-off ferries operating to and from British ports came into force in April 1997.

The lighthouse authorities, which control about 350 lighthouses and other lights and buoys, are:

- the Corporation of Trinity House, which covers England, Wales and the Channel Islands;

- the Northern Lighthouse Board, for Scotland and the Isle of Man; and

- the Commissioners of Irish Lights for Northern Ireland and the Irish Republic.

They are funded mainly by light dues levied on shipping in Britain and Ireland. Responsibility for some lights and buoys used for local navigation and for pilotage within harbours rests with harbour authorities.

PORTS

There are about 80 ports of commercial significance in Great Britain. In addition, several hundred small harbours cater for local cargo, fishing vessels, island ferries or recreation. There are three broad types of port—trust ports owned and run by boards constituted as trusts, those owned by local authorities and company-owned ports. Most operate with statutory powers. Major ports controlled by trusts include Aberdeen, Dover, Milford Haven and Tyne. Local authorities own many small ports and a few much larger ports, including Portsmouth and the oil ports in Orkney and Shetland. Seven trust ports have been privatised: Clyde, Dundee, Forth, Ipswich, Medway, Tees and Hartlepool, and Tilbury.

Associated British Ports (ABP), Britain's largest port owner, operates 23 ports, including Cardiff, Grimsby and Immingham, Hull, Newport, Southampton and Swansea. In March 1997 it acquired the port of Ipswich. Together its ports (excluding Ipswich) handled 118 million tonnes of cargo in 1996. Other major ports owned by private sector companies include Felixstowe, Liverpool, Manchester and a group of ferry ports, including Harwich (Parkeston Quay) and Stranraer.

Port Traffic

In 1996 traffic through major British ports amounted to a record 513 million tonnes. This comprised 168 million tonnes of exports, 181 million tonnes of imports and 164 million tonnes of domestic traffic (which included offshore traffic and landings of sea-dredged aggregates). The smaller ports handled an additional 38 million tonnes.

Britain's main ports, in terms of total tonnage handled, are shown in Table 19.4. Forth, Milford Haven and Sullom Voe (Shetland) mostly handle oil, while the principal ports for non-fuel traffic are London, Felixstowe, Grimsby and

Table 19.4: Traffic through the Principal Ports of Great Britain				*million tonnes*
	1992	1993	1994	1995	1996
London	48.9	50.9	51.8	51.4	52.9
Grimsby and Immingham	40.8	41.3	42.9	46.8	46.8
Forth	23.3	26.4	44.4	47.1	45.6
Tees and Hartlepool	43.4	42.7	43.0	46.1	44.6
Sullom Voe	41.4	39.4	38.6	38.3	38.2
Milford Haven	35.6	35.7	34.3	32.5	36.6
Southampton	29.8	30.9	31.5	32.4	34.2
Liverpool	27.8	30.5	29.5	30.0	34.1
Felixstowe	18.0	20.3	22.1	24.0	25.8
Medway	14.3	13.6	14.7	14.2	14.1

Source: DETR

Immingham, Tees and Hartlepool, and Liverpool.

Container and roll-on roll-off traffic in Britain was 108 million tonnes in 1996 and now accounts for 20 per cent of non-bulk traffic. The most important ports for container traffic are Felixstowe, Southampton and London. Dover is Britain's leading port for roll-on roll-off traffic. It is also the major passenger port, handling around half of international sea passenger movements to and from Britain.

Northern Ireland has four main ports, at Belfast, Larne, Londonderry and Warrenpoint. Belfast is the principal freight port, handling 15.7 million tonnes in 1996.

Development

Most recent major port developments have been at east- and south-coast ports. For example, Dover has a £100 million programme to develop its western docks to meet competition from the Channel Tunnel. ABP invests about £70 million a year in developing its port and transport facilities. New terminals for the steel traffic are planned at its ports at Hull, Goole and Newport, while major developments are planned at Immingham, Hull and Southampton.

Purpose-built terminals for oil from the British sector of the North Sea have been built at Hound Point on the Forth, on the Tees, at Flotta and at Sullom Voe (one of the largest oil terminals in the world). Supply bases for offshore oil and gas installations have been constructed at several ports, notably Aberdeen, Great Yarmouth, Montrose, Dundee and Heysham.

CIVIL AVIATION

British aviation authorities are negotiating new international rights and improving facilities such as air traffic control. British airlines are entirely in the private sector, as are many of the major airports.

Air Traffic

British airlines flew a record 1,102 million aircraft kilometres in 1996, 71 per cent higher than in 1986: 735 million kilometres on scheduled services and 367 million kilometres on non-scheduled flights. They carried 51 million passengers on scheduled services and 26 million on charter flights. Passenger seat occupancy was 78 per cent, being much higher on charter flights (nearly 89 per cent) than on scheduled services (73 per cent). It is also higher for international flights (79 per cent) than internal services (64 per cent).

Air freight is important for the carriage of goods with a high value-to-weight ratio, especially where speed is essential.

British Airways

British Airways is one of the world's leading airlines and in terms of international scheduled services it is the largest in the world. During 1996–97 its turnover from airline operations was £8,359 million. The

British Airways group, which employs 60,000 people worldwide, carried 38.2 million passengers on scheduled and charter flights both within Britain and internationally.

British Airways' scheduled route network serves almost 200 destinations in nearly 90 countries. Its main operating base is London's Heathrow Airport, with services also operational from Gatwick and regional centres such as Birmingham, Glasgow and Manchester. The airline has a fleet of 309 aircraft, one of the largest in Western Europe, including seven Concordes, 67 Boeing 747s and eight Boeing 777s.

Other Airlines

Other major British airlines operating internationally include:

- Air UK;
- Britannia Airways, the world's biggest charter airline, which carried 7.5 million passengers in 1996 and has 28 aircraft;
- British Midland, which operates a large network of scheduled services and has 34 aircraft;
- Monarch Airlines; and
- Virgin Atlantic, which has scheduled services to several overseas destinations including eight in North America, Johannesburg, Hong Kong and Tokyo.

Helicopters and Other Aerial Work

Helicopters are engaged on a variety of work, especially operations connected with Britain's offshore oil and gas industry. The main offshore operators in Britain are Bond Helicopters, British International Helicopters and Bristow Helicopters. Light aircraft and helicopters are also used in other important activities, such as charters, search and rescue services, load-lifting, aerial surveying and photography, and police and air ambulance operations.

Aviation Policies

The Government's main aviation policies are designed to promote efficient and safe air services within, to and from Britain; and to advance the interests of British airlines and passengers abroad. Day-to-day responsibility for the regulation of civil aviation rests with the Civil Aviation Authority (CAA), which also provides air traffic control services.

The Government's aim is to create an innovative climate in which both new and established airlines can compete equally to offer services to meet the needs of consumers. To achieve this, the Government negotiates with other governments to replace old, highly regulated arrangements by a new approach providing the opportunity for fair competition. Within the European Union, the Government has been in the forefront in pressing for measures to liberalise air transport, and now attaches priority to the elimination of state aid which distorts competition between EU airlines.

The Government wishes to ensure that airport capacity can be made available in response to future demand, but in a way that recognises, and takes reasonable account of, the effects on the environment.

Airports

Of over 140 licensed civil aerodromes in Britain, about one-fifth handle more than 100,000 passengers a year each. In 1996 Britain's civil airports handled a total of 137.3 million passengers (135.9 million terminal passengers and 1.4 million in transit), and 1.7 million tonnes of freight.

Heathrow is the world's busiest airport for international passengers and is Britain's most important airport for passengers and air freight, handling 56 million passengers (including transit passengers) and 1 million tonnes of freight in 1996. Gatwick is also one of the world's busiest international airports.

Ownership and Control

Seven airports—Heathrow, Gatwick, Stansted and Southampton in southern England, and Glasgow, Edinburgh and Aberdeen in Scotland—are owned and operated by BAA plc. Together they handle about 71 per cent of air passenger traffic and 81 per cent of air cargo in Britain. BAA is the world's largest commercial

Table 19.5: Passenger Traffic at Britain's Main Airports[a]				_million passengers_	
	1986	1991	1994	1995	1996
London Heathrow	31.3	40.2	51.4	54.1	55.7
London Gatwick	16.3	18.7	21.0	22.4	24.1
Manchester	7.5	10.1	14.3	14.5	14.5
Glasgow	3.1	4.2	5.5	5.4	5.5
Birmingham	2.1	3.2	4.8	5.2	5.4
London Stansted	0.5	1.7	3.3	3.9	4.8
Edinburgh	1.6	2.3	3.0	3.3	3.8
Newcastle	1.2	1.5	2.4	2.5	2.4
Luton	2.0	2.0	1.8	1.8	2.4
Belfast International	1.9	2.2	2.0	2.3	2.4
Aberdeen	1.5	2.0	2.2	2.2	2.4
East Midlands	1.1	1.1	1.6	1.9	1.8

Source: Civil Aviation Authority
[a] Terminal passengers.

operator of airports. It has overseas interests in the United States and Australia, is a member of a consortium which owns Melbourne Airport, and is a majority shareholder in the company running Naples Airport.

Some other airports are controlled by companies, such as Belfast International and Cardiff airports which are owned by TBI, and East Midlands which is run by National Express. A number of other airports, including Manchester, Luton and Newcastle, are owned by local authorities.

The CAA has responsibility for the economic regulation of the larger airports. It has powers to take action to remedy practices considered to be unreasonable or unfair, in particular any abuse of an airport's monopoly position, and also to limit increases in charges to airlines at certain airports. All airports used for public transport and training flights must be licensed by the CAA for reasons of safety. Stringent requirements, such as the provision of adequate fire-fighting, medical and rescue services, have to be satisfied before a licence is granted.

Strict security measures are in force at Britain's airports. Regulations require airlines to account for, and authorise for carriage, every item of hold baggage placed on board international flights originating in Britain.

Airport Development

Improvement schemes are in progress at many airports. At Heathrow, current developments include a £20 million new baggage reclaim hall in Terminal 1 and work in connection with the new Heathrow Express rail link to Central London (see p. 312). A planning inquiry is being held into a proposed fifth terminal at Heathrow, which could eventually cater for 30 million passengers a year. If approved, the terminal would probably open in 2004. BAA is spending £50 million on extending Edinburgh Airport, including providing a centralised check-in hall with greater capacity and a new international arrivals hall.

In 1997 the Government granted planning permission for a second runway at Manchester Airport. The 3,050-metre (10,000-ft) runway will be the first full-length runway to be built in Britain for 20 years and is expected to open in 2000.

Civil Aviation Authority

The CAA is responsible for promoting high standards of safety and service in civil aviation while minimising the regulatory burden on the industry. It certifies aircraft and air crews, licenses air operators and air travel organisers, and approves certain air fares and airport charges. The CAA also provides civilian air traffic control services in British airspace, the North Atlantic and at a number of airports through its subsidiary National Air Traffic Services Ltd (NATS). Co-ordination with military air traffic control is provided by an operating agreement between the Ministry of Defence and NATS.

Air Traffic Control and Navigation Services

Civil and military air traffic control over Britain and the surrounding seas, including much of the North Atlantic, is undertaken by NATS, working in collaboration with military controllers. Britain plays a major role in European air traffic control developments by participating in international forums. It has supported several European initiatives, including the establishment of a unit to manage traffic flows throughout Europe centrally, and a programme to harmonise and integrate European air traffic control.

Air traffic control facilities are dealing with the continuing growth in air traffic, while ensuring that delays to airlines are minimised. In 1996, only 1 per cent of flights arriving at Heathrow and Gatwick were delayed by over 20 minutes and the average delay in Britain for all aircraft was 2.8 minutes. Action is being taken by NATS to develop air traffic control capacity. All civil and military *en route* air traffic control operations in Britain will be concentrated at two sites:

- a new air traffic control centre, which is nearly complete, at Swanwick (Hampshire), to handle traffic over England and Wales; and

- a new Scottish centre to be built at Prestwick, under the Private Finance Initiative (see p. 160), which will handle traffic over Scotland and Northern Ireland and will replace the existing Prestwick centre.

Air Safety

British airlines have a good safety record. In all but two of the 15 years to 1997, there were no passenger fatalities in accidents involving large commercial British-registered aircraft in British airspace. During this period no crew or passenger fatalities associated with British-registered large commercial aircraft occurred in foreign airspace.

The DETR's Air Accidents Investigation Branch is responsible for the investigation of accidents and serious incidents occurring in British airspace and for those that happen overseas to aircraft registered or manufactured in Britain. In 1996 it investigated 362 accidents and serious incidents in Britain, and participated in 29 accident investigations overseas.

Every company operating aircraft used for commercial air transport purposes must possess an Air Operator's Certificate, which the CAA grants when it is satisfied that the company is competent to operate its aircraft safely. The CAA's flight operations inspectors, who are experienced civilian pilots, together with airworthiness surveyors, check that satisfactory standards are maintained. All aircraft registered in Britain must be granted a certificate of airworthiness by the CAA before being flown. In fulfilling its responsibilities, the CAA works closely with the Joint Aviation Authorities, a European grouping of aviation safety regulation authorities.

Each member of the flight crew of a British-registered aircraft, every ground engineer who certifies an aircraft fit to fly, and every air traffic controller must hold the appropriate licence issued by the CAA. To qualify for a first professional licence, a pilot must undertake a full-time course of instruction approved by the CAA—or have acceptable military or civilian flying experience—and pass ground examinations and flight tests.

To help safeguard aircraft against terrorist attacks, the Government is funding research, due to be completed during 1997, into ways of strengthening aircraft to withstand explosions.

Communications

Telecommunications is one of the most rapidly expanding sectors of the British economy. As well as basic telecommunications services, there has been growth in new services, such as services provided over the Internet—there are an estimated 5 million Internet or on-line users in Britain. Postal

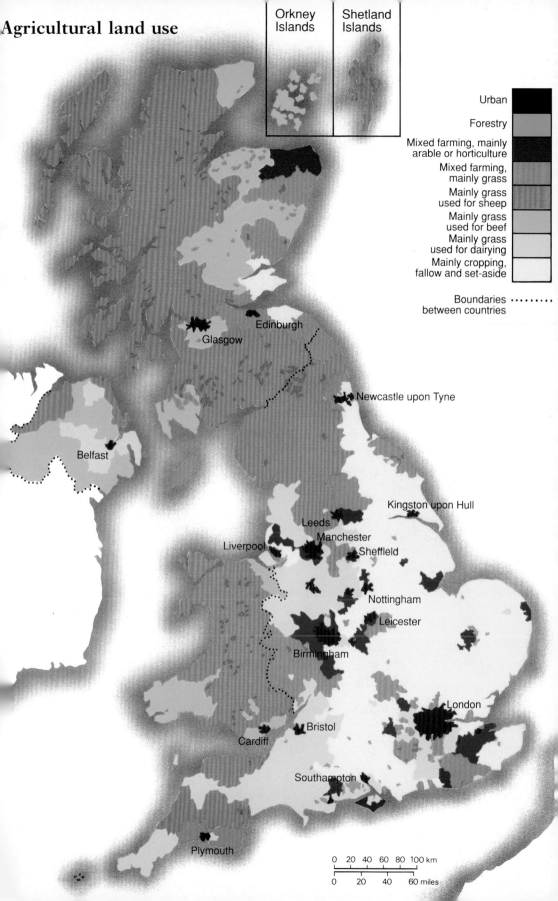

Agricultural land use

Orkney Islands

Shetland Islands

Urban

Forestry

Mixed farming, mainly arable or horticulture

Mixed farming, mainly grass

Mainly grass used for sheep

Mainly grass used for beef

Mainly grass used for dairying

Mainly cropping, fallow and set-aside

Boundaries between countries ·········

Glasgow

Edinburgh

Newcastle upon Tyne

Belfast

Kingston upon Hull

Leeds

Manchester

Liverpool

Sheffield

Nottingham

Leicester

Birmingham

London

Bristol

Cardiff

Southampton

Plymouth

0 20 40 60 80 100 km

0   20   40   60 miles

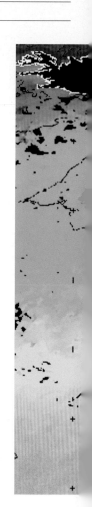

The symbol for Britain's Presidency of the European Union (January to June 1998) was created by bringing together children from all 15 EU countries. Working in pairs—one British child with a child from each of the other EU countries—they created artworks for stars which represent each of the member states. The central star was created by three British children working together.

UK Presidency of the European Union

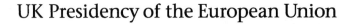

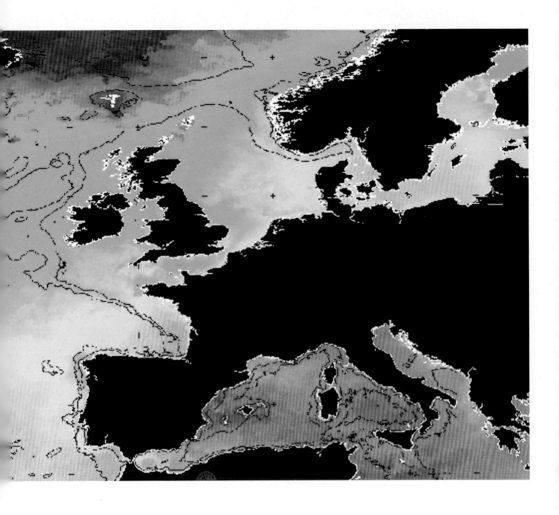

Two sea-surface temperature images
from a meteorological satellite,
one showing western Europe,
and the other the south west of England.
The data for these images were processed
by the Remote Sensing Group
of the Plymouth Marine Laboratory
in Devon: they show colour variations
relating to different water temperatures.

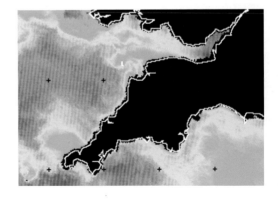

Major conservation and recreation areas

Orkney Islands

Shetland Islands

National Parks (Regional Parks in Scotland)

Forest Parks

Areas of Outstanding Natural Beauty (National Scenic Areas in Scotland)

Heritage Coast (Coastal Conservation Zones in Scotland)

National Trails

World Heritage Sites

SCOTLAND

Speyside Way

West Highland Way

Southern Upland Way

NORTHERN IRELAND

Northumberland

North York Moors

Cleveland Way

Wolds Way

Lake District

Yorkshire Dales

Pennine Way

Peak District

Snowdonia

Offa's Dyke Path

The Broads

Peddars Way and Norfolk Coast Path

(Special protected area)

WALES

ENGLAND

Pembrokeshire Coast

Brecon Beacons

Pembrokeshire Coast Path

Ridgeway

Thames Path

North Downs Way

South Downs Way

Exmoor

Dartmoor

South West Coast Path

South West Coast Path

0 20 40 60 80 100 km

0 20 40 60 miles

services remain important, and the volume of mail continues to increase.

TELECOMMUNICATIONS

Britain was one of the first countries to introduce competition in its telecommunications network. It has one of the world's most open telecommunications markets, with over 200 licences issued to more than 150 different providers. In late 1996 the market for international services was opened up, with the granting of over 50 licences. Within the EU, full liberalisation of telecommunications services and networks across most markets will take effect on 1 January 1998.

Effective competition exists in most larger urban areas of Britain, especially in commercial centres such as the City of London, as new fixed link operators have extended their networks. International calls have also been opened up to competition as new operators offer services over leased lines. This has resulted in improved choice for users, with lower prices, greater choice of supplier, and lower levels of call failure. Investment is running at around £6,000 million a year.

> Negotiations in the World Trade Organisation (see p. 206) on trade in basic telecommunications services were concluded in February 1997. The agreement, covering 69 countries responsible for 92 per cent of the world market, is expected to facilitate further expansion of the rapidly growing world telecommunications market—now worth some US$600,000 million a year—and to lead to substantial opportunities for British operators and suppliers.

Office of Telecommunications

OFTEL, a non-ministerial government department, is the independent regulatory body for the telecommunications industry. It is headed by the Director General of Telecommunications, whose functions include:

- ensuring that licensees comply with the conditions of their licences;
- promoting effective competition in the telecommunications industry;
- providing advice to the President of the Board of Trade on telecommunications matters; and
- investigating complaints against public telecommunications operators.

Rapid developments in the telecommunications sector are changing the emphasis of OFTEL's work. It is moving away from detailed regulation in basic domestic telecommunications services and looking to ensure that competition applies in international and mobile services, and to consider the effects of the convergence of the telecommunications and broadcasting sectors.

BT

BT, which has been a private sector company since 1984, is Britain's biggest telecommunications company, running one of the world's largest public telecommunications networks, including:

- over 20 million residential lines;
- 7 million business customer connections;
- 7,500 local telephone exchanges and 69 main switching units;
- over 136,000 public payphones; and
- a wide range of specialised voice, data, text and visual services.

BT handles an average of 103 million local, national and international telephone calls a day. International direct dialling is available from Britain to more than 230 countries, representing 99 per cent of the world's telephones.

BT has invested over £27,000 million since 1984 in the modernisation and expansion of its network, to meet increasing demand and to introduce specialised services. The company has over 2 million kilometres of optical fibre laid in its network in Britain. Modern digital exchanges now serve a large majority of BT's customers. The combination of digital exchange switching and digital transmission techniques, using optical fibre cable and microwave radio links, is improving the quality of telephone services substantially. It also makes possible the provision of a wider range of services through the company's main network.

BT's services include:

- a free facility for emergency calls to the police, fire, ambulance, coastguard, lifeboat and air–sea rescue services;
- directory enquiries;
- public payphone services;
- various chargeable operator–connected services, such as reversed–charge ('collect') calls;
- an operator-handled 'Freefone' service and automatic Freefone and 'Lo-call' facilities that enable callers to contact organisations anywhere in Britain, either free or at local call rates;
- premium–rate services which allow callers to obtain information from independent providers; and
- select network services such as caller display, reminder calls, three-way calling, call waiting and call diversion, which are available to customers on digital exchanges.

BT has also been developing its Internet and other multimedia activities, for example, as an Internet service provider. Its 'Campus' facilities cater for education and training needs, while trials of many healthcare activities, such as remote foetal scanning, have taken place over BT's network. It is participating with BSkyB, Midland Bank and Matsushita in British Interactive Broadcasting, which has been set up to offer interactive services, such as home shopping, to television viewers.

BT is the second largest shareholder in the International Telecommunications Satellite Organisation (INTELSAT), of which 141 countries are members, and a major investor in the European Telecommunications Satellite Organisation (EUTELSAT). It is also the second largest shareholder in the International Maritime Satellite Organisation (INMARSAT), and has interests in several other consortia.

BT operates satellite earth stations in London Docklands and at Goonhilly Downs (Cornwall), Madley (near Hereford), Aberdeen, and Mormond Hill (Grampian). In-flight operator-controlled telephone call facilities for air passengers are provided via Portishead radio station near Bristol. Digital transmission techniques have been introduced for services to the United States, Japan, Hong Kong and Australia via the Madley and Goonhilly stations.

Cable & Wireless

Cable & Wireless plc supplies a wide range of telecommunications services in over 50 countries. Its main business is the provision and operation of public telecommunications services in more than 30 countries and territories, under franchises and licences granted by the governments concerned. Over one-third of its turnover of £7,000 million in 1996-97 came from its interests in Hong Kong. In June 1997 the company reached agreement to reduce its majority stakeholding in Hong Kong Telecom. Eventually, it will have an equal stake with China Telecom in Hong Kong Telecom, and in return will participate in a new venture allowing access to the telecommunications market in China.

Cable & Wireless also supplies and manages telecommunications services and facilities for public and private sector customers, and undertakes consultancy work worldwide. Its fleet of cableships and submersible vehicle systems for laying and maintaining submarine cables is the largest in the world.

Cable & Wireless Communications

A major change in the telecommunications sector in Britain took place in October 1996 with the formation of Cable & Wireless Communications plc from the merger of Bell Cablemedia, Mercury Communications, NYNEX CableComms and Videotron. It is the largest integrated supplier in Britain of telecommunications, information and entertainment services, and is the operating arm of Cable & Wireless plc.

Cable & Wireless Communications has around 10 per cent of the telecommunications market in Britain, and serves about 1.1 million private telephone customers and 80,000 businesses. It is offering local, national and international telecommunications services, including data, television and Internet services, and is planning to develop interactive multimedia services.

Other Operators

Other public telecommunications operators include:

- COLT, which focuses on business customers in the Greater London area;
- Energis, which is using the electricity infrastructure as a platform for installing new optical fibre networks;
- Ionica, which in 1996 launched a service using radio to provide the final connection to customers, initially in East Anglia;
- Kingston Communications, the long-established network operator for the Kingston upon Hull area in Yorkshire;
- Sprint, a major long-distance telephone company in the United States, which is seeking to expand its domestic and international services in Britain; and
- Vodafone, the biggest mobile operator, which also has a licence for fixed services.

Nearly all of the 134 local cable television franchises in operation also offer voice telephony services. By April 1997 cable operators had installed nearly 2.5 million telephone lines in Britain, and over 9 million homes were able to receive broadband cable services.

Mobile Communications

There are now over 7 million mobile telephone users in Britain, one of the most extensive networks in the world. Vodafone and Telecom Securicor Cellular Radio (Cellnet) are the two largest operators, running competing national cellular radio systems. They have 3 million and 2.8 million subscribers respectively.

Britain was the first country to offer personal communications network (PCN)

services, which are intended to allow the same telephone to be used at home, at work and as a portable within the network's coverage. There are two PCN operators: Orange (controlled by Hutchison Whampoa), with around 1.1 million customers, and One-2-One (owned by Cable & Wireless and Cable West), with some 800,000 subscribers.

National Band Three Ltd is licensed to offer a nationwide trunked radio service, while 33 licences have been awarded for London and regional services. National Band Three and Tetra Link have been licensed to offer significantly enhanced digital radio services to companies. Other licences awarded include four to operate mobile data networks, four to run nationwide paging networks, three to run national digital broadband services and two to serve remote rural areas.

In July 1997 the Government issued a consultation document about the arrangements for licensing the third generation of mobile telephones, which will provide high-speed access to a large number of entertainment and information services.

POSTAL SERVICES

The Post Office, founded in 1635, pioneered postal services and was the first to issue adhesive postage stamps as proof of advance payment for mail. Royal Mail delivers to 26 million addresses in Britain, handling over 72 million letters each working day. This comes to around 18,000 million items a year, while Parcelforce handles over 140 million items. Mail is collected from over 120,000 sites, including posting boxes, post offices and large postal users.

The Government is reviewing options for giving the Post Office greater commercial freedom. It wants the Post Office to be able to take advantage of new opportunities and reach its full potential, both within Britain and internationally, while ensuring fair competition with the private sector.

Royal Mail has invested substantially in the latest mail-sorting technology, and mechanisation has been introduced at all stages of the sorting process. New high-speed mail-handling machinery—the Integrated Mail Processor—was introduced in 1997 and should enable automatic handling of 90 per cent of letter mail by 2000. Automatic sorting utilises the information contained in the postcode; the British postcode system is one of the most sophisticated in the world, allowing mechanised sorting down to part of a street on a postman's round and, in some cases, to an individual address. Royal Mail has recently invested £150 million in new high-speed mail trains, with eight terminals, including a new road-rail interchange in north London.

Royal Mail International dispatches 805 million items a year. It has its own mail-handling centre at Heathrow, which handles about four-fifths of outward airmail. It uses 1,400 flights a week to send mail direct to over 300 destinations worldwide.

Post Office Counters Ltd handles a wide range of transactions; it acts as an agent for Royal Mail and Parcelforce, government departments, local authorities and Alliance & Leicester Giro banking services. Several new services have been developed, such as bureaux de change. There are just over 19,300 post offices, of which around 600 are operated directly by the Post Office. The remainder are franchise offices or are operated on an agency basis by sub-postmasters.

Post Office Specialist Services

The Post Office offers a variety of specialist services. Parcelforce 'Datapost', a door-to-door delivery service, provides overnight delivery throughout Britain and an international service to 140 countries. 'Datapost Sameday' provides a rapid delivery within or between major cities in Britain. The Philatelic Bureau in Edinburgh is an important outlet for the Post Office's philatelic (postage stamp) business, including sales to overseas collectors or dealers. The British Postal Consultancy Service offers advice and assistance on all aspects of postal business to overseas postal administrations, and over 50 countries have used its services since 1965.

Private Courier and Express Service Operators

Private sector couriers and express operators are allowed to handle time-sensitive door-to-door deliveries, subject to a minimum fee of £1. The courier/express service industry has grown rapidly and the revenue earned by the carriage of these items is estimated at over £3,000 million a year. Britain is one of the main providers of monitored express deliveries in Europe, with London an important centre for air courier/express traffic.

Further Reading

Developing an Integrated Transport Policy: An Invitation to Contribute. Department of the Environment, Transport and the Regions, Department of the Environment for Northern Ireland, The Scottish Office and the Welsh Office, 1997.

Transport Statistics Great Britain, annual report. The Stationery Office.

20 Science and Technology

Britain has a long tradition of research and innovation in science, engineering and technology in universities, research institutes and industry. With just 1 per cent of the world's population, it carries out more than 5 per cent of global research and development (R & D). British-based scientists are second only to those of the United States in the production of published papers and achievement of citations. They have won more Nobel Prizes for science—over 70—than any country except the United States. The most recent British winners are Professor Sir Harold Kroto of Sussex University, who shared the 1996 chemistry prize with two US scientists for discovering the fullerene molecule; Professor James Mirrlees, who shared the economics prize with William Vickery of Canada; and John Walker of the Medical Research Council's Laboratory of Molecular Biology, who shared the 1997 chemistry prize with Jens Skou of Denmark and Paul Boyer of the USA.

Innovation—the successful exploitation of new ideas—is vital to the health of the economy. Many of these new ideas stem from R & D. Hence Government policy seeks to re-invigorate the science and engineering base (see p. 328) and to maintain Britain's international position of scientific excellence, so as to maximise the contribution of science, engineering and technology to economic competitiveness and improving the quality of life. A key role is played by the public sector as the prime funder of purely curiosity-driven (or basic) science: as well as playing a crucial part in advancing scientific knowledge and producing well-trained researchers, such research can often lead to unexpectedly exploitable results.

Business has the prime responsibility for researching and developing new and improved products and services, while government tries to create the climate for the development of new ideas and to facilitate technology transfer and access. The Government aims to encourage industry to invest more in R & D and take a longer-term view of R & D investment.

Government policies on science, engineering and technology will be developed in the light of the overall public spending review and of its findings of the Dearing Committee Report on the financing of higher education (see p. 451). The Government aims to improve the way in which science is used to formulate and execute policy across government departments. Britain's participation in European Union (EU) co-operative R & D will be strengthened; negotiations are in progress regarding the content and organisation of the EU Fifth Framework Programme, due to run from 1998 to 2002 (see p. 336).

BACKGROUND

British achievements in science and technology in the 20th century include fundamental contributions to molecular genetics through the discovery of the three-dimensional molecular structure of DNA (deoxyribonucleic acid) by Francis Crick, Maurice Wilkins, James Watson and Rosalind Franklin in 1953 and of cholesterol, vitamin D, penicillin and insulin by Dorothy Hodgkin.

Notable contributions in other areas over the past 25 years have been made by Stephen Hawking in improving the understanding of the nature and origin of the universe; Brian Josephson in superconductivity (abnormally high electrical conductivity at low temperatures); Martin Ryle and Antony Hewish in radio astrophysics; and Godfrey Hounsfield in computer-assisted tomography (a form of radiography) for medical diagnosis.

Other pioneering work includes the discovery in 1985 by British Antarctic Survey scientists of the hole in the ozone layer over the Antarctic. Researchers at the Laboratory of Molecular Biology, Cambridge, produced the first monoclonal antibodies—proteins produced by genetic engineering with enormous potential in the diagnosis and treatment of disease. More recently there have been several British breakthroughs in genetics research, including the identification of the gene in the Y chromosome responsible for determining sex, and the identification of other genes linked to diseases such as cystic fibrosis and a form of breast cancer. The world's first pig with a genetically modified heart was bred by scientists at Cambridge University, an important milestone in breeding animals as organ donors for people. In 1997 scientists at the Roslin Institute in Edinburgh succeeded in 'cloning' a sheep using a cell from the sheep's mammary gland.

Other examples of notable R & D successes in the chemicals, electronics, software and aerospace sectors, all areas where Britain excels, are given below. (For R & D work in materials, see chapter 15, p. 224.)

Chemicals

Research undertaken by the chemicals industry over the past few years has led to many significant technological and commercial breakthroughs. New synthetic fibres, detergent formulations and catalytic processes have been developed in Britain. Pharmaceuticals is the most research-intensive sector of the chemicals industry. British firms have been responsible for discovering and developing five of the world's 20 best-selling drugs (see p. 219). Research conducted by ICI, Glaxo Wellcome, SmithKline Beecham and Fisons led to the development of the first successful beta blockers, drugs used in the treatment of cardiovascular conditions; semi-synthetic penicillins; vaccines; and treatments for cancer, asthma, migraine, arthritis and HIV/AIDS. More than 200 potential new medicines are currently under development in British laboratories.

The biotechnology sector continues to grow, with an increasing number of specialist companies contributing to scientific breakthroughs. Many research projects focus on the application of biotechnology to pharmaceuticals and chemicals, food and agriculture, and the environment industries.

Electronics

British firms and research organisations have led in the development and application of semiconductors, including the 'three-five' semiconductor materials (such as gallium arsenide). These materials have many uses, including lasers for optical fibre communications, microwave devices for satellite communications, and high-efficiency solar cells.

Firms such as BT have been at the forefront in developing optical fibre cable; BT produced the first all-optical repeater. Software engineering for telecommunications and other applications is another area where Britain excels. Engineers are developing 'virtual reality' techniques used for designing buildings, vehicles, pharmaceuticals and a host of other products. Electronic medical equipment made in Britain is sold all over the world; Britain pioneered magnetic resonance imaging.

Aerospace

Pioneering British achievements since the 1930s include radar, jet engines, Concorde (with France), automatic landing, vertical take-off and landing, flight simulators, ejector seats and head-up displays. British Aerospace, with Marconi and Dowty Boulton Paul, devised a system known as 'fly-by-wire', in which flying control surfaces are moved by electronic rather than mechanical means. British Aerospace is currently working with government and academic laboratories on the use of 'smart materials' in aircraft. These are structures within the aircraft which can continuously monitor for signs of damage or wear and communicate with the pilot through fibre optic cables, thereby improving safety and lowering maintenance costs.

Among overseas private sector companies with major R & D investments in Britain are Daewoo, Du Pont, Psizer, IBM, Johnson & Johnson, Nissan, Sharp and Sony. Eight of the United States' top ten software firms, including Microsoft (see p. 340), have large-scale R & D facilities in Britain. South-east England has the highest concentration of R & D operations. The strong industry-academic links that exist in Britain are one of the main reasons quoted for locating in the country.

RESEARCH AND DEVELOPMENT EXPENDITURE

Total expenditure in Britain on scientific R & D in 1995 was £14,300 million, 2.05 per cent of gross domestic product (compared with 2.11 per cent in 1994). Expenditure on civil R & D was £12, 200 million in 1995, the rest going to defence projects. Since the ending of

Table 20:1 Company Spending on R&D

	R & D annual investment (£ million)	R & D as % of sales
Glaxo Wellcome	1,161	13.9
SmithKline Beecham	764	9.6
Zeneca	602	11.2
Unilever	600	1.8
Shell Transport & Trading	449	0.5
General Electric	432	6.9
Ford Motors	320	4.5
BT	282	2.0
Reuters	202	6.9
Rolls-Royce	199	4.6
ICI	191	1.8
British Aerospace	156	2.4

Source: *The 1997 UK R & D Scoreboard*, DTI
Note: R & D spending includes spending overseas.

the Cold War, there has been a marked shift in the balance between civil and defence-related R & D, reflected, for example, in a reduction in real terms in aerospace R & D. As a percentage of GDP, defence spending on R & D declined from 0.5 to 0.3 per cent between 1990 and 1995.

About 48 per cent of total funding was provided by industry and 33 per cent by government; a further 14 per cent came from abroad. Significant contributions were also made by private endowments, trusts and charities. As well as financing R & D carried out in industry itself, industry also supports university research and finances contract research at government establishments. Some charities have their own laboratories and offer grants for outside research. Contract research organisations carry out R & D for companies and are playing an increasingly important role in the transfer of technology to British industry.

Total spending on R & D in industry amounted to £9,400 million in 1995. Of this total, British industry's own contribution was 69 per cent, with 12 per cent from government and the rest from overseas. The chemistry and biotechnology-based sectors—chemicals, pharmaceuticals and healthcare—account for 28 per cent of R & D spending by listed companies; electronics and aerospace are also big investors in R & D. The three biggest investors in R & D—Glaxo Wellcome, SmithKline Beecham and Zeneca—are all in the pharmaceuticals sector (see Table 20:1).

GOVERNMENT ROLE

Science and technology issues as a whole are the responsibility of a Cabinet Minister at the Department of Trade and Industry (DTI), assisted by a Minister of State; they are supported by the Office of Science and Technology (OST), a separate entity within the DTI. The OST is headed by the Government's Chief Scientific Adviser. It provides a central focus for the development of government policy on science, engineering and technology, both nationally and internationally. In addition, it co-ordinates science and technology policy across government departments. The Director General of Research Councils reports directly to the Cabinet on the Science Budget and other matters. The Science Budget covers expenditure in the academic sector, Research Council institutes and units, certain international research centres funded by the six funding Research Councils and from grant in aid to the Royal Society and the Royal Academy of Engineering.

The term 'science and engineering base' is used to describe the research and postgraduate training capacity based in the universities and colleges of higher education and in establishments operated by the Research Councils and government departments, together with the national and international central facilities (such as CERN—see p. 336) supported by the Councils and available for use by British scientists and engineers. There are also important contributions from private institutions, chiefly those funded by charities. The science and engineering base is the main provider of basic research and much of the strategic research (research likely to have practical applications) carried out in Britain. It also collaborates with the private sector in the conduct of specific applied research. Nearly two-thirds of the Government's spending on

The Government works to help Britain strengthen its position as a world leader in the global information society.

- *ISI: Programme for Business* is designed to help British business exploit the potential of information and communication tools and technology. Through awareness projects, award schemes and a network of local support centres, the programme encourages the development and delivery of information technologies and their adoption by businesses, especially smaller firms.

- *IT for All* aims to remove social, educational and psychological barriers facing non-users of IT, by raising awareness of the new technologies and providing access to them.

The programmes involve partnership between government, business, trade associations, professional institutions, voluntary groups and the general public. Current participants include Microsoft, BT, IBM, Dixons and ICL, as well as the Open University and the British Deaf Association.

civil R & D supports basic and strategic research undertaken in the science and engineering base.

The OST has specific responsibility for the Science Budget and the government-financed Research Councils (see pp. 337–40): the Engineering and Physical Sciences Research Council (EPSRC); the Medical Research Council (MRC); the Particle Physics and Astronomy Research Council (PPARC); the Natural Environment Research Council (NERC); the Biotechnology and Biological Sciences Research Council (BBSRC); the Economic and Social Research Council (ESRC); and the Council for the Central Laboratory of the Research Councils (CCLRC). OST funding provides assistance for research, through the Research Councils, in the following ways: by awarding grants and contracts to universities and other higher education establishments and to research units; funding Research Council establishments to perform research or to provide facilities and expertise in support of research supporting postgraduate study; and subscribing to international scientific organisations. The OST also provides funding for some programmes administered through the Royal Society and the Royal Academy of Engineering (see p. 341). The other main sources of finance for universities are the higher education funding councils (see p. 452).

Strategy and Finance

Government finance goes to research establishments, higher education institutions and private industry, as well as collaborative research programmes. Total net government expenditure on science and technology (both civil and defence) in 1997–98 is £6,300 million, of which £3,800 million will be devoted to civil science. The Science Budget totals £1,330 million for 1997–98. Among government departments, the Ministry of Defence (MoD—see p. 332) has the largest research budget. The main civil departments are the Department of Trade and Industry (DTI—see p. 331), the Department of the Environment, Transport and the Regions (DETR—see p. 333) and the Ministry of Agriculture, Fisheries and Food (MAFF—see p. 333).

The funding and organisation of British science, engineering and technology have changed considerably in recent years, in accordance with the White Paper, *Realising Our Potential: A Strategy for Science, Engineering and Technology*. Published in 1993, this was the first major review of science for over 20 years. It aimed to create a closer partnership between government, industry and the scientific community in developing strengths in areas of importance to the future economic well-being of Britain. It established the **Foresight Programme** for the public and private sectors to work together to identify opportunities in markets and technologies likely to emerge over the next 10 to 20 years, and the actions to be taken to exploit them. Government priorities in science, engineering and technology programmes, and in government regulation and

training responsibilities, are being guided by the Programme.

The Foresight Programme is co-ordinated by a joint industry/academic steering group headed by the Government's Chief Scientific Adviser. The steering group identified six cross-sectoral themes or priority areas:

- communications and computing power (with applications in all economic sectors);
- new organisms, products and processes from genetics (with applications in health, agriculture, food and environmental protection);
- materials science, engineering and technology;
- production processes and services;
- pollution monitoring and control technologies, and technologies for conserving energy and other resources; and
- social trends (improving understanding of human factors involved in markets and scientific advance).

Sixteen sector panels, made up of people from industry, academia and government, examine opportunities in specific branches of science, engineering and technology. Government departments, universities and higher education funding councils, as well as the Research Councils, are reflecting Foresight priorities in their research spending allocations. The private sector is encouraged to take account of the priorities both in its participation in collaborative research programmes and in its own strategic planning. The Government is providing £30 million over four years for the first round of the Foresight Challenge Competition, to fund collaborative R & D projects which address priorities identified by the Foresight panels. This is complemented by a further £62 million from private sector project participants. An additional £200 million or so has already been channelled into other Foresight initiatives.

ROPA AND CASE

The Realising Our Potential Award (ROPA) scheme focuses on researchers already working closely with industry. Managed by the Research Councils, it provides funding for separate 'curiosity-driven' research. To date, the total value of ROPA awards amounts to £109 million for more than 1,200 projects; this includes government funding of £19.5 million for 1997. The Government also makes funds available through the Research Councils for the Co-operative Awards in Science and Engineering (CASE) scheme, which supports students on research projects jointly supervised with industry.

EQUAL—Extend Quality Life

One of the principal issues facing Britain in the years ahead is a growing elderly population. Life expectancy has risen, but has not been matched by an increase in years free from disability. The EQUAL scheme aims to examine the effects of lifestyle and diet on health, and to develop technologies to enhance the quality of life of an ageing population.

LINK

The LINK scheme provides a government-wide framework for collaborative research in support of wealth creation and improvement of the quality of life. It aims to promote partnerships in commercially relevant research projects between industry and higher education institutions and other research base organisations. Under the scheme, government departments and Research Councils fund up

---

Government is contributing £5 million to a LINK research programme concerned with promoting sustainable production of cereals and other arable crops. It is being supported by the Ministry of Agriculture, Fisheries and Food, The Scottish Office, the Department of the Environment, Transport and the Regions, and the BBSRC, in conjunction with industry. Priority research areas include 'precision farming'; alternative methods of pest, disease and weed control; sustainable soil management systems; and control of resistance to pesticides.

---

to 50 per cent of the cost of research projects, with industry providing the balance. So far there have been 56 LINK programmes; more than 800 projects worth over £410 million have been started, with the participation of 1,100 companies and 180 research base institutions. Since 1995, 17 new programmes have been announced in response to priorities identified by the Foresight Programme: for instance, in 1996 the DTI and the EPSRC launched an £8 million LINK programme on sensors and sensor systems for industrial applications.

SMART—Small Firms Award for Research and Technology

Following a review of government support for R & D by small businesses, a new locally operated single SMART scheme was introduced in England in April 1997. Under this, financial assistance is available for feasibility studies into innovative technology (up to £45,000 for independent firms with fewer than 50 employees) and for development up to pre-production prototype stage of new products and processes involving a significant technological advance (in most cases, up to 200,000 ECUs for independent businesses with fewer than 250 employees). The new scheme reflects the objectives of the Foresight Programme. Business Links (see p. 195) have an important role in generating suitable R & D projects, assisting firms to submit applications for SMART awards and ensuring assisted projects are fully exploited commercially. Separate schemes are operated in Scotland, Wales and Northern Ireland.

Public Awareness

The Government seeks to raise the status of science, engineering and technology among the general public, by increasing awareness of the contribution that they make to Britain's economic wealth and quality of life; and by improving the understanding of scientific terms, concepts and issues, so that public debate on controversial scientific and technological issues becomes better informed. Raising awareness is also important in encouraging young people to pursue careers in science and engineering. To this end, it supports activities such as the annual science festival of the British Association for the Advancement of Science (BAAS) and the National Week of Science, Engineering and Technology. The fourth of these Weeks, held in March 1997, consisted of 1,600 events held all over Britain, attracting more than 1 million visitors.

The year 1997 was designated the *Year of Engineering Success* (*YES*). This initiative is intended to increase public awareness of the role of engineers in wealth creation and life enhancement and is fully supported by both the engineering profession and industry.

Science festivals are a growing feature of local co-operative efforts to further understanding of the contribution made by science to everyday life. Schools, museums, laboratories, higher education institutions and industry contribute to a variety of special events. The oldest festival is the British Association Annual Festival of Science, held at a British university. The BAAS helps organise the National Science, Engineering and Technology Week. The largest science festival in one place is the annual Edinburgh International Science Festival; in 1997 it included 260 events and attracted about 175,000 visitors.

The Committee on the Public Understanding of Science (COPUS), set up by the Royal Society, the BAAS and the Royal Institution (see p. 342), acts as a co-ordinator for those fostering public understanding and promotes best practice in the field. COPUS awards small grants on behalf of both OST and the Royal Society and, jointly with the Science Museum, administers the Rhone-Poulenc Prize for Science Books.

Role of Women

A Development Unit was set up in the OST in response to an independent report which found that women were still under-represented in the science, engineering and technology sectors, especially at senior levels. It also disclosed that many women drop out of a science career, often to raise children, and do not return. The Unit has highlighted the economic and other benefits to business of providing a working environment sensitive to the needs of women scientists and engineers who combine a career and family responsibilities. It seeks to ensure that careers information for girls and women is widely available and to promote good employment practices. Measures are being taken by government and others to publicise best practice in childcare facilities, job sharing, flexible working and career breaks.

GOVERNMENT DEPARTMENTS

Department of Trade and Industry

In 1997–98 DTI's planned expenditure on science, engineering and technology is £363 million. This covers innovation and technology, aeronautics, space (see p. 334), and nuclear and non-nuclear energy. In supporting these activities, DTI's overall aim is to work in partnership with business, the science and technology base, the education sector, other government departments and interested organisations, to bring about improved innovation performance across the whole range of business sectors and thereby help companies compete more effectively in global markets. DTI's role includes working to change attitudes in favour of innovation in industry; encouraging partnerships and the exchange of people and knowledge between companies, colleges and universities; improving the accessibility of finance for emerging technology based firms with growth potential; and to help small firms overcome obstacles to growth.

For the DTI, innovation frequently involves not only a commitment to research and development and the adoption or adaptation of new and existing technologies, but also the improvement of every other aspect of business, including finance, marketing, design, management of people and people skills. Through its Innovation Unit, a mixed team of seconded industrialists and government officials, DTI seeks to encourage and facilitate business, education, the media, government and the general public to adopt innovation as a vital contribution to improved performance, international competitiveness and sustainable growth. In Northern Ireland the Industrial Research and Technology Unit has a similar role to that of the DTI, supporting industrial R & D, technology transfer and innovation.

Academic-Business Partnerships

The DTI is spending almost £50 million on technology transfer and access in 1997–98. It aims to increase the number and quality of partnerships between the science, engineering and technology base and industry; improve access to sources of technology and technological expertise; improve the capacity of industry to use technology effectively; and increase the uptake of the latest technology and best practice techniques.

An example of a technology transfer programme is TCS (formerly known as the Teaching Company Scheme), which has 11 government department and Research Council sponsors, and for which DTI has the main responsibility. Currently, over 1,000 graduates have places on TCS programmes, which enable them to work in industry, normally for two years, on technology transfer projects under the joint supervision of academic and company staff. There are also 19 TCS Centres for Small Firms designed to make it easier for small firms to gain access to technology in universities and to demonstrate the benefits of employing graduates.

Aeronautics

The DTI's Civil Aircraft Research and Demonstration Programme (CARAD) supports research and technology demonstration in aeronautics, enabling the industry to compete effectively in world markets (see p. 226). In 1997–98 the provision for aeronautics research and technology demonstration is £23 million. The programme is an essential part of a national aeronautics research effort, with over half of the supported research work being conducted in industry and the universities, and the remainder at the Defence Evaluation and Research Agency

(DERA—see below). CARAD and earlier programmes have supported projects across the range of aeronautics technologies, including compressors, turbines, noise, nacelles and materials. They have helped Rolls-Royce to increase its share of the large civil engine market (see p. 228), and British Aerospace has become Europe's foremost designer and manufacturer of wings for large civil aircraft. Launch Aid is a means of providing government assistance for specific development projects in the aerospace industry.

Measurement Standards

The DTI finances the development of new measurement standards under the National Measurement System (NMS—see p. 194) and materials metrology programmes. Most of the work is carried out at the National Physical Laboratory (NPL), the Laboratory of the Government Chemist (LGC) and the National Engineering Laboratory (NEL). Spending about £34 million a year, the NMS provides an infrastructure to ensure that measures can be made on a consistent basis throughout Britain. The accelerating pace of technological change and the greater awareness of the importance of quality and innovation have led to increasing demands for measurement standards and calibrations which has been met, in part, through increases in efficiency.

Ministry of Defence

The Ministry of Defence has the largest government research budget—£2,133 million for 1997–98, of which about £572 million is for medium- and long-term applied research relevant to military needs. With the ending of the Cold War, the Government is committed to achieving a gradual reduction in real terms in spending on defence R & D.

The Defence Evaluation and Research Agency (DERA) is the largest single scientific employer in Britain. Its role is to supply scientific and technical services primarily to the Ministry but also to other government departments. DERA has set up five dual-use (civil-military) technology centres in subjects ranging from structural materials to high-performance computing, to enhance the degree of collaboration between DERA, industry and the academic science base.

DERA subcontracts research to industry and universities, ensuring that their know-how is harnessed to meeting military requirements. It also works closely with industry in order to see that scientific and technological advances are integrated at an early stage into development and production. This technology transfer is not just confined to the defence industry but has also led to important 'spin-offs' into civil markets, in fields ranging from new materials and electronic devices to advanced aerodynamics. The latter in particular has been instrumental in giving Britain a leading role in civil aircraft design.

Department of the Environment, Transport and the Regions

The Department of the Environment, Transport and the Regions funds research in the following broad policy areas: environmental protection, including water, radioactive substances, chemicals and environmental technology; planning and the countryside; local government; housing; construction; transport congestion; the environmental impact of transport; transport safety and security; and mobility for elderly and disabled people. Some of the biggest programmes are those on pollution-related climate change, regional and urban air quality, construction, best practice in energy efficiency and primary and secondary safety of transport users. Total expenditure for 1997–98 is about £140 million, including the Environment Agency (see p. 348) R & D programme of £10 million in 1997–98. British scientific expertise is being made available in developing countries to protect threatened species of plants and animals as part of the Darwin Initiative (see p. 366). The Department has committed £12 million to 116 projects in nearly 60 countries. The Department is also responsible for the Health and Safety Commission and Executive.

Ministry of Agriculture, Fisheries and Food

MAFF co-ordinates its research programme with The Scottish Office Agriculture,

Environment and Fisheries Department, the Department of Agriculture for Northern Ireland and the Research Councils. It also covers the research interests of the Welsh Office Agriculture Department.

The programme reflects the Ministry's wide-ranging responsibilities for protecting and enhancing the rural and marine environment; protecting the public, especially in food safety and quality, flooding and coastal defence, and animal health and welfare; and improving the economic performance of the agriculture, fishing and food industries.

The budget for research expenditure in 1997–98 is £139 million, including support for the Royal Botanic Gardens, Kew (see p. 342). Research is contracted increasingly through open competition with Research Councils, the Ministry's agencies, non-departmental public bodies, higher education institutions and other organisations.

Department of Health

The Department of Health's R & D strategy comprises two complementary programmes: the Policy Research Programme and the National Health Service R & D Programme. The Department also oversees the research programmes of the health-related non-departmental public bodies. It will spend about £68.1 million in 1997–98. In addition, the centrally and regionally funded R & D programmes of the NHS Executive will spend around £61.8 million that year. NHS Trusts (see chapter 24) spent £334 million in 1995–96, covering 39,000 projects. The Department promotes strong links between its programmes and the science base, and with Research Councils, charities, industry and the European Union. Together with the Medical Research Council, it helped shape the EU's Biomedicine and Health Research Programme within the Fourth Framework Programme (see p. 336).

Department for International Development

The Department for International Development commissions and sponsors technology development and research (TDR) on topics relevant to those geographical regions designated as the primary targets of the aid programme and of benefit to the poorest people in those countries. Provision for TDR in 1997–98 is £79 million. Its support for strategic TDR is organised into five main programmes, covering renewable natural resources and the environment; engineering-related sectors (water and sanitation, energy efficiency and geoscience, urbanisation and transport); health and population; economic and social development; and education. TDR is also carried out as part of Britain's bilateral aid to particular countries.

The Department also contributes to international centres and programmes undertaking TDR aimed at solving problems faced by developing countries. These contributions include support for the EU's Science and Technology for Development programme, which sponsors research in renewable natural resources, agriculture, health and information technologies.

Scottish Office

The annual value of government-financed (non-military) research in Scotland is about £335 million. Some £135 million goes to Scottish research institutions from British bodies, mainly the Research Councils. Around £200 million is administratively controlled by The Scottish Office. The Scottish Higher Education Funding Council grants £106 million for research in higher education institutions. This enables them to sustain a research infrastructure, and gives some discretion to determine their own priorities.

The Scottish Office also funds research in support of its main responsibilities in light of current priorities, and the programmes of other research funders, including other government departments, Research Councils and industry. For instance, the Scottish Office Agriculture, Environment and Fisheries Department invests about £50 million in research each year, largely in the Scottish Agricultural and Biological Research Institutes and the Scottish Agricultural

College. In many areas—medicine, agriculture and biological sciences, fisheries and marine science—public sector research in Scotland has an international reputation.

The Scottish Office Education and Industry Department encourages the development of science-based industry, for example, by promoting and administering government industrial R & D schemes, and promoting participation in, and dissemination of results from, EU R & D programmes. The enterprise network in Scotland—Scottish Enterprise, Highlands and Islands Enterprise and LECs (see chapter 14)—addresses the need for innovation and technology transfer, both through grant support for product and process innovation and through a wide range of initiatives. In August 1996, Scottish Enterprise, together with the Royal Society of Edinburgh (see p. 341), launched the Technology Ventures Initiative which aims to improve the exploitation of research in Scotland and is the result of a two-year inquiry and research programme which involved business, academia, financial institutions and the public sector. Since its launch, a number of specific projects are being pursued and work is underpinned by an awareness raising campaign on the importance of commercialising science and technology.

Space Activities

Britain's space programme is brought together through the British National Space Centre (BNSC), a partnership between government departments and the Research Councils. BNSC's key aims are to develop practical and economic uses of space, to promote the competitiveness of British space companies in world markets and to maintain Britain's position in space science. These are realised primarily by collaboration with other European nations through the European Space Agency (ESA).

Through BNSC, the Government spends around £200 million a year on space activities. About two thirds of this is channelled through ESA for collaborative programmes on Earth observation, telecommunications and space science, much of which returns to

Britain through contracts awarded to British industry. The rest is spent on international meteorological programmes carried out through the European Meteorological Satellite Organisation (EUMETSAT) and the national programme which is aimed at complementing the R&D supported through ESA.

Around half of Britain's space programme is concerned with satellite-based Earth observation (remote-sensing) for commercial and environmental applications. Britain contributed strongly to ESA's ERS-1 and ERS-2 satellites, which were launched respectively in 1991 and 1995. It provided two of the instruments on both satellites. The first, a Synthetic Aperture Radar, is capable of supplying high-resolution images of the Earth with 24-hour coverage irrespective of cloud cover conditions; the second, an Along Track Scanning Radiometer, measures global sea surface temperature to a very high degree of accuracy.

Britain is also a major contributor to the development of ESA's latest Earth observation satellite, ENVISAT, due to be launched in 1999. This will carry a new generation of radar and radiometer systems as well as other scientific environmental instruments, some of which have either been designed or constructed in Britain. The complete satellite is being assembled at a purpose-built factory in Bristol, operated by the Anglo-French space company, Matra Marconi Space. British companies are also leading the development of microsatellites. Surrey Satellite Technology Ltd, based at the University of Surrey, and Satellite Innovations Ltd, have both developed and successfully launched scientific and commercial microsatellites for British and overseas customers.

Britain has a world-class reputation in space science. A quarter of its space budget is devoted to space science, in support of astronomy, planetary science and geophysics. Contributions have been made to missions ranging from the Hubble Space Telescope to the Ulysses solar space probe. Britain is contributing substantially to the SOHO mission to study the Sun; to the Infrared Space Observatory, which is investigating the birth and death of stars; and also to the Cassini Huygens mission, a seven-year programme to send a probe to Saturn and its moon Titan, launched in October 1997. It is also participating in XMM, ESA's X-ray spectroscopy mission, which will investigate X-ray emissions from black holes, due to be launched in 1999.

Britain has many bilateral agreements for scientific research with other countries, such as Russia, Japan and the United States. British scientists developed, for example, the widefield camera for ROSAT (the German, British and US X-ray satellite), and a spectrometer for the Japanese-built Yohkoh satellite. They are also providing an X-ray telescope for the Russian Spectrum-X mission, expected to be launched in 1998.

Another major area of British space expertise is satellite communications and navigation. In Europe, Britain is both a leading producer and user of satellite communications technology (see p. 229). It is taking a leading role in preparations for future ESA satellite communications missions, including ARTEMIS, which will provide important communications links for the ENVISAT programme. Britain is also contributing to the development of a global navigation satellite system within Europe which will augment the United States GPS system to provide increased accuracy and reliability required for civil aviation global navigation.

Through the PPARC (see p. 338), Britain is taking a leading role in the current largest international project in ground-based astronomy. The Gemini project involves building two 8m telescopes at Mauna Kea (Hawaii) and Cerro Pachon (Chile). These are due to be completed respectively in 1999 and 2001. The other partners are the United States, Canada, Argentina, Brazil and Chile. Britain has a 25 per cent stake in the work, with major responsibility for the primary mirror support system and much of the control software.

INTERNATIONAL COLLABORATION

European Union

Since 1984 the EU has operated a series of R & D framework programmes in several strategic sectors, with the aim of strengthening the scientific and technological basis of European industry and supporting the development of EU policies. The Fourth Framework Programme runs from 1994 to 1998. It has a budget of about £10,000 million and provides funds for international collaborative research in fields such as biotechnology, industrial materials and information technology. In the main part of the programme, more than half of all projects include British participation—in areas such as bio-medicine, agriculture, transport, and social and economic research.

Two examples of the many EU research activities involving British organisations, both of which are part of the Fourth Framework Programme, are:

- the EU's Information Technology Programme, which is a shared cost collaborative programme designed to help build the services and technologies that underpin the information society. The programme is open to companies, academic institutions and research bodies. Britain is currently participating in over 500 projects in the programme; and

- the Training and Mobility of Researchers (TMR) programme, which aims to develop human resources for science and technology through promoting high-level training for researchers and encouraging their mobility across the community. Britain is the most popular destination under the programme, with over 30 per cent of TMR fellows opting to train in British laboratories.

Other International Activities

Over 800 British organisations have taken part in EUREKA, an industry-led scheme to encourage European co-operation in developing and producing advanced products and processes with worldwide sales potential.

There are 26 members of EUREKA, including the 15 EU countries and the European Commission. Around 670 projects are in progress, involving around 3,000 firms, universities and research organisations. One British-led project is concerned with developing glass-reinforced polymers that could replace steel in vehicle suspensions, leading to the production of more comfortable and more fuel-efficient cars which would cause less damage to road surfaces. As strong as steel, these polymers are lighter and can bend further.

The COST programme (European Co-operation in the field of Science and Technical research) encourages co-operation in national research activities across Europe, with participants from industry, academia and research laboratories. Transport, telecommunications and materials have traditionally been the largest areas supported. New areas include physics, chemistry, neuroscience and the application of biotechnology to agriculture, including forestry. There are 25 member states and Britain takes part in almost all of about 140 current COST actions.

Other examples of international collaboration include the European Space Agency (see p. 334), and CERN, the European Laboratory for Particle Physics, based in Geneva, where the proposed Large Hadron Collider (LHC) is due to be completed by 2005. Scientific programmes at CERN aim to test, verify and develop the 'standard model' of the origins and structure of the universe. There are 19 member states. Britain's programme is co-ordinated through the CCLRC and the subscription is paid by the PPARC. Contributions to the high-flux neutron source at the Institut Laue-Langevin and the European Synchrotron Radiation Facility, both in Grenoble, are paid by the EPSRC. The PPARC is a partner in the European Incoherent Scatter Radar Facility within the Arctic Circle, which conducts research on the ionosphere. NERC has a major involvement in international programmes of research into global climate change organised through the World Climate Research Programme and the International Geosphere-Biosphere Programme. It also supports Britain's subscription to the Ocean Drilling Program.

Through the MRC, Britain participates in the European Molecular Biology Laboratory (EMBL), based in Heidelberg, Germany. Britain was chosen as the location for the European Bioinformatics Institute, an outstation of the EMBL. The Institute, based at Hinxton, near Cambridge, provides up-to-date information on molecular biology and genome sequencing for researchers throughout Europe. The MRC pays Britain's contribution to the Human Frontier Science Programme, which supports international collaborative research into brain function and biological function through molecular level approaches. It also pays Britain's subscription to the International Agency for Cancer Research.

Britain is a member of the science and technology committees of international organisations such as the OECD and NATO, and of various specialised agencies of the United Nations, including UNESCO. The Research Councils, the Royal Society and the British Academy are members of the European Science Foundation, and a number of British scientists are involved in its initiatives.

The British Government also enters into bilateral agreements with other governments to encourage closer collaboration in science, engineering and technology. Staff in British Embassies, High Commissions and British Council offices (see below) conduct government business on, and promote contacts in, science, engineering and technology between Britain and overseas countries; and help to inform a large number of organisations in Britain about science, engineering and technology developments and initiatives overseas. There are science and technology sections in British Missions in Paris, Tokyo, Washington, Peking, Bonn, Moscow, Seoul and Rome.

The British Council (see p. 140) promotes better understanding and knowledge of Britain, including its scientific and technological achievements. As well as supplying information on science and science policy, it fosters co-operation in research, training and education through, for example,

exchange of specialists. The Council also identifies and manages technological, scientific and educational projects in developing countries. The Research Councils maintain, with the British Council, a joint office in Brussels to promote European co-operation in research.

RESEARCH COUNCILS

Each Research Council is an autonomous body established under Royal Charter, with members of its governing council drawn from the universities, professions, industry and government. The Councils support research, study and training in universities and other higher education institutions, and carry out or support research, through their own institutes and at international research centres, often jointly with other public sector bodies and international organisations. They provide awards to about 15,000 postgraduate students in science, social sciences, engineering and technology. In addition to funding from the OST, the Councils receive income from research commissioned by government departments and the private sector; such income is particularly important for the BBSRC, NERC and CCLRC.

Engineering and Physical Sciences Research Council

The EPSRC, the Research Council with the largest budget—£386 million in 1997–98—has responsibility for developing and sustaining basic, strategic and applied research in engineering and the physical sciences. Its remit is delivered through eight programme areas: physics, chemistry and mathematics, the generic technologies of information technology and materials, and three engineering programmes. The latter comprise general engineering (concentrating on strengthening the health of the engineering disciplines), engineering for manufacturing (enhancing industrial competitiveness), and engineering for infrastructure, the environment and healthcare (improving quality of life).

In July 1997 EPSRC launched four pilot Faraday Partnerships, each with initial funding of up to £50,000 and additional funding of up to £1 million for specific collaborative research and training. The partnerships aim to improve the links between the research base and industry, particularly small and medium-sized enterprises. Areas covered in the pilot partnerships are: products comprising interdependent mechanical and electronic parts; enhanced packaging technology; intelligent sensors for control technologies; and 3D multimedia applications and technology integration.

Medical Research Council

The MRC, with a budget of £289 million for 1997–98, is the main source of public funds for biomedical research. It supports research and training aimed at improving human health to meet the needs of user communities, including the providers of healthcare and the biotechnology, food, healthcare, medical instrumentation, pharmaceutical and other biomedical-related industries. About half the MRC's expenditure is allocated to its own institutes and units, the rest going mainly on grant support of research in universities, including training awards. The Council has two large institutes—the National Institute for Medical Research at Mill Hill in London and the Laboratory of Molecular Biology in Cambridge; it also runs the Clinical Sciences Centre at the Royal Postgraduate Medical School, London. It has more than 40 research units and a number of smaller teams.

Research financed by the MRC is conducted in seven broad areas:

- macromolecules, cells, and development biology (including basic studies of molecular structures and properties, cell biology, developmental biology and biochemistry);

- genetic blueprint and health (including human genome mapping, structure and function of genes, gene therapy and genetic diagnosis and screening);

- environment and defences: nutrition, chemicals, radiation and trauma (including toxicology, environmental toxins, nutritional and lifestyle effects on

health, and factors influencing healthy growth and development;

- environment and defences: infections, immunity and inflammation (including basic studies of disease-causing organisms, the function and development of the immune system, autoimmune diseases, vaccination, and antibiotics);

- neurosciences and mental health (including all basic and applied studies relating to the nervous system, and psychology);

- organ systems and cancer (including heart disease and stroke, ageing, diabetes, reproduction, musculo-skeletal system, as well as cancer); and

- health services and public health research (including evaluative and social studies, clinical trials, evaluation of new treatments, and studies of social factors in health).

Particle Physics and Astronomy Research Council

The main task of the PPARC, which has a budget of £199 million for 1997–98, is to sustain and develop research into fundamental physical processes. It maintains four research establishments: the Royal Greenwich Observatory at Cambridge, the Royal Observatory at Edinburgh and overseas observatories on La Palma in the Canary Islands and on Hawaii. The PPARC supports research in three main areas: particle physics—theoretical and experimental research into elementary particles and the fundamental forces of nature; astronomy (including astrophysics and cosmology)—studying the origin, structure and evolution of the universe, and the life-cycle and properties of stars and galaxies; and planetary science (including solar terrestrial physics)—studying the origin and evolution of the solar system and the influence of the Sun on planetary bodies, particularly Earth.

The Council's work is in fields where international co-operation is particularly important: for example, it makes substantial contributions to the European Space Agency and CERN (see pp. 334 and 336).

Biotechnology and Biological Sciences Research Council

The BBSRC has a budget of £183 million for 1997–98. It supports basic and strategic research and research training related to the understanding and exploitation of biological systems, which underpin the agriculture, bioprocessing, chemical, food, healthcare, pharmaceutical and other biotechnology-related industries. The scientific themes are biomolecular sciences; genes and developmental biology; biochemistry and cell biology; plant and microbial sciences; animal sciences; agrifood; and engineering and biological systems. As well as funding research in universities and other research centres throughout Britain, the BBSRC sponsors eight research institutes: the Babraham Institute, the Institute of Arable Crops Research, Institute for Animal Health, Institute of Food Research, Institute of Grassland and Environmental Research, John Innes Centre, Roslin Institute and Silsoe Research Institute.

Natural Environment Research Council

NERC is principally concerned with the themes of sustainable development, environmental protection, and the quality of life. In 1997–98 it will spend most of its budget allocation of £167 million in the following areas: understanding and protecting biodiversity; environmental risks and hazards; global change; natural resources—management of land, water and the coastal zone; pollution of air, land, sea and fresh water; and waste management—bioremediation (biological treatment of pollution), and land restoration.

The Council supports research in its own and other research establishments as well as research and training in universities. It also provides a range of facilities for use by the wider environmental science community, including a marine research fleet. NERC establishments include the British Geological Survey, the British Antarctic Survey, the

Centre for Coastal and Marine Sciences and the Centre for Ecology and Hydrology, together with a number of university-based units. A new national centre for oceanographic science and technology, the Southampton Oceanography Centre, was opened in 1996. A joint venture with Southampton University, it undertakes research, training and support activities in oceanography, geology and aspects of marine technology and engineering. NERC's Research Vessel Services are also located at the Centre.

Economic and Social Research Council

The ESRC, with an R & D provision of £65 million for 1997–98, supports research and training to meet the needs of its users and to enhance Britain's economic competitiveness, quality of life, and the effectiveness of public services and policy. All research funded by the ESRC is conducted in higher education institutions or independent research institutes. The Council has nine priority themes: economic performance and development; environment and sustainability; globalisation, regions and emerging markets; governance regulation and accountability; technology and people; innovation; knowledge, communication and learning; lifespan, lifestyles and health; and social inclusion and exclusion.

The Council has made significant investments in the area of innovation, organisations and business processes, launching three new centres in 1996–97: the Centre for Research on Innovation and Competition, in Manchester; the Centre for Organisation and Innovation at the University of Sheffield; and the Complex Product Systems Innovation Research Centre at the Universities of Sussex and Brighton.

Council for the Central Laboratory of the Research Councils

The CCLRC promotes scientific and engineering research by providing facilities and technical expertise primarily to meet the needs of the other Research Councils. Its R & D budget for 1997–98 is £110 million, of which £86 million comes through agreements with other Research Councils and the remaining £24 million from contracts and agreements with the EU, overseas countries, and other industries and organisations. It covers a broad range of science and technology, including materials and biological science using accelerators and lasers, satellite instrumentation and data processing, remote-sensing, electronics, sensor technology, computing and informatics, micro-engineering and particle physics.

The CCLRC is responsible for three research establishments: the Rutherford Appleton Laboratory at Chilton in Oxfordshire; the Daresbury Laboratory near Warrington in Cheshire; and the Chilbolton Observatory in Hampshire. These centres provide facilities too large or complex to be housed by individual academic institutions. Among the facilities are ISIS (the world's leading source of pulsed neutrons and muons), some of the world's brightest lasers and the United Kingdom Synchrotron Radiation Source.

RESEARCH IN HIGHER EDUCATION INSTITUTIONS

Universities carry out most of Britain's long-term strategic and basic research in science and technology. The higher education funding councils in England, Scotland and Wales (see p. 452) provide the main general funds to support research in universities and other higher education institutions in Great Britain. These funds pay for the salaries of permanent academic staff, who usually teach as well as undertake research, and contribute to the infrastructure for research. In Northern Ireland academic institutions are funded by the Department of Education for Northern Ireland. The quality of research performance is a key element in the allocation of funding. In 1996 the funding councils carried out a research assessment exercise to assess the quality of research in each subject across all higher education institutions in Britain.

Basic and strategic research in higher education institutions are also financed by the Research Councils. Institutions undertaking research with the support of Research Council grants have the rights over the commercial exploitation of their research, subject to the prior agreement of the sponsoring Research Council. They may make use of technology transfer experts and other specialists, such as BTG, to help exploit and license commercially the results of their research. The other main channels of support are industry, charities, government departments and the European Union. Institutions are expected to recover the full cost of commissioned research. The high quality of research in higher education institutions, and their marketing skills, have enabled them to attract more funding from a larger range of external sources, especially in contract income from industry and charities.

Measures are being taken to improve the quality of research training and to make it more relevant to the needs of both students and industry. For instance, pilot schemes for two new qualifications, the engineering doctorate (EngDoc) and the research masters degree (MRes), have been introduced.

Science Parks

Science parks are partnerships between higher education or research centres and industry to promote commercially focused research and advanced technology. There are around 50 such parks, hosting more than 1,300 companies. The majority are engaged in computing, biotechnology, chemicals, electrical engineering and robotics. Technology transfer and R & D are the most common activities, rather than large-scale

Microsoft of the United States, the world's leading computer software company, plans to construct a £50 million research facility in Cambridge, to be headed by Professor Roger Needham. Cambridge scientists have been at the forefront of electronics from the initial discovery of the electron by J.J. Thomson at the beginning of the century and the beginnings of transistors and integrated circuits through to the birth of nano-technology, which deals with even smaller components.

manufacturing. A growing number of universities offer industry interdisciplinary research centres, with exploitable resources. These include access to analytical equipment, library facilities and worldwide databases as well as academic expertise.

OTHER ORGANISATIONS

Industrial Research and Technology Organisations

Research and Technology Organisations (RTOs) are independent organisations carrying out commercially relevant research and other services on behalf of industry, often relating to a specific industrial sector. Britain has the largest RTO sector in Europe, consisting of around 50 organisations, which together employ almost 10,000 people.

Charitable Organisations

Medical research charities are a major source of funds for biomedical research in Britain. Their combined contribution in 1997–98 will be about £440 million. The three largest are the Wellcome Trust—the world's biggest medical charity—with a contribution of £250 million, the Imperial Cancer Research Fund (£53 million) and the Cancer Research Campaign (£47 million).

Professional Institutions

There are numerous technical institutions, professional associations and learned societies in Britain, many of which promote their own disciplines or the education and professional well-being of their members. The Council of Science and Technology Institutes has ten member institutes representing biology, biochemistry, chemistry, environment, food science and technology, geology, hospital physics and physics.

The Engineering Council promotes the study of all types of engineering in schools and other organisations, in co-operation with its 200 industry affiliates, which include large private sector companies and government departments. Together with 39 professional engineering institutions, the Council accredits courses in higher education institutions. It also advises the Government on academic, industrial and professional issues.

Royal Society

The Royal Society, founded in 1660, is Britain's academy of science and has some 1,200 Fellows and 100 Foreign Members. Many of its Fellows serve on governmental advisory councils and committees concerned with research. The Society has a dual role, as the national academy of science and as the provider of a range of services, including research fellowships and grants, for the scientific community. It also offers independent advice to government on science matters, acts as a forum for discussion of scientific issues and fosters public awareness of science and science education. Its estimated net expenditure on science and technology in 1997–98 is £25 million.

Royal Academy of Engineering

The national academy of engineering in Britain is the Royal Academy of Engineering, which has 1,060 Fellows. It promotes excellence in engineering for the benefit of society, and advises government, Parliament and other official organisations. The Academy's programmes are aimed at attracting first-class students into engineering, raising awareness of the importance of engineering design among undergraduates, developing links between industry and higher education, and increasing industrial investment in engineering research in higher education institutions. Net expenditure on engineering in 1997–98 will be approximately £11 million.

Other Societies

In Scotland the Royal Society of Edinburgh, established in 1783, promotes science by offering postdoctoral research fellowships and studentships, awarding prizes and grants, organising meetings and symposia, and publishing journals. It has been engaged with Scottish Enterprise in developing a strategy to increase the extent of commercial use of the products of the Scottish research base (see p. 334), and has been active in the Foresight process. It also acts as a source of independent scientific advice to the Government and others.

Three other major institutions publicise scientific developments by means of lectures and publications for specialists and schoolchildren. Of these, the British Association for the Advancement of Science (BAAS), founded in 1831, is mainly concerned with science, while the Royal Society of Arts, dating from 1754, deals with the arts and commerce as well as science. The Royal Institution, which was founded in 1799, also performs these functions and runs its own research laboratories.

Zoological Gardens

The Zoological Society of London, an independent conservation, science and education body founded in 1826, runs London Zoo, which occupies about 15 hectares (36 acres) of Regent's Park, London. It also runs Whipsnade Wild Animal Park (243 hectares/600 acres) near Dunstable in Bedfordshire. The Society is responsible for the Institute of Zoology, which carries out research in support of conservation. The Institute's work covers topics such as ecology, behaviour, reproductive biology and conservation genetics. The Society also operates in field conservation and consultancy, and is concerned with practical field conservation, primarily in East and Southern Africa, the Middle East and parts of Asia. Other well-known zoos in Britain include those in Edinburgh, Bristol, Chester, Dudley and Marwell (near Winchester).

Botanic Gardens

The Royal Botanic Gardens, Kew, founded in 1759, covers 121 hectares (300 acres) at Kew in south-west London and a 187-hectare (462-acre) estate at Wakehurst Place, Ardingly, in West Sussex. They contain one of the largest collections of living and dried plants in the world. Research is conducted into all aspects of plant life, including

physiology, biochemistry, genetics, economic botany and the conservation of habitats and species. In 1997–98 Kew is to build the Millennium Commission Seed Bank containing the world's most comprehensive collection of plants at Wakehurst Place. The Millennium Commission is donating up to £30 million towards the estimated £75–£80 million cost of the project. Staff are also active in programmes to return endangered plant species to the wild. Kew participates in joint research programmes in some 52 countries.

The Royal Botanic Garden in Edinburgh was originally established in 1670, and is the national botanic garden of Scotland. Together with its three associated specialist gardens which were acquired to provide a range of different climatic and soil conditions, it has since become an internationally recognised centre for taxonomy (classification of species); the conservation and study of living and preserved plants and fungi; and as a provider of horticultural education.

A national botanic garden and research centre for Wales is to be developed on a 230-hectare (570-acre) site on the Middleton Hall estate at Llandeilo, near Swansea. The £43 million project is backed by a consortium of public and private organisations and individuals. It has been awarded £21.7 million by the Millennium Commission.

Scientific Museums

The Natural History Museum in South Kensington, London has 68 million specimens, ranging from a blue whale skeleton to minute insects. It is one of the world's principal centres for research into natural history, offering an advisory service to institutions all over the world. The Science Museum, also in South Kensington, promotes understanding of the history of science, technology, industry and medicine. Its extensive collection of scientific instruments and machinery is complemented by interactive computer games and audio-visual equipment for visitors to use. In this way, the museum explains scientific principles to the general public and documents the history of science, from early discoveries to space age technology. Other important collections include those at the Museum of Science and Industry in Birmingham, the Museum of Science and Industry in Manchester, the Museum of the History of Science in Oxford, and the Royal Scottish Museum, Edinburgh.

Further Reading

Forward Look of Government-funded Science, Engineering and Technology 1996. The Stationery Office, 1996.

A Guide to the Governmental Organisation of Science and Technology in Britain. British Council, 1995.

Progress through Partnership: First Progress Report on the Technology Foresight Programme 1996. The Stationery Office, 1996.

Realising Our Potential: A Strategy for Science, Engineering and Technology. Cm 2250. HMSO, 1993.

Science and Technology. Aspects of Britain series, HMSO, 1995.

Science, Engineering and Technology Statistics 1997. Cm 3695. The Stationery Office, 1997.

Winning through Foresight. A Strategy taking the Foresight Programme to the Millennium. OST. 1996.

21 Environmental Protection

Britain pursues policies of sustainable development and engages fully in international co-operation on matters of environmental protection. It develops much of its legislation on pollution control and the conservation of wildlife in collaboration with its partners in the European Union (EU) and bodies such as the Organisation for Economic Co-operation and Development (OECD) and the United Nations (UN). The built environment is protected by the designation of conservation areas and the listing of buildings of interest.

The Departments of the Environment and of Transport were merged in June 1997 to form a single Department of the Environment, Transport and the Regions (DETR—see also chapter 19). The Government believes that this new 'super-ministry' will be able to tackle environmental issues and sustainable development in a more integrated way. In addition, the other major government departments each have a 'Green Minister' who looks after the environmental dimension to their own department's area of responsibility.

Sustainable Development

The aim of sustainable development is to meet the needs of the present without compromising the ability of future generations to meet their own needs. Britain's strategy on sustainable development was first published in 1994, as one of the documents that arose from the Rio de Janeiro 'earth summit' in 1992 (the United Nations Conference on Environment and Development—UNCED). The new Government intends to revise this strategy to reflect its overall aim of combining economic and social goals with environmental sustainability, and to provide a more practical framework for sustainable development.

The most recent follow-up report on sustainable development—*This Common Inheritance: UK Annual Report 1997*—was published in February 1997. It describes progress made during 1996 towards meeting about 650 commitments specified in earlier reports and in the original 1994 strategy document. It also sets out priorities for action in 1997. These include implementing the new National Air Quality Strategy (see p. 353); increasing international protection of the oceans, fish stocks and other marine resources; and providing better information for consumers about the environmental impacts of the goods they buy.

> At the United Nations Special Session on the Environment and Sustainable Development in New York in June 1997 ('earth summit 2'), the Government committed itself to reversing the recent gradual decline in the flow of British aid to developing countries, especially those in Africa, and to concentrating its aid efforts on combating world poverty. It also set the target of reducing greenhouse gas emissions in Britain to 20 per cent below their 1990 levels by 2010, through more efficient use of transport, improved energy conservation and greater use of renewable sources of energy.

Under the Government's national strategy on sustainable development, four bodies were set up to help formulate policy in this area:

- The Government Panel on Sustainable Development, an independent panel which advises on issues of major strategic importance to sustainable development;
- *UK Round Table on Sustainable Development*, which brings together interests such as business, local government and academics to discuss these matters with government ministers;
- *Going for Green*, an independent committee which seeks to persuade individuals and groups to commit themselves to sustainable development (in Scotland, this role is taken by 'Forward Scotland'); and
- The Secretary of State for Scotland's *Advisory Group on Sustainable Development*, which published its first report in August 1997.

In January 1997 the *Government Panel on Sustainable Development* published its third annual report. This identified four main issues which the Panel considered needed higher priority: official procurement policy; government subsidies; climate change and long-term energy supplies; and the impact of agriculture on biodiversity. For example, the Panel called on the Government to make the environmental dimension more central to its own procurement policies (government guidance on this subject was published in July 1997). Likewise, it advised the Government to draw up new aims and principles for the use of subsidies, with the same purpose in mind.

The UK Round Table on Sustainable Development consists of about 30 members, drawn from central and local government, business, environmental organisations and other sectors of the community. It was established in 1995, originally for two years, but will now continue until at least 1999. Its second annual report, issued in March 1997, draws together conclusions from its first two years' work. Much of the Round Table's business is carried out in subgroups, set up to consider specific topics. For example, the second annual report summarises and includes recommendations on five recently completed topics:

- 'Making Connections' (overcoming the barriers to transfers within passenger and freight journeys, and trying to make such journeys as attractive as door-to-door car and lorry trips);
- 'Getting Round Town' (looking at obstacles to sustainable transport policies: a case study based in the Northampton area);
- 'Housing and Urban Capacity' (recommending a target of 75 per cent of new housing to be built on previously developed land);
- 'Freshwater' (looking at the national water resource from the perspective of sustainable development); and
- 'Energy and Planning' (a study of land use planning controls over energy developments, especially power stations and renewable energy projects).

Going for Green has been established as a private company, and from April 1996 it took responsibility for a campaign which aims to promote sustainable development to the general public. In 1996–97, the Government provided £1.5 million of funding, with £0.7 million subject to matching funding from the private sector. Among its recent activities have been a study to see how the message of waste minimisation can best be transmitted to the public, and the relaunch of the 'Green Code'. The Code outlines five 'green' goals—cutting down waste, saving energy and natural resources, travelling sensibly, preventing pollution, and looking after the local environment—and explains how they can be achieved on an individual basis.

Indicators of Sustainable Development

Indicators of Sustainable Development for the United Kingdom was published in 1996. It lists 118 indicators, grouped into 21 broad headings. The broad headings are: the economy; transport use; leisure and tourism; overseas trade; energy; land use; water resources; forestry; fish resources; climate change; ozone layer depletion; acid deposition; air; freshwater quality; marine; wildlife and habitats; land cover and landscape; soil; minerals extraction; waste; and radioactivity.

Where possible, the indicators track trends over the last 20 to 25 years. They are already making a major contribution to the measurement of progress in attaining sustainable development, and are helping to inform the Government, business and the public about the ways in which the environment is changing and how these changes are linked to economic development.

Business and Consumer Involvement

The Government has launched a number of initiatives designed to help business improve its environmental performance, ensure business concerns are taken into account when policy is made, and help consumers assess firms' environmental credentials. For example, the Environmental Technology Best Practice Programme encourages British industry and commerce to adopt the best environmental technology, and to give greater attention to waste minimisation. The Government's contribution to the Programme amounts to £32 million over the eight years to 2001–2. Other initiatives include the Energy Efficiency Best Practice Programme (which is aimed at, among others, those responsible for industrial production and processes) and the Small Company Environmental and Energy Management Assistance Scheme (SCEEMAS—see p. 259).

Advisory Committee on Business and the Environment

The Advisory Committee on Business and the Environment is made up of business leaders, appointed by the Government and serving in a personal capacity. Its roles are:

● to advise the Government on environmental issues of concern to business;

● to provide a link with international business initiatives on the environment; and

● to help mobilise the business community through demonstrating good environmental practice.

In February 1997, the Committee published guidance for business on good practice in environmental reporting, which showed how business can benefit from greater openness about its environmental performance.

Standards on Environmental Management

In 1992 the British Standards Institution (see p. 194) published BS 7750, the world's first standard for environmental management systems. Since then an international set of standards based on the British standard has come into operation, one of which, ISO 14001, has now superseded BS 7750. ISO 14001 allows organisations to evaluate how their activities, products and services affect the environment, and gives them a structure through which they can achieve improvements in overall environmental performance.

The Eco-Management and Audit Scheme (EMAS) is a voluntary scheme for individual industrial sites, which was established by EU law in April 1995. EMAS and ISO 14001 are complementary systems, the main difference between them (apart from restrictions on eligibility for EMAS) being the requirement under EMAS for a published environmental management statement. This statement provides the public with independently validated information on the organisation's environmental performance. To date, nearly 40 organisations in Britain are registered to EMAS, including Vauxhall, Woodcote Industries, Ciba Clayton and the London Borough of Sutton (under the British extension of the scheme to local government). Government grants are available to help small businesses meet the cost of employing environmental experts to assist with registration.

Ecolabelling

Increasingly, consumers wish to take environmental considerations into account when buying goods. Britain has played a leading role in developing the EU ecolabelling scheme. This voluntary scheme aims to help consumers identify those products which are less harmful to the environment over their whole lifecycle, from raw materials and manufacture to final disposal. In 1993 Britain awarded the first European ecolabels to Hoover for washing machines in its 'New Wave' range. Since then, other products have started to carry labels, including brands of kitchen towel and toilet paper (Nouvelle and Co-Op), and paints. Environmental criteria have been agreed for a number of other product groups, such as laundry detergents, copying paper and refrigerators.

There is also a Europe-wide energy label scheme, which rates the energy-efficiency performance of 'white goods' such as refrigerators. The manufacturers themselves are responsible for the accuracy of these labels.

Most products, however, still lie outside these schemes. In February 1997, the Government published a Consultation Paper, *Green Claims*, which seeks to improve the quality of environmental information given to consumers by proposing a code of practice on the making of 'green claims' for products.

Often such claims are confusing, and the Government hopes that the establishment of ground rules will help consumers to make better-informed environmental choices about the products they buy.

Environmental Research

Research into environmental protection is essential to the formulation of the Government's environmental policies. Several government departments—such as the Ministry of Agriculture, Fisheries and Food and The Scottish Office—have substantial research programmes. The Department of the Environment, Transport and the Regions has allocated nearly £29 million for 1997–98 to research and monitoring in the following eight broad areas:

- the global atmosphere (climate change and depletion of the ozone layer);
- air quality and emissions;
- noise as an environmental pollutant;
- chemicals and biotechnology (including pesticides and genetically modified organisms);
- radioactive substances (both man-made and natural);
- water and land (including water quality and health, marine quality and contaminated land);
- waste policy; and
- economics and statistics.

Among the most important non-departmental official bodies that carry out research in this area are the Meteorological Office (including the Hadley Centre—see p. 354), and the Environment Agency (see p. 348), whose R & D budget for 1997–98 is £12.3 million, including £2.5 million on water pollution control. The Natural Resources Institute in Chatham, Kent, also has an important role in environmental research, as do many of Britain's universities. The Climatic Research Unit at the University of East Anglia is regarded by many as the most important of its kind in the world. Nearly 100 British universities and colleges run courses on environmental studies or natural resource management.

Research Councils

Basic and strategic research is carried out by government-funded research councils (see pp. 337–40). Most have a role in environmental protection research, but the Natural Environment Research Council (NERC) is particularly important. It has a Science Budget allocation of £166.6 million in 1997–98, plus about £43 million from other sources. NERC undertakes and supports research in the environmental sciences and funds postgraduate training. Its programmes encompass the marine, earth, terrestrial, freshwater, polar and atmospheric sciences, and science-based archaeology. NERC puts particular emphasis on international collaborative work on global environmental issues.

One of the research projects funded by NERC has resulted in a new way of tracking how wild salmon use landmarks and environmental cues to orient themselves, find food and shelter, and respond to droughts or floods. The implications for better management of wild salmon fisheries are considerable.

The research, carried out by the University of Glasgow and Freshwater Fisheries Lab, Pitlochry, has also produced an unexpected application in aquaculture. The discovery that landmarks are used in setting up territories has suggested a new way to reduce aggression in farmed salmon.

Pollution Control

Administration

Executive responsibility for pollution control is divided between local authorities and central government agencies. Central government makes policy, promotes legislation and advises pollution control authorities on policy implementation. In England, the Secretary of State for the Environment, Transport and the Regions has general responsibility for co-ordinating the work of the Government on environmental protection. In Scotland and Wales, the respective Secretaries of State are responsible for co-ordinating pollution control. In Northern Ireland, responsibility rests with the Department of the Environment for Northern Ireland—DOENI.

Local authorities also have important duties and powers. They are responsible for such matters as:

- collection and disposal of domestic wastes;
- keeping the streets clear of litter;
- control of air pollution from domestic and from many industrial premises; and
- noise and general nuisance abatement.

The Environment Agency for England and Wales (EA) is a non-departmental public body that combines the functions of the former National Rivers Authority, Her Majesty's Inspectorate of Pollution and the local waste regulation authorities. Through the mechanism of 'integrated pollution control' (IPC—see below), it has a central role in the control of particular industrial emissions to land, air and water. Other discharges to water are subject to discharge consents (see p. 350).

The Scottish Environment Protection Agency (SEPA) combines the functions formerly carried out by Her Majesty's Industrial Pollution Inspectorate and the Scottish river purification authorities. Waste regulation and some air pollution functions of the unitary local authorities have also been taken over by SEPA. In Northern Ireland, the Environment and Heritage Service, an executive agency of DOENI, exercises pollution control functions relating to emissions to land, water and air.

An independent standing body, the Royal Commission on Environmental Pollution, advises the Government. It has produced 20 reports on a variety of topics, the last two being on the sustainable use of soil, and on transport and the environment.

Integrated Pollution Control

Integrated Pollution Control (IPC) is applied to certain categories of industrial pollution. The potentially most harmful processes are specified for IPC and require authorisation from the EA, in England and Wales. Emissions to air from more minor processes are controlled by local authorities under a parallel system of local air pollution control (LAPC). In granting authorisation for releases under IPC, the EA requires the use of the best available techniques, not entailing excessive cost, to prevent or minimise polluting emissions and to ensure that any releases are made harmless.

In Scotland, IPC and LAPC are administered by SEPA. In Northern Ireland broadly similar controls are exercised by the Environment and Heritage Service, and proposals have been formulated for the introduction of a system of pollution control similar to IPC in 1998.

A new EC Integrated Pollution and Prevention and Control (IPPC) directive will greatly extend the scope of IPC, both in the number of installations and processes covered, and in the range of environmental impacts that will need to be considered before a permit is issued. Britain is committed to implementing the directive by the end of 1999.

Land and Waste

Certain local authorities are designated as waste collection and/or waste disposal authorities, responsible for different parts of the process of dealing with wastes that are subject to specific controls. Waste regulation, formerly a local authority responsibility, now rests with the EA, SEPA and, with the implementation of new legislation, with the Environment and Heritage Service in Northern Ireland. A licensing system regulates waste disposal sites, treatment plants and storage facilities receiving controlled wastes. 'Special'—that is, hazardous—wastes are subject to additional controls, which have been tightened by new regulations that came into force in 1996. Responsibility for proper handling of waste falls on everyone who has control of it from production to final disposal or reclamation. Operators of landfill sites remain responsible for them, even after closure, until the EA is satisfied that no future hazard is likely to arise.

In Scotland, the new unitary councils (see p. 22) are responsible for the collection and disposal of refuse, with SEPA acting as waste regulation authority for both the public and private sectors. In Northern Ireland, responsibility for the collection, disposal and regulation of waste currently rests with the district councils. However, proposed legislative changes will centralise waste regulation.

In 1995–96, the Department of the Environment estimated that 26 million tonnes of waste was collected by local authorities in England and Wales. A little over 90 per cent of this waste came from households. Only 6.5 per cent of household waste was separately collected for recycling and composting.

In the case of municipal waste, 83 per cent was reported as disposed of to landfill sites, 12 per cent had value recovered from it through recycling, composting or energy recovery, and the remaining 5 per cent was incinerated without any energy recovery.

There is still some way to go to achieve the targets set out in the waste strategy White Paper issued in 1995, *Making Waste Work*:

- to recycle or compost 25 per cent of household waste by 2000;
- to encourage 40 per cent of homes with a garden to carry out home composting by 2000;
- to recover value from 40 per cent of municipal waste by 2005; and
- to reduce the proportion of controlled waste going to landfill sites to 60 per cent by 2005.

The Government introduced a landfill tax in October 1996, which provided a tax incentive for waste minimisation and recycling. However, it may also lead to 'fly tipping' of waste, as an illegal way of avoiding the tax. A co-operative exercise is therefore planned between the environment agencies, local authorities and the Tidy Britain Group (the national agency for tackling litter) to survey the incidence of fly tipping since the introduction of the tax. A report will be published in the first half of 1998.

There is an ongoing programme of government financial support for capital costs incurred by local authorities and the environment agencies in the investigation and 'remediation' of contaminated land (including old landfill sites), so that it can be brought back into use. In 1996–97, £14 million was allocated, covering over 230 projects.

Recycling and Materials Reclamation

The reclamation and recycling of waste materials is encouraged whenever this is the best practicable environmental option. Local authorities are obliged to make plans for the recycling of waste. Waste disposal authorities in England must pay 'recycling credits' to waste collection authorities when they collect and return household waste for recycling. These credits are based on savings in disposal costs that have been avoided. In Wales and Scotland, the same authorities handle waste collection and disposal, so that the need for payments does not arise.

Under the EC directive on packaging and packaging wastes, at least 50 per cent of Britain's packaging waste must be re-utilised through recycling and other recovery methods by the year 2001. Meanwhile, the newspaper industry has already exceeded a voluntary target of using 40 per cent of recycled content in British newspapers.

The general public can deposit used glass containers in bottle banks for recycling. There were 15,000 bottle bank sites in Britain by 1995, 1,400 steel can banks and 8,700 can banks accepting aluminium cans. A variety of other materials, such as textiles, paper and plastics, are also recycled. One of the Government's waste strategy targets is to have easily accessible recycling facilities for 80 per cent of households by 2000.

Litter and Dog Fouling

Under the Environmental Protection Act 1990, it is a criminal offence to leave litter in any public place in the open air or to dump rubbish except in designated places. The litter fixed penalty fine was increased from £10 to £25 in January 1997, and the maximum fine for a prosecution is £2,500 under the Dogs (Fouling of Land) Act 1996. Local authorities have a duty to keep their public land free of litter and refuse, including dog faeces, as far as is practicable. Members of the public have powers to take action against authorities which fail to comply with their responsibilities. Local authorities also have powers to make it an offence not to clear up after one's dog in specified places. In Scotland outdoor venues which host events that attract large numbers of people are now obliged to clear up all litter within twelve hours.

In 1997–98, the Department of the Environment, Transport and the Regions allocated £2.7 million to the Tidy Britain Group, which provides a comprehensive anti-litter programme in collaboration with local authorities and the private sector. In a 1995 survey, the Group found that 90 per cent of littering offences recorded by the police were committed by males, most of whom were teenagers.

Water

All discharges to water in Britain require the consent of the appropriate regulatory authority. In England and Wales the EA's principal method of controlling water pollution is through the regulation of all effluent discharges into groundwaters, inland and coastal waters. The EA maintains public registers containing information about water quality, discharge consents, authorisations and monitoring. Applicants for consents to discharge have the right of appeal if they are dissatisfied with the EA's decision; most of these appeals are dealt with by the Planning Inspectorate. In Scotland control is exercised by SEPA. In Northern Ireland the Environment and Heritage Service is responsible for controlling water pollution.

The Government introduced regulations for a new system of classifying water quality in England and Wales in 1994. This provides the basis for setting statutory water quality objectives (SWQOs), which will specify for each individual stretch of water the standards that should be reached and the target date for achieving them. In 1996 the EA began consultations on eight pilot SWQOs to see if they can be successfully extended to other water catchment areas.

More than 95 per cent of the population in Britain live in properties connected to a sewer, and sewage treatment works serve over 80 per cent of the population. In England and Wales, the water industry is committed to an investment programme of some £11,000 million over ten years for improvements to water quality. Progressively higher treatment standards for industrial waste effluents and new measures to combat pollution from agriculture are expected to bring further improvements in water quality. In Scotland, responsibility for the provision of all water and sewerage services lies with three Water and Sewerage Authorities, covering the north, east and west of the country.

Over the past 30 years, notable progress has been made in cleaning up the previously heavily polluted major estuaries of the east coast of Britain, including the Forth, Tees, Thames and Tyne. In 1995, the chemical quality of 91 per cent of rivers and canals in England and Wales was graded as 'good' or 'fair' under the EA's General Quality Assessment scheme. Nearly 88 per cent of Northern Ireland's freshwater rivers were graded 'good' or 'fair' under the same scheme, and in Scotland, under a different scheme, 99 per cent of rivers or canals were graded as 'unpolluted' or of 'fairly good' quality.

There are currently 68 designated Nitrate Vulnerable Zones in England and Wales, whose aim is to protect water against pollution caused by nitrates used in agriculture.

Another risk to water quality comes from pollution from water in abandoned coal and other mines, although the scale of the problem is comparatively small—only 1.5 per cent of the total river length monitored by the EA is affected by such discharges. In 1996, the EA and the Coal Authority identified for further study a priority list of 35 serious mine water discharges from abandoned coal mines in England and Wales which need remedial pollution treatment, and which are being monitored by the EA during 1997. Following discussions with the EA and SEPA, the Coal Authority has undertaken 14 detailed feasibility studies on the most environmentally damaging discharges and allocated over £2 million principally to tackle four priority sites during 1997–98.

Bathing Waters and Coastal Sewage Discharges

The water industry is investing roughly £2,000 million to provide treatment of coastal sewage discharges and improve the quality of Britain's bathing waters. In the 1996 tests of bathing water quality, 90 per cent of identified bathing waters (423 out of 472) in Britain met the mandatory bacteria standards of the EC bathing water directive, compared with 80 per cent of beaches in 1993, and 66 per cent in 1988. The current programme of improvements to bathing waters is set to continue so that the remaining problems can be identified and put right.

The Tidy Britain Group publishes a Seaside Awards booklet which describes Britain's award-winning beaches (there were 224 in 1997). All seaside award beaches are regularly assessed for cleanliness and safety, and to ensure that the bathing water complies with current EU legislation.

Marine Environment

An international Convention for the Protection of the Marine Environment of the North East Atlantic was agreed in 1992. It covers inputs and discharges of harmful substances from both land and sea, sets targets for the introduction of additional safeguards for the area, and requires parties to the Convention to take all possible steps to prevent or eliminate pollution. Britain is also a leading participant in the series of North Sea Conferences, the most recent of which was held in Denmark in 1995. Good progress is being made in meeting North Sea Conference targets for reducing the input of hazardous substances into the sea. For example, direct and riverine inputs of lead and mercury to coastal waters were reduced by 75 and 77 per cent respectively between 1985 and 1995.

The Marine Pollution Control Unit (MPCU), part of the Coastguard Agency (see p. 315), is responsible for dealing with spillages of oil or other hazardous substances

Emissions of Carbon Dioxide

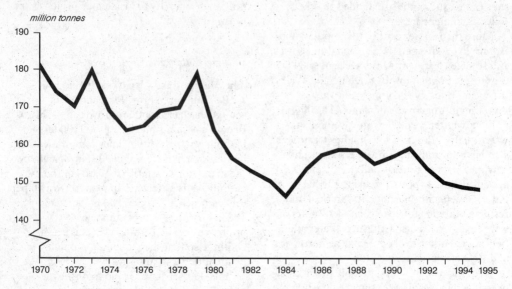

Source: Department of the Environment, Transport and the Regions

from ships at sea. The MPCU has various counter-pollution facilities, including: remote-sensing surveillance aircraft; aerial and seaborne spraying equipment; stocks of oil dispersants; mechanical recovery and cargo transfer equipment; and specialised beach cleaning equipment.

The Government's national contingency plan details arrangements for dealing with pollution. The plan is currently being reviewed in consultation with all interested parties and will, among other things, take account of the lessons learned from the grounding of the tanker *Sea Empress* off south Wales in 1996. The review is due to be completed in 1998.

Licences for oil and gas exploration include special conditions designed to protect the environment. These conditions are agreed with the Joint Nature Conservation Committee (see p. 359). Applicants for licences must demonstrate that they have addressed environmental concerns when developing their work programme. Draft regulations to implement the EC environmental impact assessment directive for offshore oil and gas activities were issued for consultation in August 1997 and are likely to

be brought into force before the end of the year.

Before starting offshore operations, operators are required to have approved oil spill contingency plans in place. In addition, all discharges that contain oil are controlled by legislation, and limits are specified for the permissible level of oil discharged. In response to commitments made at the North Sea Conferences, progressively tighter limits on oil discharged with drill cuttings have been set, which have resulted in an effective ban on their discharge from January 1997. The quantity of oil discharges from this source from installations in British waters fell from 18,500 tonnes in 1988 to 3,180 tonnes in 1995.

. Britain ended the dumping of industrial waste at sea in 1992, and waste has not been licensed for incineration at sea since 1990. The disposal at sea of most other types of waste will be phased out over the next few years. Britain has accepted an internationally agreed indefinite ban on the sea dumping of low- and intermediate-level radioactive waste—the sea dumping of high-level waste is also prohibited. After the phasing out of sewage sludge dumping in 1998, the only category of waste which Britain will routinely dispose of at sea will be silt dredged from ports, harbours and the like. Even this will only be approved if no beneficial use for the material is available.

Air

Air quality in Britain has improved considerably in the last 30 years. Total emissions of smoke in the air have fallen by over 85 per cent since 1960. London and other major cities no longer have the dense smoke-laden fogs, or 'smogs', of the 1950s, and in central London winter sunshine has increased by about 70 per cent since the late 1950s. However, there are still some areas of Britain, most notably parts of Northern Ireland and some areas associated with coal mining, where the use of domestic solid fuel is widespread and contributes to episodes of poor air quality. Furthermore, new concerns have arisen, especially over the emissions from the growing number of motor vehicles, which can produce summertime smogs that can have an adverse impact on health. Measures have consequently been adopted to reduce emissions from road vehicles (see pp. 355–7).

Industrial processes with the greatest potential for producing harmful emissions are controlled under the Environmental Protection Act 1990—enforced in England and Wales by the EA, and in Scotland by SEPA—and are subject to IPC. Processes with a significant but lesser potential for air pollution require approval, in England and Wales from local authorities, and in Scotland from SEPA. Local authorities also control emissions of dark smoke from commercial and industrial premises, and implement smoke control areas to deal with emissions from domestic properties. In Northern Ireland, regulations are in preparation to make illegal the sale of unauthorised fuel in smoke contol areas, and to limit the sulphur content of all domestic solid fuel.

In July 1997, the Government adopted the National Air Quality Strategy, which had been published in March. This sets out objectives for the air pollutants of main concern: nitrogen dioxide, airborne particles, ground-level ozone, sulphur dioxide, carbon monoxide, lead, benzene and 1,3 butadiene. The Strategy, the first of its kind in Europe,

sets air quality objectives to be achieved by 2005 and will start being implemented by the end of 1997.

The Environment Act 1995 places new duties on local authorities in Great Britain to review and assess air quality and prepare remedial action plans where appropriate. Corresponding legislation will shortly be prepared for Northern Ireland. The Government will provide local authorities with guidance and financial assistance, in order to enable them to fulfil their new responsibilities.

Britain has an automatic air quality monitoring network with sites covering much of the country, in both urban and rural areas. It is being extended and upgraded at a cost of over £4 million a year, while local authority sites are being integrated into the national network. The automated urban network currently includes over 135 sites.

Since 1990, daily Air Quality Bulletins have made air pollution data from the monitoring network available to the public. These give the concentrations of the main pollutants, together with an air pollution forecast. The information features in television and radio weather reports, and appears in many national and local newspapers. Information, updated hourly from the automatic monitoring sites, is also available directly on an interactive free telephone number, on videotext systems and on the Internet.

In July 1997 the Government announced a £1 million research programme to find out more about the effects of air pollutants commonly found in the home. Such pollutants, when combined with air pollution seeping in from outside sources, may have adverse health effects. Among the areas of investigation are the interactions between tobacco smoke, allergens and other indoor pollutants; the relationship between indoor and outdoor air pollutants; and the health effects of damp in the home. The key pollutants of interest are particulate matter, carbon monoxide, oxides of nitrogen and organic compounds.

Climate Change

Several gases naturally present in the atmosphere keep the Earth at a temperature suitable for life by trapping energy from the sun—the greenhouse effect. Emissions from human activities are increasing the atmospheric concentrations of several important greenhouse gases, which in turn is thought to be leading to additional global warming. Easily the most significant greenhouse gas in Britain is carbon dioxide (CO_2), followed by methane and nitrous oxide. Some other gases, such as hydrofluorocarbons, have high global warming potential but low levels of emission.

In 1996, the Intergovernmental Panel on Climate Change (IPCC) concluded that the balance of evidence suggested a discernible human influence on global climate. It estimated that between 1990 and 2100 there might be an increase in global surface temperatures of about 2°C—a greater average rate of warming than any seen in the last 10,000 years.

Britain is conducting extensive research into climate change. The research programme includes the construction of an advanced climate change detection instrument for launch on a satellite towards the end of the 1990s, and the work of the Hadley Centre for Climate Prediction and Research.

The Framework Convention on Climate Change was signed by more than 150 nations at the 'earth summit' in Rio de Janeiro (see p. 344). Its objective is to achieve stabilisation of greenhouse gas concentrations in the atmosphere at a level which would prevent dangerous man-made interference with the climate system. Britain is one of a handful of developed countries on course to meet its Convention commitments. By the year 2000, emissions of CO_2 are expected to be between 4 and 8 per cent below 1990 levels; emissions of methane 22 per cent below; and emissions of nitrous oxide 62 per cent below. This achievement would reflect the measures in Britain's *Climate Change Programme*, which was published in 1994 and is based on a partnership between the Government and those who contribute to greenhouse gas emissions.

The Programme includes:

- the removal of subsidies on the use of fossil fuels;

- an annual increase in road fuel duties of 5 per cent in real terms (although the July 1997 budget went further than that, increasing the duty by nearly 7 per cent—see p. 157), and improved fuel efficiency in cars;

- the introduction of value added tax on domestic fuel (although the July 1997 budget reduced the tax from 8 to 5 per cent);

- the promotion of new and renewable sources of energy to enable them to compete in energy markets;

- programmes to improve industrial, commercial and domestic energy efficiency; and

- the adoption of EU minimum efficiency standards for electrical appliances.

Other key factors which have put Britain on course to exceed its targets are a fall in emissions of methane from coal mining and landfill waste; and a 95 per cent cut in emissions of nitrous oxide from the manufacture of chemicals used in the production of nylon (overall levels were 21 per cent lower in 1995 than in 1990).

In 1995 the first conference of parties to the Framework Convention met in Berlin and set in hand a process for agreeing new commitments for the period beyond 2000. The resulting 'Berlin Mandate' is aimed primarily at strengthening commitments from developed nations. Another meeting is due to be held in Kyoto, Japan, at the end of 1997, where a protocol should be agreed to fulfil the Berlin Mandate. The EU is proposing that developed countries should aim to reduce their total emissions of a group of greenhouse gases to at least 7.5 per cent below their 1990 levels by 2005 and 15 per cent below by 2010. In June 1997, Britain set itself the further challenge of reducing its own CO_2 emissions by 20 per cent by the year 2010.

Stratospheric Ozone Layer

Stratospheric ozone forms a layer of gas about 10 km to 50 km (6 to 30 miles) above the Earth's surface, protecting it from the more harmful effects of solar radiation. However, there is evidence for ozone losses over much of the globe, including a 'hole' in the ozone layer over Antarctica, first discovered by British scientists in 1985. Over Britain itself, the ozone layer tends to become thinner in the spring, and the current trend suggests a decrease in total ozone of 5 to 6 per cent a decade. Ozone depletion is caused by man-made chemicals containing chlorine or bromine, such as chlorofluorocarbons (CFCs) or halons, which have been used in aerosol sprays, refrigerators and fire extinguishers.

The Government has made a commitment to the earliest possible phasing out of all ozone-depleting substances. Britain was one of the first 25 signatories to the 1987 Montreal Protocol, which deals with the protection of the stratospheric ozone layer. This required the phasing out of the production of halons by the end of 1993, and the phasing out of CFCs, 1,1,1 trichloroethane and carbon tetrachloride by the end of 1995 in all developed countries. This has been substantially achieved in Britain apart from exemptions for a small number of essential uses, for example in medical inhalers. Consumption of CFCs in the EU as a whole in 1995 was 87 per cent lower than in 1994 and 2 per cent of the 1986 level.

The Protocol has also placed controls on hydrochlorofluorocarbons, which are transitional substances with much lower ozone-depleting potential than CFCs. They are needed in a number of areas to allow industry to cease using CFCs more quickly, but must be phased out in new equipment by 2020. Production and consumption of methyl bromide must be phased out by 2010, although the EU proposed in Montreal in September 1997 that consumption of methyl bromide in developed countries should be reduced to 50 per cent of 1991 levels by 2001 and phased out in 2005.

The Montreal Protocol also imposes controls on developing countries, which are committed to phasing out CFCs by 2010. A multilateral fund has been established to assist developing countries to comply with the controls on ozone-depleting substances; Britain contributes towards this.

Thanks to international action taken under the Montreal Protocol, the ozone layer, though continuing to suffer damage over the next few years, is expected to begin recovering within the next decade.

Emissions of Sulphur Dioxide and Oxides of Nitrogen

Sulphur dioxide (SO_2) and oxides of nitrogen (NO_x) are the main gases that lead to acid rain. The principal sources are combustion plants that burn fossil fuels, such as coal-fired power stations, and, for NO_x, road vehicles. By the end of 1995, national SO_2 emissions had fallen by 52 per cent since 1980. Under an EC directive on the control of emissions from large combustion plants, the Government has published a National Plan setting out further phased reductions in emissions from existing plants: NO_x is to be reduced by 30 per cent by 1998; and SO_2 by 60 per cent by 2003 (in both cases compared with the level in 1980). The latest figures, for 1995, show that Britain has achieved a reduction of 45 per cent for NO_x and 55 per cent for SO_2 (15 per cent ahead of the 1998 target level). Britain has also met the targets set in the first United Nations Economic Commission for Europe (UNECE) protocol on NO_x, and is currently involved in development of a new UNECE NO_x protocol. In 1996 it ratified the second UNECE sulphur protocol, and agreed to secure a reduction of at least 80 per cent in SO_2 emissions from all sources by 2010.

The damaging effect of acid depositions from combustion processes on freshwaters and soils has been demonstrated by scientific research. Lower emissions of SO_2 over the past 20 years (see graph on p. 356) have, however, led to the first signs of a decrease in acidification in some lochs in south-west Scotland.

Vehicle Emissions

Stringent emission standards for passenger cars require new petrol-engined cars to be fitted with catalytic converters. These typically reduce emissions by over 75 per cent. Diesel cars are also subject to strict controls on particulate emissions. Since 1994, vans have had to meet a limit of equivalent severity to cars. Stricter controls for heavy diesel vehicles, including lorries and buses, were

Emissions of Sulphur Dioxide

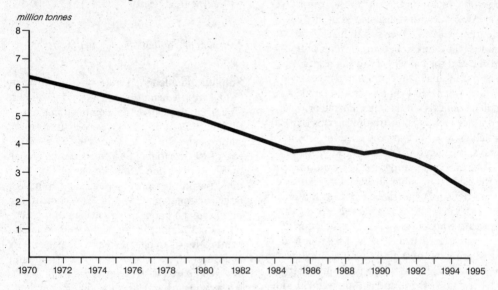

million tonnes

Source: Department of the Environment, Transport and the Regions

introduced in 1993. Further cuts in permitted emission levels from all vehicles were introduced in 1996 and 1997.

Compulsory tests of emissions from vehicles in use are a key element in Britain's strategy for improving air quality. Britain has introduced metered emission tests and smoke checks into the annual 'MoT' roadworthiness test. Limits for vehicles in service were further tightened in 1995, and special tests have been applied to catalyst-fitted vehicles from January 1996. Enforcement checks carried out at the roadside or in operators' premises also include at least a visual check for excessive smoke. Wherever possible, a smoke meter is used for borderline cases. The Vehicle Inspectorate (see p. 307) carried out 125,000 roadside emissions checks in 1996–97 (on cars, coaches, lorries and buses) and 180,000 roadworthiness checks. As a result of these measures, a marked and progressive decline in regulated pollutants is expected, which will continue until well into the first decade of the 21st century.

Sales of unleaded petrol have risen from virtually nothing in the mid-1980s to about 70 per cent of all petrol sold in 1997. This is due mainly to:

- a differential in duty between leaded and unleaded petrol;
- the requirement for all new cars from 1990 onwards to be capable of running on unleaded petrol; and
- the necessity for cars fitted with catalytic converters to use unleaded petrol.

Emissions of lead from petrol-engined road vehicles declined from 7,500 tonnes in 1980 to 1,000 tonnes in 1996.

Regulations introduced in 1994 set compulsory limits to the volatility of petrol for the first time. In 1996 the former Department of the Environment issued guidance on controlling air pollution when storing, loading and unloading petrol at terminals, and unloading petrol into storage at petrol stations. The Government is also consulting on new measures that will reduce the levels of pollutants emitted during refuelling of petrol vehicles at petrol stations. These initiatives should substantially reduce the emission of volatile organic compounds contained in petrol vapour.

The 1994 regulations also brought in a new EU standard for low sulphur diesel fuel, which has further reduced particulate emissions from all diesel vehicles from 1996. In addition, the Government has introduced, from August 1997, a duty differential of 1p per litre between ultra low sulphur diesel and conventional diesel fuel.

For a description of the new Government's proposed integrated transport policy, designed to encourage the wider use of alternative forms of transport to road vehicles, see chapter 19.

Internationally developed standards have been implemented in Britain to control the emission of smoke and unburned hydrocarbons from civil aircraft. International standards to control NO_x and carbon monoxide will be incorporated into domestic legislation.

Noise

Local authorities have a duty to inspect their areas for noise nuisance from premises and vehicles, machinery or equipment in the street, and to investigate complaints. They must serve a noise abatement notice where the noise is judged to be a statutory nuisance. They can also designate noise abatement zones, within which registered levels of noise from certain premises may not be increased without their permission. There are also specific provisions in law to.

- control noise from construction and demolition sites;
- control the use of loudspeakers in the streets; and
- enable individuals to take independent action through the courts against noise nuisance.

The Government believes that, wherever possible, attempts should be made to resolve problems informally. It promotes increased public awareness of neighbour noise issues and also encourages the use of community mediation, funding an umbrella organisation, Mediation UK. However, informal resolution is not always possible. The Noise Act 1996 strengthens the law in England, Wales and Northern Ireland on action that can be taken against noisy neighbours. For example, local authorities can seize noise-making equipment

and may also enforce a discretionary new night noise offence. In addition, the Housing Act 1996 (see chapter 23) gives them new powers to deal with anti-social behaviour by tenants, which includes noise nuisance. Complaints made to Environmental Health Officers in local authorities in England and Wales about noise from domestic premises increased by almost 300 per cent between 1983–84 and 1994–95.

Regulations set out the permissible noise levels for various classes of new vehicle, and a new EC noise directive was implemented in Britain in 1996. Compensation may be payable for loss in property values caused by physical factors, including noise from new or improved public works such as roads, railways and airports. Highway authorities are required to make grants available for insulation of homes that would be subject to specified levels of increased noise caused by new or improved roads. Noise insulation may also be provided where construction work for new roads will seriously affect nearby homes for a substantial period of time. Equivalent regulations have been introduced for new railways.

Britain has played a leading role in negotiations aimed at phasing out older, noisier subsonic jet aircraft. The phased implementation of a complete ban on the operation of 'Chapter 2' aircraft (noisier planes, as classified by international agreement) began in 1995, and it is intended to phase out all these types by 2002. Various operational restrictions have been introduced to reduce noise disturbance further at London's Heathrow, Gatwick and Stansted airports. These measures include:

- restrictions on the type and number of aircraft operating at night;
- the routeing of departing aircraft to minimise noise nuisance; and
- quieter take-off and landing procedures.

The Government has introduced a control system for night flights combining a noise quota with a ceiling on the total number of movements. The population disturbed by aircraft noise[1] at Heathrow airport fell from

---

[1] That is, living within the 57 Leq noise contour, which is generally regarded as the onset of disturbance.

591,000 in 1988 to 319,000 in 1994, even though the number of air transport movements increased. This was largely because of the phasing out of older, noisier aircraft.

'Light pollution' is becoming more widely acknowledged as a problem that needs to be addressed. It is felt that the intrusiveness of artificial light at night, particularly in rural areas, needs to be kept to a minimum, not just because of the nuisance value to humans, but because it disrupts the natural rhythms of the countryside and shuts out the clear night skies. The Government is currently considering ways of raising public awareness of the issue, and, in July 1997, it published a good practice guide for lighting in the countryside.

Radioactivity

Man-made radiation represents only a small fraction—about 15 per cent—of what the population is exposed to; most occurs naturally. A large proportion of the man-made radioactivity comes from medical treatments, such as X-rays. Nevertheless, man-made radiation is subject to stringent control. Users of radioactive materials must be registered by the EA in England and Wales and its equivalents in Scotland and Northern Ireland. Authorisation is also required for the accumulation and disposal of radioactive waste. The Health and Safety Executive (HSE—see p. 185), through its Nuclear Installations Inspectorate, is responsible for granting nuclear site licences for major nuclear installations. No installation may be constructed or operated without a licence granted by the HSE.

In 1987 the Government first announced measures to deal with the problem of radon, a naturally occurring radioactive gas which can accumulate in houses, and which accounts for half of the total average population radiation dose. The measures included a free survey by the National Radiological Protection Board (NRPB) for householders living in areas mostly likely to be affected by radon —Cornwall, Devon, Somerset, Northamptonshire and Derbyshire. Since then, other areas with an above-average number of houses likely to be affected by radon have been identified. As a result of earlier surveys, the NRPB can now predict with much greater accuracy the areas most likely to have substantial numbers of homes above the level that requires action. Free tests are being offered to householders in those areas. In 1996–97, almost 300,000 invitations went out to householders to have free radon measurements, and the NRPB published a detailed map showing areas likely to have high radon levels.

In Northern Ireland, survey work undertaken by the Environment and Heritage Service resulted in the identification of a radon-affected area in South Down/Armagh in 1993. Since then all householders in the area have been offered a free survey. To date some 12,000 houses have been monitored, and since 1994 building control regulations have required the inclusion of radon prevention measures in new dwellings.

Radioactive Waste Disposal

The disposal of radioactive waste is regulated under the Radioactive Substances Act 1993 (as amended by the Environment Act 1995). Radioactive wastes vary widely in nature and level of activity, and the methods of disposal reflect this. Most solid low-level waste (LLW), material of low radioactivity, is disposed of at the shallow disposal facility at Drigg in Cumbria. Some small quantities of LLW are disposed of at authorised landfill sites.

Intermediate-level waste (ILW) is currently stored. UK Nirex Ltd was recently charged with developing a disposal route for ILW. As part of its site investigation programme for a repository, Nirex proposed to construct a Rock Characterisation Facility (RCF) near the British Nuclear Fuels site at Sellafield, in Cumbria (see p. 271). Cumbria County Council refused planning permission for the RCF, and Nirex's appeal against the refusal was dismissed by the Secretary of State for the Environment in March 1997. The

Government is now considering the implications of that decision for radioactive waste management policy. Nirex has no plans to begin investigations at any sites.

The Government is developing a research strategy for the disposal of high-level or heat-generating waste. This waste will first be converted into a glasslike form and then stored for at least 50 years to allow the heat and radioactivity to decay.

Genetically Modified Organisms

Genetically modified organisms (GMOs) have many potentially beneficial uses, such as better and larger supplies of food and advances in health care. As with any new technology, it is important to make sure that there are no significant risks to mankind or the environment. This is done through the Environmental Protection Act 1990 and subsequent regulations. Advice on all applications to release or market GMOs is provided by a statutory advisory committee. Britain participated in drawing up draft international guidelines on safety in biotechnology, which were adopted by the United Nations Environment Programme in 1995. It also supports the development of a safety protocol to the Convention on Biological Diversity, which would focus on transboundary movements of living modified organisms.

Conservation

Britain has a long tradition of conservation, and for many years has had policies and laws designed to protect both its natural environment and its built heritage. A wide variety of designations are used to protect areas, sites and monuments that are of special interest, and various organisations work towards the conservation of different aspects of Britain's national heritage.[2]

The Department of the Environment, Transport and the Regions is responsible for countryside policy and environmental

protection in England; the Department for Culture, Media and Sport has responsibility for the listing of buildings and for the protection, through scheduling, of ancient monuments in England. The Welsh Office, The Scottish Office and the Department of the Environment for Northern Ireland have broadly equivalent responsibilities. These departments delegate many of their conservation responsibilities to the agencies described below. In addition, local authorities and a wide range of voluntary organisations are actively involved in environmental conservation and protection.

The Countryside and Nature Conservation

Five government agencies are responsible for countryside policy and nature conservation in Britain:

- the Countryside Commission and English Nature, which both operate in England, the former being responsible for countryside policy and the latter for nature conservation;
- the Countryside Council for Wales (CCW);
- Scottish Natural Heritage (SNH); and
- the Environment and Heritage Service in Northern Ireland.

English Nature, the CCW and SNH fulfil their responsibilities for international nature conservation matters and those affecting Great Britain as a whole through the Joint Nature Conservation Committee (JNCC). The JNCC also undertakes research in connection with these responsibilities and sets standards for data, monitoring and other matters concerning nature conservation. It includes representatives from Northern Ireland and independent members, and has a supporting specialist staff. Its budget for 1997–98 is £4.5 million.

Countryside Agencies

The Countryside Commission, the CCW, SNH and the Environment and Heritage Service are responsible for promoting the

---

[2] For protection of the countryside and wildlife in an agricultural context, see chapter 18, pp. 293–4.

enhancement of the natural beauty and amenity of the countryside and encouraging the provision of facilities for open-air recreation—while respecting the needs of those who live and work in the countryside. Activities undertaken by these bodies include:

● advising the Government on countryside matters;

● assisting the provision by local authorities and others of facilities for recreation in the countryside, often within easy reach of towns;

● designating and improving recreational rights of way;

● undertaking research projects; and

● ensuring the protection of special landscapes.

Total funding for the countryside agencies in 1997–98 is £24 million for the Countryside Commission, £23 million for the CCW, £37 million for SNH and £21.5 million for the Environment and Heritage Service.

The Countryside Commission recognises over 210 country parks and over 250 picnic sites in England. A further 36 country parks in Wales are recognised by the CCW. In Scotland there are also 36 country parks, and many local authority and private sector schemes for a variety of countryside facilities have been approved for grant aid by SNH.

Nature Conservation Agencies

English Nature, the CCW and SNH are the Government's statutory advisers on nature conservation in their areas. Their work includes:

● establishing and managing National Nature Reserves and encouraging the establishment of Local Nature Reserves;

● advising the Government;

● identifying and monitoring Sites of Special Scientific Interest (SSSIs—see below);

● providing general nature conservation information and advice;

● giving grants; and

● supporting and conducting research.

English Nature's funding for 1997–98 is nearly £39 million.

In March 1997 there were 343 National Nature Reserves in Britain covering more than 200,000 hectares (over 490,000 acres), and three statutory Marine Nature Reserves. Nearly 6,200 SSSIs had been notified in Great Britain for their plant, animal, geological or physiographical features. Some are of international importance and have been designated for protection under the EC Birds Directive or the Ramsar Convention (see p. 366). Local authorities have declared over 500 Local Nature Reserves in England, 23 in Scotland and 38 in Wales.

In England, the Countryside Commission and English Nature have jointly mapped and described areas of distinct landscape and ecological character, covering the whole country (English Nature's 'Natural Areas' and the Commission's Countryside Character Programme). Their *Character Map of England* was launched in December 1996. This framework will underpin the separate programmes of the two agencies and guide countryside policies. The Northern Ireland *Countryside Survey*, published in June 1997, records resources such as woodland, semi-natural vegetation, field boundaries and agricultural land in selected areas across the Province.

English Nature enters into land management agreements with owners and occupiers of SSSI land, increasingly to support management that benefits its wildlife and natural features. Overall, English Nature's grant schemes provide more than £2.2 million a year to assist local action to sustain biodiversity and geodiversity. SNH and the CCW also enter into land management agreements.

Nature conservation in Northern Ireland is the responsibility of the Environment and Heritage Service of DOENI. The NI Council for Nature Conservation and the Countryside advises the DOENI on nature conservation matters, including the establishment and management of land and marine nature reserves and the declaration of Areas of Special Scientific Interest. In all, 129 Areas of Special Scientific Interest had been declared by August 1997, covering 79,260 hectares

(196,000 acres), and 45 statutory nature reserves had been established.

Wildlife Protection

The principal legislation protecting wildlife in Great Britain is the Wildlife and Countryside Act 1981. This:

- extended the list of protected species;
- restricted the introduction into the countryside of animals not normally found in the wild in Britain (in July 1997 the Government proposed to make it illegal to keep non-native *fish* in, or release them into, any waters in England and Wales without a licence—again, to protect native species); and
- afforded greater protection for SSSIs than previously and made provision for Marine Nature Reserves.

There is also provision for reviews of the list of protected species to be conducted by the three official nature conservation agencies, acting jointly through the JNCC, every five years, and for recommended changes to be submitted to the Secretary of State for the Environment, Transport and the Regions (see p. 2). In Northern Ireland separate legislation on species and habitat protection is in line with the rest of Britain.

The Partnership for Action Against Wildlife Crime (PAW) was launched in 1995. In March 1997 PAW made recommendations for action to strengthen the powers of the police and the enforcement of legislation against wildlife crime. It proposed that courts be given the option of imprisoning criminals who steal or kill endangered species, and that greater use should be made of DNA testing in combating crime of this kind. In May 1997, two egg collectors were fined a record £90,000 each for illegally targeting protected birds on a nature reserve on the Scottish island of Orkney.

County wildlife trusts, urban wildlife trusts and the Royal Society for the Protection of Birds (RSPB) play an important part in protecting wildlife throughout Britain, and between them have established over 2,000 reserves. The county and urban trusts are affiliated to a parent organisation, 'RSNC The Wildlife Trusts'. The RSPB is the largest voluntary wildlife conservation body in Europe.

Species Recovery and Reintroduction

Extensive research and management are carried out to encourage the recovery of populations of species threatened with extinction. The three nature conservation agencies have also set up recovery programmes for a number of threatened species of plants and animals. During 1996–97, English Nature's programme covered 49 species, including the bittern, dormouse, lady's-slipper orchid, sand lizard and fen raft spider. The aim is to ensure the survival of self-sustaining populations of these threatened species in the wild. SNH has a programme initially covering 17 species, and the CCW one covering 15 species.

Projects have also been established to reintroduce species into areas in which they used to be found. For example, the red kite had died out in England and Scotland, although it was still found in Wales and mainland Europe. An international project is now being co-ordinated by English Nature, SNH and the RSPB to bring nestling red kites from Sweden, Spain and Germany and release them into the wild in areas which the species had previously inhabited. By 1997, breeding populations had been established in southern England and Northern Scotland. Sand lizards were recently reintroduced to sand dunes on the Welsh west coast, having not been recorded in Wales since the 1950s; and in 1995–96, the natterjack toad was reintroduced to Talacre Warren in Clwyd, where there had previously been strong colonies.

The Royal Botanic Gardens at Kew (see p. 342) holds seeds from about 3,000 plant species which are extinct or under severe threat in the wild, and has been successful with reintroduction projects. Its new Millennium Seed Bank is looking to hold seeds of all seed-bearing plants in Britain by the year 2000, and 10 per cent of flowering

Broadleaved Tree-planting 1980–81 to 1995–96

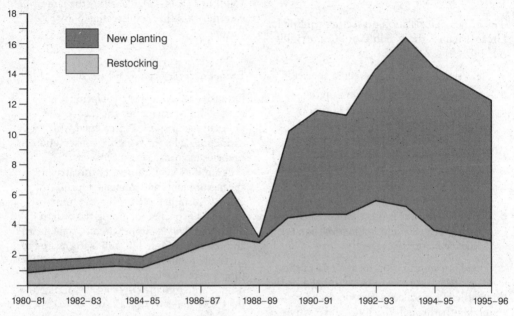

Thousands of hectares

New planting

Restocking

Source: Forestry Commission, Department of Agriculture for Northern Ireland

plants from the arid regions of the world by 2010. The Royal Botanic Gardens in Edinburgh (see p. 342) also plays a significant role.

Tree Preservation and Planting

Tree Preservation Orders enable local authorities to protect trees and woodlands. Once a tree is protected, it is in general an offence to cut down or reshape it without permission. Courts can impose substantial fines for breaches of such orders. Where protected trees are felled in contravention of an order or are removed because they are dying, dead or dangerous, replacement trees must be planted. Local authorities have powers to enforce this.

Tree planting is encouraged through various grant schemes. The planting of broadleaved trees has greatly increased since the 1980s (see graph above). Major afforestation projects involving the DETR and the Countryside Commission include the

creation of 12 community forests near major cities. The Woodland Trust is a voluntary body which protects existing woodland and plants new trees for the future. It now owns 839 woods across Britain, and has planted well over a million trees in the past ten years or so. In Scotland, the Central Scotland Woodland Trust is promoting a major tree-planting and environmental improvement scheme.

In 1997 about 85,000 broadleaved and deciduous trees were planted in a new community woodland at Oughtrington near Warrington, in the north west of England. The land for the tree-planting was bought by the Woodland Trust with the help of a £91,000 grant from the Countryside Commission. Local people raised £20,000 towards the venture. The new woodland will add to the three million trees already planted in the Mersey Community Forest.

Hedgerows

Hedgerows are more than just field boundaries. They are wildlife corridors sheltering a wealth of plant, insect and animal life. For example, three-quarters of Britain's native lowland mammals and birds, and half its butterfly species, breed in hedges. The survival of hedgerows is essential to the promotion of biodiversity.

In recent years, the scale of hedgerow removal has provoked wide concern. Between 1984 and 1993, for example, 67,800 km (42,375 miles) were 'grubbed out' from the countryside of England and Wales. Although the Hedgerows Regulations 1997 were introduced in June, to control the removal of important hedgerows, the new Government believes more should be done to conserve and expand this valuable element of our natural heritage. It has therefore formed a group, including representatives from statutory agencies, local authorities and the main farming and conservation bodies, to review how the Regulations might be strengthened to provide greater protection for hedgerows.

The Coast

Local planning authorities are responsible for planning land use at the coast; they also aim to safeguard and enhance the coast's natural attractions and preserve areas of scientific interest. The protection of the coastline against erosion and flooding is administered centrally by the Ministry of Agriculture, Fisheries and Food, the Welsh Office and The Scottish Office. Operational responsibility lies with local authorities and the EA (see p. 348). The Coastal Forum, administered by the DETR, promotes discussion among key bodies in England with interests in the coast. A similar forum exists in Wales, and the Scottish Coastal Forum provides a national focus, advice and guidance on coastal issues in Scotland. In 1996, the Government published *Coastal Zone Management: Towards Best Practice*, which looks towards identifying the best ways of securing more integrated and sustainable management of the coast.

Certain stretches of undeveloped coast of particular beauty in England and Wales are defined as Heritage Coast. Jointly with local authorities, the countryside agencies have designated 45 Heritage Coasts, protecting 1,530 km (956 miles), about 35 per cent of the total length of coastline.

English Nature provides funds for groups setting up voluntary marine nature reserves and producing or implementing management plans for England's estuaries. So far, 13 reserves have been grant-aided and 29 estuary management plans produced, covering more than 85 per cent of England's total estuarine area. There are also 29 informal marine consultation areas in Scotland. Statutory bodies taking decisions that affect these areas are asked to consult SNH. In addition, SNH has established the Focus on Firths initiative to co-ordinate management of the main Scottish estuaries.

The National Trust, through its Enterprise Neptune campaign, raises funds to acquire and protect stretches of coastline of great natural beauty and recreational value. About £24 million has been raised since 1965 and the Trust now protects 904 km (565 miles) of coastline in England, Wales and Northern Ireland. The National Trust for Scotland also owns large parts of the Scottish coastline and protects others through conservation agreements.

National Parks, Areas of Outstanding Natural Beauty and National Scenic Areas

The Countryside Commission and the CCW can designate National Parks and areas of outstanding natural beauty (AONBs), subject to confirmation by the Secretaries of State for the Environment, Transport and the Regions and for Wales respectively.

Ten National Parks have been established in England and Wales. Their aims are to conserve and enhance the natural beauty, wildlife and cultural heritage they contain, and to promote opportunities for the understanding and enjoyment by the public of the areas they cover. They are 'national' in the sense that they are of special value to the nation as a whole. However, most of the land remains in private hands. The Parks are each administered by an independent National Park Authority which, among other things:

Table 22.1: National Parks and Other Designated Areas, December 1995

	National Parks area (sq km)	Percentage of total area	Areas of Outstanding Natural Beauty (sq km)[a]	Percentage of total area
England	9,630[b]	7	20,393	16
Wales	4,130	20	832	4
Scotland	–	–	10,018	13
Northern Ireland	–	–	2,849	20

Sources: Countryside Commission, Countryside Council for Wales, Scottish Natural Heritage, Department of the Environment for Northern Ireland
[a] National Scenic Areas in Scotland.
[b] This figure excludes The Broads and relates only to those National Parks designated under Section 7 of the National Parks and Access to the Countryside Act 1949.

- acts as the development control authority for its area;
- negotiates land management agreements and encourages farmers to manage their land in the traditional way;
- looks after footpaths and negotiates agreements for public access;
- sets up information centres; and
- employs rangers.

The Norfolk and Suffolk Broads are also administered by their own independent authority and enjoy protection equivalent to that of a National Park. Since 1994 the planning policies that apply to the National Parks have also applied to the New Forest area in Hampshire.

A total of 41 AONBs have been designated, covering around 20,400 sq km (7,900 sq miles) in England and 830 sq km (320 sq miles) in Wales. They comprise parts of the countryside which lack extensive areas of open country suitable for recreation and hence National Park status, but which nevertheless have an important landscape quality. Local authorities are encouraged to give special attention to AONBs in their planning and countryside conservation work.

In Scotland, there are four regional parks and 40 National Scenic Areas, covering more than 11,000 sq km (4,300 sq miles), where certain kinds of development are subject to consultation with SNH and, in the event of a disagreement, with the Secretary of State for Scotland. In addition, the Cairngorms and

Loch Lomond and the Trossachs are two areas of outstanding natural importance in Scotland. For the former, the Government has established a Cairngorms Partnership; in the latter case, the local authorities are considering establishing a joint committee to manage the area.

In Northern Ireland the Council for Nature Conservation and the Countryside advises the Government on the preservation of amenities and the designation of areas of outstanding natural beauty. In all, nine such areas have been designated, covering over 2,800 sq km (1,100 sq miles).

There are 17 forest parks in Great Britain, covering nearly 3,000 sq km (1,150 sq miles) which are administered by the Forestry Commission. There are nine in Northern Ireland, where they are administered by the Forest Service of the Department of Agriculture.

Public Rights of Way and Open Country

Unitary, county and district councils in England and Wales (see p. 80) are responsible for keeping public rights of way signposted and free from obstruction. Public paths are usually maintained by these 'highway authorities', which also supervise landowners' duties to repair stiles and gates. In Scotland, planning authorities are responsible for asserting and protecting rights of way. Subject to public consultation, local authorities in Great Britain can undertake legal procedures to create paths, close paths no longer needed for public use, and divert paths to meet the needs of either the public or landowners. Farmers in England and Wales are required by law to restore any public paths damaged or erased by agricultural operations. England has about 169,000 km (106,000 miles) of rights of way and Wales has about 40,000 km (24,000 miles).

The Countryside Commission is helping authorities with the enormous task of bringing all rights of way in England into good order, and the Parish Path Partnership scheme, introduced in 1992, is designed to stimulate local involvement and improvement. Meanwhile, the CCW is recording public rights of way on a Geographical Information System (GIS) computer database. Information about path conditions is being collected for communities throughout Wales through the Community Path Survey. In Scotland a major new 'Paths for All' initiative has been started by SNH to promote better access to countryside close to towns and cities.

There are ten approved national trails open in England, stretching about 2,800 km (1,740 miles), two in Wales, and three approved-long-distance routes in Scotland, covering about 550 km (345 miles). A new national trail following the route of Hadrian's Wall will be ready in 2001, and proposals for the Cotswold Way national trail have been submitted by the Countryside Commission. A new Pennine Bridleway, designed for horseriders and mountain bikers, was approved in 1995. In Wales, Glyndŵr's Way (a roughly circular route in Powys), and in Scotland a new Great Glen Way, are at an advanced stage of planning.

Horse-riding and cycling in the countryside are encouraged, for both health and environmental reasons. Dozens of volunteers are currently trying to identify 'lost' bridleways in an effort to claim them back for riders as legally defined rights of way. Meanwhile, the National Cycle Network, a nationwide construction project for the Millennium, is being co-ordinated by the charity Sustrans with the help of Lottery funds (see p. 47). One of the aims of the Network, which should have 6,500 miles (10,400 km) of cycleway when completed, is to popularise cycling as a viable alternative to the car.

> **The 1996 UK Day Visits Survey showed that:**
>
> - two-thirds of the population visited the countryside during the course of the year;
> - of the 1,200 million day visits in 1996, 55 per cent were by car, a 5 per cent decrease on the 1994 figure;
> - walking was the single most popular activity, with half the walks involving a distance of over two miles; and
> - each visitor spent on average £5 per visit.

There is no automatic right of public access to open country, although many landowners allow it more or less freely. Local planning authorities in England and Wales can secure access by means of agreements with landowners. If agreements cannot be reached, authorities may acquire land or make orders for public access. Similar powers cover Scotland and Northern Ireland; in Northern Ireland, the primary responsibility lies with district councils. In Scotland, there is a tradition of freedom to roam, based on tolerance between landowners and those seeking reasonable recreational access to the hills.

Common land totals an estimated 550,000 hectares (1.4 million acres) in England and Wales, but a legal right of public access exists for only one-fifth of this area. Common land is usually privately owned, but people other than the owner may have rights over it, for example, as pasture land. There is also a widespread tradition of public enjoyment of such land. Commons are protected by law and cannot be built on or enclosed without government consent in England and Wales. There is no common land in Scotland or Northern Ireland.

The Countryside Commission is hoping to establish at least 250 new 'millennium greens' for local communities in England by the year 2000. By August 1997, 94 communities had progressed to the second step towards creating their own millennium green.

Voluntary Sector

Many voluntary organisations work to preserve the amenities of the countryside, including the National Trust, the Council for the Protection of Rural England, the Campaign for the Protection of Rural Wales, the Association for the Protection of Rural Scotland and the Ulster Society for the Preservation of the Countryside.

The Government assists both these and other voluntary bodies covering the whole spectrum of environmental activity, including the preservation and appreciation of buildings (see p. 368). For example, the Department of the Environment, Transport and the Regions makes grants through the Environmental Action Fund, and The Scottish Office Environment Department makes funds available to organisations to help them carry out conservation, improvement and education work.

International Action

Britain's international obligations to conserve wildlife include the Berne Convention on the conservation of European wildlife and natural habitats, the Bonn Convention on the conservation of migratory species, and EC directives on the conservation of wild birds and of natural habitats and wild fauna and flora. The implementation of the habitats directive, which was adopted into British regulations in 1994, includes the designation of protected sites called Special Areas of Conservation (SACs). Together with Special Protection Areas (SPAs) classified under the EC wild birds directive, SACs will form an EU-wide network of protected sites known as Natura 2000. To date over 100 sites have been identified as possible SACs, and some 74 sites have been classified as SPAs. Britain is also party to the Ramsar Convention on wetlands of international importance, and has over 100 Ramsar sites.

Britain is a party to the Convention on International Trade in Endangered Species of Wild Fauna and Flora (CITES), which strictly regulates trade in endangered species by means of a permit system. In May 1997, the new European Wildlife Trade Regulation was launched, which will ban or control the trade in more than 25,000 species of animals, birds and plants.

The Convention on Biological Diversity was signed by over 150 countries, including Britain, at the 1992 Rio 'earth summit'. It required countries to develop national strategies for the conservation and sustainable use of biological diversity. Britain published its biodiversity action plan in 1994; it provides a strategy for conserving and enhancing biodiversity over the next ten and twenty years.

Follow-up action is now being carried forward by Country Groups in England, Wales, Scotland and Northern Ireland, and a Local Issues Group is providing guidance for the development of Local Biodiversity Action Plans. In Scotland, further guidance based on the practical experience of four pilot local authority areas will be issued in the autumn of 1997. The first progress report on the Action Plans is due in 2000.

The Darwin Initiative forms part of the measures announced by Britain at the first 'earth summit'. It is intended to make British experience, and financial support, available to developing countries with important biological resources, with the aim of assisting the conservation and sustainable use of species there. A committee of experts advises the Government on the Initiative. Nearly 150 projects have been funded so far, including a study of tall grassland habitats in Nepal; the conservation of coral reef fish in Kenya and Egypt; an inventory of the Mbaracayu Forest Nature Reserve in Paraguay; and plant biodiversity conservation training in Eastern Europe.

A new species of bat has been found breeding in Northern Ireland. Nathusius's Pipistrelle, which had previously been only an occasional visitor to the British Isles, was discovered by researchers working with Queen's University, Belfast. In May 1997, they found a nursery roost of these rare bats, with a full complement of females and juveniles, in buildings near Antrim.

Buildings and Monuments

Lists of buildings of special historic or architectural interest are compiled by the Government, in England with the advice of English Heritage. In Scotland and Wales, buildings are listed by Historic Scotland and Cadw: Welsh Historic Monuments, executive agencies of The Scottish and Welsh Offices respectively. It is against the law to demolish, extend or alter the character of any 'listed' building without prior consent from the local planning authority or the appropriate Secretary of State (or from Historic Scotland in Scotland). The local planning authority can issue 'building preservation notices' to protect for six months unlisted buildings that are at risk, while the Government considers whether they should be listed. In Northern Ireland, DOENI, advised by the Environment and Heritage Service and the Historic Buildings Council, is responsible for the listing of buildings.

In England, details of each listed building are contained in about 2,000 volumes (now available on a computerised database as well) which can be inspected at the offices of the Royal Commission on the Historical Monuments of England in Swindon and London. The lists for specific local authorities are also held by the local council planning authorities, where they are available for consultation, and at some public libraries.

Ancient monuments are similarly protected through a system of 'scheduling'. English Heritage, the government agency responsible for the conservation of historic remains in England, is currently engaged in a systematic assessment of all archaeological sites in England, in order to identify which of them

(out of some 600,000) should be afforded statutory protection. Similar efforts are being made to increase the number of listed buildings and ancient and historic scheduled monuments in Wales and in Northern Ireland, where a resurvey of historic buildings began in 1997.

Many of the royal palaces and parks are open to the public; their maintenance is the responsibility of the Secretary of State for Culture, Media and Sport, and Historic Scotland. Historic Royal Palaces and the Royal Parks Agency are the executive agencies which carry out this function outside Scotland.

English Heritage cares for 408 properties on the Government's behalf, advises the Government on certain categories of application for consent to alter or demolish scheduled monuments and listed buildings, and gives grants for the repair of ancient monuments and historic buildings in England. Most of its monuments are open to the public. There were a record 11.3 million visitors to English Heritage properties in 1997, and the number of paying members rose by 13 per cent. Core government funding for English Heritage is £105 million in 1997–98.

In Scotland and Wales, Historic Scotland, which cares for 330 monuments, and Cadw, with 131, perform similar functions. An Ancient Monuments Board and an Historic Buildings Council advise the Secretaries of State. In Northern Ireland, DOENI has 182 historic monuments in its care, managed by the Environment and Heritage Service. DOENI is also advised by a Historic Buildings Council and a Historic Monuments Council.

Local planning authorities have designated more than 8,600 'conservation areas' of special

Table 22.2: Scheduled Monuments and Listed Buildings, 1997		
	Listed buildings	Scheduled monuments
England	365,500[a]	17,087[b]
Wales	19,161	2,985
Scotland	42,200	6,542
Northern Ireland	8,586	1,230

Sources: Department for Culture, Media and Sport, Welsh Office, Environment and Heritage Service of DOENI, The Scottish Office
[a] This is the number of list entries, some of which include more than one building. There are about 450,000 listed buildings in England.
[b] This is the number of schedule entries, some of which cover more than one site. There are approximately 26,000 individual sites in England.

architectural or historic interest in England; there are 478 in Wales, 601 in Scotland and 54 in Northern Ireland, designated by DOENI. These areas receive additional protection through the planning system, particularly over the proposed demolition of unlisted buildings.

The National Heritage Memorial Fund helps towards the cost of acquiring, maintaining or preserving land, buildings, works of art and other items of outstanding interest which are of importance to the national heritage. Government funding for 1997–98 is £5 million. The Fund is also used for distributing the heritage share of the proceeds from the National Lottery (see p. 47). By August 1997, £686 million had been awarded to projects from the Heritage Lottery Fund.

Among the voluntary organisations which campaign for the preservation and appreciation of buildings are:

- the Society for the Protection of Ancient Buildings;
- the Ancient Monuments Society;
- the Georgian Group;
- the Victorian Society;
- the Twentieth Century Society;
- the Architectural Heritage Society of Scotland;
- the Ulster Architectural Heritage Society;
- the Architectural Heritage Fund; and
- the Council for British Archaeology.

Although they are funded largely by subscription and private donations, some of these societies have statutory responsibilities, in recognition of which they receive government support.

The National Trust (for Places of Historic Interest or Natural Beauty), a charity with 2.4 million members, owns and protects well over 300 properties open to the public, in addition to 272,600 hectares (673,300 acres) of land in England, Wales and Northern Ireland. Scotland has its own National Trust, which owns 40 historic buildings, including a number of castles, and 74,800 hectares (184,700 acres) of land.

The Civic Trust makes awards for development and restoration work which enhance surroundings. It undertakes urban regeneration projects and acts as an umbrella organisation for nearly 1,000 civic societies. There are associate trusts in Scotland, Wales and north-east England. In Northern Ireland, there are currently 11 building preservation trusts.

Industrial, Transport and Maritime Heritage

Britain was the first country in the world to industrialise on a large scale, and many advances in manufacturing originated in Britain. The resulting rich industrial heritage includes such sites as the Ironbridge Gorge, where Abraham Darby (1677–1717) first smelted iron using coke instead of charcoal. This has now been designated a World Heritage Site (see below). Many other museums devoted to the preservation of industrial buildings and equipment have been set up, such as the Newcastle Discovery Museum and the Carrickfergus Gasworks Museum.

Britain also pioneered railways, and has a fine heritage of railway buildings and structures. A large number of disused railway lines have been bought by railway preservation societies, and several railway museums have been established, for example, the Steamtown Railway Museum in Carnforth, Lancashire.

The National Heritage Memorial Fund recently awarded £25 million to secure the structure, operation and environment of an 87-mile section of the Kennet and Avon Canal, an important part of Britain's inland waterway heritage (see p. 314).

Reminders of Britain's maritime past are also preserved. Portsmouth is home to HMS *Victory* (Admiral Nelson's flagship), HMS *Warrior* (the world's first iron battleship), and the remains of the *Mary Rose*, the world's only surviving 16th-century warship, raised from the seabed in 1982. The Imperial War Museum has opened the cruiser HMS *Belfast* to the public on the river Thames in London. Isambard Kingdom Brunel's SS *Great Britain*, the world's first large screw-driven ship, is preserved in Bristol. A voluntary body, the Maritime Trust, has been established to preserve vessels and other maritime items of historic or technical interest. The Trust's vessels include the clipper *Cutty Sark* at Greenwich, in London. In all, it is estimated that some 400 historic ships are preserved in Britain, mostly in private hands.

World Heritage Sites

So far, Britain has 14 sites in the World Heritage List, which was established under the World Heritage Convention to identify and secure lasting protection for those parts of the world heritage of outstanding universal value. These sites are:

- Canterbury Cathedral, with St Augustine's Abbey and St Martin's Church, in Kent;
- Durham Cathedral and Castle;
- Studley Royal Gardens and Fountains Abbey, in North Yorkshire;
- Ironbridge Gorge, with the world's first iron bridge and other early industrial sites, in Shropshire;
- the prehistoric stone circles at Stonehenge and Avebury, in Wiltshire;

- Blenheim Palace, in Oxfordshire;
- the city of Bath, in north-east Somerset;
- Hadrian's Wall, the former Roman frontier in northern England;
- the Tower of London;
- the Palace of Westminster, Westminster Abbey and St Margaret's, Westminster, also in London;
- the islands of St Kilda, in Scotland;
- Edinburgh Old and New Towns;
- the castles and town walls of King Edward I, in north Wales; and
- the Giant's Causeway and Causeway Coast, in Northern Ireland.

A fifteenth site has been proposed to UNESCO: Maritime Greenwich in London, including the old Royal Observatory, the National Maritime Museum, the Royal Naval College and the town centre. In addition, Britain has two natural sites in its overseas Dependent Territories (see p. 121): Gough Island (part of Tristan da Cunha) in the South Atlantic; and Henderson Island in the South Pacific.

Further Reading

Digest of Environmental Statistics. Annual report. The Stationery Office, 1997.

Indicators of Sustainable Development for the United Kingdom. HMSO, 1996.

Making Waste Work: A Strategy for Sustainable Waste Management. HMSO, 1996.

The National Air Quality Strategy. The Stationery Office, 1997.

The 1997 Seaside Awards. Tidy Britain Group, 1997.

This Common Inheritance: UK Annual Report 1997. The Stationery Office.

22 Local Development

Economic trends in recent decades have altered traditional patterns and locations of employment. Inner-city areas have suffered from the closure of long-established industries, leaving problems of dereliction and unemployment. Unemployment also affects farming and other industries in the countryside. Government policy seeks to address these problems, as part of a wider strategy for reducing inequalities in British society, using a range of regeneration programmes to stimulate business, employment and physical renewal in deprived urban and rural areas. Through the use of the statutory system of land-use planning and development control it aims for sustainable development, balancing demands for land from business, housing, transport, farming and leisure, while protecting the environment.

A comprehensive review of regeneration policies throughout the country is in progress. Legislation will establish a network of Regional Development Agencies in England with considerable local autonomy to co-ordinate regional economic and social development, which will be aided by an integrated transport policy at national, regional and local levels. The main priorities for planning are decentralisation, giving greater powers to the regions; creating a more integrated approach to policy formulation; and improving efficiency in the working of the planning system.

GOVERNMENT ROLE

The Government's regeneration policies stand alongside programmes for health, education, social services and housing in its overall strategy for reducing economic and social inequalities. The Government Offices for the Regions (GORs—see pp. 6 and 9) carry out many local regeneration and development functions, working in partnership with local communities, including local government, to maximise economic prosperity and quality of life. The aim is to overcome the causes of local and regional social and economic decline— unemployment, bad housing, crime, poor health and a degraded environment.

Policy is guided by five key principles: integration, decentralisation, regeneration, partnership and sustainability. The Government plans to adopt a more coherent and integrated approach to regional economic development and planning, and to improve regional accountability. Together with devolution for Scotland and Wales (see pp. 21–9), the Government is to set up Regional Development Agencies throughout England and also a strategic authority for London. The new Agencies will formulate local priorities, and there will be greater local decision-making. Some regeneration programmes will retain the competitive element introduced by the last Government. Existing partnerships between the private and public sectors will be strengthened. Sustainability will be a central focus, including a strong commitment to a 'green approach'.

The new Regional Development Agencies, which are expected to be operational from April 1999, will have several functions— including promoting inward investment, helping small businesses and co-ordinating regional economic development and wider regeneration. They will work closely with the GORs (sharing for the most part the same boundaries), local authorities and Training and Enterprise Councils (see p. 175).

A major new strategy document for the development of Northern Ireland up to 2025 *Shaping Our Future*—was released in June 1997. Following extensive consultation, a Regional Strategic Framework will be published in 1998, taking into account the need for a coherent and integrated approach towards economic, social, environmental and community development.

REGENERATION

A Single Regeneration Budget (SRB), brings together 20 previous programmes. Several of the more important ones are described below. Urban issues in Scotland, Wales and Northern Ireland are being tackled by Programme for Partnership, the Programme for the Valleys and the Making Belfast Work initiative respectively, as well as by various other government programmes (see pp. 374–7). Another set of programmes and policies are directed at addressing the needs of rural areas.

The National Millennium Exhibition will take place at Greenwich in London from December 1999 on a 320-hectare (800-acre) derelict site on the banks of the River Thames, with funding from government, the National Lottery (see p. 47) and private sponsorship. Education and technology for the future will be key features of the exhibits. Current plans also include the development, on adjacent land, of 5,000 homes, a business district, and industrial and retail areas. Seven of the most deprived boroughs in Britain surround the exhibition area. Between 10 and 12 million paying visitors are expected to attend the Exhibition, which will last at least 12 months. The Exhibition's centrepiece will be a 320m-wide, 50m-high Millennium Dome, designed by the Richard Rogers Partnership. Parks, lakes and riverside walks will be a permanent legacy. Projects and events celebrating the new millennium will take place in many other parts of Britain (see p. 47).

Single Regeneration Budget

The Secretary of State for the Environment, Transport and the Regions has overall responsibility for the SRB, which came into operation in 1994 and has a budget of over £1,300 million for 1997–98. The aim is to promote flexible and locally responsive forms of regeneration. The main programmes funded by the SRB are administered by the GORs. The SRB Challenge Fund supports bids for local regeneration initiatives. The first two bidding rounds were for schemes starting in 1995 and 1996; further schemes, commencing in 1997, were given approval in the third round. A fourth bidding round was launched in March 1997, with supplementary guidance for the round published in July. In total, some £1,700 million will be available for new regeneration projects during the three years to 1999–2000. These, it is hoped, will create or safeguard 650,000 jobs, support over 90,000 new businesses, complete or improve 250,000 homes and support over 40,000 voluntary or community groups. On average, every £1 of Challenge Fund money is estimated to attract £2.50 of private investment.

The Urban Forum, a national body, brings together voluntary organisations engaged in urban policy and regeneration. Its aims are to act as a communication channel between the voluntary sector and the Government; develop new ideas; and encourage local communities and voluntary groups to engage in regeneration partnerships.

City Challenge

Under the City Challenge initiative, local authorities were invited, in partnership with the private and voluntary sectors, local communities and government agencies, to submit plans for regenerating key urban neighbourhoods by tackling problems of physical decay, lack of economic opportunity and poor quality of life. There have been two rounds of the City Challenge competition, with 31 successful partnerships each receiving government funding of £37.5 million over five years. In the six-year period to 1997–98, when the initiative will end, £1,162 million of City Challenge money is expected to attract over £4,700 million of private sector investment.

In addition, it is forecast that these partnerships will improve over 98,000 dwellings, create or preserve over 147,000 jobs, create or improve over 3.3 million sq metres of business or commercial floor space and assist over 8,000 new business start-ups. Many principles of the City Challenge initiative have been taken forward in the SRB Challenge Fund programme.

Urban Development Corporations

Twelve urban development corporations (UDCs) were set up in England to reverse large-scale urban decline. The first two, London Docklands and Merseyside, started operations in 1981. Ten others were subsequently established: Birmingham Heartlands, Black Country (West Midlands), Bristol, Leeds, Central Manchester, Plymouth, Sheffield, Trafford Park (Greater Manchester), Teesside, and Tyne and Wear. At their peak, the UDCs covered about 16,000 hectares (about 40,000 acres). The Bristol, Leeds and Central Manchester development corporations have been closed down; all the other UDCs are scheduled to be wound up by March 1998. Public expenditure on the programme will amount to £3,900 million over the lifetime of the UDCs, including spending on the Docklands Light Railway (see p. 313).

English Partnerships

The key objectives of English Partnerships, a government agency, are to create job opportunities, attract inward investment and improve the environment, through the reclamation and development of vacant, derelict and contaminated land throughout England. It works with other public bodies and the private and voluntary sectors. English Partnerships has negotiated the transfer of 56 non-operational coal sites from British Coal, and has announced a ten-year package of regeneration plans with the potential to generate more than 50,000 jobs in coalfield areas. In 1996–97 a total of 468 new projects were approved, which English Partnerships estimate to be creating 24,200 jobs, reclaiming 1,100 hectares (2,700 acres) and attracting £630 million in private finance. The budget for 1997–98 is about £300 million. Assistance is available from the European Regional Development Fund (ERDF—see p. 199).

Compacts

Over 100 school/industry Compacts have been introduced in England during the past 15 years (see p. 447). They aim to motivate young people to achieve more at school and to continue in further education and training after age 16. Over 224,000 young people, 1,600 schools and 21,000 employers participated in Compacts in 1995–96.

Regional Enterprise Grants

The DTI's Regional Enterprise Grant programme has been supporting investment and innovation projects in small firms in certain designated areas. A total of £14.8 million was allocated to small businesses in 1996–97.

Other Measures

The first of a network of City Technology Colleges was opened near Birmingham in 1988; 15 are currently operating. Intended to raise educational standards, the colleges have been established jointly by government and industry. Training programmes (see chapter 12) are also helping many people in the inner cities. In addition, over 100 Employment Service 'outreach' staff are based in, or regularly visit, inner-city areas, where they help unemployed people look for jobs and encourage them to participate in employment and training programmes. This activity supplements normal Jobcentre services.

The Government encourages tourism as a force for improving inner-city areas, and a number of major projects which create a cultural and artistic focus for inner-city regeneration have been undertaken. Examples include the development of the Royal Armouries Museum at Clarence Dock in Leeds, which opened in 1996 at a cost of over £40 million, and the International Convention Centre in Birmingham. The English Tourist Board and regional tourist boards encourage promotional activities in inner-city areas through local initiatives bringing together tourist boards, local authorities, the private sector and other agencies.

Groundwork Trusts

Groundwork Trusts seek to alleviate environmental problems arising from dereliction and vandalism and to increase public awareness of opportunities to change and improve local environments. They work in partnership with public bodies, the private sector, other voluntary organisations and individuals. Over 100 local authorities are involved, including eight in London and 23 metropolitan districts. The Groundwork Foundation is a national body providing the Trusts with advice and support.

Housing Action Trusts

The six Housing Action Trusts (HATs) are non-departmental public bodies charged with the task of regenerating severely rundown housing estates in north Hull, Liverpool, Birmingham (Castle Vale estate) and the London boroughs of Waltham Forest, Tower Hamlets and Brent (Stonebridge estate). The HATs manage 16,700 existing properties, and have ten-year programmes in which to complete their work. HATs' integrated approach to regeneration includes programmes to provide homes, education, training, employment and recreational facilities for their 38,000 residents. Since 1991 the HATs have provided 1,406 new and 3,545 renovated homes, found training places for over 4,000 residents and created or preserved 3,200 jobs, 83 per cent of which have been filled by estate residents.

European Union Programmes

Rundown areas in Britain benefit from EU Structural Funds (see p. 126). These come mainly from the ERDF, which finances infrastructure projects and support for industry, among other things. Objectives for the Funds include regenerating areas affected by industrial decline and combating long-term unemployment. The Department of the Environment, Transport and the Regions (DETR) is responsible for co-ordinating ERDF programmes in England. About £1,000 million from the ERDF has been allocated to declining industrial (Objective 2) regions in England during the period 1997–99. England has also been allocated £200 million and £130 million under Objectives 1 and 5b (see p. 199) for the same period. Scotland, Wales and Northern Ireland also receive ERDF (£400 million, £180 million and £290 million respectively in 1997–98) under Objectives 1, 2 and 5b. The EU Special Support Programme for Peace and Reconciliation is allotting Northern Ireland projects a total of £56.7 million during 1997–98 (see p. 377).

Rural Development

The British countryside continues to undergo considerable change. Employment in traditional sectors such as agriculture, mining and rurally based defence establishments is in decline and small firms are increasingly important to the rural economy. The need remains for more diverse employment opportunities; the tourism industry, for example, provides work openings for many areas. Rapid technological change is giving new chances for industry to overcome problems of remoteness arising from a rural location, though availability of advanced telecommunications infrastructure is still far from universal. Faxes, modems, the Internet and other IT equipment now make it much easier for people to work at home. Some rural areas have been successful in recent years in attracting high-technology industries. Other areas, however, have fragile economies which require diversity to become robust.

Low wages remain a characteristic of many rural areas and the decline of local services causes major problems for many people. The movement of people into the countryside from the towns has increased the demand for housing and, with a major projected growth in the number of households, this is likely to continue.

The Rural Development Commission is the government agency concerned with the economic well-being of the people who live and work in rural England. During 1997–98 it expects to spend some £45 million. The bulk of this money is targeted at 31 Rural Development Areas (RDAs), which cover 35 per cent of the land area of England and 2.75 million people. Expenditure within the RDAs is used to diversify the rural economy and strengthen rural communities through projects developed in partnership with the private, public and voluntary sectors. The Commission also supports the voluntary sector and key services countrywide. Nationally, the Commission has an important role in advising and influencing government and other organisations.

Wales, Scotland and Northern Ireland

Wales

The Welsh Capital Challenge (WCC), introduced in April 1997, is designed to support an integrated approach to capital expenditure which promotes economic, environmental and social development, and which benefits disadvantaged urban and rural areas in Wales. In 1997–98 the WCC awarded £20 million for projects commencing in that year and an additional £12 million for forward commitments, generating over £27 million of private sector investment. In the longer term this assistance is expected to stimulate further investment of nearly £80 million by the private sector and create an additional 1,800 jobs.

The Strategic Development Scheme (SDS) is designed to support local authority strategies and projects for economic, environmental and social development, and gives particular backing to comprehensive local regeneration plans based on local partnerships involving the voluntary and private sectors. Over a three-year period, from 1997–98, the SDS is in the process of transferring to the control of local authorities, until some £38 million is at their disposal. The delegated funding for 1997–98 is £11.6 million. Ministers are due to announce arrangements for the 1998–99 WCC and SDS shortly after their review of all economic grant schemes administered by the Welsh Office, local authorities, development agencies, and other bodies.

The Programme for the Valleys for 1993–98 built on previous programmes for the south Wales valleys and introduced new initiatives for social, economic and environmental regeneration. Its objective was to create jobs; improve training, education and transport; enhance the quality of the environment; widen the quality and choice of housing; and improve the health of local people. In 1997 the Government announced proposals for creating job opportunities in the Valleys through the development of industrial villages—new small and medium-sized high-technology companies supplying larger factories near the M4 motorway in Wales.

As part of its economic and environmental development activities, the Welsh Development Agency (WDA; see p. 31), together with local authorities and the private sector, is working to regenerate and revitalise towns and cities throughout Wales. Attracting inward investment is a key priority. In urban areas, through infrastructure and environmental improvement schemes during the last three years, it estimates that it has brought in £268 million of private sector investment. Urban Investment Grant encourages private sector developments on derelict and rundown sites in urban areas; the 1997–98 budget is £6.8 million. Other capital development programmes have also played a vital role in the expansion of the economy. For example, the property development programme provides readily available industrial premises, both for local businesses and inward investment projects.

Development is also encouraged by the Land Authority for Wales, a statutory body with powers to make land available for urban progress, employment and social housing in circumstances where the private sector would find this difficult on its own. It is a self-financing land trading body which ploughs back its profits for future investment.

The Cardiff Bay Development Corporation was set up in 1987 to promote renewal in part of south Cardiff, once the city's commercial centre. Government support for the Corporation will be £53 million in 1997–98. The Corporation's regeneration strategy includes a barrage project, which will create a large freshwater lake within Cardiff Bay and 12 km (7 miles) of waterside frontage; a 400-hectare (990-acre) bird reserve is to be provided nearby to help compensate for the loss of the Cardiff Bay habitat. Work on the barrage is scheduled for completion in December 1998; the bird reserve should be ready before then. The regeneration targets are for the creation of 29,000 new jobs in the Cardiff Bay area, 5,900 new homes and over £1,500 million of private investment.

The Development Board for Rural Wales builds industrial and commercial premises, provides a range of services to business and promotes rural Wales abroad as a suitable location for inward investment. In 1997–98 it has a government budget of £20 million.

The 1997 White Paper *A Voice for Wales*, which set out the Government's plans for a Welsh Assembly, contained proposals to create a new 'economic powerhouse' agency for Wales in advance of the establishment of an Assembly. A transfer of the functions and responsibilities of the Land Authority for Wales and the Development Board for Rural Wales to the WDA would form the nucleus of the powerhouse. The intention is that the expanded WDA should cover urban and rural Wales; offer a range of services to business; provide the land, sites and premises needed by new and expanding businesses; and act as a single point of contact for inward investors.

Scotland

Programme for Partnership, the current urban regeneration policy framework, was introduced in 1996. Under Programme for Partnership, council-wide partnerships have been formed in areas where there is significant deprivation to develop broad regeneration strategies. Each of these partnerships comprises the local council, Scottish Homes (see p. 385), the Local Enterprise Company (see p. 175), other relevant agencies, and representatives from the private sector, the community and the voluntary sector. The partnerships have in turn developed proposals for Priority Partnership Areas (PPAs) and Regeneration Programmes (RPs). A PPA is a comprehensive regeneration initiative, lasting up to ten years. An RP is a connected series of regeneration proposals, backed by an overview of an area's needs, and lasts for up to five years.

Programme for Partnership builds on the experience gained from four partnerships.[1] Set up in 1988, three of these are still operational, led by the Scottish Office and involving Scottish Enterprise (see p. 197), Scottish Homes, local authorities, the private sector and local communities. Their objectives include plans to better the quality and tenure mix of housing available to local people; improve employment prospects by providing more opportunities for training and further education; and tackle social and environmental problems on housing estates.

Progress has been made by each Partnership in implementing its individual strategy. That at Whitfield met its objectives early, and the Scottish Office withdrew from it in May 1995. However, the remaining partners have pledged to carry forward and sustain the regeneration process. The Scottish Office will withdraw from the three remaining

---

[1] Whitfield (Dundee), Castlemilk (Glasgow), Wester Hailes (Edinburgh) and Fergustie Park (Paisley).

partnerships, after about ten years, during 1997–2000. As the progress made in these areas must be protected, forward planning groups have been set up to consider how this can be done.

Local Enterprise Companies (LECs—see p. 175), working under contract to Scottish Enterprise, have substantial budgets and a range of powers and functions to improve the environment and encourage business and employment in their areas. Responsibility for derelict land reclamation also rests with Scottish Enterprise, LECs and Highlands and Islands Enterprise. They may acquire and reclaim land either by agreement or compulsorily; they seek to work more closely with the private sector to bring land back into use.

Many employers and business organisations participate in Education Business Partnerships in Scotland. The Training and Employment Grants scheme is designed to increase access to employment opportunities for young and long-term unemployed people.

A Partnership Fund, established in 1996, supports rural partnerships of government departments and agencies, private sector bodies and voluntary groups with responsibilities in rural areas. A National Rural Partnership has been established to encourage the formation of such local associations and to advise on spending priorities for the Partnership Fund.

Northern Ireland

The Department of the Environment for Northern Ireland (DOENI) leads an urban regeneration drive through its Urban Regeneration Group (URG). The URG has a budget of about £52 million for 1997–98 and aims to improve economic, social and environmental conditions, its main focus of activity being deprived and rundown areas. It operates either with other government and public sector bodies or through grants to the private sector, including community and voluntary groups. It also works with the International Fund for Ireland (IFI) and implements parts of several EU programmes; these sources provide additional financial assistance.

The URG plans to spend £10.8 million in 1997–98 through Urban Development Grant,

Comprehensive Development Schemes and Environmental Improvement Works. The first is Northern Ireland's principal urban regeneration measure. Its objective is the economic and physical renovation of inner-city areas of Belfast and Londonderry, by encouraging private enterprise and investment in property development, leading to job creation and improvement of the environment. Since 1983, £66 million of Urban Development Grant is estimated to have generated £240 million of private sector investment in Belfast, while in Londonderry grant worth £27 million has brought in some £71 million of private funding. Projected Urban Development Grant expenditure for the two cities in 1997–98 is £5.4 million.

The Community Economic Regeneration Scheme (CERS), launched in 1989 to focus on Belfast and Londonderry and larger towns, and the Community Regeneration and Improvement Special programme (CRISP), launched in 1990, for small towns, are designed to provide facilities such as workshops and commercial outlets, and help to boost local employment in areas where the private sector is reluctant to invest. Both schemes are funded by the DOENI with the IFI (see p. 19). Some 16 CERS and 49 CRISP schemes have been implemented with some £30 million of URG funds and about £41 million from the IFI. Planned URG expenditure in 1997–98 is £3 million, which should be matched or perhaps exceeded by the IFI.

In Belfast the Laganside Development Corporation is charged with regenerating the once derelict area around Belfast docks and the city's waterfront. Its annual DOENI grant is about £7.6 million. The estimated investment in Laganside since 1989 has been about £100 million, in addition to the Corporation's own expenditure. Recent events include the opening of the Waterfront Concert Hall/Conference Centre, owned by Belfast City Council. The Making Belfast Work initiative (MBW) aims to strengthen and more precisely target community, private and public sector efforts to tackle the problems of the city's most disadvantaged areas—by increasing employability and improving the quality of life. By March 1997 the MBW had received some £200 million; planned spending in 1997–98 is £20.7 million. Belfast also has a Partnership Board, with public, private, trade union and voluntary sector interests, to promote a long-term vision of, and policies for, urban renewal. The work of the DOENI's Belfast Development Office and of the MBW are to be merged into a Belfast Regeneration Office.

The Londonderry Regeneration Initiative (LRI) addresses dereliction, social deprivation and economic difficulties. By March 1997 some £23 million had been allocated to the LRI, with estimated spending in 1997–98 of £2.7 million. Londonderry also has a Partnership Board.

EU programmes implemented through the URG include the Special Support Programme for Peace and Reconciliation, whose sub-programmes seek to promote urban regeneration and to improve the social and physical environment, develop derelict sites, enhance areas where sectarian conflict has been marked, and provide amenities supported by local communities and new employment opportunities in areas of greatest need. Under sub-programme 6, a District Partnership to harness the energies and talents of local groups has been established in each district council area of Northern Ireland. The Physical and Social Environment sub-programme 2 targets need at community level. The Urban Community Initiative in Belfast and Londonderry seeks solutions to socio-economic problems. Its Belfast sub-programme especially targets Shankhill and Upper Springfield; that for Londonderry focuses on the Creggan estate, the Fountain area and the Bogside/Brandywell districts.

Public Sector Land

The Department of the Environment, Transport and the Regions (DETR) promotes the sale and development of vacant and under-used public sector land in England. Information is being assembled on potential key sites and, where there are no firm plans to market or develop them, action will be taken to promote their sale. Under the 'Public Request to Order Disposal' scheme, members of the public are encouraged to ask the Government to instruct public bodies to dispose of vacant or under-used land on the open market. In 1994 the rules governing the way local authorities can spend the proceeds of asset sales were altered to encourage the sale of surplus land.

PLANNING

Direct responsibility for land-use planning in Great Britain lies with local authorities. The Secretaries of State for the Environment, Transport and the Regions, Wales and Scotland have overall responsibility for the operation of the system. The DETR brings together the major responsibilities for land-use planning, housing and construction, countryside policy and environmental protection, and transport in England. The Welsh and Scottish Offices have broadly equivalent responsibilities. In Northern Ireland, the DOENI, through the Planning Service Agency, is in charge of planning matters, liaising with the district councils.

In England, the DETR provides national and regional guidance on planning, while strategic planning is the responsibility of the county councils and unitary district authorities. In Scotland, the Scottish Office issues National Planning Policy Guidelines and Planning Advice Notes. At present in England, most district councils are responsible for local plans and development control. In London and the metropolitan counties, and in some non-metropolitan unitary areas, districts prepare unitary development plans and are responsible for development control. In Wales and Scotland, planning responsibilities rest with the new unitary authorities and council areas (see p. 80).

Development Plans

Development plans have a central role in shaping patterns of progress in an area, as planning decisions must be made in accordance with the development scheme unless 'material considerations' indicate otherwise. In England and Wales, the preparation of a district-wide development plan is mandatory. The Government is considering further measures to speed up plan adoption.

The present system in England comprises structure, local and unitary development plans. Structure plans set out broad policies for the development and use of land, which are adopted by county councils and some unitary councils. In some cases planning arrangements for local authorities require structure planning to be carried out over an area wider than that of an individual authority. In these circumstances, unitary authorities are given structure plan responsibility for their own area so that they can work jointly with neighbouring authorities to maintain a joint scheme covering their combined areas. Local plans are prepared in general conformity with the adopted structure plan, and provide detailed guidance for development; these are adopted by most district councils and National Park authorities. Unitary development plans, setting out both strategic and detailed land-use and development policies, are adopted by metropolitan districts, London boroughs and some non-metropolitan unitary authorities. County and unitary councils also draw up local plans for minerals and waste issues, for which they are the development control authority.

In Wales, the new unitary authorities have taken over responsibility for plan preparation and will be drawing up unitary development plans for their areas. It is intended to have these plans in place by the year 2000. In Scotland, where unitary development plans are not a feature of the system, the new councils have also undertaken responsibility for plan preparation; in some cases, structure plans will be taken forward by a number of councils working together. Under Northern Ireland's single-tier system, plans are prepared by the DOENI.

Members of the public are encouraged to participate in the formulation of plan policies and proposals. They can formally object and, in the case of local and unitary development plans, make their case in public to an independent inspector (reporter in Scotland). When devising plans, the authorities must take account of any national or regional guidance issued by the Government; regional guidance exists only in England.

An important element of the Government's strategy for sustainable development (see chapter 21) is for full use to be made of urban land in existing towns and cities, while having regard to the quality of the urban environment, in order to avoid the need to develop 'greenfield' sites and to reduce transport demands. In 1996 the previous Government announced new planning guidance aimed at revitalising town centres in England. It encouraged a plan-led approach to promoting development in town centres, emphasised the importance of a coherent town centre parking strategy in maintaining urban vitality, and required a clearer assessment of out-of-town retail proposals that could have an impact on the viability of town centres. When putting forward out-of-town retail proposals, developers are expected to demonstrate that they have first thoroughly examined more central sites. While broadly similar guidance for Scotland also came out in 1996, the then Government issued for consultation in March 1997 draft revised guidance directed at clarifying the policy to secure more consistent interpretation of the original principles. The finalised guidance emphasises government commitment to town centres.

Green Belts

Green Belts are areas of land meant to be left open and free from inappropriate development. The aims are to check the sprawl of large built-up areas; safeguard surrounding countryside from encroachment; prevent neighbouring towns from merging; preserve the special character of historic towns; and assist in urban regeneration by encouraging the re-use of derelict and other urban land.

Green Belts have been established around major cities and conurbations, including London, Aberdeen, Edinburgh, Glasgow, Merseyside, Greater Manchester and the West Midlands, as well as several smaller towns. Some 1.5 million hectares (3.8 million acres) are designated as Green Belt in England and 155,000 hectares (380,000 acres) in Scotland. The Government attaches great importance to the protection of Green Belts, which have been a cornerstone of the planning system for over 40 years. Planning guidance on Green Belts in England was revised in 1995 to strengthen the strict controls over development and to secure greater benefits for the environment. Guidance on Green Belts in Wales was introduced in 1996.

Development Control

Most development requires specific planning permission. Applications are dealt with in the light of development plans and other relevant planning considerations, including national and regional guidance. Currently, about 450,000 applications for planning permission are received by district councils in England each year, of which some 88 per cent are approved. The Government is keen to speed up the planning process, and local authorities in Great Britain have been set the target of deciding 80 per cent of applications within eight weeks. In Scotland, planning authorities have been set a target of determining at least 80 per cent of applications within two calendar months. However, an increased target of 85 per cent has been set for minor business and industry, and other minor development applications. This target rises to 90 per cent for householder applications within the same two-month deadline.

Local planning authorities in England and Wales have a duty to publicise planning applications in their areas. Methods commonly used include site notices, newspaper advertising and notifying neighbours. In Scotland applicants are required to notify owners, occupiers and, in some cases, lessees of neighbouring land and buildings when an application is submitted to the planning authority. Newspaper advertising is required for certain types of development. Applicants have a right of appeal to the relevant Secretary of State if a local authority refuses planning permission, grants it with conditions attached, or fails to decide an application within eight weeks[2] (or whatever longer period is agreed with the applicant). The majority of appeals are decided on the basis of written submissions. However, either party has the right to be heard by an inspector (reporter in Scotland) at a public local inquiry or at a hearing. A local inquiry is usually held for more complicated or controversial applications. In Northern Ireland, neighbour notification and newspaper advertising are carried out by the DOENI Planning Service Agency. Appeals are determined by the Planning Appeals Commission, which is also responsible for holding public local inquiries.

The Secretaries of State can decide that a planning application should be referred to them for decision. They generally only use this power to 'call in' proposals which raise planning issues of national or regional importance. In such circumstances, applicants and local planning authorities have the right to be heard by a person appointed by the Secretary of State, and a public inquiry will normally be held. Examples of major proposals considered at public inquiry include a fifth terminal at London's Heathrow Airport and the proposed superquarry at Lingerabay on Harris (Outer Hebrides). In Northern Ireland, major planning applications can be referred to a public inquiry in certain circumstances.

The Scottish Office has launched a 1997 Quality Awards Scheme which will highlight excellence in the planning service.

Environmental Impact Assessment

Planning applications for certain types of development must be accompanied by an environmental statement. This should describe the likely adverse environmental effects and measures to minimise them.

In the next 20 years some 4 million houses and flats may have to be built in England to accommodate people in need of decent housing. The Government has stressed that the countryside should not normally be used for constructing houses for needy urban dwellers; these people should be housed in towns and cities in accordance with overall plans for sustainable urban development. Any additional new housing in rural areas ought to be in keeping with the traditional character of the countryside and not be prejudicial to the environment.

---

[2] Two calendar months in Scotland.

Statements are available to the public and statutory bodies such as the Countryside Commission and English Nature (see pp. 359–60). Planning authorities must consider the environmental statement, and any representations received on it, before granting planning permission.

Architectural Standards and the Built Environment

The Government emphasises the importance of good design and architectural quality, both in individual buildings and in the built environment as a whole. The appearance of new developments, and their relationship to their surroundings, are issues that should be addressed through the style of individual buildings and through the urban pattern. While local planning authorities are expected to reject designs which are out of scale or character with their surroundings, the Government's view is that they should not seek to control the detailed composition of buildings unless the sensitive character of their location justifies it, nor should they seek arbitrarily to impose a particular architectural taste or look. Guidance on architectural competitions has been updated by the DETR and the Department for Culture, Media and Sport. The Royal Fine Art Commissions for England and Scotland advise government departments, local planning authorities and other public bodies on questions of quality, public amenity and artistic importance.

The new Architects Registration Board, together with the architects' professional bodies—the Royal Institute of British Architects, the Royal Incorporation of Architects in Scotland and the Royal Society of Ulster Architects—exercises control over standards in architectural training and encourages high standards in the profession. The Royal Town Planning Institute carries out similar functions for the planning profession.

Further Reading

Assessing the Impact of Urban Policy. HMSO, 1994.

Environmental Appraisal of Development Plans: A Good Practice Guide. HMSO, 1993.

Environmental Assessment: A Guide to the Procedures. HMSO, 1989.

Urban Regeneration. Aspects of Britain series. HMSO, 1995.

23 Housing

In all, 181,100 new dwellings were constructed in Great Britain in 1996, compared with 189,900 in 1995. Owner-occupation has increased from 50 per cent in 1971 to 67 per cent at the end of 1996. The public, charitable and private sectors all build housing for sale or rent, with about four-fifths of new dwellings being constructed by the private sector for sale to owner-occupiers. Local authorities, housing associations and the private sector provide low-cost housing for rent or sale. Supporting home ownership and ensuring an adequate provision of social and private rented housing are key government objectives. The release of receipts from the sale of council houses will provide additional resources for building and refurbishing homes to meet need. Further measures to tackle homelessness are being taken.

Government Policies

The Secretary of State for the Environment, Transport and the Regions in England and the Secretaries of State for Wales, Scotland and Northern Ireland are responsible for formulating housing policy and supervising the housing programme. The Government is working towards stability in the housing market. Building societies, banks and other providers of mortgages are encouraged to offer flexible mortgages for home owners, and there will also be greater protection for consumers against the sale of unfair mortgage packages.

Measures are planned to prevent the problem of 'gazumping': this refers to a situation in which the vendor of a property breaks an agreement with a would-be purchaser and accepts a higher purchase price from someone else, the original would-be purchaser having already incurred legal, survey and other costs. Gazumping does not occur in Scotland, which operates a system of sealed bids for buying properties.

Rented Housing

The Government supports partnership between the public sector, registered social landlords (RSLs) and the private sector as providers of good quality 'social housing'— housing provided at rents affordable to people on low incomes, usually substantially below market rents. Social rented housing is usually owned either by local authorities or by RSLs, and accounts for over a fifth of all homes. Set-aside receipts from the sale of council housing stock by local authorities are to be re-invested gradually in building new houses and rehabilitating existing properties.

Schemes to utilise private finance to improve the public housing stock and provide greater choice of housing will be encouraged; however, such schemes will only go ahead with the consent of the tenants concerned. Greater protection will be given to tenants of private rented houses in multiple occupation (HMOs). The Government will publish an approved code of practice setting out the amenity and fire safety standards required in HMOs and bring into effect a new duty on HMO landlords to keep their properties fit for the number of occupants. The Government also intends to introduce a national mandatory licensing system for HMOs.

A new form of tenure, 'commonhold', will be introduced in England and Wales, enabling leaseholders of flats to own their homes individually and the common parts of the buildings containing their homes collectively. Commonhold and other similar tenure systems have been working successfully in Australia and other countries for many years; they overcome many of the problems associated with the leasehold system. Additionally, the Government intends to make it easier for leaseholders of flats to buy their freehold.

Homelessness

Local authorities have a duty to secure accommodation for families and vulnerable individuals who are homeless through no fault of their own. The problem of homeless people living rough on the streets, often without any family support, is being tackled in central London and other areas through the Rough Sleepers Initiative (see p. 388).

Home Ownership

The number of owner-occupied dwellings in Great Britain amounted to 16 million at the end of 1996, compared with 15.9 million in 1995.

Mortgage Loans

Most people buy their homes with a mortgage loan, using the property as security. These are obtained through building societies, banks or

Tenure in Great Britain, 1996

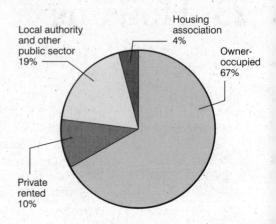

Source: *Department of the Environment, Transport and the Regions*

other financial institutions such as specialist mortgage lenders. There are three main types of mortgage—repayment (a straightforward loan), endowment (a loan combined with life insurance) and the new PEP mortgages (loans combined with investment earnings). Additionally, some companies grant loans for house purchase to their employees. The amount that lenders are prepared to advance to a would-be house purchaser is generally calculated as a multiple of his or her annual income, typically up to two-and-a-half or three times earnings, and the term of the loan is approximately 25 years. Owner-occupiers can claim tax relief on interest payments on the first £30,000 of their mortgages on their main home (see p. 163).

In the recession in the early 1990s, many homeowners saw a fall in the value of their homes, and some have had trouble keeping up with mortgage payments. The Government is encouraging the mortgage lending industry to develop flexible mortgages which allow borrowers to pay more than their normal monthly payments and then make lower payments, or else take a payment holiday, during periods of financial pressure. This arrangement can be particularly helpful to self-employed people and others whose income tends to fluctuate, and it can help prevent temporary gaps in mortgage payments being treated as arrears.

House prices 1983–1996

£ 000

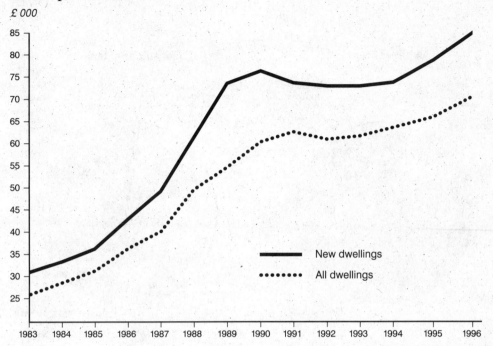

Source: *Housing and Construction Statistics*

Right to Buy and Low-Cost Ownership

With a few exceptions, in England and Wales public tenants with secure tenancies of at least two years' standing are entitled to buy their house or flat at a discount dependent upon the length of the tenancy. Similar provisions apply in Scotland and Northern Ireland. Nearly 2.2 million council, housing association and New Town development corporation houses have been sold into owner-occupation in Great Britain. Sales are continuing at a rate of about 55,000 a year.

Other schemes which aim to increase low-cost home ownership include shared ownership schemes[1] and discounted sales of empty properties owned by local authorities. In addition, £60 million is being made available to local authority tenants in England in 1997–98 under the Cash Incentive Scheme, under which tenants of social housing are

given cash help to buy in the private sector. Over 5,000 local authority tenants a year are receiving this assistance, thereby opening up new lettings for those in greatest need.

In Wales, local authorities and housing associations operate a low-cost home ownership scheme which allows purchasers to buy a home for 70 per cent of its value, the balance being secured as a charge on the property. Scottish Homes operates a scheme to encourage private developers to build for owner-occupation in areas they would not normally consider; in 1997–98 some £1.33 million will be devoted to the scheme. A shared ownership scheme in Northern Ireland is administered by the Northern Ireland Co-ownership Housing Association.

Rented Sector

Local authorities work with RSLs and the private sector to increase the supply of low-cost housing without necessarily providing it

---

[1] These involve the homeowner buying a share of a property from a registered social landlord (RSL) and paying rent for the remainder.

Type of Accommodation Occupied

All households

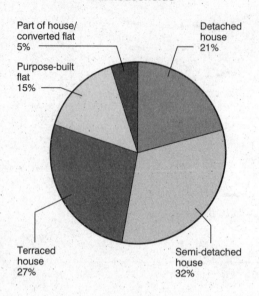

Part of house/converted flat 5%

Detached house 21%

Purpose-built flat 15%

Terraced house 27%

Semi-detached house 32%

Local authority tenants

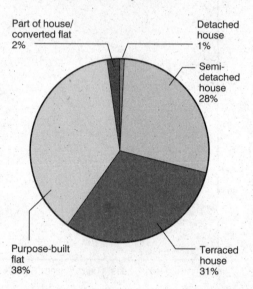

Part of house/converted flat 2%

Detached house 1%

Semi-detached house 28%

Purpose-built flat 38%

Terraced house 31%

Source: *General Household Survey 1996*

themselves. RSLs are the main supplier of new social housing. Rents on new private sector lettings in Great Britain were deregulated (freed from controls) in 1988, with the aim of stimulating the private rented sector, which had been declining for most of this century.

Privately Rented Housing

Around 10 per cent of households rent from a private landlord, and the Government wants to see a healthy private rented sector. Assured and assured–shorthold tenancies enable landlords to charge a reasonable market rent and recover possession of their property when they need to. Assured and short assured tenancies in Scotland are broadly similar. The Housing Act 1996 has introduced measures to encourage small landlords in England and Wales to let property, by reducing paperwork for letting on an assured shorthold tenancy

and by speeding up action on rent arrears. A 'Rent a Room' scheme enables homeowners to let rooms to lodgers without having to pay tax on rents up to a level of about £80 a week. Housing investment trusts, set up to own residential property for rent, benefit from tax provisions designed to encourage institutional investment in the private rented sector.

In Northern Ireland the private rented sector accounts for approximately 4 per cent of total housing stock; only a third of this is subject to statutory control on rents. Rent levels of controlled properties are linked to those of the Northern Ireland Housing Executive. Shorthold tenancies and assured tenancies are available.

Social Housing

Social rented housing is usually owned either by local authorities or by RSLs. It accounts for over a fifth of all homes.

The ladybird spider is one of Britain's rarest, and is now only found in a single tiny patch of heath, about 50 metres square, in Dorset (left).

English Nature has a project with the Zoo Federation and Forest Enterprise to save and re-establish it. Removal of rhododendron plants has already allowed it to expand its single colony, and a small number of spiders have been imported from Denmark to gain experience of rearing them in captivity.

If successful, captive rearing of native spiders should start soon with a probable first release date into the wild in about 2003.

Eurotunnel has taken a leading role in funding the White Cliffs Countryside Project on land it acquired before building the Channel Tunnel, but did not need for its operations. The site, near Folkestone in Kent, is designated as one of special scientific interest (SSSI). Sensitive land management has allowed plants and insects to flourish on the previously poorly maintained site, and Eurotunnel's financial contribution has been recognised by a 1997 SSSI Award from English Nature.

The common blue,
one of the dozen or so butterflies recorded so far.

One of the ponds, looking towards Folkestone.

The Heritage Lottery Fund has awarded a grant to restore and improve the seafront and Marine Gardens in Clacton, Essex. The Gardens, designed by Daniel J. Bowe, were originally created in the 1920s. The work should be completed in time for the 1998 summer season.

The North Pennines Area of Outstanding Natural Beauty
is characterised by large expanses of heather moorland,
such as Blanchland Moor (below).
Northumberland County Council helps to protect
the natural and industrial heritage of this area and promotes sustainable tourism.
In 1997, the unusual combination of a warm, dry May and a wet June
created ideal conditions for the heather to flower,
and it proved to be a particularly spectacular year.

Public Housing

Most social housing in Great Britain is provided by local housing authorities—the structure of local authorities in England, Wales and Scotland is outlined on pp. 80–1. Public housing is also provided by Scottish Homes, which currently has a stock of about 29,000 houses. It is, however, in the process of transferring its houses to alternative landlords such as housing associations. The Northern Ireland Housing Executive is responsible for the supply and management of public housing there.

Public housing authorities in Great Britain own about 4.5 million houses and flats; the Northern Ireland Housing Executive has some 142,000 homes. Some local authorities no longer have any housing stock, having transferred all of it to housing associations. Other authorities have transferred part of their stock. By August 1997, 57 authorities had transferred their stock, involving 250,000 properties and raising over £4,000 million in private finance.

Local authorities meet the capital costs of modernising their housing stock from central government grants, their own resources and from loans from the Public Works Loan Board (an independent statutory body) and private sector financial organisations. They must maintain housing revenue accounts on a 'ring-fenced' basis to keep them separate from other council funds. The Government grants English and Welsh local authorities Housing Revenue Account Subsidy, worth around £3,900 million in 1997–98. In Scotland, Housing Support Grant of about £15 million is available in 1997–98 for those authorities which are in deficit on their housing revenue accounts.

Local authorities in England have been allocated nearly £900 million in 1997–98 through the Housing Investment Programme. Welsh authorities have been allocated £35 million. In Scotland, local authorities have received net capital allocations amounting to £172 million for investment in council homes. The Northern Ireland Housing Executive's capital programme is financed mainly by borrowing from government and receipts from house sales; in 1997–98 borrowing will total £53 million. Revenue expenditure is funded from rental income and by a government grant, which in 1997–98 is about £143 million.

Registered Social Landlords (RSLs)

RSLs, which are non-profit-making, are the main suppliers of new low-cost housing for rent and for sale to those on low incomes and in the greatest housing need. Some provide supported housing to meet the special needs of those with, for example, learning difficulties (mental handicap), drug and alcohol problems, young people at risk and frail elderly people. RSLs own, manage and maintain 1,091,000 homes in England, including 140,000 units of sheltered accommodation (see p. 415) and 60,000 of supported housing.

In Great Britain new housing schemes carried out by RSLs may qualify for Social Housing Grant if the social landlord concerned is one of about 2,230 registered with the Housing Corporation (in England), Scottish Homes or, in Wales, Tai Cymru. These three organisations are statutory bodies which regulate and pay grant to RSLs in their respective parts of Great Britain. Broadly similar assistance is available to RSLs in Northern Ireland. The Housing Corporation's programme has provision for around £690 million in grants in 1997–98. Housing Corporation funding will make possible an additional 35,000 lettings for rent or shared ownership in 1997–98.

For 1997–98, expenditure on Scottish Homes' development funding programme, which includes grants to private developers and landlords, is £208 million, while the target for the amount of private finance attracted is £130 million. Tai Cymru is managing a net capital programme of £60 million in 1997–98, with a target of making 2,900 new homes available. Government provision to the housing association movement in Wales was £601 million between 1992–93 and 1996–97. Private sector finance generated over the same period reached £362 million.

Northern Ireland's registered housing associations are expected to start 1,450 units of accommodation in 1997–98. They now have a stock of about 17,150 units for rent. The budget for building for rent is £43 million in 1997–98, which, with an additional £19 million of private finance, will provide a further 400 units of rented accommodation. Government plans allow for total funding of £284 million over the period 1993–94 to 1998–99.

Tenants' Rights

Local authority tenants in England, Scotland and Wales have security of tenure and other statutory rights, which are set out in the Council Tenant's Charter. In addition to the right to buy (see p. 383), these include the right to have certain urgent repairs done quickly at no cost to themselves and the right to be paid for improvements made when they move home. Tenants must be kept closely involved in the process of letting tenders to manage council estates. They also have the right to take over the running of their estates through tenant management organisations (TMOs). Over 140 TMOs are operational and about 100 more are in the process of development.

In England the rights which RSLs are required to give their residents will, from early 1998, be set out in the rights standard of the Housing Corporation's regulatory standards, and will be explained in a series of residents' charters. The standard covers equal opportunities, occupancy agreements, information, consultation, participation and influence, complaints, and redress. In Wales, the rights of housing association tenants are protected through the Tenants' Guarantee, issued by Tai Cymru, which covers matters such as tenancy terms, principles for setting rent levels, equal opportunities, information and consultation. Similar non-statutory guidance, based on arrangements agreed between Scottish Homes and the Scottish Federation of Housing Associations, has been implemented in Scotland. In Northern Ireland, the Department of the Environment for Northern Ireland has issued a Tenants' Guarantee, similar to the English and Welsh versions, for tenants of registered housing associations.

The Housing Association Tenants' Ombudsman Service in England, under the auspices of the Housing Corporation, allows independent investigation of tenants' complaints against their housing association, giving them a right similar to that for council tenants through the local government ombudsman (see p. 84). Similar schemes have been launched in Scotland and Northern Ireland, and a scheme is due to be launched in Wales in 1998.

Housing for Older People

Sheltered housing provides specialised facilities for elderly people, such as common and laundry rooms, alarm systems and resident or non-resident warden support. Increasing emphasis is being placed on schemes to help them continue to live in their own homes by, for example, adapting their present homes to meet particular needs. In England, government-funded home improvement agencies help the elderly, people with disabilities and those on low incomes to carry out repairs and improvements to their properties. Some £4.5 million of government assistance will go to support 143 home improvement agencies in 1997–98. Care and Repair Ltd is the national co-ordinating and monitoring body. Parallel arrangements apply in Wales, where £976,000 of government funding has been allotted to 243 home improvement agencies in 1997–98, including Care and Repair Cymru, the national body. Corresponding provision is made for Scotland under the Care and Repair scheme co-ordinated by Scottish Homes, which expects to cover 600 homes in 1997–98 involving capital expenditure of £610,000.

Rural Housing

Where there is a clear need for low-cost housing in rural areas, local authorities can permit housing in localities where development would not normally be allowed, so long as the new housing can be reserved to meet that need. The Housing Corporation also funds a special rural programme to build houses in villages with a population of 3,000 or below; between 1989–90 and 1996–97 it approved funding from this for the building of 13,500 such homes.

Tai Cymru has a major role in rural housing provision, with about a quarter of its programme devoted to rural areas. The Welsh Office also supports low-cost schemes for rural housing. In Scotland, considerable progress is being made through a range of initiatives as part of the Scottish Homes Rural Strategy. Scottish Homes has invested £411 million in countryside areas between 1989–90 and 1996–97, providing 13,000 homes. In 1997–98 it will spend £40 million in rural areas, making 900 homes available. The Northern Ireland Housing Executive operates a rural strategy, involving action both in public housing (new building and improvements) and, through the house renovation grant scheme, in private housing.

Improving Existing Housing

In urban areas of Britain, slum clearance and redevelopment used to be major features of housing policy, but there has been a trend in recent years towards the modernisation and conversion of sub-standard homes in order to help maintain existing communities. Housing conditions have improved considerably, but problems remain in some areas where there are concentrations of dwellings requiring substantial repairs. In some cases, however, clearance may still be the most satisfactory course of action. To help overcome objections to clearance, local authorities can pay a new discretionary relocation grant to those displaced by clearance to enable them to buy at least a part share in a new home in the same area.

Social Housing

Run-down estates are being improved through the Single Regeneration Budget Challenge Fund, which encourages local partnerships in England to tackle social and economic problems, including housing improvements. A £380 million Estate Renewal Challenge Fund is being made available over three years to help renovate poor-quality estates by speeding their transfer to housing associations and other new landlords. In all, 20 local authorities are receiving finance to improve the condition of 41,000 homes.

In Wales, Estate Partnership funding is used to combat the problem of run-down estates; £10.6 million of central government support has been allocated for this purpose in 1997–98, to supplement local authority and private sector contributions. The Government's policy on urban regeneration in Scotland is also based on the partnership approach. In the Urban Partnerships in Dundee, Edinburgh, Glasgow and Paisley (see p. 375), 3,180 new houses have been built and another 5,510 refurbished.

Private Housing

The Government offers assistance through house renovation grants to owners of private housing who are on low incomes and unable to afford necessary repairs and improvements. Specific help is available to disabled people needing adaptations to their homes. Grants provide up to 100 per cent support for essential repairs and improvements to the poorest homeowners. In all, 529,700 grants have been made in England since 1991, totalling £2,563 million. In Wales some 64,000 grants were completed between April 1991 and March 1997, at a cost of £861 million. In addition, some 32,000 minor works assistance grants were completed at a cost of £26.5 million.

Scottish local authorities award grants for improvement and repair. Scottish Homes also has the power to provide grants to complement the role of local authorities in private house renewal. In Northern Ireland, funding is allocated through the house renovation grants scheme, administered by the Northern Ireland Housing Executive, on a similar basis to that in England and Wales. In isolated rural areas, financial assistance to replace dwellings which cannot be restored is also on offer under this scheme. Legislation is being considered to apply to Northern Ireland the principles of the grants provisions of the Housing Grants, Construction and Regeneration Act 1996.

Homelessness

Many people to whom local authorities owe a housing duty have some form of accommodation, even though it is often temporary, overcrowded or otherwise unsatisfactory. Those entitled to rehousing are found accommodation by local authorities. Local authorities have a legal duty to secure accommodation for households which are eligible for assistance and accepted as unintentionally homeless and in priority need. The latter category includes pregnant women, people with dependent children, and those who are vulnerable due to old age, mental or physical handicap or other special reasons. Legal provisions, which came into force in England and Wales in 1997, reformed the law on homelessness and the allocation of council housing. The aim was to ensure fairer access to long-term social housing by creating a single route to such accommodation—the local authority housing register—while ensuring a safety net for families and vulnerable people who lose their home through no fault of their own. In Scotland, a new code of guidance on homelessness was issued in 1997, to which by law local authorities must have regard in applying the homelessness legislation in the Housing (Scotland) Act 1997. Northern Ireland policy on homelessness is under review and will take account of any changes to policies or legislation in England and Wales.

The Rough Sleepers Initiative was established in 1990 in central London, where the problem of people sleeping rough on the streets was especially acute; it has a government grant of £73 million for 1996–97 to 1998–99. So far the scheme has provided about 1,150 places in short-term hostels including places for clients with drink problems, and at least 3,300 permanent and 970 leased places in 'move-on'

Table 23.1: Households in England Accepted as Homeless

1991	144,780
1992	142,890
1993	132,380
1994	122,460
1995	121,280
1996	116,870

Source: Department of the Environment, Transport and the Regions

Table 23.2: Rough Sleepers Counted in Central London

Month and year	Number
March 1992	440
June 1993	358
May 1994	268
November 1994	288
May 1995	270
May 1996	288
November 1996	286

Source: Department of the Environment, Transport and the Regions

accommodation. In addition, 40 beds in permanent high-care accommodation for people with mental ill health and a winter shelter programme with approximately 400 beds each winter have been provided. The Initiative has been extended to other areas in England. In Bristol, 150 new permanent homes, 24 beds in high-care accommodation, 40 hostel places, a winter shelter and additional outreach and resettlement have been provided. A voluntary sector count, held in November 1996, found that 286 people were sleeping rough in central London, compared with estimates of over 1,000 people before the Rough Sleepers Initiative began. The Department of Health operates the Homeless Mentally Ill Initiative to supply accommodation and psychiatric care for mentally ill people who have been sleeping rough in central London and Bristol. It also funds projects designed to ensure that homeless people have access to health services. A Scottish Rough Sleepers Initiative has been introduced, inviting bids for expenditure in the second half of 1997 and the following two years. A total amount of £16 million over the three years has been allocated. In addition, a further £2 million has been allocated to tackle the problem of empty properties in Scotland with a view to increasing the supply of housing available to those in need.

The Government is providing £8 million in 1997–98 to voluntary groups helping single homeless people in England; grants of £600,000 for 1997–98 are being made to voluntary organisations tackling homelessness in Scotland, and £623,000 in Wales. The Northern Ireland Housing Executive is providing £367,000 to voluntary groups involved with homelessness there.

Housing Advice

Under the Housing Act 1996, local authorities have a duty to secure the provision of advice to prevent homelessness. As well as housing associations, other voluntary sector bodies have a role to play in housing matters. Such groups undertake a number of roles, for example advising people about their rights under housing law or encouraging energy efficiency in the home. The Government allocates grants to assist the work of such bodies. In England the largest project currently funded is the Homelessness Advice Service, with £2 million in 1997–98; in Scotland, aid worth £1.4 million in 1997–98 is being given to about 25 voluntary bodies, including the Scottish Homelessness Advisory Service, for work on homelessness and other housing matters. In Wales, £500,000 is being provided to support national tenant organisations and other bodies involved in housing management education and training. In Northern Ireland, the Government is providing about £208,000 to the Housing Rights Service, a voluntary organisation which offers advice on all aspects of housing, and £188,000 to the Northern Ireland Tenants Action Project, which promotes the participation of tenants in the management of their homes.

Further Reading

Housing. Aspects of Britain series. HMSO, 1993.
Our Future Homes. HMSO, 1995.

Annual Reports
Building Societies Commission. The Stationery Office.
Housing and Construction Statistics. The Stationery Office.
The Housing Corporation. Housing Corporation.

24 Health and Social Services

Since taking office in May 1997, the Government has launched a new public health strategy, setting goals for improving the overall health of the nation which recognise the impact that poverty, poor housing, unemployment and a polluted environment have on health. It has also announced reforms to reduce the administrative costs of running the National Health Service (NHS), and has commissioned a new hospital building programme. Three White Papers are to be issued: two in late 1997, setting out a framework for the future of the NHS and outlining the Government's strategy for reducing smoking; and a third in summer 1998, on the public health strategy.

The National Health Service (NHS) provides a full range of medical services, available to all residents, regardless of their income. Local authority personal social services and voluntary organisations provide help and advice to the most vulnerable members of the community—elderly, physically disabled and mentally ill people, those with learning disabilities, and children in need of care.

Central government is directly responsible for the NHS, which is administered by a range of health authorities and health boards throughout Britain. The Secretary of State for Health in England and the Secretaries of State for Scotland, Wales and Northern Ireland are responsible for all aspects of the health services in their respective territories. The Department of Health is responsible for national strategic planning in England, and within that department, the NHS Executive— with its eight regional offices—is responsible

for developing and implementing policies for the provision of high quality health services. The Scottish Office Department of Health, the Welsh Office and the Department of Health and Social Services in Northern Ireland have similar responsibilities.

There are 100 health authorities in England and 5 in Wales, 15 health boards in Scotland and 4 health and social services boards in Northern Ireland, all of which are responsible for identifying the healthcare needs of the people living in their area. They secure hospital and community health services and arrange for the provision of services by doctors, dentists, pharmacists and opticians, as well as administering their contracts. The health authorities and boards co-operate closely with local authorities responsible for social work, environmental health, education and other services. There are community health councils (local health councils in

Scotland and area health and social services councils in Northern Ireland) covering all parts of the country, representing local opinion on the services provided.

Personal social services are administered by local authorities but central government is responsible for establishing national policies, issuing guidance and overseeing standards. Joint finance and planning between health and local authorities aims to prevent overlapping of services and to encourage the development of community services.

Major Policy Developments

PUBLIC HEALTH

The Existing Approach

The White Paper *The Health of the Nation*, published by the previous administration in 1992, laid out a strategy for improving health in England. It set targets for improvements in the following areas:

- coronary heart disease and stroke (major single causes of premature death in England);

- cancers (now the biggest cause of death across all ages);

- accidents (the commonest cause of death in those under 30);

- mental illness (a leading cause of ill-health and also a cause of many suicides); and

- HIV/AIDS and sexual health.

Targets were set for reducing death rates, ill-health, and behaviour that poses a risk to health. In most areas there has been steady progress towards the targets but in a few cases—such as teenage smoking, obesity and excess alcohol consumption in women—figures are on the increase. Strategies have also been developed for Scotland, Wales and Northern Ireland which reflect the health variations in the different parts of Britain.

Central activity in England has included, for example, interdepartmental taskforces on accident prevention, smoking, the workplace and physical activity. At local level, agencies, such as the NHS, local authorities, voluntary organisations and the private sector, have been encouraged to form 'health alliances'. Good practice in this kind of collaborative working has been rewarded through the Health Alliance Award scheme. Progress towards the Health of the Nation targets has been monitored regularly and formally reviewed, and periodic progress reports published. Similar initiatives have been taken in Scotland, Wales and Northern Ireland.

Proposals for a New Public Health Strategy

In July 1997 the Government outlined its plans for a wide-reaching public health strategy to tackle the underlying causes of ill health. It proposes to set new goals for improving the overall health of the nation by recognising the impact that poverty, poor housing, unemployment and a polluted environment can have on health. Persistent inequalities in health exist between different occupational and ethnic groups, between geographical areas and between men and women in Britain. There is evidence that people who live in disadvantaged circumstances have more illness, greater distress, and shorter lives than those who are more affluent. The Government has said that it hopes that by tackling the wider influences on health it can have an impact on health inequalities. Immediate action includes plans to improve food safety (see chapter 18), to discourage smoking (see p. 408), and to find out more about the effects of air pollutants commonly found in the home (see chapter 21).

The new Government considers there are lessons to be learnt from the existing approach: that it has been sensible to concentrate on the biggest killers and causes of avoidable ill health. It intends to continue to work towards the existing targets, though some may need to be modified. However, it thinks that the Health of the Nation policy ignored health inequalities and did little to promote collaboration across government. It also failed to consider population groups separately—children, the working-age population, elderly people. By focusing on disease and services, the policy cast the burden back onto the NHS, and the policy's emphasis on lifestyle issues cast too much responsibility back onto the individual.

The Government's new approach to health is marked by the appointment of a Minister for Public Health, one of whose roles will be to ensure that policies across government can be evaluated for their potential impact on people's health: an agenda which challenges every department of government.

The Government has stated that it intends to produce a coherent strategy with clear targets to guide action at local level, involving health and local authorities as well as voluntary organisations and community groups, the private sector and individuals. It plans to develop the health promoting roles of the local authority departments dealing with social services, education, housing, recreation, public transport, traffic, environmental health and consumer protection. A consultation paper on the new strategy for England will be published in late 1997. Similar action is being taken in other parts of Britain.

The Government has commissioned an independent review of the latest available information on inequalities in health and expectation of life in England. The review will identify the priority areas in which the Government needs to develop policy, and will publish a report in 1998.

REFORMS IN MANAGEMENT

The Present System

Management reforms introduced under the NHS and Community Care Act 1990 created a form of competition in the running of the NHS—the so-called 'internal market'. This was done by making a division between purchasers and providers of health care.

Under this system:

Health authorities/health boards and some general practitioners (GPs—see below) have become *purchasers*, responsible for assessing local health care needs and choosing between rival providers to give patients the best available service. Each health authority/health board is now funded to buy health care for its local residents through arranging contracts with hospitals and other health service units in either the public or the private sector.

Hospitals and other health service units (for example, ambulance services and community health services) have become *providers*.

Hospitals, which are now directly funded for the number of patients they treat, have become self-governing NHS Trusts, independent of local health authority control but remaining within the NHS. They are accountable to the relevant health department, and derive their income largely through contracts to provide the services that health authorities/health boards and GP fundholders (see below) wish to buy.

Since 1990 GPs from larger medical practices have been able to apply to join the GP fundholding scheme, under which they receive an annual budget directly from the health authority/health board, enabling them to choose between hospitals and consultants to buy certain non-urgent hospital services for their patients. More recently all GPs have been able, if they wish, to hold a budget to buy community-based services, such as those of district nurses, from NHS Trusts.

By April 1997 all NHS hospitals in Britain (other than in the Scottish Islands) had become Trusts, and over 50 per cent of GPs—serving about 60 per cent of the population—had become fundholders.

Broadly similar changes were introduced under separate legislation in Northern Ireland, where health and personal social services are provided on an integrated basis by health and social services boards.

The New Government's Proposed Reforms

Abolishing the Internal Market

In May 1997 the new Government announced its decision to replace the 'internal market', in which GP fundholders and health authorities/health boards buy services from NHS Trusts. It will set out its proposals for replacing the internal market in a White Paper in late 1997. The Government considers that the excessive administrative costs of buying care, with each transaction the subject of a separate invoice, have undermined the provision of care, and that the market system has distorted clinical priorities.

The Government considers that the internal market has led to a two-tier health service in which fundholding practices and their patients enjoy unfair financial advantages over non-fundholding practices, allowing hospitals to give preference to fundholder patients at the expense of other patients with greater clinical need.

To address this problem, the Government has announced measures aimed at ensuring equality in waiting lists by giving priority to patients solely on the basis of clinical need. From April 1998—when current contracts run out—all health authorities and their GPs will have to establish common waiting-time standards for all patients living in their area. From the same date NHS Trusts will not be allowed to offer preferential admission to the patients of GP fundholders, and fundholders will not be able to press for faster treatment except on clinical or social grounds.

NHS Efficiency Task Force

In England the Government has begun to cut the NHS administration budget—by £100 million in the current financial year—and has redirected the funds into patient care, starting with screening for women at risk of breast cancer (see p. 410) and new intensive care facilities for children (see p. 400). In June 1997 it set up a task force as part of its campaign to redirect funds towards patient care. The task force will explore more effective and efficient ways of delivering patient care across the NHS within the next 12 months.

Areas to be examined include, among others:

- the £500 million which health authorities and Trusts spend each year with the private sector, with consideration being given to whether some of this could be better spent with the NHS;

- the scope to bring forward plans to dispose of land and buildings worth £1,200 million over a five-year period;
- better use of clinically effective techniques;

- the scope for further reductions in the prices paid for utilities, such as water, electricity and gas; and

- controlling growth in the NHS drugs budget.

Health Action Zones

The Government is considering proposals for targeting a small number of areas where it believes the health of local people could be improved by better integrated arrangements for treatment and care. The areas would be designated 'Health Action Zones'. Within these zones, health authorities, NHS Trusts, GPs, nurses, health visitors, midwives, pharmacists, dentists, opticians and all others involved in delivering NHS services at local level, would be brought together to develop a health strategy in partnership with local authorities, community groups, the voluntary sector, and local businesses. Working closely with the Department of Health, the participants would explore mechanisms for breaking through current organisational boundaries to tackle inequalities, and delivering better services and better health care, building upon and encouraging co-operation across the NHS. Funding for the zones would be met from existing resources. A similar initiative to encourage local health care partnerships has been launched in Scotland. Further details on the future framework of the NHS will be set out in the White Paper to be published in late 1997.

Review of London's Health Services

A review of health services in London was announced in June 1997. This will establish the current state of services in the capital and will review health authority and Trust plans, including plans for capital investment, to ensure that all residents have ready access to high quality healthcare. The review will also take account of the Government's new strategy to improve public health through better health promotion and prevention (see p. 391). It will report by autumn 1997. The programme of hospital closures in London carried out under the previous government will be suspended during the period of the review.

The National Health Service

The NHS is based upon the principle that there should be a full range of publicly funded

Health in England 1996

The 1996 *Health in England* report[1] was published in May 1997. This was the second in a series of annual studies monitoring trends in the health-related knowledge, attitudes and behaviour of adults in England. Some of its findings show:

- 31 per cent of men and 29 per cent of women were current cigarette smokers. The average number of cigarettes smoked each day was 12.9 for women and 15.3 for men—no change from 1995. Almost two-thirds of current smokers would like to give up smoking. As in 1995, smokers aged 25 to 44 and those who smoked 10 cigarettes or more a day were most likely to want to quit.

- Alcohol consumption for both men and women was higher in the 16 to 24 age group than in any other age group, average consumption being 22.4 units a week for men and 14.4 for women.

- 25 per cent of respondents were classed as sedentary, that is, they took part less than once a week in 30 minutes or more of exercise of moderate intensity. Lack of time was the most common reason given by people when asked what stopped them exercising more.

- 38 per cent of adults aged 16 to 74 reported eating bread; fruit, vegetables or salad; and potatoes, rice or pasta every day (important constituents in a healthy diet). When asked about their attitudes to diet, 32 per cent said they were confused about 'what is supposed to be healthy and what isn't'. Older men were the most likely to say they were confused.

- 32 per cent of respondents aged 16 to 54 said they had at some time used drugs which were not prescribed by a doctor; 14 per cent had done so in the past year and 9 per cent in the past month. Drug use was most likely to be reported by those aged 19 to 21. Seventy-four per cent of men and 50 per cent of women in this group said they had at some time tried a drug. Of the people who reported using a drug in the past month, 18 per cent said they intended to stop in the next month. Ten per cent said they did not see the need ever to stop taking drugs.

- Over a third of men and over a quarter of women aged 16 to 24 reported having more than one sexual partner in the 12 months before the interview, compared with 6 per cent of men and 3 per cent of women in the 45 to 54 age group. When asked whether they would use a condom with a new partner, 67 per cent of women and 58 per cent of men said that they would always do so, while 17 per cent of women and 31 per cent of men said it would 'depend'. Only 1 per cent of people said that they would never use a condom. These findings do not differ significantly from those recorded in 1995.

- The proportion of people who thought a suntan was important decreased slightly between 1965 and 1996, from 28 per cent to 25 per cent. The prevalence of sunburn decreased with age from 41 per cent of those aged 16 to 24 to only 8 per cent of those aged 65 to 74.

services designed to help the individual stay healthy. The services are intended to provide effective and appropriate treatment and care where necessary while making the best use of available resources. All taxpayers, employers and employees contribute to its cost so that those members of the community who do not require health care help to pay for those who do. Some forms of treatment, such as hospital care, are generally provided free; others (see p. 395) may be charged for.

Growth in real spending on the health service is being used to meet the needs of increasing numbers of elderly people and to take full advantage of advances in medical technology. It is also used to provide more

[1] *Health in England: what people know, what people think, what people do.* The Stationery Office, 1997.

appropriate types of care, often in the community rather than in hospital, for priority groups such as elderly and mentally ill people and those with learning disabilities. Increased spending has, in addition, been allocated to combat the growing problems arising from alcohol and drug misuse; and to remedy disparities in provision between the regions of Britain.

ADMINISTRATION

Expenditure

The Health Programme is funded mainly by central government and consists of:

- NHS Hospital and Community Health Services (HCHS), providing all hospital care and a wide range of community services;

- NHS Family Health Services (FHS), providing general medical, dental, pharmaceutical and some ophthalmic services, and covering the cost of medicines prescribed by GPs;

- Central Health and Miscellaneous Services (CHMS), providing services most effectively administered centrally, such as welfare food (which includes free milk and vitamins to families with children under five, and pregnant women, on Income Support) and support to the voluntary sector; and

- the administrative costs of the health departments.

The Personal Social Services Programme consists largely of spending by local authorities. The programme is financed partly by central government but most local authority personal social services spending depends on decisions by individual local authorities on how to spend the resources available to them.

The Voluntary Sector

Government grant aid to voluntary organisations working in health and personal social services in England (£59 million in 1996–97) goes primarily to national

Health Service Expenditure in England, 1996–97

Total: £34,900m

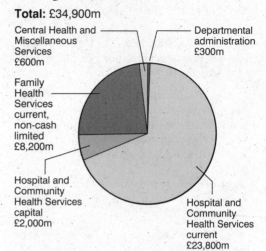

Central Health and Miscellaneous Services £600m

Departmental administration £300m

Family Health Services current, non-cash limited £8,200m

Hospital and Community Health Services capital £2,000m

Hospital and Community Health Services current £23,800m

Source: *Department of Health. The Government's Expenditure Plans 1997–98 to 1999–2000*

organisations dealing with children, elderly people, carers and people from ethnic minorities, as well as those looking after people with mental illness, physical or learning disabilities, or suffering from the effects of HIV/AIDS or the misuse of alcohol or drugs. In Scotland central government grants to voluntary organisations in social welfare amounted, in 1996–97, to almost £9 million. In Northern Ireland the Department of Health and Social Services spent £6.4 million in support of a wide range of voluntary activity during 1996–97.

Health authorities/boards and local authorities also make grants to local organisations.

Finance

About 82 per cent of the cost of the health service is paid for through general taxation. The rest is met from:

- the NHS element of National Insurance contributions (see chapter 25), paid by employed people, their employers, and self–employed people (12.2 per cent);

- charges towards the cost of certain items such as drugs prescribed by family doctors, and general dental treatment (2.3 per cent);

- capital refunds to NHS Trusts (2.5 per cent); and

- other receipts, including land sales and the proceeds of income generation schemes (0.9 per cent).

Health authorities may raise funds from voluntary sources. Certain hospitals increase revenue by taking private patients, who pay the full cost of their accommodation and treatment.

In 1996–97 an estimated 85 per cent of medical prescription items were supplied free. Prescription charges are not paid by:

- children under 16 years (or young people under 19 who are in full-time education);

- pregnant women and women who have had a baby in the past year;

- people aged 60 and over;

- patients with certain medical conditions;

- war and armed forces disablement pensioners (for prescriptions which relate to the disability for which they receive a war pension); and

- people in families who are receiving Income Support, income-based Jobseeker's Allowance or Disability Working Allowance (see chapter 25); and people or families with low incomes.

Over 480 million prescriptions, worth almost £4,000 million, are dispensed each year in England and Wales.

There are proportional charges for most types of NHS dental treatment, including examinations. However, the following people are entitled to free treatment: women who begin a course of treatment while pregnant or within 12 months of having a baby, children up to 18, full-time students under 19; and those who receive, or whose partners receive, Jobseeker's Allowance, Income Support or Disability Working Allowance. Others on low incomes may be entitled to free treatment or to help with charges.

Since 1989 the availability of free NHS sight tests has been restricted to children, full-time students under the age of 19, people in

> A government report on prescription fraud published in June 1997 has revealed that between £70 million and £100 million in England and Wales is lost **each year** through prescription charge evasion and some £15 million through theft and forgery. The Government has announced a number of measures to tackle this. These include developing proposals for a new criminal offence of evading prescription charges; rewarding pharmacies for detecting stolen or counterfeited prescription forms; and greater use of information technology to improve investigation and detection of fraud by NHS contractors.

families receiving Income Support, income-based Jobseeker's Allowance or Disability Working Allowance, and those at particular risk of eye disease. Following a report by the Royal National Institute for the Blind, which suggested that since 1989 people have been having their eyes tested less often, the Government has announced that it will be reviewing the current arrangements.

Family practitioners (doctors, dentists, optometrists and community pharmacists) are self-employed (or, in the case of pharmacists, employed by a pharmacy company) and have contracts with the NHS. GPs are paid by a system of fees and allowances designed to reflect responsibilities, workload and practice expenses. Dentists providing treatment in their own surgeries are paid by a combination of set-rate fees for treating children, continuing care payments for adults registered with the practice, and a prescribed scale of fees for individual treatments. Community pharmacists dispense from their own or their company's premises and are refunded the cost of the items supplied, together with professional fees. Ophthalmic medical practitioners and ophthalmic opticians taking part in the general ophthalmic service receive approved fees for each sight test carried out.

The NHS is one of the largest employers in the world, with a workforce of nearly 1 million people. Staff costs account for approximately 70 per cent of current spending on hospitals and community health services. Figures for

England and Scotland between 1985 and 1995 show that:

- the number of hospital medical and dental staff in England rose from 43,000 to 55,300; in Scotland it rose from 5,588 to 6,642;

- the number of professional and technical staff in England rose by 29 per cent to 94,000, while in Scotland the increase was 27 per cent to 12,594;

- the number of nursing and midwifery staff decreased by 13 per cent to 349,800. This reflects the growth in bursaried students under the Project 2000 nurse training scheme—see p. 412. (Project 2000 trainees have full student status and are not NHS employees.) The change masks an underlying trend of an increase of 3 per cent in the number of qualified nursing and midwifery staff since 1985. In Scotland during the same period the number of nursing and midwifery staff rose by 2.7 per cent to 52,416—an increase of 7.1 per cent since 1985;

- in England managerial and other administrative staff increased from 110,900 to 161,000; in Scotland they rose from 14,315 to 19,778; and

- in England ancillary staff and maintenance and works staff fell from 183,400 to 102,400, while in Scotland they fell from 29,015 to 14,106—the sharp fall reflecting the continuing effect of competitive tendering (see chapter 7, p. 83). Many of these jobs are now carried out by the private sector.

Openness in the NHS

The Code of Practice on Openness in the NHS came into force in 1995. Designed to make NHS organisations more accountable and provide greater public access to information, the Code applies to NHS Trusts, health authorities/boards and local health practitioners such as GPs, dentists and pharmacists. It sets out the information that NHS Trusts and health authorities/health boards should publish or otherwise make available.

The NHS Code contains, among other things:

- information about what services are provided, the targets and standards set and results achieved, and the costs and effectiveness of the service;

- details of important proposals on health policies or proposed changes in the way the services are delivered; and

- information about how people can have access to their own personal health records.

NHS Complaints System

Complaints about all NHS-funded services are dealt with in a similar fashion at two distinct levels. The procedures aim to resolve complaints speedily at a local level; where complainants are dissatisfied with the response at local level, a new system of review by an independent panel is an option. Patients can refer complaints to the Health Service Commissioner (see below) if they are dissatisfied with the response from the NHS.

Health Service Commissioners

Health Service Commissioners (one each for England, Scotland and Wales) are responsible for investigating complaints directly from members of the public about health service bodies. The three posts are at present held by one person (with a staff of about 250), who is also Parliamentary Commissioner for Administration (Ombudsman—see p. 70). As Health Service Commissioner, he or she reports annually to Parliament. In Northern Ireland the Commissioner for Complaints has a similar role.

The Health Service Commissioner can investigate complaints that a person has suffered hardship as a result of:

- a failure in a service provided by a health service body;

- a failure to provide a service which the patient was entitled to receive; or

- maladministration by an NHS authority—that is, something that the

NHS authority failed to do or did in the wrong way.

Complaints must be sent to the Commissioner in writing, and the health service body concerned should first have been given a reasonable opportunity to respond. Legislation passed in 1996 extended the Health Service Commissioner's jurisdiction to include complaints against all family health service practitioners and their staff, and about the exercise of clinical judgment.

In 1996–97 the Commissioner received a record 2,219 complaints about the NHS—24 per cent more than the previous year. He completed 238 investigations.

Patient's Charters

Patient's Charters set out the rights of patients and the standards of service they can expect to receive from the NHS. The responsibility for implementing the Patient's Charters rests with all parts of the NHS, English regional offices (see p. 390), and purchasers and providers of services (see p. 392).

The original Patient's Charter in England came into force in 1992 and an expanded version was issued in 1995, covering dental, optical and pharmaceutical services and the hospital environment. In England subsequent leaflets have set out how the Patient's Charter applies to specific services. These are: maternity services (published in 1994); a blood donor's charter (1995); services for children and young people (1996), and mental health services (1997).

In England the Patient's Charter sets national charter standards, which are not legal rights but specific standards of service that the NHS aims to provide. These cover respect for the individual patient; waiting times for ambulances, clinical assessment in Accident and Emergency departments and appointments in out-patient clinics; and cancellation of operations. Separate but similar Patient's Charters have been developed for Scotland, Wales and Northern Ireland.

All health authorities in England and health boards and NHS Trusts in Scotland have also produced local charters, with statements of the standards of service patients can expect to receive. GP practices are encouraged to produce their own charters, setting out the standards of service they offer their patients.

Planned Changes

The new Government sees the existing Charter as simplistic, concentrating too much on the easily measurable. It considers that it fails to give proper weight to the quality of clinical care and patients' own experiences of how well the service has been delivered. The existing Patient's Charter will remain in place for the time being, but the Government intends to make changes to its current provisions. In particular from October 1997 it plans to introduce in England a new national standard on immediate assessment in Accident and Emergency departments of hospitals to ensure that patients are properly assessed, and treated according to clinical priority.

FAMILY HEALTH SERVICES

The Family Health Services are those given to patients by doctors (GPs), dentists, opticians and pharmacists of their own choice. They remain the first point of contact most people have with the NHS. Every year there are about 250 million consultations with GPs and about 6 million people visit a pharmacy every day. Often those who visit their GP or dentist need no clinical treatment but healthy lifestyle counselling and preventive health care advice instead. The last decade has seen continued growth of the Family Health Services in line with longstanding government policy to build up and extend these services in order to improve health and relieve pressure on the far more costly secondary care sector (that is, hospital and specialist services).

GPs provide the first diagnosis in the case of illness, give advice and may prescribe a suitable course of treatment or refer a patient to the more specialised services and hospital consultants. About four-fifths of GPs in Britain work in partnerships or group practices. Primary healthcare teams also include health visitors and district nurses, midwives, and sometimes social workers and other professional staff employed by the health authorities. Most GPs in Great Britain and about half in Northern Ireland work in health centres. As well as providing medical and nursing services, health centres may also have facilities for health education, family planning, speech therapy, chiropody, assessment of hearing, physiotherapy and remedial exercises. Dental, pharmaceutical and ophthalmic services, hospital out-patient and supporting social work services may also be provided.

There have been substantial increases in primary health care staff in recent years. For example, between 1986 and 1996 the number of GPs in England rose by 9 per cent (to 29,000); and average patient list size fell by 8 per cent (to just under 1,900). During the same period, however, the number of GP trainees fell by 21 per cent.

Special funds have been earmarked by the Government for improving the quality of primary health care in some inner city areas.

Planned Improvements in Primary Care

In recent years GPs have gained powers on behalf of their patients in a changed relationship with consultants. The new Government acknowledges that the GP fundholding schemes have produced benefits in terms of improved patient care and is keen to work in partnership with them to build better services. It intends to retain the lead role for primary care but remove the disadvantages that have come from the present system. Details of the Government's plans for primary care will be set out in the White Paper on the future of the NHS to be published in late 1997.

Primary Care Pilot Schemes

The NHS (Primary Care) Act, passed in March 1997, has introduced greater flexibility in the delivery of primary health care services for patients. It enables GPs, dentists, NHS Trusts and NHS employees to work with health authorities and health boards to develop new ways of delivering primary care under local contracts.

In July 1997 the Government announced plans to set up a number of pilot schemes under the NHS (Primary Care) Act. Two types of scheme are proposed, both to be sited in areas which experience high levels of illness and where there are often problems in recruiting GPs:

- The first type of scheme will enable NHS Trusts or GP practices to employ GPs on a salaried basis. (At present GPs are employed on individual contracts.) This is designed to give patients in areas of high health risk access to a flexible family doctor service on their doorstep.

- The second type of scheme will create primary health care 'one-stop shops', where GPs, community nurses and other professionals work as a single team in the community offering a range of services from eye tests to lay counselling.

The Government has received over 500 proposals from health professionals interested in taking part in the projects. About 200 of the applications are expected to be chosen to become pilot schemes in April 1998. Proposals for pioneering schemes to improve primary care dentistry will be announced shortly and the first schemes are expected to come into operation from October 1998.

Pilot Schemes for GP Locality Commissioning

From April 1998 the Government will run about 20 pilot schemes throughout England which will test new approaches to securing high-quality health services for all patients in their areas. The pilot schemes will bring together GPs and other primary care professionals, in partnership with their health authority, to explore how each can best play their part in developing a local health strategy and putting it into practice together with local NHS Trusts and the wider community. Reflecting the Government's commitment to local flexibility, the schemes will be chosen to cover a range of areas and approaches.

Midwives, Health Visitors and District Nurses

Midwives provide care and support to women throughout pregnancy, birth and the postnatal period (up to 28 days after the baby is born). Midwives work in both hospital and community settings.

Under a number of pilot schemes in England and Scotland, district nurses and health visitors are able to prescribe from a limited list of drugs and medical appliances. These schemes, based in GP practices, are intended to reduce significantly the time patients have to wait for relief of their symptoms. Nurse prescribing will be extended throughout the country from April 1998.

Health visitors are responsible for the preventive care and health promotion of families, particularly those with young children. They have a public health role, identifying local health needs and working closely with GPs, district nurses and other professions. District nurses give skilled nursing care to people at home or elsewhere outside hospital; they also play an important role in health promotion and education.

HOSPITAL AND SPECIALIST SERVICES

District general hospitals offer a broad range of clinical specialities, supported by a range of other services such as anaesthetics, pathology and radiology. Almost all have facilities for the admission of emergency patients, either through Accident and Emergency departments or as direct referrals from GPs. Treatments are provided for in-patients, day cases, out-patients and patients who attend wards for treatment such as dialysis. Some hospitals also provide specialist services which cover more than one region or district. These are known in England as supra-regional or supra-district services covering, for example, heart and liver transplants, and craniofacial services and rare eye and bone cancers. (In Scotland similar services are contracted for centrally.) There are also specialist hospitals such as the world-famous Hospital for Sick Children at Great Ormond Street, Moorfields Eye Hospital, and the National Hospital for Neurology and Neurosurgery, all in London. These hospitals combine specialist treatment facilities with the training of medical and other students, and international research.

Many of the hospitals in the NHS were built in the 19th century; some trace their origins to much earlier charitable foundations. Much has been done to improve and extend existing hospital buildings and many new hospitals have been or are being opened. Recent policy has been to provide a balanced hospital service centred around a district general hospital, complemented as necessary by smaller, locally based hospitals and facilities.

Private Finance Initiative

The Private Finance Initiative (PFI) was launched in 1992 to promote partnership between the public and private sectors on a commercial basis (see chapter 11). In the health service it involves the use of private finance in NHS capital projects for the design, construction and operation of buildings and support services. The new Government has stated that it is determined to make the PFI work, and in May 1997 introduced legislation designed to reinvigorate the system by clarifying powers of NHS Trusts to sign PFI agreements. Following a review of major PFI acute hospital building schemes in England, in July 1997 it announced a major new hospital building programme. Under this, 14 major acute hospital schemes in England—with a capital value of around £1,300 million—have been approved to proceed. Two major PFI schemes in Wales worth around £75 million and 13 worth £646 million in Scotland are also proceeding. The hospitals will be designed, built, maintained and owned by the private sector, which will lease the completed facilities back to the NHS. Clinical services will continue to be provided by NHS staff, and the NHS will remain in control of the key planning and clinical decisions.

The Government is currently reviewing the PFI's procurement process and also its application and will report its findings at the beginning of 1998.

Mobile Intensive Care Service for Children

In July 1997 the Government announced plans to improve paediatric intensive care (PIC) services in England. These include the development of a 24-hour retrieval service, to ensure that critically ill children needing transfer to a PIC unit are accompanied by doctors and nurses trained in paediatric intensive care. The Government has provided funding of £5 million for 1997–98 to assist in improving PIC services in England.

Greater Accountability for NHS Trusts

Each NHS Trust (see p. 392) is run by a board of executive and non-executive directors. Trusts are free to employ their own staff and set their own rates of pay, although staff transferring to Trust employment retain their existing terms and conditions of service. Trusts are also free to carry out research and provide facilities for medical education and other forms of training. They may treat private patients to generate income provided this does not interfere with NHS obligations.

In June 1997 the new Government announced that it would in future require all Trust board meetings to be open to the public. It has also taken measures to make boards more representative of the local communities they serve, by ensuring that appointments procedures include representatives of ordinary NHS users, patients and carers.

Organ Transplantation

The United Kingdom Transplant Support Service Authority (a Special Health Authority of the NHS), provides a 24-hour support service to all transplant units in Britain for the matching and allocation of organs for transplant. During 1996, 1,683 kidney transplants were performed. A similar service exists for corneas and, in 1996, over 2,600 were transplanted.

There are eight designated heart transplant centres in England, and one in Scotland. Programmes for lung and combined heart and lung transplantation are in progress and in 1996, 291 heart, 117 lung, and 53 heart/lung transplants were performed. The world's first combined heart, lungs and liver transplant operation was carried out at Papworth in 1987. There are six designated liver transplant units in England and one in Scotland. In 1996, over 600 liver transplants were performed.

A voluntary organ donor card system enables people to indicate their willingness to become organ donors in the event of their death. The NHS Organ Donor Register, a computer database of those willing to be organ donors, was launched in 1994. By June 1997 it contained over 4 million names.

Commercial dealing in organs for transplantation is illegal.

Blood Transfusion Services

Blood transfusion services are run by the National Blood Authority in England, the Scottish National Blood Transfusion Service, the Welsh Blood Service and the Northern Ireland Blood Transfusion Agency. Britain is self-sufficient in blood and blood products.

In England alone around 2.4 million donations are given each year by voluntary unpaid donors and separated into many different life-saving products for patients. Red cells, platelets and other products with a limited 'shelf life' are prepared at blood centres. The production of plasma products is undertaken at the Bio Products Laboratory in Elstree (Hertfordshire) and the Protein Fractionation Centre in Edinburgh.

Each of the four national bodies co-ordinates programmes for donor recruitment, retention and education, and donor sessions are organised regionally, in towns, villages and workplaces. Donors are normally aged between 18 (17 in Scotland) and 65. Blood centres are responsible for blood collection, screening, processing and supplying hospital blood banks. They also provide wide-ranging laboratory, clinical, research, teaching and advisory services and facilities. These are subject to nationally co-ordinated quality audit programmes.

Ambulance and Patient Transport Services

NHS emergency ambulances are available free of charge for cases of sudden illness or collapse, for accidents and for doctors' urgent calls. Rapid response services, in which paramedics use cars and motorcycles to reach emergency cases, have been introduced in a number of areas, particularly London and other major cities with areas of high traffic density. Helicopter ambulances serve many parts of England and an integrated air ambulance service is available throughout Scotland.

Non-emergency patient transport services are available free of charge to NHS patients considered by their doctor (or dentist or midwife) to be medically unfit to travel by other means. The principle applied is that each patient should be able to reach hospital in a reasonable time and in reasonable comfort, without detriment to his or her medical condition. In many areas the ambulance service organises volunteer drivers to provide a hospital car service for non-urgent patients.

Patients who are on, or dependants of people on, Income Support or Disability Working Allowance are eligible for reimbursement of costs of travelling to hospital. People on low incomes may also be eligible.

Rehabilitation

Rehabilitation services are available for elderly, young, and mentally ill people, and for those with physical or learning disabilities who need such help to resume life in the community. These services are offered in hospitals, centres in the community and in people's own homes through co-ordinated work by a range of professionals.

Medical services may provide free artificial limbs and eyes, hearing aids, surgical supports, wheelchairs, and other appliances. Following assessment, very severely physically disabled patients may be provided with environmental control equipment which enables them to operate devices such as alarm bells, radios and televisions, telephones, and heating appliances. Nursing equipment may be provided on loan for use in the home.

Local authorities may provide a range of facilities to help patients in the transition from hospital to their own homes. These include the provision of equipment; help with cleaning, shopping and cooking; care from domestic help workers; and professional help from occupational therapists and social workers. Voluntary organisations also provide services, complementing the work of the statutory agencies and widening the range of services.

Hospices

Hospice or palliative care is a special type of care for people whose illness may no longer be curable; it enables them to achieve the best possible quality of life during the final stages. The care may be provided in a variety of settings: at home (with support from specially trained staff), in a hospice or palliative care unit, in hospital or at a hospice day centre.

Hospice or palliative care focuses on controlling pain and other distressing symptoms and providing psychological support to patients, their families and friends, both during the patient's illness and into bereavement.

Palliative care was first developed in Britain in 1967 by the voluntary hospices and continues to be provided by them in many areas, but is now also provided within NHS palliative care units, hospitals and community services.

Hospices and palliative care services mostly help people with cancer, although patients with other life-threatening illnesses are also cared for. There are also several hospices providing respite care for children from birth to 16 years of age.

The National Council for Hospices and Specialist Palliative Care Services is an umbrella organisation which brings together both voluntary and health service providers in order to provide a co-ordinated view of the service and work; it covers England, Wales and Northern Ireland. Its Scottish counterpart is the Scottish Partnership Agency for Palliative and Cancer Care.

Private Medical Treatment

Some NHS hospitals share expensive equipment with private hospitals, and NHS patients are sometimes treated (at public expense) in the private sector where it is considered that this will represent value for money. The scale of private practice in relation to the NHS is, however, relatively small.

It has been estimated that about three-quarters of those receiving acute treatment in private hospitals or NHS hospital pay beds are funded by health insurance schemes, which make provision for private health care in return for annual subscriptions. Over 3 million people subscribe to such schemes, about half of them within group schemes, some arranged by firms on behalf of employees. Subscriptions often cover more than one person (for example, members of a family); about 11 per cent of the population in Britain is covered by private medical insurance. A survey carried out in 1994 showed that 36 per cent of households with an annual gross income of £26,000 or more had private medical insurance, compared with only 3 per cent of those with an annual gross income of less than £8,000. Those on higher incomes were also more likely to have the majority of the costs of their private medical insurance met by their employer.

In July 1997 the Government announced that it would abolish the tax relief given for premiums on private health insurance paid by people aged 60 and over. In 1996–97 approximately 550,000 people aged over 60 received this tax relief at the cost of some £110 million.

Many overseas patients come to Britain for treatment in private hospitals and clinics, and Harley Street in London is an internationally recognised centre for medical consultancy.

Parents and Children

Special preventive services are provided under the NHS to safeguard the health of pregnant women and of mothers with young children. Services include free dental treatment; health education; and vaccination and immunisation of children against certain infectious diseases (see p. 409).

A woman is entitled to care throughout her pregnancy, the birth and the postnatal period. Care may be provided by a midwife, a community-based GP, a hospital-based obstetrician, or a combination of these. The birth may take place in a hospital maternity unit, a midwife/GP-led unit, or at home. After the birth, a midwife will visit until the baby is at least ten days old and after that a health visitor's services are available. Throughout her pregnancy and for the first year of her baby's life, a woman is entitled to free prescriptions and dental care.

A comprehensive programme of health surveillance is provided for pre-school

children in clinics run by the community health trusts, and increasingly by GPs. This enables doctors, dentists and health visitors to oversee the physical and mental health and development of pre-school children. Information on preventive services is given and in some clinics welfare foods are distributed. The school health service offers health care and advice for schoolchildren, including medical and dental inspection and treatment where necessary.

Child guidance and child psychiatric services provide help and advice to families and children with psychological or emotional problems. In recent years special efforts have been made to improve co-operation between the community-based child health services and local authority education and social services for children. This is particularly important in the prevention of child abuse and for the health and welfare of children in care (see p. 418).

Human Fertilisation and Embryology

The world's first 'test-tube baby' was born in Britain in 1978, as a result of the technique of *in vitro* fertilisation. This opened up new horizons for helping with problems of infertility and for the science of embryology. The social, ethical and legal implications were examined by a committee of inquiry under Baroness Warnock (1984) and led eventually to the passage of the Human Fertilisation and Embryology Act 1990, one of the most comprehensive pieces of legislation on assisted reproduction and embryo research in the world.

The Human Fertilisation and Embryology Authority (HFEA), set up under the 1990 Act, licenses and controls centres providing certain infertility treatments, undertaking human embryo research or storing gametes or embryos. The HFEA maintains a code of practice giving guidance to licensed centres and reports annually to Parliament.

The law prohibits surrogacy arrangements made on a commercial basis and prohibits any advertising concerning surrogacy. An independent review of aspects of surrogacy law was set up in June 1997. Its terms of reference are to consider whether payments, including expenses, to surrogate mothers should continue to be allowed and, if so, on what basis; to examine whether there is a case for regulating surrogacy arrangements through a recognised body; and, in the light of the above, to advise whether changes are needed to the present legislation.

Ethical Issues

The Advisory Committee on Genetic Testing was set up in 1996 to consider the ethical, social and scientific aspects of genetic testing. In November of the same year the Committee issued for consultation a draft code of practice on genetic testing supplied to the public; the document was published in September 1997. The establishment of a Human Genetic Advisory Commission was announced in 1996, and met for the first time in February 1997. The Commission will take a broad view of developments in human genetics and foster public confidence in its application.

Family Planning

Free family planning advice and treatment is available from GPs or from family planning clinics. Clinics are also able to provide condoms and other contraceptives free of charge. The Government's public health strategy aims to ensure the provision of effective family planning services for those who want them.

Abortion

Under the Abortion Act 1967, as amended, a time limit of 24 weeks applies to the largest category of abortion—risk to the physical or mental health of the pregnant woman—and also to abortion because of a similar risk to any existing children of her family. There are three categories in which no time limit applies: to prevent grave permanent injury to the physical or mental health of the woman; where there is a substantial risk of serious foetal handicap; or where continuing the pregnancy would involve a risk to the life of the pregnant woman greater than if the pregnancy were terminated. The Act does not apply in Northern Ireland.

In 1996:

- the number of legal abortions in England and Wales rose by 8.3 per cent to 177,225 compared with 163,638 in 1995;

- abortions on women resident in England and Wales increased by 13,333 to 167,648, an increase of 8.6 per cent compared with 1995;

- abortions carried out under the NHS increased by 12,570 (11.5 per cent) to 121,512, while non-NHS abortions also increased: by 1,017 (1.9 per cent) to 55,713; and

- abortions for non-resident women rose by 254 to 9,577, an increase of 2.7 per cent. These abortions represented 5.4 per cent of all abortions carried out in England and Wales.

Drug Misuse

The misuse of drugs, such as heroin, cocaine and amphetamines, is a serious social and health problem, and the new Government is making the fight against such misuse a priority. It is reviewing current anti-drugs work and will be drawing up a new drugs strategy for England. (See chapter 8 for details of the present drugs strategy, including the work of Drug Action Teams). A separate drug and alcohol strategy for Wales was launched in 1996. It involves a drug and alcohol unit (see below), an advisory committee on drug and alcohol misuse, and five drug and alcohol action teams, one in each Welsh health authority area.

Research on various aspects of drug misuse is funded by several government departments. The Government is advised on matters relating to drug misuse and connected social problems by the Advisory Council on the Misuse of Drugs (in Scotland the Scottish Advisory Committee on Drug Misuse).

Prevention

Government national mass media publicity campaigns have been run since 1985 to persuade young people not to take drugs, and to advise parents, teachers and other professionals on how to recognise and combat the problem. Since 1991–92 the focus has changed to give greater emphasis to locally based campaigns and includes work on solvent misuse. A £5 million-a-year publicity campaign, which aims to increase public awareness of the risks of drug-taking, was launched in 1995 and will run until 1998.

The Home Office Drugs Prevention Initiative provides funding for local drugs prevention teams in 12 areas in England. The teams aim to show what local communities working together can do to tackle problems associated with drugs misuse. The 1997–98 budget for the Initiative is some £2 million and funding will continue until March 1999. At present over 70 local projects are being implemented. They are aimed at young people (including some projects within the criminal justice system designed to confront the links between drugs and crime); at parents; and at whole communities. The Initiative is underpinned by an extensive programme of research and the findings will be made widely available to enable people at all levels to take action within the community against drug misuse.

In Wales the Welsh drug and alcohol unit has prepared a drug prevention action plan, and a prevention campaign was launched in 1997.

The Government makes funds available through local education authorities in England and Wales to provide in-service training for teachers involved in drug-prevention work in schools. As part of the National Curriculum in England and Wales (see chapter 26), children in primary and secondary schools receive education on the dangers of drug misuse. A circular on drug prevention and schools, containing guidance to help schools provide effective drug education programmes, was issued in 1995.

Separate measures have been introduced in Scotland to discourage drug misuse through publicity campaigns and action in the education service and the community. Some £3 million has been made available to the Scotland Against Drugs Campaign, launched in 1996. This initiative aims to deliver a fundamental change in attitudes to drugs and personal responsibility, closely involving both the business community and the media.

National Drugs Helpline

A national drugs and solvents telephone helpline provides a 24-hour free confidential advice, counselling and information service throughout Britain to anyone concerned about the health implications of drugs or solvent misuse. The telephone number is 0800 77 66 00.

Treatment and Rehabilitation

Treatment for drug dependence includes: residential detoxification and rehabilitation; community drug dependency services; needle and syringe exchange schemes to combat the spread of HIV/AIDS and other blood-borne infections; advice and counselling; and after-care and support services. Facilities are provided by both statutory and independent agencies.

A task force set up to review the effectiveness of treatment services for drug misusers in England reported in May 1996. It recommended that:

- services which are a first point of contact for drug misusers should offer basic health checks;
- the process of 'shared care' with appropriate support for GPs should be made available as widely as possible;
- steps should be taken to ensure drug misusers who inject or are at risk of injecting have better access to Hepatitis B vaccinations; and
- counselling and support services should be recognised as core components of drug treatment and not as subsidiary to other treatments.

The total amount available to health authorities in England for drug treatment services in 1997–98 is over £37 million. In addition, a grant is payable each year to local authorities to enable them to support voluntary organisations providing services to drug and alcohol misusers. In Scotland, £9.8 million is being made available in 1997–98 for the support of drug misuse and drug-related HIV/AIDS services.

An increasing number of GPs treat drug misusers, but only a limited number of doctors are licensed to prescribe certain controlled drugs to them, such as heroin and cocaine. However, any doctor may prescribe methadone as a substitute drug for drug misusers. All doctors must notify the authorities of any patient they consider to be addicted to certain controlled drugs, and guidelines on good medical practice in the treatment of drug misuse have been issued to doctors.

Other Services

A number of non-statutory agencies work with, and complement, health service provision. Advice and rehabilitation services, including residential facilities, for example, are provided by many voluntary organisations. Support in the community is provided by the probation service and local social services departments (social work departments in Scotland).

Solvent Misuse

Government policy aims to prevent solvent misuse through educating young people, parents and professionals about the dangers and signs of misuse, and, where practicable, restricting the sales of solvent-based liquefied gas and aerosol products to young people.

In England, Wales and Northern Ireland it is an offence to supply such substances to children under 18 if the supplier knows or has reason to believe they are to be used to induce intoxication. In Scotland proceedings can be taken under the common law.

The Department of Health funds a hospital-based unit in London to collect and publish annual mortality statistics associated with solvent misuse. The statistics for 1995 show the number of deaths having risen to 68, an increase over the 58 deaths in 1994, which had been the lowest since 1981.

Alcohol Misuse

Alcohol is consumed by over 90 per cent of the adult population. In 1994, 27 per cent of

men and 13 per cent of women in England and Wales were drinking above the then recommended sensible limits (21 units a week for men and 14 units for women). In England alone, this is the equivalent of around 9 million adults. Between 8.8 and 14.8 million working days each year are lost through alcohol-related absence. The most widely accepted estimate of the cost of alcohol misuse in England and Wales is £2,700 million a year.

The Government seeks to tackle alcohol-related problems through a co-ordinated programme of action across government departments, and involving health and local authorities, the independent sector, employers and the alcohol industry.

Concern over alcohol misuse by young people was heightened following the appearance on the market from mid-1995 of a range of new alcoholic drinks known as 'alcopops'. After examining the measures needed to prevent or inhibit the inappropriate marketing, promotion and sale of alcoholic drinks to those aged under 18, in July 1997 the Government set out the action it expected the alcohol industry to take in order to tackle the problem over the coming year.

Part of the funds allocated to the Health Education Authority (see p. 410) are for promoting the sensible drinking message in England, and equivalent bodies are similarly funded in other parts of Britain. In Scotland, pilot projects have been launched at local level to tackle underage drinking.

Treatment and rehabilitation within the NHS include in-patient and out-patient services in general and psychiatric hospitals and specialised alcoholism treatment units. Primary care teams (GPs, community psychiatric nurses and social workers) and voluntary organisations providing treatment and rehabilitation in hostels, day centres and advisory services also play an important role.

The development of services to help problem drinkers and their families is being taken forward within the framework of community care. Local authorities are required to identify the need for alcohol misuse services in their area, and to list the services provided in their community care plans (see p. 414). They are then responsible for arranging for the needs of individuals with alcohol problems to be assessed, and for buying an appropriate course of care.

There is close co-operation between statutory and voluntary organisations. In England the voluntary agency Alcohol Concern plays a prominent role in improving services for problem drinkers and their families; increasing public awareness of alcohol misuse and harm-free drinking; and improving training for professional and voluntary workers.

Between 1990–91 and 1997–98 a total government contribution of £9 million was allocated to Alcohol Concern for improving and extending the network of care, advisory and counselling services. In addition, a grant of £2.5 million is being paid to local authorities during 1997–98 to help voluntary agencies improve and extend provision for alcohol and drug misusers in England. The Scottish Council on Alcohol undertakes similar work in Scotland. Research and surveys on various aspects of alcohol misuse are funded by several government departments.

Smoking

Cigarette smoking is the greatest single cause of preventable illness and death in Britain. It is associated with around 120,000 premature deaths a year and costs the NHS an estimated £610 million a year for the treatment of related diseases (for example, heart disease, lung cancer and bronchitis). In Scotland alone, for example, over 10,600 people die each year as a result of their smoking—that is, one in six of all deaths in Scotland. The largest increase in smoking rates is seen in teenagers and especially girls (see p. 408). Studies of smoking in pregnancy shows a relationship between maternal smoking and the risk of sudden infant deaths as well as low birth weight in infants.

Education on the harmful effects of smoking is included in the National Curriculum for all pupils in publicly maintained schools in England and Wales. A new three-year anti-smoking campaign for teenagers was launched in July 1996, with extensive magazine advertising. In response, over 175,000 young people applied for an information pack about smoking and adopting a positive alternative lifestyle. In Scotland the Health Education Board for Scotland (see p. 410) operates a free telephone helpline, 'Smokeline', which has received almost 318,300 calls since 1992. The Board is spending some £610,000 on smoking initiatives in 1997–98. Its telephone number is 0800 84 84 84.

The Government also supports the work of the voluntary organisation Action on Smoking and Health (ASH), whose services include a workplace consultancy, offering advice and help to employers in formulating anti-smoking policies.

The Tobacco Control Alliance, founded in 1994 and supported by over 40 organisations, calls for a concerted effort to eliminate tobacco use in Britain, to create an environment where children are relieved of the pressure to start smoking, and to encourage and help smokers to stop.

Tobacco Advertising and Promotion Controls

All tobacco advertising is banned on television, and cigarette advertisements are banned on radio. At present other forms of advertising and promotion of tobacco products are regulated by two voluntary agreements between the Government and the tobacco industry.

The first agreement bans tobacco advertising in cinemas and in young women's magazines. It prohibits outdoor poster advertising within 200 metres of schools; places an upper limit on poster advertising expenditure; and bans all permanent shopfront advertising. It also requires that government health warnings appear on all tobacco advertising, alerting the consumer to the risks associated with smoking.

The second voluntary agreement, on sports sponsorship by tobacco firms, covers levels of spending, restrictions on sponsorship of events chiefly for spectators under 18 years, and controls over the siting of advertising at televised events.

The health warnings which appear on packets of tobacco products are governed by law and not by voluntary agreement. Packets of cigarettes and rolling tobacco must carry one of six specified health warnings (for example, 'smoking causes cancer'). All tobacco products must also carry the warning 'tobacco seriously damages health'.

Smoking among Secondary School Children 1996

The preliminary results of a government survey of smoking among children in England and Scotland aged 11 to 15 were published in July 1997. This was the latest in a series of national surveys carried out every two years since 1982.

- In England in 1996 13 per cent of secondary school children aged 11 to 15 were regular smokers (that is, smoking at least one cigarette a week), compared with 10 per cent in 1986. Throughout the 1990s girls have been more likely to smoke than boys, and in 1996 11 per cent of boys and 15 per cent of girls were regular smokers.

- In Scotland 14 per cent of 12 to 15 year-olds were smokers in 1996 compared with 12 per cent in 1986. Up to 1996 the overall prevalence of smoking among boys in Scotland was lower than among girls, and had remained at about the same level since the mid-1980s. The overall increase in 1996 was mainly due to the rise in the proportion of boys who were smokers, from 11 per cent in 1994 to 14 per cent in 1996.

- Very few children are smokers when they start secondary school, but, by the time they are 15, about three out of every ten in England and Scotland smoke at least one cigarette a week.

Legislative Proposals

The Government is to publish a White Paper in late 1997 setting out its strategy for reducing smoking, and therefore reducing smoking-related disease and death, using every possible lever of government—changes in the law, taxation, education and publicity. As an essential first step, it intends to introduce legislation to ban tobacco advertising altogether.

As one immediate measure aimed at reducing tobacco consumption, the Government is to raise the tax payable on cigarettes by 5 per cent in real terms from December 1997.

AIDS

Up to the end of June 1997 a total of 14,431 cases of AIDS had been reported in Britain, of whom 9,937 (69 per cent) were homosexual or bisexual males. The total number of recognised HIV infections was 29,599, of whom 24,942 (85 per cent) were male. The majority—17,489 (59 per cent)—were homosexual or bisexual males, but 5,804 (20 per cent) were heterosexual non-injecting drug users.

The latest report of the monitoring programme in England and Wales[2] (published in December 1996) confirms that HIV infection is found throughout England and Wales among those groups at greatest risk, but rates are much higher in London than elsewhere. Transmission is still occurring in some homosexual/bisexual men, and injecting drug users are still taking part in high-risk behaviour, with younger users and women in particular sharing injecting equipment. Prevalence in pregnant women in London has remained relatively high at one in 556. The results of this monitoring are used to plan services, inform policy and develop HIV/AIDS projections.

Government Strategy

Key elements of the Government's strategy include:

- encouraging appropriate behaviour change by increased targeting of sections of the population at particular risk, including homosexual and bisexual men and drug misusers;

- sustaining and improving general public awareness;

- continuing to make HIV testing facilities more widely known, and encouraging health authorities to commission additional accessible HIV testing sites; and

- continued funding for the voluntary sector.

[2] Unlinked Anonymous HIV Prevalence Monitoring Programme: England and Wales Summary of the Data to the end of 1995. Department of Health. 1996.

A concerted approach is being maintained, spanning government, the NHS, local authorities and the voluntary sector (including women's groups, religious communities and organisations working with ethnic minorities).

In England NHS funding for HIV/AIDS treatment and care amounted to £199.6 million in 1997–98, and local authority funding amounted to £13.7 million. In Scotland £9.6 million has been made available to health boards for HIV/AIDS treatment and care in 1997–98. Details of Britain's contribution to international co-operation on AIDS are given in chapter 9.

Voluntary Organisations

Voluntary agencies concerned with HIV/AIDS include the Terrence Higgins Trust, London Lighthouse, Body Positive and the National AIDS Trust. Both London Lighthouse and the Mildmay Mission Hospital, in London, provide hospice care and community support. The Government distributes grants on a yearly basis, taking into account developing health priorities and the ability of voluntary bodies to raise funds from other sources for HIV/AIDS work.

Infectious Diseases

Health authorities/health boards carry out programmes of immunisation against diphtheria, measles, mumps, rubella, poliomyelitis, tetanus, tuberculosis, whooping cough and haemophilus influenzae type B infection ('Hib'). Immunisation is voluntary, but parents are encouraged to protect their children. The proportion of children being vaccinated has been increasing since 1978. GPs who achieve targets of 70 and 90 per cent uptake of child immunisation receive special payments.

By September 1996 immunisation uptake in Britain was 96 per cent for diphtheria, tetanus and polio, 95 per cent for Hib (a major cause of meningitis in children under five years), 94 per cent for whooping cough, and 92 per cent for measles, mumps and rubella for children by their second birthday. The incidence of such childhood diseases is at its lowest ever level. Since the introduction of the Hib vaccine in 1992, Hib meningitis

has been almost completely eliminated in young children.

Health authorities/boards have a key responsibility for prevention and control of outbreaks of infectious disease, liaising closely with colleagues in environmental health departments of local authorities. They are assisted by the Public Health Laboratory Service, which aims to protect the population from infection through the detection, diagnosis, surveillance, prevention and control of communicable diseases in England and Wales. Similar facilities are provided in Scotland by the Scottish Centre for Infection and Environmental Health and, in Northern Ireland, by the Department of Health and Social Services, the Northern Ireland Public Health Laboratory and other hospital microbiology laboratories.

In response to the worldwide resurgence of TB (tuberculosis) in recent years, a working group was set up in 1994 to consider policies for TB control. The group issued two reports in 1996: the first spelt out the essential elements of a successful local control and prevention policy; the second recommended strategies for identifying, treating and preventing TB in homeless people, a group at particular risk.

Cancer Care

Care and treatment of cancer forms an enormous part of the NHS's work, consuming nearly 7 per cent of its total budget. A framework for the future development of cancer services was announced in 1995. This recommended that services should be organised at three levels, with *primary care* seen as the initial focus of care; *cancer units* created in many local hospitals of a sufficient size to support a multidisciplinary team with the expertise and facilities to treat commoner cancers; and *cancer centres* situated in larger hospitals to treat less common cancers and to support smaller cancer units by providing services not available in all local hospitals. Health authorities/health boards are now planning to implement the changes recommended.

The new Government is committed to improving the provision and availability of high-quality cancer services and is directing savings achieved from cuts in the cost of the NHS internal market (see p. 392) into patient care. As a first step, £10 million has been made available for breast cancer services to speed up access to diagnosis, reduce waiting times for treatment and support networks of specialist breast cancer teams.

Cancer Screening

Breast cancer is recognised as a major health problem in Britain. In England and Wales some 13,000 women die from it each year and 1 in 12 women in England (1 in 10 in Scotland) will develop it. Britain was the first country in the European Union to introduce a nationwide breast screening programme, under which women aged between 50 and 64 are invited for mammography (breast X-ray) every three years by computerised call and recall systems. In 1995–96:

- 76 per cent of women in England (74 per cent in Scotland) aged 50 to 64 invited for screening were screened;

- over one million women of *all ages* were screened within the programme;

- 5,569 cases of cancer were diagnosed among women screened in England (522 cases in Scotland).

The nationwide cervical screening programme aims to reduce death from cancer of the cervix by inviting women aged between 20 and 64 (20 and 60 in Scotland) to take a free smear test at least every five years. Health authorities must ensure that the results of a smear test are returned from the laboratory to the patient within a month.

Special payments are made to GPs who achieve targets of 50 and 80 per cent for the uptake of smear tests. The Government estimates that almost all GPs now earn bonus payments for meeting cervical screening targets. In Scotland over 83 per cent of eligible women have been screened over the last five years.

Deaths from cervical cancer in England and Wales have fallen since the programme began, dropping from 1,942 in 1988 to 1,369 in 1994, and in Scotland from 191 in 1988 to 138 in 1996.

Health Education

Responsibility for health education in Britain lies with four separate health education authorities, which work alongside the national health departments. All four authorities are part of the NHS. They are the Health Education Authority; Health Promotion Wales; The Health Education Board for Scotland; and the Health Promotion Agency for Northern Ireland. All have broadly similar responsibilities. Their aims are:

- to provide information and advice about health directly to members of the public;

- to support other organisations and health professionals who provide health education to members of the public; and

- to advise the Government on health education.

In addition, the Health Education Authority has the major executive responsibility for public education in Britain about AIDS. It also assists in the provision of training for HIV/AIDS workers, and provides a national centre of information and advice on health education. Major campaigns carried out by the health education authorities include those focusing on coronary heart disease, cancer, smoking and alcohol misuse.

Almost all NHS health authorities/health boards have their own health education service, which works closely with health professionals, health visitors, community groups, local employers and others to determine the most suitable local programmes. Increased resources in the health service are being directed towards health education and preventive measures. GPs receive special payments for health promotion programmes.

Healthier Eating

There has been growing public awareness in recent years of the importance of a healthy diet. Medical research has shown that a diet which is low in fats, especially saturates, and rich in fruits, vegetables and starchy foods contributes to good health and can reduce the risk of certain serious illnesses, such as coronary heart disease and stroke.

The *Health of the Nation* White Paper followed the recommendations of the Committee on the Medical Aspects of Food and Nutrition Policy (COMA) that people should reduce their average intakes of total fat and saturated fatty acids and avoid obesity in order to reduce cardiovascular disease. It contained dietary targets for reducing these two nutrients and for reducing adult obesity, and the Nutrition Task Force was established in 1992 to devise a programme to achieve them. The programme was implemented through a number of project teams in information and education, catering, the NHS and the food chain. The Task Force published its final report in April 1996 and its programme was devolved to the wider community and to those considered best placed to ensure progress towards the targets.

In July 1996 the Scottish Diet Action Group published an action plan designed to deliver, over 10 years, the changes recommended in a 1993 working party report on the improvements required in the Scottish diet. The plan highlights the steps that the food industry and other interests can take voluntarily to improve the Scottish diet. The Food and Nutrition Strategy Group is developing a plan for Northern Ireland.

Nutritional labelling indicating the energy, fat, protein and carbohydrate content of food is being encouraged on a voluntary basis. The major supermarket chains and most food manufacturers have already introduced voluntary labelling schemes. Nutrition labelling is compulsory on products for which a nutritional claim is made. The food industry is exploring ways of making the labelling information easier to understand.

ENVIRONMENTAL HEALTH

Environmental health provides public health protection through control of: physical environment; atmospheric pollution and noise; contaminated land, food and water; unfit housing; health and safety; communicable diseases; and statutory nuisances. In Britain no single government department is responsible for environmental health as a whole, although the Department of Health advises other government departments on the

health implications of their policies. The role of central government departments includes the formulation of policy, drafting and processing of legislation on environmental health services, provision of guidance on the legislation, and, in some areas, enforcement. Environmental health services are mainly operated at local level through regional and district local government units.

Professionally trained environmental health officers are mainly employed by local authority councils. They are concerned with inspection, health education and regulation.

The Institute for Environment and Health, established by the Medical Research Council, is concerned mainly with research and management of research into the hazards to which people may be exposed through the environment. In Scotland the Scottish Centre for Infection and Environmental Health provides surveillance and advisory services on environmental health matters.

The Department of Health, Welsh Office and Scottish Office have established the national Focus for Work on response to chemical incidents and surveillance of health effects of environmental chemicals. Located in Cardiff, the Focus is concerned with co-ordinating expert advice to health professionals at the time of incidents, and providing support to the NHS on emergency planning, surveillance and training issues.

Safety of Food

Under the Food Safety Act 1990 it is illegal to supply food that is unfit for human consumption or falsely or misleadingly labelled. Treatments or processes must not make food harmful to health. Places where food or drink is prepared, handled, stored or sold must comply with hygiene provisions. Local authorities enforce food law and environmental health officers may take away for examination, samples of food on sale for human consumption. In addition to general regulations laying down hygiene requirements, there are specific regulations for milk and milk products, meat and meat products, eggs, fish products and shellfish, covering labelling, composition, additives and contaminants.

See chapter 18 for details of the Government's plans to set up an independent Food Standards Agency.

CJD and Public Health

In 1996 the Government announced the identification of a new variant of CJD (Creutzfeldt-Jakob disease), an extremely rare spongiform encephalopathy in humans. The government Spongiform Encephalopathy Advisory Committee (SEAC) concluded that the most likely explanation, in the absence of any credible alternative, is that these cases are linked to exposure to BSE (bovine spongiform encephalopathy) before the introduction of the ban on specified bovine offals in 1989.

While there remains no unequivocal scientific evidence that CJD is linked to BSE, the Government is providing additional funding for research into CJD and BSE, including for that carried out at the national CJD Surveillance Unit in Edinburgh, which monitors the incidence of the disease.

See chapter 18 for details of government measures to control the spread of BSE.

SAFETY OF MEDICINES

Only medicines that have been granted a marketing authorisation issued by the European Medicines Evaluation Agency (EMEA) or the Medicines Control Agency (MCA) may be sold or supplied to the public. Marketing authorisations are issued following scientific assessment on the basis of safety, quality and efficacy.

A number of committees provide independent advice to the Medicines Control Agency and the EMEA, for example the Committee on Safety of Medicines in Britain.

THE HEALTH PROFESSIONS

Doctors and Dentists

Only people on the medical or dentists' registers may practise as doctors or dentists in the NHS. University medical and dental schools are responsible for undergraduate teaching; the NHS provides hospital and community facilities for training. Full registration as a doctor requires five or six years' training in a medical school and hospital, and the community, with a further year's experience in a hospital. For a dentist, five years' training at a dental school is required.

An extensive review of specialist medical training was carried out in 1992–93 and its recommendations are now being implemented. The Government considers that the introduction of a new specialist registrar grade, which reduces from three to two the number of specialist training grades, will, in future mean that doctors will increasingly complete their training at an earlier age. The changes, together with other policies to increase consultant numbers and reduce junior doctors' hours, are expected to increase the amount of service provided to NHS patients by consultants.

The regulating body for the medical profession is the General Medical Council and, for dentists, the General Dental Council. The main professional associations are the British Medical Association and the British Dental Association.

Nurses, Midwives and Health Visitors

There are two routes to registration as a nurse or midwife: either through a higher education diploma or through a degree course.

Nursing students undertake the pre-registration Diploma in Higher Education (Project 2000) programme, which emphasises health promotion as well care of the sick and enables students to work either in hospitals or in the community. The programme lasts three years and consists of periods of college study combined with practical experience in hospital and in the community.

Midwifery education programmes for registered general/adult nurses take 18 months, but the direct entry programme lasts three years.

Health visitors are registered general/adult nurses who have completed a programme in health visiting. By 1998 all programmes will be at degree rather than at diploma level. District nurses are registered general/adult nurses who provide care for clients in the community. As with health visitors, all community nursing programmes will be at degree rather than at diploma level from October 1998. In Northern Ireland health visitors, district nurses and schools nurses, community psychiatric, community mental handicap and occupational health nurses undertake a one-year diploma course.

The United Kingdom Central Council for Nursing, Midwifery and Health Visiting is responsible for regulating and registering these professions. Four National Boards—for England, Wales, Scotland and Northern Ireland—are responsible for ensuring that the education and training policies of the Council are carried out. The main professional associations are the Royal College of Nursing and the Royal College of Midwives.

Pharmacists

Only people on the register of pharmaceutical chemists may practise as pharmacists. Registration requires three or four years' training in a school of pharmacy, followed by one year's practical experience in a community or hospital pharmacy approved for training by the Royal Pharmaceutical Society of Great Britain or the Pharmaceutical Society of Northern Ireland (regulatory bodies for the profession).

Opticians

The General Optical Council regulates the professions of ophthalmic optician and dispensing optician. Only registered ophthalmic opticians (or registered ophthalmic medical practitioners) may test sight; training for the former takes four years, including a year of practical experience under supervision. Dispensing opticians take a two-year full-time course with a year's practical experience, or follow a part-time day-release course while employed with an optician.

Other Health Professions

Chiropodists, dieticians, medical laboratory scientific officers, occupational therapists, orthoptists, physiotherapists and radiographers, and most recently, orthotists and prosthetists may, after graduating, apply for state registration. Each profession has its own board under the general supervision of the Council for Professions Supplementary to Medicine. An application to create a further board for arts therapists was approved in March 1997. State registration is mandatory for employment in the NHS and local authorities.

Dental therapists and dental hygienists are almost exclusively recruited from certified dental nurses who have taken at least one year's training. Dental therapists then take a two-to-three-year training course and dental hygienists take a two-year training course; both carry out specified dental work under the supervision of a registered dentist.

National and Scottish Vocational Qualifications (NVQs and SVQs—see pp. 448–9) have been developed for health care support workers, ambulance personnel, operating department practitioners, physiological measurement technicians and administrative and clerical staff.

Complementary Medicine

Complementary medicine (or complementary therapies) can cover a range of therapies and practices, the best known being osteopathy, chiropractic, homoeopathy, acupuncture and herbalism.

Complementary medicine, with the exception of homoeopathy, is usually available only outside the NHS and is not commonly included in private health insurance schemes.

HEALTH ARRANGEMENTS WITH OTHER COUNTRIES

The member states of the European Economic Area (EEA—see p. 126) have special health arrangements under which EEA nationals resident in a member state are entitled to receive emergency treatment, either free or at a reduced cost, during visits to other EEA countries. Treatment is provided, in most cases, on production of a valid Form E111, which in Britain, people should obtain from a post office before travelling. There are also arrangements for people who go to another EEA country specifically for medical care, or who require continuing treatment for a pre-existing condition. Unless covered by the

E111 arrangements, visitors to Britain are generally expected to pay for routine, non-emergency treatment, or if the purpose of their visit is to seek specific medical treatment. In addition to the EEA health arrangements, Britain has a number of separate bilateral agreements with certain other countries, including Australia and New Zealand.

Personal Social Services

Personal social services help elderly people, disabled people, children and young people, people with mental illness or learning disabilities, their families and carers. Major services include skilled residential and day care, help for people confined to their homes, and the various forms of social work. The statutory services are provided by local government social services authorities in England and Wales, social work departments in Scotland, and health and social services boards in Northern Ireland. Alongside these providers are the many and varied contributions made by independent private and voluntary services. Much of the care given to elderly and disabled people is provided by families and self-help groups. There are an estimated 7 million informal carers in Britain, at least 1.5 million of whom provide over 20 hours of care a week. Carers who provide (or intend to provide) substantial care on a regular basis have the right, on request, to an assessment of their own needs.

Demand for personal social services is rising because of the increasing number of elderly people, who, along with disabled and mentally ill people, and those with learning disabilities, have the opportunity to lead more normal lives in the community, if they are given suitable support and facilities.

In response to the piecemeal way regulation in social services has developed, in 1995 the then Government launched a wide-ranging review of the regulation and inspection of children's and adults' personal social services. The review issued its report—the Burgner Report—in October 1996. It recommended that:

- local authority responsibility for inspecting care homes should be removed

from the social services department and placed elsewhere;

- local authority provision should be subject to the same registration and enforcement rules as voluntary and private sector provision;

- regulation should be extended to include small children's homes and domiciliary care; and

- all inspection reports should be available to the public.

Management Reforms

Reforms in community care provision, which came into force between 1991 and 1993, established a new financial and managerial framework intended to enable vulnerable groups in the community to live as independently as possible in their own homes for as long as they are able and wish to do so, and to give them a greater say in how they live and how the services they need should be provided.

Local authorities increasingly act as enablers and commissioners of services, as well as the actual providers, after assessing their populations' needs for social care. They are now responsible for funding and arranging social care in the community for people who require public support. This includes the provision of home helps or home care assistants to support people in their own homes, and making arrangements for residential and nursing home care for those no longer able to remain in their own homes.

Local authorities' community care charters, first published in 1996, give local people more information about the services and standards they can expect under the community care reforms.

Elderly People

Older people represent the fastest growing section of the community. The proportion of the population aged 75 and over has risen from 4.7 per cent 25 years ago to 7.1 per cent in 1996. The number of elderly people in the population is expected to grow less quickly in the next decade than it has in the previous decade.

Services for elderly people are designed to help them live at home whenever possible. These services may include advice and help given by social workers, domestic help, the provision of meals in the home, sitters-in, night attendants and laundry services as well as day centres, lunch clubs and recreational facilities. Adaptations to the home can overcome a person's difficulties in moving about, and a wide range of equipment is available for people with difficulties affecting their hearing or eyesight. Alarm systems have been developed to help elderly people obtain assistance in an emergency. In some areas 'good neighbour' and visiting services are arranged by the local authority or a voluntary organisation. Elderly people who live in residential care homes or nursing homes are subject to charging with a means test. Those who cannot afford to pay have their costs met by the State. Local authorities in England, Scotland and Wales may also levy charges for domiciliary services.

The most marked trend in residential care provision over recent years has been the continuing increase in the number of places provided in the private and voluntary sector and the corresponding fall in the number provided in local authorities' own homes.

As part of their responsibility for social housing, local authorities provide homes designed for elderly people ('sheltered accommodation'); some of these developments have resident wardens. Housing associations and private builders also build such accommodation.

Many local authorities provide free or subsidised travel for elderly people within their areas.

Disabled People

Britain has an estimated 6 million adults with one or more disabilities, of whom around 400,000 (7 per cent) live in communal establishments. Over the past ten years there has been increasing emphasis on rehabilitation and on the provision of day, domiciliary and respite support services to enable disabled people to live independently in the community wherever possible.

Local social services departments help with social rehabilitation and adjustment to disability. They are required to identify the number of disabled people in their area and to publicise services. These may include advice on personal and social problems arising from disability, as well as on occupational, educational, social and recreational facilities, either at day centres or elsewhere. Other services provided may include adaptations to homes (such as ramps for wheelchairs, stairlifts and ground-floor toilets), the delivery of cooked meals, and help with personal care at home. In cases of greatest need, help may be given with installing a telephone or a television. Local authorities and voluntary organisations may provide severely disabled people with residential accommodation or temporary facilities to allow their carers relief from their duties. Special housing may be available for those able to look after themselves.

Some authorities provide free or subsidised travel for disabled people on public transport, and they are encouraged to provide special means of access to public buildings.

The Disability Discrimination Act 1995 is designed to tackle discrimination against disabled people in Britain by providing them with a more accessible environment. The Act:

- provides a right for disabled people not to be discriminated against in employment and places a duty on employers with 20 or more staff to consider reasonable adjustments to the terms on which they offer employment where these would help to overcome the practical effects of a disability;

- provides a right of access to goods and services which will make it unlawful to refuse to serve a disabled person and may require service providers to make reasonable adjustments to their services to make them more accessible. The provisions requiring 'reasonable adjustments' have yet to be implemented; and

- has established the National Disability Council to advise the Government on eliminating discrimination against disabled people.

The new Government has transferred responsibility for disability issues from the

Department of Social Security to the Department for Education and Employment. This is intended to signal a move away from treating disabled people merely as recipients of benefits towards a culture which will value their wide role in society as people willing and able to take advantage of education, training and employment opportunities.

People with Learning Disabilities (Mental Handicap)

The Government's policy is to encourage the development of local services for people with learning disabilities and their families through co-operation between health authorities, local authorities, education and training services, and voluntary and other organisations.

Local authority social services departments are the leading statutory agency for planning and arranging services for people with learning disabilities. They provide or arrange short-term care, support for families in their own homes, residential accommodation and support for various types of activities outside the home. The main aims are to ensure that as far as possible people with learning disabilities can lead full lives in their communities and are admitted to hospital only when it is necessary on health grounds. People with learning disabilities form the largest group for local authority-funded day centre places and the second largest group in residential care.

The NHS provides for the primary health care needs of people with learning disabilities as it does for the general population. It also provides specialist services when the ordinary NHS services cannot meet health care needs. Residential care is provided for those with severe or profound disabilities whose needs can only effectively be met by the NHS.

Mentally Ill People

Government policy aims to ensure that people with mental illnesses should have access to all the services they need as locally as possible. The cornerstone of community care policy for mentally ill people is the Care Programme Approach. Under this, each patient in contact with the specialist services should receive an assessment and a care plan, have a key worker appointed to keep in touch with him or her, and be given regular reviews. The Care Programme Approach is subject to audit, enabling health authorities to identify any problems with the quality of its implementation.

While the total number of places for mentally ill people in the large hospitals has continued to fall, this has been matched by increasing provision of alternative places in smaller NHS hospitals, local authority accommodation and private and voluntary sector homes.

Arrangements made by social services authorities for providing preventive care and after care for mentally ill people in the community include day centres, social centres and residential care. Social workers help patients and their families with problems caused by mental illness. In some cases they can apply for a mentally disordered person to be compulsorily admitted to and detained in hospital. In England and Wales the Mental Health Act Commission (in Scotland the Mental Welfare Commission and in Northern Ireland the Mental Health Commission) provide important safeguards for patients to ensure that the law is used appropriately.

A grant of £67.3 million for 1997–98 to local authorities in England (£18 million in Scotland) is designed to encourage them to increase the level of social care available to mentally ill patients, including those with dementia who need specialist psychiatric care in the community.

Supervision registers for discharged patients most at risk are maintained by the providers of services for mentally ill people and allow hospital staff to keep track of them. For details of the Government's homeless mentally ill initiative, see chapter 23.

There are many voluntary organisations concerned with those suffering from mental illness (such as MIND and SANE), or learning disabilities (such as MENCAP), and they play an important role in providing services for both groups of people.

Help to Families

Local authorities must safeguard the welfare of any child in need, and promote the upbringing of such children by their families, by providing a range and level of services appropriate to those children's needs. These services can include advice, guidance, counselling, help in the home, or family centres and can be provided for the family of the child in need or any member of the family, if this will safeguard the child's welfare. Local authorities can provide these services directly or arrange for them to be provided by, for example, a voluntary organisation. Local authorities are also required to publicise the help available to families in need. Many local authorities or specialist voluntary organisations run refuges for women, often with young children, whose home conditions have become intolerable, through, for example, domestic violence. The refuges provide short-term accommodation and support while attempts are made to relieve the women's problems.

Day Care for Children

Day care facilities for children under five are provided by local authorities, voluntary agencies and privately. In allocating places in their day nurseries and other facilities, local authorities give priority to children with special social, learning or health needs. Local authorities also register and inspect childminders, private day nurseries and playgroups in their areas and provide support and advice services.

Day care figures for England up to the end of March 1996 show:

- 5,700 day nurseries with 178,000 places—an increase of 6 per cent and 10 per cent respectively over 1995.

- 103,000 registered childminders, providing 376,000 places—an increase of 6 per cent and 1 per cent respectively over 1995.

- There was a small fall in playgroup provision, with under 17,000 playgroups providing just under 400,000 places—equivalent to one place at a weekly session for each child aged 2 to 4.

- There was a considerable increase in facilities for younger school age children: places at out of school clubs increased by 57 per cent (to 70,000) and those at holiday schemes by 7 per cent (to 205,000).

The Government has begun work on a comprehensive review of the provision of education and care for children aged under five.

National Strategy for Childcare

In July 1997 the new Government announced plans to develop an integrated childcare system to match the requirements of the modern labour market and help parents, especially women, to balance family and working life. See chapter 6, p. 44, for details of out-of-school childcare facilities for children over age 5.

Child Protection

Cases of child abuse are the joint concern of a number of different agencies and professions. Area child protection committees provide forums for discussion and co-ordination and draw up policies and procedures for handling cases. The Government's central initiative on child abuse has provided funding for a variety of projects, including training for health visitors, school nurses, and local authority social services staff. In Scotland the Government provides support for child protection training at the University of Dundee and through a grant scheme for local authorities.

The number of children and young people on child protection registers in England show that by the end of March 1996:

- There were about 32,000 children on registers, a decrease of 7 per cent compared with 1995.

- About 28,000 names were added to the register during the year, a decrease of 7 per cent since 1995; and about 30,000 names were removed from the register, an increase of 1 per cent compared with the previous year.

- About 40 per cent of registrations related to those considered at risk of physical injury. Those considered at risk of neglect accounted for 33 per cent; those considered at risk of sexual abuse, for 22 per cent. Boys accounted for 54 per cent of those registered under 'physical injury'; girls accounted for 61 per cent of those registered under 'sexual abuse'.

Children in Care

Local government authorities must provide accommodation for children who have no parent or guardian, who have been abandoned, or whose parents are unable to provide for them.

In England and Wales a child may be brought before a family proceedings court if he or she is neglected or ill-treated, exposed to moral danger, beyond the control of parents, or not attending school. The court can commit children to the care of a local authority under a care order. Certain preconditions have to be satisfied to justify an order. These are that the children are suffering or are likely to suffer significant harm because of a lack of reasonable parental care or because they are beyond parental control. However, an order is made only if the court is also satisfied that this will positively contribute to the children's well-being and be in their best interests. In court proceedings children are entitled to separate legal representation and the right to have a guardian to protect their interests. All courts have to treat the welfare of children as the paramount consideration when reaching any decision about their upbringing. The law requires that wherever possible children should remain at home with their families.

Parents of children in care retain their parental responsibilities but act as far as possible as partners with the authority. Local authorities are required to prepare a child for leaving their care and to continue to advise him or her up to the age of 21; they are also required to have a complaints procedure with an independent element to cover children in their care.

Recent concerns over standards of care in certain local authority children's homes prompted a number of official inquiries between 1992 and 1993; their recommendations are now being implemented.

In Scotland children who have committed offences or are in need of care and protection may be brought before a children's hearing, which can impose a supervision requirement on a child if it thinks that compulsory measures are appropriate. Under these requirements most children are allowed to remain at home under the supervision of a social worker, but some may live with foster parents or in a residential establishment while under supervision. Supervision requirements are reviewed at least once a year until ended by a children's hearing.

In Northern Ireland the juvenile court may place children who are in need of care, protection or control into the care of a fit person (including a health and social services board or trust), or may make them subject to a supervision order.

Fostering and Children's Homes

Local authorities have a duty to ensure that the welfare of children being looked after away from home is properly safeguarded as regards their health, education, contact with their families and general quality of life. Local authorities are required to produce a plan for the future of each child in their care. When appropriate, children in care are placed with foster parents, who receive payments to cover the child's living costs. Alternatively, the child may be placed in residential care. Children's homes are provided for a range of purposes and may also be registered as schools. They may be run by local authorities, voluntary or private organisations and are subject to formal inspections.

Adoption

Local authority social services departments are required by law to provide an adoption service, either directly or by arrangement with approved voluntary adoption societies. Agencies may offer adoptive parents an allowance in certain circumstances if this would help to find a family for a child. Under adoption law it is illegal to receive an unrelated child for adoption through an unapproved third party. The Registrars-General keep confidential registers of adopted children.

Adopted people may be given details of their original birth record on reaching the age of 18 (or 16 if adopted in Scotland), and counselling is provided to help them understand the circumstances of their adoption. An Adoption Contact Register enables adopted adults and their birth parents to be given a safe and confidential way of making contact if that is the wish of both parties. A person's details are entered only if they wish to be contacted. In Scotland a similar service is provided through BirthLink.

The number of children, healthy babies in particular, who are available for adoption is far exceeded by those people wishing to adopt. In recent years fewer than 7,000 children have been adopted annually. Of those, about half are adopted by one legal parent and a new partner, following marriage or remarriage.

The Government intends to introduce new adoption legislation as soon as parliamentary time allows.

Finance

In 1994–95 nearly 50 per cent of local authorities' spending on personal social services was on elderly people (see pie chart). The biggest single item of expenditure was residential care for older people, which accounted for 25 per cent of all gross personal social services spending.

During the same period the greater part of local authorities' spending on children's services involved the provision of community homes, fostering and field social work.

Social Services Staff

The effective working of the social services depends largely on professionally qualified social workers. Training programmes leading to a Diploma in Social Work (DipSW) are provided by partnerships between universities and colleges of higher and further education and employing agencies. The Central Council for Education and Training in Social Work (CCETSW) is the statutory body responsible for promoting and regulating social work

training. The range of qualifications available include National Vocational Qualifications (NVQs and, in Scotland, SVQs), the DipSW and two further awards—the Post Qualifying Award in Social Work and the Advanced Award in Social Work. The range of qualifications is relevant for staff working in all sectors, including those in residential, day and domiciliary care service.

Professional social workers (including those in the NHS) are employed mainly by the social services departments of local authorities (local authority social work departments in Scotland and Health and Social Services Trusts in Northern Ireland). There is also a growing independent sector.

Each of the four countries of Britain has a personal social services training strategy whose objectives include increasing the supply of qualified social workers, and improving the quality of both qualifying training and the training of the existing workforce.

Local Authority Spending on Personal Social Services in England

Total: £7,503m

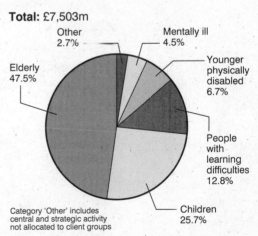

Other 2.7%
Mentally ill 4.5%
Elderly 47.5%
Younger physically disabled 6.7%
People with learning difficulties 12.8%
Children 25.7%

Category 'Other' includes central and strategic activity not allocated to client groups

Source: *Department of Health. The Government's Expenditure Plans 1997–98 to 1999–2000*

Further Reading

Health Education in Scotland: A National Policy Statement. The Scottish Office, 1991.

Health for All in Wales: Strategies for Action. Health Promotion Authority for Wales, 1990.

The Health of the Nation: A Strategy for Health in England. Cm 1986. HMSO, 1992.

A Regional Strategy for the Health and Personal Social Services in Northern Ireland 1992–97. Northern Ireland Department of Health and Social Services, 1992.

Scotland's Health: A Challenge to Us All. The Scottish Office, 1992.

Social Welfare (2nd edn). Aspects of Britain series, HMSO, 1995.

Annual Publications

Health and Personal Social Services Statistics for England. The Stationery Office.

A Regional Strategy for Health and Social Wellbeing. Northern Ireland Department of Health and Social Services.

The NHS in Scotland Annual Report. The Scottish Office.

Scottish Health Statistics. The Scottish Office.

Welsh Health: Annual Report of the Chief Medical Officer. The Welsh Office.

On the State of the Public Health. The Annual Report of the Chief Medical Officer of the Department of Health. The Stationery Office.

25 Social Security

Social security is the Government's largest expenditure programme. Planned spending in 1997–98 is almost one-third of public expenditure (see p. 159). The Government elected in May 1997 has stated its commitment to a far-reaching overhaul of the social security system. This is based on the key objectives of promoting incentives to work, reducing poverty and welfare dependency, and strengthening community and family life. Measures already being taken include a wide-ranging review of pensions, a Bill at present before Parliament to modernise the way in which social security is delivered, and the Welfare-to-Work programme to help young people, the long-term unemployed and lone mothers back into work.

As the largest single area of government spending, social security amounts to about 30 per cent of all public expenditure, compared with 13.5 per cent in 1949-50, the first full year after the introduction of the Welfare State (see p. x).

There are many reasons for this growth, not least the increasing number and range of benefits, as social security has expanded to cover both a wider range of contingencies and the changing shape and expectations of society. The system of 'safety net' benefits is now far more comprehensive than when the Welfare State began. Medical advances have

increased life expectancy. Between 1951 and 1995 the proportion of the population over pension age rose from around 13.5 per cent to 18.5 per cent. People who become disabled are now leading long and active lives. Fifty years ago, they might not have survived the onset of their disability. These and other factors have meant that both the numbers receiving benefits and the amounts that they receive have increased far beyond what was expected when the Welfare State was conceived.

The social security system is designed to secure a basic standard of living for people in financial need by providing income during periods of inability to earn (including periods of unemployment), help for families and assistance with costs arising from disablement.

There are four broad categories of social security benefit:

- **contributory benefits**, where entitlement depends on a satisfactory record of payment of contributions to the National Insurance Fund,[1] from which benefits are paid;

- **income-related benefits**, available to people whose income falls below a certain level, depending on their family circumstances. These benefits take account of capital, as well as income;

- **Jobseeker's Allowance** (see p. 427), which has both contributory and income-related components; and

- **other benefits**, which depend on qualifying conditions such as disability or family needs.

Contributory benefits account for about one half of programme expenditure; income-related benefits for almost a third; and other non-contributory benefits for about a sixth. General taxation provides over half the income for the social security programme, with employers' National Insurance contributions around a quarter and employees' National Insurance contributions about a fifth. Appeals about claims for benefits are decided by independent tribunals.

ADMINISTRATION

Administration in Great Britain is handled by five separate executive agencies of the Department of Social Security, together employing a total of around 94,000 staff:

- the Benefits Agency administers and delivers the majority of benefits;

- the Child Support Agency assesses and collects maintenance payments for children (see p. 428);

- the Contributions Agency handles National Insurance contributions;

- the Information Technology Services Agency computerises the administration of social security; and

- the War Pensions Agency delivers services to war pensioners.

The Housing and Council Tax Benefit schemes are administered by local authorities, which recover most of the cost from the Government.

In Northern Ireland, National Insurance contributions and social security benefits are administered by the Social Security Agency. The Housing Benefit scheme is administered by the Northern Ireland Housing Executive and the Rate Collection Agency; council tax does not apply in Northern Ireland, where domestic 'rates' are still collected.

Advice about Benefits

The Department of Social Security produces a range of leaflets and posters providing general information on entitlement and liability. These are available in English and a number of other languages. The Benefit Enquiry Line is a confidential telephone service offering general advice to people with disabilities and their carers. The number is: 0800 88 22 00.

Proposed Legislative Changes

The Social Security Bill at present before Parliament is designed to modernise the way social security is delivered. It aims to overhaul complex legal arrangements that have grown up piecemeal over the years and to create a streamlined and integrated service.

Its provisions include, among others:

- creating a simpler process for deciding claims and appeals for all social security benefits, and increasing accountability for the administration of the appeals process;

- introducing changes in the National Insurance scheme to ensure that employers, employees, and the self-employed do not avoid payment;

- simplifying the award and review of Social Fund budgeting loans (see p. 429); and

---

[1] The National Insurance Fund is a statutory fund into which all National Insurance contributions payable by employers, employees and self-employed people are paid and from which expenditure on contributory benefits is met.

- simplifying administrative details by ensuring that certain taxes on benefits and expenses are dealt with in the same way by the tax and National Insurance systems.

Counter-fraud Measures

A range of measures is being introduced to improve the prevention and detection of fraud in the social security system:

- The Social Security Administration (Fraud) Act, passed in March 1997, includes powers to deal with landlord and Housing Benefit fraud. The Act, among other measures:
  - creates a new offence of obtaining benefit by false representation;
  - permits certain government departments to share information with each other;
  - allows local authorities to share information with each other and with government departments;
  - permits local authorities to require certain landlords to provide information about their residential properties;

    enables local authority investigators to gain entry to business premises and to examine business records;
  - makes preparations to stop fraudulent landlords and claimants getting benefit re-directed from one property to another;
  - introduces financial penalties as an alternative to prosecution for those who defraud the system; and
  - enables the Benefit Fraud Inspectorate (see below) to inspect and report on local authorities' administration of Housing Benefit and Council Tax Benefit.

- The Benefit Fraud Inspectorate was established in April 1997 to examine and report on standards of counter-fraud and security performance in the administration of all social security benefits.

- A government-funded pilot scheme was launched in July 1997 to investigate organised benefit fraud in London which involves more than one local authority. The scheme, which is concentrating on fraud involving organised gangs, landlords and managing agents, will run until March 1999 when its success will be evaluated.

- Phonelines have been established to provide members of the public with a means of reporting suspected benefit fraud and avoidance of tax and contributions payments.

CONTRIBUTIONS

Entitlement to National Insurance benefits such as Retirement Pension, Incapacity Benefit, contributory Jobseeker's Allowance, Maternity Allowance and Widow's Benefit, is dependent upon the payment of contributions. There are five classes of contributions. **The rates given below are effective from April 1997 to April 1998:**

- Class 1—paid by employees and their employers. Employees with earnings below £62 a week do not pay Class 1 contributions. Contributions on earnings of £62 a week and over are at the rate of 2 per cent of the first £62 of total earnings and 10 per cent of the balance, up to the upper earnings limit of £465 a week. Employers' contributions are subject to the same threshold. On earnings above the threshold, contributions rise in stages from 3 per cent of total earnings up to a maximum of 10 per cent when earnings are £210 or more a week; there is no upper earnings limit. The contribution is lower if the employer operates a 'contracted-out' occupational pension scheme (see p. 426).

- Class 1A—paid by employers who provide their employees with fuel and/or a car for private use. A Class 1A contribution is payable on the cash equivalent of the benefit provided.

- Class 2—paid by self-employed people. Class 2 contributions are at a flat rate of £6.15 a week. The self-employed may claim exemption from Class 2 contributions if their profits are expected to be below £3,480 for the 1997–98 tax year. Self-employed people are not eligible for unemployment and industrial injuries benefits.

- Class 3—paid voluntarily to safeguard rights to some benefits. Contributions are at a flat rate of £6.05 a week.

- Class 4—paid by the self-employed on their taxable profits over a set lower limit (£7,010 a year), and up to a set upper limit (£24,180 a year) in addition to their Class 2 contribution. Class 4 contributions are payable at the rate of 6 per cent.

Employees who work after pensionable age (60 for women and 65 for men) do not pay contributions but the employer continues to be liable. Self-employed people over pensionable age do not pay contributions.

Social Security Expenditure, Great Britain 1996–97: benefit expenditure by broad groups of beneficiaries

Total: £92,850m

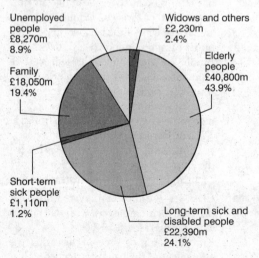

Unemployed people
£8,270m
8.9%

Widows and others
£2,230m
2.4%

Elderly people
£40,800m
43.9%

Family
£18,050m
19.4%

Short-term sick people
£1,110m
1.2%

Long-term sick and disabled people
£22,390m
24.1%

Source: *Social Security Departmental Report:*
The Government's Expenditure Plans 1997–98 to 1999–2000

BENEFITS

For most contributory benefits there are two conditions. First, before benefit can be paid at all, a certain number of contributions must have been paid. Second, the full rate of benefit cannot be paid unless contributions have been paid or credited to a specific level over a set period. A reduced rate of benefit is payable dependent on the level of contributions paid or credited. For example, a great many of those receiving retirement pensions and widows benefits receive a percentage-based rate of benefit. Benefits are increased annually in line with percentage increases in retail prices. The main benefits (payable weekly) are summarised on pp.424–33. **Rates given are those effective from April 1997 until April 1998.**

Retirement

A state **Retirement Pension** is a taxable weekly benefit payable, if the contribution conditions have been met, to women at the age of 60 and men at the age of 65. The Sex Discrimination Act 1986 protects employees of both sexes in a particular occupation from being required to retire at different ages. This, however, has not affected the payment of the state retirement pension at different ages for men and women.

Legislation was introduced in 1995 to equalise the state pension age for men and women at 65. The change will be phased in over ten years, starting from April 2010. Women born before 6 April 1950 will not be affected; their pension age will remain at 60. The new pension age of 65 will apply to women born on or after 6 April 1955. Pension age for women born between these dates will move up gradually from 60 to 65.

The state pension scheme consists of a basic weekly pension of £62.45 for a single person and £99.80 for a married couple, together with an additional earnings-related pension (sometimes called 'SERPS'—state earnings-related pension). Pensioners may have unlimited earnings without affecting their pensions. Those who have put off their retirement during the five years after state pension age may earn extra pension.

Table 25.1: Estimated Numbers Receiving Benefits in Great Britain 1997–98 (forecast)[a]

Benefit	Contributory (C) or non-contributory (NC)	Thousands
Retirement Pension	C	10,620
Widows' Benefit	C	294
Jobseeker's Allowance		
contributory	C	263
non-contributory	NC	1,538
Incapacity Benefit	C	
short term (lower rate)		121
short term (higher rate) and long term		1,550
Maternity Allowance	C	11
Non-contributory Retirement Pension	NC	27
War Pension	NC	311
Attendance Allowance	NC	1,287
Disability Living Allowance	NC	2,017
Disability Working Allowance	NC	16
Invalid Care Allowance	NC	407
Severe Disablement Allowance	NC	395
Industrial Injuries Disablement Benefit[b]	NC	265
Reduced Earnings Allowance[b]	NC	142
Industrial Death Benefit	NC	17
Income Support	NC	4,133
Child Benefit	NC	
number of children		12,935
number of families		7,150
Family Credit	NC	813
Housing Benefit	NC	
rent rebate		2,744
rent allowance		1,848
Council Tax Benefit	NC	5,793

Source: *Social Security Departmental Report: The Government's Expenditure Plans 1997–98 to 1999–2000*
[a] Figures are for beneficiaries at any one time.
[b] Figures refer to the number of pensions and in payment, and not to the number of recipients.

A *non-contributory retirement pension* of £37.35 a week is payable to people aged 80 or over who have lived in Britain for at least 10 years since reaching the age of 60, and who have not qualified for a contributory pension. People whose pensions do not give them enough to live on may be entitled to Income Support (see p. 427). Over 10.6 million people in Great Britain received a basic state pension in 1996.

Rights to basic pensions are safeguarded for people whose opportunities to work are limited while they are looking after a child or a sick or disabled person. Men and women may receive the same basic pension, provided they have paid full-rate National Insurance contributions when working. From April 1999 the earnings-related pension scheme will be based on a lifetime's revalued earnings instead of on the best 20 years. It will eventually be calculated as 20 per cent rather than 25 per cent of earnings, to be phased in over ten years from 1999. The pensions of people retiring this century will be unaffected.

As part of its plan to improve the income of women in retirement, the new Government is to introduce a Bill to enable the courts to divide pension rights between divorcing couples. The arrangements are expected to be in force by 2000.

Occupational and Personal Pensions

Employers may 'contract out' their employees from the state scheme for the additional earnings-related pension and provide their own occupational pension instead. Their pension must be at least as good as the state additional pension. Joining an employer's contracted-out scheme is voluntary: employers are not free to contract out employees from the earnings-related pension scheme without the employees' consent. The State remains responsible for the basic pension.

Occupational pension schemes have 9.2 million members. The occupational pension rights of those who change jobs before pensionable age, who are unable or who do not want to transfer their pension rights, are now offered some protection against inflation. Workers leaving a scheme have the right to a fair transfer value. The trustees or managers of pension schemes have to provide full information about their schemes.

Increasing numbers of pensioners receive income from occupational pensions and investment income. Around two-thirds of all pensioners now receive an occupational pension worth, on average, £80.80 a week, while more than three-quarters have some form of income from their investments, receiving an average of £38.40 a week.

As an alternative to their employers' scheme or the state additional earnings-related pension scheme, people are entitled to choose a personal pension available from a bank, building society, insurance company or other financial institution. In 1994–95, 5.6 million people contracted out of the state earnings-related pension scheme and took out personal pensions. Legislation passed in 1995 requires occupational schemes to provide equal treatment between men and women and to make personal pensions more flexible and attractive to a broader age-range.

A Pensions Ombudsman deals with complaints about maladministration of pension schemes and adjudicates on disputes of fact or law. A pensions registry helps people trace lost benefits. A new regulatory authority for occupational pensions came into force in April 1997 (see chapter 16).

Pensions Review

In July 1997 the new Government announced a wide-ranging review of pensions. It considers that the failure over the last 20 years to develop an adequate pensions strategy has resulted in widening inequalities among pensioners. Its long-term objective is to ensure that everyone has the opportunity to build up an adequate pension to guarantee security in retirement.

The review will look at the central areas of insecurity for elderly people including all aspects of the basic pension and its value, and second pensions including SERPS (see p. 424). The Government intends to retain the basic state pension as the foundation of pension provision and SERPS for those who wish to remain in it. It will aim to achieve a broad-based agreement for the long-term future of pensions.

It has also said that it wants to support and strengthen the framework for occupational pensions. It will develop its proposals for stakeholder pensions, offering secure, flexible and value-for-money second pensions for those who cannot join an employer's occupational pension scheme, whose pay is low or intermittent, and for whom personal pensions are usually unsuitable. Proposals will also be developed for citizenship pensions for carers who are unable to contribute to pensions in their own right.

As part of the review, the Government has commissioned a report on the state of pension provision in Britain and likely future trends. It is also setting up a working group to look at how improvements can be made to raising awareness of pension issues.

The Government intends to publish an initial framework for change in the first part of 1998.

Unemployment

Welfare-to-Work Programme

See chapter 12 for details of the Government's Welfare-to-Work programme, which offers opportunities to work for all people of working age who have, in its opinion, been left to depend on benefit for too long. This includes young people, the long-term unemployed, lone parents and people who are disabled or on Incapacity Benefit who want training or work.

Jobseeker's Allowance

Jobseeker's Allowance (JSA) is a benefit for people needing financial support because of unemployment. To get JSA, claimants must be actively looking for work, and be capable of, and available for, work. They must normally be aged at least 18 years and under pension age; and have paid enough National Insurance contributions *or* have income and savings below a certain level. All claimants are also required to have a valid Jobseeker's Agreement, which sets out a plan of action to seek work. Benefit is paid at rates determined by family circumstances on a basis similar to Income Support (see below). JSA can be either contribution-based or income-based.

- *Contribution-based JSA*: those who have paid enough National Insurance contributions are entitled to a personal JSA for up to six months, regardless of any savings or partner's income.
- *Income-based JSA*: those on a low income are entitled to an income-based JSA, payable for as long as the jobseeker requires support and continues to satisfy the qualifying conditions. The amount a claimant receives comprises an age-related personal allowance, allowances for dependent children, premium payments for those with children or special needs, and mortgage interest payments.

Back to Work Bonus

To enhance incentives to take up or keep part-time work, and encourage people to move off benefit and into employment, recipients of JSA and people aged under 60 who receive Income Support can benefit from a Back to Work Bonus. People who have been unemployed for three months or more and are working part-time may keep the first £5 of their earnings (£10 for couples, £15 for lone parents, disabled people and some people in

special occupations) in any week in which they work while receiving benefit. An amount equal to half of any earnings above that level counts towards the build-up of a bonus amount. When the unemployed person moves off benefit and into work, he or she will be able to claim a tax-free lump sum of up to £1,000. The part-time (up to 24 hours a week) earnings of a partner can also contribute towards building up a Back to Work Bonus, which can be paid if the couple leave benefit as a result of the partner moving into work.

The new Government is to evaluate the effectiveness of the Back to Work Bonus in contributing to its Welfare-to-Work objectives.

Income Support

Income Support is payable to certain people aged 16 or over who are not required to be available for work, and whose income is below certain set levels. They include lone parents, pensioners, carers and long-term sick and disabled people. Income Support is made up of: a personal allowance based on age and on whether the claimant is single, a lone parent or has a partner; age-related allowances for dependent children and additional sums known as premiums; and housing costs. From this total amount other income, including some other social security benefits, is deducted.

The Income Support scheme sets a limit to the amount of capital a person may have and still remain entitled to claim it. People with savings or capital worth more than £8,000 are ineligible; savings between £3,000 and £8,000 will reduce the amount received. People living permanently in residential care or a nursing home with savings over £16,000 are ineligible; and savings between £10,000 and £16,000 will affect the amount received.

The new Government has stated that it is concerned that up to one million pensioners currently fail to claim the income support to which they are entitled and is commissioning research into the reasons for this.

Earnings Top-up

While Family Credit (see p. 429) helps people with dependent children to be better off in work, there has been no similar provision for single people and couples without children. In 1996 a new benefit—Earnings Top-up—was introduced on a pilot basis to test whether topping up wages for workers without dependent children helps them get jobs and stay in work. The new benefit is being tested at two different levels, with different rates for couples and single people. It is available in eight pilot areas and is the first social security benefit to be introduced on a pilot basis. An intensive research and evaluation programme has already begun.

Families

Most pregnant working women receive **Statutory Maternity Pay** directly from their employer. It is paid for a maximum of 18 weeks to any woman who has been working for the same employer for 26 weeks and who earns on average at least £62 a week. She will receive 90 per cent of her average weekly earnings for the first 6 weeks and a lower rate of £55.70 a week for the remaining 12 weeks.

Women who are not eligible for Statutory Maternity Pay because, for example, they are self-employed, or have recently changed jobs or given up their job, may qualify for a weekly **Maternity Allowance**, which is payable for up to 18 weeks. This amounts to £55.70 a week for employees and £48.35 a week for the self-employed and those not in work. All pregnant employees have the right to take 14 weeks' maternity leave.

A payment of £100 from the Social Fund (see p. 429) may be made if the mother or her partner receive Income Support, income-related Jobseeker's Allowance, Family Credit or Disability Working Allowance. It is also available if a woman adopts a baby.

The main social security benefit for children is **Child Benefit**. This is a tax-free, non-contributory payment of £11.05 a week for the eldest qualifying child of a couple, and £9.00 for each other child. A higher rate of £17.05 is payable for the eldest qualifying child of a person bringing up a child on their own, whether they are the child's parent or not. Child Benefit is payable for children up to the age of 16, and for those up to 19 who

continue in full-time non-advanced education. It is generally not payable to people whose entry to Britain is subject to immigration control.

A person claiming Child Benefit for an orphaned child they have taken into their family may be entitled to **Guardian's Allowance**. This is a tax-free non-contributory benefit of £11.20 a week, reduced to £9.90 a week if a higher rate of Child Benefit is in payment. In certain circumstances Guardian's Allowance can be paid when only one parent is dead.

At the end of 1996 Child Benefit was paid for 12,790,000 children, an increase on the previous year of 60,000.

Child Support Agency

An estimated 1 million lone parents in Britain bring up 1.7 million children in households without work. The Child Support Agency (CSA), set up in 1993, has now virtually replaced the court system for obtaining basic child maintenance. The CSA is responsible for assessing child maintenance and, where requested by either parent, collecting and enforcing child maintenance payments and for tracing absent parents.

If any person is living with and caring for a child, and one, or both, of the child's parents are living elsewhere in Britain, he or she may apply to have child support maintenance assessed and collected by the CSA. If that person or their present partner claims Income Support, income-based Jobseeker's Allowance, Family Credit or Disability Working Allowance, they may be required to apply for child support maintenance if asked to do so by the CSA.

Assessments for child support maintenance are made using a formula which takes into account each parent's income and which makes allowance for essential outgoings. Legislation passed in 1995 introduced a system of departures from the formula assessment of child support to allow the amount of maintenance payable to be varied in a small proportion of cases. A child maintenance bonus worth up to £1,000 may be payable to parents with care who have been in receipt of Income Support or income-based

Jobseeker's Allowance and in receipt of child maintenance when they leave benefit for work.

In Northern Ireland the child support maintenance scheme is operated by the Northern Ireland Child Support Agency, established at the same time as the CSA.

The Government intends to review all aspects of the CSA to ensure that maintenance is assessed and collected as quickly as possible.

Childcare Costs

At present families claiming Family Credit, Disability Working Allowance, Housing Benefit and Council Tax Benefit, and who pay for childcare for children under 11, can have up to £60 a week in formal childcare costs offset against their earnings when their benefit entitlement is worked out. In July 1997 the Government announced measures designed to make it easier for lone parents and breadwinners with disabled partners to return to work: from April 1998 the disregard for childcare costs will be increased from a maximum of £60 to £100 a week, where there are more than two or more children in the family, and the maximum eligible age will be increased from 11 to 12.

As part of its Welfare-to-Work programme (see chapter 12), the Government is implementing a national childcare strategy that will help lone mothers to get out and work instead of being dependent on benefits. A pilot scheme was launched in eight areas in July 1997 in which lone parents with children of school age are being invited into jobcentres to be given advice and information about voluntary work, training and work. This will be accompanied by measures to increase the supply of, and help with, childcare-for example, by providing a network of school clubs throughout the country. A national programme will be fully implemented in 1998. See chapter 6, p. 44 for details of the Government's plans for improving childcare.

Family Credit

Family Credit is a tax-free benefit payable to low-income working families with children. It is payable to couples or lone parents. At least

one parent must work for at least 16 hours a week. The amount payable depends on a family's net weekly income; the number and ages of the children in the family; the amount of certain childcare charges paid, and the number of hours worked.

A maximum amount of Family Credit (consisting of an adult credit, plus a credit for each child varying with age, and an extra credit if one parent works for at least 30 hours a week), is payable if the family's net weekly income is less than £77.15. If income is more than £77.15, 70 p of every £1 of the excess is deducted from the maximum payable.

Child Benefit, Child Benefit (Lone Parent) and the first £15 of any maintenance in payment are not counted as income. And certain childcare charges of up to £60 a week can be offset against earnings before entitlement to Family Credit is calculated. The capital limit for Income Support (see p. 427) also applies to Family Credit.

In 1994-95 the total amount of Family Credit paid was £1,441 million; total amount unclaimed was estimated at £270 million. The number of people receiving Family Credit was estimated at 602,000 and the average number not claiming although entitled was estimated to be 220,000.

Social Fund

The Social Fund helps people with expenses which are difficult to pay for out of regular income. It consists of *regulated payments*, which are not cash-limited, and *discretionary payments*, which are paid out of an annual budget (£467.5 million in 1997–98).

The regulated payments are:

- maternity payment—£100 for each baby born, adopted or subject to a parental order. Payable to those on Income Support, income-based Jobseeker's Allowance, Family Credit or Disability Working Allowance;

- funeral payment—includes up to £600 for funeral expenses, plus the reasonable costs of all burial or cremation expenses. Available to those on Income Support and income-based Jobseeker's Allowance, Family Credit, Housing Benefit, Council

Tax Benefit or Disability Working Allowance; and

- cold weather payment—£8.50 a week towards additional heating costs during sustained periods of very cold weather between November and March. Payable to those on Income Support or income-based Jobseeker's Allowance, who have a pensioner or disability premium, or who have a child under 5 years old.

The discretionary payments are:

- community care grants to help, for example, people resettle into the community from care, or to remain in the community, to ease exceptional pressure on families and to meet certain travel expenses. Available to those on Income Support or income-based Jobseeker's Allowance or due to receive it on discharge from care;

- budgeting loans for important intermittent expenses after 26 weeks on Income Support or income-based Jobseeker's Allowance; and

- crisis loans to help people in an emergency or as a result of a disaster where there is serious damage or serious risk to health or safety. There is no qualifying benefit for this loan.

Widows

Widows' Payment. Widows under the age of 60—or those over 60 whose husbands were not entitled to a state retirement pension when they died—receive a tax-free single payment of £1,000 following the death of their husbands, provided that their husbands had paid a minimum number of National Insurance contributions. Women whose husbands have died of an industrial injury or prescribed disease may also qualify, regardless of whether their husbands had paid National Insurance contributions.

A widowed mother with at least one child for whom she is getting Child Benefit receives a **Widowed Mother's Allowance** of £62.45 a week, with a further £9.90 for a child for whom the higher rate of Child Benefit is payable, and £11.20 for each subsequent child.

Widow's Pension. A taxable, weekly benefit of £62.45 a week is payable to a widow who is 55 years or over when her husband dies or when her entitlement to Widowed Mother's Allowance ends. A percentage of the full rate is payable to widows who are aged between 45 and 54 when their husbands die or when their entitlement to Widowed Mother's Allowance ends. Special rules apply for widows whose husbands died before 11 April 1988. Entitlement continues until the widow remarries or begins drawing retirement pension. Payment ends if she lives with a man as his wife. Widows also benefit under the Industrial Injuries scheme (see p. 431).

A man whose wife dies when both are over pension age inherits his wife's pension rights just as a widow inherits her husband's rights.

Sickness and Disablement

A variety of benefits are available for people unable to work because of sickness or disablement. Employers are responsible for paying **Statutory Sick Pay** to employees from the fourth day of sickness for up to a maximum of 28 weeks. There is a single rate of Statutory Sick Pay for all qualifying employees provided their average weekly earnings are at least equivalent to the lower earnings limit for the payment of National Insurance contributions. The weekly rate is £55.70.

Incapacity Benefit is for people below state pension age who cannot work because of an illness or disability. Entitlement to Incapacity Benefit begins when entitlement to Statutory Sick Pay ends or, for those who do not qualify for Statutory Sick Pay, from the first day of sickness. The benefit has three rates:

- a lower rate of £47.10 a week for the first 28 weeks (for those not entitled to statutory sick pay);

- a higher rate of £55.70 a week between the 29th and 52nd week; and

- a long-term rate of £62.45 a week from the 53rd week of incapacity.

Extra benefits may be paid for adult and child dependants. Incapacity Benefit is taxable from the 29th week of incapacity.

The medical test of incapacity for work usually applies after 28 weeks' sickness. It assesses ability to perform a range of work-related activities rather than the ability to perform a specific job.

Severe Disablement Allowance is a tax-free benefit for people who have not been able to work for at least 28 weeks because of illness or disability but who cannot get Incapacity Benefit because they have not paid enough National Insurance contributions. The benefit is £37.75, plus additions of up to £13.15 a week depending on the person's age when they became incapable of work. Additions for adult dependants and for children may also be paid. Claims may be made by people aged between 16 and 65. Once a person has qualified for the allowance, there is no upper limit for receipt. New claimants must satisfy the same incapacity test as that used in Incapacity Benefit (see above).

People who become incapable of work after their 20th birthday must also be medically assessed as at least 80 per cent disabled for a minimum of 28 weeks. People already in receipt of certain benefits, such as the higher rate of the Disability Living Allowance care component, will automatically be accepted as 80 per cent disabled.

Other Benefits

Disability Living Allowance is a non-contributory tax-free benefit for adults aged under 65 years and children with an illness or disability who need help with personal care and/or with getting around. It has two components: a care component which has three weekly rates—£49.50, £33.10 and £13.15; and a mobility component which has two weekly rates—£34.60 and £13.15, payable from age 5 and over.

Attendance Allowance, a non-contributory tax-free benefit of £49.50 or £33.10 a week, may be payable to people severely disabled at or after age 65, who have personal care needs, depending upon the amount of attention they require.

A non-contributory **Invalid Care Allowance** of £37.35 weekly may be payable to people between 16 and 65 who cannot take up a full-time paid job because they are caring for at least 35 hours a week for a person receiving either Attendance Allowance or the higher or middle care component of Disability Living Allowance. An additional carer's premium may be paid if the recipient is also receiving Income Support, income-related Jobseeker's Allowance, Housing Benefit or Council Tax Benefit. About 1.5 million adults in Great Britain care for a disabled person for at least 20 hours a week.

Disability Working Allowance is a tax-free, income-related benefit for people aged 16 or over who work an average of 16 hours a week or more and have an illness or disability that limits their earning capacity. Awards are for fixed periods of six months. To qualify a person must either:

- be getting Disability Living Allowance, or an analogous benefit, such as Constant Attendance Allowance under the War Pensions or Industrial Injuries Disablement scheme; or

- have an invalid three-wheel vehicle supplied by the Department of Social Security; or

- have been entitled to one of the following in at least one of the 56 days before the date of claim: higher rate short-term Incapacity Benefit; long-term Incapacity Benefit; Severe Disablement Allowance; or the disability premium or higher pensioner premium with Income Support, income-based Jobseeker's Allowance, Housing Benefit or Council Tax Benefit.

The allowance is available to single people, lone parents and couples. The rate depends on the person's income and size of family, and the ages of any children. The allowance is not payable if capital or savings exceed £16,000.

Motability, an independent charitable organisation, helps disabled drivers to obtain vehicles or powered wheelchairs on favourable terms by using the higher rate mobility component of Disability Living Allowance or the War Pension mobility supplement.

Industrial Injuries Disablement Benefits/Reduced Earnings Allowance

Various benefits are payable for disablement caused by an accident at work or a prescribed disease caused by a particular type of employment. The main benefit is the tax-free **Industrial Injuries Disablement Benefit**: up to £101.10 a week is usually paid after a qualifying period of 15 weeks if a person is at least 14 per cent or more physically or mentally disabled as a result of an industrial accident or a prescribed disease.

Basic Disablement Benefit can be paid in addition to other National Insurance benefits, such as Incapacity Benefit. It can be paid whether or not the person returns to work and does not depend on earnings. The degree of disablement is assessed by an independent adjudicating medical authority and the amount paid depends on the extent of the disablement and on how long it is expected to last. Except for certain progressive respiratory diseases, disablement of less than 14 per cent does not attract Disablement Benefit. In certain circumstances additional allowances, such as **Constant Attendance Allowance** and **Exceptionally Severe Disablement Allowance**, may be payable. In some cases **Reduced Earnings Allowance** may be payable.

Housing and Council Tax Benefits

Housing Benefit is an income-related, tax-free benefit which helps people on low incomes meet the cost of rented accommodation, using general assessment rules and benefit levels similar to those for Income Support (see p. 427). It can pay up to 100 per cent of rent, depending on the claimant's circumstances. Unlike Income Support, the Housing Benefit scheme sets a limit of £16,000 on the amount of capital a person may have and still remain entitled to claim benefit.

Housing Benefit for most private sector tenants is calculated by reference to the general level of rents for properties with the same number of rooms in the locality. This is designed to ensure that private sector tenants receiving benefit have an incentive to choose better value accommodation at the outset of a tenancy.

Most single people aged under 25 who are not lone parents and who are renting privately have their Housing Benefit limited to the average cost of non-self-contained accommodation in the locality; this is intended to reduce disincentives to work, and to discourage young people from leaving home before they can afford to do so.

In 1996–97 a total of £11,523 million of Housing Benefit was paid. An average 4.7 million people claimed.

Council Tax Benefit helps people to meet their council tax payments (the tax set by local councils to help pay for services—see chapter 11, p. 167). The scheme offers help to those claiming Income Support and income-based Jobseeker's Allowance and others with low incomes. Subject to rules broadly similar to those governing the provision of Income Support and Housing Benefit (see above), people may receive rebates of up to 100 per cent of their council tax. In 1996–97, 5.6 million households received such help. A person who is solely liable for the council tax may also claim benefit (called 'second adult rebate') for a second adult who is not liable to pay the council tax and who is living in the home on a non-commercial basis.

In 1996–97 the total amount of Council Tax Benefit paid was £2,361 million. An average 5.6 million people claimed.

War Pensions and Related Services

Pensions are payable for disablement as a result of service in the armed forces or for certain injuries received in the merchant navy or civil defence during wartime, or to civilians injured by enemy action. The amount paid depends on the degree of disablement: the pension for 100 per cent disablement is £107.20 a week.

There are a number of extra allowances. The main ones are for unemployability, restricted mobility, the need for care and attendance, the provision of extra comforts, and as maintenance for a lowered standard of occupation. An age allowance of between £7.15 and £22.10 is payable weekly to war pensioners aged 65 or over whose disablement is assessed at 40 per cent or more.

Pensions are also paid to war widows and other dependants. (The standard rate of

25.2: Tax Liability of Social Security Benefits

Not Taxable	*Taxable*
Attendance Allowance	Incapacity Benefit
Child Benefit	(long term or short term higher rate)
Child's Special Allowance	Industrial Death Benefit Pensions
Council Tax Benefit	Invalid Care Allowance
Disability Living Allowance	Jobseeker's Allowance[a]
Disability Working Allowance	Retirement Pension
Family Credit	Statutory Maternity Pension
Guardian's Allowance	Statutory Sick Pay
Housing Benefit	Widowed Mother's Allowance
Incapacity Benefit (short term lower rate)	Widow's Pension
Income Support	(Income Support paid in certain
Industrial Disablement Benefit/Reduced	trade dispute cases)
Earnings Allowance	
Maternity Allowance	
Severe Disablement Allowance	
War Disablement Pension	
War Widow's Pension	

Source: Inland Revenue
[a] That part of the Jobseeker's Allowance equivalent to the individual or couple rate of personal allowance, as appropriate.

pension for a private's widow is £81.00 a week.) War Widow's Pension is also payable to a former war widow who has remarried and then become widowed again, divorced or legally separated.

The War Pensioners' Welfare Service helps and advises war pensioners, war widows and other dependants. It works closely with ex-Service organisations and other voluntary bodies which give financial help and personal support to those disabled or bereaved as a result of war.

Concessions

Other benefits for which unemployed people and those on low incomes may be eligible include exemption from health service charges (see p. 398), grants towards the cost of spectacles, free school meals and free legal aid (see p. 112). In families which are on Income Support, pregnant women and children under 5 years old are entitled to free milk and vitamins.

People on low incomes, as well as all pensioners, widows and long-term sick people on Incapacity Benefit, receive extra help to meet the cost of VAT on their fuel bills. In 1997–98 the cost of this help will be about £750 million.

Reduced charges are often made to unemployed people, for example, for adult education and exhibitions, and pensioners are usually entitled to reduced transport fares.

Taxation

The general rule is that benefits which replace lost earnings are subject to tax, while those intended to meet a specific need are not (see Table 25.2). Various income tax reliefs and exemptions are allowed on account of age or a need to support dependants.

Benefit Controls on People from Abroad

Residence Test

A residence test requires claimants to establish that they are habitually resident in the Common Travel Area (that is, Britain, the Republic of Ireland, the Channel Isles and the Isle of Man) before a claim for income-based Jobseeker's Allowance, Housing Benefit or Council Tax Benefit can be paid. The test brings Britain into line with most other European countries, which already limit access to their benefit systems to those who have lived in the country for some time.

Asylum Seekers

Only people who claim refugee status *as soon as* they arrive in Britain can claim income-based Jobseeker's Allowance, Income Support, Housing Benefit and Council Tax Benefit. Their eligibility to receive this will stop if their asylum claim is refused by the Home Office. People who claim asylum after they have arrived in Britain are not entitled to benefit.

ARRANGEMENTS WITH OTHER COUNTRIES

As part of the European Union's efforts to promote the free movement of labour, regulations provide for equality of treatment and the protection of benefit rights for employed and self-employed people who move between member states. The regulations also cover retirement pensioners and other beneficiaries who have been employed, or self-employed, as well as dependants. Benefits covered include Child Benefit and those for sickness and maternity, unemployment, retirement, invalidity, accidents at work and occupational diseases.

Britain has reciprocal social security agreements with a number of other countries which also provide cover for some National Insurance benefits and family benefits.

In 1996, 759,400 British National Insurance pensions were paid overseas, at a cost of some £950 million.

Further Reading

Social Security Statistics 1996. The Stationery Office, 1996.

Social Welfare (2nd edn). Aspects of Britain series, HMSO, 1995.

The Government's Expenditure Plans 1997–98 to 1999–2000. Social Security Departmental Report. Cm 3613. The Stationery Office, 1997.

26 Education

It was in the late 1970s that serious concern began to be expressed about the quality of school education and the lack of a national curriculum. Since then major changes have taken place, including the introduction of various forms of school curriculum, the testing and assessment of pupils' progress and the provision of much more information about school performance to parents.

Education is the top priority of the new Government. Its policy is being focused on improvements in school standards and creating partnerships between the local education service, the schools inspectorates and central government.

INTRODUCTION

Despite the reforms which have taken place to date, test results have shown that many pupils still leave school with few or no qualifications and that standards of literacy have not changed significantly since 1945. In order to deal with this problem, a programme of legislation for England and Wales has been drawn up to improve school standards for pupils in their first years of education. This is designed to ensure education for all 4 year olds whose parents want it, effective assessment of all those starting primary school and more time devoted to literacy and numeracy in primary schools. Training for teachers on best practice in teaching these subjects will be provided. In addition, it is government policy to reduce class sizes over the next five years to fewer than 30 for all 5, 6 and 7 year olds. A new Standards and Effectiveness Unit has been established to spread best practice throughout the education service in England.

Administration

Four government departments, each headed by a Secretary of State, are responsible for education. These are the Department for Education and Employment in England, the Scottish Office Education and Industry Department, the Welsh Office Education Department and the Department of Education for Northern Ireland.

In England, Scotland and Wales most state school education is provided by local government education authorities and the rest by self-governing and grant-maintained schools. However, there are only two self-governing state schools in Scotland. In Northern Ireland five education and library boards own, manage and run all controlled schools; they also fund most voluntary schools (see p. 438) and provide finance for advisory and support services for all schools in their areas.

The education service in Great Britain is financed in the same way as other local government services (see chapter 7, p. 84), education authorities providing funds to schools largely on the basis of pupil numbers. In Northern Ireland the costs of the education and library boards are met by the Department of Education. There are, however, some further resources allocated to education authorities in England and Wales for specific purposes, such as training to improve school performance in literacy and numeracy, support for information technology and funds for inner city schools facing particularly severe problems. Additional government grants are made for capital expenditure at voluntary aided schools (see p. 437).

Grant-maintained schools in England are financed by the Funding Agency for Schools, which distributes central government grants to them. Similar schools in Wales are financed by the Welsh Office.

SCHOOLS

Parents are required by law to see that their children receive full-time education, at school or elsewhere, between the ages of 5 and 16 in England, Scotland and Wales and 4 and 16 in Northern Ireland. About 93 per cent of pupils receive free education from public funds, while the others attend independent schools financed by fees paid by parents.

Nursery Schools

Over half of 3 and 4 year olds attend nursery schools, nursery classes or reception classes in primary schools. In addition, many children attend pre-school playgroups, most of which are organised by parents.

The new Government aims to secure high-quality nursery education for 4 year olds whose parents want it. Proposals have been published under which English and Welsh local education authorities (LEAs), in partnership with private and voluntary providers, will draw up early years development plans, setting out how this aim will be achieved. The plans are designed to show how co-operation between private nurseries, playgroups and schools can best serve the interests of children and their parents by dovetailing education with top-quality childcare. In addition the Government will work with local authorities and others to establish early excellence centres designed to demonstrate good practice in education and childcare.

In Scotland a new system of planning and funding for nursery education will be introduced from August 1998; this is intended to support the Government's objective of providing a part-time place for every pre-school age child whose parents want it.

The previous Government's nursery voucher scheme for providing nursery places, which was launched in 1996, is being abolished.

Primary Schools

Compulsory education starts in infant primary schools or departments; at the age of 7 many pupils transfer to separate junior primary schools or departments. The usual age for transfer from primary to secondary school is 11 in England, Wales and Northern Ireland and 12 in Scotland. Some LEAs in England have first schools for pupils aged 5 to 8, 9 or

Table 26.1: Number of Schools and Pupils in Britain, 1995–96

Type of school	Number	Pupils
State Nursery	1,486	1,102,000
State Primary	23,451	5,309,500
State Secondary	4,462	3,675,600
Independent Schools and City Technology Colleges	2,436	603,100
Special Schools	1,567	115,700
Total	33,402	9,814,100

Source: Department for Education and Employment

10 and middle schools for age ranges between 8 and 14.

It is government policy to reduce the size of primary school classes for 5, 6 and 7 year olds to 30 or below within the next five years. LEAs are being invited to begin drawing up action plans to ensure that this target is met.

Secondary Schools

The majority of state secondary pupils in England and Wales attend comprehensive schools. These mostly take pupils without reference to ability or aptitude, providing a wide range of secondary education for all or most of the children in a district. Schools include those taking the 11 to 18 age-range, middle schools, and schools with an age range of 11 or 12 to 16. Most other state-educated children attend grammar or secondary modern schools, to which they are allocated after selection procedures at the age of 11.

Scottish secondary education is non-selective, consisting of comprehensive schools covering the age-range 12 to 18.

In Northern Ireland secondary education is organised largely along selective lines, with grammar schools admitting pupils on the basis of tests in English, maths and science. Most pupils attend non-grammar secondary schools.

City Technology Colleges

There are 15 city technology colleges in England and Wales, which are non-fee-paying secondary independent schools created by a partnership of government and private sector sponsors. The promoters own or lease the schools, employ teachers and other staff, and make substantial contributions to the costs of building and equipment. The National Curriculum (see p. 439) is taught with an emphasis on maths, technology and science.

Specialist Schools

The specialist schools programme in England was launched in 1993 with the creation of technology colleges. These are state secondary schools which teach the National Curriculum (see p. 439) with a special emphasis on technology, science and maths. A network of language colleges concentrates on teaching modern foreign languages while continuing to deliver the full National Curriculum. Specialist arts and sports colleges, too, have been opened.

A specialist school must have the backing of private sector sponsors if it wishes to become specialised. Capital and annual grants are available from public funds to complement business sponsorship. There are 194 technology colleges, 47 language colleges, 6 arts and 11 sports colleges in England.

School Management

England and Wales

At present there are four main types of state school:

- county schools owned and funded by LEAs;

- voluntary schools (of which there are three categories), established by church and other foundations and funded mainly by LEAs;

- grant-maintained (GM) schools funded by central government; and

- special schools (LEA and grant-maintained) for pupils with special educational needs.

The Government intends to establish a new framework for school organisation. There will be five categories of state school—community, foundation, voluntary, community special and foundation special. All state schools will work in partnership with and receive their recurrent funding from LEAs. The LEA's job will be to support and challenge schools to raise educational standards, not to control them.

Schools will be run by governing bodies, as they are now. The number of parent governors will be increased. Other governors will represent the local community, school staff and the LEA. The governing bodies of church schools will also include church representatives.

Schools will manage their own budgets and staffing, as they do now. The new framework for local management of schools will be based on a clear distinction between functions that LEAs must carry out and fund centrally and those for which schools are responsible, using their delegated budgets.

Scotland

In Scotland over 75 per cent of schools have school boards consisting of elected parent and staff members as well as co-opted members. They are required to promote contact between parents, the school and the community, and are involved in the appointment of senior staff and the community use of school premises. Devolved management (from the education authority to the school) is in place in primary, secondary and special schools.

Northern Ireland

The main categories of school supported by public funds are:

- controlled schools, which are owned by the education and library boards and wholly financed from public funds;

- voluntary maintained schools, most of which are owned by the Roman Catholic Church; the majority of these schools are wholly financed from public funds;

- voluntary grammar schools, which may be owned by denominational or non-denominational bodies and, with the exception of a small capital fee in some schools, are wholly financed from public funds; and

- grant-maintained or controlled integrated schools, which take Protestant and Roman Catholic pupils and are wholly financed from public funds.

All publicly financed schools are managed by boards of governors, which include elected parents and teachers among their members.

Although all schools must be open to pupils of all religions and there is some crossover between schools, most Roman Catholic pupils attend Catholic maintained schools or Catholic voluntary grammar schools, and most Protestant children are enrolled at controlled schools or non-denominational voluntary grammar schools.

The Government has a statutory duty to encourage integrated education as a way of breaking down sectarian barriers. There are 32 integrated schools with some 7,000 pupils (about 2 per cent of the school population). Integrated schools are financed by the Government. Existing controlled, maintained and voluntary grammar schools can apply to become integrated following a majority vote by parents.

Virtually all schools have delegated budgets under which school governors decide spending priorities.

Rights and Duties of Parents

Parents must be given general information about a school through a prospectus and the school's annual report or, in Scotland, the school's handbook. They also have a statutory right to express a preference for a particular school for their child, and there is an appeal system if their choice is not met.

In England and Wales parents choosing a local secondary school have the right to see:

- national performance tables showing the latest public examination results, vocational qualification results and rates of absence on a school-by-school basis; and

- information in each local school's prospectus on its public examination results, vocational qualification results, attendance rates and the destinations of school leavers.

All state schools in England and Wales have to give parents a written annual report on their child's achievements, containing details about:

- the child's progress in all subjects and activities;

- the child's attendance record;

- the results of National Curriculum assessments and of public examinations taken by the child;

- comparative results of pupils of the same age in the school and nationally; and

- the arrangements for discussing pupils' school reports with teachers.

Under new proposals, these school performance tables will be made more useful by showing the rate of progress made by pupils as well as their absolute levels of achievement.

All parents are invited to an annual meeting to discuss the governors' annual report.

Under new proposals, parents in England and Wales will become more involved with their child's education through a written home-school agreement setting out clearly what is expected of the school, parents and pupils. All schools will be required to have such agreements. The Government is also planning to increase the number of elected parent governors and to ensure that at least one elected parent governor will serve on LEA policy-making education committees. In addition, home-school associations of parents and teachers will be encouraged in England, and will be a requirement in Wales.

The Government has stated that homework for pupils is an essential part of a good education and the school's approach to this may form part of the home-school agreement. Following consultation, national guidelines will be issued giving details about the amount of homework pupils are expected to do.

In Scotland information is published for parents on school costs, examination results, pupil attendance and absence, and the destinations of school leavers. Inspection reports are published for parents. National guidelines to schools on reporting to parents advise that they should provide them with information about their children's attainment in the various subjects, teachers' comments on their progress and details about steps to build on success or overcome difficulties. One main school report each year is advised, together with one brief update report.

The Northern Ireland system for reporting to parents is broadly similar to that in England and Wales.

School Curriculum

England and Wales

The National Curriculum consists of statutory subjects for 5 to 16 year olds. English, maths and science are core subjects for 5 to 11 year olds in England; other statutory subjects are design and technology, information technology, geography, history, physical education, arts and music. A modern foreign language is added for pupils aged between 11 and 14. Statutory subjects at ages 14 to 16 are English, maths, science, technology, a foreign language and physical education. Religious education and, at secondary level, sex education are not prescribed in the curriculum but are requirements (see p. 440). Careers education is also statutory at secondary level.

There is a separate curriculum for Wales reflecting not only the Welsh language but the different circumstances of Wales. Nearly all primary schools in Wales teach Welsh as a first or second language and about a quarter use Welsh as the sole or main medium of instruction. In secondary schools, Welsh is compulsory for pupils aged 11 to 16 in Welsh-speaking schools and for pupils aged 11 to 14 in other schools. English is not a statutory language in Welsh-speaking schools catering for pupils aged 5 to 7. The Government is proposing to extend opportunities to be educated through the medium of Welsh.

The Government has announced targets to improve literacy and numeracy for 11 year olds in England in order to provide them with a more satisfactory preparation for secondary education. By 2002, the targets are for 80 per cent of 11 year olds to reach the standards for their age in English and 75 per cent in maths. In addition, all primary schools will, from 1998, be expected to devote an hour to English during each teaching day. Local literacy consultants will train teachers in all the primary schools in their area, and the project will be managed by the Government's Standards and Effectiveness Unit. The Government has established a Numeracy Task Force to advise on a new programme for maths teaching, including a daily numeracy hour for primary school pupils from 1998.

Targets set out for Wales are different from those in England. The Government is consulting on targets for English, Welsh and maths. The schools inspectorate will publish advice to teachers on how to manage time in order to give due weight to literacy and numeracy. Other measures are being explored to raise standards in these subjects.

For each National Curriculum subject, programmes of study lay down what pupils should be taught, with attainment targets setting out expected standards of performance. Pupils' performance is assessed at the ages of 7, 11 and 14 by their teachers in the core subjects of English, maths and science. Fourteen year olds are also assessed in National Curriculum statutory non-core subjects. In addition, 7 year olds take National Curriculum tests in English and maths, and most 11 and 14 year olds are tested in the core subjects. In Welsh-speaking schools the three age-groups are tested in Welsh.

The Government is proposing to introduce a scheme under which effective assessment will be made of the abilities of all children starting primary school.

All state schools must provide religious education, each LEA being responsible for producing a locally agreed syllabus which has to be reviewed every five years. Syllabuses must reflect Christianity while taking account of the other main religions practised in Britain. Parents have the right to withdraw their children from religious education classes.

All state secondary schools are required to provide sex education for all pupils, including education about HIV/AIDS and other sexually transmitted diseases. In primary schools the governors decide whether sex education should be offered beyond the requirements of the National Curriculum Science Order. Parents are entitled to withdraw their children from sex education classes other than those required by the National Curriculum. All state schools must provide information to parents about the content of their sex education courses.

The General Certificate of Secondary Education (GCSE) is the main qualification taken by pupils at the end of compulsory schooling at the age of 16. There are also GCSE (Short Course) qualifications taking half the time allotted to a GCSE; these are available in modern foreign languages, physical education, religious education, geography, history, design and technology, and information technology. In Wales a Short Course GCSE is available in Welsh as a second language.

The Qualifications and Curriculum Authority (QCA) is an independent government agency, which brings together the work of the National Council for Vocational Qualifications and the School Curriculum and Assessment Authority, with additional powers and duties, giving it an overview of the curriculum, assessment and qualifications across the whole of education and training in England. The QCA is responsible for ensuring that the curriculum and qualifications available to young people and adults are of high quality, coherent and flexible. There is a similar organisation in Wales called the Qualifications, Curriculum and Assessment Authority for Wales.

All GCSE and other qualifications offered to pupils in state schools must be approved by the Government. Associated syllabuses and assessment procedures must comply with national guidelines and be approved by the relevant qualifications authority.

Scotland

Content and management of the curriculum are not prescribed by statute, responsibility resting with education authorities and headteachers. Guidance is available from the Secretary of State and the Scottish Consultative Council on the Curriculum, which has recommended that secondary school pupils should have a broad and balanced curriculum.

A major review programme has been carried out on the curriculum for 5 to 14 year olds. Government guidance has been issued on English, maths, expressive arts, Latin, Gaelic, modern languages, environmental studies, and religious and moral education. Standardised tests in English and maths are given to pupils whenever they complete one of five levels. A major programme to extend modern language teaching to primary schools is in progress.

Provision is made for teaching in Gaelic in Gaelic-speaking areas and in some other areas where education authorities have identified this as a priority. More resources are being put into Gaelic teaching.

Scottish education authorities are required to ensure that pupils are given religious instruction although parents can withdraw their children if they wish. Some schools provide for Roman Catholic children, but in all schools there are safeguards for individual conscience.

Government guidance on sex education is provided to education authorities and headteachers, who are responsible for the content of the curriculum.

Pupils take the Scottish Certificate of Education (SCE) at Standard Grade after four years of secondary education at the age of 16. The proportion of pupils leaving school with no SCE qualification has fallen from one in four in 1983–84 to fewer than one in ten. SCE Standard Grade examinations are conducted by the Scottish Qualifications Authority.

Northern Ireland

The Northern Ireland curriculum, compulsory in all publicly financed schools, consists of religious education and six broad areas of study: English, maths, science and technology, the environment and society, creative and expressive studies and, in secondary schools, language studies. A core syllabus for religious education has been approved by the four main churches and this must be taught in all grant-aided schools.

The curriculum also includes four cross-curricular themes: cultural heritage, education for mutual understanding, health education and information technology. Secondary schools have two additional themes, namely, economic awareness and careers education.

Sex education is taught through the compulsory science programme of study and the health education cross-curricular theme.

Following reviews of the curriculum, its overall content has been reduced in primary schools and more flexibility in subject choice has been given to secondary schools. Teaching of the compulsory curriculum takes up about 85 per cent of teaching time in primary schools and 60 to 65 per cent in secondary schools.

Pupil assessment, which is statutory, takes place at the ages of 8 and 11 for English and maths; if a pupil is taught in the Irish language, he or she is assessed in Irish and maths at the age of 8 and in English, Irish and maths at the age of 11. Fourteen year olds are additionally assessed in science. As in England and Wales, the GCSE exam is used to assess 16 year old pupils.

Information Technology

Curricular requirements in all parts of Britain place a strong emphasis on the use of information and communications technology (ICT). The Government is proposing to create a new National Grid for Learning for the Millennium throughout Britain in order to unlock the potential of computers and communication networks for school education and to equip pupils and other learners for this new world. Its objective is to create a society where, within ten years, information and communication technology (ICT) has permeated every aspect of education. Hitherto, education has been affected relatively marginally by these new technologies, although recent publicly funded programmes have considerably increased the installation and use of micro-computers in schools.

The proposed Grid will provide curriculum support for schools and help train teachers. It will also link closely with the proposed University for Industry (see p. 454). In addition, national and local museums, galleries and libraries will be an essential part of the Grid which, using the Internet, will open up learning to individuals by taking it beyond school classrooms or lecture halls.

In addition, the Government is proposing to:

- ensure that all new teachers are ICT-literate and retrain all existing teachers with funds from the National Lottery (see chapter 6, pp. 47–8);

- work with the cable and telecommunications companies to connect schools, colleges and libraries and to keep access charges as low as possible;

- develop plans for a public/private partnership to deliver educational software and services to teachers, pupils and other learners; and

- ensure equality of access for all, including people in isolated rural areas, those with special educational needs and those in areas of urban deprivation.

The four government education departments jointly fund the National Council for Educational Technology which promotes and evaluates the use of new technologies in education and training. The Scottish Council for Educational Technology also develops software and other applications geared to the curriculum and school organisation in Scotland.

The British Broadcasting Corporation (BBC—see chapter 29) transmits television and radio programmes for schools. The independent Channel 4 (see chapter 29) also broadcasts educational television programmes. Teachers' notes, pupils' pamphlets and computer software accompany many of these broadcasts.

Raising School Standards

England and Wales

The newly created Standards and Effectiveness Unit within the Department for Education and Employment has been set up to ensure that all parts of the education service in England contribute fully to the raising of standards in schools. It is staffed by civil servants and practitioners from schools, local authorities and other areas of education. The Welsh Office Education Department fulfils this function in Wales.

The principles underlying the Government's school improvement strategy are that:

- the prime responsibility for improvement lies with the schools themselves;
- the role of central government, supported by national agencies and local government, is to provide the right balance of support for, and pressure on, schools; and
- intervention in a school should be in inverse proportion to its success.

In England the independent Office for Standards in Education (OFSTED) and in Wales the Office of Her Majesty's Chief Inspector advise the Government on quality, standards and efficiency. The two inspectorates also organise and regulate a system of school inspections. Each school is regularly inspected by a team of independent inspectors containing educationalists and lay people. Parents are sent a summary of the

report, which is also published in full. The school governing body must prepare an action plan to follow it up and report back to parents on progress.

From 1998–99 each school will have its own targets to raise standards and will be responsible for achieving them. Each school will be inspected every six years, but more often where weaknesses are apparent. Between inspections, school performance will be regularly monitored by LEAs, which will ensure that the school's improvement plans meet national guidelines set out by the Government. Consultation on changes to the system in Wales is taking place.

Each LEA will be working to a development plan agreed with its schools and approved by the Government. OFSTED and its Welsh counterpart will inspect the operations of LEAs to ensure that they are driving up educational standards.

The Government is taking steps to ensure the rapid improvement of schools where standards are a cause for concern. The LEA will be able to issue formal warnings and, if necessary, appoint additional governors and withdraw the school's delegated budget. Where a school found failing by inspectors does not make adequate progress, central government can either put the school under new management or require the LEA to close it, or make a fresh start by opening a reconstituted school.

Education Action Zones

The Government is planning a pilot programme of up to 25 education action zones to be set up in areas with a mix of underperforming schools and the highest levels of disadvantage. The zones will comprise groups of schools working together with local partners and agencies with the aim of improving standards in education. Zones will be areas of innovation, both in ways of working and in the provision of education. A forum would be responsible for running each zone and ensuring that ambitious targets for improvement are met. The forum could include representatives of parents, the business and social community, schools and the LEA. In addition, the Secretary of State would appoint one or two representatives to provide advice and support. The Government intends that in most circumstances at least one school in the zone would be a specialist technology, language, sports or arts college which would become a magnet for excellence in the area.

Scotland

In Scotland HM Inspectors of Schools (HMI) are responsible for independent evaluation of education standards and for advising the Secretary of State. Reports are published on inspections and given to parents. Inspectors return to the school between one and two years after the publication of the report to assess progress in meeting their recommendations. Their conclusions about progress are published together with an indication of any further action which may be required. The school continues to be monitored by HMI until the recommendations have been satisfactorily addressed.

HMI's Audit Unit collects, analyses and publishes evidence about the performance of schools and education authorities, and recommendations are made for action and improvement. It also publishes information for parents about schools.

An action group has been appointed to advise the Government on steps necessary to raise standards, including the setting by schools of targets for their own improvement.

Northern Ireland

In Northern Ireland the Education and Training Inspectorate evaluates, reports and advises the Department of Education on quality and standards in schools. Inspection reports are published and a summary prepared for parents. Where an inspection has identified important weaknesses, school governors are required to prepare an action plan and submit details to the Department. In such cases, a follow-up inspection will take place about a year after the original inspection and, if sufficient improvement has not been made, a report will be published. The governors will be required to submit a further

action plan and the school's work will continue to be monitored and evaluated by the Inspectorate and the Department in order to ensure that improvement takes place.

The Department is planning additional measures to improve schools, based on a recent three-year programme of evaluation and support which was targeted on the 29 lowest achieving secondary schools and some of their contributory primary schools.

Ethnic Minority Children

Children from ethnic minority backgrounds form a tenth of the school population in England and smaller proportions in Wales and Scotland. While the achievements of some groups are exceptional, others are underperforming and efforts are being made to improve matters.

English language teaching continues to receive priority for pupils without English as their first language. Schools may also teach the main ethnic minority community languages at secondary level in England and Wales as part of the National Curriculum. Schools should take account of the ethnic and cultural backgrounds of pupils, and curricula should reflect ethnic and cultural diversity. The annual school census in England contains questions about the ethnic backgrounds of pupils.

The new Government is committed to taking action to:

- spread successful teaching methods of schools that have raised ethnic minority pupils' achievements;

- provide guidance on tackling racial harassment and stereotyping; and

- review the level and delivery of specialist support designed to raise the participation and achievement of ethnic minority pupils.

Children with Special Needs

Special educational needs comprise learning difficulties of all kinds, including mental and physical disabilities which hinder or prevent learning. LEAs in England and Wales must identify children whose learning difficulties are very severe or complex, assess and meet their needs, and involve parents in decisions about their child's education.

If the LEA believes that it should determine the education for the child, it must draw up a formal statement of the child's special educational needs and the action it intends to take to meet them. There are statutory time limits governing this procedure. A state school named in the statement is required to admit the child. The Government has stated that over time more resources should be put into direct support for children and less emphasis placed on bureaucratic statementing procedures.

In England and Wales parents have a right of appeal to the Special Educational Needs Tribunal if they disagree with the LEA decisions about their child. The Tribunal's verdict is final and binding on all parties. The Government has stated that it would like to see more mediation between parents and LEAs to reduce the need for disputes to be taken to the Tribunal.

Wherever possible, children with special educational needs are taught in ordinary schools, where placement must be compatible both with the needs of the child and the provision of efficient education for the other children in the school. The LEA is required to comply with parents' choice of school unless this is inappropriate for the child, involves an inefficient use of resources or is incompatible with the efficient education of other children.

A Government Code of Practice offers practical guidance to all LEAs and state schools in England and Wales on how to identify, assess and monitor all pupils with special educational needs. Each school in England and Wales must provide information to parents about its policies on meeting special educational needs.

The Government has established a National Advisory Group to oversee the implementation of programmes designed to improve education for children with special needs. It includes members from schools, LEAs, voluntary bodies representing children and parents, and others.

In Scotland the choice of school is a matter for agreement between education authorities and parents. Education authorities are required to take special educational needs fully into account when making provision for pupils in their areas. There are a small number of pupils (about 2 per cent of the school population) whose needs are such that the authority is required to open a record describing the special education necessary to meet them. A 1995 report by school inspectors sets out basic principles emphasising the importance of partnership between all involved. The Government has increased resources for in-service training of staff.

In Northern Ireland legislation has been passed under which similar arrangements to those in England and Wales, including an appeal system, are being introduced.

There are some 1,570 special schools (both day and boarding) in Britain for pupils with special educational needs. Some of these are run by voluntary organisations and some are established in hospitals. They cater for some 115,700 pupils.

Health and Welfare of Schoolchildren

Physical education, including organised games, is part of the curriculum of all state schools. In England and Wales playing fields must be available for pupils over the age of 8.

Government health departments are responsible for the medical inspection of schoolchildren and for advice on, and treatment of, medical and dental problems. The education service seeks to help prevent and deal with juvenile drug misuse and to help prevent the spread of AIDS. In England government funds support the training of teachers with responsibility for anti-drug education.

The Government has also issued guidance on drug prevention in England's schools, outlining how to teach pupils about the dangers of drug misuse, advising schools on drug education and prevention, and giving advice on how to deal with drug-related incidents on school premises.

In Scotland similar curriculum advice is made available to every school. School drug education programmes are subject to monitoring by school inspectors.

In Northern Ireland a drug education, advice and resource pack has been issued to all schools and colleges. All schools must have a drug education policy and publish details about it in their prospectus.

Schools are responsible for providing school meals for pupils, taking account of local circumstances. The Government is proposing to specify minimum nutritional standards for inclusion in school meals contracts.

Free meals are provided for children whose parents receive a social security benefit called income support or another known as income-based Jobseeker's Allowance (see p. 427); all other pupils are charged for meals. LEAs and GM schools may provide milk to pupils. Where they choose to do so they must provide it free to pupils of parents in receipt of these social security benefits. Milk to all other pupils must be charged for.

In Northern Ireland school meals must be provided for primary, special and grant-aided nursery school pupils.

LEAs provide free of charge the transport they consider necessary to enable pupils to attend school and they may help other pupils with their fares. LEAs must publish annually details about their policy on free and assisted transport.

Independent Schools

Fee-paying independent schools providing full-time education for five or more pupils of compulsory school age must register by law with the Department for Education and Employment and are subject to inspection. They can be required to remedy serious shortcomings in their premises, accommodation, teaching or staffing and, in the case of boarding schools, welfare of pupils. They must exclude anyone who has been barred from teaching in, or owning, a school. About 7 per cent of schoolchildren attend independent schools.

There are about 2,420 independent schools in Britain educating 600,000 pupils of all ages. They charge fees varying from around £300 a term for day pupils at nursery age to over £4,000 a term for senior boarding pupils. Many offer bursaries to help pupils from less well-off families as well as academic, music, art and other scholarships. The Assisted Places Scheme under which financial assistance is given from public funds

according to parental income is being phased out in order to channel the money saved into cutting class sizes for all 5, 6 and 7 year olds in state schools to 30 or below within the next five years. The Government gives income-related help with fees to pupils at eight music and ballet schools; there are a limited number of similar scholarships at cathedral choir schools.

Independent schools range from small kindergartens to large day and boarding schools, and from new and, in some cases, experimental schools to ancient foundations. The 600 boys', girls' and mixed preparatory schools prepare children for entry to senior schools. The normal age-range for these preparatory schools is from 7+ to 11, 12 or 13, but many have pre-preparatory departments for younger children. A number of independent schools have been established by religious orders and ethnic minorities. Independent schools for older pupils from 11, 12 or 13 to 18 or 19 include about 550 which are often referred to as 'public schools'.

In Northern Ireland there are only 21 small independent schools, educating about 1,000 pupils. They are subject to inspection by the Department of Education for Northern Ireland.

The Government is to start consultations on ways of bridging the gap between independent and state schools. In particular it is suggesting that independent schools, as an expression of their charitable status, could offer opportunities for more children by sharing their facilities with the local community. Many existing examples of this co-operation include afternoon homework classes and holiday arts, sports and language courses.

Teachers

England and Wales

Teachers in state schools in England and Wales are appointed by LEAs or school governing bodies. They must hold qualifications approved by the Government.

Almost all entrants to teaching in state schools in England and Wales complete an approved course of teacher training. These courses are offered by university departments of education as well as other higher education establishments (see p. 451) and groups of schools. One of the two main qualifications is the three- or four-year Bachelor of Education (BEd) honours degree. The other is the successful completion of a three- or four-year degree course, topped up by a one-year Postgraduate Certificate in Education (PGCE) course.

Schools play an important role in initial teacher training by helping to plan and manage courses and select, train and assess students, usually in partnership with colleges and universities. Schools are able to train students to teach their specialist subjects, assess pupils and manage classes. Consortia of schools can run courses for postgraduate students if they wish to do so. Other courses, including all undergraduate courses, are run by universities and colleges in partnership with schools.

The Teacher Training Agency (TTA) is responsible for accrediting training providers and for financing initial teacher training courses in England. It also ensures that national standards are met and promotes teaching as a career. In Wales, initial teacher training is funded by the Higher Education Funding Council for Wales, which also accredits institutions and schools providing courses.

The TTA has launched a national qualification for headteachers, and the Government expects this to form the basis of a new mandatory qualification for future appointees as heads. In addition the TTA has developed its HEADLAMP programme in England, which provides leadership and management training for heads appointed to their first posts. The Welsh Office has recently consulted on plans to increase headteacher training in Wales.

The Government has published details of a new core curriculum in English and maths, setting out the knowledge, understanding and skills which all those training to teach these subjects in primary schools must meet. In Wales, Welsh will be included in this new curriculum. More rigorous requirements have also been announced for all primary and secondary courses of initial teacher training and will apply from 1998. In addition, the Government is to introduce an induction year for newly qualified teachers to consolidate their skills. There are also plans to pilot the development of laboratory schools in which trainees will observe good and experienced teachers at work.

In order to help experienced teachers to stay in the profession, the Government intends to introduce a new career grade of Advanced Skills Teacher to reward the best teachers willing to help raise standards by supporting trainee and newly qualified teachers in the classroom.

The Government is undertaking an urgent review of existing arrangements for appraising teachers' performance. It has stated that key elements in such arrangements should be classroom observation, assessment of results achieved by pupils in a teacher's care and an annual performance review linked to targets for improved pupil performance.

LEAs, teacher trade unions and school governor organisations have been asked to work with the Government at national level in order to solve the problem of the small minority of incompetent teachers.

The Government has stated that it wants teachers' professional standing to be enhanced by the creation of a General Teaching Council which would speak for the profession and also reflect the interests of parents, employers, LEAs and the wider community. This Council would ensure that teaching is a profession based on high standards and would raise the status of teaching and promote it as a career. The Government intends to set up the Council by 2000.

Scotland

All teachers in education authority schools must be registered with the General Teaching Council (GTC) for Scotland. The GTC is responsible for disciplinary procedures under which teachers guilty of professional misconduct may be removed temporarily or permanently from the register. Advice is given by the GTC to the Secretary of State on teacher supply and the professional suitability of teacher training courses.

All entrants to the teaching profession are graduates. New primary teachers qualify either through a four-year BEd course or a one-year postgraduate course at a higher education teacher training institution. Teachers of academic subjects at secondary schools must hold a degree with at least two passes in each subject that they wish to teach. Secondary school teachers must undertake a one-year postgraduate training course or an undergraduate course combining subject studies, study of education and school experience.

Guidelines for initial teacher training courses stress the importance of partnership between teacher training institutions and schools, and the competences required in the classroom for teachers beginning their careers.

All pre-service courses must be approved by The Scottish Office Education and Industry Department. They must also be validated by a higher education institution and accredited by the GTC as leading to registration. National guidelines for staff development and appraisal are being reviewed. Newly qualified teachers must serve a two-year probationary period at the beginning of their teaching careers.

Northern Ireland

All new entrants to teaching in grant-aided schools are graduates and hold an approved teaching qualification. Arrangements are being developed under which initial teacher training would be integrated with induction/early in-service training, the latter covering a period of three years. In addition, work is under way on a recognised qualification for headteachers, equivalent to the arrangements in England and Wales. The Government is committed to the establishment of a General Teaching Council in Northern Ireland.

Teacher training is provided by Queen's University, in Belfast, the University of Ulster, two colleges of education and the Open University (see p. 453). The principal courses are BEd Honours (four years) and the one-year Postgraduate Certificate of Education. The Open University course is part-time and lasts 18 months. Education and library boards have a statutory duty to provide curricular support services and in-service training.

Schools, Careers and Business

The Government has stated that improved school-business links can help raise pupils' levels of achievement and enable them to see the relevance of what they learn at school. It is therefore strengthening existing links such as the *Education Business Partnerships* and wants to see the best of EBP practice spread throughout the country. The Partnerships consist of representatives from industry, education and the wider community, and aim to bring about closer links between education and industry in order to ensure that young people develop the skills to help them succeed in the labour market.

One of the main schemes managed by the Partnerships is the *Teacher Placement Service* (TPS), funded by the Government. The TPS organises placements in business for teachers and lecturers to extend their professional and personal development, improve learning opportunities for young people, and provide better careers education services.

Compacts bring together employers, young people, schools, colleges and other bodies involved in training in order to help young people achieve more at school, and to continue their education and training after the age of 16. Under Compact schemes, young people work towards agreed goals, while employers provide incentives for achieving them.

The Government's *Project Business* scheme offers young people the opportunity to learn how business works and acquire the work skills needed by employers. Business volunteers work with teachers and business/works visits are arranged for young people.

Careers

All young people in full-time education are entitled to impartial careers guidance. Most secondary schools have a written policy statement on careers education and guidance, a careers co-ordinator and an agreement with their local careers guidance service about the co-ordinated contribution they will make to student development. LEAs are active participants in the majority of careers service organisations.

In Northern Ireland careers education is one of the six compulsory education themes forming part of the secondary school curriculum (see p. 441). The Careers Service is part of the Training and Employment Agency.

All state secondary schools in England and Wales provide leavers with a National Record of Achievement setting out their school attainments, including public examination and National Curriculum assessment results. In Scotland the Record is not compulsory.

In Northern Ireland all pupils in secondary education are issued with a Record of Achievement on leaving school, and from 1997–98 this applies to primary schools as well.

EDUCATION AND TRAINING AFTER 16

The Government plans to ensure that all young people will have access to high-quality education and training after the age of 16. Under the new Investing in Young People programme, young people will have two routes that they can follow—one based on school and college education, and the other on work-based learning. In addition, under the Welfare-to-Work programme (see p. 173), all young unemployed people will be guaranteed education and training opportunities, while those with poor basic skills will have the option of participating in full-time study on an approved course.

About 70 per cent of 16 year old pupils choose to continue in full-time education in school sixth forms, sixth-form colleges, further education colleges, universities and other higher education institutions. The percentage for 17 and 18 year olds is 59 per cent and 40 per cent respectively.

Broadly speaking, education after 16 outside schools is divided into further and higher education. Further education is largely vocational and in England covers courses up to and including GCE A level and AS qualifications, and GNVQ Advanced level or their equivalents (see below). Higher education covers advanced courses at levels higher than GCE A level or equivalent.

Youth credits are on offer from Training and Enterprise Councils in England and Wales and from Local Enterprise Companies in Scotland (see p. 195). These enable 16 and 17 year olds leaving full-time education to obtain vocational education and training through their employer or a specialist trainer.

In many English and most Welsh post-school establishments, parts of each course attract credits which can be accumulated by the student and transferred between institutions. In Scotland a credit accumulation scheme covers courses in all further and higher education. Similar schemes in higher education in Northern Ireland are compatible with those of institutions in the rest of Britain.

The national computer-based Educational Counselling and Credit Transfer Information Service (ECCTIS) provides prospective students and their advisers with free access to information on course opportunities at universities and colleges throughout Britain. ECCTIS can be found in the majority of secondary schools with sixth forms, as well as most further education colleges, universities, careers offices, Training and Enterprise Councils, and, in other countries, British Council offices.

Schools and Sixth-form Colleges

Having completed compulsory school education, students in England, Wales and Northern Ireland can stay on at school, be educated in a further education or sixth-form college, or choose to take paid employment. If they continue in education, they study for examinations which lead to higher education, professional training or vocational qualifications. These include the academic General Certificate of Education (GCE) Advanced (A) level, the Advanced Supplementary (AS) examination, General National Vocational Qualifications (GNVQs) and National Vocational Qualifications (NVQs). The GCE A level is usually taken at the age of 18 or 19 after two years' study; part of the qualification is based on course work and the rest on written test papers. AS levels usually involve one year's study and enable sixth-form pupils to study a wider range of subjects. A level arts students, for example, can still study science subjects at AS level.

The new GNVQs, mainly undertaken by young people in full-time education between the ages of 16 and 18, provide a broad-based preparation for a range of occupations and higher education. There are three GNVQ levels—Advanced, Intermediate and Foundation. An Advanced GNVQ requires a level of achievement broadly equal to two GCE A levels. GNVQs may also be taken in combination with other qualifications, such as GCE A levels or GCSEs.

GNVQs are awarded by the City and Guilds of London Institute, the RSA (Royal Society of Arts) Examinations Board and Edexcel (formerly the Business and Technology Education Council).

Skills valued by employers are being given a higher priority in education and training. More young people will also be offered the opportunity to gain a qualification in the three key skills of communication, application of number and information/communication technology, which are already compulsory in GNVQs and some publicly funded youth training schemes.

The Qualifications and Curriculum Authority is responsible for supervising academic and vocational qualifications in England as well as the school curriculum (see p. 440). A similar organisation has been established in Wales (see p. 440).

Scotland

Pupils staying on at school after the end of compulsory education study for the Higher Grade Scottish Certificate of Education examination ('Highers') between the ages of 16 and 18; passes at this grade are the basis for entry to higher education or professional training. The Certificate of Sixth Year Studies (CSYS) is for pupils who have completed their Higher Grade main studies and who wish to continue studies in particular subjects.

A flexible system of vocational courses for 16 to 18 year olds has been introduced in schools and colleges in subjects such as business and administration, engineering and industrial production. These courses are also intended to meet the needs of many adults entering training or returning to education. The courses lead to the award of the non-advanced National Certificate for students over 16 who have successfully completed a programme of vocational courses based on short study units. Similar unit-based courses are also available at advanced levels, leading to the award of a Higher National Certificate or Diploma.

General Scottish Vocational Qualifications (General SVQs) are designed to meet the needs of 16 to 19 year olds at school or in further education colleges. Broadly compatible with the GNVQs in the rest of Britain, General SVQs are a stepping-stone to higher education or further training. They are accredited and awarded by the Scottish Qualifications Authority.

A new five-level system of courses and awards for fifth- and sixth-year pupils—'Higher Still'—will be introduced in August 1999. Under this, Highers remain as one of the levels, but courses are based on units of study of 40 or 80 hours. The recommended study time for each Higher is extended from 120 hours to 160 hours. Advanced Higher courses are being developed, incorporating the current Certificate of Sixth Year Studies and building on Highers to provide a two-year 320-hour course. Group awards will be available at all five levels. The Scottish Qualifications Authority validates and awards course certificates.

Further Education Colleges

People over the age of 16 can also take courses in further education colleges, where much of the study is work-related. Further education institutions supply much of the education in government-sponsored training programmes.

Table 26.2: Further Education Students in Britain 1995–96	
Full-time and Sandwich	764,000
Part-time, including day and evening students	2,803,000
Total	3,567,000

Source: Department for Education and Employment

Many students on further education courses attend part-time, either by day release or block release from employment or during the evenings. The system has strong ties with commerce and industry, and co-operation with business is encouraged by the Government and its agencies. Employers are normally involved in designing courses.

Courses are run by some 550 institutions of further education, many of which also offer higher education courses (see p. 451). In England and Wales each is controlled by an autonomous corporation and governing body with substantial representation from business. Public funding is allocated to institutions by further education funding councils, part of it being directly related to student numbers.

The Scottish Office Education and Industry Department distributes funds to colleges in Scotland which are controlled by autonomous boards of management.

In Northern Ireland further education colleges are financed through the education and library boards by the Department of Education; in April 1998 the colleges will become free-standing institutions financed directly by the Department.

Funding councils in England and Wales send out independent inspectors to assess the quality of the education provided by colleges. They publish reports containing quality assessments, and colleges are obliged to explain how they will put things right if there are major criticisms. Each college has to publish information about its examination results annually. Colleges in Scotland are inspected by the Schools Inspectorate and in Northern Ireland by the Education and Training Inspectorate.

Vocational Qualifications

England, Wales and Northern Ireland have a wide range of National Vocational Qualifications (NVQs), awards which recognise work-related skills and knowledge and provide a path for lifelong learning and achievement. Prepared by industry and commerce, including representatives from trade unions and professional bodies, NVQs are based on national standards of competence and can be achieved at levels 1 to 5. Level 1 awards cover routine tasks carried out under supervision, while Level 5 NVQs encompass complex work roles, often involving detailed technical knowledge and a high level of responsibility.

In Scotland there is an analogous system of Scottish Vocational Qualifications (SVQs). NVQs and SVQs have mutual recognition throughout Britain.

Awarding Bodies

NVQs are offered by awarding bodies approved by the appropriate qualifications and assessment authority. The awarding bodies are approved to offer a qualification for a set period of time, after which they must seek reaccreditation from the authority to offer that particular award. This ensures that the standards of competence on which awards are based are kept up to date and relevant.

In Scotland the Scottish Qualifications Authority is the national accreditation body and the main awarding organisation.

National Targets for Education and Training

The National Targets for Education and Training, originally launched in 1991 and revised in 1995, aim to raise standards and improve Britain's international competitiveness. Progress towards these targets is monitored by the independent National Advisory Council for Education and Training Targets and by the Advisory Scottish Council for Education and Training Targets. The Targets, which relate to the year 2000, cover young people and the workforce as a whole. The 'Foundation Learning' Targets are that:

- by the age of 19, 85 per cent of young people should achieve five GCSEs at grade C or above, an intermediate GNVQ or NVQ level 2;
- 75 per cent of young people should achieve NVQ level 2 competence in communication, numeracy and information technology by the age of 19, with 35 per cent reaching level 3 by the age of 21; and

- by 21, 60 per cent of young people should achieve two GCE A levels, an Advanced GNVQ or NVQ level 3.

The 'Lifetime Learning' Targets are that:

- 60 per cent of the workforce should be qualified to the standard of NVQ level 3, an Advanced GNVQ or two GCE A levels;

- 30 per cent of the workforce should have a vocational, professional, management or academic qualification at NVQ level or above; and

- 70 per cent of organisations employing 200 or more people and 35 per cent of those employing 50 or more should be recognised as Investors in People.

Targets in Scotland are that:

- by the age of 19, 85 per cent of young people should attain SVQ standard level II or five standard SCE grades 1–3 or equivalent; and

- by the age of 21, 70 per cent of young people should achieve SVQ level III or three Highers (grades A–C).

The Government plans to conduct an extensive consultation exercise from November 1997 to February 1998 which will assess how appropriate these Targets are and consider developing new ones which fully reflect its priorities.

Investors in People

The Investors in People standard helps companies and other employers to improve their performance by linking the training and development of all employees directly to the achievement of business objectives (see p. 175).

Youth Training

The objectives of the Government's youth training schemes are to provide participants with training leading to NVQ/SVQ vocational qualifications and the acquisition of broad-based skills.

As part of the new Investing in Young People programme, *National Traineeships* for training to NVQ levels 1 and 2 will take effect from the autumn of 1997 for young people in England and Wales. They offer a broad and flexible learning programme, including the skills of communication, numeracy and information technology.

Modern Apprenticeships are designed to increase significantly the number of young people trained to technician, supervisory and equivalent levels. More than 100,000 of them have begun these apprenticeships, which operate in over 70 industry sectors (see p. 176).

Higher Education

There are six times as many pupils taking part in higher education now than in the early 1960s. One in three young people now enter higher education compared with one in six in 1989. Over half of all entrants are mature students (aged 22 or over) and just over a third are part-timers. Since 1989 full-time students have increased by almost 70 per cent.

Dearing Committee Report

The Government is planning to publish a White Paper on Lifelong Learning in response to the conclusions of the National Committee of Inquiry into Higher Education, which was set up February 1996 under the chairmanship of Sir Ron Dearing. The committee was established to make recommendations on the purposes, structure, size and funding of higher education throughout Britain. Its report, published in July 1997 and welcomed by the Government, supported a further

Students in Higher Education in Britain, 1995–96	
Full-time Students	
Undergraduates	946,000
Postgraduates	90,000
Part-time students	
Undergraduates	454,000
Postgraduates	136,000
Open University	122,000
Total	**1,748,000**

Source: Department for Education and Employment

expansion of up to 40 per cent in higher education over the next 20 years. The main recommendations covered the local and regional role of higher education, the qualifications framework, academic standards, the role of information technology, management and government of institutions, and the quality of teaching and research.

In Scotland a separate committee has made recommendations on the distinctive nature of the Scottish higher education system.

Finance

Higher education is largely financed by public funds and income received by institutions from research contracts and other sources. Tuition fees for students are at present paid through the students awards system (see below).

Government finance for higher education institutions in England, Scotland and Wales is distributed by higher education funding councils responsible to their respective Secretary of State. In Northern Ireland grant is paid direct to the two universities by the Department of Education, following advice from the Northern Ireland Higher Education Council. The private University of Buckingham receives no public grants.

The funding councils and the Department of Education for Northern Ireland help to meet the costs of teaching, research and related activities in all publicly funded universities and higher education colleges. In addition to teaching students, institutions undertake paid training, research or consultancy for commercial firms. Many establishments have endowments or receive grants from foundations and benefactors. Some 30 per cent of higher education income originates from private sources.

Student Finance

Over 95 per cent of full-time students resident in England and Wales on first degree and other comparable higher education courses receive mandatory awards covering tuition fees and a maintenance grant. The level of the grant depends on the income of the student and of the student's parents or spouse. Awards are made by LEAs in England and Wales. The Government reimburses in full the amount spent by education authorities on mandatory awards. Similar schemes are administered by the Student Awards Agency for Scotland and the Northern Ireland education and library boards.

Most students on courses of full-time, non-postgraduate higher education can also take out a loan to help pay their maintenance costs. Loans are not means-tested and repayments are indexed to inflation. The scheme is designed to share the cost of student maintenance more equitably between students, parents and the taxpayer.

Limited access funds administered by universities and colleges are available to students facing real financial difficulties. In 1996–97 there is provision of £27.7 million in England, £4.3 million in Scotland, £1.7 million in Wales and £868,000 in Northern Ireland for this purpose.

The Government has announced plans to reform the system of student finance from October 1998 in order to share the costs of higher education with those who benefit from it. The plans include the introduction of an annual tuition fee representing about a quarter of the average cost of a course. Tuition will continue to be free for students from lower income families. Other full-time students will pay up to £1,000 a year depending on parental income. All students will be eligible for 100 per cent loans for maintenance, a part of which will be related to parental income. The total parental contribution will be no more than is expected at present. Loans will be repaid by graduates, contributions being related to their income. The average repayment period will be much longer than at present, ensuring that average repayments will be at a lower annual level.

Grants for postgraduate study are offered by the government education departments and by the research councils (see pp. 337–40). Increasing numbers of scholarships are available from research charities, endowments and particular industries or companies.

Access Courses

Access and foundation courses provide a preparation before enrolment on a course of higher education for prospective students who do not have the standard entry qualifications. Many of these students are from the ethnic minority communities.

The Scottish Wider Access Programme (SWAP) promotes greater participation in higher education by mature students and those without the normal entry requirements. Successful completion of a SWAP course guarantees a higher education place.

Universities

There are some 90 universities, including the Open University, which enjoy academic freedom, appoint their own staff, decide which students to admit and award their own degrees. The universities of Oxford and Cambridge date from the 13th century, and the Scottish universities of St Andrews, Glasgow and Aberdeen from the 15th century. The University of Edinburgh was established in the 16th century. All the other universities were founded in the 19th and 20th centuries. The 1960s saw considerable expansion in new universities. The number of universities also jumped considerably in 1992, when polytechnics and their Scottish equivalents were given their own degree-awarding powers and were allowed to take the university title. At the same time, similar provision was made for higher education colleges which met certain criteria.

Applications for first degree courses are usually made through the Universities and Colleges Admission Service (UCAS), in Cheltenham, Gloucestershire.

First degree courses are mainly full-time and usually last three years in England, Wales and Northern Ireland. However, there are some four-year courses, and medical and veterinary courses normally require five years. All traditional first degree courses in Scotland require a minimum of three years' study (or four years to honours level). The ratio of staff to full-time students in England is about 1 to 16.5. The number of postgraduates has increased by over a half in the last decade.

Universities offer courses in a wide range of subjects, including traditional arts subjects and science and technology. Some courses lead to the examinations of the chief professional bodies. Many universities have close links with commerce and industry; some students have a job and attend on a part-time basis.

Degree titles vary according to each university. In England, Wales and Northern Ireland the most common titles for a first degree are Bachelor of Arts (BA) or Bachelor of Science (BSc) and for a second degree Master of Arts (MA), Master of Science (MSc), or Doctor of Philosophy (PhD). In the older Scottish universities Master is used for a first degree in arts subjects. Uniformity of standards between universities is promoted by employing external examiners for all university examinations.

Some universities are responsible for validating degrees at higher education institutions without degree-awarding powers.

The Government is encouraging universities to co-operate closely with industry on research. Around 50 science parks have been set up by higher education institutions in conjunction with industrial scientists and technologists to promote the development and commercial application of advanced technology (see chapter 20, p. 340).

The Open University

The Open University is a non-residential university offering degree and other courses for adult students of all ages in Britain, the European Union, Gibraltar, Slovenia and Switzerland.

The University uses a combination of specially produced printed texts, correspondence tuition, television and radio broadcasts, audio/video cassettes and computing. For some courses there are residential schools. There is a network of study centres for contact with part-time tutors and counsellors, and with fellow students. Formal academic qualifications are not required to register for most courses. Its first degrees are the BA (Open) or the BSc (Open), which are general degrees awarded on a system of credits for each course completed. There is also an MMath degree for students who have taken an approved combination of courses specialising in mathematics, and an MEng degree for those who have studied an approved combination of courses to achieve the highest professional status of Chartered Engineer. In 1997 there were about 135,000 registered undergraduates, and in all 200,000 first degrees have been awarded since the University started its courses in 1970.

The University also has a programme of higher degrees. About 15,000 students were registered on higher degree courses in 1997. In addition, there are programmes for professionals in a variety of fields.

The University has advised many other countries on setting up similar institutions, and has contributed to projects such as the European Distance Education Network. It is financed by the Higher Education Funding Council for England.

University for Industry

The Government has announced plans to set up a new University for Industry which will collaborate with the Open University. It is designed to increase opportunities for adults wishing to develop their potential and will bring government, industry and education together in a public/private partnership. It will use new technology to increase skills and extend lifelong learning.

Further Education for Adults

Further education for adults is provided by further education institutions, adult centres and colleges run by LEAs, and voluntary bodies such as the Workers' Educational Association. The duty to secure such education is shared by the further education funding councils, The Scottish Office Education and Industry Department and LEAs. University departments of continuing education also provide courses for adults.

The councils and The Scottish Office Education and Industry Department fund formal academic and vocational courses, courses providing access to higher education and courses in basic literacy and numeracy, including English for speakers of other languages. LEAs are responsible for the less formal leisure and recreational courses. The councils, The Scottish Office Education and Industry Department and the LEAs must take

account of adult students with special educational needs.

Basic Skills Agency

The Basic Skills Agency is concerned with adult literacy, numeracy and related basic skills in England and Wales. It provides consultancy and advisory services; funds local development projects, including research; publishes materials for teachers and students; and organises and sponsors staff training. The Agency also covers basic skill training in the workplace for unemployed and young people. Government funding of the Agency was worth about £4 million in 1995–96.

NIACE (The National Organisation for Adult Learning)

NIACE represents all interests in the education and training of adults. It is a membership body and a registered charity. It convenes conferences, seminars and meetings, collects and disseminates information, conducts inquiries and research, undertakes special projects and works with other organisations.

Open and Distance Learning

The terms 'open' and 'distance' learning broadly mean learning undertaken through use of various media, such as television, without the direct supervision of a tutor. More further education colleges are incorporating many distance learning materials and methods in their mainstream courses.

Scottish Community Education Council

The Scottish Community Education Council advises the Government and promotes all community education matters, including adult literacy and basic education, and youth work.

Educational Research

Educational research is supported financially by government departments, the Economic and Social Research Council, charities, higher education institutions, teachers' associations and other agencies. The major research institutions outside the universities are the autonomous National Foundation for Educational Research in England and Wales, and the Scottish Council for Research in Education.

LINKS WITH OTHER COUNTRIES

Large numbers of people come to Britain from other countries to study, and many British people work and train overseas. The British aid programme (see chapter 9, p. 136) encourages links between educational institutions in Britain and developing countries.

There has been an expansion of interest in European studies and languages in recent years, with exchanges of teachers, schoolchildren and students taking place.

European Union Schemes

Exchange of students is promoted by the EU SOCRATES programme, through which grants are provided to enable EU students and those from other countries belonging to the European Economic Area (see p. 126) to study in other states. The programme covers all academic subjects, and the period of study normally lasts between three and 12 months. In 1996–97 about 11,000 British students were studying in other EU member states.

The SOCRATES programme also promotes competence in foreign languages. It offers funding which contributes towards in-service training methods. Other parts of the programme support partnerships between schools, study visits by senior educationalists and a range of multinational projects including open and distance learning, adult education and education for the children of migrant workers, gypsies and travellers.

Youth for Europe III aims to bring together young people from different cultural and social backgrounds in the European Union through a wide range of exchanges.

The LEONARDO DA VINCI programme supports and complements vocational training policies and practices in member states, fostering transnational co-operation and innovation in training through pilot projects, exchanges and research projects.

EU member states have created nine European schools, including one at Culham, Oxfordshire, for pupils aged between four and 19, to provide a multilingual education for the children of staff employed in EU institutions.

Overseas Students in Britain

British universities and other higher and further education establishments have built up a strong reputation overseas by offering tuition of the highest standards and maintaining low student-to-staff ratios.

In 1995–96 there were some 500,000 overseas students at publicly funded higher and further education institutions in Britain. Most overseas students following courses of higher or further education pay fees covering the full cost of their courses.

Nationals of other member countries of the European Union generally pay the lower level of fees applicable to British students; if their courses are designated for mandatory awards, they may be eligible for fees-only awards from LEAs. Students attending Scottish institutions apply to either the Student Awards Agency for Scotland, the appropriate local council or one of the 43 Scottish incorporated further education colleges, depending on the place and level of the course.

Government Scholarship Schemes

The Government makes considerable provision for foreign students and trainees through its overseas aid programme and other award and scholarship schemes. In 1996–97 some 4,500 overseas students were supported.

The Foreign & Commonwealth Office (FCO) finances the British Chevening Scholarships, a worldwide programme offering outstanding graduate students and young professionals the opportunity to spend time studying at British universities and other academic institutions. In 1996–97 the FCO spent some £32 million on over 3,000 scholarships for students from 150 countries. These included jointly funded scholarships for overseas students co-sponsored by the FCO, business and industry, grant-giving foundations, the Churches and universities;

some 750 scholarships were provided under these arrangements.

Outside the aid programme, the Overseas Research Students Awards Scheme, funded by the higher education funding councils, provides assistance for overseas full-time postgraduate students with outstanding research potential.

Other Schemes

Many public and private scholarships and fellowships are available to students from overseas and to British students who want to study overseas. Among the best known are the British Council Fellowships, the Commonwealth Scholarship and Fellowship Plan, the Fulbright Scholarship Scheme, the British Marshall Scholarships, the Rhodes Scholarships, the Churchill Scholarships and the Confederation of British Industry Scholarships. Most British universities and colleges offer bursaries and scholarships for which graduates of any nationality are eligible.

THE YOUTH SERVICE

The youth service—a partnership between local government and voluntary organisations—is concerned with the informal personal and social education of young people aged 11 to 25 (5 to 25 in Northern Ireland).

Local authorities maintain their own youth centres and clubs and provide most of the public support for local and regional voluntary organisations. The service is said to reach around 5 million young people, the voluntary organisations contributing a significant proportion of overall provision.

The Department for Education and Employment's Youth Service Unit gives grants to the national voluntary youth organisations to meet 50 per cent of the cost of programmes designed to promote access to the youth service, support training for voluntary youth workers and help improve the effectiveness of the organisations.

Funded primarily by local government, England's National Youth Agency provides:

- support for those working with young people; and

- information and publishing services.

The Welsh Office sponsors the Wales Youth Agency, which is the agent for payment of grant aid to national youth service bodies with headquarters in Wales; it is also responsible for the accreditation of training and staff development for youth workers.

In Scotland the youth service forms part of the community education provision made by local authorities. It is also promoted by the Scottish Community Education Council. The Scottish Office gives grants to voluntary youth organisations to assist them with their headquarters expenditure and staff training.

In Northern Ireland the education and library boards provide and fund youth clubs and outdoor activity centres. They assist with the running costs of registered voluntary youth units and provide advice and support to youth groups. Boards also assist young people visiting the rest of Britain, Ireland and overseas. The Youth Council for Northern Ireland advises the education system on the development of the youth service. It promotes the provision of facilities, encourages cross-community activity and pays grants to the headquarters of voluntary bodies.

Voluntary Youth Organisations

National voluntary youth organisations undertake a significant share of youth activities through local groups, which raise most of their day-to-day expenses by their own efforts. Many receive financial and other help from LEAs, which also make available facilities in many areas. The voluntary organisations vary greatly in character and include the uniformed organisations, such as the Scouts and Girl Guides. Some organisations are church-based. Some also represent Jews and Muslims. Sport and the arts are catered for by various bodies. In Wales, Urdd Gobaith Cymru (the Welsh League of Youth) provides cultural, sporting and language-based activities for young Welsh speakers and learners.

Thousands of youth clubs encourage their members to participate in sport, cultural and other creative activities. Some youth clubs provide information, counselling and advice.

Many local authorities and voluntary youth organisations make provision for the young unemployed, young people from the ethnic minorities, young people in inner cities or rural areas and those in trouble or especially vulnerable. Other areas of concern are homelessness and provision for handicapped young people.

Many authorities have youth committees on which official and voluntary bodies are represented. They employ youth officers to co-ordinate youth work and to arrange in-service training.

Youth Workers

In England and Wales a two-year training course at certain universities and higher education colleges produces qualified youth and community workers; several undergraduate part-time and postgraduate courses are also available. In Scotland one-, two- and three-year courses are provided at colleges of education. Students from Northern Ireland attend courses run in universities and colleges in Britain and the Irish Republic.

Other Organisations

Finance is provided by many grant-giving foundations and trusts for activities involving young people. The Prince's Trust and the Royal Jubilee Trust provide grants and practical help to individuals and organisations; areas of concern include urban deprivation, unemployment, homelessness, and young offenders. Efforts are also made to assist ethnic minorities.

The Duke of Edinburgh's Award Scheme challenges young people from Britain and other Commonwealth countries to meet certain standards in activities such as community service, expeditions, social and practical skills and physical recreation.

Voluntary Service by Young People

Thousands of young people voluntarily undertake community service designed to help those in need, including elderly and disabled people. Many schools also organise community service work as part of the curriculum.

Further Reading

Excellence in Schools,. Department for Education and Employment. The Stationery Office, 1997.

Building Excellent Schools Together, Welsh Office. The Stationery Office, 1997.

The Government's Expenditure Plans 1997–98 to 1999–2000, Department for Education and Employment and Office for Standards in Education. The Stationery Office, 1997.

Standards and Quality in Scottish Schools 1992–95. Scottish Office Education and Industry Department, 1996.

27 Religion

Everyone in Britain has the right to religious freedom without interference from the community or the State. Religious organisations and groups may own property, conduct their rites and ceremonies, run schools, and promote their beliefs in speech and writing, within the limits of the law. There is no religious bar to the holding of public office.

INTRODUCTION

Although Britain is predominantly Christian, most of the world's religions are represented in the country. There are large Hindu, Jewish, Muslim and Sikh communities, and also smaller communities of Baha'is, Buddhists, Jains and Zoroastrians, as well as followers of new religious movements and pagans. Non-religious alternatives for humanists and atheists are offered by organisations such as the British Humanist Association and the National Secular Society, although most humanists and atheists do not belong to organised groups. Many Britons would class themselves as agnostic.

There has been a fall in recent years in the number of full-time ministers and the number of adults recorded as members of most of the larger Christian churches. At the same time there has been significant growth in a range of independent churches, and in new religious movements. Surveys have also revealed that many people who do not belong to religious groups claim to be religious and say they believe in God.

Religious Freedom

Freedom of conscience in religious matters was achieved gradually from the 17th century onwards. The older laws discriminating against minority religious groups were gradually enforced less harshly and then finally repealed. Heresy ceased to be a legal offence with the passage of the Ecclesiastical Jurisdiction Act 1677, and the Toleration Act 1688 granted freedom of worship to Protestant minority groups, such as the Religious Society of Friends (Quakers—see p. 462) and other non-conformists.

In 1828 the repeal of the Test and Corporation Acts gave nonconformist Protestant Christians full political rights, making it possible for them to be appointed to public office. Roman Catholics gained political rights under the Roman Catholic Relief Act 1829, and the Jewish Relief Act 1858 enabled Jews to become Members of Parliament. The religious tests imposed on prospective students and academic staff of the universities of Oxford, Cambridge and Durham were successively abolished by Acts of 1854, 1856 and 1871. Similar restrictions on the staff of Scottish universities were formally removed in 1932.

The past 30 years have seen an increasingly diverse pattern of religious belief and affiliation in Britain. This has been linked both to patterns of immigration and to new religious directions among some of the indigenous population. Social structures have been gradually changing to accommodate this. For example, arrangements are made at many places of work to allow the members of the various faiths to follow their religious observances.

Relations with the State

There are two established churches in Britain, that is, churches legally recognised as official churches of the State: in England the Anglican *Church of England*, and in Scotland the Presbyterian *Church of Scotland*. The Monarch is pledged by the coronation oath to defend each Church in its respective territory. There is no longer an established Church in Wales or in Northern Ireland. Ministers of the established churches, as well as clergy belonging to other religious groups, work in services run by the State, such as the armed forces, national hospitals and prisons, and may be paid a state salary for such services. Voluntary schools provided by religious denominations may be wholly or partly maintained from public funds. Religious education in publicly maintained schools is required by law, as is a daily act of collective worship (see p. 440). Religious broadcasting is subject to some legislative controls (see p. 497).

The State does not contribute to the general expenses of church maintenance, although some state aid does help repair historic churches. In 1996–97, for instance, English Heritage grants to churches totalled £10.3 million as compared with the £100 million spent on the buildings by parishes. Assistance is also given to meet some of the costs of repairing cathedrals; some £4 million was made available in 1996–97. This funding is not restricted to Church of England buildings.

The Government shares with the Church of England the upkeep of over 300 churches of special architectural or historic importance which are no longer required for regular parish use and for which no alternative use can be found. The contribution for the period 1995 to 1998 is about £7.5 million. The Historic Chapels Trust, launched in 1993, aims to preserve the redundant chapels and places of worship of other denominations and faiths, including synagogues and temples, which are of particular architectural or historic interest.

Involvement in Social Issues

Religious involvement in broader social issues was highlighted in the Church of England's report *Faith in the City: A Call for Action by Church and Nation*, published in 1985. This led to the establishment of the Church of England's Church Urban Fund, an independent charity which raises money to enable people living in urban priority areas to found projects which alleviate the effects of poverty on their lives. By June 1997 it had made grants totalling £27.1 million to 1,250 different projects.

The General Assembly of the Church of Scotland debates annual reports from its Committee on Church and Nation on social, economic, and political matters; and, through its Board of Social Responsibility, is the largest voluntary social work agency in Scotland.

Organisations belonging to other churches and religious groups are also closely involved with a wide range of social issues (see, for example, the work of the Salvation Army, p. 462).

The Inner Cities Religious Council, formed in 1992 and based in the Department of the Environment, Transport and the Regions, is a forum for discussion between the faiths and the Government, and encourages practical regeneration in the inner cities and run-down housing estates elsewhere. Chaired by a government minister, the Council comprises senior leaders of the Hindu, Jewish, Muslim, Sikh and Christian faiths, including the majority Black churches.

Unemployment and the Future of Work: an Enquiry for the Churches—a major report examining the problems of unemployment— was published by the Council of Churches for Britain and Ireland (see p. 463) in April 1997. Proposed solutions to unemployment include support for a statutory minimum wage, the implementation of a maximum 48-hour week, and an increase in taxes for high earners.

The Sacred Land Project

The Sacred Land Project, launched in April 1997, plans to conserve or create over 2,000 sacred sites in Britain during the next five years. Sponsored by the World Wildlife Fund for Nature, the Project will work with local communities, religious groups, and conservation and environmental organisations to re-open ancient pilgrim routes, create new pilgrim paths, help restore old shrines and sacred sites and develop sacred gardens. It not only celebrates Britain's multi-faith society but also demonstrates practical ways to improve quality of life through care of the natural environment. The Project has the support of all the major Christian churches, as well as most of the other faiths practised in Britain.

An example of a current project is the Holy Island Interfaith Centre and Garden, Scotland. This island, which is the site of the cave of a 6th-century hermit and of a 13th-century Christian monastery, is now owned by the Samye Ling Tibetan Buddhist Centre. The Sacred Land Project is helping the Centre to replant over 27,000 trees on the island and is advising on the creation of a new monastic garden incorporating Christian and Buddhist sacred garden traditions.

Statistics on Religious Affiliation

There is no standard information about the number of members of religious groups, since questions are not normally asked about religious beliefs in censuses or for other official purposes, except in Northern Ireland. Each group adopts its own way of counting its members, and the membership figures in this chapter—often supplied by the religious groups themselves—are therefore approximate.

THE CHRISTIAN COMMUNITY

Church of England

The Church of England became the established church during the Reformation in the 16th century. Conflicts between Church and State culminated in the Act of Supremacy in 1534, which repudiated papal supremacy and declared Henry VIII to be Supreme Head of the Church of England. The Church of England's form of worship was set out in successive versions of the Book of Common Prayer from 1549 onwards. The Church's relationship with the State is one of mutual obligation, since the Church's privileges are balanced by certain duties it must fulfil.

The Monarch is the 'Supreme Governor' of the Church of England and must always be a member of the Church, and promise to uphold it. Church of England archbishops, bishops and deans of cathedrals are appointed by the Monarch on the advice of the Prime Minister, although the Crown Appointments' Commission, which includes lay and clergy representatives, plays a key role in the selection of archbishops and diocesan bishops. All clergy swear allegiance to the Crown. The Church can regulate its own worship. The two archbishops (of Canterbury and York), the bishops of London, Durham and Winchester, and 21 other senior bishops sit in the House of Lords. Clergy of the Church, together with those of the Church of Scotland, the Church of Ireland and the Roman Catholic Church, may not sit in the House of Commons.

The Church of England is divided into two provinces: Canterbury, comprising 30 dioceses, including the Diocese in Europe; and York, with 14 dioceses. The dioceses are divided into archdeaconries and deaneries, which are in turn divided into about 13,000 parishes, although in practice many of these are grouped together. There are, altogether, about 10,000 full-time stipendiary Church of England clergy—men and women—working within the diocesan structure, excluding mainland Europe. In 1995 an estimated 194,300 people were baptised into the Church in the two provinces, excluding the Diocese in Europe; of these, 148,000 were under one year old, representing 24 per cent of live births. In the same year there were 29,500 confirmations. Attendances at services on a normal Sunday are just over one million. In 1993, 91,214 marriages were solemnised in the Church of England. These accounted for 66 per cent of all marriages with religious ceremonies, and 32 per cent of all marriages in England. Many people who rarely, if ever, attend services still regard themselves as belonging to the Church of England.

The central governing and legislative body is the General Synod, which comprises separate houses of bishops, clergy and lay members. Lay people are also involved with church government in the parishes. The Synod is the centre of an administrative system dealing with missionary work, inter-church relations, social questions, and recruitment and training for the ministry. It also covers other church work in Britain and overseas, the care of church buildings and their contents, church schools (which are maintained largely from public funds), colleges and institutes of higher education, and voluntary and parish education.

The Church Commissioners are responsible for managing the greater part of the Church of England's assets. The Prime Minister appoints an MP to the unpaid post of Second Church Estates Commissioner to represent the Commissioners in Parliament. There are plans to transfer certain powers of the Commissioners to the newly created Archbishops' Council, chaired by the Archbishops of Canterbury and York.

Apart from the Church Commissioners' income, most of the remainder of the Church's income is provided by local voluntary donations. The average annual stipend of a Church of England priest is about £13,450; the average value of additional benefits, including free housing and a non-contributory pension, is £7,015.

The first women priests were ordained in 1994 and there are now 859 stipendiary women clergy. Women priests can now be appointed to all offices in the Church, except those of archbishop or bishop. Three bishops have been appointed to provide additional pastoral care to those members and parishes of the Church who remain opposed to the ordination of women to the priesthood.

Other Anglican Churches

The Church of England is part of a worldwide communion of Anglican churches. These are similar in organisation and worship to the Church of England and originated from it. There are four distinct Anglican Churches in the British Isles, each governed separately by its own institutions: the Church of England, the Church in Wales, the Episcopal Church in Scotland, and the Church of Ireland (which operates in both Northern Ireland and the Irish Republic). The Church of Ireland was disestablished in 1869 and the Church in Wales in 1920.

The Anglican Communion comprises 36 autonomous Churches in Britain and abroad, and three regional councils overseas, with a total membership of about 70 million. Links between the components of the Anglican Communion are maintained by the Lambeth Conference of Anglican bishops, which is held every ten years, the next Conference being held in Canterbury in 1998. Presided over by the Archbishop of Canterbury, the Conference has no executive authority, but enjoys considerable influence. The Anglican Consultative Council, an assembly of lay people and clergy as well as of bishops, meets every two or three years to allow consultation within the Anglican Communion. The Primates Meeting brings together the senior bishops from each Church at similar intervals.

A new museum on the site of St Augustine's Abbey in Canterbury opened in May 1997, to mark the 1,400th anniversary of the arrival of St Augustine in England. The museum contains decorated mediaeval stonework and tiles, shrines and reliquaries excavated on the site of the Abbey, most of them on display for the first time.

Church of Scotland

The Church of Scotland has a presbyterian form of government, that is, government by church courts, composed of ministers and elders (presbyters), all of whom are ordained to office, and also deacons. It became the national church following the Scottish Reformation in the late 16th century and legislation enacted by the Scottish Parliament. The Church's status was then consolidated in the Treaty of Union of 1707 and by the Church of Scotland Act 1921, the latter confirming its complete freedom in all spiritual matters. It appoints its own office bearers, and its affairs are not subject to any civil authority.

The adult communicant membership of the Church of Scotland is over 680,000; there are about 1,200 ministers serving in parishes. Both men and women may join the ministry. The 1,292 churches are governed locally by Kirk Sessions, consisting of ministers and elders. Above the Kirk Session is the Presbytery. The General Assembly, consisting of elected ministers, elders and deacons, meets annually under the chairmanship of an elected moderator, who serves for one year. The Monarch is normally represented at the General Assembly by the Lord High Commissioner.

There are also a number of independent Scottish Presbyterian churches, largely descended from groups which broke away from the Church of Scotland. They are particularly active in the Highlands and Islands.

Free Churches

The term 'Free Churches' is often used to describe those Protestant churches in Britain which, unlike the Church of England and the Church of Scotland, are not established churches. Free Churches have existed in various forms since the Reformation, developing their own traditions over the years. Their members have also been known as dissenters or nonconformists. While this historical experience has given these churches a certain sense of shared identity, they otherwise vary greatly in doctrine, worship and church government. All the major Free Churches—Methodist, Baptist, United Reformed and Salvation Army—allow both men and women to become ministers.

The Methodist Church, the largest of the Free Churches, with almost 380,270 adult full members and a community of more than 1.2 million, originated in the 18th century following the Evangelical Revival under John Wesley (1703–91). The present church is based on the 1932 union of most of the separate Methodist Churches. It has 3,660 ministers and 6,678 places of worship.

MAYC, the youth service of the Methodist Church, serves over 60,000 young people aged 13 to 25. Each year MAYC organises London Weekend, one of the largest youth events in Europe, bringing together dance, drama, rock music and worship produced and performed by youth groups from all over Great Britain.

The Baptists first achieved an organised form in Britain in the 17th century. Today they are mainly organised in groups of churches, most of which belong to the Baptist Union of Great Britain (re-formed in 1812), with about 152,600 members, 2,418 ministers and 2,130 places of worship. There are also separate Baptist Unions for Scotland, Wales and Ireland, and other independent Baptist Churches.

The third largest of the Free Churches is the United Reformed Church, with some 97,500 members, 1,818 ministers and 1,750 places of worship. It was formed in 1972 following the merger of the Congregational Church in England and Wales (the oldest Protestant minority in Britain, whose origins can be traced back to the Puritans of the 16th century) with the Presbyterian Church of England (a church closely related in doctrine and worship to the Church of Scotland). In 1981 there was a further merger with the Re-formed Association of the Churches of Christ.

Alongside these churches are other historic Free Church bodies. The Salvation Army was founded in the East End of London in 1865 by William Booth (1829–1912). Within Britain it is second only to the Government as a provider of social services. It is the largest provider of hostel accommodation, offering almost 3,355 beds every night. Other services include work with alcoholics, prison chaplaincy and a family tracing service which receives 5,000 enquiries each year. The Salvation Army in Britain is served by around 1,732 officers (ordained ministers) and runs some 986 worship centres.

The Religious Society of Friends (Quakers), with about 17,500 adult members and 9,000 attenders in Britain and 460 places of worship, was founded in the middle of the 17th century under the leadership of George Fox (1624–91). It has no ordained ministers and no formal liturgy or sacraments. Silent worship is central to its life as a religious organisation. Emphasis is also placed on social concern and peacemaking.

Among the other Free Churches are: the Presbyterian Church in Ireland, the largest

Protestant church in Northern Ireland, where it has 304,000 members; the Presbyterian (or Calvinistic Methodist) Church of Wales, with 51,720 members and the largest of the Free Churches in Wales; and the Union of Welsh Independents (42,440 members).

A recent development has been the rise of Pentecostalism and the charismatic movement. A number of Pentecostalist bodies were formed in Britain at the turn of the century. The two main Pentecostalist organisations operating in Britain today are the Assemblies of God (approximately 55,000 members, over 900 ministers and over 660 places of worship) and the Elim Pentecostal Church. Since the Second World War immigration from the Caribbean has led to the growth of a significant number of majority Black Pentecostalist churches.

In the early 1960s a Pentecostalist charismatic movement began to influence some followers in both the Church of England and the Roman Catholic Church; it remains a growing influence in both these churches, and in the historic Free Churches. The Christian 'house church' movement (or 'new churches') began in the early 1970s, when some charismatics began to establish their own congregations. Services were originally held in private houses although many congregations have now acquired their own buildings. The movement, whose growth has been most marked in England, is characterised by lay leadership and is organised into a number of loose fellowships, usually on a regional basis, such as the Ichthus Fellowship in south-east London.

Roman Catholic Church

The formal structure of the Roman Catholic Church in England and Wales, which ceased to exist after the Reformation, was restored in 1850. The Scottish Roman Catholic Church's formal structure went out of existence in the early 17th century and was restored in 1878. However, throughout this period Catholicism never disappeared entirely. There are now seven Roman Catholic provinces in Great Britain, each under an archbishop, and 30 dioceses, each under a bishop (22 in England and Wales and eight in Scotland, independently responsible to the Pope). There

are 3,319 parishes and about 4,800 priests (only men may become priests). Northern Ireland has six dioceses, some with territory partly in the Irish Republic. About one British citizen in ten claims to be a Roman Catholic.

The Roman Catholic Church attaches great importance to the education of its children and requires its members to try to bring up their children in the Catholic faith. Some 1.5 per cent of the teachers in Britain's 2,438 Catholic schools are members of religious orders. These orders also undertake other social work, such as nursing, childcare and running homes for elderly people. There are approximately 12,000 members of religious orders in England, Scotland and Wales. Most Catholic schools are maintained out of public funds.

Other Christian Churches

Other Protestant Churches include the Unitarians and Free Christians, whose origins are traceable to the Reformation.

The Christian Brethren are a Protestant body organised in their present form by J. N. Darby (1800–82). There are two branches: the Open Brethren and the Closed or Exclusive Brethren.

Many Christian communities founded by migrant communities, including the Orthodox, Lutheran and Reformed Churches of various European countries, the Coptic Orthodox Church and the Armenian Church, have established their own centres of worship, particularly in London. All these churches operate in a variety of languages. The largest is probably the Greek Orthodox Church, many of whose members are of Cypriot origin. It is represented in many cities throughout Britain.

There are also several other religious groups in Britain which were founded in the United States in the last century. These include the Jehovah's Witnesses, the Church of Jesus Christ of the Latter-Day Saints (the Mormon Church), the Christadelphians, the Seventh-Day Adventists, the Christian Scientists and the Spiritualists.

Co-operation among the Churches

The Council of Churches for Britain and Ireland (formerly the British Council of

Churches) is the main overall body for the Christian churches in Britain. The Council co-ordinates the work of its 32 member churches and associations of churches, in the areas of social responsibility, international affairs, church life, world mission, racial justice and inter-faith relations. The Council's member churches are also grouped in separate ecumenical bodies, according to country: Churches Together in England, Action of Churches Together in Scotland, Churches Together in Wales, and the Irish Council of Churches.

The Free Church Federal Council, with 19 member denominations, includes most of the Free Churches of England and Wales. It promotes co-operation among the Free Churches (especially in hospital chaplaincy and in education matters).

The Evangelical Alliance, with a membership of individuals, churches or societies drawn from within 20 denominations, represents over 1 million evangelical Christians.

Inter-church discussions about the search for Christian unity take place internationally, as well as within Britain, and the main participants are the Roman Catholic, Orthodox, Anglican, Lutheran, Methodist, Reformed and Baptist Churches. In 1995 the Church of England and the Methodist Church started informal meetings to consider moves towards unity.

The Anglican Churches and the Church of Scotland are among the 14 British Churches which are members of the World Council of Churches. This organisation links some 332 churches in over 120 countries around the world.

OTHER FAITH COMMUNITIES

The Buddhist Community

The Buddhist community in Britain consists largely of adherents of British or Western origin. There are well over 500 Buddhist groups and centres, including some 50 monasteries and temples. All the main schools of Buddhism are represented. The Buddhist Society, founded in 1924, promotes the principles of Buddhism; it does not belong to any particular school of Buddhism.

The Hindu Community

The Hindu community in Britain comprises around 320,000 members and originates largely from India. The largest groups of Hindus are to be found in Leicester, different areas of London, Birmingham and Bradford. The first Hindu temple, or mandir, was opened in London in 1962 and there are now over 150 mandirs in Britain, a number of which are affiliated to the National Council of Hindu Temples.

The Swaminarayan Hindu Mission, in north London, has the largest Hindu temple to be built outside India, together with an extensive cultural complex which has provision for conferences, exhibitions, marriages, sports, and health clinics.

The Jewish Community

Jews first settled in England at the time of the Norman Conquest and remained until banished by royal decree in 1290. The present community in Britain dates from 1656, having been founded by Jews of Spanish and Portuguese origin, known as Sephardim, who now account for some three per cent of the community. Later more settlers came from Germany and Eastern Europe; they are known as Ashkenazim.

The Jewish community in Britain numbers about 285,000 and is, after that in France, the largest in Western Europe. The main groups are to be found in the Greater London area (183,000), Manchester and Salford (28,000), Leeds (10,000), and Brighton and Hove (6,000). About 70 per cent are affiliated to synagogues. Most Ashkenazi Jews (63 per cent), acknowledge the authority of the Chief Rabbi, while the more strictly observant (7 per cent) have their own spiritual leaders, as do the Sephardim. The Reform movement (founded in 1840), the Liberal and Progressive movement (founded in 1901), and the recently established Masorti movement, account for most of the remaining 30 per cent of synagogue members.

Jewish congregations in Britain number about 360. The Board of Deputies of British Jews is the officially recognised representative body for all these groups. Founded in 1760, it is mainly elected by synagogues. The Board serves as the voice of the community to both government and the wider non-Jewish community.

A large-scale survey of British Jews, conducted by the Institute of Jewish Policy Research, was published in 1996. This reports that 44 per cent of Jewish men aged under 40 are married, or living with, non-Jewish partners, and that among Jewish women in this age range, 20 to 25 per cent marry outside the Jewish community.

Roughly one in three Jewish children attend Jewish day schools, some of which are supported by public funds. Several agencies care for elderly and handicapped people.

The Muslim Community

Figures given for the size of the Muslim community in Britain range from three-quarters of a million to 2 million. Recent estimates, based on extrapolations from the 1991 census, suggest the population is between 1 million and 1.5 million, while estimates from within the Muslim community suggest between 1.5 million and 2 million. The largest number originate from Pakistan and Bangladesh, while sizeable groups have come from India, Cyprus, the Arab world, Malaysia and parts of Africa. There is a growing number of British-born Muslims, mainly the children of immigrant parents, but including an increasing number of converts to Islam.

There are over 600 mosques and numerous Muslim prayer centres throughout Britain. Mosques are not only places of worship; they also offer instruction in the Muslim way of life and facilities for educational and welfare activities.

The first mosque in Britain was established at Woking, Surrey, in 1890. Mosques now range from converted houses in many towns to the Central Mosque in Regent's Park, London, and its associated Islamic Cultural Centre, one of the most important Muslim institutions in the Western world. The Central Mosque has the largest congregation in Britain, and during festivals it may number over 30,000. The Islamic Cultural Centre's activities include a weekend school for children, and regular lectures, seminars and conferences. Pastoral care includes free legal advice, counselling, marriage and funeral services, and prison and hospital visiting.

There are also important mosques and cultural centres in Liverpool, Manchester, Leicester, Birmingham, Bradford, Cardiff, Edinburgh and Glasgow.

Many of the mosques are administered by various local Muslim organisations, and both the Sunni and the Shi'a traditions within Islam are represented among the Muslim community in Britain. Members of some of the major Sufi traditions have also developed branches in British cities. The Ismaili Centre in London provides wide-ranging pastoral care and a place of worship for Shi'a Imami Ismaili Muslims, whose current Imam is Prince Karim Aga Khan.

The Sikh Community

A large British Sikh community (estimates range from 400,000 to 500,000) originates mainly from India, and particularly from the Punjab. The largest groups of Sikhs are in Greater London, Manchester, Birmingham, Nottingham and Wolverhampton. Sikh temples, or gurdwaras, cater for the religious, educational, social welfare and cultural needs of their community. A granthi is normally employed to take care of the building and to conduct prayers. The oldest gurdwara in London was established in 1908 and the largest is in Hounslow, Middlesex (to the west of London). There are over 200 gurdwaras in Britain.

Other Faiths

Small communities of other faiths include that of the Jains, mainly living in London, Leicester and Coventry. Jainism is an ancient religion brought to Britain by immigrants from India. A Jain temple (or derasar) opened in Leicester in 1988. The Zoroastrian religion, or Mazdaism, which originated in ancient Iran, is mainly represented in Britain by the Parsi community, whose ancestors left Iran in the 10th century and settled in north-west India. The Baha'i movement originated in 19th-century Iran; there are an estimated

6,000 Baha'is in Britain, organised in 500 local assemblies and administered by the National Spiritual Assembly in London.

There are also several thousand members of the Ahmadiyya movement in Britain, who consider themselves Muslim although are not generally recognised as such by the Muslim community.

A more recent development is Rastafarianism. This emerged out of the back to Africa movement in the West Indies early this century, and arrived in Britain through Jamaican immigration in the 1950s. It has no single creed, but draws heavily on the Old Testament.

New Religious Movements

A large number of new religious movements are active in Britain. Sometimes popularly referred to as cults they have been established since the Second World War and often have overseas origins. Examples include the Church of Scientology, the Transcendental Meditation movement, the Unification Church (popularly known as the 'Moonies') and various New Age groups. INFORM (Information Network Focus on Religious Movements), which is supported by the main churches, carries out research and seeks to provide objective information about new religious movements. It was founded in response to public concern about the activities of some of these cults.

CO-OPERATION BETWEEN FAITHS

A number of national organisations work to promote good relations between different religions in Britain. They include the Inter Faith Network for the United Kingdom, which links a wide range of organisations with an interest in inter-faith relations, including representative bodies from the Baha'i, Buddhist, Christian, Hindu, Jain, Jewish, Muslim, Sikh and Zoroastrian faith groups. The Network runs a public advice and information service on inter-faith issues.

Other national organisations include the Council of Christians and Jews, which works for better understanding among members of the two religions and deals with issues in the educational and social fields.

Within each faith tradition are organisations and individuals working to further good relations with other faiths. For example, the Council of Churches for Britain and Ireland (see p. 463) has a Commission on Inter Faith Relations.

Further Reading

Religion. Aspects of Britain series, HMSO, 1992.

Religions in the UK: A Multi-Faith Directory. Ed. Paul Weller, University of Derby and The Inter Faith Network for the United Kingdom, 1997.

Unemployment and the Future of Work: an Enquiry for the Churches. Council of Churches for Britain and Ireland, 1997.

28 The Arts

Britain's artistic and cultural heritage is one of the richest in the world. The origins of English literature, one of the world's most influential bodies of writing, can be traced back to medieval times, its texts among the oldest specimens of vernacular writing in Europe, while over the centuries Britain has amassed some of the finest collections of works of art. The performing arts also have a long and distinguished history. With the advent of the National Lottery, arts funding in Britain has undergone the biggest change since the system of support for the arts was established fifty years ago.

INTRODUCTION

London is one of the leading world centres for the arts. Other large cities, including Birmingham, Leeds, Manchester, Edinburgh, Glasgow and Cardiff, have also sustained and developed their reputations as centres of artistic excellence in recent years. Arts festivals attract wide interest. Many British playwrights, craftspeople, composers, film-makers, painters, writers, actors, singers, musicians and dancers enjoy international reputations. They include, for example, Harold Pinter, Sir Colin Davis, Andrew Lloyd Webber, David Hockney, Sir V.S. Naipaul, Vanessa Redgrave, Sir Ian McKellen and Sir Anthony Hopkins. Television and radio bring a range of arts events to a large audience. At an amateur level, millions of people devote their time and their talents to the benefit of local communities.

Cultural industries play an important part in Britain's economy. An analysis of the 1991 Census, *Employment in the Arts and Cultural Industries*,[1] shows that the total number of people in the cultural sector was 648,900, representing 2.4 per cent of the economically active population. The arts are a thriving industry: it is estimated that the performing and contemporary visual arts have an annual turnover of well over £1,000 million.

Department for Culture, Media and Sport

In May 1997 the former Department for National Heritage was renamed the Department for Culture, Media and Sport. The Department (see p. 534), whose head now becomes the Secretary of State for Culture, Media and Sport, determines government policy and administers expenditure on national museums and art galleries in England, the Arts Council of England (see p. 468), the British Library and

---

[1] Research Report No 2, Arts Council of England, 1995.

other national arts and heritage bodies. Other responsibilities include the regulation of the film industry, broadcasting and the press, the National Lottery and the export licensing of antiques. Under the new Government, the Department has also acquired responsibility for oversight of the music industries, previously undertaken by the Department of Trade and Industry.

The Secretaries of State for Wales, Scotland and Northern Ireland are responsible for the arts in their countries, including the national museums, galleries and libraries and their respective Arts Councils (see below).

The Department for Culture, Media and Sport and the home departments provide funds and advice, and encourage partnership with the private sector, including business sponsorship. The national museums and galleries are also encouraged to increase their resources through other means—for example, trading. An important concept in funding policy is the 'arm's length' principle, by which government funds are distributed to arts organisations indirectly, through bodies such as the Arts Councils, the British Film Institute and Scottish Screen. This principle helps to avoid political influence over funding decisions by ensuring that funds are allocated by those best qualified to do so.

New Government Policy Towards Cultural Activity

The new Government has announced four major principles behind its support for cultural activity:

1. Culture must be made more accessible to the many, not just to the few. (Proposals already made include plans to pilot open theatre nights and an artscard scheme for young people, as well as reviewing the case for admission charges to core collections in national museums and galleries.)

2. Culture must become more a part of everyday life, with encouragement given to public culture projects, for example bringing live art and contemporary painting and sculpture to public spaces.

3. The need to recognise the enormous economic importance of cultural activity

and its role in working towards high and sustainable levels of employment.

4. The need to ensure that culture is made an integral part of the education service.

A new interdepartmental Taskforce, whose members include prominent figures in business and culture, has been set up to improve economic performance in the creative industries.

Arts Councils

The main channels for government aid to the contemporary and performing arts are the independent Arts Councils of England, Scotland, Wales and Northern Ireland. Their aims are to: develop and improve the knowledge and practice of these activities; make them more accessible to the public; and advise and co-operate with central government departments, local authorities and other organisations.

The Arts Councils give financial assistance and advice to organisations ranging from the major arts centres and opera, dance and drama companies to small touring theatre companies and experimental performance groups. They also provide funds for the training of arts administrators and help arts organisations to develop other sources of income, including sponsorship and local authority support. They promote education, access and participation in the arts through a variety of art forms, including ballet and contemporary dance, drama, literature, music, opera, visual arts and photography, working with creative writers, dramatists, choreographers, dancers, actors, musicians, composers, artists and photographers.

The Arts Council of England provides the main funding for the ten *Regional Arts Boards*, which offer financial assistance to artists and arts organisations across England and advise on, and sometimes help to promote, arts activities. Other sources of funding for the Boards come from the British Film Institute and the Crafts Council, as well as from local authorities. The Boards are responsible for most of the funding of organisations within their region.

The Arts Council of England also funds the national companies—the Royal Opera, Royal

Ballet and Birmingham Royal Ballet, English National Opera, Royal Shakespeare Company, Royal National Theatre and South Bank Centre. It also funds touring companies without a regional base and other arts organisations with a national strategic role.

Finance

In England planned central government expenditure through the Department for Culture, Media and Sport in 1997–98 amounts to £221 million for museums and galleries; £195 million for the contemporary and performing arts; £103 million for libraries; and £43 million for broadcasting and the media. The grant for the arts is channelled mainly through the Arts Council of England, the Crafts Council and the National Heritage Pairing Scheme for the Arts (see p. 470). In addition the Arts Councils distribute National Lottery proceeds to the arts, amounting to approximately £250 million a year.

Planned 1997–98 expenditure by the Arts Councils for Scotland, Wales and Northern Ireland is respectively £27 million, £13 million and £7.4 million.

The Scottish Office is also providing £40.4 million for Scotland's National Galleries and Museums and National Library, while the Welsh Office is providing some £17 million for Wales's National Museum and National Library. Planned spending by the Department of Education for Northern Ireland on the three major museums there amounts to about £8.9 million in 1997–98.

National Lottery

The National Lottery (see p. 47) is providing a major new source of funds to support arts projects of all kinds in Britain. Its effects are permeating all sectors of the arts.

By 1 July 1997, grants of almost £782.4 million had been distributed by the Arts Councils and the Heritage Lottery Fund (see p. 368) to a wide range of arts projects, from major schemes such as £3.8 million to The Tate Gallery in Merseyside and £3 million to Armagh City and District Council, Northern Ireland, for a new theatre/arts centre, to much smaller grants for theatre restoration and providing musical instruments to local bands and youth clubs.

> Two major new National Lottery schemes run by the Arts Council of England were launched in November 1996.
>
> - The Arts for Everyone Main programme is for projects ranging from £500 to £500,000. The programme is aimed at arts organisations—professional and amateur—which have an established track record and which may have previously received funding from the Arts Council, Regional Arts Boards or local authorities.
>
> - The Arts for Everyone Express programme is for projects ranging from £500 to £5,000, and is aimed primarily at youth or voluntary groups, or small professional arts organisations putting together their first creative project. It has begun to put small-scale grants in place at community and neighbourhood level, fostering local artistic activity in a way that has an impact on people's ordinary lives.

NESTA

The Government proposes to set up a National Endowment for Science, Technology and the Arts (NESTA) with funding from the National Lottery to help talented young people develop their skills in the creative industries and in science and technology, and help turn creativity into products and services which are effectively exploited with rights effectively protected.

NESTA, which will be independent of government, will encompass science, technology and design, film, broadcasting and the audio-visual and music industries, architecture, the arts and information and communications technology. The Government believes that NESTA should place particular emphasis on multimedia and other areas where the arts and science and technology meet.

Local Authorities

Local authorities maintain around 1,000 local museums and art galleries and a network of over 4,000 public libraries. They also support many other buildings, organisations and events for cultural activity in their areas, providing grant aid for professional and voluntary bodies, including orchestras, theatres, and opera and dance companies. They undertake direct promotions of cultural activity and contribute to the cost of new or converted buildings for the sector. In England net revenue support from local authorities for 1996–97 was around £194.6 million.

The Corporation of London—the local authority for the City of London—is the third largest sponsor of culture in Britain (the largest are the Government and the BBC), with a budget of £37 million in 1997–98. The Corporation owns and manages the Barbican Centre (Europe's largest multi-arts and conference centre); is principal patron of the London Symphony Orchestra and the Royal Shakespeare Company; and funds and manages the Guildhall School of Music and Drama, where over 700 performing arts students from more than 40 countries are studying.

Business Sponsorship

Industrial and commercial companies offer vital sponsorship to a wide range of cultural activity. The Pairing Scheme for the Arts, managed by the Association for Business Sponsorship of the Arts (ABSA), on behalf of the Department for Culture, Media and Sport, aims to encourage businesses in Britain to sponsor cultural activity. Under the scheme, government funding of between £500 and £75,000 is awarded to culture organisations to complement the sponsorship from businesses. Launched in 1984, the scheme has brought over £124 million into culture (including a government contribution of over £40 million). In 1997–98 government funding for the Scheme was £5.05 million.

Under ABSA's Business in the Arts programme, the private sector gives part-time management expertise to arts organisations.

Foundation for Sport and the Arts

The Foundation for Sport and the Arts was set up in 1991 by the Pool Promoters Association to channel funds into sport and the arts. Almost £20 million of the Foundation's annual revenue is used to benefit the arts and is distributed in the form of awards to a variety of organisations.

The Government Art Collection

The Government Art Collection comprises over 12,000 works and covers principally historical, modern and contemporary British art. It is displayed in 500 government buildings in Britain and overseas and provides a showcase for Britain's creative talent. See colour plates between pp. 256 and 257 and the Foreword (p. vii).

Cultural Diversity and Disability

Cultural Diversity

The Arts Council of England and the Regional Arts Boards support African, Caribbean and Chinese work as one of their stated priorities and expect such work to be built into mainstream provision of arts centres, galleries and so on. In addition they fund the Asian Arts Development Agency; the African Asian Visual Arts Archive; and the British Chinese Artists Association. Leading companies receiving support include the African people's dance company, Adzido; the theatre group, Black Mime; the British-Malaysian dance group, Bi-Ma; and the numerous costume bands taking part in the annual Notting Hill Carnival—the largest street festival in Europe.

Arts and Disability

The National Disability Arts Forum and other national agencies are funded by the Arts Council of England, as are creative organisations, such as CandoCo, a company of disabled and non-disabled dancers. The Council also supports an apprenticeship scheme for disabled people in major arts organisations, such as the Royal Shakespeare Company, which is part of an initiative aimed at increasing employment opportunities in the arts for disabled people.

Other schemes supported by the Arts Council of England include an audit of deaf arts conducted by Deafworks and projects involving disabled artists in schools. The Scottish Arts Council supports Art Link and Project Ability, which provide opportunities for people with disabilities to develop creativity in a range of art forms.

The provision of access for disabled people to arts buildings is a basic criterion for all grants made from the National Lottery. The Department for Culture, Media and Sport funds the ADAPT Trust which advises on and provides funds for improvements in access (physical or sensory) to a range of leisure and arts venues.

Arts Centres

Over 200 arts centres in Britain give people the chance of enjoying and taking part in a range of activities, with educational projects becoming increasingly important. Nearly all arts centres are professionally managed, while using the services of volunteers. They are assisted mainly by the Arts Councils, Regional Arts Boards and local authorities, while the Arts Council of England funds two national centres the South Bank Centre and the Institute of Contemporary Arts. Many theatres and art galleries also provide a focal point for other community arts facilities.

The British Council

The British Council (see p. 140) promotes British creativity internationally in the arts, literature and design, and highlights Britain's cultural diversity. The Visiting Arts Office of Great Britain and Northern Ireland, is a joint venture of the British Council with the Foreign & Commonwealth Office, the four national Arts Councils and the Crafts Council. It encourages the inward flow to Britain of arts from other countries.

Broadcasting

BBC radio and television and the independent companies (see chapter 29) broadcast a variety of drama, opera, ballet and music, as well as general arts magazine programmes and documentaries. These have won many international awards at festivals such as the Prix Italia and Montreux International Television Festivals. Independent television companies also give grants for arts promotion in their regions.

Broadcasting is a major medium for making the arts available to the public and is a crucial source of work for actors, musicians, writers, composers, technicians and others in the arts world. It has created its own forms—nothing like the arts documentary or drama series, for instance, exists in any other medium. Broadcasters commission and produce a vast quantity of new work. Television and radio provide critical debate, information and education about the arts.

The BBC has five orchestras, which employ many of Britain's full-time professional musicians. Each week it broadcasts about 100 hours of classical and other music (both live and recorded) on its Radio 3 (FM 90.2–92.4) channel. BBC Radio 1 (FM 97.6–99.8) broadcasts rock and pop music, along with a range of other programming, 24 hours a day, and a large part of the output of BBC Radio 2 (FM 88.0–90.2) is popular and light music. There are at present two national commercial radio stations which broadcast music: Classic FM (FM 100–102), which broadcasts mainly classical music; and Virgin Radio (FM 105.8; MW 1197,1215), which plays broad-based rock music. Much of the output of Britain's local radio stations consists of popular and light music.

The BBC regularly commissions new music, particularly by British composers, and sponsors concerts, competitions and festivals. Each summer it presents and broadcasts the BBC Promenade Concerts (the 'Proms'), the world's largest music festival, at the Royal Albert Hall.

Festivals

Some 650 professional arts festivals take place in Britain each year. The annual Edinburgh International Festival, featuring a wide range of arts, is held in August and September and is the largest of its kind in the world. Other festivals held in Edinburgh include the annual International Jazz Festival, the International Film and Television Festivals and the annual Book Festival. Some well-known festivals concentrating on music are the Three Choirs Festival, which has taken place annually for more than 260 years in Gloucester, Worcester or Hereford; the Cheltenham International Festival of Music, largely devoted to contemporary British music; and the Aldeburgh festival.

Among other festivals catering for a number of art forms are the Royal National Eisteddfod of Wales, the Royal National Gaelic Mod in Scotland, the Belfast Festival at Queen's University, and the festivals in Brighton, Buxton, Chester, St Davids, Harrogate, Llangollen, Malvern, Perth and York. Pop music festivals include Glastonbury, Phoenix (at Stratford-upon-Avon) and Womad (Reading). Many smaller towns also hold arts festivals. A major event in London is the Notting Hill Carnival, which is organised largely by the Afro-Caribbean community.

Arts 2000

Arts 2000 is an Arts Council initiative which celebrates the approach of the millennium. During each year between 1992 and 2000, one city, town or region in Britain has been nominated, through competition, to celebrate a particular art form. The Eastern Region was the Region of Opera and Musical Theatre in 1997; Yorkshire and Humberside is the Region of Photography and the Electronic Image for 1998; and Glasgow, the City of Architecture and Design for 1999.

Winners use a combination of Arts Council and matching funds to create a wide-ranging and imaginative programme including a strong international content.

DRAMA

Britain is one of the world's major centres for theatre, and has a long and rich dramatic tradition. There are companies based in London and in many other cities and towns; in addition, numerous touring companies visit theatres, festivals and other venues, including arts and sports centres and social clubs.

Contemporary British playwrights who have received international recognition, with examples of their works, include:

- David Hare: *Skylight; Racing Demon; Amy's View*;
- Alan Ayckbourn: *The Revengers' Comedies; A Chorus of Disapproval*;
- John Godber: *Up 'N Under; On the Piste*;
- Caryl Churchill: *Serious Money; The Skriker*; and
- Tom Stoppard: *Travesties; Arcadia; Indian Ink*.

Among the best-known directors are Sir Peter Hall, Richard Eyre, Nicholas Hytner, Trevor Nunn, Adrian Noble, Jonathan Miller, Deborah Warner and Terry Hands, while the many British performers who enjoy international reputations include Eileen Atkins, Kenneth Branagh, Dame Judi Dench, Ralph Fiennes, Sir John Gielgud, Sir Alec Guinness, Paul Scofield, Sir Ian McKellen, Helen Mirren, Vanessa Redgrave, Dame Diana Rigg, Dame Maggie Smith and Juliet Stevenson. British stage designers such as John Bury, Ralph Koltai and Carl Toms are internationally acclaimed.

Britain has about 300 theatres intended for professional use which can seat between 200 and 2,300 people. Some are privately owned, but most are owned either municipally or by non-profit-making organisations. Over 40 of these have resident theatre companies receiving subsidies from the Arts Councils and Regional Arts Boards. In summer there are also open air theatres, including one in London's Regent's Park and the Minack Theatre, which is on a clifftop near Land's End in Cornwall. Most theatres are commercially run and self-financing, relying on popular shows and musicals to be profitable. By contrast, companies funded by the Arts Councils tend to offer a variety of traditional and experimental productions. Experimental or innovative work is often staged in 'fringe theatres' in London and other cities; these are smaller theatres which use a variety of buildings, such as rooms in pubs.

London

London has about 100 theatres, 15 of them permanently occupied by subsidised companies. These include:

- the Royal National Theatre, which stages a range of modern and classical plays in its three auditoriums on the South Bank;

- the Royal Shakespeare Company, which presents plays mainly by Shakespeare and his contemporaries, as well as some modern work, has two auditoriums in the City's Barbican Centre. The Company's main base is in Stratford-upon-Avon; it also tours other parts of Britain for six months of the year; and

- the English Stage Company, which stages the work of many new playwrights. (Normally sited at the Royal Court Theatre in Sloane Square, at the time of writing the company was based at the Duke of York and Ambassadors theatres while the Royal Court was being renovated.)

The largest concentration of London's commercial theatres is around Shaftesbury Avenue. West End theatre attendance was over 11 million in 1996.

In 1989 the partial remains of the Globe Theatre, where Shakespeare acted, and the Rose Theatre, where his plays were performed during his lifetime, were excavated on the south bank of the Thames; both have since been listed as ancient monuments. A modern, part Lottery-funded reconstruction of the Globe Theatre, near its original site, opened its first season in 1997.

Regional Theatres

Outside London most cities and many large towns have at least one theatre. Older theatres which have been restored include the Theatre Royal, Newcastle upon Tyne, which dates from the 18th century; the Alhambra, Bradford; the Lyceum, Sheffield; the Theatre Royal, Bristol; and the Grand Opera House, Belfast, all dating from the 19th century. Others, such as the West Yorkshire Playhouse, Leeds, and the Theatre Royal, Plymouth, have been built to modern designs. Edinburgh's rebuilt and restored Empire Theatre—now the Edinburgh Festival Theatre—provides an international venue for large-scale productions. A custom-built theatre for new writing recently became the new home of the Traverse Theatre in Edinburgh. Several universities have theatres which house professional companies playing to the public.

Most regional repertory companies mount about eight to ten productions a year; several have studio theatres in addition to the main auditorium, where they present new or experimental drama and plays of specialist interest. Repertory theatres also often function as social centres by offering concerts, poetry readings and exhibitions, and by providing restaurants, bars and shops.

Regional theatre companies with major reputations include the Citizens' Theatre, Glasgow; the Royal Exchange, Manchester; Bristol Old Vic; West Yorkshire Playhouse; the Festival Theatre, Chichester; and the Nottingham Playhouse, one of the first modern regional theatres. Successful productions from regional theatre companies often transfer to London's West End. In addition, the largest regional theatres receive visits from the Royal National Theatre or the Royal Shakespeare Company, which has three theatres at its base in Stratford-upon-Avon. The Cambridge Theatre Company, Oxford Stage Company and English Touring Theatre Company tour the English regions and worldwide.

Table 28.1: West End Theatres, 1986 and 1996		
	1986	1996
Attendances	10.2m	11.1m
Increase/decrease on previous year	−5.17%	−6.35%
Average number of theatres open during the year	42	41
Number of performances	16,543	16,084
Number of productions	213	186

Source: *The Society of London Theatre Box Office Data Report 1996*

Theatre for Young People

The Unicorn Theatre for Children and Polka Children's Theatre, both in London, present plays specially written for children; and the Whirligig Theatre tours throughout Britain. The Young Vic Company in London and Contact Theatre Company in Manchester stage plays for young people. Numerous Theatre-in-Education companies perform in schools. Some of these companies operate independently—Theatre Centre, for example, plays in London and tours further afield. Others are attached to regional repertory theatres such as the Wolsey Theatre, Ipswich, and Greenwich Theatre. Most regional repertory theatres also mount productions for younger audiences, and concessionary ticket prices are generally available for those at school, college or university.

There has been a marked growth in youth theatres, which number more than 500 in England alone; both the National Youth Theatre in London and the Scottish Youth Theatre in Glasgow offer early acting opportunities to young people.

Dramatic Training

Training for actors, directors, lighting and sound technicians and stage managers is provided mainly in drama schools, among them the Royal Academy of Dramatic Art (RADA), the Central School of Speech and Drama, the London Academy of Music and Dramatic Art (LAMDA), and the Drama Centre (all in London); the Bristol Old Vic School, the Royal Scottish Academy of Music and Drama (Glasgow) and the Welsh College of Music and Drama (Cardiff). Theatre design courses, often based in art schools, are available for people wanting to train as stage designers. A number of universities and colleges offer degree courses in drama.

Amateur Theatre

There are several thousand amateur dramatic societies throughout Britain. They use a variety of buildings, including schools and public halls. Their work is encouraged by a number of organisations, including the Central Council for Amateur Theatre, the National Drama Conference, the Scottish Community Drama Association and the Association of Ulster Drama Festivals. Amateur companies sometimes receive financial support from local government and other bodies.

MUSIC

People in Britain are interested in a wide range of music, from classical to different forms of rock, country and pop music. Jazz, folk and world music, and brass bands also have substantial followings.

Throughout the year Britain's arts festivals, many of which have a strong music focus, attract thousands of people—residents and tourists alike.

Orchestral and Choral Music

Seasons of orchestral and choral concerts are promoted every year in many large towns and cities. The principal concert halls in central London are the Royal Festival Hall in the South Bank Centre, next to which are the Queen Elizabeth Hall and the Purcell Room, which accommodate smaller-scale performances; the Barbican Hall (part of the Barbican Centre for Arts and Conferences in the City of London); the Royal Albert Hall in Kensington; the Wigmore Hall, a recital centre; and St John's, Smith Square. Birmingham has its own recently built concert hall, the Symphony Hall, while the 2,400-seat Bridgewater Hall opened in 1996 for Manchester's Hallé Orchestra and one of a similar size opened in Belfast in 1997.

The leading symphony orchestras in London are the London Symphony, the Philharmonia, the London Philharmonic, the Royal Philharmonic and the BBC Symphony. Important regional orchestras in England include the Royal Liverpool Philharmonic, the Hallé, the City of Birmingham Symphony and the Bournemouth Symphony, while in the other countries of Britain the leading orchestras are: the Ulster Orchestra, the Royal Scottish National Orchestra and the BBC National Orchestra of Wales. The BBC's five orchestras give broadcast concerts which are often open to the public. There are also chamber orchestras, such as the City of London Sinfonia, the Academy of St Martin-in-the-Fields, the Northern Sinfonia, the Bournemouth Sinfonietta and the Scottish Chamber Orchestra. Specialised ensembles include the Orchestra of the Age of Enlightenment, the English Baroque Soloists and the English Concert. The London Sinfonietta and the Birmingham Contemporary Music Group specialise in contemporary music.

British conductors such as Sir Colin Davis, Vernon Handley, Trevor Pinnock, John Eliot Gardiner, Andrew Davis, Sir Simon Rattle, Sir Neville Marriner, Christopher Hogwood, Jane Glover and Richard Hickox reach a wide audience through their recordings as well as by their performances. The works of living composers such as Sir Michael Tippett, Sir Peter Maxwell Davies and Sir Harrison Birtwistle enjoy international acclaim. Other well-established British composers include Michael Berkeley, John Tavener, Sir Malcolm Arnold, Oliver Knussen, Nicola le Fanu, George Lloyd, David Matthews, Mark Anthony Turnage, John Casken, James MacMillan and Judith Weir. The Master of the Queen's Music, Malcolm Williamson, holds an office within the Royal Household with responsibility for organising and writing music for state occasions. Percussionist Evelyn Glennie and clarinettist Emma Johnson are among solo performers currently enjoying great acclaim.

The principal choral societies include the Bach Choir, the Royal Choral Society, the Huddersfield Choral Society, the Cardiff Polyphonic Choir, the Edinburgh International Festival Chorus and the Belfast Philharmonic Society. Almost all the leading orchestras maintain their own choral societies. The English tradition of ecclesiastical choral singing is exemplified by choirs such as those of King's College Chapel, Cambridge, and Christ Church Cathedral, Oxford, while other choirs such as the Roman Catholic Westminster Cathedral choir are also well known. There are many male-voice choirs in Wales and in certain parts of England.

The Leeds International Pianoforte Competition for young pianists is one of the most prestigious events in the musical calendar; and the biennial Cardiff Singer of the World Competition attracts outstanding young singers from all over the world.

Pop and Rock Music

Hundreds of hours of pop and rock music are broadcast through BBC and independent radio stations every week. Television programmes of both live and recorded music also feature pop and rock, which is by far the most popular form of music in Britain. It covers a diversity of styles, ranging from dance to heavy metal.

British groups continue to be popular throughout the world and are often at the forefront of new developments in music. Some of the more recent groups include the Spice Girls, Oasis, Blur, and Manic Street Preachers. Well-known performers include George Michael, Gabrielle, Annie Lennox and Paul Weller. In May 1997 the Spice Girls became the first British group for 15 years to top the US charts with a debut album. Worldwide sales of the album *Spice* have exceeded 12 million.

The pop and rock music industry contributes significantly to Britain's overseas earnings through the sale of recordings, concert tours, and promotional material, including clothing and books.

Britain's first National Centre for Popular Music is being built in Sheffield, with a National Lottery grant of £11 million. This interactive arts and education centre, celebrating the global influence of pop music, is expected to open in 1998.

Jazz

Jazz has a large and growing following in Britain and is played in numerous clubs and pubs, and increasingly in the leading concert halls. There is also a jazz radio station, Jazz FM, which broadcasts in London and in the north west of England. The London Jazz Festival attracts international stars, such as the bandleader Django Bates, saxophonists Pharoah Saunders and Joshua Redman, and the singer Jean Carn. British musicians such as Barbara Thompson, Stan Tracey, Julian

Joseph, David Jean Baptiste, Tommy Smith and Courtney Pine have established international reputations. Festivals of jazz music are held throughout Britain, including Brecon, Cardiff Bay, Edinburgh, Glasgow, Birmingham, Cheltenham and Bath.

Training

Professional training in music is given at universities and colleges of music, known as conservatoires. The leading London conservatoires are the Royal Academy of Music, the Royal College of Music, the Guildhall School of Music and Drama, and Trinity College of Music. Outside London the main conservatoires are the Royal Scottish Academy of Music and Drama in Glasgow, the Royal Northern College of Music in Manchester, the Welsh College of Music and Drama, Cardiff, and the Birmingham Conservatoire.

The City University's music industry course provides training in business practice aimed specifically at musicians and music administrators.

Other Educational Schemes

Many children learn to play musical instruments at school, and some take the examinations of the Associated Board of the Royal Schools of Music or Trinity College of Music. Music is one of the foundation subjects in the National Curriculum (see chapter 26), with a focus on creative music making. The national youth orchestras of Great Britain, Scotland, Ulster and Wales, and other youth orchestras have established high standards. Nearly a third of the players in the European Community Youth Orchestra come from Britain. There is also a National Youth Jazz Orchestra and a network of other youth jazz orchestras and wind bands around the country.

Youth and Music, an organisation affiliated to the international Jeunesses Musicales, offers subsidised tickets for young people to attend opera, dance and concert performances.

OPERA

Interest in opera has been growing markedly in Britain. In a recent survey[2] in 1996–97 over 3 million adults said they attended opera performances. A number of British singers— Thomas Allen, Anne Evans, Philip Langridge, Felicity Lott, Felicity Palmer and Bryn Terfel, for example—have now established themselves in the international opera houses.

Regular seasons of opera are held at the Royal Opera House, Covent Garden, London, although from July 1997 the Royal Opera House will be closed for two years for redevelopment. This is being done with the help of a National Lottery grant of £78 million, and during the two-year closure both the Royal Opera and the Royal Ballet will perform in a number of alternative venues in London.

English National Opera stages opera in English at the London Coliseum. Scottish Opera has regular seasons at the Theatre Royal in Glasgow, and tours mainly in Scotland and northern England. Welsh National Opera presents seasons in Cardiff and tours extensively in England and Wales. Music Theatre Wales has become well known for its contemporary work. Leeds-based Opera North tours mainly in the north of England and has gained an international reputation. The Almeida Opera in London develops much new work. English Touring Opera takes opera to towns throughout England. Opera Northern Ireland presents seasons at the Grand Opera House, Belfast, and tours the Province.

The National Opera Studio provides advanced training for young singers, seeking to bridge the gap between colleges and the profession.

An opera season for which international casts are specially assembled is held every summer at Glyndebourne in East Sussex. This is followed by an autumn tour by Glyndebourne Touring Opera, using casts drawn from the chorus of the festival season.

DANCE

An estimated 6 million people take part in dance, making it one of Britain's leading participatory

---

[2] Source: Target Group Index, BMRB International.

activities, and audiences are attracted to a widening range of professional dance.

Subsidised Dance Companies

Subsidised dance companies include the Royal Ballet and Birmingham Royal Ballet, English National Ballet, Northern Ballet Theatre and Rambert Dance Company, which rank among the world's leading companies and are supported by professional orchestras. Birmingham Royal Ballet tours widely in Britain and overseas; English National Ballet divides its performances between London and the regions; Northern Ballet Theatre is based in Leeds and also tours. Other subsidised companies include the Cardiff-based Diversions Dance Company and the Scottish Dance Theatre.

The Arts Councils also subsidise a wide range of other companies and dance organisations, including the Adzido Pan African Dance Ensemble, Shobana Jeyasingh Dance Company, Richard Alston Dance Company, and Dance Umbrella, which promotes an annual festival of contemporary dance in London. Matthew Bourne, Christopher Bruce, Richard Alston, Lloyd Newson, Ashley Page, Shobana Jeyasingh, Siobhan Davies and Jonathan Burrows are among the foremost British choreographers. Leading dancers include Darcey Bussell, Gill Clarke, Adam Cooper and Deborah Bull.

National Dance Agencies

A network of eight agencies for professional and community dancers has been established across England. The agencies, which receive Arts Council, Regional Arts Board and local authority funding, offer classes, provide information and advice, help to co-ordinate activities and commission dance artists to create work.

Training

Professional training for dancers and choreographers is provided mainly by specialist schools, which include the Royal Ballet School, the Central School of Ballet, the Northern School of Contemporary Dance (Leeds) and the London Contemporary Dance School; these, with many private schools, have helped to raise British dance to its present standard. Dance is a subject for degree studies at a number of institutions, including the Laban Centre (University of London), the University of Surrey, Dartington College of Arts in Devon and Middlesex University.

Other Educational Schemes

The Arts Council of England runs Taped, a scheme to finance dance videos for use in education, while the Video Place provides a library of videotape documentation of dance performances for viewing by promoters, choreographers, dancers, teachers and students. The Scottish Arts Council supports Dance Base, which offers a range of classes.

All government-funded dance companies provide dance workshops and education activities. Many have won awards for major projects, such as Phoenix Dance Company's 'Urban Exchange' and English National Ballet's 'Striking a Balance'. Ludus Dance Company, based in Lancaster, works mainly with young people.

The National Youth Dance Company provides opportunities for young dancers to work with professionals and to create and perform dance. Similar opportunities exist for young people to join youth dance companies throughout the country.

FILMS

The British film industry has recovered from its doldrums of the early 1980s, and by late 1996 cinema attendances and domestic film production were at their highest levels for over 20 years. Commercial successes like *Four Weddings and a Funeral*, *Trainspotting*, *Mrs Brown* and *The Full Monty* have helped to draw attention back to British films, which also continue to win a large share of awards at major international festivals and events. In 1996 more than £420 million was taken at the box office.

British films, actors, and producers as well as the creative and technical services supporting them are widely acclaimed. British performers who enjoy international reputations include Kenneth Branagh, Michael Caine, Sean Connery, Ralph Fiennes, Hugh Grant, Richard E Grant, Sir Anthony Hopkins, Jeremy Irons, Liam Neeson, Miranda Richardson, Alan Rickman, Greta Scacchi and Emma Thompson. Successful British directors include Alan Parker, Mike Newell, Sally Potter, Michael Radford, Ken Loach, Mike Leigh, whose film *Secrets and Lies* won the Palme d'Or at the 1996 Cannes Film Festival, and Anthony Minghella, who won the 1997 Oscar for best director with *The English Patient*.

There are about 2,200 cinema screens in Britain, and estimated attendances are currently running at about 2.5 million a week; cinema admissions have more than doubled (to 124 million a year) since 1984. In London and other large cities a number of art or repertory cinemas show films which have not been more widely distributed. These include films from Britain and abroad; other foreign films, often with English subtitles; and older films which are being shown again, sometimes in a newly edited form.

Animation

The resurgence of interest in animation in Britain is due in part to the pioneering work of British animators, who have created 3D animation and computer animation. British animations have won six Oscars for Best Animated Short Film in recent years, including David Fine and Alison Snowdon's *Bob's Birthday* in 1995 for Channel 4, Nick Park's *A Close Shave* (his third Oscar), in 1996, and Peter Law's *Wat's Pig* in 1997. Television has proved an important source of production finance.

Government Support

Government support for the British film industry has historically focused on promoting film as an art form rather than as an industrial process competing in a highly developed international market. The new Government has announced that it will concern itself increasingly with the economic development of the industry, helping it to become more competitive in the international market. In July 1997 it introduced a 100 per cent tax write-off on the production and acquisition costs for British films with budgets of up to £15 million.

An action plan to boost the film industry was announced in May 1997. The Government has set up a film policy review group consisting of leading figures from the film industry to formulate an agenda for action. The group will examine six areas:

- broadening the audience and improving access to good cinema;
- increasing the market share of British films;
- developing the skills and talents of those who wish to work in the audio–visual industry;
- improving the current financial and fiscal framework;
- promoting exports of films and marketing technical skills abroad; and
- assisting the work of the British Film Commission and the regional and local commissions (see p. 479) in attracting inward investment and film-making in their areas.

The group will aim to double the availability of British films to British audiences and encourage the film industry to achieve its creative and economic potential. A Minister for Film has been appointed to develop policy.

National Lottery Funding

As in other areas of the arts, the National Lottery has already made a huge impact on the film sector. By the end of June 1997, £90.5 million had already been allocated to 209 film-related projects. An award of £13.8 million went to the British Film Institute for the development of its National Film and Television Archive.

In May 1997 the Arts Council of England, supported by National Lottery funding of £92.2 million, awarded three new film franchises. The production companies, Pathé Productions, which includes producers responsible for *Gandhi* and *The Killing Fields*,

The Film Consortium, whose producers worked on *Land and Freedom* and *The Crying Game*, and DNA Film Ltd, formed by Duncan Kenworthy, the producer of *Four Weddings and a Funeral*, and Andrew MacDonald, the producer of *Trainspotting*, will receive funding which is designed to provide the financial security to plan ahead and the ability to maximise distribution. The franchises are expected to produce over 90 British films in the six-year period, with a possible total investment of £460 million.

Government Sponsorship in 1996

The Government supports a number of organisations which promote the film industry. Its largest grants go to the British Film Institute (see below) and to Scottish Screen (see p. 480). Major grants go to three other organisations:

The British Film Commission (BFC), launched in 1991, markets the British film and television production service industry to overseas production executives in order to attract inward investment. Productions helped by the BFC have contributed over £300 million to the British production industry and the British economy. (Government grant in 1996: £800,000.) Productions supported by the BFC include *Mission. Impossible*; *101 Dalmations*; *Saving Private Ryan*, and the forthcoming *New Star Wars*.

The BFC also works alongside the UK Film Commission Network, which currently comprises 24 area or city offices. The growth of this network over the past five years illustrates both the increase in production in Britain and the recognition by local and central government of the effectiveness of such organisations in stimulating increased production.

In 1996 the BFC helped to set up the London Film Commission, while the Northern Ireland Film Commission was launched in April 1997 as the successor to the Northern Ireland Film Council.

British Screen Finance, a private sector company, provides loan finance for new film-makers with commercially viable productions who have difficulty in attracting funding. Loans are for the production of low- and medium-budget films involving largely British talent. Total investment to date on 120 films is £45.5 million. (Government grant in 1996: £2 million.) Successful films supported by British Screen Finance include *The Crying Game* and *Orlando*.

The European Co-Production Fund offers loans of up to 30 per cent of a film's budget, enabling British producers to collaborate in the making of films in Europe. It has invested more than £13.2 million in 41 feature films, with a total value of more than £110.5 million. (Government grant in 1996: £2 million.) Successful films include the Oscar-winning *Antonia's Line* and *Damage*.

Reflecting its support for the trend of international co-productions, Britain has seven official bilateral co-production agreements (with Australia, Canada. France, Germany, Italy, New Zealand and Norway), and has ratified the Council of Europe Convention on Cinematographic Co-Production, which fosters further opportunities for European co-production.

British Film Institute

The development of film, video and television as art forms is promoted by the British Film Institute (BFI) and in Scotland by Scottish Screen.

The BFI runs the National Film Theatre in London and the National Film and Television Archive, which contains over 350,000 films and television programmes, including newsreels, animation, feature and short films dating from 1894. The BFI also has the world's largest library of information on film and television, holding extensive international collections of books, periodicals, scripts, stills and posters.

The BFI's activities on the South Bank comprise: the Museum of the Moving Image, which traces the history of film and television; the London IMAX cinema (see below); and the National Film Theatre. The last named has three cinemas showing films of historical, artistic or technical interest, and is unique in offering regular programmes unrestricted by commercial considerations. In 1996–97 about 2,000 films, television and video programmes were shown, attracting attendances of over 209,000. In November each year the BFI hosts the London Film Festival at the National

Film Theatre and in London's West End, at which some 250 new films from all over the world are screened. In 1996 over 107,000 people attended Festival screenings.

Building is in progress on the nine-storey London IMAX cinema, which will contain a 500-seat auditorium housing a seven-storey screen, making it the largest screen in Europe.

The BFI supports a network of regional film theatres across Britain, and gives grants to arts, media and film organisations through the Regional Arts Boards (see p. 468).

Scottish Screen

Scottish Screen was set up in April 1997, bringing together the functions of four existing film agencies: the Scottish Film Council, previously responsible for supporting regional film theatres, promoting and providing material for media education and administering the Scottish Film Archive; the Scottish Film Production Fund, offering financial assistance to develop film scripts; Scottish Screen Locations, providing advice to film-makers on suitable locations for film productions in Scotland; and Scottish Broadcast and Film Training. The new organisation has been restructured to take on an increased emphasis on production.

Children's Film

The Children's Film and Television Foundation produces and distributes entertainment films for children, shown largely through video and television.

The Children's Film Unit makes feature films for children (mainly for Channel 4) and runs weekly workshops for children on all aspects of film-making. The Unit caters for about 80 children at any time and has produced 15 feature films.

The Northern Ireland Film Council runs Cinemagic, an award-winning international film festival for young people.

Training in Film Production

The National Film and Television School is financed jointly by the Government and by the film, video and television industries. It offers postgraduate and short course training for directors, editors, camera operators, animators and other specialists. The School enrols about 30 full-time students a year and about 500 on short course programmes. In 1996–97 it received a government grant of £1.9 million. The School is planning to move from its present location in Buckinghamshire to the former BBC film studios in west London in 2000.

The London International Film School, the Royal College of Art, and some universities and other institutions of higher education also offer courses in film production.

Cinema Licensing and Film Classification

Cinemas showing films to the public must be licensed by local authorities, which have a legal duty to prohibit the admission of children to unsuitable films, and may prevent the showing of any film. In assessing films the authorities normally rely on the judgment of an independent non-statutory body, the British Board of Film Classification (BBFC), to which all films must be submitted. The Board was set up on the initiative of the cinema industry to ensure a proper standard in films shown to the public. It does not use any written code of censorship, but can require cuts to be made before granting a certificate; on rare occasions, it refuses a certificate.

Films passed by the Board are put into one of the following categories:

- U (universal)—suitable for all;
- PG (parental guidance), in which some scenes may be unsuitable for young children;
- 12, 15 and 18, for people of not less than those ages; and
- Restricted 18, for restricted showing only at premises to which no one under 18 is admitted—for example, licensed cinema clubs.

Videos

The BBFC is also legally responsible for classifying videos under a system similar to

Right: a young mother brings her 11-week-old son to a Bristol clinic in 1948 for his weekly check-up.

Below: a nurse gives a girl a faradaic current bath for flat feet, while the other girl has a sinusoidal footbath at an orthopaedic department (1948).

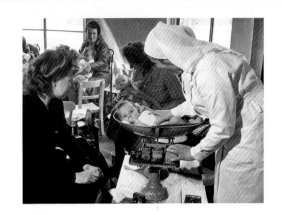

Children at Aylesford, Kent, visit a mobile clinic in 1949. It had a waiting room for six people, a surgery and a combined recovery room and laboratory.

Listening to a lecture at Florence Nightingale's first school for nurses at St Thomas' Hospital in London, on its 100th anniversary in 1960. Only 200 out of 2,000 applicants were chosen every year to train.

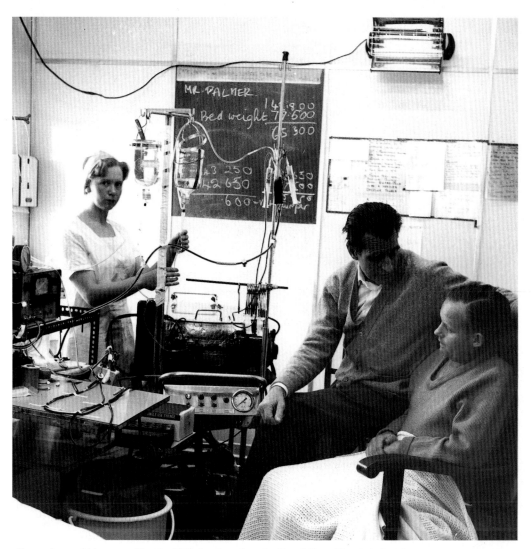

Above: A new kidney machine in 1963 developed at the Royal Free Hospital, London. It helped to save the lives of the two patients.

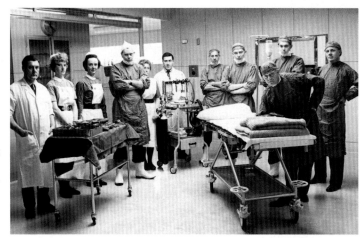

Right: The surgeons, doctors, technicians and nurses who made up the M1 Accident Unit of Luton and Dunstable Hospital, Bedfordshire, in 1964. The previous year, they had dealt with 1,200 road accident cases, many of them from the M1.

Above: a laboratory technician at the Monklands Hospital at Airdrie displays a culture sample of the E-coli 157 virus. As a result of an outbreak of E-coli 157 food poisoning in the Lanarkshire region of Scotland recently, ten people died and hundreds were made ill.

Left: The NHS is the largest purchaser in Britain of equipment and products for healthcare. A CAT scanner, shown here, produces three-dimensional computer-generated images, and is used extensively as a major diagnostic tool.

that for films. It is an offence to supply commercially a video which has not been classified or to supply it in contravention of its classification—for example, to sell or hire a video classified 18 to a person under 18.

MUSEUMS AND GALLERIES

About 110 million people a year, across all social groups, visit more than 2,500 museums and galleries open to the public, which include the major national collections, around 1,100 independent museums, and museums receiving support from local authorities.

Museums and galleries in Britain receive about £440 million a year in public expenditure. All national museums and galleries are financed chiefly from government funds; they may charge for entry to their permanent collections and special exhibitions. Most of the national collections are managed by independent trustees.

Museums and galleries maintained by local authorities, universities, independent museums and private funds may receive help in building up their collections through grants administered by the Museums and Galleries Commission (see below) and the museum councils in Scotland, Wales and Northern Ireland. Support to national and regional public and independent museums and galleries is also given by the Arts Councils and by trusts and voluntary bodies, including the Henry Moore Foundation, the Calouste Gulbenkian Foundation and the National Art Collections Fund.

The Museums and Galleries Commission promotes co-operation between national and regional museums and galleries and provides funds to the seven area museum councils, which supply a variety of services, advice, and their own small grants to individual museums.

Many National Lottery (see chapter 6) awards are being used to improve the infrastructure of the museums and galleries sector. By July 1997, 222 awards totalling more than £404 million had been granted in support of museum and gallery projects. Museum goers are already beginning to benefit: the first phase of the new Earth Galleries opened at the Natural History Museum in July 1996, and the Imperial War Museum's new American Air Museum at Duxford, Cambridgeshire, opened in August 1997.

The Museums and Galleries Commission administers a system whereby pre-eminent works of art may be accepted by the Government in settlement of inheritance tax and allocated to public galleries; items accepted in 1996–97 include: a Queen Anne longcase clock by Daniel Quare; furniture and lamps by Giacometti; and three 18th-century watercolours by Thomas Girtin.

The Government encourages the loan of objects from national and regional collections so that works of art can be seen by as wide a public as possible. The Arts Council of England is also broadening access to the national collections, through a National Collections Touring Scheme and the National Touring Exhibition Service.

British artists, photographers, architects and sculptors with international reputations include David Hockney, Lucian Freud, Howard Hodgkin, David Bailey, Jane Bown, Sir Richard Rogers, Sir Anthony Caro and Phillip King. Younger artists with a similar standing include Richard Deacon, Tony Cragg, Damien Hirst, Rachel Whiteread and Anish Kapoor. The work of these artists is shown in the independent galleries funded by the Arts Council of England: the Arnolfini in Bristol; the Ikon, Birmingham; the Museum of Modern Art, Oxford; and the Serpentine, London.

A review of museums policy in England, *Treasures in Trust*, was published in 1996. This provided a new framework for museums, with increased emphasis on care of collections, public participation and quality of service. It proposed that up to 30 non-national museums be designated as holding pre-eminent collections. Its recommendations are now being implemented. In June 1997 the new Government announced that 26 museums were so designated. They range from the National Tramway Museum in Derbyshire to the Ashmolean Museum in Oxford. A further 20 museums will be designated in 1998.

Overall 1995–96 saw a further increase in the number of visits to the national museums and galleries in England (see Table 28.2).

The Independent Museums Association, to which many museums and art galleries and their staffs belong, facilitates exchange of information and discussion of matters relating to museums and galleries. The Association, which has many overseas members, provides training, seminars and research; its publications include the monthly *Museums Journal* and a new technical periodical, *Museum Practice*.

The Museum Training Institute is responsible for developing training standards and programmes within museums.

National Collections

The national museums and art galleries, many of them located in London, contain some of the world's most comprehensive collections of objects of artistic, archaeological, scientific, historical and general interest. The English national museums are:

- the British Museum (including the ethnographic collections of the Museum of Mankind);
- the Natural History Museum;
- the Victoria and Albert Museum (the V&A, which displays fine and decorative arts);

- the National Museum of Science and Industry, including the Science Museum and its two regional institutes—the National Railway Museum (York) and the National Museum of Photography, Film and Television (Bradford);
- the National Gallery (which houses western painting from around 1260 to 1900);
- the Tate Gallery, with collections in London (British painting and modern art), Liverpool and St Ives (St Ives School and contemporary art);
- the National Portrait Gallery;
- the Imperial War Museum;
- the Royal Armouries;
- the National Army Museum;
- the Royal Air Force Museum;
- the National Maritime Museum;
- the Wallace Collection (which includes paintings, furniture, arms and armour, and objets d'art); and
- the National Museums and Galleries on Merseyside.

The Royal Armouries, Britain's oldest museum, has collections in the Tower of London (items relating to the Tower's history), Leeds (arms and armoury) and Fort

Table 28.2: Visits to National Museums and Galleries 1996–97 in England

	Number of visits *million*	percentage increase/ decrease over 1995–96
British Museum	6.8	+11.5
Imperial War Museum	1.3	−1.5
National Gallery	5.0	+11.1
National Maritime Museum	0.48	−17.2
National Museums and Galleries on Merseyside	1.22	−0.8
National Portrait Gallery	0.86	+4.9
Natural History Museum	1.80	+23.3
National Museum of Science and Industry	2.53	−6.4
Tate Gallery	2.48	−19.1
Victoria and Albert Museum	1.59	+3.2
Wallace Collection	0.18	+12.5
Royal Armouries	0.79	+229.1[a]

[a]Opened in 1995.
Source: Department for Culture, Media and Sport

Nelson, near Portsmouth (artillery). The Tate Gallery is to create Britain's first national museum of modern art, situated on the south bank of the Thames. Awarded £50 million by the Millennium Commission, the new museum will house a collection of 20th-century art of international importance and is expected to open in 2000. The Imperial War Museum, which has three sites in London and one in Cambridgeshire, plans to open a branch on the banks of the Manchester Ship Canal. The new museum will concentrate on social history since 1914 and is expected to open by 2002.

In Scotland the national collections are held by the National Museums of Scotland and the National Galleries of Scotland. The former include the Royal Museum of Scotland, the Scottish United Services Museum and the Scottish Agricultural Museum, in Edinburgh; the Museum of Flight, near North Berwick; and the Museum of Costume at Shambellie House near Dumfries. A new Museum of Scotland is being built next to the Royal Museum to house the National Museums' Scottish collection.

The National Galleries of Scotland comprise the National Gallery of Scotland, the Scottish National Portrait Gallery and the Scottish National Gallery of Modern Art. The National Galleries of Scotland also have collections at Paxton House near Berwick and Duff House in Banff.

In 1996–97 the National Museums of Scotland attracted 1.5 million visitors, and the National Galleries of Scotland some 1.6 million.

The National Museum of Wales, which has opened new galleries at its main building in Cardiff, has a number of branches, including the Museum of Welsh Life at St Fagans, the Welsh Slate Museum at Llanberis and the Industrial and Maritime Museum in Cardiff's Bay development.

From April 1998 Northern Ireland's three major museums—the Ulster Museum in Belfast; the Ulster Folk and Transport Museum in County Down; and the Ulster-American Folk Park in County Tyrone—will merge to form the National Museums of Northern Ireland.

Other Collections

Other important collections in London include the Museum of London; Sir John Soane's Museum; the Courtauld Institute Galleries; and the London Transport Museum. The Queen's Gallery in Buckingham Palace has exhibitions of pictures from the extensive royal collection.

Most cities and towns have museums devoted to art, archaeology and natural and local history, often administered by the local authorities but sometimes by local learned societies or by individuals or trustees. Many are associated with their universities, such as the Ashmolean Museum in Oxford and the Fitzwilliam Museum in Cambridge.

Many collections of art and antiques in historic family houses, including those owned by the two National Trusts (see p. 368) and English Heritage (see p. 367), are open to the public.

There are also a number of national art exhibiting societies, the most famous being the Royal Academy of Arts at Burlington House in London. The Academy holds an annual Summer Exhibition and other important exhibitions during the rest of the year. The Summer Exhibition is the world's largest open contemporary art exhibition and brings together a wide range of work by established artists and by others exhibiting for the first time. The Royal Scottish Academy holds annual exhibitions in Edinburgh. There are also children's exhibitions, including the National Exhibition of Children's Art. The Arts Council of England funds the National Touring Exhibitions Service organised by the Hayward Gallery, London, which draws on the Arts Council's major loan collection of modern and contemporary British art.

An increasing number of open air museums depict the regional life of an area or preserve early industrial remains. These include the Weald and Downland Museum in West Sussex, and the Ironbridge Gorge Museum in Shropshire. Skills of the past are revived in a number of 'living' museums, such as the Gladstone Pottery Museum near Stoke-on-Trent and the Quarry Bank Mill at Styal in Cheshire.

The Burrell Collection in Glasgow houses world-famous tapestries, paintings and objets d'art. The Design Museum in London's Docklands contains a collection of 20th-century mass-produced consumer objects.

Crafts

The crafts in Britain have an annual turnover estimated at £400 million. Government aid for the crafts, amounting to £3.2 million in 1997–98, is administered in England and Wales by the Crafts Council. The Council supports craftspeople by promoting public interest in their work, and encouraging the creation of works of contemporary craftsmanship. Grants are available to help with setting up workshops and acquiring equipment. The Crafts Council runs the National Centre for Crafts in London, organises the annual Chelsea Crafts Fair, and co-ordinates British groups at international trade fairs. Crafts Council exhibitions tour nationally and internationally, and grants are made to encourage exhibitions, projects and organisations. The Council has an Education Unit, which runs lectures, seminars and workshops for students, teachers and the public and provides research in crafts education. It also runs a bi-monthly magazine, *Crafts*.

Craftworks, an independent company, is the crafts development agency for Northern Ireland, providing training, marketing and business counselling for the crafts sector. The Arts Council of Northern Ireland also funds crafts promotion, as does the Scottish Office through the Scottish Arts Council.

Training in Art and Design

Most practical education in art and design is provided in the art colleges and fine and applied art departments of universities (these include the Slade School of Art and Goldsmith's College of Art, London); and in further education colleges and private art schools. Many of these institutions award degrees at postgraduate level. Art is also taught at an advanced level at the four Scottish Central (Art) Institutions.

Courses at universities concentrate largely on academic disciplines, such as the history of art. The leading institutions include the Courtauld and Warburg Institutes of the University of London and the Department of Classical Art and Archaeology at University College London. The Open University also offers courses in art history and theory of art. Art is one of the foundation subjects in the National Curriculum. The Society for Education through Art encourages, among other activities, the purchase by schools of original works of art by organising an annual Pictures for Schools exhibition.

The Open College of the Arts offers correspondence courses in art and design, painting, sculpture, textiles, photography and creative writing to people wishing to study at home.

Export Control of Works of Art

London is a major centre for the international art market, and sales of works of art take place in the main auction houses (two of the longest established being Sotheby's and Christie's), and through private dealers. Certain items are covered by export control; guidance is provided by the Export Licensing Unit of the Department for Culture, Media and Sport. A licence is required before such items can be exported, and if the Department's advisers object to the granting of a licence, the matter is referred to the Reviewing Committee on the Export of Works of Art. If the Committee considers a work to be of national importance, it can advise the Government to defer a decision on the licence application for a specified time to provide an opportunity for an offer to be made to buy at or above the recommended fair market price.

Objects saved for the nation in 1997 include: a 17th century painting, *Cup of Water and a Rose* by Zurbarán, acquired by the National Gallery; a Neolithic stone ball acquired by Aberdeen Museum; and an 18th-century gold box by G.M. Moser acquired by the Royal Museum of Scotland.

LITERATURE AND LIBRARIES

English literature is taught extensively at schools, colleges and universities throughout

Britain. Creative writing is also taught at a variety of institutions, one of the best known being the University of East Anglia, in Norwich. The University also houses the British Centre for Literary Translation. There are free public libraries throughout Britain (see p. 486), private libraries and several private literary societies.

Outstanding literary merit is recognised by a number of awards, some of the most valuable being the Booker and Whitbread prizes. The David Cohen British Literature Prize for a lifetime's achievement by a living writer was won by Muriel Spark in 1997. A part of the £40,000 prize, which is awarded every two years, enables winners to commission new works from younger writers. Other awards to encourage young authors include those of the Somerset Maugham Trust Fund and the E.C. Gregory Trust Fund.

Ulster-born poet Seamus Heaney was awarded the Nobel Prize for Literature in 1995. Other distinguished contemporary British poets include Ted Hughes (the Poet Laureate), James Berry, Gillian Clarke, Carol Ann Duffy, U.A. Fanthorpe, Tony Harrison, Geoffrey Hill, Elizabeth Jennings, R.S. Thomas and Carol Rumens. As the Poet Laureate, Ted Hughes is a member of the Royal Household and receives an annual stipend from the Civil List (see p. 55)

Many British writers are internationally recognised. Well-known living novelists, with examples of their works, include:

- Martin Amis: *London Fields*; *Money*; *The Information*;

- A.S. Byatt: *Still Life*; *Possession: A Romance*; *Babel Tower*;

- Julian Barnes: *Flaubert's Parrot*; *Love, Etc.*; *Cross Channel*;

- Kazuo Ishiguro: *An Artist of the Floating World*; *The Remains of the Day; The Unconsoled*; and

- Ruth Rendell: *Crocodile Bird*; *Demon in my View*; *Simisola*.

Many writers from overseas, often from Commonwealth countries, live and work in Britain, writing books in English which have a wide circulation in Britain and overseas.

Authors' Copyright and Performers' Protection

Original literary works (including computer programs and databases), and dramatic, musical or artistic works, films, sound recordings and broadcasts are automatically protected by copyright in Britain. This protection is also given to works from countries party to international copyright conventions. The copyright owner has rights against unauthorised reproduction, public performance, broadcasting and issue to the public of his or her work; and against dealing in unauthorised copies. In most cases the author is the first owner of the copyright, and the term of copyright in literary, dramatic, musical and artistic works is the life of the author and a period of 70 years after death. For films the term is 70 years from the last death among the following: principal director, authors of the screenplay and dialogue, or composer of music for the film. Sound recordings are protected for 50 years from the year of making or release, and broadcasts for 50 years from the year of broadcast.

Performers are also given automatic protection against broadcasting and recording of live performances, and reproduction of recordings. This lasts for 50 years from the year of performance or release of a recording of it. A new right against the extraction and re-utilisation of the contents of a database is to be introduced from 1 January 1998.

Literary and Philological Societies

Societies to promote literature include the English Association and the Royal Society of Literature. The leading society for studies in the humanities is the British Academy for the Promotion of Historical, Philosophical and Philological Studies (the British Academy).

Other specialist groups are the Early English Text Society, the Bibliographical Society and several others devoted to particular authors, the largest of which is the Dickens Fellowship. Various societies, such as the Poetry Society, sponsor poetry readings and recitals. London's South Bank Centre runs a programme of literary events.

Libraries

Public Libraries

Local authorities in Great Britain and education and library boards in Northern Ireland have a duty to provide a free lending and reference library service. There are 5,000 public libraries in Britain, nearly 700 libraries in higher and further education and over 3,000 specialised libraries in other organisations, as well as three national libraries (see p. 487). Altogether these employ some 42,500 people. A further 1,400 are employed in schools and 18,000 in the provision of electronic information. In England about 60 per cent of adults are members of their local library and about half of these borrow a least once a month.

The services that public libraries and the British Library supply provide important support to a range of business interests, from multi-national companies to individual entrepreneurs. Public libraries also offer individuals the opportunity to acquire new skills and knowledge, and by working with organisations such as TECs (see chapter 12, p. 175) can play an important part in the labour market.

Many libraries have collections of compact discs, records, audio- and video-cassettes, and musical scores for loan to the public, while a number also lend from collections of works of art, which may be originals or reproductions. Most libraries hold documents on local history, and nearly all provide children's departments, while reference and information sections and art, music, commercial and technical departments meet a growing demand. The information role is one of increasing importance for many libraries, and greater use is being made of information technology, including personal computers, CD-ROMs and reference databases.

The new Government has reaffirmed its commitment to the principle of public libraries providing free access to core services such as book lending and reference. In its review of the distribution of National Lottery proceeds (see chapter 6), it will examine the case for supporting activity in libraries as part of its policy to refocus the Lottery so that more people can feel its benefits. One of its first initiatives under the Lottery's New Opportunities Fund includes training and support for some 10,000 librarians in the effective use of information and communications technology.

The Government is advised by the Library and Information Commission, which is a forum for policy on library and information provision in general, and the Advisory Council on Libraries, which advises on public libraries in England. In June 1997 the new Government announced that the Commission's Working Group on Information Technology, established by the previous administration, would continue to report on how public libraries can respond effectively to the challenge of new information and communication technology.

A new challenge fund to develop library services has been set up: the Public Libraries Challenge Fund, run by the Department for Culture, Media and Sport and the Wolfson Foundation, will provide £6 million in 1997–98—£2 million from the Government and £1 million from the Wolfson Foundation, to be matched by a further £3 million from library authorities. Projects in the following categories are eligible for support:

- the development and application of information technology;
- the improvement of reference sections; and
- the renovation and refurbishment of library buildings.

The Library Association

The Library Association is the principal professional organisation for those engaged in library and information services. Founded in 1877, the Association has 26,000 members. It maintains a Register of Chartered Librarians and publishes books, pamphlets and an official journal.

The Library Association is the designated authority for the recognition of qualifications gained in other EU member states.

Public Lending Right Scheme

The Public Lending Right Scheme gives registered authors the right to receive payment from a central fund (totalling £4.9 million in 1997–98) for the loans made of their books from public libraries in Britain. Payment is made in proportion to the number of times the authors' books are lent out. The maximum payment an author can receive is £6,000.

The British Library

The British Library, the national library of Britain, is one of the world's greatest libraries, with a collection of more than 150 million separate items. These include books, journals, manuscripts, newspapers, stamps, maps and recorded sound. British publishers should deposit a copy of most of their output at the Library.

The Library's collection grows by about two shelf miles a year and consists of bequests, donations and purchases collected over a period of more than 200 years. It is also the guardian of treasures such as the Magna Carta and Shakespeare's First Folio. Some 450,000 reader visits are made to the Library each year. Some of the Library's reading rooms are open to all without formality; others are open to those who need to see material not readily available elsewhere or whose work or studies require the facilities of the national library; access to all reading rooms is free.

The Library's Document Supply Centre at Boston Spa (West Yorkshire) is the national centre for inter-library lending within Britain and between Britain and countries overseas. It dispatches over 4 million documents a year. The Research and Information Centre, based in London, is a major source of funding for research and development in library and information services.

A new building for the British Library has been constructed at St Pancras, London, at a cost of £511 million. The St Pancras building will offer, for the first time, a purpose-built home for Britain's national library with environmentally controlled storage, increased reader space and seating, and greatly improved public facilities, including three exhibition galleries, an auditorium and a bookshop. The Humanities Reading Room, the largest, will open in November 1997. Other reading rooms will open during 1998 and early 1999.

Other Libraries

The National Libraries of Scotland and Wales, the Bodleian Library of Oxford University and the Cambridge University Library can also claim copies of all new British publications under legal deposit. At the National Library of Scotland the second phase of a new building, accommodating a map library, lending services and the Scottish Science Library, was opened in May 1995. A major extension of the National Library of Wales was completed in the same year.

University and other Non-public Libraries

As well as public and national libraries there are over 600 libraries in higher and further education, about 5,600 school libraries and 2,220 specialised libraries within other public and private sector organisations (for example companies with research facilities and government departments).

The university libraries of Oxford and Cambridge are unmatched by those of the more recent foundations. However, the combined library resources of the colleges and institutions of the University of London total 9 million volumes, the John Rylands University Library of Manchester contains 3.5 million volumes, Edinburgh 2.5 million, Leeds 2.3 million, and Birmingham, Glasgow, Liverpool and Aberdeen each have over 1 million volumes. Many universities have important research collections in special subjects—the Barnes Medical Library at Birmingham and the British Library of Political and Economic Science at the London School of Economics, for example.

Besides a number of great private collections, such as that of the London Library, there are the libraries of the learned societies and institutions, such as the Royal Institute of International Affairs, the Royal Geographical Society and the Royal Academy of Music. The Poetry Library in the South Bank Centre, owned by the Arts Council of England, is a collection of 20th-century poetry written in or translated into English; the library houses about 60,000 volumes.

The Public Record Office in London and in Kew, Surrey, houses the records of the superior courts of law of England and Wales and of most government departments, as well as famous historical documents. The Office has many millions of documents, dating from the time of the Norman Conquest to the present day. Public records, with a few exceptions, are available for inspection by members of the public 30 years after the end of the year in which they were created. The Scottish Record Office in Edinburgh and the Public Record Office of Northern Ireland, Belfast, serve the same purpose.

Books

In 1996 British publishers issued about 100,000 separate titles. The British publishing industry devotes much effort to developing overseas markets, and in 1996 the estimated value of exports of British books amounted to over £1,100 million.

Among the leading organisations representing publishing and distribution interests are the Publishers Association, which has 200 members; and the Booksellers Association, with 3,300 members. The Publishers Association, through its International Division, promotes the export of British books. The Welsh Book Council supports the production of books in the Welsh language. The Book Trust encourages reading and the promotion of books through an information service and a children's library.

Historical Manuscripts

The Royal Commission on Historical Manuscripts locates, reports on, and gives information and advice about historical papers outside the public records. It also advises private owners, grant-awarding bodies, record offices, local authorities and the Government on the acquisition and maintenance of manuscripts. The Commission maintains the National Register of Archives (the central collecting point for information about British historical manuscripts) and the Manorial Documents Register, which are available to researchers.

Further Reading

Department of National Heritage Annual Report 1996. The Government's Expenditure Plans 1997–98 to 1999–2000. Cm 3611. The Stationery Office, 1997.

29 The Media

The media play a central role in daily life in Britain, informing and educating, questioning and challenging—and, of course, entertaining. Over 97 per cent of British households have at least one television set. People spend an average of 25 hours a week watching television and over 16 hours listening to the radio. Britain's newspapers and magazines, at national, regional and local level, offer readers greater diversity of content than in probably any other country in Europe.

Television and Radio

Broadcasting in Britain has traditionally been based on the principle that it is a public service accountable to the people. While retaining the essential public service element, it now also embraces the principles of competition and choice.

Three public bodies have the main responsibility for television and radio services. These authorities work to broad requirements and objectives defined or endorsed by Parliament, but are otherwise independent in their day-to-day conduct of business. They are:

- the BBC (British Broadcasting Corporation), which broadcasts television and radio programmes;

- the ITC (Independent Television Commission), which licenses and regulates commercial television services including cable and satellite services, whether delivered by digital or analogue technology; and

- the Radio Authority, which licenses and regulates commercial radio services, including cable and satellite.

The Department for Culture, Media and Sport (DCMS—which changed its name from the Department of National Heritage in July 1997) is responsible for overseeing the broadcasting system as a whole; the Secretary of State for Culture, Media and Sport is answerable to Parliament on broad policy questions.

Television

There are currently five terrestrial television channels offering a mixture of drama, light entertainment, films, sport, educational, children's and religious programmes, news and current affairs, and documentaries. The BBC provides two national networks which are financed almost wholly by a licence fee (see p. 492), while the ITC licenses and regulates three commercial terrestrial television services—ITV (Channel 3),

Channel 4 and Channel 5—which are funded by advertising and sponsorship. In Wales, S4C (Sianel Pedwar Cymru) broadcasts programmes on the fourth channel.

Satellite television and cable services, also licensed and regulated by the ITC, account for over 11 per cent of total viewing. Their main source of funding is subscription income.

Radio

In recent years there has been a proliferation of local and national radio stations. The BBC has five national networks, which together transmit all types of music, news, current affairs, drama, education, sport and a range of features programmes. There are three national commercial radio stations (see p. 496).

There are 38 BBC local radio stations serving England and the Channel Islands, and national regional radio services in Scotland, Wales and Northern Ireland, including Welsh and Gaelic language stations. About 200 independent local radio (ILR) services are also in operation. Stations supply local news and information, sport, music and other entertainment, education and consumer advice.

CHANGES IN REGULATION

Broadcasting in Britain has been undergoing radical change. The availability of more radio frequencies, together with satellite, cable and microwave transmissions, has already made a greater number of local, national and international services possible. The transition from analogue to digital transmission technology has the potential to expand this capacity enormously. Digital broadcasting is a new, more effective way of transmitting radio and television services. It allows much more information than before to be transmitted, and can offer many more channels, extra services, interactivity and higher quality picture and sound to viewers and listeners willing to invest in new receiving equipment.

Broadcasting Act 1996

In recognition of this potential, the Government passed legislation in 1996 setting out a flexible regulatory framework for the introduction of digital terrestrial broadcasting and paving the way for more broadly-based competitive media groups. There were four key objectives:

- to safeguard plurality of media ownership and diversity of viewpoint;

- to preserve Britain's unique tradition of public service broadcasting;

- to support the competitiveness of the British broadcasting industry and give Britain the opportunity to lead the world in the exploitation of digital technology; and

- to ensure broadcasters maintain appropriate standards of impartiality, taste and decency.

Digital Terrestrial Broadcasting

The 1996 Act provides for:

- the licensing of at least 18 national digital terrestrial television channels, transmitted on six frequency channels or 'multiplexes',[1] and serving, in the medium term, from 60 to over 90 per cent of the population; and

- the licensing of at least 12 digital radio services on two national multiplexes, with at least one multiplex available for local services in most areas of Britain, and an additional multiplex for extra local services in areas of greatest demand.

The Act guarantees capacity on three of the six digital television multiplexes and on one national radio multiplex for the existing public service broadcasters. This is to enable them to improve their services in the digital age and ensure that British broadcasting maintains its current standards of programming. The ITC and Radio Authority are both required to award national multiplex licences to those

---

[1]Through the process known as multiplexing, the signals of several broadcasters are combined into a single stream on a single-frequency channel. There is therefore no longer a direct one-to-one relationship between a television service and a frequency. The signals are finally received and decoded by digital receivers or set-top boxes attached to existing television sets.

applicants whose plans will best promote the development of digital broadcasting—by installing the new transmission network as quickly as possible, making consumer receiver equipment as affordable as possible, and broadening consumer choice of programming.[2]

The Government will review the take-up of digital receivers within five years into the first multiplex licence period, and at that point will determine whether it can set a date for switching off analogue television frequencies.

Many of the new services on digital television will be available on a subscription or pay-per-view basis. Any broadcaster wishing to offer pay-television needs to use a 'conditional access' system (covering encryption, scrambling and subscription management services) to ensure that only those who have paid for a particular service receive that service. Since any dominant provider of such systems would have the power to determine who can, or cannot, enter the pay-television market, it is important that providers are subject to effective regulation. The Government has implemented European Union regulations to ensure that all broadcasters can gain access on 'fair, reasonable and non-discriminatory terms' to any digital set-top boxes which can receive their signal. OFTEL (see p. 321) has powers to intervene over anti-competitive behaviour.

Media Ownership

Legislation in 1990 laid down rules enabling the ITC and Radio Authority to keep ownership of the broadcasting media widely spread and to prevent undue concentrations of single and cross-media ownership, in the wider public interest. A government review of ownership regulation issued in 1995 concluded that there was a continuing case for specific regulations beyond those which are applied by the general competition law. It said that the existing rules needed to be relaxed, both within and across different media sectors; this would reflect the needs and aspirations of

the industry against the background of accelerating technological change. Following on from those recommendations, the 1996 Act:

- allows greater cross-ownership between newspaper groups, television companies and radio stations, at both national and regional levels; and

- introduces 'public interest' criteria by which the regulatory authorities can assess and approve (or disallow) mergers or acquisitions between newspapers and television and radio companies.

The legislation removes the two-licence limit on the control of ITV (Channel 3) licences, replacing it by a television ownership limit of 15 per cent share of the total television audience. It also allows local newspapers with more than a 50 per cent share of their market to own a local radio station, providing at least one other independent local radio station is operating in that area.

Other Measures

The Act also introduced a number of other significant measures including:

- a new restricted television service licence, which allows specialist and community broadcasters to provide a service for a particular event or local area;

- provisions which prevent certain sporting events being shown exclusively on pay-per-view or subscription television without prior consent of the ITC;

- new power for the ITC to protect regional programming in the event of a merger or acquisition of an ITV (Channel 3) licence; and

- the creation of the Broadcasting Standards Commission (see p. 498).

THE BBC

A Royal Charter and Agreement govern the constitution, finances and obligations of the BBC. The Corporation's Board of Governors, including the Chairman, Vice-Chairman and a National Governor each for Scotland, Wales

---

[2]Licences to operate commercial digital television multiplexes were awarded by the ITC in June and July 1997. The Radio Authority will advertise commercial radio multiplex licences in 1998.

and Northern Ireland, is appointed by the Queen on the advice of the Government. The Board of Governors is ultimately responsible for all aspects of broadcasting by the BBC. The Governors appoint the Director-General, the Corporation's chief executive officer who heads the Executive Committee and Board of Management—the bodies in charge of the daily running of the Corporation.

The BBC has a regional structure throughout Britain. The three English regions—BBC North, BBC Midlands & East and BBC South—and BBC Scotland, BBC Wales and BBC Northern Ireland make programmes for their local audiences as well as contributing to the national network.

The National Broadcasting Councils for Scotland, Wales and Northern Ireland advise on the policy and content of television and radio programmes intended mainly for reception in their areas. Ten Regional Councils in England advise the Board of Governors on the needs and concerns of audiences.

BBC Charter and Agreement

In 1996 a new Royal Charter came into effect, enabling the BBC to continue as Britain's main public service broadcaster until 2006. The new Agreement between the BBC and the Secretary of State for Culture, Media and Sport, which runs concurrently with the Charter, formally establishes the Corporation's editorial independence in all matters of programme content, scheduling and management. It also provides for the licence fee to remain the chief source of finance for the BBC's public service activities until at least 2002.

The new Charter and Agreement maintain the BBC's essential characteristics as a public corporation; preserve its primary objectives of providing broadcasting services of information, education and entertainment; and reinforce the duties placed on the Governors to maintain programme standards and to ensure the Corporation's accountability to its audiences. They also allow for the development of the BBC's commercial activities, in partnership with the private sector, in Britain and abroad (although these must be funded, operated and accounted for separately from its licence-fee-funded services).

Finance

The domestic services of the BBC are financed predominantly by a licence fee. All households or premises with a television set must buy an annual licence (costing £91.50 for colour and £30.50 for black and white in 1997–98).

Licence income is supplemented by profits from BBC Worldwide commercial activities (see p. 499), such as television programme exports, sale of recordings, publications and other merchandise connected with BBC programmes, hire and sale of educational films, film library sales, and exhibitions based on programmes. The BBC World Service's radio broadcasting operations are financed by a grant-in-aid from the Foreign & Commonwealth Office, while BBC Worldwide Television is self-financing.

In early 1997 the BBC's transmission network was privatised, providing new funds for investment in digital television.

Reorganisation

In 1996 the BBC announced a radical reorganisation of its management structure in order to strengthen its existing channels and services and develop additional digital services for the licence-fee payer. The changes involve the separation of broadcasting (scheduling and commissioning) from production (television, radio and multimedia) and the creation of a single national and international news operation. Since April 1997 the new organisation has comprised six major components:

- BBC Broadcast, which schedules channels and commissions services for audiences in Britain and abroad;

- BBC Production, which develops the BBC's in-house radio and television production capability across all genres and media;

- BBC News, which is responsible for an integrated national and international news operation across the full range of BBC news and current affairs services;

- BBC Worldwide, which is responsible for generating income in Britain and abroad, and for the World Service;

- BBC Resources, which provides support facilities and expertise to BBC programme-makers and broadcasters; and

- the Corporate Centre, which provides strategic services to the BBC as a whole.

BBC Television

The BBC broadcasts around 20,000 hours of television each year on its two domestic channels to national and regional audiences:

- BBC 1 is the channel of broad appeal. In 1996–97 it broadcast over 1,000 hours of features, documentaries and current affairs programmes, together with nearly 1,000 hours of drama and entertainment, over 650 hours of sport and almost 400 of children's programmes.

- BBC 2 is the channel of innovation and flexibility. It caters for special audience interests, with a variety of programmes including documentaries, late-night comedy and leisure and lifestyle shows.

Programmes are made at, or acquired through, Television Centre in London and six major bases throughout Britain (Glasgow in Scotland, Cardiff in Wales, Belfast in Northern Ireland, and Birmingham, Bristol and Manchester in England). Or they are commissioned from independent producers—the BBC is obliged to make sure that at least 25 per cent of its original programming comes from the independent sector.

Education is a central component of the BBC's public service commitment. A wide range of educational programmes is broadcast for primary and secondary schools (over 90 per cent of which use BBC schools television), further education colleges and the Open University (see p. 453), while programmes for adults cover numeracy, literacy, language learning, health, work and vocational training. Books, pamphlets, computer software, and audio and video cassettes are produced to supplement the programmes. A night-time

> The BBC is developing plans for new digital television services to be available free-to-air on all digital delivery systems. These services, which will increase choice for licence-fee payers, will include an extended widescreen BBC 1 and BBC 2, extra digital TV services supplementing BBC 1 and BBC 2 output (BBC Choice), 24-hour television news, enhanced coverage and access to regional news and information (BBC Inform TV), and extensive opportunities for interactive learning in the school, workplace and home. In addition, from November 1997 there will be themed subscription services (operated by BBC Worldwide and Flextech and called UKTV) for those prepared to pay for them. These services will not be funded by the licence fee.

education and training service—The Learning Zone—was launched on BBC 2 in 1995, and the BBC provides specialist programming for further education colleges through FETV (Further Education TV).

BBC Network Radio

BBC Network Radio, broadcasting to the whole of Britain, serves an audience of 29 million each week, transmitting over 42,000 hours of programmes each year on its five networks:

- BBC Radio 1 is a leading contemporary music station (24 hours a day), serving a target audience of 15- to 24-year-olds. It plays top-selling, new and specialist music, covers live performances, social action campaigns and broadcasts music, documentaries and news programmes.

- BBC Radio 2 provides a 24-hour service of popular music (including folk, country, gospel, rhythm & blues, brass band, and light classics), comedy, arts and speech.

- BBC Radio 3 offers a wide repertoire of classical music and jazz, more than half of which is performed live or is specially recorded, together with drama, documentaries and discussion (also for 24 hours a day).

● BBC Radio 4 (broadcast with some differences on FM and Long Wave) has a backbone of authoritative news and current affairs coverage, complemented by drama, science, the arts, religion, natural history, medicine, finance and gardening; it also carries parliamentary coverage, cricket in season on Long Wave and BBC World Service (see p. 499) overnight.

● Radio 5 Live has news and sports coverage 24 hours a day.

INDEPENDENT BROADCASTING

Independent Television Commission

The ITC is responsible for licensing and regulating commercial television services operating in, or from, Britain. These include ITV (Channel 3), Channel 4, Channel 5, cable and other local delivery services, independent teletext services, and satellite services based in Britain or whose main establishment is in Britain. Under the provisions of the Broadcasting Act 1996, the ITC also has powers to license and regulate commercial digital terrestrial television and BBC commercial television services. The ITC does not make, broadcast or transmit programmes itself.

The ITC must see that a wide range of commercial television services is available throughout Britain and that they are of a high quality and appeal to a variety of tastes and interests. It must also ensure fair and effective competition in the provision of these services, and adherence to the rules on media ownership.

The ITC regulates the various television services through licence conditions, codes and guidelines. The codes cover programme content, advertising, sponsorship and technical standards. If a licensee does not comply with the conditions of its licence or the codes, the ITC can impose penalties. These range from a formal warning or a

requirement to broadcast an apology or correction, to a fine. In extreme circumstances, a company's licence may be shortened or revoked.

ITC staff regularly monitor programmes, and take into account comments from viewers and audience research. They are also advised by 11 Viewer Consultative Councils, and by committees on educational broadcasting, religious broadcasting, charitable appeals and advertising.

ITV (Channel 3)

The first regular ITV programmes began in London in 1955 (19 years after the BBC launched the world's first regular television service in 1936). ITV is made up of 15 regionally based television companies which are licensed to supply programmes in the 14 independent television geographical regions. There are two licences for London, one for weekdays and the other for the weekend. An additional ITC licensee provides a national breakfast-time service, transmitted on the ITV network.

The ITV licences for Channel 3 are awarded for a 10-year period by competitive tender to the highest bidder (who has to have passed a quality threshold). Licensees must provide a diverse programme service designed to appeal to a wide range of viewers' tastes and interests. They have a statutory duty to present programmes made in, and about, their region, and there is also a requirement for district and regional programming to be aimed at different areas within regions.

Each company plans the content of the programmes to be broadcast in its area. These are produced by the company itself, by other programme companies, or are bought from elsewhere. As with the BBC, at least 25 per cent of original programming must come from the independent sector. About one-third of the output is made up of informative programmes—news, documentaries, and coverage of current affairs, education and religion—while the remainder covers drama, entertainment, sport, arts and children's programmes. Programmes are broadcast 24 hours a day throughout the country. A common national and international news service is provided by Independent Television News (ITN).

Channel 3 companies are obliged to operate a national programme network. The ITV Network Centre, which is owned by the companies, independently commissions and schedules programmes.

Operating on a commercial basis, licensees derive most of their income from selling advertising time. Their financial resources and programme production vary considerably, depending largely on the population of the areas in which they operate. Newspaper groups can acquire a controlling interest in Channel 3 companies, although safeguards exist to ensure against any undue concentrations of media ownership (see p. 491).

Channel 4 and S4C

Channel 4, which began broadcasting in 1982, provides a national 24-hour television service throughout Britain, except in Wales, which has a corresponding service—S4C (Sianel Pedwar Cymru). Channel 4 is a statutory corporation, licensed and regulated by the ITC, and funded by selling its own advertising time.

Channel 4's remit is to provide programmes with a distinctive character and to appeal to tastes and interests not generally catered for by Channel 3. It must present a suitable proportion of educational programmes and encourage innovation and experiment. Channel 4 commissions programmes from the ITV companies and independent producers and buys programmes from overseas.

The fourth channel in Wales is allocated to S4C, which is regulated by the Welsh Fourth Channel Authority. Members of the Welsh Authority are appointed by the Government. S4C must ensure that a significant proportion of programming—particularly between 18.30 and 22.00 hours—is in the Welsh language. At other times S4C transmits national Channel 4 programmes. Like Channel 4, S4C sells its own advertising. Roughly 10 per cent of its income comes from this source, with the remainder coming from a government grant, the level of which is fixed in statute.

Channel 5

Britain's newest national terrestrial channel went live in March 1997, its 10-year licence having been awarded by competitive tender to Channel 5 Broadcasting Limited. Channel 5 serves about 70 per cent of the population.

Before the service went on air, the licensee had to make arrangements to re-tune domestic equipment such as video recorders and satellite receivers to eliminate interference caused by the new channel's transmissions. This operation affected between four and five million homes and the licensee was required to carry it out at no cost to the viewer.

Like Channel 3, the new service is subject to positive programming requirements. It must show programmes of quality and diversity, with a wide range of original productions and commissions from independent producers. The new channel is supported by advertising revenue.

Gaelic Broadcasting Fund

The Gaelic Broadcasting Committee is an independent body committed to ensuring that a wide range of quality television and radio programmes is broadcast in Gaelic for reception in Scotland. Its members are appointed by the ITC, in consultation with the Radio Authority. The Committee distributes government money to programme makers through the Gaelic Broadcasting Fund. Gaelic television programmes funded in this way have been transmitted since 1993. The Fund was extended to radio from April 1997.

The Radio Authority

The Radio Authority's licensing and regulatory remit covers all independent radio services, including national, local, cable and satellite services. Its three main tasks are to plan frequencies, appoint licensees with a view to broadening listener choice, and regulate programming and advertising.

Like the ITC, the Radio Authority has to make sure that licensed services are of a high quality, and offer programmes which will appeal to many different tastes and interests. It has published codes covering engineering, programmes, news and current affairs, and advertising and sponsorship, to which licensees must adhere.

Independent National Radio (INR)

There are three independent national radio services (licences having been awarded by the Radio Authority through competitive tender), which all broadcast 24 hours a day:

- Classic FM, which broadcasts mainly classical music, together with news and information;

- Virgin 1215, which plays broad-based rock music (and is supplemented by a separate Virgin station which operates under a local London licence); and

- Talk Radio UK, which is a speech-based service.

Independent Local Radio (ILR)

Independent local radio stations have been broadcasting in Britain since 1973. ILR stations broadcast a wide variety of programmes and news of local interest, as well as music and entertainment, traffic reports and advertising. There are also stations serving ethnic minority communities. The Radio Authority awards independent local licences, although not by competitive tender; the success of licence applications is in part determined by the extent to which applicants widen choice and meet the needs and interests of the people living in the area and in part by whether they have the necessary financial resources to sustain programme plans for the eight-year licence period.

Some of the locations for stations have been selected with small-scale radio in mind. As part of its brief to develop a wide range of radio services, the Authority is licensing a number of more specialist stations.

The Authority also issues restricted service licences (RSLs)—short-term RSLs, generally for periods of up to 28 days, for special events or trial services, and long-term RSLs, primarily for student and hospital stations, to broadcast to specific establishments.

TELETEXT, CABLE AND SATELLITE SERVICES

Teletext Services

The BBC and independent television each operate a teletext service, offering constantly updated information on a variety of subjects, including news, sport, travel, weather conditions and entertainment. The teletext system allows the television signal to carry additional information which can be selected and displayed as 'pages' of text and graphics on receivers equipped with the necessary decoders. The BBC and Channels 3, 4 and 5 provide subtitling for people with hearing difficulties.

The ITC awards teletext licences in Channels 3,4, and 5 by competitive tender for a period of ten years. Applicants have to satisfy certain statutory requirements before their cash bid can be considered.

Cable Services

Cable services are delivered to consumers through underground cables and are paid for by subscription. The franchising of cable systems and the regulation of cable television services are carried out by the Programmes and Cable Division of the ITC, while the Radio Authority issues cable radio licences.

'Broadband cable' systems can carry between 30 and 65 television channels using analogue technology (including terrestrial broadcasts, satellite television and channels delivered to cable operators by landline or videotape), as well as a full range of telecommunications services. Digital technology is being introduced which will support up to 500 television channels. Interactive services such as video-on-demand, home shopping, home banking, security and alarm services, electronic mail and high-speed Internet access (see p. 507) are also possible on cable and trials are being carried out in some locations. Cable can additionally supply television services tailored specifically for local communities; cable operators are testing varying programming concepts to find out what works best at the local level.

Cable franchises have been granted covering areas which include 80 per cent of all homes and nearly all urban areas in Britain. Regulation is as light as possible to encourage the development of a wide range of services, and flexible enough to adapt to new technology. The ITC awards only one broadband cable franchise in each area. In mid-1997 there were about 9.5 million homes able to receive broadband cable services and nearly 2.75 million subscribing homes.

ITC licences are required for systems capable of serving more than 1,000 homes. They are awarded for each area on the basis of competitive tendering. Systems extending beyond a single building and up to 1,000 homes require only an individual licence from OFTEL. Cable investment must be privately financed.

There are no specific quality controls on cable services. However, if cable operators also provide their own programme content as opposed to just conveying services, they require a programme services licence from the ITC, which includes consumer protection requirements.

Direct Broadcasting by Satellite

Direct broadcasting by satellite (DBS), by which television is transmitted directly by satellite into people's homes, has been available throughout Britain since 1989. The signals from satellite broadcasting are received through specially designed aerials or 'dishes'. Most services are paid for by subscription.

Many British-based satellite television channels have been set up to supply programmes to cable operators and viewers with dishes in Britain and, in some cases, throughout Europe. Some offer general entertainment, while others concentrate on specific areas of interest, such as sport, music, children's programmes, and feature films.

Over 30 English language channels were available to viewers with standard satellite dishes at the end of 1996. The ITC also licenses a number of foreign language services, some of them designed for ethnic minorities within Britain and others aimed primarily at audiences in other countries. Viewers in Britain may also receive a variety of television services from other European countries. The largest satellite programmer is BSkyB (British Sky Broadcasting) which, with over 5 million subscribers, dominates paid-for television in Britain.

Satellite services must comply with the ITC's programmes, advertising and sponsorship codes, but they are not subject to any positive programming obligations.

Satellite radio services must be licensed by the Radio Authority if they are transmitted from Britain for general reception within the country, or if they are transmitted from outside Britain but are managed editorially from within it.

OTHER ASPECTS

Advertising and Sponsorship

The BBC may not obtain revenue from broadcasting advertisements or from commercial sponsorship of programmes on its public service channels. Its policy is to avoid giving publicity to any firm or organised interest except when this is necessary in providing effective and informative programmes. It does, however, cover sponsored sporting and artistic events. Advertising and sponsorship are allowed on commercial television and radio services, subject to controls. The ITC and the Radio Authority operate codes governing advertising standards and programme sponsorship, and can impose penalties on broadcasters failing to comply with them.

Advertisements on independent television and radio are broadcast between programmes as well as in breaks during programmes. Advertisers are not allowed to influence programme content. Advertisements must be distinct and separate from programmes. Advertising on terrestrial television is limited to an average of seven minutes an hour during the day and seven and a half minutes in the peak evening viewing period. Advertising is prohibited in broadcasts of religious services and in broadcasts to schools. Political advertising and advertisements for betting (other than the National Lottery, the football pools and bingo) are prohibited. All tobacco advertising is banned on television and cigarette advertisements are banned on radio. Religious advertisements may be broadcast on commercial radio and television, provided they comply with the guidelines issued by the ITC and the Radio Authority.

Sponsorship in Independent Broadcasting

In Britain sponsorship is a relatively new way of helping to finance commercial broadcasting, although the practice has long been established in other countries. In return for their financial contribution, sponsors receive a credit associating them with a particular programme.

The ITC's Code of Programme Sponsorship and the Radio Authority's Advertising and Sponsorship Code aim to ensure that sponsors do not exert influence on the editorial content of programmes and that sponsorships are made clear to viewers and listeners. News and current affairs programmes may not be sponsored. Potential sponsors for other categories of programme may be debarred if their involvement could constrain the editorial independence of the programme maker in any way. References to sponsors or their products must be confined to the beginning and end of a programme and around commercial breaks; they must not appear in the programme itself. All commercial radio programmes other than news bulletins may be sponsored.

Government Publicity

Government publicity material to support non-political campaigns may be broadcast on independent television and radio. This is paid for on a normal commercial basis. Short public service items, concerning health, safety and welfare, are transmitted free by the BBC and independent television and radio. All government advertisements and public service information films are subtitled via electronic text to support people with hearing difficulties.

Broadcasting Standards

The independence enjoyed by the broadcasting authorities carries with it certain obligations over programme content. Broadcasters must display, as far as possible, a proper balance and wide range of subject matter, impartiality in matters of controversy and accuracy in news coverage, and must not offend against good taste. Broadcasters must also comply with legislation relating to obscenity and incitement to racial hatred.

The BBC, the ITC and the Radio Authority apply codes providing rules on impartiality, the portrayal of violence and standards of taste and decency in programmes, particularly during hours when children are likely to be viewing or listening. By convention, television programmes broadcast before 21.00 hours (or 20.00 hours on certain cable and satellite services) are expected to be suitable for a general audience, including children.

Complaints can be made to the regulators, including the BBC, which opened its own Programme Complaints Unit in 1994 to investigate serious complaints about BBC television or radio programmes.

Broadcasting Standards Commission (BSC)

In April 1997 the Broadcasting Standards Commission (BSC) was set up, replacing the Broadcasting Standards Council and the Broadcasting Complaints Commission, and combining their functions. The BSC is required to:

- draw up and review guidance for the avoidance of unjust or unfair treatment and unwarranted infringement of privacy in television and radio;

- draw up and review a code on the portrayal of violence and sexual conduct and on standards of taste and decency (which television and radio broadcasters would have to take into account when drawing up their own guidelines);

- monitor and report on the portrayal of violence, sexual conduct and standards of taste and decency in programmes generally;

- consider and adjudicate on complaints about fairness and standards;

- represent the Government at international bodies concerned with setting standards for broadcasting; and

- make arrangements for undertaking research into matters related to, or connected with, fairness and taste and decency in broadcasting.

Parliamentary and Political Broadcasting

The proceedings of both Houses of Parliament may be broadcast on television and radio, either live or, more usually, in recorded and edited form on news and current affairs programmes. The BBC has a specific Charter and Agreement obligation to transmit an impartial account day by day of the proceedings in both Houses of Parliament.

The BBC and some of the commercial services provide time on national radio and television for an annual series of party political broadcasts. Party election broadcasts are arranged following the announcement of a General Election. In addition, the Government may make ministerial broadcasts on radio and television, with opposition parties also being allotted broadcast time.

Audience Research

Both the BBC and the commercial sector are required to keep themselves informed on the state of public opinion about the programmes and advertising that they broadcast. This is done through the continuous measurement of the size and composition of audiences and their opinions of programmes. For television, this work is undertaken through BARB (the Broadcasters' Audience Research Board),

owned jointly by the BBC and the ITV Network Centre. For radio, joint research is undertaken for BBC radio and for commercial radio by RAJAR (Radio Joint Audience Research).

Both the BBC and the commercial sector conduct regular surveys of audience opinion on television and radio services. Public opinion is further assessed by the BBC and ITC through the work of their advisory committees, councils and panels.

INTERNATIONAL SERVICES

BBC Worldwide

In 1994 the international and commercial interests of the BBC were brought together in BBC Worldwide, to enable the BBC to develop its role in the fast-expanding broadcast and media world. BBC Worldwide comprises BBC World Service Radio, funded by a government grant, and BBC Worldwide Limited.

World Service

BBC World Service broadcasts by radio in English and 45 other languages worldwide. It has a global weekly audience of at least 140 million listeners. This excludes any estimate for listeners in countries where it is difficult to survey audiences. The core programming of news, current affairs, business and sports reports is complemented by a wide range of cultural programmes, including drama, literature and music.

BBC World Service programmes in English and many other languages are made available by satellite for rebroadcasting by agreement with local or national radio stations, networks and cable operators. BBC World Service Radio International sells recorded programmes to other broadcasters in over 100 countries.

BBC Monitoring, the international media monitoring arm of BBC World Service, provides transcripts of radio and television broadcasts from over 140 countries. As well as providing a vital source of information to the BBC, this service is also used by other media organisations, government departments, the commercial sector and academic institutions.

Worldwide Limited

With responsibility for the BBC's commercial television activity, BBC Worldwide Television is a major international broadcaster and a leading distributor and co-producer of BBC programmes.

In 1996–97 BBC Worldwide Television licensed more than 27,000 hours of programming to 550 broadcasters in 69 countries, making the BBC the largest European exporter of television programmes. Notable recent successes have been *Pride and Prejudice*, *People's Century* and *Dancing in the Streets*.

BBC Worldwide works closely with BBC production departments, independent producers and its network of international offices to determine commercial strategies for key programmes with international licensing potential. It is also developing premium channels to compete in the international marketplace. Its core service is BBC World, an advertiser-funded, 24-hour international news and information channel. The channel provides news bulletins, in-depth analysis and reports, and is available to over 50 million homes around the world. BBC Prime, an entertainment and drama channel for Europe, has 5 million subscribers.

BBC Worldwide also operates a large-scale publishing and licensing operation covering magazines, books, video, audio sales, CD-Roms and a commercial on-line service.

Foreign & Commonwealth Office

British Satellite News is an international satellite news service, produced by WTN (Worldwide Television News) for the Foreign & Commonwealth Office. The service, under FCO editorial control, transmits programmes five days a week. These are distributed, either by satellite or on hard copy compilations, free to television stations throughout Eastern Europe, the Middle East, Latin America and Asia for use in news bulletins.

London Radio Services, also produced through WTN, provides daily radio bulletins in English, Spanish and Arabic for overseas distribution by ISDN line and satellite. There are also a number of radio magazine programmes available on tape in several languages. London Television Services is the marketing arm of the FCO, distributing the television programmes and videos produced by the Department. These include *UK Today*, *Inside Britain*, *Perspective* and many special productions on topical subjects.

International Relations

European Agreements

Britain has implemented two important European agreements on cross-border broadcasting: the European Community Broadcasting Directive (which was revised in 1997) and the Council of Europe Convention on Transfrontier Television. Under these, countries have to allow the retransmission of programmes originating from other participating countries. They must also ensure that their own broadcasters observe certain minimum standards on advertising, sponsorship, taste and decency and the portrayal of sex and violence on television. The revised Directive also provides Community-wide protection for national measures securing public access to major events on free-to-air television.

Audiovisual Eureka (AVE), which has a membership of 33 European countries including Britain, aims to help improve aspects of the European audiovisual industry through practical measures to enhance training, development and distribution. It concentrates its work on the countries of Central and Eastern Europe. Another important task of AVE has also been to establish an Audiovisual Observatory based in Strasbourg which collects, disseminates and standardises European audiovisual data for the industry.

Britain plays an active part in the European Community MEDIA II programme. The programme (which succeeded MEDIA I on 1 January 1996) is aimed at enhancing the strength of member states' national audiovisual industries by encouraging greater collaboration between them and wider distribution of their products.

European Broadcasting Union

The BBC and the Radio Authority are members of the European Broadcasting Union, which manages Eurovision, the international network of television news and programme exchange. The Union is responsible for co-ordinating the exchange of programmes and news over the Eurovision network and intercontinental satellite links. It provides a forum linking the major public services and national broadcasters of Western Europe and other parts of the world, and co-ordinates joint operations in radio and television.

The Press

More daily newspapers, national and regional, are sold for every person in Britain than in most other developed countries. On an average day nearly 60 per cent of people over the age of 15 read a national morning newspaper; over 65 per cent read a Sunday newspaper. Around 90 per cent of people read a regional or local newspaper.

National papers have an average total circulation of over 13 million on weekdays and 15 million on Sundays, although the total readership is considerably greater. Men are more likely to read newspapers than women, and more people in the 25–44 age group read a daily newspaper than in any other age group.

There are about 1,400 regional and local newspaper titles and over 6,500 periodical publications.

Several newspapers have had very long and distinguished histories. *The Observer*, for example, first published in 1791, is the oldest national Sunday newspaper in the world, and *The Times*, Britain's oldest daily national newspaper, began publication in 1785.

The press caters for a range of political views, interests and levels of education. Newspapers are almost always financially independent of any political party. Where they express pronounced views and show obvious political leanings in their editorial comments, these may derive from proprietorial and other non–party influences. Nevertheless, during general election campaigns many newspapers recommend their readers to vote for a particular political party. Even newspapers which adopt strong political views in their editorial columns sometimes include feature and other types of articles by authors of different political persuasions.

In order to preserve their character and traditions, some newspapers and periodicals are governed by trustee–type arrangements. Others have management arrangements that try to ensure their editors' authority and independence.

In recent years working practices throughout the newspaper industry have undergone major changes in response to the challenges posed by computer–based technology and the need to contain costs.

Newsprint, more than half of which is imported, forms about a quarter of average national newspaper costs; labour represents over half. In addition to sales revenue, newspapers and periodicals earn considerable amounts from their advertising. Indeed, the press (including newspapers, magazines and directories) is by far the largest advertising medium in Britain. Unlike most of its European counterparts the British press receives no subsidies and relatively few tax and postal concessions.

NATIONAL AND REGIONAL TITLES

Ownership of the national, London and many regional daily newspapers lies in the hands of a number of large corporations, most of which are involved in the whole field of publishing and communications.

The National Press

The national press consists of 10 morning daily papers and 9 Sunday papers (see Table 29.1). At one time London's Fleet Street was the centre of the newspaper industry, but now all the national papers have moved their editorial and printing facilities to other parts of London or away from the capital altogether. Editions of several papers, for example the *Financial Times* and *The Guardian*, are also printed in other countries.

National newspapers are often described as 'quality', 'mid-market' or 'popular' papers on the basis of differences in style and content. Five dailies and four Sundays are usually described as 'quality' newspapers, which are directed at readers who want full information on a wide range of public matters. Popular newspapers appeal to people wanting news of a more entertaining character, presented more concisely. 'Mid-market' publications cover the intermediate market. Quality papers are normally broadsheet (large-sheet) in format and mid-market and popular papers tabloid (small-sheet).

Many newspapers are printed in colour and most produce colour supplements as part of the Saturday or Sunday paper, with articles on travel, food and wine, and other leisure topics.

Regional Newspapers

Most towns and cities throughout Britain have their own regional or local newspaper. These range from morning and evening dailies to Sunday papers and others which are published just once or twice a week. They mainly include stories of regional or local attraction, but the dailies also cover national and international news, often looked at from a local viewpoint. They also provide a valuable medium for local advertising.

England

Examples of the top regional daily newspapers by circulation in England include the *Express & Star* (197,500) in the West Midlands, Birmingham's *Evening Mail* (191,700), *Manchester Evening News* (171,500), and *Liverpool Echo* (159,700). Of the bigger regional Sunday papers, the *Sunday Mercury* in Birmingham sells 145,000 copies and the *Sunday Sun* in Newcastle upon Tyne sells 119,000.

Table 29.1: National Newspapers

Title and foundation date	Controlled by	Circulation average February–July 1997[a]
Dailies		
'Populars'		
Mirror (1903)	Mirror Group plc	2,355,285
Daily Star (1978)	United News & Media plc	741,220
The Sun (1964)	News International plc	3,875,329
'Mid market'		
Daily Mail (1896)	Daily Mail & General Trust plc	2,163,676
Express (1900)	United News & Media plc	1,227,971
'Qualities'		
Financial Times (1888)	Pearson	316,578
The Daily Telegraph (1855)	Telegraph Group Ltd	1,117,439
The Guardian (1821)	Guardian Media Group plc	407,870
The Independent (1986)	Mirror Group Consortium	257,594
The Times (1785)	News International plc	747,054
Sundays		
'Populars'		
News of the World (1843)	News International plc	4,434,856
Sunday Mirror (1963)	Mirror Group plc	2,268,263
The People (1881)	Mirror Group plc	1,932,237
'Mid market'		
The Mail on Sunday (1982)	Daily Mail & General Trust plc	2,137,872
Express on Sunday (1918)	United News & Media plc	1,159,759
'Qualities'		
Sunday Telegraph (1961)	Telegraph Group Ltd	886,337
The Independent on Sunday (1990)	Mirror Group Consortium	275,078
The Observer (1791)	Guardian Media Group plc	450,831
The Sunday Times (1822)	News International plc	1,314,576

[a]Circulation figures are those of the Audit Bureau of Circulations (consisting of publishers, advertisers and advertising agencies) and are certified average daily or weekly net sales for the period.

London has one paid-for evening paper, the *Evening Standard*, with a circulation of about 435,000. It provides Londoners with news and features covering events in the capital and of national and international interest. There are local weekly papers for every district in Greater London; these are often different local editions of one centrally published paper.

Wales

The daily morning paper, the *Western Mail*, which is published in Cardiff, circulates throughout Wales (60,300), as does *Wales on Sunday* (57,400). Many others give more local coverage of Welsh events, and the weekly press includes Welsh-language and bilingual papers. Welsh community newspapers receive an annual grant as part of the Government's wider financial support for the Welsh language.

Scotland

Daily morning papers, with circulations ranging up to around 700,000, include the *Daily Record* (sister paper of the *Mirror*), the *Scotsman* (published in Edinburgh), the *Herald*, (published in Glasgow), the *Dundee Courier and Advertiser* and the *Aberdeen Press and Journal*. Daily evening papers, with circulations up to 138,000, include the Edinburgh *Evening News*, Glasgow's *Evening Times*, Dundee's *Evening Telegraph* and Aberdeen's *Evening Express*. The Sunday papers are the *Sunday Mail*, the *Sunday Post* and a quality broadsheet paper, *Scotland on Sunday*.

Northern Ireland

Northern Ireland has two morning newspapers, one evening and two Sunday papers, all published in Belfast, with circulations ranging from about 46,000 to 137,000. They are the *News Letter* (unionist), the *Irish News* (nationalist), the evening *Belfast Telegraph*, *Sunday Life* and *Sunday World* (Northern Ireland edition). There are just over 50 weeklies. Newspapers from the Irish Republic, as well as the British national press, are widely read in Northern Ireland.

Free Distribution Newspapers

Several hundred free distribution newspapers, mostly weekly and financed by advertising, are published in Britain. They have enjoyed rapid growth in recent years.

Ethnic Minority Publications

Many newspapers and magazines in Britain are produced by members of ethnic minorities. Most are published weekly, fortnightly or monthly. A Chinese newspaper, *Sing Tao*, the Urdu *Daily Jang* and the Arabic *Al-Arab*, however, are dailies.

Afro-Caribbean newspapers include the *Gleaner* and *West Indian Digest*. The *Voice* and *Caribbean Times*, both weeklies, are aimed at the black population in general. *The Weekly Journal*, launched in 1992, is the first 'quality' broadsheet aimed at Britain's black community.

The *Asian Times* is an English language weekly for people of Asian descent; the *Sikh Courier* is produced quarterly. Examples of ethnic language newspapers include the Urdu *Daily Jang*, and the weeklies *Garavi Gujarat* and *Gujarat Samachar*. Publications also appear in Bengali, Hindi and Punjabi. The fortnightly *Asian Trader* and *Asian Business* are both successful ethnic business publications, while *Cineblitz International* targets those interested in the Asian film industry.

Many provincial papers print special editions for their local ethnic minority populations.

THE PERIODICAL PRESS

There are about 6,500 separate periodical publications which carry advertising. They are generally defined as either 'consumer' titles, providing readers with leisure-time information and entertainment, or 'business and professional' titles, which provide people with material of relevance to their working lives. Within the former category, there are general consumer titles, which have a wide appeal, and consumer specialist titles, aimed specifically at groups of people with particular interests, such as motoring or classical music. A range of literary and political journals, appearing monthly or quarterly, cater for a more academic readership. There are also many in-house and customer magazines produced by businesses or public services for their employees and/or clients.

The weekly periodicals with the highest sales are those which carry full details of the forthcoming week's television and radio programmes, including satellite schedules. *What's on TV*, *Radio Times* and *TV Times* each have circulations in excess of 1 million. *Reader's Digest*, which covers just about any subject, has the highest circulation (1.5 million) among monthly magazines.

Women's magazines also traditionally enjoy large readerships. The top-selling title is *Take a Break* with a weekly circulation of around 1.4 million. Old favourites like *Woman's Weekly*, *Woman's Own*, *Woman*, *Woman's Realm* and *My Weekly* have circulations ranging from 250,000 to over 800,000. Several women's magazines owned by overseas publishing houses have attracted large followings; *Prima* and *Best*, for instance, each sell over 500,000 copies, while *Bella* and *Hello!* are also widely read.

> A recent phenomenon has been the upsurge in the market for men's general interest magazines—for example, *FHM*, *Loaded*, *Sky Magazine*, *GQ*, *Men's Health* and *Maxim*. Circulations range from about 149,000 to 365,000.

Children are well served with an array of comics and papers, while magazines like *Smash Hits*, *Sugar*, *Top of the Pops* and *Bliss*, with their coverage of the pop music scene and features of interest to young people, are very popular with teenagers.

Leading journals of opinion include the *Economist*, an authoritative, independent commentator on national and international affairs, finance and business, and science and technology; *New Statesman*, which reviews social issues, politics, literature and the arts from an independent socialist point of view; and the *Spectator*, which covers similar subjects from a more conservative standpoint. A rather more irreverent approach to public affairs is taken by *Private Eye*, a satirical fortnightly with a loyal following.

Weekly 'listings' magazines like *Time Out* provide details of cultural and other events in London and other large cities.

There are some 4,300 business and professional titles, with the highest concentrations in medicine, business management, sciences, architecture and building, social sciences, and computers. *New Scientist*, for example, is extending its readership beyond the strictly scientific audience, and now has a circulation of over 120,000. Controlled (free) circulation titles represent about two-thirds of the business and professional magazine market. Ninety five per cent of business and professional people regularly read the publications relevant to their sector.

NEWS AGENCIES

The top international news agencies operating in Britain are Reuters, Associated Press and United Press International. The main agency which gathers news inside Britain is the Press Association (PA), which is owned by the regional newspaper publishers. A number of other British and foreign agencies and news services have offices in London (for example, Agence France Presse), and there are smaller agencies based in other British cities.

The Press Association

The Press Association operates through the following companies.

PA News, the national news agency for Britain and the Irish Republic, provides comprehensive coverage to the national and regional print, broadcast and electronic media. Around 1,500 stories and 100 pictures and graphics are transmitted each day by satellite and telecommunications links. PA's national and regional coverage includes live coverage from Parliament, business, the courts and major international events with a British or Irish interest. PA customers include Teletext, on-line information providers and Internet sites (for information on the Internet see p. 507). Other services include a press cuttings archive, a photo library with over 5 million pictures, and NewsFile, an on-line news service.

PA Sport provides comprehensive coverage of British and Irish sport, including fixtures, reports, results, statistics and graphics. Specialist writers provide in-depth coverage of all major sports, from national leagues to local clubs.

PA Listings specialises in delivering formatted listings data and editorial copy to the print, broadcast and electronic media, covering TV and radio, finance, arts and entertainment guides, bars and restaurants, and seasonal events.

PA WeatherCentre supplies and interprets weather information, including forecasts, maps, charts and statistics, for a variety of media and non-media customers.

PA New Media provides tailored news, sport and listings information for Internet and other electronic formats, supported by a range of design and management services.

PRESS INSTITUTIONS

Trade associations include the Newspaper Publishers Association, whose members publish national newspapers, and the Newspaper Society, which represents British regional and local newspapers. The Scottish Daily Newspaper Society represents the interests of daily and Sunday newspapers in Scotland; the Scottish Newspaper Publishers' Association acts on behalf of the owners of weekly newspapers in Scotland; and Associated Northern Ireland Newspapers is made up of proprietors of weekly newspapers in Northern Ireland. The membership of the Periodical Publishers Association includes most independent publishers of business, professional and consumer journals.

Organisations representing journalists are the National Union of Journalists and the Chartered Institute of Journalists. The main printing union is the Graphical, Paper and Media Union, with a membership of around 200,000.

The Foreign Press Association was formed in 1888 to help the correspondents of overseas newspapers in their work by arranging press conferences, tours, briefings, and other services and facilities.

The Guild of Editors is the officially recognised professional body for newspaper editors and their equivalents in radio and television. It has approximately 500 members and exists to defend press freedom and to promote high editorial standards. The British Association of Industrial Editors is the professional organisation for editors of house journals. The Association of British Editors represents the whole range of media, including radio, television, newspapers and magazines.

Training

A wide range of newspaper training courses are accredited by the National Council for the Training of Journalists (NCTJ), while magazine courses are accredited by the Periodical Training Council (the training arm of the Periodical Publishers Association). Courses for regional newspapers in such subjects as newspaper sales, advertising and management are provided by training services endorsed by the Newspaper Society. Some newspaper publishers carry out journalist training independently of the NCTJ. The Newspaper Society is the leading body for the development of National Vocational Qualifications (see p. 448) in the newspaper industry.

PRESS CONDUCT AND LAW

The Press Complaints Commission

In a free society, there is a delicate and sometimes difficult balance in the relationship between the responsibilities of the press and the rights of the public. The Press Complaints Commission, a non-statutory body, was set up in 1991 by the newspaper and periodical industry following recommendations in a report on privacy and the press by an independent committee. This was in response to growing criticism of press standards, with allegations of unjustified invasion of privacy and inaccurate and biased reporting, which resulted in calls for government regulation of the press.

In 1995 the Government rejected proposals for statutory regulation and for legislation to give protection to privacy. Instead, it endorsed self-regulation under the

Commission, and recommended tougher measures to make self-regulation more effective.

The Commission's membership is drawn from both the public and the press. It deals with complaints about the content and conduct of newspapers and magazines, and operates a code of practice agreed by editors covering such failings as inaccuracy, invasion of privacy, harassment and discrimination by the press.

The industry and the Commission have introduced measures to reinforce voluntary regulation. These include an increase in the number of independent members of the Commission to ensure a lay majority, the incorporation of the code of practice into the contracts of employment of most editors and journalists, and the appointment of a Privacy Commissioner with special powers to investigate complaints about invasion of privacy.

The Press and the Law

There is no state control or censorship of the newspaper and periodical press, and newspaper proprietors, editors and journalists are subject to the law in the same way as any other citizen. However, certain statutes include sections which apply to the press.

There are laws governing:

- the extent of newspaper ownership in television and radio companies (see p. 491);
- the transfer of newspaper assets; and
- the right of press representatives to be supplied with agendas and reports for meetings of local authorities, and reasonable facilities for taking notes and telephoning reports.

There is a legal requirement to reproduce 'the printer's imprint' (the printer's name and address) on all publications, including newspapers. Publishers are legally obliged to deposit copies of newspapers and other publications at the British Library (see p. 487).

Publication of advertisements is governed by wide-ranging legislation, including public

health, copyright, financial services and fraud legislation. Legal restrictions are imposed on certain types of prize competition.

Laws on contempt of court, official secrets and defamation are also relevant to the press. A newspaper may not publish comments on the conduct of judicial proceedings which are likely to prejudice the reputation of the courts for fairness before or during the actual proceedings, nor may it publish before or during a trial anything which might influence the result. The unauthorised acquisition and publication of official information in such areas as defence and international relations, where such unauthorised disclosure would be harmful, are offences under the Official Secrets Acts 1911 to 1989. However, these are restrictions on publication—that is, on dissemination to the public by any means— not just through the printed press.

Most legal proceedings against the press are libel actions brought by private individuals.

Defence Advisory Notices

Government officials and representatives of the media form the Defence, Press and Broadcasting Advisory Committee, which has agreed that in some circumstances the publication of certain categories of information might endanger national security. Details of these categories are contained in Defence Advisory Notices (DA Notices) circulated to the media, whose members are asked to seek advice from the Secretary of the Committee, a retired senior military officer, before publishing information in these areas. Compliance with any advice offered by the Secretary is expected but there is no legal force behind it and the final decision on whether to publish rests with the editor, producer or publisher concerned.

The Notices were published for the first time in 1993 to promote a better understanding of the system and to contribute to greater openness in government.

Advertising Practice

Advertising in all non-broadcast media, such as newspapers, magazines, posters, sales promotions, cinema, direct mail, and electronic media such as CD-ROM and the Internet, is regulated by the Advertising Standards Authority (ASA). The ASA is an independent body which sees that everyone who prepares and publishes advertisements conforms to the British Codes of Advertising and Sales Promotion. The Codes are written and enforced by the advertising industry through the Committee of Advertising Practice (CAP). They require that advertisements and promotions:

- are legal, decent, honest and truthful;
- are prepared with a sense of responsibility to the consumer and society; and
- respect the principles of fair competition generally accepted in business.

The ASA monitors advertisements to ensure their compliance with the Codes and investigates any complaints received. Pre-publication advice is provided by CAP's copy advice team to assist publishers, agencies and advertisers. If an advertisement is found to be unacceptable because it is misleading or offensive, the ASA can ask the advertiser to change or remove it. Failure to do so can result in damaging adverse publicity in the ASA's monthly report of its judgments, the refusal of advertising space by publishers, and the loss of trading privileges. In the rare cases of deliberate or persistent offending, the ASA can also refer misleading advertisements to the Director General of Fair Trading, who has the power to seek an injunction to prevent their publication.

THE MEDIA AND THE INTERNET

The Internet is among the most far-reaching of recent developments in electronic communications. It plays a new and increasingly important role in the provision and dissemination of information and entertainment. Broadly, it is a loose collection of computer networks around the world—it links thousands of academic, government, military and public computer systems, giving millions of people access to a wealth of stored information and other resources. No one owns it—there is no centralised controlling or regulating body. To access, or send out, information an Internet user needs only a computer with the necessary software, a telephone and a modem (which allows computers to talk to each other over a telephone line).

The system dates from the 1960s, when it began life in the military and academic communities in the United States. It has only assumed widespread significance in commercial and consumer terms during the present decade. It is the World Wide Web (WWW or Web) which has given the Internet its user appeal and accessibility. The Web consists of tens of thousands of pages or 'sites' on the Internet, which can be viewed by a browser (a programme that provides a window in a computer screen on which the pages are displayed). Users can move from page to page in search of whatever information or service they are after.

For an increasingly computer-literate generation of consumers, the Internet could become a real alternative to more traditional media. Aware of this possibility, many publishers and broadcasters have established sites on the World Wide Web. British press interests which have a presence on the system include the *Daily Mail, The Times, The Guardian, The Daily Telegraph*, the Mirror Group, and the Press Association—and also prominent magazine publishers, like Emap, IPC and *Time Out*. There are over 100 regional newspaper Websites, offering a range of editorial, directory and advertising services. Broadcasters, such as the BBC and Channel 4, are also represented.

Further Reading

Department of National Heritage Annual Report 1997: The Government's Expenditure Plans 1997–98 to 1999–2000. Cm 3611. The Stationery Office, 1997.

Privacy and Media Intrusion: The Government's Response. Cm 2918. HMSO, 1995.

Media Ownership Regulation: an explanatory guide to the provisions in the Broadcasting Acts 1990 and 1996. Department of National Heritage, 1996.

Digital Terrestrial Broadcasting: an explanatory guide to the provisions introduced by the Broadcasting Act 1996. Department of National Heritage, 1996.

Extending Choice in the Digital Age. BBC, 1996.

Reaching the Regions: a guide to Britain's regional and local press. The Newspaper Society, 1997.

30 Sport and Active Recreation

Over 100 British sportsmen and women currently hold world championship titles. Britain won a total of 15 medals at the 1996 Olympics in Atlanta and 122 at the subsequent Paralympics. The National Lottery is now making a significant contribution towards financing sport, both at grass roots and elite levels, and will be helping to finance major developments such as the planned new national stadium in England and the British Academy of Sport. The Government intends to extend opportunities for participation through a national sports strategy, now being developed, which will embrace all sections of the community.

About 29 million people in Britain over the age of 16 regularly take part in sport or exercise. The most popular participation sports or activities are walking (including rambling and hiking), swimming, snooker/pool, keep fit/yoga and cycling.

ORGANISATION AND ADMINISTRATION

The Secretary of State for Culture, Media and Sport is responsible for the Government's policies on sport and recreation in England. The Secretaries of State for Wales, Scotland and Northern Ireland have similar responsibilities in their countries. Responsibility for aspects of government sports policy of benefit to Britain as a whole rests with the Secretary of State for Culture, Media and Sport, in association with the respective home country Secretaries of State.

Within its overall policy of 'Sport for All', the Government is developing a national sports strategy, and intends to work in partnership with local authorities, sports governing bodies and sporting agencies, to produce an integrated approach to sports provision. The strategy is intended to improve sporting performance at all levels and to extend opportunities for participation in sport.

Sports Councils

Government responsibilities in sport and recreation are largely channelled through the Sports Councils. There are separate sports councils for England, Scotland, Wales and Northern Ireland, while the United Kingdom Sports Council (UKSC) takes the lead on all aspects of sport and physical recreation which require strategic planning, administration, co-ordination or representation for Britain as a whole. The UKSC currently has nine members, including the chairmen of the home country Sports Councils and key individuals from amateur and professional sport.

The UKSC is particularly concerned with providing support for top-level athletes, to ensure that British sport in future produces a constant flow of world-class performers and winners. Key functions include:

- identifying sporting policies for Britain as a whole;

- identifying areas of unnecessary duplication and waste in the administration of sport;

- developing and delivering appropriate grant programmes for sports bodies covering Britain or Great Britain as a whole and for sports which have potential for success at an international level;

- managing the development of the British Academy of Sport;

- co-ordinating policy for bringing major international sports events to Britain;

- representing British sporting interests overseas and increasing influence at international level; and

- working to develop a fair and ethical sporting environment for all.

The home country Sports Councils operate wide-ranging grant programmes, from encouraging the development of sport for young people to developing sporting excellence on a national basis. They also manage the National Sports Centres (see p. 514), and are responsible for distributing the National Lottery Sports Fund (see p. 519).

As part of its new approach to sport, the Government has concluded that there is a need to review the way in which the Sports Councils are working, to ensure that they operate efficiently for the future in the best interests of sport.

Local Authorities

Local authorities are the main providers of basic sport and recreation facilities for the

In November 1996 the World Class Performance Programme was launched to provide support across Britain to the most talented athletes competing up to Olympic and world championship level. The funds are expected to be available to some 4,500 top sportspeople. Three further programmes are planned:

- the World Class Events Programme, designed to attract and stage major international events in Britain;

- the World Class Start Programme, to provide community coaching and leadership schemes; and

- the World Class Potential Programme, to develop talent in schools and sports clubs.

These initiatives will be funded from the National Lottery Sports Fund. The programmes should contribute around £50 million a year to sport in Britain when they are all under way.

local community. In England they manage over 1,500 indoor sports centres. Other facilities include parks, lakes, playing fields, tennis courts, artificial pitches, golf courses and swimming/leisure pools. Many local authorities employ full-time sports development officers. The Government intends to encourage each local authority to develop a leisure strategy in which sport would have a prominent role, with the aim of ensuring that the provision of sporting facilities meets local needs.

Sports Clubs

Local sports clubs provide a wide variety of recreational facilities. Some cater for indoor recreation, but more common are those providing sports grounds, particularly for cricket, football, rugby, hockey, tennis and golf. Over 150,000 voluntary sports clubs are affiliated to the national governing bodies of sport. Many clubs linked to business firms cater for sporting activities. Commercial facilities include fitness centres, tenpin bowling centres, ice and roller-skating rinks, squash courts, golf courses and driving ranges, riding stables and marinas.

National Sports Associations

The Central Council of Physical Recreation (CCPR) is the largest sport and recreation federation in the world. It comprises 209 British bodies and 68 English associations, most of which are governing bodies of sport. The Scottish Sports Association, the Welsh Sports Association and the Northern Ireland Sports Forum (NISF) are related associations. Their primary aim is to represent the interests of their members to the appropriate national and local authorities, including the Sports Councils, from which they receive funding. Award schemes run by the associations include the CCPR's Community Sports Leaders Award scheme, which attracts some 36,000 youngsters each year, and the NISF's Service to Sport Awards.

British Olympic Association

The British Olympic Association (BOA) is the National Olympic Committee for Britain and comprises representatives of the 35 governing bodies of Olympic sports. It organises the participation of British teams in the Olympic Games, determines the size of British Olympic teams, sets standards for selection and raises funds. It is supported by sponsorship and by donations from the private sector and the public. Over 300 competitors represented Britain in the 1996 Olympics and won 15 medals: one gold, eight silver and six bronze.

The BOA also makes important contributions to the preparation of competitors in the period between Games, such as arranging training camps. The Association's British Olympic Medical Centre at Northwick Park Hospital in north London supplies a medical back-up service for competitors before and during the Olympics.

The BOA is investigating the possibility of a British bid for the Olympic Games in the early part of the 21st century.

Sports Governing Bodies

Individual sports are run by over 400 independent governing bodies. Their functions include drawing up rules, holding events, regulating membership, and selecting and training national teams. Governing bodies receiving long-term funding from the Sports Councils are required to produce four-year development plans, from the grass roots to the highest competitive levels. In order to have access to Lottery funds, they now need also to prepare 'world-class performance' plans, with specific performance targets. There are also organisations representing people who take part in more informal physical recreation, such as walking and cycling. Most sports clubs in Britain belong to, or are affiliated to, the appropriate governing body.

National Coaching Foundation

The National Coaching Foundation (NCF) works closely with sports governing bodies, local authorities, and higher and further education. Supported by the Sports Councils, it provides a comprehensive range of education and development services for coaches in all sports. It has ten regional offices in England, and one each in Scotland, Wales and Northern Ireland.

The NCF also runs Champion Coaching, one of the elements of the National Junior Sport Programme (see p. 512). Champion Coaching provides after-school coaching in a variety of sports in England, Wales and Northern Ireland. In 1997–98 there will be 150 local authority schemes, with about 11,500 children and 1,000 coaches participating.

Sport in Schools and for Young People

The Government is planning to develop further the sporting opportunities for young people. It has set up a new Youth Sports Unit in the Department for Culture, Media and Sport. Sport for young people is given a high priority by the Sports Councils.

Physical education (PE), which includes sport, is a compulsory subject in the National Curriculum (see p. 439) for all pupils aged 5 to 16 in state-maintained schools in England and Wales and in the common curriculum in Northern Ireland. All schools have to include in their prospectuses details of their sporting aims and provision for sport, and to record in their governors' reports how they have met these aims.

> The Government believes that sport should be a fundamental part of school life and it will be looking at ways of promoting sport in schools. The Government also intends to introduce after-school clubs, which would be funded through the National Lottery Sports Fund and include provision for additional sporting opportunities for children.

In Scotland the National Guidelines contain programmes of study and attainment targets for physical activity for pupils aged 5 to 14. The Scottish Sports Council is preparing a national scheme under which each school would have a school sports co-ordinator.

A new initiative designed to encourage young people to participate in sport was launched in 1997. Leading sports figures will be visiting schools and local clubs to set out the benefits of a wide range of sports. Lottery funds will also be made available to schools for additional sports coaching.

Assessment of Sporting Facilities

Two new schemes have been set up to assess the sporting merits of schools:

- a Sportsmark scheme to recognise schools that have effective policies for promoting sport; and
- 'Sportsmark Gold' awards for the most innovative schools or those showing exceptional achievement.

Playing Fields

The Government is looking at the options to meet its commitment of ensuring that playing fields needed by schools and their local communities are not sold in the future. In the meantime, the respective national Sports Councils must be consulted on planning proposals affecting all playing fields in Great Britain.

Links with the Local Community

Links between schools and the local community are being encouraged so that, for example, children have access to the sports amenities which clubs and associations can make available outside school hours. A £2 million challenge fund was established in England in 1996 to promote links between schools and sports clubs or governing bodies.

National Junior Sport Programme

The National Junior Sport Programme in England aims to encourage sporting participation and to develop children's sports skills. It is run by the English Sports Council (ESC). Key partners include the Youth Sport Trust, the physical education profession, local authorities, youth clubs, the National Coaching Foundation and national governing bodies of sport. An important component is the TOP programme designed to provide 4 million children with sports equipment, qualified coaches and places to play. Over the three years to 1998 about £14 million is being provided by the National Lottery Sports Fund, the ESC and private sector funding including business sponsorship.

The scheme has several elements, including:

- Top Play, for those aged four to nine, aims to develop core skills, such as co-ordination, ball skills and teamwork;
- BT Top Sport, for those aged 7 to 11, introduces children to specific sports, such as cricket, football, rugby and tennis;
- Champion Coaching (see p. 511), run by the National Coaching Foundation;
- Top Club, a programme which assists clubs in developing junior coaching and competitive opportunities for young people; and
- Sports Fair, a programme to promote sporting activity with youth groups.

Women and Sport

The Government is keen to improve opportunities for women in sport, where their participation has been at a significantly lower rate than that of men. This will be an important aspect of the national sports strategy.

Sporting agencies, including the Sports Councils and the Women's Sports Federation (WSF), promote the interests of women and girls in sport and active recreation. The WSF encourages the establishment of women's sports groups throughout Britain and organises events and activities. It runs both the Sportswomen of the Year Awards and an annual nationwide awards scheme for girls and young women between the ages of 11 and 19.

Organisations are required to include ways of encouraging the participation of women when applying for support from the National Lottery Sports Fund. This is helping to increase participation of women, especially in sports that have traditionally been dominated by men.

Sport for Disabled People

The governing bodies of sport are increasingly taking responsibility for disabled people. There is close liaison with the Sports Councils, which provide advice to governing bodies on encouraging the integration of people with disabilities.

The key organisations for people with disabilities are:

- Disability Sport England (formerly the British Sports Association for the Disabled), a national body working across all the disabilities, which organises regional and national championships in many sports and also runs training courses, coaching courses and development days. The Scottish and the Welsh Sports Associations for the Disabled and the Northern Ireland Committee on Sport for People with Disabilities have similar co-ordinating roles;

- the United Kingdom Sports Association for People with Learning Disability (UKSAPLD), a co-ordinating body with a membership of over 20 national organisations, which promotes and develops opportunities in sport and recreation for people with learning disability; and

- the British Paralympic Association (BPA), which organises Britain's participation in the Paralympics, in close liaison with the British Olympic Association. The UKSAPLD is responsible, in partnership with the BPA, for the preparation and training of the Paralympic team. In 1996, 244 competitors represented Britain in the Paralympics and won 122 medals: 39 gold, 42 silver and 41 bronze.

There are also bodies concerned with individual disabilities and single sports. The Riding for the Disabled Association, for example, caters for some 25,000 riders, and there are five national disability sports organisations concerned with individual disabilities: the British Amputee and Les Autres Sports Association; British Blind Sport; the British Deaf Sports Council; the British Wheelchair Sports Foundation; and Cerebral Palsy Sport. They provide coaching and help to organise national competitions in conjunction with the governing bodies of sport and Disability Sport England.

Other Organisations

The Countryside Commission (for England), the Countryside Council for Wales and Scottish Natural Heritage are responsible for conserving the natural beauty of the countryside, and for encouraging the provision of facilities for open-air recreation. They are working with the Sports Councils to ensure that outdoor recreation and sport are managed according to the principles of sustainable development.

British Waterways is a publicly owned body responsible for managing and developing much of Great Britain's inland waterways. Many leisure and recreational pursuits, such as angling and various types of sailing and boating, are enjoyed on waterways and reservoirs.

In Northern Ireland the Environment and Heritage Service, an agency within the Department of the Environment, is responsible for protecting the natural environment and promoting its appreciation.

MAJOR SPORTS FACILITIES

Britain has a range of world-class sporting facilities including 13 National Sports Centres, run by the Sports Councils. Wembley Stadium in London is to be redeveloped as the new national stadium for England, and up to £80 million is being provided to support facilities in Manchester, which will host the Commonwealth Games in 2002. These include £60 million for a new sports stadium and nearly £20 million for an Olympic-sized swimming complex.

British Academy of Sport

A British Academy of Sport is to be established. It is a key element of the proposal to provide customised support services to top-level sportsmen and women, including the integrated development and delivery of sports science, sports medicine and coaching. The Academy will provide world-class services and training facilities, and will co-ordinate a network of regional centres of sporting excellence.

Three sites have been selected as possible locations from an original list of 26 bids. The Government is considering its preferred site.

National Stadium

A new national 80,000 all-seater stadium for England is to be located at Wembley (London). This will involve rebuilding the existing stadium, and it is expected to be ready in time for the FA (Football Association) Cup Final in 2002. Facilities of the highest standard will be provided and the stadium will be capable of hosting major world sporting events. It will cost around £210 million, of which £120 million will be provided from Lottery funding.

National Sports Centres

First priority at the National Sports Centres is given to the governing bodies of sport for national squad training and for the training of coaches. Centres also make their facilities available to top sportsmen and women for individual training and to the local community. Most Centres provide residential facilities.

England

The English Sports Council (ESC) runs six major National Sports Centres. Crystal Palace in London is a leading competition venue for a wide range of sports and a major training centre for national squads, clubs and schools, and serious enthusiasts. It is a regional centre of excellence for athletics, netball, weightlifting and swimming. Crystal Palace stadium is Britain's major international athletics venue, with capacity for 17,000 spectators. Other facilities include Olympic-size swimming and diving pools and a sports injury centre. The Centre also houses the National Boxing Academy. The long-term future of Crystal Palace is being reviewed, partly in the light of the redevelopment of Wembley as a new national stadium and the forthcoming establishment of the British Academy of Sport.

Bisham Abbey in Berkshire caters for a number of sports, including tennis, football, hockey, weightlifting, squash, rugby union and golf. The England football and rugby union squads train at the Centre. Bisham Abbey has long-standing partnerships with the British Amateur Weightlifting Association and the Lawn Tennis Association (LTA), which has helped to develop the Abbey as the National Tennis Training Centre and the home of the LTA Rover Tennis School.

Lilleshall National Sports Centre in Shropshire offers extensive sports facilities, which are used by a variety of national teams. Facilities include the Olympic Gymnastics Centre, regularly used by the British gymnastic squads, and extensive playing fields for football and hockey. The Football Association uses Lilleshall as its base for major coaching activities. Lilleshall also houses the Olympic Archery Centre.

The National Water Sports Centre at Holme Pierrepont in Nottinghamshire is one of the most comprehensive water sports centres in the world. It has facilities for rowing, canoeing, water-skiing, powerboating, ski-racing, angling and sailing. Its main features are a 2,000-metre regatta course and the only purpose-built floodlit canoe slalom course in the world.

The National Cycling Centre, opened in Manchester in 1994, is Britain's first indoor velodrome. It was the venue for the World Cycling Championships in 1996.

Wales

The Sports Council for Wales runs two National Sports Centres:

- The Welsh Institute of Sport in Cardiff is the country's premier venue for top-level training and for competition in many sports. Facilities include a world-standard gymnastics hall, a sports science laboratory and a sports injury clinic.
- The National Watersports Centre at Plas Menai in north Wales is a centre of excellence for sailing and canoeing; activities include dinghy and catamaran sailing, offshore cruising and powerboat training.

Plas y Brenin National Mountain Centre, a third centre, is run by the English Sports Council. Situated in Snowdonia National Park in north Wales, it offers courses in rock climbing, mountaineering, canoeing, orienteering, skiing and most other mountain-based activities. It is Britain's leading training institution for the development of mountain instructors.

Scotland

Scotland has three National Sports Centres, which are run by the Scottish Sports Council:

- The Scottish National Outdoor Centre at Glenmore Lodge near Aviemore caters for a range of activities, including hill walking, rock climbing, mountaineering, skiing, kayaking and canoeing. Its main purpose is to provide top-quality training for those who intend to lead or instruct others in outdoor activities.
- The Scottish National Sports Centre— Inverclyde—at Largs, has a large number of facilities, including a gymnastics hall, a golf training facility and a laboratory for fitness assessment. The Centre also acts as an important venue for major championships. Inverclyde was used by 32 governing bodies of sport in 1996–97,

many of them using it as their national training and coaching base.

- The Scottish National Water Sports Centre—Cumbrae—on the island of Great Cumbrae in the Firth of Clyde, offers an extensive range of courses catering for all levels of ability. It has a comprehensive range of modern craft for a variety of sailing activities, as well as sub-aqua diving equipment. Cumbrae hosts major sailing championships.

Northern Ireland

The Northern Ireland Centre for Outdoor Activities at Tollymore in County Down, run by the Sports Council for Northern Ireland, offers courses in mountaineering, rock climbing, canoeing and outdoor adventure. Leadership and instructor courses resulting in nationally recognised qualifications are also available.

A Northern Ireland Outdoor Team Sports Training Centre is under development in Belfast. The first phase, involving two new synthetic pitches, was opened in 1995 at Queen's University of Belfast Playing Fields.

SPORTS MEDICINE AND SCIENCE

Sports Medicine

The National Sports Medicine Institute, funded by the UKSC and ESC, is responsible for the co-ordination of sports medicine services. Based at the medical college of St Bartholomew's Hospital, London, its facilities include a physiology laboratory, library and information centre. Work is in progress to develop a network of regional centres to provide both clinical and educational services, which will be linked with new support services at the National Sports Centres.

In Scotland a network of 33 sports medicine centres provides specialist help with sports injuries. The Scottish Institute of Sports Medicine and Sports Science, opened in 1995, aims to form partnerships with national governing bodies to provide athletes and coaches with high-quality medical and scientific support.

A Northern Ireland Sports Medicine Centre was established in 1996 as a partnership between the Sports Council for Northern Ireland and a local healthcare trust.

Sports Science

The development of sports science support services for the national governing bodies of sport is being promoted by the Sports Councils, in collaboration with the British Olympic Association and the National Coaching Foundation, in an effort to raise the standards of performance of national squads. The type of support provided may cover biomechanical (human movement), physiological or psychological factors. There are 24 national governing bodies involved in the UKSC's Sports Science Support Programme. The Sports Council for Wales has established a sports science service at the Welsh Institute of Sport with support from the Welsh Office.

Drug Misuse

The UKSC aims to prevent doping in sport and achieve a commitment to drug-free sport and ethical sporting practices. Its Ethics and Anti-Doping Directorate co-ordinates a drug-testing programme and conducts a comprehensive education programme aimed at changing attitudes to drug misuse.

In running its drug-testing programme, the UKSC is responsible for the collection of samples; arranging their analysis at a laboratory accredited by the International Olympic Committee, at King's College, University of London; and reporting the results to the appropriate governing body. The UKSC's programme involves nearly 80 national governing bodies and 24 international sporting federations from 47 sports. Nearly 4,500 tests were conducted in 1996–97—over 2,800 in competition and 1,650 out of competition—and 98 per cent were negative. The UKSC provides a Drug Information Line to allow athletes to check whether a licensed medication is banned or permitted under their governing body's regulations.

Anabolic steroids and other anabolic substances (such as growth hormones) have recently become controlled drugs, and greater penalties for their unauthorised supply have been introduced. This is expected to help to eliminate their misuse in sport and other leisure activities such as bodybuilding.

Britain has implemented the Council of Europe's Anti-doping Convention, designed to ensure minimum national standards for the organisation of doping control. Five countries—Britain, Australia, Canada, New Zealand and Norway—have signed the International Anti-Doping Arrangement to facilitate the development of high-quality domestic anti-doping programmes and of internationally recognised standards in anti-doping programmes.

SPECTATOR SAFETY

Safety at sports grounds in Great Britain is governed by legislation. The main instrument of control is a safety certificate which is issued by the relevant local authority. When determining the conditions of a safety certificate, the local authority is expected to comply with the Guide to Safety at Sports Grounds produced by the Department for Culture, Media and Sport and The Scottish Office. Similar legislation in Northern Ireland is under discussion.

The Taylor Report

Following the Hillsborough stadium disaster in Sheffield in 1989, when 96 spectators died, the Taylor Report was published in 1990. Its major recommendation was that standing accommodation should be eliminated at all grounds designated under the Safety of Sports Grounds Act 1975. The Government accepted the report but limited the all-seating requirement to football.

In England and Wales the all-seater policy is being enforced through licences issued by the Football Licensing Authority. These require all clubs in the Premier League and those in the First Division of the Football League to have all-seater grounds; these conditions have now largely been satisfied. Clubs in the Second and Third Divisions of the Football League are permitted to keep some standing accommodation, providing that the terracing is safe. In Scotland the all-seating policy is being implemented through a voluntary agreement under the direction of the Scottish football authorities.

The Football Trust

The Football Trust provides grant aid to help football clubs at all levels. It is funded partly by contributions from football governing bodies and partly from reductions in pool betting duty which will continue until 2000. These concessions have provided over £144 million to assist football clubs with projects to improve the comfort and safety of spectators in line with the Taylor Report recommendations. In June 1997 further funding of £55 million over the next four years was announced to enable the Trust to continue its programme of football ground safety and improvement work. This extra funding will come from the ESC's Lottery Fund, the Football Association and the FA Premier League.

The Football Trust also administers funding of safety work at rugby league, rugby union and cricket grounds under the Sports Grounds Initiative.

Crowd Control

The Government has worked closely with the police, football authorities and the governments of other European countries to implement crowd control measures. Extensive measures ensured that Euro 96—the final of the European Championship (see p. 523)—was not disrupted by violence or disorder. Strict crowd control and surveillance measures were taken at the eight grounds in England where matches were held.

Legislation has made it an offence in England and Wales to throw objects at football matches, run onto the playing area or chant indecent or racist abuse. There are also controls on the sale and possession of alcohol at football grounds and on transport to and from grounds. Courts in England and Wales have the power to prohibit convicted football hooligans from attending football matches, and to impose restriction orders to prevent

them travelling abroad to attend specified matches. In Northern Ireland similar legislation is under consideration.

The Government has established a Football Task Force to investigate and recommend new measures to deal with public concerns on a range of issues, including racism, ticket prices and access for the disabled. Measures are also being considered by the Government on crowd violence and racist abuse, including higher penalties for such abuse at football matches.

SPONSORSHIP AND OTHER FUNDING

Sport is a major industry in Britain. In addition to professional sportsmen and women, over 450,000 people are employed in the provision of sports clothing, publicity, ground and club maintenance and other activities connected with sport. Consumer expenditure on sport in Britain is estimated at some £10,400 million a year. The private sector makes a substantial investment in sport, with more than 2,000 British companies involved.

Sports sponsorship reached a record level in 1996, at £340 million, 19 per cent higher than in 1995 This reflected a boost from Euro 96 to which sponsors contributed £38.5 million. Nearly 1,000 separate sports sponsorship deals were reported in 1996.

Sponsorship may take the form of financing specific events or championships, such as horse races or cricket leagues, or of grants to sports organisations or individual performers. Motor sport and football receive the largest amounts of private sponsorship. Sponsorship is encouraged by a number of bodies, including:

- the Institute of Sports Sponsorship, set up by the Central Council of Physical Recreation (CCPR) and which comprises some 80 British companies involved in sponsoring sport; and

- the Sports Sponsorship Advisory Service, administered by the CCPR and funded by the ESC, and similar advisory services of the Scottish Sports Council and the Sports Council for Wales.

Legislation is planned to ban all forms of tobacco advertising and promotion (see p. 408), and the Department of Health is consulting the Department for Culture, Media and Sport to ensure that the ban is implemented in a way which minimises any damage to sport. Early in 1998 a White Paper will set out the Government's plans to tackle tobacco consumption. These will include a transitional period to allow sports bodies to identify and secure alternative sponsors.

Sportsmatch

Sportsmatch aims to increase the amount of business sponsorship going into 'grass roots' sport and physical recreation. It offers matching funding for new sponsorships and extension of existing ones. Priority is given to projects involving the young, disabled people and ethnic minorities and to projects in deprived areas.

In England the Institute of Sports Sponsorship runs the scheme on behalf of the Department for Culture, Media and Sport. Between 1992 and July 1997 Sportsmatch approved over 1,800 awards in England, totalling £14.7 million and covering nearly 70 different sports. Football, rugby union, cricket, tennis and basketball have received most awards. Minority sports, such as korfball, orienteering and trampolining, have also received awards. About half the companies involved are sponsoring sport for the first time. In Scotland and Wales the scheme is managed by the appropriate Sports Council's Sponsorship Advisory Service.

Sports Aid Foundation

The Sports Aid Foundation raises funds to help talented British individual sportspeople to meet their personal training expenses. Assistance is given to those needing financial help and is concentrated on individuals who do not qualify for awards from the National Lottery Sports Fund. The Foundation raises its funds by commercial sponsorship and by donations from companies, local authorities, voluntary organisations and members of the public. The Scottish and Welsh Sports Aid Foundations and the Ulster Sports and Recreation Trust have similar functions.

Foundation for Sport and the Arts

The Foundation for Sport and the Arts was set up by the football pools promoters in 1991 to channel funds into sport and the arts. This followed the Budget in which pool betting duty was reduced by 2.5 per cent, provided that the money forgone by the Government was paid into the new Foundation. In addition, the pools promoters passed on an additional 5 pence in the pound levy on pools coupons to the Foundation. About £33 million was given to sports schemes in 1995–96. The Foundation has made awards to schemes benefiting over 100 sports and totalling £200 million.

Betting and Gaming

Most betting in Britain takes place on horse racing and greyhound racing. Bets may be made at racecourses and greyhound tracks, or through about 8,500 licensed off-course betting offices, which take about 90 per cent of the money staked. A form of pool betting—totalisator betting—is organised on racecourses by the Horserace Totalisator Board (the Tote). Racecourse bets may also be placed with on-course bookmakers. Betting on other sporting events, such as football, is becoming more popular.

Bookmakers and the Tote contribute an annual levy—a fixed proportion of their turnover—to the Horserace Betting Levy Board. The amount of levy payable is decided by the racing and bookmaking industries or, if agreement cannot be reached, by the Home Secretary. The Levy Board promotes the improvement of horse breeds, advancement of veterinary science and the improvement of horse racing.

In 1996–97 the total money staked in all forms of gambling, excluding gaming machines, was over £14,700 million. Various measures have recently been taken to provide new opportunities for the industry and the consumer. These include relaxation on membership conditions of casinos (of which there are around 120 in Great Britain), and broadcast advertising of commercial bingo.

National Lottery Awards

Sport is one of five good causes to receive awards from funds raised by the National Lottery. By June 1997 awards of £630 million had been made to some 3,200 projects in Britain. Projects have ranged from the provision of small items of equipment and floodlight facilities at grass roots level to the building of major sports venues. Around 50 sports have benefited from Lottery funding. The largest single award from the National Lottery Sports Fund has been for nearly £20 million for the swimming complex in Manchester (see p. 514). Changes to the Lottery distribution regulations now mean that some £50 million a year is being used for programmes as well as building projects. The Government's White Paper on the Lottery (see p. 47) outlines further changes in the ways in which the Sports Councils are able to encourage applications and plan strategically for the deployment of Lottery funds.

Some of the funds from the Millennium Commission (see p. 47) are also for sporting and recreational developments. Major schemes include:

- £46 million for the Millennium Stadium in Cardiff, which will be ready for the 1999 Rugby World Cup (see p. 527);
- £42.5 million for a new national cycle network; and
- £23 million for the development of the national football stadium in Scotland at Hampden Park (Glasgow).

SPORT ON TELEVISION AND RADIO

Major sporting events receive extensive television and radio coverage and are watched or heard by millions of viewers or listeners. Sports receiving the most coverage on terrestrial television are football, horse racing, snooker and cricket. Euro 96 attracted a peak viewing figure of 26 million, spread over two channels.

Since 1988 the amount of sport on television has grown considerably, to over 12,000 hours a year, primarily as a result of the development of satellite and cable broadcasting including channels devoted exclusively to sport. Some major events, such as certain football, rugby union and cricket matches, are now shown live only on these channels. As a result, there has been considerable discussion about public accessibility to sport on television, including the pay-per-view service, whereby subscribers pay an additional amount to watch particular events—BSkyB introduced pay-per-view in 1996, mainly for top boxing contests.

Certain important sporting events—'listed' events—are not permitted to be shown on television solely on pay-per-view or subscription terms unless they have first been offered to terrestrial channels:

- the FIFA World Cup football finals;
- the FA Cup Final;
- the Scottish FA Cup Final;
- the finals weekend of the Wimbledon Tennis Championships;
- the Olympic Games;
- the Grand National;
- the Derby; and
- Test cricket matches involving England.

The Government has set up an urgent review of the listed events. Its aim is to ensure that major sporting events are available to the greatest number of potential viewers and listeners.

A TO Z OF POPULAR SPORTS

Some of the major sports in Britain, many of which were invented by the British, are described below.

Angling

Angling is one of the most popular countryside sports. There are an estimated 3 million anglers in Britain. Many fish for salmon and trout, particularly in the rivers and lochs of Scotland and in Wales. In England and Wales the most widely practised form of angling is for coarse fish (freshwater fish other than salmon or trout). Separate organisations represent game, coarse and sea fishing clubs in England, Wales, Scotland and Northern Ireland, and there are separate competitions in each of the three angling disciplines. A number of options for a national centre for angling are under discussion by the governing bodies; the ESC has indicated that it will consider a bid for Lottery funding and also provide technical advice and assistance.

In 1996 Alan Scotthorne won the world freshwater fishing championships, while Chris Clark won the world shore championships and England took the team title in the latter event.

Athletics

A recent development in athletics has been a significant growth in mass participation events, notably marathons and half marathons. The largest is the London Marathon, which takes place every spring. About 29,000 runners took part in the 1997 event. Many of the runners are sponsored, raising considerable amounts for charities and other good causes.

British athletes held world records in two events in October 1997: Jonathan Edwards in the triple jump, achieved in 1995 when he became the first man to jump beyond 18 metres; and Colin Jackson in the 110 metre hurdles (achieved in 1991). British athletes won six medals in the 1996 Olympics in Atlanta, with silver medals for Jonathan Edwards and for Roger Black (400 metres), Steve Backley (javelin) and the men's 4 x 400 metres relay team (Jamie Baulch, Roger Black, Mark Richardson and Iwan Thomas); and bronze medals for Denise Lewis (heptathlon) and Steve Smith (high jump). Paula Radcliffe finished second in the 1997 world cross-country championships in Turin. At the world athletics championships in Athens in August 1997, British athletes won five silver medals—Steve Backley, Jonathan Edwards, Colin Jackson, Denise Lewis and the men's 4 x 400 metres relay team (with the same line-up as the Olympics)—with a bronze medal for the men's 4 x 100 metres relay team of Darren Braithwaite, Darren Campbell, Julian Golding and Doug Walker.

Badminton

Badminton takes its name from the Duke of Beaufort's country home, Badminton House, where the sport was first played in the 19th century. The game is organised by the Badminton Association of England and the Scottish, Welsh and Irish (Ulster Branch) Badminton Unions. Around 5 million people play badminton in Britain and there are over 5,000 clubs. The Badminton Association of England has a modern coach education system to develop coaches for players of all levels.

The world championships were held in Glasgow in May–June 1997. The All England Badminton Championships, held at the National Indoor Arena in Birmingham, is a leading tournament in the world grand prix circuit.

A mini version of the game—Short Badminton—and badminton for the disabled have been introduced in recent years.

Basketball

In Britain over 3 million people participate in basketball. The English Basketball Association is the governing body in England, with similar associations in Wales, Scotland and Ireland (Ulster Branch). All the associations are represented on the British and Irish Basketball Federation, which acts as the co-ordinating body for Britain and the Irish Republic.

The leading clubs play in the National Basketball Leagues, which cover four divisions for men and two for women, while there are also leagues for younger players. Mini-basketball has been developed for players under the age of 13. Wheelchair basketball is played under the same rules, with a few basic adaptations, and on the same court as the running game.

The English Basketball Association runs various development schemes for young people which aim to increase participation and improve the quality of basketball throughout England. There is also a scheme to provide 10,000 outdoor basketball goals in parks and play areas in England to encourage recreational participation in the sport.

Bowls

The two main forms of bowls are lawn (flat green and crown green) and indoor bowls. About 4,000 lawn bowling clubs are affiliated to the English, Scottish, Welsh and Irish Bowling Associations, which, together with Women's Bowling Associations for the four countries, play to the rules of the World Bowls Board. Crown green bowls and indoor bowls have their own separate associations.

British bowlers have achieved considerable success in international championships. At the world outdoor championships (held every four years) the winners at the most recent event, held in Adelaide in 1996, included Tony Allcock, who became the first man to defend the singles title successfully, and Scotland, winners of the overall team title. At the 1997 world indoor championships, held in Preston, Hugh Duff won his second world title in the singles, while Tony Allcock and Mervyn King won the pairs title. Norma Shaw was the winner of the 1997 women's world indoor singles championship, held at Llanelli.

Boxing

Boxing in its modern form is based on the rules established by the 9th Marquess of Queensberry in 1865. In Britain boxing is both amateur and professional, and in both strict medical regulations are observed.

All amateur boxing in England is controlled by the Amateur Boxing Association of England. There are separate associations in Scotland and Wales, and boxing in Northern Ireland is controlled by the Irish Amateur Boxing Association. The associations organise amateur boxing championships as well as training courses for referees, coaches and others. Headguards must be used in all British amateur competitions.

Professional boxing is controlled by the British Boxing Board of Control. The Board appoints inspectors, medical officers and representatives to ensure that regulations are observed and to guard against overmatching and exploitation.

Britain currently has seven world champions: Naseem Hamed, who holds the World Boxing Organisation (WBO) featherweight title; heavyweights Lennox Lewis (who holds the World Boxing Council—WBC—version) and Herbie Hide (WBO); super-middleweights Robin Reid (WBC) and Joe Calzaghe (WBO); Robbie Regan (WBO bantamweight); and Carl Thompson (WBO cruiserweight).

Chess

There are local chess clubs and leagues throughout Britain, and chess is also played widely in schools and other educational establishments. Domestic competitions include the British Championships, the National Club Championships and the County Championships. The Hastings Chess Congress, which started in 1895, is the world's longest running annual international chess tournament.

The governing bodies are the British Chess Federation (responsible for England and for co-ordinating activity among the home nations), the Scottish Chess Association and the Welsh and Ulster Chess Unions.

England won the European Team Championship for the first time in May 1997. Earlier in the year Luke McShane, at 13, became the world's youngest international master.

Cricket

The earliest extant set of laws for cricket, which was first played in south-east England, are dated 1744. The rules of the game became the responsibility, in the 18th century, of the Marylebone Cricket Club (MCC), which still frames the laws today. The MCC is based at Lord's cricket ground in north London, the administrative centre of the English game.

Cricket is played in schools, colleges and universities, and amateur teams play weekly games in cities, towns and villages. Throughout Britain there is a network of cricket consisting of first-class, minor counties and club games with a variety of leagues.

The main competition in professional cricket is the Britannic Assurance County Championship, played by 18 first-class county teams in four-day matches. There are currently three one-day competitions: the Benson & Hedges Cup, the NatWest Trophy and the AXA Life League.

A major change in the administration of cricket took effect in January 1997 when the England and Wales Cricket Board was established, succeeding a number of bodies, including the Test and County Cricket Board. In August 1997 the new Board produced a strategic plan for the future of cricket. Following discussions, a number of changes to the main cricket competitions have been decided, including a new knockout cup in 1999 replacing the Benson & Hedges Cup and which will involve the top eight counties in the County Championship in 1998; and a new National League, with two divisions, which will succeed the AXA Life League in 1999.

Every year there is a series of five-day Cornhill Insurance Test matches played between England and one or more touring teams from Australia, India, New Zealand, Pakistan, South Africa, Sri Lanka, the West Indies or Zimbabwe. A team representing England usually tours one or more of these countries in the British winter. England will host the 1999 World Cup.

The governing body of cricket for women and girls is the Women's Cricket Association. Women's cricket is played at local, county and international level.

Cycling

Cycling, one of Britain's fastest growing activities, includes road and track racing, time-trialling, cyclo-cross (cross country racing), touring and bicycle moto-cross (BMX). All-terrain or mountain bikes are increasingly popular.

The British Cycling Federation has 16,000 members and is the internationally recognised governing body for British cycling as a sport. The Road Time Trials Council (to which 1,019 cycling clubs are affiliated) controls road time trials. The CTC (Cyclists' Touring Club), with 65,000 members and affiliates, is the governing body for recreational and urban cycling, and

holds the CTC rally each year in York. CTC Scotland represents cyclists in Scotland, Wales has its own Cyclists' Union and Northern Ireland also has separate federations for competitive cycling.

In 1996 Chris Boardman won the 4,000 metres pursuit title at the World Cycling Championships at the Manchester Velodrome, in a new world record of 4 minutes 11 seconds. He later regained the world record for the distance covered in 1 hour, when at the Velodrome he rode for over 56 km. At the Atlanta Olympics he had won a bronze in the time trial, while Max Sciandri also won a bronze, in the road race.

Equestrianism

The arts of riding and driving are promoted by the British Horse Society, which is concerned with the welfare of horses, road safety, riding rights of way and training. It runs the British Equestrian Centre at Stoneleigh in Warwickshire. With some 63,000 members, the Society is the parent body of the Riding Club movement, which holds rallies, meetings and competitions culminating in annual national championships.

Leading horse trials, comprising dressage, cross-country and show jumping, are held at a number of locations. The Badminton Horse Trials is one of Britain's largest sporting events, attracting around 250,000 spectators.

Show jumping is regulated and promoted by the British Show Jumping Association. The major events include the Horse of the Year Show at Wembley in London and the Hickstead Derby at Hickstead (West Sussex). John Whitaker has won the Volvo World Cup twice, in 1990 and 1991, and was runner-up in May 1997, riding Virtual Village Welham.

The authority responsible for equestrian competitions (other than racing) at international and Olympic level is the British Equestrian Federation, which co-ordinates the activities of the British Horse Society and the British Show Jumping Association.

Football

Association football is controlled by separate football associations in England, Wales,

Football has seen an influx of money during the 1990s, particularly into the top clubs. This has arisen primarily as a result of the agreements on television coverage, notably with BSkyB, while several leading clubs, such as Manchester United, are listed on the London Stock Exchange. More leading international footballers—from most European countries and from South America, Africa, Australia and elsewhere—are now playing in the top divisions as clubs have been able to finance their purchase. Transfer fees have also risen—a then world record fee was set in 1996 when Alan Shearer was signed by Newcastle United from Blackburn Rovers for £15 million.

Scotland and Northern Ireland. In England 340 clubs are affiliated to the Football Association and more than 42,000 clubs to regional or district associations. The FA, founded in 1863, and the Football League, founded in 1888, were both the first of their kind in the world. In Scotland there are 78 full and associate clubs and nearly 6,000 registered clubs under the jurisdiction of the Scottish Football Association.

A new FA Premier League was started in England in 1992 and now comprises 20 clubs. A further 72 full-time professional clubs play in three main divisions run by the Football League. During the season, which lasts from August until May, over 2,000 English League matches are played. In June 1997 a £40 million scheme to establish new centres of excellence for coaching and developing young players was announced, with a contribution of £20 million from the FA Premier League being matched by £20 million from the English Sports Council's Lottery Fund.

Three Welsh clubs play in the Football League, while the National League of Wales contains 20 semi-professional clubs. In Scotland the Scottish Football League has 40 clubs, equally divided into four divisions. In Northern Ireland, 16 semi-professional clubs play in the Irish Football League.

The major annual knock-out competitions are the FA Cup sponsored by Littlewoods and the Coca-Cola Cup (the League Cup) in England, the Tennents Scottish Cup, the Coca-Cola Cup (the Scottish League Cup), the Irish Cup and the Welsh FA Cup.

Euro 96, the final stage of the European Championship, was held in June 1996. This was the biggest football tournament to have been held in Britain since the 1966 World Cup. About 1.2 million spectators watched Euro 96 and the event was televised in 195 countries. Following the success of the event, the FA announced its intention of putting in a bid to host the World Cup in 2006. England and Scotland have both qualified for the 1998 World Cup finals in France.

Gaelic Games

Gaelic Games, increasingly popular in Northern Ireland, cover the sports of Gaelic football, handball, hurling, camogie (women's hurling) and rounders. There are over 700 clubs in Northern Ireland affiliated to the Gaelic Athletic Association and the Camogie Council, the official governing bodies responsible for Gaelic Games.

Golf

Golf originated in Scotland and is ruled by the Royal and Ancient Golf Club (R & A), which is situated at St Andrews on the east coast of Scotland. The Golfing Union of Ireland and parallel unions in Wales, Scotland and England are the national governing bodies for men's amateur golf. These bodies are affiliated to the R & A and are represented on the Council of National Golf Unions, which is the British co-ordinating body responsible for handicapping and organising home international matches. Women's amateur golf in Great Britain is governed by the Ladies' Golf Union. Club professional golf is governed by the Professional Golfers' Association (PGA) and tournament golf by the European PGA Tour and the Women Professional Golfers European Tour. Women's golf in Northern Ireland is governed by the Irish Ladies Golf Union.

The main tournament of the British golfing year is the Open Championship, one of the world's four 'major' events. Other important events include the World Matchplay Championship at Wentworth; the Walker Cup and Curtis Cup matches for amateurs, played between Great Britain and Ireland and the United States; and the Ryder Cup and Solheim Cup matches for men and women professionals respectively, played every two years between Europe and the United States. Europe retained the Ryder Cup in September 1997, winning in Valderrama (Spain) by 14.5 to 13.5 points.

There are nearly 2,000 golf courses in Britain. Some of the most famous include St Andrews, Royal Lytham and St Anne's, Muirfield and Troon (which staged the 1997 British Open Championship).

Nick Faldo won the US Masters tournament at Augusta in 1996, his third win in the event and his sixth 'major' title. Colin Montgomerie headed the European list of money winners in 1997 for the fifth year running and finished second in the 1997 US Open. In the women's game Alison Nicholas won the US Women's Open in July 1997 and Laura Davies is ranked number three in the world.

Greyhound Racing

Greyhound racing is one of Britain's most popular spectator sports, with about 5 million spectators a year. Meetings are usually held three times a week at each track, with at least ten races a meeting. The main event of the year is the Greyhound Derby, run in June at Wimbledon Stadium, London. Tracks are licensed by local authorities. There are 32 major tracks and around 45 smaller tracks, although the number of tracks has fallen recently.

The rules for the sport are drawn up by the National Greyhound Racing Club, the sport's judicial and administrative body. The representative body is the British Greyhound Racing Board.

Gymnastics

Gymnastics is divided into five main disciplines: artistic (or Olympic) gymnastics, rhythmic gymnastics, sports acrobatics, general gymnastics and sports aerobics.

The governing body for the sport is British Gymnastics. Over the past decade the number of affiliated clubs has nearly doubled. The sport is particularly popular with schoolchildren and young adults. It is estimated that between 3 and 4 million schoolchildren take part in some form of gymnastics every day.

Highland Games

Scottish Highland Games cover a wide range of athletic competitions, including running, cycling, dancing and solo piping. The heavyweight events are the most popular and include throwing the hammer, tossing the caber and putting the shot. Over 70 gatherings of various kinds take place throughout Scotland, the most famous being the annual Braemar Gathering.

The Scottish Games Association is the official governing body responsible for athletic sports and games at Highland and Border events in Scotland.

Hockey

The modern game of hockey was started by the Hockey Association (of England), which was founded in 1886. The Irish Ladies Hockey Union was the first women's governing body and assisted in the formation of the controlling body of women's hockey in England, the All England Women's Hockey Association. A single association—the England Hockey Association—was formed in June 1997 to govern all hockey in England; there are similar single associations in Scotland and Wales. Cup competitions and leagues exist at national, divisional or district, club and school levels, both indoors (six-a-side) and outdoors, and there are regular international matches and tournaments. A National Hockey Stadium in Milton Keynes, opened in 1996, is now the venue for all major hockey matches in England.

Horse Racing

Horse racing takes two forms—flat racing and National Hunt (steeplechasing and hurdle) racing. The turf flat race season runs from late

March to early November, but all-weather flat racing and National Hunt racing take place throughout the year. Britain has 59 racecourses and about 12,000 horses currently in training.

The Derby, run at Epsom, is the outstanding event in the flat racing calendar. Other classic races are: the 2,000 Guineas and the 1,000 Guineas, both run at Newmarket; the Oaks (Epsom); and the St Leger (Doncaster). The most important National Hunt meeting is the National Hunt Festival held at Cheltenham in March, which features the Gold Cup and the Champion Hurdle. The Grand National, run at Aintree, near Liverpool, is the world's best-known steeplechase and dates from 1839.

> British-trained racehorses have won several important events overseas in recent years. Singspiel, trained by Michael Stoute, won the Canadian International and the Japan Cup in 1996, and the Dubai World Cup in 1997.

The British Horseracing Board is the governing authority for racing in Britain. Its responsibilities include the fixture list, race programmes, relations with the Government and the betting industry, and central marketing. The Jockey Club, as the regulatory authority, is responsible for licensing, discipline and security.

Ice Skating

Ice skating has four main disciplines: ice figure (single and pairs), ice dance, speed skating and precision skating. The governing body is the National Ice Skating Association of UK Ltd. There are 68 rinks in Britain, with plans in hand for a number of new rinks. A £16 million project for a new ice arena in Sheffield will receive funding from the National Lottery Sports Fund.

British couples have won the world ice dance championship 17 times, the most recent being Jayne Torvill and Christopher Dean, who won four consecutive world championships between 1981 and 1984. They returned to amateur competition briefly in 1994, winning a gold medal at the European Championships and a bronze medal at the Winter Olympics.

Judo

Judo is popular not only as a competitive sport and self-defence technique, but also as a means of general fitness training. An internationally recognised grading system is in operation through the sport's governing body, the British Judo Association. In October 1997 Kate Howey won the world middleweight title. The world championships in 1999 will be staged in Birmingham.

Keep Fit

Keep fit encompasses various forms of movement and exercise activities. The Keep Fit Association (KFA), one of the largest governing bodies in England, has 1,500 teachers and a membership of 12,000. It promotes fitness through movement, exercise and dance for people of all ages and abilities. Its national certificated training scheme is recognised by local education authorities throughout Britain. Autonomous associations serve Scotland, Wales and Northern Ireland. The Exercise Association of England is a health-promoting organisation concerned with raising professional standards and advising the public.

Martial Arts

A broad range of martial arts, mainly derived from the Far East, is practised in Britain. There are recognised governing bodies for karate, ju-jitsu, aikido, Chinese martial arts, kendo, taekwondo and tang soo do. The most popular martial art is karate, with over 100,000 participants.

Motor-car Sports

The main four-wheeled motor sports include motor racing, autocross, rallycross, rallying and karting. In motor racing the Grand Prix Formula 1 World Championship is the major form of the sport.

The governing body for four-wheeled motor sport in Britain is the RAC (Royal Automobile Club) Motor Sports Association. The Association issues licences for a variety of competitions. It also organises the RAC Rally, an event in the World Rally Championship, and the British Grand Prix, which is held at Silverstone as part of the Formula 1 World Championship.

Britain has had more Formula 1 world champions than any other country. The most recent is Damon Hill (son of Graham Hill, a previous world champion), who won the 1996 Formula 1 World Championship and has won 21 Grand Prix.

British car constructors, including Williams and McLaren, have enjoyed outstanding success in Grand Prix racing and many other forms of racing. Most of the cars in Formula 1 have been designed, developed and built in Britain. A new team to enter Formula 1 in 1997 is the Stewart Grand Prix team (headed by a previous world champion, Jackie Stewart, and his son Paul). The motor sport industry in Britain is estimated to generate an annual turnover of £1,300 million (of which exports account for 60 per cent) and to employ more than 50,000 people.

In 1995 Colin McRae became the first British driver to win the World Rally Championship.

Motor-cycle Sports

Motor-cycle sports include road racing, moto-cross, grass track, speedway, trials, drag racing, enduro (endurance off-road racing) and sprint. There are between 40,000 and 50,000 competitive motor cyclists in Britain.

The governing bodies of the sport are the Auto-Cycle Union in England and Wales, the Scottish Auto-Cycle Union and the Motor Cycle Union of Ireland (in Northern Ireland). The major events of the year include the Isle of Man TT races and the British Road Race Grand Prix. The Auto-Cycle Union also provides off-road training by approved instructors for riders of all ages.

Carl Fogarty won the World Superbike Championships in 1994 and 1995, and in 1997 finished runner-up, winning six races. In 1996 Darren Dixon and Alex Hetherington won their second successive world sidecar title. Joey Dunlop has a record 22 wins in the Isle of Man TT races.

Mountaineering

The representative body is the British Mountaineering Council (BMC), which works closely with the Mountaineering Councils of Scotland and Ireland. The main areas of work include access and conservation. A survey has estimated that climbing is one of the fastest growing sports in Britain. The BMC estimates that the number of active participants is around 150,000, while there are many more hill walkers. There are over 300 mountaineering and climbing clubs in Britain, and three National Centres for mountaineering activities run by the Sports Councils (see p. 515). Organisations such as the Scottish Mountain Safety Group help to promote the safe enjoyment of the hills.

British mountaineers have played a leading role in exploring the world's great mountain ranges. The best-known is Sir Chris Bonington, who has climbed Everest and led many other expeditions, including an expedition in 1997 to the unclimbed Sepu Kangri in Tibet. Some of the world's hardest rock climbs are found on cliffs in Britain.

Netball

More than 60,000 adults play netball regularly in England and a further 1 million young people play in schools. The sport is played almost exclusively by women and girls.

The All England Netball Association is the governing body in England, with Scotland, Wales and Northern Ireland having their own separate organisations. National competitions are staged annually for all age groups. The world championships are held every four years—in 1995 they were staged at the National Indoor Arena in Birmingham.

Rowing

Rowing is taught in many schools, universities and rowing clubs throughout Britain. The main types of boats are single, pairs and double sculls, fours and eights. The governing body in England is the Amateur Rowing Association; similar bodies regulate the sport in Scotland, Wales and Ireland (Ulster Branch).

The University Boat Race, between eight-oared crews from Oxford and Cambridge, has been rowed on the Thames almost every spring since 1836. The Head of the River Race, also on the Thames, is the largest assembly of racing craft in the world, with more than 420 eights racing in procession. At the Henley Regatta in Oxfordshire crews from all over the world compete each July in various kinds of race over a straight course of 1 mile 550 yards (about 2.1 km).

Steven Redgrave and Matthew Pinsent won the gold medal in the coxless pairs in both the 1992 and 1996 Olympics. Steven Redgrave has now won four successive Olympic gold medals, a feat achieved by only a very few people in Olympic history. They have now joined up with one of the team who won a bronze medal in 1996 in the coxless fours—Tim Foster—and with James Cracknell to form a new coxless four with the long-term aim of competing in the Olympic Games in Sydney in 2000. They won one of two gold medals for Britain at the world championships in Aiguebelette (France) in September 1997, with the women's coxless four also winning gold. Britain won a record eight medals, with two silver medals—in the women's double sculls and the men's lightweight eight—and four bronze medals.

Rugby League

Rugby league (a 13-a-side game) originated in 1895 following the breakaway from rugby union (see below) of 22 clubs in the north of England, where the sport is still concentrated.

The governing body of the professional game is the Rugby Football League, while the amateur game is governed by the British Amateur Rugby League Association. The major domestic club match of the season is the Challenge Cup Final, played at Wembley Stadium in London. Rugby league's centenary world cup took place in England and Wales in 1995, when England were runners-up to Australia.

Rugby league was transformed in 1996 with the creation of a Super League. This consists of 12 clubs: ten from the north of England,

one from London and one representing Paris. There are two other divisions, with 11 and 12 clubs respectively. A new World Club Championship, involving the Super League teams and teams from Australia and New Zealand, began in June 1997, and the final was held in Australia in October 1997.

Rugby Union

Rugby union football (a 15-a-side game) is thought to have originated at Rugby School in the first half of the 19th century. The sport is played under the auspices of the Rugby Football Union (RFU) in England and parallel bodies in Wales, Scotland and Ireland (Ulster Branch). Each of the four countries has separate national league and knock-out competitions for its domestic clubs.

An annual Five Nations Championship is contested by England, Scotland, Wales, Ireland and France. Overseas tours are undertaken by the national sides and by the British Lions, a team representing Great Britain and Ireland. Tours are made to Britain by teams representing the major rugby-playing nations.

The Rugby World Cup is held every four years. Wales has been selected by the International Rugby Board to host the finals of the 1999 World Cup. The Cardiff Arms Park Stadium is being substantially rebuilt in time for this event, with a significant financial contribution from the Millennium Commission (see p. 47). Other matches in the competition will be shared among England, Scotland, Ireland and France.

Rugby union is going through a period of change following the decision in 1995 to end its amateur status and as a result of the renegotiation of television contracts for international matches at much higher levels than before. Players may now be paid and, as with football (see p. 523), new money has been attracted into several of the top clubs.

Skiing

Skiing takes place in Scotland from December to May and also at several English locations when there is sufficient snow. The five established winter sports areas in Scotland are Cairngorm, Glencoe, Glenshee, the Lecht and

Nevis Range. All have a full range of ski-lifts, prepared ski runs and professional instructors.

There are over 115 artificial or dry ski-slopes throughout Britain, and 1.5 million people take part in the sport. The British Ski and Snowboard Federation is the representative body for international competitive skiing and snowboarding. The home country ski councils are responsible for the development of the sport in their appropriate country, mainly through coaching, race training and arranging competitions.

Snooker and Billiards

Snooker was invented by the British in India in 1875 and is played by approximately 7 million people in Britain. British players have an outstanding record in the game and have dominated the major professional championships. The main tournament is the annual Embassy World Professional Championship, held in Sheffield. The outstanding player of the 1990s is Stephen Hendry, who has won the world title six times (including five years in a row up to 1996) and was runner-up in 1997.

The controlling body for the non-professional game in England is the English Association for Snooker and Billiards. Scotland, Wales and Northern Ireland have separate associations. The World Professional Billiards and Snooker Association organises all world-ranking professional events and holds the copyright for the rules. The representative body for women is the World Ladies' Billiards and Snooker Association.

Squash

Squash derives from the game of rackets, which was invented at Harrow School in the 1850s. The governing body for squash in England is the Squash Rackets Association; there are separate governing bodies in Wales, Scotland and Northern Ireland. The British Open Championships is one of the major world events in the sport.

The number of players in Britain is estimated at over 2 million, of whom more than 500,000 compete regularly in inter-club league competitions. There are nearly 9,000 squash courts in England, provided mainly by squash clubs, commercial organisations and local authorities.

In 1997 England retained the world team championships when the team beat Canada in the final in Kuala Lumpur. The England team consisted of Del Harris, Peter Marshall, Simon Parke and Chris Walker.

Swimming

Swimming is a popular sport and form of exercise for people from all age groups. Competitive swimming is governed by the Amateur Swimming Association (ASA) in England and by similar associations in Scotland and Wales. Together these three associations form the Amateur Swimming Federation of Great Britain, which co-ordinates the selection of Great Britain teams and organises international competitions. Northern Ireland forms part of the Irish Amateur Swimming Association. Instruction and coaching are provided by qualified teachers and coaches who hold certificates awarded mainly by the ASA.

In the 1996 Olympics Paul Palmer won a silver medal in the 400 metres freestyle and Graeme Smith a bronze medal in the 1,500 metres freestyle. James Hickman won the 200 metres butterfly at the World Short Course Championships in Gothenburg in April 1997.

Table Tennis

Table tennis was developed in Britain in the second half of the 19th century. It is popular with all sections of the community, and is played in a variety of venues and among all age groups. The sport is also a major recreational and competitive activity for people with disabilities. The governing body in England is the English Table Tennis Association, while there are separate associations in Scotland, Wales and Northern Ireland.

The 1997 World Table Tennis Championships were held in Manchester.

Tennis

The modern game of tennis originated in England in 1873 and the first championships were played at Wimbledon in 1877. The governing body for tennis in Great Britain is the Lawn Tennis Association (LTA), to which the Welsh and Scottish LTAs are affiliated. Tennis in Northern Ireland is governed by Tennis Ireland (Ulster Branch).

The Wimbledon Championships, held within the grounds of the All England Club, are one of the four tennis 'Grand Slam' tournaments. Prize money totalled £6.9 million in 1997. An extensive redevelopment of the All England Club is in progress and the new No 1 Court was used for the 1997 Championships. In 1997 the Championships generated £31 million for British tennis.

In September 1997 Greg Rusedski was runner-up in the US Open, and by October he was ranked fourth in the world, the highest rating by a British player since the start of open tennis in 1968, while Tim Henman was also in the world's top 20. In the 1996 Olympics Neil Broad and Tim Henman were runners-up in the men's doubles. David Sherwood and James Trotman won the junior boys' doubles title at the 1997 Australian Open.

Players can take part in national and county championships. National competitions are organised for schools, and short tennis has been introduced for children aged five and over. The game is played in over 3,000 schools and in leisure centres. About 5 million people play tennis in Britain.

The LTA has a five-year plan for developing tennis in Great Britain in the period to 2001. It is working in partnership with county tennis associations, clubs, schools, further and higher education institutions, and local authorities. The aim is to expand participation, encourage regular competition and produce more world-class tennis players.

Volleyball

The English Volleyball Association and parallel associations in Scotland, Wales and Northern Ireland act as the sport's governing bodies. The Association organises national, regional and area championships for a variety of ages. Mini-Volley is a three-a-side version of the game adapted for children under 13. Grass and beach volleyball tournaments are proving very popular with children and are leading to an increase in the number of schools playing volleyball.

Yachting

Yachting comprises sailing, powerboating and windsurfing on both inland and offshore waters. Racing in sailing boats takes place between one-design classes or under handicap, which provides level racing for boats of different size and shape. Among well-known ocean races are the Round The World Yacht Race and the Fastnet Race.

The Royal Yachting Association is the governing body for all yachting in Britain. About 3 million people participate in the sport.

At the 1996 Olympics silver medals were won by Ben Ainslie in the Laser class and by John Merricks and Ian Walker in the 470 (double-handed dinghy) class. Shirley Robertson is ranked as the world number one in the Europe class.

Further Reading

The History of Cricket: From The Weald to the World, by Peter Wynne-Thomas. The Stationery Office, 1997.

Sport and Leisure. Aspects of Britain series. HMSO, 1994.

Annual Reports

The United Kingdom Sports Council, the English Sports Council, the Sports Council for Wales, the Scottish Sports Council and the Sports Council for Northern Ireland.

Appendix 1:
Government Departments and Agencies

An outline of the principal functions of the main government departments and a list of their executive agencies is given below.

Cabinet ministries are indicated by an asterisk. Executive agencies are normally listed under the relevant department, although in some cases they are included within the description of the department's responsibilities.

The work of many of the departments and agencies listed below covers Britain as a whole. Where this is not the case, the following abbreviations are used:

- (GB) for functions covering England, Wales and Scotland;
- (E,W & NI) for those covering England, Wales and Northern Ireland;
- (E & W) for those covering England and Wales; and
- (E) for those concerned with England only.

The principal address and telephone and fax numbers of each department are given. For details of the addresses of executive agencies see the annual *Civil Service Year Book*.

Cabinet Office (Office of Public Service)
70 Whitehall, London SW1A 2AS   Tel: 0171 270 1234 Fax: 0171 270 0618

The Cabinet Office and the responsibilities of the Office of Public Service—OPS—are described on p. 73.

Executive Agencies

The Buying Agency
CCTA: Central Computer and
  Telecommunications Agency
Civil Service College
Property Advisers to the Civil Estate
Security Facilities Executive

One further agency—the Central Office of Information—reports to the Chancellor of the Duchy of Lancaster but is a department in its own right and not part of OPS (see p. 535).

Her Majesty's Stationery Office, since September 1996 a division of the Cabinet Office, is responsible for printing legislation and for control and administration of Crown copyright and administration of parliamentary copyright.

ECONOMIC AFFAIRS

*Ministry of Agriculture, Fisheries and Food
3–8 Whitehall Place, London SW1A 2HH
Tel: 0171 270 3000   Fax: 0171 270 8443

Policies for agriculture, horticulture, fisheries and food; responsibilities for related environmental and rural issues (E); food policies.

Executive Agencies

Central Science Laboratory
Intervention Board
Meat Hygiene Service
Pesticides Safety Directorate
Veterinary Laboratories Agency
Veterinary Medicines Directorate

*Department of Trade and Industry
1–19 Victoria Street, London SW1H 0ET
Tel: 0171 215 5000   Fax: please phone for best fax number

Industrial and commercial affairs; science and technology; promotion of new enterprise and competition; information about new business methods and opportunities; investor protection and consumer affairs. Specific responsibilities include innovation policy; regional industrial policy and inward investment promotion; small businesses; management best practice and business/education links; industrial relations and employment legislation; deregulation; international trade policy; commercial relations and export promotion; competition policy; company law; insolvency; radio regulation; patents and copyright protection (GB); the development of new sources of energy and the Government's relations with the energy industries.

Executive Agencies

Companies House
Employment Tribunals Service
Insolvency Service
National Weights and Measures Laboratory
Patent Office
Radiocommunications Agency

Office of Fair Trading
Field House, Breams Buildings, London EC4A
1PR Tel: 0171 242 2858   Fax: 0171 269 8961

A non-ministerial department which aims to
promote and safeguard the economic interests of
consumers. It administers a wide range of
competition and consumer protection legislation.

*Department of Transport
See under Department of the Environment,
Transport and the Regions, p. 534.

*HM Treasury
Parliament Street, London SW1P 3AG
Tel: 0171 270 3000   Fax: 0171 270 5244

Oversight of the framework for monetary policy;
tax policy; planning and control of public spending;
government accounting; international financial
relations; and the regime for regulation of financial
services.

HM Customs and Excise
New King's Beam House, 22 Upper Ground,
London SE1 9PJ   Tel: 0171 620 1313   Fax: 0171
865 5625

Collecting and accounting for Customs and Excise
revenues, including VAT (value added tax); agency
functions, including controlling certain imports and
exports, policing prohibited goods, and compiling
trade statistics.

**ECGD (Export Credits Guarantee
Department)**
PO Box 2200, 2 Exchange Tower, Harbour
Exchange Square, London E14 9GS
Tel: 0171 512 7421   Fax: 0171 512 7021

Access to bank finance and provision of insurance
for British project and capital goods exporters
against the risk of not being paid for goods and
services; political risk insurance cover for British
investment overseas; reinsurance to private sector
insurance companies offering insurance for British
consumer type exports.

Inland Revenue
Somerset House, Strand, London WC2R 1LB
Tel: 0171 438 6622   Fax: 0171 438 6971

Administration and collection of direct taxes;
valuation of property (GB).

Executive Agency

The Valuation Office

National Savings
Charles House, 375 Kensington High Street,
London W14 8SD   Tel: 0171 605 9300   Fax: 0171
605 9438

An executive agency, reporting to the Chancellor of
the Exchequer, which aims to raise funds for the
Government by selling a range of investments to
members of the public.

Office for National Statistics
1 Drummond Gate, London SW1V 2QQ
Tel: 0171 233 9233   Fax: 0171 533 5719

An executive agency created in April 1996 by the
merger of the Central Statistical Office and the
Office of Population, Censuses and Surveys. It is
responsible for the full range of functions previously
carried out by both former offices. This includes:

- preparing and interpreting key economic
  statistics for government policy; collecting
  and publishing business statistics; publishing
  annual and monthly statistical digests;

- providing researchers, analysts and those in
  education and other customers with a
  statistical service that assists their work and
  promotes the functioning of industry and
  commerce;

- administration of the marriage laws and local
  registration of births, marriages and deaths
  (E & W); provision of population estimates
  and projections and statistics on health and
  other demographic matters (E & W); Census
  of Population (E & W). Surveys for other
  government departments and public bodies
  (GB); and

- promoting these functions within Britain, the
  European Union and internationally to
  provide a statistical service to meet European
  Union and international requirements.

Royal Mint
Llantrisant, Pontyclun, Mid Glamorgan CF72 8YT
Tel: 01443 222111   Fax: 01443 623185

An executive agency responsible for producing and
issuing coinage for Britain. It also produces
ordinary circulation coins and coinage blanks for
around 100 countries as well as special proof and
uncirculated quality collectors' coins,
commemorative medals, and royal and official seals.

REGULATORY BODIES

Office of Electricity Regulation (OFFER)
Hagley House, Hagley Road, Birmingham B16 8QG   Tel: 0121 456 2100   Fax: 0121 454 7622

Regulating and monitoring the electricity supply industry; promoting competition in the generation and supply of electricity; ensuring that companies comply with the licences under which they operate; protecting customers' interests (GB).

Office of Gas Supply (OFGAS)
Stockley House, 130 Wilton Road, London SW1V 1LQ   Tel: 0171 828 0898   Fax: 0171 932 1664

Responsible for protecting the interests of gas consumers by regulating British Gas Trading and Transco's prices and for introducing competition to the domestic gas market.

Office of the National Lottery (OFLOT)
2 Monck Street, London SW1P 2BQ   Tel: 0171 227 2000   Fax: 0171 227 2005

Responsible for the grant, variation and enforcement of licences to run the National Lottery and promote lotteries as part of it.

Office of Passenger Rail Franchising (OPRAF)
Golding's House, 2 Hay's Lane, London SE1 2HB Tel: 0171 940 4200   Fax: 0171 940 4259

Responsible for letting, monitoring performance, and managing grant support for the 25 former British Rail passenger rail franchises; encourages railway investment (GB).

Office of the Rail Regulator (ORR)
1 Waterhouse Square, 138–142 Holborn, London EC1N 2ST   Tel: 0171 282 2000   Fax: 0171 282 2040

Regulating the rail industry, including: the licensing of operators of railway assets; the approval of agreements for access by those operators to track, stations and light maintenance depots; the enforcement of domestic competition law; and consumer protection (GB).

Office for Standards in Education (OFSTED)
29–33 Kingsway, London WC2B 6SE   Tel: 0171 421 6800   Fax: 0171 421 6522

Improving standards of achievement and quality of education through regular independent inspection of schools, public reporting and informed advice (E).

Office of Telecommunications (OFTEL)
50 Ludgate Hill, London EC4M 7JJ   Tel: 0171 634 8700   Fax: 0171 834 8842

Monitoring telecommunications operators' licences; enforcing competition legislation; representing users' interests.

Office of Water Services (OFWAT)
Centre City Tower, 7 Hill Street, Birmingham B5 4UA   Tel: 0121 625 1300   Fax: 0121 625 1346

Monitoring the activities of companies appointed as water and sewerage undertakers; regulating prices, promoting economy and efficiency, protecting customers' interests and facilitating competition (E & W). Ten regional customer service committees represent customer interests and investigate complaints. The OFWAT National Customer Council speaks for customers at a national level.

LEGAL AFFAIRS

* Lord Chancellor's Department
Selborne House, 54–60 Victoria Street, London SW1E 6QW   Tel: 0171 210 8500

Responsibility, through the Court Service, for the administration of the Supreme Court, county and crown courts and a number of tribunals. Also oversees the locally administered magistrates' courts and the Official Solicitor's Department. All work relating to judicial appointments. Overall responsibility for civil and criminal legal aid, for the Law Commission and for the promotion of general reforms in the civil law. Main responsibility for private international law. Responsibility for the Public Record Office and the Public Trust Office (E & W). The Lord Chancellor also has responsibility for the Northern Ireland Court Service.

The Legal Services Ombudsman and the Advisory Committee on Legal Education and Conduct are independent of the Department but report to the Lord Chancellor.

Executive Agencies

The Court Service
HM Land Registry
Public Record Office
Public Trust Office

Crown Prosecution Service
50 Ludgate Hill, London EC4M 7EX   Tel: 0171 273 8000   Fax: 0171 329 8377

An independent organisation responsible for the prosecution of criminal cases resulting from police investigations, headed by the Director of Public Prosecutions and accountable to Parliament through the Attorney General, superintending minister for the service (E & W).

Legal Secretariat to the Law Officers
Attorney General's Chambers, 9 Buckingham Gate,
London SW1E 6JP   Tel: 0171 828 7155
Fax: 0171 233 9206

Supporting the Law Officers of the Crown (Attorney
General and Solicitor General) in their functions as
the Government's principal legal advisers (E, W &
NI). The Attorney General, who is also Attorney
General for Northern Ireland, is the minister
responsible for the Treasury Solicitor's Department
(see below), and has a statutory duty to superintend
the Director of Public Prosecutions and the Director
of the Serious Fraud Office (see below), and the
Director of Public Prosecutions for Northern Ireland.

Parliamentary Counsel
36 Whitehall, London SW1A 2AY   Tel: 0171 210
6633   Fax: 0171 210 6637

Drafting of government Bills (except those relating
exclusively to Scotland); advising departments on
parliamentary procedure (E, W & NI).

Treasury Solicitor's Department
Queen Anne's Chambers, 28 Broadway, London
SW1H 9JS   Tel: 0171 210 3000   Fax: 0171 210
3004

Provision of legal services to a large number of
government departments, agencies, and public and
quasi-public bodies. Services include litigation;
giving general advice on interpreting and applying
the law; instructing Parliamentary Counsel on Bills
and drafting subordinate legislation; and, through
an executive agency, providing conveyancing
services and property-related legal work (E & W).

Executive Agency

Government Property Lawyers

**Lord Advocate's Department and Crown
Office** (see p. 537)

Serious Fraud Office
Elm House, 10–16 Elm Street, London WC1X 0BJ
Tel: 0171 239 7272   Fax: 0171 837 1173

Investigating and prosecuting serious and complex
fraud under the superintendence of the Attorney
General (E, W & NI).

EXTERNAL AFFAIRS AND DEFENCE

*Ministry of Defence
Main Building, Whitehall, London SW1A 2HB
Tel: 0171 218 9000   Fax: 0171 218 6460

Defence policy and control and administration of
the armed Services.

Defence Agencies

Army Base Repair Organisation
Army Base Storage and Distribution Agency
Army Individual Training Organisation
Army Personnel Centre
Army Technical Support Agency
Defence Analytical Services Agency
Defence Animal Centre
Defence Bills Agency
Defence Clothing and Textiles Agency
Defence Codification Agency
Defence Dental Agency
Defence Evaluation and Research Agency
Defence Intelligence and Security Centre
Defence Postal and Courier Services Agency
Defence Secondary Care Agency
Defence Transport and Movements Executive
Disposal Sales Agency
Duke of York's Royal Military School
Hydrographic Office
Joint Air Reconnaissance Intelligence Centre
   Agency
Logistic Information Systems Agency
Medical Supplies Agency
Meteorological Office
Military Survey
Ministry of Defence Police
Naval Aircraft Repair Organisation
Naval Bases and Supply Agency
Naval Manning Agency
Naval Recruiting and Training Agency
Pay and Personnel Agency
Queen Victoria School
RAF Logistics Support Services
RAF Maintenance Group
RAF Signals Engineering Establishment
RAF Training Group
Service Children's Education
Ships Support Agency

*Foreign & Commonwealth Office
King Charles Street, London SW1A 2AH
Tel: 0171 270 1500   Fax: 0171 270 6340

Conduct of Britain's overseas relations, including
advising on policy, negotiating with overseas
governments and conducting business in
international organisations; promoting British
exports and investment into Britain; presenting
British ideas and policies to the people of overseas
countries; administering the remaining Dependent
Territories; and protecting British interests abroad,
including the welfare of British citizens.

Executive Agency

Wilton Park Conference Centre

*Department for International Development
94 Victoria Street, London SW1E 5JL   Tel: 0171 917 7000   Fax: 0171 917 0019

Responsibility for all aspects of international development policy and for promoting more coherent British and international polices in support of sustainable development in partnership with governments of developing countries, with international organisations, and with voluntary bodies in Britain and overseas. Also handles Britain's contribution to the international effort to tackle global environmental problems and provides assistance for those affected by disasters.

SOCIAL AFFAIRS, THE ENVIRONMENT AND CULTURE

*Department for Culture, Media and Sport
2–4 Cockspur Street, London SW1Y 5DH
Tel: 0171 211 6200   Fax: 0171 211 6270

The arts; public libraries; national museums and galleries; tourism; sport; the built heritage (E); broadcasting; press regulation; film industry; export licensing of antiques; the National Lottery.

Executive Agencies

Historic Royal Palaces Agency
Royal Parks Agency

*Department for Education and Employment
Sanctuary Buildings, Great Smith Street, London SW1P 3BT   Tel: 0171 925 5000   Fax: 0171 925 6000

Overall responsibility for school, college and university education (E). The Careers Service (E); Employment Service; youth and adult training policy and programmes; sponsorship of Training and Enterprise Councils; European social policies and programmes; co-ordination of government policy on women's issues and equal opportunities issues in employment (GB).

Executive Agency

Employment Service

*Department of the Environment, Transport and the Regions

Environment and the Regions:

Eland House, Bressenden Place, London SW1E 5DU   Tel: 0171 890 3333   Fax: 0171 890 4556

Policies for local government, Regional Development Agencies, regional governance and regeneration; housing, construction, planning and countryside affairs; and environmental protection and water. It is responsible for sponsoring the Health and Safety Executive and Commission (E).

Executive Agencies

Planning Inspectorate
Queen Elizabeth II Conference Centre

Transport

Eland House, Bressenden Place, London SW1E 5DU
Tel: 0171 890 3333 Fax: 0171-276 4556

Land, sea and air transport; domestic and international civil aviation; international transport agreements; shipping and the ports industry; marine pollution; regulation of drivers and vehicles (including road safety); regulation of the road haulage industry; transport and the environment. Motorways and trunk roads; oversight of local authority transport (E). Sponsorship of London Transport (E); British Rail; Railtrack (GB) and the Civil Aviation Authority.

Executive Agencies

The Coastguard Agency
Driver and Vehicle Licensing Agency
Driving Standards Agency
Highways Agency
Marine Safety Agency
Vehicle Certification Agency
Vehicle Inspectorate

*Department of Health
Richmond House, 79 Whitehall, London SW1A 2NS   Tel: 0171 210 3000   Fax: 0171 210 5433

National Health Service, including Health Education Authority; personal social services provided by local authorities; and certain aspects of public health, including hygiene (E).

Executive Agencies

Medical Devices Agency
Medicines Control Agency
NHS Estates
NHS Pensions Agency

*Home Office
50 Queen Anne's Gate, London SW1H 9AT
Tel: 0171 273 4000   Fax: 0171 273 4660

Administration of justice; criminal law; treatment of offenders, including probation and the prison service; the police; crime prevention; fire service and emergency planning; licensing laws; regulation of firearms and dangerous drugs; electoral matters and local legislation (E & W). Gaming (GB).

Passports, immigration and nationality; race relations; royal matters. Responsibilities relating to the Channel Islands and the Isle of Man.

Executive Agencies

Fire Service College
Forensic Science Service
HM Prison Service
United Kingdom Passport Agency

*Department of Social Security
Richmond House, 79 Whitehall, London SW1A 2NS   Tel: 0171 238 0800   Fax: 0171 238 0763

The social security system (GB).

Executive Agencies

Benefits Agency
Child Support Agency
Contributions Agency
Information Technology Services Agency
War Pensions Agency

OTHER OFFICES AND AGENCIES

Central Office of Information
Hercules Road, London SE1 7DU   Tel: 0171 928 2345   Fax: 0171 928 5037

An executive agency procuring publicity material and other information services on behalf of government departments and publicly funded organisations.

Ordnance Survey
Romsey Road, Southampton SO16 4GU
Tel: 01703 792000   Fax: 01703 792452

An executive agency, which reports to the Secretary of State for the Environment, Transport and the Regions, providing official surveying, mapping and associated scientific work covering Great Britain and some overseas countries.

Office of the Data Protection Registrar
Wycliffe House, Water Lane, Wilmslow, Cheshire SK9 5AF   Tel: 01625 545745   Fax: 01625 524510

The Data Protection Registrar is an independent officer who reports directly to Parliament. The Officer maintains a public register of electronic data users and computer bureaux; enforces the data protection principles; encourages the development of codes of practice to help data users comply with the principles; and considers complaints about breaches of the principles and other provisions of the Data Protection Act. Data users must be registered with the Data Protection Registrar.

NORTHERN IRELAND

*Northern Ireland Office
Stormont Castle, Belfast BT4 3ST   Tel: 01232 520700   Fax: 01232 528473
Whitehall, 11 Millbank, London SW1P 4QE
Tel: 0171 210 6454   Fax: 0171 210 8254

Responsibilities

The Secretary of State for Northern Ireland is the Cabinet minister responsible for Northern Ireland. Through the Northern Ireland Office the Secretary of State has direct responsibility for constitutional developments, law and order, security, and electoral matters.

Executive Agencies

The Compensation Agency
Forensic Science Agency of Northern Ireland
Northern Ireland Prison Service

The work of the Northern Ireland departments, whose functions are listed below, is also subject to the direction and control of the Secretary of State.

Department of Agriculture for Northern Ireland
Development of agri-food, forestry and fisheries industries; veterinary, scientific and development services; food and farming policy; agri-environment policy and rural development.

Department of Economic Development for Northern Ireland
Promotion of inward investment and development of larger home industry (Industrial Development Board); promotion of enterprise and small business (through the Local Enterprise Development Unit); training and employment services; promotion of industrially relevant research and development and technology transfer (through the Industrial Research and Technology Unit); promotion and development of tourism (through the Northern Ireland Tourist Board); energy; mineral development; company regulation; consumer protection; health and safety at work; industrial relations; equal opportunity in employment; and Northern Ireland-wide co-ordination of deregulation.

Executive Agencies

Industrial Research and Technology Unit
Training and Employment Agency (Northern Ireland)

Department of Education for Northern Ireland
Control of the five education and library boards and education from nursery to further and higher

education; youth services; sport and recreation; the arts and culture (including libraries); and the development of community relations within and between schools.

Department of the Environment for Northern Ireland

Most of the Department's functions are carried out by executive agencies. These include: planning, roads, water and construction services; environmental protection and conservation services; land registries, public records, ordnance survey, rate collection, driver and vehicle testing and licensing. Core departmental functions include: overall responsibility for housing and transport policies; fire services; certain controls over local government; disposal and management of the Department's land and property holdings; and urban regeneration.

Executive Agencies

Construction Service
Driver and Vehicle Licensing (Northern Ireland)
Driver and Vehicle Testing Agency
Environment and Heritage Service
Land Registers of Northern Ireland
Ordnance Survey of Northern Ireland
Planning Service
Public Record Office of Northern Ireland
Rate Collection Agency
Rivers Agency
Roads Service
Water Service

Department of Finance and Personnel

Control of public expenditure; personnel management of the Northern Ireland Civil Service; provision of central services and advice and responsibilities for promoting fair, co-ordinated and cohesive government.

Executive Agencies

Business Development Service
Government Purchasing Agency
Northern Ireland Statistics and Research Agency
Valuation and Lands Agency

Department of Health and Social Services for Northern Ireland

Health and personal social services and social legislation. Responsibility for the administration of all social security benefits and the collection of National Insurance contributions.

Executive Agencies

Northern Ireland Child Support Agency
Northern Ireland Health and Social Services
 Estates Agency
Northern Ireland Social Security Agency

SCOTLAND

*The Scottish Office

St Andrew's House, Edinburgh EH1 3DG
Tel: 0131 244 1111   Fax: 0131 244 2918
Dover House, Whitehall, London SW1A 2AU
Tel: 0171 270 6744   Fax: 0171 270 6730

Responsibilities

The Secretary of State for Scotland is responsible for a wide range of statutory functions administered by The Scottish Office in Scotland and which in England and Wales are the responsibility of a number of departmental ministers. The Secretary of State has overall responsibility for legal services in Scotland and is advised by the two Scottish Law Officers—the Lord Advocate and the Solicitor General for Scotland. He also works closely with ministers in charge of Great Britain departments on topics of special significance to Scotland within their fields of responsibility. Other Scottish departments for which the Secretary of State has responsibility include the Registers of Scotland and the Scottish Record Office, which are executive agencies, the General Register Office for Scotland and the Scottish Courts Administration (together with its executive agency the Scottish Courts Service), which is also responsible to the Lord Advocate for certain legal functions.

The Scottish Office's responsibilities are discharged principally through its five departments (which include seven executive agencies).

Relations with Other Government Departments

Other government departments with significant Scottish responsibilities have offices in Scotland and work closely with The Scottish Office.

An outline of the functions of the main Scottish departments is given below.

Scottish Office Agriculture, Environment and Fisheries Department

Promotion and regulation of agriculture: safeguarding public, food, plant and animal health and welfare; land use and forestry; livestock subsidies and commodities. Environment, including environmental protection, nature conservation and the countryside; water and sewerage services; sustainable development. Promotion and regulation of fisheries; protection of the marine environment; research on and monitoring of fish stocks; enforcement of fisheries laws and regulations.

Executive Agencies

Scottish Agricultural Science Agency
Scottish Fisheries Protection Agency
Scottish Fisheries Research Services

Scottish Office Development Department
Housing and area regeneration; new towns; local government organisation and finance; transport and local roads, Roads Directorate; co-ordination of Scottish Office European interests; land-use planning; building control; protection and presentation to the public of historic buildings and ancient monuments.

Executive Agency

Historic Scotland

Scottish Office Education and Industry Department
Industrial and regional economic development matters; exports, technology; Highlands and Islands co-ordination; enterprise and tourism; industrial expansion; energy; training; education; student awards; arts (including the National Institutions), libraries, museums and galleries, Gaelic language; sport and recreation.

Executive Agencies

The Scottish Office Pensions Agency
Student Awards Agency for Scotland

Scottish Office Department of Health
National Health Service; Chief Scientist's Office; Public Health Policy Unit.

Scottish Office Home Department
Central administration of law and order (includes police service, criminal justice and licensing, legal aid and the Scottish Prison Service); civil law, fire, home defence and civil emergency services; social work services.

Executive Agency

Scottish Prison Service

Central services are provided to the five Scottish departments. Services include the office of the Solicitor to the Secretary of State, The Scottish Office Information Directorate, the Directorate of Administrative Services, Finance and Personnel Groups.
The following departments are directly responsible to the Law Officers and are not part of The Scottish Office.

Lord Advocate's Department
2 Carlton Gardens, London SW1Y 5AA   Tel: 0171 210 1010   Fax: 0171 210 1025

Provision of legal advice to the Government on issues affecting Scotland; responsibility for drafting government primary legislation relating to Scotland and adapting for Scotland other primary legislation. Provision of advice in matters of parliamentary procedures affecting Scotland.

Crown Office
25 Chambers Street, Edinburgh EH1 1LA
Tel: 0131 226 2626   Fax: 0131 226 6564

Control of all prosecutions in Scotland.

WALES

*Welsh Office
Cathays Park, Cardiff CF1 3NQ   Tel: 01222 825111   Fax: 01222 823807
Gwydyr House, Whitehall, London SW1A 2ER
Tel: 0171 270 3000   Fax: 01222 823807

Responsibilities

The Welsh Office is responsible for many aspects of Welsh affairs, including health, community care and personal social services; education, except for terms and conditions of service, student awards and the University of Wales; Welsh language and culture; agriculture and fisheries; forestry; local government; housing; water and sewerage; environmental protection; sport; land use, including town and country planning; countryside and nature conservation; new towns; ancient monuments and historic buildings; arts, museums and libraries.
    The Department's responsibilities also include roads; tourism; enterprise and training; selective financial assistance to industry; the Urban Programme and urban investment grants in Wales; the operation of the European Regional Development Fund in Wales and other EU matters; women's issues; non-departmental public bodies; civil emergencies; all financial aspects of these matters, including Welsh revenue support grant; oversight responsibilities for economic affairs and regional planning in Wales.

Executive Agency

CADW: Welsh Historic Monuments

Appendix 2:
Recent Legislation

The public Acts of Parliament passed since autumn 1996 are listed below. Twenty-three Acts were introduced by Private Members; these are indicated by asterisks. All are available from The Stationery Office.

1996

Channel Tunnel Rail Link Act 1996. Ch 61.

Consolidated Fund (No 2) Act 1996. Ch 60.

Hong Kong Economic and Trade Office Act 1996. Ch 63.

*Public Order (Amendment) Act 1996. Ch 59.

*Theft (Amendment) Act 1996. Ch 62.

1997

Appropriation Act 1997. Ch 31.

Appropriation (No 2) Act 1997. Ch 57.

Architects Act 1997. Ch 22.

Birds (Registration Charges) Act 1997. Ch 55.

*British Nationality (Hong Kong) Act 1997. Ch 20.

Building Societies Act 1997. Ch 32.

*Building Societies (Distributions) Act 1997. Ch 41.

Civil Procedure Act 1997. Ch 12.

*Confiscation of Alcohol (Young Persons) Act 1997. Ch 33.

Consolidated Fund Act 1997. Ch 15.

Contract (Scotland) Act 1997. Ch 34.

Crime and Punishment (Scotland) Act 1997. Ch 48.

Crime (Sentences) Act 1997. Ch 43.

*Criminal Evidence (Amendment) Act 1997. Ch 17.

*Dangerous Dogs (Amendment) Act 1997. Ch 53.

Education Act 1997. Ch 44.

Education (Schools) Act 1997. Ch 59.

Finance Act 1997. Ch 16.

Finance (No 2) Act 1997. Ch 58.

Firearms (Amendment) Act 1997. Ch 5.

Flood Prevention and Land Drainage (Scotland) Act 1997. Ch 36.

*Horserace Totalisator Board Act 1997. Ch 1.

*Knives Act 1997. Ch 21.

Justices of the Peace Act 1997. Ch 25.

*Land Registration Act 1997. Ch 2.

Law Officers Act 1997. Ch 60.

Lieutenancies Act 1997. Ch 23.

Local Government and Rating Act 1997. Ch 29.

*Local Government (Gaelic Names) (Scotland) Act 1997. Ch 6.

Merchant Shipping and Maritime Security Act 1997. Ch 28.

National Health Service (Primary Care) Act 1997. Ch 46.

National Health Service (Private Finance) Act 1997. Ch 56.

National Heritage Act 1997. Ch 14.

Northern Ireland Arms Decommissioning Act 1997. Ch 7.

Nurses, Midwives and Health Visitors Act 1997. Ch 24.

*Pharmacists (Fitness to Practise) Act 1997. Ch 19.

Planning (Consequential Provisions) (Scotland) Act 1997. Ch 11.

Planning (Hazardous Substances) (Scotland) Act 1997. Ch 10.

Planning (Listed Buildings and Conservation Areas) (Scotland) Act 1997. Ch 9.

Police Act 1997. Ch 50.

Police and Firemen's Pensions Act 1997. Ch 52.

*Police (Health and Safety) Act 1997. Ch 42.

*Police (Insurance of Voluntary Assistants) Act 1997. Ch 45.

*Police (Property) Act 1997. Ch 30.

*Policyholders Protection Act 1997. Ch 18.

*Prisons (Alcohol Testing) Act 1997. Ch 38.

Protection from Harassment Act 1997. Ch 40.

*Public Entertainments Licences (Drug Misuse) Act 1997. Ch 49.

Referendums (Scotland and Wales) Act 1997. Ch 61.

*Road Traffic Reduction Act 1997. Ch 54.

Scottish Legal Services Ombudsman and Commissioner for Local Administration in Scotland Act 1977. Ch 35.

*Sea Fisheries (Shellfish) (Amendment) Act 1997. Ch 3.

Sex Offenders Act 1997. Ch 51.

*Sexual Offences (Protected Material) Act 1997. Ch 39.

Social Security Administration (Fraud) Act 1997. Ch 47.

Social Security (Recovery of Benefits) Act 1997. Ch 27.

*Telecommunications (Fraud) Act 1997. Ch 4.

Town and Country Planning (Scotland) Act 1997. Ch 8.

Transfer of Crofting Estates (Scotland) Act 1997. Ch 26.

*United Nations Personnel Act 1997. Ch 13.

Welsh Development Agency Act 1997. Ch 37.

Appendix 3: Obituaries

Diana, Princess of Wales
Born 1 July 1961, the youngest daughter of the 8th Earl Spencer and the Hon. Mrs Shand-Kydd. Married the Prince of Wales on 29 July 1981, the first Englishwoman to marry an heir to the throne for over 300 years. Died 31 August 1997, after a car crash in Paris. Her two sons, Prince William, born 1982, and Prince Harry, born 1984, are respectively second and third in line of succession to the throne. During her marriage, she was patron or president of over 100 organisations, but after her divorce in July 1996, she reduced her charity work to six areas: young homeless people; leprosy sufferers; HIV/AIDS; English National Ballet; cancer sufferers; and sick children. During the last year of her life she gave her support to the British Red Cross Anti-Personnel Land Mines Campaign. To mark her humanitarian work, The Diana, Princess of Wales Memorial Fund has been set up to channel donations to the causes she championed during her lifetime.

Brother Adam, OBE
World-famous expert on beekeeping
Born 1898, died September 1996

Robert Appleby, CBE
Chairman of the British subsidiary of Black and Decker, 1956–75
Born 1913, died November 1996

The Revd W Awdry, OBE
Clergyman and author; creator of *Thomas the Tank Engine*
Born 1911, died March 1997

Quentin Bell, FRSA, FRSL
Artist and author
Born 1910, died December 1996

Michael Bentine, CBE
Radio and television comedian
Born 1922, died November 1996

Raymond Berry
Former chairman of Berry's Electric and manufacturer of the Magicoal electric fire
Born 1911, died December 1996.

Sir Rudolf Bing
Opera impresario and former General Manager of New York's Metropolitan Opera
Born 1902, died September 1997

Professor Sir Malcolm Brown, FRS
Geologist; Director of the British Geological Survey, 1979–85
Born 1925, died March 1997

Professor Robert Browning, FBA
Classicist and Byzantine scholar
Born 1914, died March 1997

Norman de Bruyne, FRS
Scientist, inventor and aircraft designer
Born 1904, died March 1997

Heather Child, MBE
Calligrapher
Born 1911, died June 1997

Denis Compton, CBE
England and Middlesex Cricketer
Born 1918, died April 1997

Reggie Cooke, OBE
Mountaineer, naturalist and engineer
Born 1901, died December 1996

Air Marshal Sir Denis Crowley-Milling, KCB, CBE, DSO, DFC and Bar
Wartime fighter ace
Born 1919, died December 1996

Lieutenant-Colonel Samuel Derry, DSO, MC
Organiser of wartime escapes from Italy by Allied servicemen
Born 1914, died December 1996

Carl Dolmetsch, CBE
Musician and recorder virtuoso
Born 1911, died July 1997

Peter Earle
Investigative reporter
Born 1925, died April 1997

Professor Hans Eysenck
Psychologist
Born 1916, died September 1997

Hugh Faulkner, OBE
Director (1961–83) and founding member of Help the Aged
Born 1916, died April 1997

Eric Fenby, OBE
Musician and amanuensis to Frederick Delius
Born 1906, died February 1997

Jack Fishman
Journalist, author and songwriter
Born 1920, died April 1997

Ronald Fowler, CBE
Economic statistician who established the Retail Prices Index and the Family Expenditure Survey
Born 1910, died January 1997

Lord Gladwyn, GCMG, GCVO, CB (formerly Gladwyn Jebb)
Diplomat (former Permanent Representative to the United Nations and British Ambassador to France)
Born 1900, died October 1996

Sir James Goldsmith
Businessman, publisher and politician
Born 1933, died July 1997

General Sir John Hackett, GCB, CBE, DSO and Bar, MC, FRSL
Commander-in-Chief, British Army of the Rhine, 1966–68
Born 1910, died September 1997

Brigadier Michael Harbottle, OBE
Soldier and peacekeeper
Born 1917, died May 1997

John Hillaby
Writer, naturalist and traveller
Born 1917, died October 1996

William Hilton
Head of Astronautics at Hawker Siddeley Aviation, 1959–62; pioneer aerospace engineer
Born 1912, died March 1997

Elspeth Huxley, CBE
Writer
Born 1907, died January 1997

Sir Michael Jaffé, CBE
Art historian and Director of the Fitzwilliam Museum, Cambridge, 1973–90
Born 1923, died July 1997

Jak (Raymond Jackson)
Cartoonist
Born 1927, died July 1997

Sir John Junor
Newspaper editor
Born 1919, died May 1997

Professor David Keith-Lucas, CBE
Aeronautical engineer and Professor of Aircraft Design, Cranfield Institute of Technology, 1965–72
Born 1911, died April 1997

Sir John Kendrew, CBE, FRS
Biochemist; joint winner with Max Perutz of the 1962 Nobel Prize for Chemistry for work on the structure of protein molecules
Born 1917, died August 1997

Professor L C Knights
Professor of English Literature, Cambridge
University, 1965–73
A founder editor of *Scrutiny, a Quarterly Review*
Born 1906, died March 1997

Professor Hans Kosterlitz, FRS
Pharmacologist who discovered opioid peptides,
the body's own painkillers
Born 1903, died October 1996

Professor H H Lamb
Climatologist
Born 1913, died June 1997

Frederick Launder
Screenwriter and film director
Born 1907, died February 1997

Tommy Lawton
Footballer (former England and Everton centre
forward)
Born 1919, died November 1996

Mary Leakey, FBA
Archaeologist and anthropologist
Born 1913, died December 1996

Laurie Lee, MBE, FRSL
Poet and novelist
Born 1914, died May 1997

Iris Lemare
First professional woman conductor in Britain
Born 1902, died April 1997

Cecil Lewis, MC
Aviator, broadcaster, author, film director; one of
the founders of the BBC
Born 1898, died January 1997

The 5th Earl of Listowel, PC, GCMG
Politician and Governor-General of Ghana,
1957–60
Born 1906, died March 1997

Alwyn McKay
Pioneer nuclear scientist
Born 1913, died July 1997

**Vice-Admiral Sir Hugh Mackenzie, KCB,
DSO and Bar, DSC**
First Chief Polaris Executive, 1963–68
Born 1913, died October 1996

Sorley MacLean (Sorhaile MacGill-Ean)
Gaelic poet
Born 1911, died November 1996

George Mandl, MBE
Paper manufacturer and founder of GT Mandl
group of companies
Born 1923, died February 1997

Dr Drummond (Drum) Matthews, FRS
Geophysicist; Scientific Director, British
Institutions Reflection Profiling Syndicate,
Cambridge University, 1981–90
Born 1931, died July 1997

Sir John May, PC
Former Lord Justice of Appeal
Born 1923, died January 1997

David Murrison
Editor of the Scottish National Dictionary, 1946–76
Born 1913, died February 1997

Denis Owen
Ecologist and geneticist
Born 1931, died October 1996

Myfanwy Piper
Art critic, and librettist for Benjamin Britten
Born 1911, died January 1997

Chris Prater
Pioneer in screen printing
Born 1924, died November 1996

Sir Victor (V S) Pritchett, CH, CBE
Author and critic
Born 1900, died March 1997

Marjorie Proops, OBE
Journalist
Born c.1911, died November 1996

Professor Stephen Rees-Jones
Pioneer in art conservation
Born 1909, died December 1996

**Lord Rippon of Hexham, PC, QC (formerly
Geoffrey Rippon)**
Former Conservative MP and Cabinet minister
Born 1924, died January 1997

Ivor Roberts-Jones, CBE, RA
Sculptor (work includes statue of Winston
Churchill, Parliament Square, London)
Born 1913, died December 1996

Neville Robinson
Physicist; a pioneer in nuclear magnetic resonance
Born 1925, died October 1996

Lord Roskill, PC
Lord Justice of Appeal, 1971–80; Lord of Appeal in
Ordinary, 1980–86
Born 1911, died October 1996

Willie Rushton
Comedian and cartoonist
Born 1937, died December 1996

Ronnie Scott, OBE
Jazz musician and night-club owner
Born 1927, died January 1997

Baroness Seear, PC
Former Deputy Leader of the Liberal Democrats
in the House of Lords
Born 1913, died April 1997

Donald Shepherd, OBE
Inventor of the Portakabin and the Portaloo
Born 1918, died March 1997

**Lord Sherfield, GCB, GCMG, FRS (formerly
Sir Roger Makins)**
British Ambassador to the United States, 1953–56
and Permanent Secretary to the Treasury, 1956–59
Born 1904, died November 1996

Sir Georg Solti
Conductor
Born 1912, died September 1997

Sir John Stow, GCMG, KCVO
Governor-General of Barbados, 1966–67
Born 1911, died October 1996

**Lord Taylor of Gosforth, PC (Peter Murray
Taylor)**
Lord Chief Justice of England, 1992–96
Born 1930, died April 1997

Lord Todd, OM (Alexander Robertus Todd)
Professor of Organic Chemistry, Cambridge
University, 1944–71 and winner of the 1957 Nobel
Prize for Chemistry
Born 1907, died January 1997

Brigadier Dame Mary Tyrwhitt, DBE, TD
Founder-director of the Women's Royal Army
Corps (WRAC)
Born 1903, died February 1997

Kenneth Watkins, OBE
Founder of the Woodland Trust
Born 1909, died November 1996

Dame Veronica Wedgwood, OM, DBE, FBA
Historian
Born 1910, died March 1997

Professor Sir Geoffrey Wilkinson, FRS
Joint winner of the 1973 Nobel Prize for Chemistry
for his work on organo-metallic compounds
Born 1921, died September 1996

Professor Glanville Williams, QC
Professor of English Law, Cambridge University,
1966–78, and eminent scholar of criminal law
Born 1911, died April 1997

Appendix 4:
Principal Abbreviations

ACAS: Advisory, Conciliation and Arbitration
Service

AONB: Area of Outstanding Natural Beauty

BAe: British Aerospace

BBC: British Broadcasting Corporation

BSE: Bovine Spongiform Encephalopathy

BT: British Telecommunications plc

CAA: Civil Aviation Authority

CAP: Common Agricultural Policy

CBI: Confederation of British Industry

CCW: Countryside Council for Wales

CFCs: Chlorofluorocarbons

CFP: Common Fisheries Policy

CJD: Creutzfeld-Jacob disease

CO$_2$: Carbon dioxide

CPS: Crown Prosecution Service

CSA: Child Support Agency

DCMS: Department for Culture, Media and Sport

DOENI: Department of the Environment for Northern Ireland

DETR: Department of the Environment, Transport and the Regions

DfEE: Department for Education and Employment

DTI: Department of Trade and Industry

EA: Environmental Agency for England and Wales

EC: European Community

ECU: European Currency Unit

EEA: European Economic Area

EMU: Economic and monetary union

ESA: Environmentally Sensitive Area

EU: European Union

FCO: Foreign & Commonwealth Office

GATT: General Agreement on Tariffs and Trade

GDP: Gross Domestic Product

GM: Grant-maintained

GNP: Gross National Product

GORs: Government Offices for the Regions

GP: General Practitioner

HSE: Health and Safety Executive

IEA: International Energy Agency

ILR: Independent Local Radio

IMF: International Monetary Fund

IPC: Integrated pollution control

ITC: Independent Television Commission

ITV: Independent television

JSA: Jobseeker's Allowance

kW (MW, GW, TW): Kilowatt (megawatt, gigawatt, terawatt)

LAPC: Local air pollution control

LEA: Local education authority

LEC: Local Enterprise Company

LFA: Less Favoured Area

LFS: Labour Force Survey

LT: London Transport

m (mm, km): Metre (millimetre, kilometre)

MAFF: Ministry of Agriculture, Fisheries and Food

MEP: Member of the European Parliament

Ml: Megalitre

MP: Member of Parliament

MW (GW) Megawatt, gigawatt

NATO: North Atlantic Treaty Organisation

NDPBs: Non-departmental public bodies

NGLs: Natural gas liquids

NHS: National Health Service

NI: Northern Ireland

NII: Nuclear Installations Inspectorate

NO$_X$: Oxides of nitrogen

OECD: Organisation for Economic Co-operation and Development

ONS: Office for National Statistics

OPS: Office of Public Service

OST: Office of Science and Technology

PE: Physical education

PEP: Personal Equity Plan

PFI: Private Finance Initiative

plc: Public limited company

PSBR: Public sector borrowing requirement

R & D: Research and Development

RAF: Royal Air Force

RPI: Retail Prices Index

SEPA: Scottish Environment Protection Agency

SERPS: State earnings-related pension scheme

SNH: Scottish Natural Heritage

SO$_2$: Sulphur dioxide

SOAEFD: Scottish Office Agriculture, Environment and Fisheries Department

SSSI: Site of Special Scientific Interest

TAC: Total allowable catch

TEC: Training and Enterprise Council

TESSA: Tax exempt special savings account

TUC: Trades Union Congress

UKCS: United Kingdom Continental Shelf

UKSC: United Kingdom Sports Council

UN: United Nations

VAT: Value added tax

WEU: Western European Union

WTO: World Trade Organisation

Appendix 5:
Public Holidays in Britain, 1998

Thursday 1 January	New Year's Day	Britain
Friday 2 January	Public Holiday	Scotland only
Tuesday 17 March	St Patrick's Day	Northern Ireland only
Friday 10 April	Good Friday	Britain
Monday 13 April	Easter Monday	Britain
Monday 4 May	May Day Bank Holiday	Britain
Monday 25 May	Spring Bank Holiday	Britain
Monday 13 July	Orangemen's Day	Northern Ireland only
Monday 3 August	Public Holiday	Scotland only
Monday 31 August	Summer Bank Holiday	Britain (except Scotland)
Friday 25 December	Christmas Day	Britain
Monday 28 December	Boxing Day Holiday	Britain

Index

Printed in the United Kingdom for the Stationery Office
J26904 C75 12/97

Travel Trends

Travel Trends reports the results of the 1996 International Passenger Survey which summarises travel patterns to and from the UK.

The survey includes analyses of overseas residents' visits to the UK and UK residents' visits abroad broken down into number of visits, purpose, length of stay, expenditure incurred and means of transport used.

The 1996 edition of _Travel Trends_ contains a series of tables and charts providing invaluable information for anyone working in the travel, tourism and leisure industries.

International Passenger Survey

To order your copy priced £30 contact, the Stationery Office on 0171-873 9090 or the Office for National Statistics on 0171-533 5678 quoting, ISBN 0 11 620 966 6

Travel*pac*....

Electronic data at your fingertips

- What proportion of business travellers to France used the Channel Tunnel?
- Where do 16-24 year olds go on holiday?
- Who comes to the UK on package holidays?
- What are the most popular off- peak holiday destinations?

**Travel*pac* answers the questions that matter to your business -
WHO GOES WHERE, WHEN, WHY AND HOW?**

Travel*pac* compact dataset is available on CD ROM[1] providing detail on
selected IPS variables, simplified and coded ready for analysis in a number of
common formats (SPSS, Excel, Lotus and Ascii).

The variables include:
- mode of travel
- purpose of visit
- country of residence for overseas visitors
- country of visit for UK residents
- time of year of travel

- age band of traveller
- gender
- expenditure
- nights spent on the visit
- sample size.

You can now answer the questions that matter to your business.

The **Travel*pac*** CD ROMs can be purchased direct from ONS in any of the
following ways:

by post : Sales Office
Zone B1/06
Office for National Statistics
1 Drummond Gate
London SW1V 2QQ

by fax: 0171 533 5689

by phone: 0171 533 5678

> **Travel*pac* Prices**
>
> 1996 CD ROM
> £75 + VAT
>
> 1993 to 1996 CD ROM
> £150 +VAT.

For further information about these products, please ring 0171 533 5765.

[1] datasets can also be supplied on floppy disks.

Main railway passenger routes

Legend:
- Electrified major lines
- Other major lines
- Other routes
- Channel Tunnel

Inverness
Aberdeen
Dundee
Perth
Stirling
Glasgow
Edinburgh
Berwick
Londonderry
Larne
Belfast
Carlisle
Newcastle upon Tyne
Darlington
Middlesbrough
Scarborough
Harrogate
York
Leeds
Hull
Bradford
Blackpool
Preston
Manchester
Doncaster
Grimsby
Liverpool
Sheffield
Holyhead
Nottingham
Crewe
Derby
Stafford
King's Lynn
Shrewsbury
Leicester
Peterborough
Norwich
Birmingham
Coventry
Worcester
Cambridge
Ipswich
Hereford
Colchester
Harwich
Fishguard
Gloucester
Oxford
Swansea
Swindon
London
Margate
Newport
Reading
Ashford
Dover
Cardiff
Bristol
Bath
Gatwick
Folkestone
Taunton
Salisbury
Hastings
Southampton
Portsmouth
Brighton
Eastbourne
Exeter
Weymouth
Bournemouth
Newton Abbot
Plymouth
Penzance

Scale: 0 20 40 60 80 100 km
0 20 40 60 miles